D1546027

949.506
GRE

The Greek revolution

DISCARD

APR 0 6 2021

THE GREEK REVOLUTION

Theodoros Vryzakis, *Hellas in Gratitude,* 1858. National Gallery-Al. Soutzos Museum, Athens.

The Greek Revolution

A CRITICAL DICTIONARY

Edited by

Paschalis M. Kitromilides
& Constantinos Tsoukalas

THE BELKNAP PRESS OF
HARVARD UNIVERSITY PRESS
Cambridge, Massachusetts
London, England   *2021*

Copyright © 2021 by Paschalis M. Kitromilides and Constantinos Tsoukalas
All rights reserved
Printed in the United States of America

First printing

Translations from Greek by Alexandra Douma.
Frontispiece: *Hellas in Gratitude,* Theodoros Vryzakis, 1858. National Gallery, Athens.

Library of Congress Cataloging-in-Publication Data
Names: Kitromilides, Paschalis, editor. | Tsoukalas, Kōnstantinos, 1937– editor.
Title: The Greek revolution : a critical dictionary / edited by Paschalis M. Kitromilides
    and Constantinos Tsoukalas.
Description: Cambridge, Massachusetts : The Belknap Press of Harvard University Press, 2021. |
    Includes bibliographical references and index.
Identifiers: LCCN 2020040853 | ISBN 9780674987432 (cloth)
Subjects: LCSH: Philhellenism. | Greece—History—War of Independence, 1821–1829.
Classification: LCC DF805 .G738 2021 | DDC 949.5 / 0603–dc23
LC record available at https://lccn.loc.gov/2020040853

*In honor of the generations of scholars
who, across two hundred years, have devoted their intellectual labor
to the study of the Greek Revolution*

Contents

Color plates follow page 390.

Note to the Reader

This book is intended as a guide to readers wishing to acquaint themselves with the events, people, and ideas that make up the drama of the 1820s in European and global history. Our point of departure and main purpose is to record the many facets of the Greek Revolution, the rising of the Greek people in 1821 after many centuries of Ottoman rule. Coming as it did at the heyday of repression in Restoration Europe following the defeat of the French Revolution, the Greek Revolution represented the earliest instance of questioning the oppressive order imposed by the Congress of Vienna on the peoples of the old Continent. Whereas the revolts in Naples and Piedmont in 1820–1821 were quickly put down, the revolution of the Greeks developed into a full-scale war of independence that lasted for more than a decade.

The Greek struggle for liberation breathed new life into the Age of Revolution and rekindled the hopes of liberal spirits throughout the continent and the rest of the world. The Philhellenic movement involved not only enthusiasm and support for the fighting Greeks, but also a broader assertion of the aspiration of freedom and the hopes of the oppressed around the world. It is not accidental that the first international recognition of the new Greek polity came from the Republic of Haiti in 1822. It was a gesture of solidarity among emerging new states, highly symbolic of the expectations of the age.

The present volume explains what actually happened in the broader Greek world, the world delimited by Greek culture and language in the eastern Mediterranean and in southeastern Europe, during the turbulent decade of revolution and war. We have attempted to demonstrate the global repercussions and impact of those events on the politics, the culture, and especially the arts of the rest of Europe and the world, particularly the Americas. The fighting Greeks provided models of action to other peoples, primarily in their immediate vicinity in southeastern and eastern Europe but also beyond. Our hope in compiling the collection has been to show that the Greek Revolution was not just about Greece and the Greeks but about the cause of freedom and social liberation, a cause with multiple meanings for all peoples and individuals.

The global significance of the struggle of the Greeks was also reflected in its major achievement, the attainment of Greek independence. After a decade of struggle, victories and defeats, dissension and civil war, and enormous suffering in terms of humanitarian catastrophes, the Greeks managed to accede to sovereign statehood, the first such achievement in European history after the French Revolution and the Congress of Vienna. The neighboring Serbs, who had revolted in 1804 and kept an intermittent revolutionary movement going for almost three decades, finally achieved the status of an autonomous principality under Ottoman sovereignty in 1831 and had to wait until the Congress of Berlin in 1878 to attain sovereign statehood. The Greeks, thanks to the persistence of their struggle, but also the weight of their ancient heritage in European culture and the Philhellenic movement, emerged as the first "new nation," to borrow Seymour Martin Lipset's expression, in Europe, setting a model for the rest of the Continent and the neighboring Middle East.

This work is intended as a wide-ranging guide, but it does not pretend to be exhaustive or to provide a general history of the Revolution. Our aspirations in this project have been much more modest. Exhaustiveness, in our judgment, would not have been a realistic ambition in a project like this, not only on account of practical considerations of feasibility but also on account of the many gaps in scholarship on the Greek Revolution that are quite noticeable after half a century of neglect of the subject, a period during which the several strands of research on modern Greek history turned their main attention to other subjects. We have thus attempted to provide, through a selection of paradigmatic topics, an overview to help prospective readers satisfy their initial curiosity and to encourage further exploration. Our intended audience includes both specialists who will turn to this volume for an initial check and control of issues in their own research and nonexperts who seek an introduction to a subject that attempts to claim a more visible place in contemporary scholarship. We offer this work as a record and *vade mecum* of what has long been known and what has been more recently produced about the Greek Revolution.

Incorporating in this single volume a new, all-inclusive history of the Greek Revolution is likewise beyond our purposes. The epic accounts of Spyridon Trikoupis, Ioannis Philimon, Anastasios Goudas, and Constantinos Paparrigopoulos in the nineteenth century, or of Dionysios Kokkinos and Apostolos Vakalopoulos in the twentieth, as well as the imposing historical works by foreign observers of the Revolution discussed by P. Vallianos in this volume, cannot be easily repeated. Instead, they have been succeeded by large-scale collective projects such as the twelfth volume of the *History of the Greek Nation* (1975) or the third volume of the *History of Modern Hellenism* (2003), both of which have been important sources for our project.

We have called our work a dictionary in order to underline its character as a record of ongoing exploration that can be revisited and enriched in future reincarnations. Of the two models available to us, both generated at the bicentennial of the French Revolution, the *Dictionnaire Critique* by François Furet and Mona Ozouf and the *Dictionnaire historique* by Albert Soboul, we chose to follow the former in order to signal our intentions to be selective rather than exhaustive and to stimulate critical reflection on the topics chosen for inclusion. The authors of individual essays were asked to identify the conventional understanding of their particular subjects and either confirm or revise that understanding taking into account recent research and debates. Readers are therefore warned that they will not find everything pertaining to the Greek Revolution, but they should use the topics covered as a foundation and entry into the event.

We present *The Greek Revolution: A Critical Dictionary* in the hope that it will fulfill its promise of both reliable information on a broad range of topics and a critical revisiting, rethinking, and understanding that remains, we trust, the primary purpose served by historical knowledge.

Note on Transliteration

The only standard system for the transliteration of the Greek alphabet into languages written in Latin characters is that used for the transliteration of classical Greek. The transliteration of ancient Greek, however, is quite inappropriate for rendering the spelling and especially the phonetics of modern Greek. Accordingly the following modifications have been introduced to make it conform more to the modern morphology and sound of the language. Diphthongs have generally been retained, except in those cases where the modern pronunciation of Greek requires a consonant to be adequately rendered (for example, "aftou" not "autou"). The Greek vowels η and ι have been uniformly rendered with *i*, and similarly ο and ω have been rendered with *o*. The Greek υ has been rendered with *y*, except when it forms part of a diphthong; then it is rendered by *u* (for example, "tou"). The rough breathing has been dropped.

Consonants have generally been rendered phonetically. Thus the Greek β has been rendered by the Latin *v* rather than *b*. The Greek consonant φ is rendered by *ph* in all words with an ancient Greek root. Conversely, Greek names with Latin roots (such as Constantinos) have been transliterated as closely as possible to their original form.

We have generally followed the monotonic accentuation system in force in Greece today for the spelling of Modern Greek, but we have respected individual authors' use of the polytonic system in cases where such a preference occurs in the text of their essays.

The names of modern Greek authors appear in the form used by the authors themselves if they have published work in a foreign language. Inevitably some inconsistencies will remain, but we hope the reader will find this understandable in a book of this nature. Place names have been used in their standard forms in the English language, otherwise they have been transliterated following the general rules adopted in this book.

Words and terms originating in the Turkish language as well as Turkish names have been used in the conventional forms established by usage in English-language writing. In some cases diacritics have been added to help pronunciation of these linguistic forms.

Abbreviations

BOA	Başbakanlık Osmanlı Arşivi (Ottoman State Archives, Istanbul)
DIEEE	*Δελτίον της Ιστορικής και Εθνολογικής Εταιρείας της Ελλάδος* (Bulletin of the Historical and Ethnological Society of Greece)
FO	Foreign Office
GSA	General State Archives (Greece)
HAT	Hatt-ı Hümayun (Imperial [Re]scripts)
IEE	*Ιστορία του Ελληνικού Έθνους*, Vol. XII: *Η Ελληνική Επανάσταση και η ίδρυση του ελληνικού κράτους* (History of the Greek Nation, Vol. XII: The Greek Revolution and the foundation of the Greek state), ed. by G. Christopoulos—I. Bastias (Athens 1975)
INE	*Ιστορία του νέου ελληνισμού*, Vol. III: *Η Ελληνική Επανάσταση 1821–1832* (History of modern Hellenism, Vol. III: The Greek Revolution 1821–1832), ed. by Vasilis Panayiotopoulos (Athens 2003)
Kitromilides—Sklavenitis	*Ιστοριογραφία της νεότερης και σύγχρονης Ελλάδας* (Historiography of modern and contemporary Greece), ed. by Paschalis M. Kitromilides and Triantaphyllos Sklavenitis (Athens 2004), Vols. I–II.
RESEE	*Revue des Études Sud-Est Européennes*
RHSEE	*Revue Historique du Sud-Est Européen*
TNA	The National Archives (London)
Vakalopoulos	Vakalopoulos Apostolos Vakalopoulos, *Ιστορία του νέου ελληνισμού* (History of Modern Hellenism), Vols. V-VI-VII (Thessaloniki 1980–1986)

Foreword

The outbreak of the revolutionary movement at various points in the Greek world during the months of February and March 1821 marked the beginning of a ten-year liberation struggle from Ottoman despotism and culminated with the establishment of an independent and sovereign Greek state after four centuries of subjugation. The Protocol of London, signed by Great Britain, France, and Russia on February 3, 1830, recognizing Greek independence, signaled a new beginning in the history of the Greek people as a modern nation. A one-sided appraisal of the Greek Revolution of 1821 would be impermissible. Based on the available historical evidence, it should be examined from a twofold perspective.

To begin with, the 1821 Revolution must be examined from the Greek point of view, as the preparation for and conduct of the liberation struggle to shake off the Ottoman yoke and establish a state that would be autonomous and sovereign. It is precisely this perspective that gives prominence to the characteristic devotion to freedom that runs through the centuries of Greek history from classical antiquity. As attested by the classical authors of Greek tragedy, freedom for the Greeks has been an existential principle and thoroughly experienced condition of their lives as historical beings. This is corroborated by the fact that no conquest or subjugation at any phase of their history had succeeded in destroying or even undermining the historical survival of the Greek people as a self-aware community.

Historical evidence suggests that the struggle for independence did not begin in 1821. Several uprisings stretching over at least half a century had preceded the Revolution, the earliest and most important being the 1769–1770 Orlov Revolt, which took place during the Russian-Turkish war of 1768–1774. All these early endeavors came to naught, since the stance of the great powers of that era—Great Britain, France, and Russia—on the Ottoman Empire was determined by conflicting interests and balance of power considerations.

Despite early setbacks, the resoluteness of the Greeks to initiate their revolution was strengthened over time, as they correctly interpreted the "signs of the times" anticipating the eventual position of the great powers on the establishment of a Greek state. The foundation of the "Society of Friends" (*Philiki Etaireia*) in Odessa on September 14, 1814, was crucial to the success of the endeavor as a whole. The plans of the Society of Friends bore fruit in early 1821 and resulted in the following watershed events in the preparation of the rising. First, the "Clandestine Council" of Vostitsa took place on January 26–29, 1821. It can hardly be disputed that, despite the initial reservations and partial objections of some participants, this council determined a number of alternative dates in the immediate future for the beginning of the national uprising of the Greeks. Second, the Mani uprising of March 17, 1821, led by Petrobey Mavromichalis, clearly heralded the eruption of the Greek Revolution. Third, the session of the "Messenian Senate" in Kalamata on March 23, 1821, rendered the declaration of revolution two days later, on March 25, 1821, an official fact in European diplomacy with the Senate's appeal to the European courts announcing the Greek struggle of liberation.

The Greeks had to wait for a further nine years for the vindication of their national revolution. This delay was caused by disastrous civil strife and the ambivalence—to say the least—of the great powers. This ambivalence is clearly evinced by their position on the uprising spearheaded by the Sacred Battalion and its leader, Alexandros Ypsilantis, which was suppressed promptly, as well as their toleration, between the years 1825 and 1827, of Ibrahim's bloody invasion of the Peloponnese at the behest of the Ottoman sultan. It was not until July 6, 1827, that the great powers made a determination on the establishment of an independent state. By that point, the atrocities perpetrated by Ibrahim Pasha's forces had taken on unprecedented proportions, while Philhellenic movements, inspired by Lord Byron, had considerably swayed public opinion, especially in Britain and France. The Battle of Navarino on October 20, 1827, strengthened the resolve of the great powers, though they continued to exhibit some ambivalence in proceeding with their final decision. Another three years would pass before the signing of the Protocol of London of February 3, 1830, establishing the independent Greek state.

Despite the nine-year delay between the outbreak of the Revolution and its conclusion, it is indisputable that the moment the Revolution broke out the Greeks had made the irrevocable decision to see it to its end, at any cost. This end could only be the shattering of the Ottoman yoke and the establishment of an independent Greek state founded on the liberal democratic principles and values of the American Revolution, outlined in the Declaration of Independence signed on July 4, 1776, and of the French Revolution, embedded in the 1789 Declaration of the Rights of Man and Citizen. This was evident in the early and rather rudimentary Declaration of the Messenian Senate, convened in Kalamata on March 23, 1821. It was even more clearly manifested in the successive initiatives of the Greeks to draft a constitution that culminated in the "Political Constitution" Greece adopted in Troezen on May 1, 1827. Despite its limited implementation due to the conditions at the time, the "Political Constitution" can still be regarded as one of the most consummate Greek constitutions, on account of its pronounced liberal democratic temper. The innovative institutional elements in the establishment of the principle of national sovereignty were one of its distinguishing features. These elements comprise the plenitude and comprehensiveness of the institutionalization of the fundamental human rights and the fully elaborated formulation of the principle of the division of powers, which is of key importance for the institutional foundations of representative democracy and the rule of law.

However, the national revolution of the Greeks and the establishment of the modern Greek state as per the 1830 Protocol of London should be also considered from the additional perspective of how and why the nascent Greek state became the herald and mold of the type of nation-state that was to become prevalent in Europe as a general model of state organization. This state model entails a form of sovereignty that ensures the state's autonomy and self-government while retaining its core national attributes. This line of inquiry is suggested by a historiographical view that points out that the modern Greek state, by virtue of its birth and of the rapid propagation of the model on which it was based, became a quasi foundation of Europe in its present form. We take the term Europe to signify indiscriminately both the member-states of the European Union as well as those that currently are not.

As we have already noted, the formative period preceding the birth of the first nation-state in Europe was anything but straightforward. Several earlier Greek attempts at independence had failed. Numerous obstacles and the attendant lamentable vicissitudes are the hallmark of post-1821 developments. To a substantial extent, this was due to the ambivalence and the ensuing irresolution of the great powers of the era, which had conflicting interests and were incapable of deciding on a clear position regarding the fate of the Ottoman Empire, even though the latter had already shown multiple and substantial signs of decline. The failure of the great powers to wean themselves from the despotic empires that had formerly been dominant in Europe was undoubtedly conducive to this unfavorable development for the Greeks. Although this may seem, prima facie, contradictory, the ideology of the Enlightenment was not a factor that could help the great powers overcome their irresolution on the Greek question. We may draw this inference from the following. No one may ignore the fact that the formation and elaboration of some sort of European "idea" and "ideology" were due to the Enlightenment; the same applies to our own contemporary endeavor to build a complete European edifice through the integration of the European Union. The Enlightenment, however, favored the reform rather than the radical transformation of the modern state model. Enlightenment exponents were aiming not at the obliteration of the model of the modern state but at its reform by introducing and consolidating representative democracy and ensuring the unimpeded exercise of fundamental human rights, especially individual rights and civil liberties.

Romanticism emerged as a response to the Enlightenment and exerted a manifold influence over diverse forms of cultural expression, asserting itself in some instances as a genuine revolutionary movement by configuring and underpinning the implementation of political change inspired by the aspirations of national movements. One of the most prominent of these changes affected, through the adoption of the model of the nation-state, the way in which the national community was conceptualized, as strongly attested by the example of the formation of the modern Greek state. The substantial Philhellenic movement, with the emblematic figure of Lord Byron at its head, grew drastically in size following the siege and exodus of Mesolonghi on April 10, 1826, and played a crucial part in the decision of the great powers to create a Greek nation-state in 1827, later formalized with the London Protocol of 1830. Within the next few decades, this newly born nation-state was to become the prevailing norm of state building in Europe, as demonstrated by subsequent developments in Belgium, Italy, Germany, and the states that emerged in Greece's immediate vicinity in southeastern Europe. Thus it can be argued that the birth of the nation-state, with the emergence of modern Greece as an emblematic early example, is deeply indebted to Romanticism and its liberal ideological claims and expressions.

The foregoing allow us to draw two conclusions. First, it was through the national revolution of 1821 and the realization of the vision to create a nation-state founded on principles of representative democracy and fundamental human rights that the Greeks eloquently and thoroughly refute, to this day, the conspicuously inaccurate views of those who dispute the fact that contemporary Greece forms, by virtue of its modern origins, part of the West. These observers claim that, even though Greece was certainly the cradle of Classical culture and therefore a fundamental pillar of Western culture, contemporary Greeks and

Greece do not belong to the West. No one is justified in disputing the fact that Greece, already at the point of attainment of its independence, was and remained part of the West and, a fortiori, a true buttress of Western culture. The history and geographical position of Greece attest to and irrefutably substantiate the first conclusion. The nation-state of Greece is the West's outer boundary to the East. This increases the significance of Greece as part of the West in proportion to the fact that, due to its geographical position and its cultural origins, it is in a position to keep its gaze turned eastward, thus facilitating the cultural dialogue between East and West. In this manner, it confutes the claims of the alleged "clash of civilizations" and channels this cultural dialogue into the protection of peace, by building bridges and enabling the unimpeded communication between cultures. All this takes on a new and cardinal importance in our turbulent times.

Our second conclusion points to the significance of the model of the Greek nation-state, established in 1830 in the form that was to become a general model of state organization, as the solid foundation on which the European edifice should be based, as the European Union progresses to its eventual complete integration. Therefore, the European Union may and should be organized as a federal state defined by the principle of representative democracy, which, in turn, is founded on the rule of law and the protection of fundamental human rights. This federal state, thus configured, would mold an authentic European consciousness in the minds of the citizens of the member states. Hence, in this framework, the central organs of European democracy will possess extensive powers customarily accorded to federal states, thus enabling the European Union to fulfill its global historical mission of defending the values of peace, democracy, and social justice. Every member state, in its capacity as a nation-state, will irrevocably retain its inalienable distinctive national characteristics that determine its autonomy and self-government and define the horizon of its historical origins and prospects. In the course of this unfolding of history, every nation-state will make consciously and generously its "European contribution" in order to ensure the perpetual enrichment of European democracy and European culture.

The Greek national revolution led to the emergence of modern Greece as a nation-state in its exemplary form and thus possessed a far-reaching significance for the European context as a whole. If we examine and assess the Greek Revolution in this perspective we might be able to appreciate it as an important turning point in the history of modern Europe and recognize further in it the dynamic of the appropriate acceleration of the construction of the European edifice as it builds toward its final completion; a completion desirable for more than one reason.

The editors and contributors to this imposing volume are to be commended and congratulated for making available this timely, comprehensive, and pluralist reference work that can serve as a reliable compass in navigating the complexities of a historical subject of global significance.

Prokopios Pavlopoulos
Former President of the Hellenic Republic

THE GREEK REVOLUTION

Introduction: In an Age of Revolution

The "age of revolution" is a historiographical concept that emerged from the work of three great historians active in the immediate post–World War II period: R. R. Palmer, Eric Hobsbawm, and Jacques Godechot. Their writing and ideas about the nature of history and historical thought left an indelible mark on twentieth-century historiography in the United States, Britain, and continental Europe. Godechot is the least well-known in English-reading scholarship, but he was the first of the three to speak of the French Revolution as a broader European and world phenomenon, not just a major upheaval in the political and social history of France. In describing France as the "Great Nation" (*la Grande Nation*), he demonstrated that what had happened in France in the 1790s, and the ramifications of those events throughout the rest of Europe and beyond, had in fact catapulted the whole world into a revolutionary upheaval of far-reaching consequences (Godechot 1956). In 1955, Godechot co-authored one of the major papers presented at the International Congress of Historical Sciences at Madrid with Yale historian R. R. Palmer, putting forward the idea of an international movement of political change and liberation that extended throughout Western civilization in the second half of the eighteenth century. In this sense, the Atlantic became the Mediterranean of the new age.

By contextualizing this early formulation of the idea of a transnational revolution in the Western world, we can recognize the political and ideological motivations connected with the Cold War that guided historical thought at the time. The idea enunciated in that early article foreshadowed the great works in which Godechot and Palmer respectively expanded and documented their historical interpretation. Thus, Godechot's *La Grande Nation: L'expansion de la France révolutionnaire dans le monde* (1956) and the two volumes of Palmer's

The Age of the Democratic Revolution (1959–1964) proved to be milestones that defined a period in world history known as the age of revolution.

Acknowledging the Cold War dimension of Palmer's conception of the "Age of the Democratic Revolution" recognizes its historicity but should not neutralize its historiographical significance. On the contrary, by elaborating the concept of the "democratic revolution," Palmer was reclaiming the revolutionary origins of the American republic, and, as Hannah Arendt also recognized at the time, he refused to concede a monopoly of revolutionary credentials to the Soviet Union. It was precisely those revolutionary origins of the American nation that the civil rights movement claimed in the 1960s, at exactly the time that Palmer was producing the second volume of his work. This broader contextualization should be borne in mind in appraising the significance of the historiographical idea of the age of revolution.

In 1962, the two pioneers of the idea were joined by another historian, Eric Hobsbawm, who used the term age of revolution in the title of what is arguably his most influential book. Hobsbawm brought the perspective of Marxism to bear on his definition and understanding of the age of revolution. For him, the two revolutions that defined the age were not the American Revolution of 1776 and the French Revolution of 1789, as was the case with Palmer's approach, but rather the Industrial Revolution and the French Revolution. The Industrial Revolution transformed European society in radical ways, beginning with its original hearth in England and spreading to the Continent with equally revolutionizing effects. Hobsbawm saw the French Revolution primarily as a political revolution that provided "the vocabulary and the issues of liberal and radical-democratic politics for most of the world" (Hobsbawm 1962, 74). Beyond this, however, Hobsbawm recognized the French Revolution, in the years 1789–1814, as a period of deep and violent class struggle, and it was the dynamic of the social conflicts that it unleashed that gave it its distinct character and shaped its legacy.

The idea of the age of revolution elicited strong and varied criticism upon its inception in the 1950s and 1960s (Armitage and Subrahmanyam 2010, xvi–xviii; Armitage 2013). It proved, nevertheless, remarkably fertile and capable of revising and renewing itself as a matrix of historical research. Perhaps its most solemn affirmation as an operational concept of historical research came in 1989 at the bicentennial of the French Revolution with the world congress at the Sorbonne and the imposing four-volume publication *L'image de la Révolution française dans le monde*, which projected the French Revolution as a global phenomenon shaping the heritage of modernity.

The Sorbonne Congress decisively placed the age of revolution in a global perspective, a development that motivated original thinking and research tracing the expressions of pertinent phenomena in multiple contexts on a global scale. Some of the most interesting and suggestive results of this broadened perspective have been produced by researching the age of revolution beyond Europe, on the eastern and southern littorals of the Mediterranean (Coller 2013), in South America and the Caribbean, and in Asia and Africa (Armitage and Subrahmanyam 2010).

The Greek world is very much part of the story of the age of revolution, even before the emergence of the globalized perspective. Greek expressions of the age of revolution, like the radical movement of Rhigas Velestinlis in the 1790s, invariably make their appearance in the works of Godechot, Palmer, and Hobsbawm. Hobsbawm brings into the picture other manifestations of revolutionary change and movement in the Greek world and its broader southeastern European context, including forms of primitive social protest expressed by banditry and various other instances of resistance to Ottoman rule, culminating in the revolutionary outbreaks and the national movements of the 1820s.

The bicentennial of the Greek Revolution (1821–2021) provides a new context to revisit events, to reappraise in greater detail the participation of the Greek world in the age of revolution, and to read the whole range of events in southeastern Europe from the 1790s to the 1820s as components of the broader picture, which has by now taken on a global dimension. To read the historical record in light of new approaches and an expanded interpretative framework, it is imperative to delve into the events that took place over the ten-year period of the Greek Revolution. The present project aspires to make accessible to international scholarship the actual events in Greece and the broader Greek world, a world delimited by Greek culture and language in southeastern Europe and the eastern Mediterranean. It is a story of heroism and tragedy, of passion and conflict, of pathos and pity, but also of resilience, hope, and an indomitable determination to win the struggle of liberty after many centuries of subjection to alien despotic rule.

In introducing the collective narrative of that ten-year drama, the first questions to ask would perhaps be the following: was it really a revolution, and does it really fit into the age of revolution? These questions are provocative but necessary, and the answers are neither obvious nor easy. If appraised by the standards and requirements of scholarship, the questions might be handled by referring to the primary authoritative theories of revolution that have been put forward by historians and social scientists in the last few decades.

The Greek Revolution, considered in its entirety, supports several contemporary theories of revolution. In the following pages we observe Crane Brinton's concept of the "eternal Figaro" in the social and political criticism articulated amid intense ideological conflict in the two decades leading up to the revolution (Brinton 1952, 72–74). Once the uprising was set in motion in the Morea and Rumeli, the revolutionary dynamic of peasant society helped spread the insurrection in those regions. This illustrates the classic analysis of the "revolution from below" in the historical sociology of revolutions by Barrington Moore, Jr., and later Theda Skocpol. Moore's comparison of England and France on the question of peasant society and its significance for the prospects of revolution is relevant in the consideration of the Greek case: the integrity of peasant society in the Morea, Rumeli, Crete, and elsewhere in the Greek lands can explain how the revolution found its necessary social bases in those regions, survived once it broke out, and persisted amid the civil wars and other adversities of the revolutionary decade.

The Greek Revolution can also be interpreted through the lens of two theoretical approaches that elaborate on Alexis de Tocqueville's idea of the revolution of rising expectations, which points out that revolutions come not when things are at their worst, but rather when they are on the road to improvement, encouraging unrealistic expectations. The resulting disappointment leads people to resort to violence and revolution. In Tocqueville's diagnosis, this was what led to the French Revolution. James Davies and Ted Gurr expanded on this theory in their own analyses of revolution, which traced the origins of revolutionary action to discontent resulting from a contraction in well-being following a period of improvement and to a sense of relative deprivation, respectively.

Although these theories were based on evidence provided by changing societies in the twentieth century, they could be tested on the basis of the historical record provided by the Greek Revolution. It should be remembered that the revolution came to the Greek world after a long period of social and cultural change in the eighteenth century and remarkable economic development during in the Napoleonic wars and the continental blockade. When all this came to an end after 1815, the disappointment of rising expectations created a climate of discontent that made possible the work of the Philiki Etaireia, the secret society founded in 1814 with the intention to prepare the revolution, as explained by C. Chatzopoulos in this volume.

The social-psychological perspective on the Greek Revolution could be greatly enriched by considering Moore's later work on the significance of the sense of injustice and the moral outrage resulting from it (Moore 1978). Such feelings may motivate resistance and revolutionary action. The literature of the Greek version of the radical democratic Enlightenment both before and during the course of the Greek Revolution, is replete with examples of how the sense of injustice experienced by Greeks with an enhanced awareness of the condition of subjection to which their society had been reduced and which they were fighting to shake off. The Greeks' sense of injustice was articulated in both social and national terms, another reminder of the revolutionary potential of national identity that has not escaped Moore's attention (Moore 1978, 484–489).

One final perspective of theories of revolution that could be reasonably applied to the Greek experience comes from the work of Charles Tilly and, more precisely, from his arguments on the geopolitical dimension of revolutionary changes. There can be little doubt that international war in the fifty years or so preceding 1821 set a broader geopolitical environment for the coming of the Greek Revolution. Multiple Russo-Turkish wars spanning the 1770s though 1812 set a context of imperial conflicts that encouraged revolutionary expectancy in southeastern Europe, as recorded in many contemporary sources. As Vasilis Molos suggests in this volume, the Russo-Turkish conflict in the Mediterranean in 1768–1774 could be seen as having planted the seeds of a movement of resistance to Ottoman rule among the Greeks.

If war in southeastern Europe in the 1770s provided an initial impulse, it was war on a continental scale brought about by Napoleon's imperial ambitions that allowed the Greeks to begin thinking concretely of their future in the new terms of national sovereignty and other political ideas emanating from revolutionary France. It would not be an exaggeration to claim that the Greek Revolution became possible only after shifting to aspirations of national statehood, thus reminding us of John Dunn's idea that revolutions are profoundly political phenomena focused on change in the structure of power and directed by a strong element of human agency. It is precisely this strong element of human agency that can be recognized in the Greek struggle for freedom, amid all the conflicts and contradictions marking the behavior of those involved.

Geopolitics not only brought about the preconditions of revolutionary change but also shaped its outcome. Great-power antagonism over predominance in the Mediterranean, which had long favored the survival of the Ottoman Empire, paradoxically also generated the first step in its gradual dismemberment with the liberation of Greece. Beyond war and power politics, geopolitics in a literal sense, in the primordial sense of the weight of geography in determining the course of historical events, remained a fundamental aspect of collective destinies in the region. In fact, one might suggest that the whole range of historical events, comprising the origins, course, and eventual outcome of the Greek Revolution, could be placed in a "neo-Braudelian" understanding, pointing to the geographical location of the Greek peninsula and its surrounding archipelagos at the center of the Mediterranean Sea, its Balkan hinterlands and the shape of its terrain, rugged and mountainous, as critical factors that set the scene of the revolution and determined its outcome.

The richness of theories of revolution, so expertly surveyed by Bailey Stone (2014), could provide many other angles for considering the Greek Revolution in a comparative perspective, allowing new insights to be gained and making possible alternative readings of events—in short, making possible a critical understanding. The recognition of the significance of events in Greece during the 1820s in the light of theories of revolution could in turn provide correctives to the theories themselves. The theories referred to above, structuralist, social-psychological, and geopolitical, tend to overlook one significant component in the dynamics of modern revolutions: nationalism. This aspect of the revolutionary phenomenon is amply illustrated by the Greek revolutionary experience.

Nationalism remains the major political force of modernity, leading societies from premodern feudal forms of organization into the modern world. This promise can explain its power and persistence. In the literature on the age of revolution, Godechot and Palmer duly recognized the significance of nationalism, but it was primarily Hobsbawm who underlined the emergence of the modern idea of the nation as one of the major developments shaping the age and the world (Hobsbawm 1962, 163–177). In discussing the phenomenon of nationalism, Hobsbawm points out that the Greek struggle for independence was a unique expression of the age of revolution in that it illustrated the way "the perennial fight of the sheepherding clansmen and bandit-heroes against *any* real government fused with the ideas of middle-class nationalism and the French Revolution" (ibid., 172–173).

According to Hobsbawm, the uniqueness of the Greek example in the age of revolution can explain its appeal as the "inspiration of nationalists and liberals everywhere." It was in Greece that "an entire people did rise against the oppressor in a manner which could be plausibly identified with the cause of the European left." The story of that rising is related in the essays that make up this critical dictionary.

The Greek Revolution was a peasant war and, as such, amounted to a social revolution in a society subjected to multiple forms of inequality and injustice. The peasant population joined the insurrection to grab land and free itself from despotism and the inequality that sustained it. At the same time, a liberal "republican" revolution aspired to overturn an *ancien régime* of unaccountable despotic autocracy and replace it with a government based on the rule of law and respect for individual rights and civil liberties. The whole project of the Greek Enlightenment essentially amounted to this objective. Finally, the Greek Revolution was largely a national revolution, in which a community claimed its rights to sovereign national statehood in the world of free nations. Under the influence of the Enlightenment, this community had become conscious of its historical lineage, in whose terms it had come to conceive of itself as a modern nation. In this sense the Greek Revolution is a paradigmatic case illustrating how nationalism remains "a persistent force in revolutions" (Goldstone 2003, 16). In fact, it was a nation-building project in a literal sense. By means of their involvement in revolutionary action, regardless of the original motivation of such involvement, or through suffering the consequences of fighting and upheaval brought about by the war of independence, diverse social groups, with multiple ethnic, linguistic, and class backgrounds, emerged as Greeks, members of the national community fighting for its freedom. One element of identity held all these groups together: their shared belonging to the Orthodox Church. This can explain both the religious overtones of the war of independence, as recorded in many sources, and the critical role of Orthodoxy in forging the modern national identity that was imprinted on the population of free Greece.

The aspiration of national liberation and the affirmation of the national identity of the country that emerged from the revolution made it intelligible to contemporary European political thought. In the midst of the climate of repression prevailing in Restoration Europe, the risings of 1820–1821 in Italy and southeastern Europe, and in the Romanian and Greek lands, were the earliest expressions of the hope of freedom in the face of the counterrevolution. Whereas all other risings proved abortive, the revolution in Greece lived on for ten years and eventually managed, amid many setbacks and sorrows, to give rise to an independent and sovereign national state, the first such achievement in post-Napoleonic Europe along with the emergence of the kingdom of Belgium in 1830 (Manessis 1959). This can explain the appeal of events in Greece to liberal public opinion in Europe and America that generated the Philhellenic movement, expertly surveyed by Roderick Beaton and Ioannis Evrigenis in this volume. It also explains the hopes it inspired in liberal political thought, whose leading exponents at the time turned their attention to revolutionary Greece. This included Benjamin Constant, who issued an *Appeal to Christian Nations in favor of the Greeks* in 1825, at the height of his political career. Most notably the nation- and state-building efforts of the Greeks attracted the interest of Jeremy Bentham, who devoted a considerable part of his preparatory work for the *Constitutional Code* to commentaries and advice to the Greeks on the construction of a democratic state in the liberated country.

In the following pages, thirty-nine authors explore the Greek aspects of the age of revolution. Our project points to an expanding historiographical horizon and tries to fill in some of the lacunae left in mainstream literature on the much-discussed subject of the age of revolution, which has been revived by new debates in contemporary scholarship (Bell and Mintzker 2018). We propose not a

complete new history of the Greek Revolution but a critical revisiting and rethinking of its main features and constituents as a broad historical phenomenon.

Before turning to the essays, readers seeking a more substantive knowledge
and critical understanding of the Greek Revolution should consider a few historiographical issues surrounding the subject.

The first issue concerns the longstanding debate over the beginning of the
revolution. Although its significance is primarily symbolic, this issue still carries considerable emotional weight. In planning the revolution, the Philiki
Etaireia and its leader, Alexandros Ypsilantis, discussed the possibility of beginning the revolt on the day of the Annunciation, March 25, a major religious
feast day for the Orthodox Church, when masses of people would be gathered
at church and thus readily available to be incited to rise against tyranny. Events
overtook these plans, however, and the revolution broke out at different geographical points over the course of February and March 1821. In February,
Ypsilantis himself initiated the rising in Moldavia and in Wallachia. The
revolt broke out in March at various places in the Morea, at Kalamata, at Vostitsa,
at Kalavryta, and at Patras, as related by Dionysis Tzakis in this volume. On
April 24 the Levant Company consul at Patras, Philip Green, reported that "a
Revolt on the part of the Greeks against the Turkish government within Morea"
was underway (TNA, SP 105, 139, f. 351).

Revolutionary events reached a symbolic climax on March 25 at Patras,
where the local archbishop, Germanos, raised the standard of revolution and the
Greek captains took an oath to either liberate their homeland or die. Already
on March 23, the "Messenian Senate," the revolutionary body that had been set
up at Kalamata by the chiefs of Mani, had issued a proclamation signed by
Petrobey Mavromichalis to "the European courts," announcing that the Greeks
had risen against tyranny and were requesting the support and advice of the
European nations in their "sacred and just struggle to renew the suffering Greek
nation" (Panagiotopoulos 1967). This amounted to the first diplomatic act whereby
the revolution was seeking international recognition. Its date, therefore, could
rightfully be considered the day Greece emerged as a free nation, claiming its
place in the world of sovereign states. The Messenian proclamation of Greek independence eventually found its way into the European press (e.g. *The Morning
Chronicle* [London], June 15, 1821).

Years later, the French historian François Pouqueville, brother of the
French consul at Patras, alleged in his history of the Greek Revolution that
the revolution had been proclaimed on March 25 by Archbishop of Old Patras
Germanos at the Monastery of Agia Lavra, near Kalavryta. This story has remained apocryphal; Archbishop Germanos says nothing about it in his memoirs. However, in the postrevolutionary period, its strong symbolism inspired

a powerful legend, which was most characteristically recorded in a highly evocative painting by Theodoros Vryzakis, a Romantic painter of the revolution, in 1865.

The fact remains, nevertheless, that on March 23–25, 1821, two highly symbolic events expressed the revolutionary will of the Greeks: the raising of the cross as the standard of revolution by Archbishop Germanos at Patras, and the Messenian declaration of Greek independence to the European courts. In view of this important symbolic legacy, therefore, it was not without foundation that in 1838, King Othon established March 25 as the national day of Greece by royal decree, marking the anniversary of the Greek Revolution. The nation-building process on the symbolic level was thus set in order.

A second, substantive issue in the history of the revolution concerns the fate and handling of the country's archaeological heritage during a decade of war, violence, and upheaval. For centuries, foreign looters preyed on the antiquities of Greece and the indifference of both the country's rulers and its inhabitants allowed time and the elements to reduce the splendid monuments of antiquity to ruin. Lord Elgin's looting of the monuments of the Acropolis (1801–1811) is only the best-known example of such operations of destruction. Ioannis Gennadios, the book lover and Greek ambassador to the Court of St. James, told the story of "archeologising" invaders and looters years ago, but it must be retold many times over in order to underline the significance of the subject. Shortly after the looting of the Acropolis, two other important monuments of classical art in the country, the temple of Athena Aphaia at Aigina and the temple of Apollo at Phygaleia in the Western Peloponnese, were looted. Their sculptures were taken away and sold and can now be seen at the Glyptotek in Munich and at the British Museum in London, respectively. Foreign diplomatic agents in Athens before and during the revolution, including Louis François Fauvel, consul of France, and Georg Christian Gropius, vice-consul of Austria, partook in the looting and illicit trade of Greek antiquities.

The story of the fate of ancient monuments and works of classical art during the years of the revolution up to the period of rule by Ioannis Capodistrias constitutes one of the serious desiderata of the historiography of the revolution. The outbreak of the revolution provoked concern in some circles about the safety of the antiquities of Greece, especially Athens. In August 1821, the British ambassador to Constantinople submitted a note to the Ottoman foreign minister, Reis Effendi, asking him to instruct Ottoman troops to respect the antiquities of Athens. The Grand Vezir complied with the request. War, however, is not a propitious environment for antiquities, and the monuments of Athens were heavily damaged during the repeated sieges of the Acropolis.

The revolutionary Greeks themselves appeared fully aware of the need to protect the antiquities of the country. The provisional legislative body of eastern central Greece, the Areopagus, issued explicit instructions in November 1821 to the minister of civil administration charging him with "the protection of antiquities." This was the first ever official declaration of the government's duty to protect the archaeological wealth of the country. A similar instruction was issued on February 27, 1822, by Ioannis Kolettis, minister of military affairs in the first national government set up by the First National Assembly, to General Voutier, directing him to take care not to damage the monuments during the siege of the Acropolis by Greek forces (Petrakos 2015, 1: 26–27).

Despite the concern shown by the revolutionary authorities, looting of antiquities in the liberated parts of the country continued in the 1820s, especially in the islands. Incidents of looting of antiquities on the island of Anafi and illegal excavations on Milos are characteristic. Adamantios Korais wrote from Paris to the Greek authorities urging them to take measures to protect the antiquities.

Throughout the revolutionary decade, concern for the archaeological heritage of the country surfaced from time to time amid the pressures of war. In 1825, the prerevolutionary Philomousos Etaireia of Athens was revived, and one of its earliest initiatives was the conservation and restoration of ancient monuments and the collections of antiquities scattered in houses in the city in order to prevent them from being sold to foreigners. The executive endorsed all these proposals. In the same year, the central government instructed local police forces in Athens and on Milos to prevent the removal and the export of antiquities.

In 1825, as minister of the interior, Grigorios Dikaios, better known as Papaflessas, issued an edict specifying the duties of the commissioner of education, who was charged with issuing instructions to local authorities and school teachers to collect antiquities from their regions so every school in the country would have its museum and thus prevent foreigners from preying on the heritage of the country.

The Third National Assembly at Troezen, which voted on the *Political Constitution of Greece* and elected Ioannis Capodistrias as the first head of state of the liberated country, in its ordinance of May 1, 1827, on administrative organization included among the duties of district commissioners the responsibility "to prevent the sale or export of antiquities" (Petrakos 2015, 1: 58–59).

One of Capodistrias's earliest measures was the establishment of the Archaeological Service in 1829 for the supervision and protection of Greek antiquities. One of the governor's first concerns was the establishment of a home on Aigina for the orphans of the struggle. He also provided for a national museum, to be housed in the orphanage building, and he appointed a fellow Corfiot scholar, Andreas Moustoxydis, as the first ephor. Under Capodistrias, Greek archaeology entered a new phase of regulation and protection and was established as one of the primary objectives of statecraft in the liberated country (Petrakos 2015, vols. 2–3).

A third aspect of the social history of the Greek Revolution, which seems marked by an unexpected topicality in the twenty-first century, is the phenomenon of refugee movements and forced migration. War, military campaigns, and Ottoman reprisals caused considerable upheaval among large populations in all parts of the Greek world and generated multiple waves of forced migration as civilians attempted to flee to safety. It is impossible to secure accurate estimates of numbers of losses and civilian casualties of the war for such a distant period, but estimates range from about 230,000 to 600,000 (Komis 2003, 235). Refugee movements are also difficult to estimate in quantitative terms, but surviving evidence allows us to follow in considerable detail the ebb and flow of forced migration during the revolution.

Refugee movements originated primarily as a consequence of the defeat of revolutionary outbreaks at various continental areas and islands. The violent suppression of revolutionary action by the Ottomans forced local populations to seek refuge in the liberated regions of mainland Greece or in neighboring islands that appeared safer. Thus large numbers of refugees left the coastal areas of western and northwestern Asia Minor, Magnesia and Pilion in Thessaly, Thrace, the areas of Arta and Souli in Epirus, the areas of Naousa and Chalkidiki in Macedonia, and the islands of Chios and Kasos following their destruction by Ottoman forces in 1822 and 1824, respectively. Successive refugee waves left Crete after every violent suppression of revolutionary action in the island, fleeing to neighboring Cycladic islands like Milos, Ios, and Syros, or to Nafplio. Refugees from Asia Minor initially sought refuge at Psara and then, after the destruction of the island, moved on and settled on other islands, notably in Amorgos but also further west at Salamina, where they encountered other refugee groups fleeing the repeated violent conflicts across the straits in Attica. Refugee groups from further north, such as in Thessaly and Macedonia, went to the Northern Sporades islands, while Epirots went to Mesolonghi and from there to other localities in Rumeli. A considerable refugee wave of noncombatants moved from the Peloponnese to the Ionian islands, especially Zakynthos.

Forced migration was not limited to Greeks. The Muslim population, both Turkish-speaking and Greek-speaking, of the main theaters of revolutionary action felt equally exposed, also resulting in refugee waves. In the Peloponnese they took refuge mostly in the major urban centers and fortified towns to be under the protection of Ottoman authorities. This also happened in Crete, where the Turko-Cretans congregated in the main cities Iraklio, Rethymno, and Chania. Peloponnesian Muslims, like their Christian compatriots, also fled to British-occupied Zakynthos seeking to escape the consequences of military confrontations.

The emergence of refugee waves and forced migration also invited relief policies. The earliest such measure was taken by the provisional administration of free Greece on April 20, 1822, in order to relieve the plight of the Chian refugees following the massacre of Chios, which shocked international public opinion at the time. In May 1824 a census was taken of persons in need on account of the war, primarily widows, orphans, and people with infirmities, including refugees. That was a step toward better-coordinated relief policies. One of Capodistrias's earliest measures as head of the government was the instruction in January 1828 to register refugees in the Nafplio area in order to better meet their needs. Relief was also distributed to refugees in Aigina and other islands. Large-scale relief also arrived from the United States on repeated occasions, on the initiative of the American Philhellenes Dr. Samuel Gridley Howe and Peckan Milles (Andriotis 2020, 13–14).

Regardless of their origin, refugees arriving in areas under the control of Greek authorities primarily sought relocation in towns. This was a decisive factor in the growth of the major urban centers in the fledgling new state. In 1825, the two largest groups in the population of Nafplio, the capital city of the new state, after those originating in various localities in the Peloponnese, were refugee groups from Asia Minor and Crete. Under Capodistrias, a special suburb for the settlement of refugees was founded next to the capital with the promising name Pronoia, meaning providence. In 1827, a refugee group from Smyrna calling itself "Free Smyrniots" requested permission from the Third National Assembly to establish a "New Smyrna" in the area of the Isthmus of Corinth. They had the support of Dr. Howe, and although their request was accepted, their plans did not ultimately materialize.

The most significant and lasting result of the relocation of refugee groups was the emergence of Ermoupolis, a major new urban center on the island of Syros. Settled primarily by Chian survivors of the 1822 massacre but also by large groups from Smyrna, Kydonies, and Constantinople, the new coastal town, named in 1825 after the ancient Greek patron god of commerce, grew into the main port and commercial city of new Greece until it was eclipsed by Pireus in the late nineteen century. Thus, the story of forced migration and refugee movements in the Greek Revolution also inaugurates the history of social change in the new nation state.

A fourth historiographical issue that needs to be addressed in building a fuller picture of the revolution is the phenomenon of civil wars. The two civil wars of the revolutionary period, the first in late 1823 and the early months of 1824, and the second in late 1824 with repercussions throughout 1825, constituted important phases in the politics of the Greek Revolution but also put the survival of the revolution in serious jeopardy. Earlier writing on the revolution treated the civil wars as serious affronts to the ideal of national unity. Although an implicit moralizing perspective may be politically edifying, it does not do much for a substantive understanding of the phenomenon of civil strife and conflict. If we turn back to the theories of revolution through which the Greek Revolution might be understood and interpreted, we will recognize the incidence of civil war as an integral part of the revolutionary process *qua* revolution, that is, a radical overturn and subversion of an established social order.

Crane Brinton was the first to recognize conflict and dissension in the ranks of the revolutionaries as an integral component of the unfolding logic of revolutionary change, while Barrington Moore, Jr., in his own classic theoretical analysis of the American Civil War, pointed out that civil war can in fact be understood as revolution. Civil or internal war also occupies a central role in the logic of revolution in the social-psychological interpretation proposed by Ted Gurr.

The insights drawn from theories of revolution can be helpful in reinterpreting and reappraising the phenomenon of civil wars in the Greek Revolution. The conflicts between regional elites over the control of the new state under construction can be understood as components of the revolutionary process itself, out of which emerged the modern community of the Greek nation. Civil wars, which represented the birth pangs of the national community, were essentially the resistance of traditional, premodern forms of organization of power and social inequality to the requirements of change, equality, and new social order immanent in the project of constructing a modern national community and state. The pertinent suggestions of John Petropulos and Nikiforos Diamandouros on the civil wars of the Greek Revolution point to this enhanced understanding of the subject.

A final historiographical issue that looms on the broader horizon of the subjects treated in this collective project has to do with the statecraft whereby the founder of the Greek *politeia,* Ioannis Capodistrias, attempted to lay the institutional foundations of a modern political order worthy of the fighting nation's sacrifices and hopes. Capodistrias was possibly the most distinguished Greek of his time, with a clear sense of the world and the requirements of modern politics. Such was the basis of his judgment as to what the still-fighting nation needed in order to truly secure its freedom following its deliverance from alien despotism: a well-ordered modern polity under the rule of law. That was the objective to which his statecraft was directed.

Many aspects of Capodistrias's statecraft are treated in the essays of this volume: his diplomacy, which secured the independence of Greece, along with his military, educational, and ecclesiastical policies. His statecraft as a whole, and his concept of the modern state that would best serve the interest of the liberated Greek people, is one of the larger projects that this collection invites scholars of modern history to undertake. Capodistrias belongs to the few select statesmen in the history of politics who had the opportunity to become founders of states, the admirable political leaders who are extolled in the history of political thought by observers ranging from Plutarch to Machiavelli to David Hume. The modern state-building to which he devoted his life and paid for with his death, and the way in which he faced up to the antinomies of politics and the responsibilities of leadership, should emerge as a primary object of reflection on the occasion of the bicentennial of the Greek Revolution.

Paschalis M. Kitromilides

References

Andriotis, Nicos. 2020. *Πρόσφυγες στην Ελλάδα 1821–1940* [Refugees in Greece 1821–1940]. Athens.

Armitage, David. 2013. Foreword to *The Age of the Democratic Revolution*, by R. R. Palmer, xv–xxiv. Princeton, NJ.

Armitage, David, and Sanjay Subranhmayam, eds. 2010. *The Age of Revolution in Global Context c. 1760–1840*. New York.

Bell, David A., and Yair Mintzaker, eds. 2018. *Rethinking the Age of Revolutions: France and the Birth of the Modern World*. Oxford.

Bentham, Jeremy. 1990. *Securities Against Misrule and Other Constitutional Writings for Tripoli and Greece*. Edited by Philip Scholfield. Oxford.

Brinton, Crane. 1952. *The Anatomy of Revolution*. New York.

Coller, Ian. 2013. "The Revolutionary Mediterranean." In *A Companion to the French Revolution*, edited by Peter McPhee, 414–434. Oxford.

Dunn, John. 1989. *Modern Revolutions*, 2nd ed. Cambridge.

Godechot, Jacques. 1956. *La Grande Nation: L'expansion de la France révolutionnaire dans le monde*. Paris.

Goldstone, Jack. 2003. *Revolutions: Theoretical, Comparative and Historical Studies*. Belmont, CA.

Gurr, Ted. 1970. *Why Men Rebel*. Princeton, NJ.

Hobsbawm, Eric. 1962. *The Age of Revolution*. New York.

Komis, C. 2003. "Προσφυγικές μετακινήσεις" ["Refugee movements"]. *INE* 3:235–244.

Manessis, A. 1959. *Deux états nés en 1830*. Brussels.

Moore, Barrington, Jr. 1966. *Social Origins of Dictatorship and Democracy: Lord and Peasant in the Making of the Modern World*. Boston.

Moore, Barrington, Jr. 1978. *Injustice: The Social Bases of Obedience and Revolt.* Boston.

Palmer, R. R. 1959–1964. *The Age of the Democratic Revolution.* 2 vols. Princeton, NJ.

Panagiotopoulos, V. P. 1967. "Δύο προκηρύξεις της Μεσσηνιακής Συγκλήτου" ["Two proclamations of the Messenian Senate"]. *Μεσσηνιακά Γράμματα* 2:591–598.

Petrakos, V. Ch., ed. 2015. *Ημερολόγιο αρχαιολογικό. Τα χρόνια του Καποδίστρια 1828–1832* [Archaeological diary: The Capodistrias years 1828–1832]. 3 vols. Athens.

Skocpol, Theda. 1979. *States and Social Revolutions: A Comparative Analysis of France, Russia and China.* Cambridge.

Stone, Bailey. 2014. *The Anatomy of Revolution Revisited.* Cambridge.

Tilly, Charles. 1993. *European Revolutions 1492–1992.* Oxford.

Vakalopoulos, Apostolos. 1939. *Πρόσφυγες και προσφυγικό ζήτημα κατά την Επανάστασιν του 1821* [Refugees and the refugee question during the revolution of 1821] Thessaloniki.

Vovelle, Michel, ed. 1989. *L' image de la Révolution française dans le monde.* 4 vols. Paris and Oxford.

I

CONTEXTS

Balkan Hinterlands: The Danubian Principalities

In this essay I first offer a recapitulation of more or less well-known facts and a framework for considering them. I then discuss the personality of the Romanian leader associated with the start of the Etaireia movement in Wallachia and an interpretation of his action through some contrasting views in Romanian historiography.

What broke out in February 1821 was intended to be the first step in the war for Greek independence, but the choice of the place and time entangled the Etaireia project with a peasant revolt and with dissensions in the Phanariot government of Wallachia and Moldavia. The anarchic development that followed was understood by a contemporary as "tyranny and rebellion," comparable in his eyes with "the American Republic of Mexico," a disorder due to "unruly people who carried on *liberté-égalité-monarchie universelle,* without prince and Church" (Stoica de Hațeg 1967, 299, 302, 306–307). The maintenance of law and order was necessary near the unstable border between the Ottoman Empire and Serbia, where, while Russian troops had fought the Turks, in 1806–1812, the involvement of Balkan raiders had been visible. Constantinos Ypsilantis, the former prince of neighboring Wallachia, who had hoped to be restored by Russia, strove to incite a rising of Christians against the Turks. His son, nineteen-year-old Alexandros, was commanding eight hundred Arnaouts (Albanian partisans) on that front; he would remember this experience in 1821 (Camariano 1964, 433–446; Panaitescu 1933; Pappas 1991; Todorov 1975, 474–477).

Actually, after 1814, the propaganda spread by the secret society Philiki Etaireia penetrated both Danubian Principalities through Greek tradesmen and monks of the many monasteries dedicated to the major sanctuaries of Orthodox Christianity. As reported in the memoirs of Emmanouil Xanthos, this network included Odessa and Kishinev after 1812, when Bessarabia became a Russian province (Clogg 1976, 182–200). Wallachia (one million two hundred thousand inhabitants) and Moldavia (about eight hundred thousand) were dependent on the sovereign Sublime Porte, under Phanariot princes surrounded by a greedy oligarchy, open to the influence of the Russian consul (Deletant 1981, 229–248). The contest between Russia and France, which used to divide the Phanariot dynasties (Dascalakis 1974, 71–76; Holban 1939; Holban 1940–1941; Oțetea 1974), had ceased after Napoleon's times; therefore, the leader of the Etaireia, Alexandros Ypsilantis, considering himself supported by the tsar, planned to go to Paris to ask for supplementary help and changed his mind only when hearing the first news from the Peloponnese (Oțetea 1960, 74–75). Ypsilantis's geostrategy lacked almost any information on the actual situation in the country where he risked his fortune. The equipment of his forces was so improvised that, to collect ammunition in Bessarabia, before the passage of the Pruth river, a Greek company gathered thousands of bullets from the ground of an old battlefield (Oțetea 1960, 291–292). An unforeseen problem was the weather in a country deprived of normal communications, in which the winter of 1820 lasted from December to the following June with terribly cold temperatures, snow, hail, and floods (Românul 1996, 158–159).

The territory claimed by Ypsilantis's forces was Ottoman in name but deprived of a Turkish army. The local population included a significant number of Greeks whose affinity with the liberation cause was assumed. But the character of the political regime was deceptive because at the court and in the boyars' council (the divan) there were men already acting for the Etaireia, or only in the interest of Russia, others too diffident of change and taking into account a future Phanariot prince to be selected among the pretenders from Constantinople. The utmost trouble was caused by the general corruption of public administration and justice, which provoked the peasants' revolt in Wallachia. The complexity of social relationships in Romanian society made it difficult to appreciate the participation in this popular rebellion. It seems beyond doubt that the first insurgents belonged to a military corps of free peasants who rejected the imposition of a tax from which they had previously been exempt.

The leader who gathered the first forty peasants (gradually the number of his followers grew a hundred times more), Tudor (Theodore) Vladimirescu, was of similar rural origin, but had bought a position of inferior boyarship, responsible for the police and defense service of a district in Oltenia (Little Wallachia). He had also served in the Russian army as a noncommissioned officer, and was praised for his gifts and skills. Many aspects of his career are controversial, but it has been convincingly proven that his own aspirations coupled with the task he was allotted to give the Etaireia much-needed support (Oțetea 1945).

The high-ranked boyars saw their properties threatened by this tumultuous movement, but, as they lacked strength, they tried a compromise with Tudor. Some of them feared that their hope that the tsar would protect them against the peasants' rising had been annihilated. At the same time (late January 1821) that Vladimirescu made known his intentions with a proclamation addressed to the whole people of Wallachia and with a petition to the sultan, the Congress of the Holy Alliance opened at Laybach (Ljubljana). Any instigation to revolution, like those which had started in Spain and Naples, could not be tolerated by the united monarchs. So, Alexander of Russia took back the discreet encouragements, in which Ypsilantis had believed. The menaces directed by Tudor against "those dragons who are swallowing us alive" indicated a social crisis inside the very regime whose cooperation had been already acquired by the Etaireia. No link to the anti-Ottoman Greeks (who were ready to join him) could ever be suspected: the sultan was called "God's proxy" and "our all-powerful emperor" by Tudor, whose apparent aim was only to redress injustices from the past (Vîrtosu 1932, 10). The accusation of the Phanariots sounded sinister in the slogans often repeated to the Wallachians by their chief about "the bloodsuckers of the people," who "during one hundred years exploited the destitute peasants," reducing them to "the bareness of corpses in the grave." The victims of misrule had a fair right to the fulfillment of promises and privileges from the Sublime Porte, which were believed to have been established when Wallachia had settled its relation to the Ottoman Empire. The legitimizing role of history was perceived by Vladimirescu no less than by the boyars. The popular leader identified the fatherland with "the common people," whose advocate he considered himself to be, and denied this status to "a fellowship of robbers," as he called those dignitaries who were violating the holy treaty with the Porte. The boyars had a different notion of the fatherland. The references to *patria*, a term introduced in Romanian in the eighteenth century, were better articulated, regarding the country as the community that shares a political meaning, based on an ancestral past (Lemny 1986). A memoir sent by the boyars to the tsar in 1821, who was then at Laybach, requesting the replacement of the Phanariots by a Romanian hereditary prince, stated that "the nation of the Dacians was known in history many centuries before our Lord Jesus Christ" (Filitti 1932, 59). A similar appeal for a Russian intervention, after invoking "the rights of men," sought an argument in the heroic fights for independence by the great Romanian leaders Mircea, Vlad and Michael (Georgescu 1972, 163–165). The 1821 memoir then referred to the rule of Trajan and then to the foundation of the principality of Wallachia in 1241, which it attributed to a legendary character, followed by the dates of the treaties of allegiance to the Ottoman Empire, which had been communicated to Russia after 1772, to support the aspiration of autonomy and of a native prince.

Now, to return to the sequence of events. In January, Vladimirescu seized the opportunity of the death of the Prince of Wallachia, Alexander Soutsos, to immediately put his plan into action. Soutzo's death had also opened up the disputes around the vacant throne of Wallachia (Pippidi 1980). While a regency council was settled as a result, Tudor's army took the form of a great assembly, quite similar to the democratic constitution adopted in Serbia under Karageorge, and proceeded toward Bucharest like a national procession. Among the demands of the discontented men who continued to flock to Bucharest were the reduction or suspension of taxes, the abolition of the general system of appointment on the basis of favoritism or bribes, freedom of commercial activity and the creation of a tax-exempt military corps; above all these demands was to be the confirmation of Tudor as "chieftain and ruler." The whole month of February passed before Tudor's arrival in Bucharest. Moreover, in the proclamation, which announced the arrival on March 16, there was not a word about Ypsilantis, who was also on his way to Bucharest.

The Etairists assembled in Bessarabia had crossed the border at the river Pruth on February 22, in full agreement with Michael Soutzo, still the prince of Moldavia. The proclamations from Jassy which, in the usual revolutionary style, promised to deliver the Hellenic fatherland (including Serbia and Bulgaria) were addressed to Greek patriots in Moldavia and Wallachia. They called upon the ancient Greek heroes, but how could Epaminondas and Thrasyboulos have any effect on the Romanians? In Jassy, the local population could not fraternize with the Etairists' men because it witnessed requisitions, recruitment of people who were unreliable as soldiers and highly dubious figures in commanding places; plunder and devastation became the daily rule of occupation from the end of March until it was succeeded in June by the Turkish troops (Drăghici 2017, 215–216).

After having spent only a week in Moldavia, Ypsilantis left with two thousand armed men and, on his way to Bucharest, when learning of the Russian disapproval, he invited "the Dacians" to join the descendants of the ancient Hellenes. He and Vladimirescu were arriving at about the same time in Wallachia and prepared their meeting by a mutual explanation of their intentions. Tudor intended to win to his cause the three estates—clergy, boyars, and what we may call bourgeoisie (artisans and tradesmen)—but he addressed his call especially to the common people. On March 20 Tudor declared that he was inspired by an optimistic faith that he could reconcile antagonisms. He used the term *neam* (nation) in order to fasten the ties among those social groups, united by love of the fatherland as a debt to their ancestors. Turning to the administrators of regions where he wanted to recruit for his army, he told them of the rights of the country and of the common people that must be defended against enemy intrusions. For guaranteed happiness, the peasants were asked to settle their last unpaid fiscal obligations.

The following days were going to be of quite considerable importance. A Russian spy who was present in Bucharest noticed, after March 22, the difference between Tudor's anticorruption program and the anti-Ottoman discourse of the Greeks. Therefore, the two armies chose for their encampment two locations on opposing edges of Bucharest. Prince Theodore, as he was already being called, made a solemn entrance on the scene on March 21. Through the eyes of a Romanian reporter, we can observe many of the intrigues of the boyars in high office. They "decided to try anything to get rid of Tudor by separating him from Ypsilantis, making them fight each other until one or the other or rather both would perish" (Râmniceanu 1987, 121–122). This was the mission of Alexandru Filipescu, who managed to persuade Tudor to be more accommodating with the boyars and the Turks and increased his reluctance to help Ypsilantis. As a result, even before meeting with Ypsilantis, Tudor was heard to say: "I can't be impelled to shed the blood of Romanians for the Greek country" (Iorga 1939, 105–106; Oțetea 1945, 227–229). On March 23 there was an exchange of fealty oaths between Tudor and the boyars. In order to ensure his legitimacy and personal safeguard, he agreed to the conditions proposed by the divan, including measures to regulate taxation. His rise to power culminated in impressive marks of respect from flatterers, who greeted him like a prince (Românul 1996, 152–153). Therefore, the interview with Ypsilantis on March 26 failed because of mutual suspicion (Românul 1996, 154). After having claimed he would grant everybody liberty and justice, Tudor's harsh ways of imposing discipline disappointed his faithful. Bucharest, with one hundred and thirty thousand inhabitants in 1819, was now deserted by most of them, who feared the inevitable invasion of Ottoman troops. The city needed to reinforce its fortifications, for which workers were assembled in a short time. It looked as though Tudor was organizing local resistance in case he might obtain the autonomy of his government, but resources were not sufficient for provisioning Ypsilantis's camp. The tension between the two centers grew at the approach of the Turkish threat and on April 10, Vladimirescu marked the point beyond which he was not prepared to go: "Indeed, what can the Dacians and the Hellenes have in common? What benefit may come to Dacians from the future prosperity of the Hellenes?" (Iorga 1939, 139; Oțetea 1945, 247).

Having moved closer to the mountains toward Transylvania, Ypsilantis wrote in a letter of April 19 to defend himself and the Greeks who followed him for being delayed in their march to the beloved fatherland. Before leaving "the noble sons of Dacia," he offered them his advice: the appropriate task that awaited them was to transform this hospitable country into a liberal and constitutional state (Oțetea 1945, 257). It would be ruled by a native (thus, not a Greek), with an elected parliament, whose one or two chambers would represent all social groups, and with a regular army. Taxation would be established by the legislative power. The prince's civil list would be the annual reward to the first citizen of the state (Hurmuzaki 1967, Doc. 1821, 5:83–86). This document is illuminating about the deficiencies of Romanian society, but no less revealing that an idealist Western education was inadequate in facing the situation. When Tudor quit the capital on May 15, a few hours before the entry of the Turkish vanguard, he intended to return to his native Oltenia where his authority was undisputed. The hangers-on of the Greek army, Macedonian detachments semidependent of Ypsilantis, closed his path of escape. The captains were unlikely to miss this occasion to take their revenge on Tudor for many conflicts in their common past. Taking as pretext Tudor's disloyalty to the Etaireia, they were certain that Ypsilantis would approve of the killing of his rival, whose overlordship had humiliated them. Though Tudor had proudly said that he was "with his sword in his country," he had become vulnerable in the middle of his combatants.

After his assassination on May 26, the full collapse of his army ensured that any effective force that could oppose the Ottoman onslaught had dwindled. The defeat at Dragatsani on June 6 marked the end of the Etairist adventure in Wallachia (Map 1). Three of the men mainly responsible for Tudor's murder, Georgios Olympios, Savvas Phokianos, and Ioannis Pharmakis, eventually ended their lives under the blows of the Turks.

The next year, the appointment of a Romanian prince by the sultan vindicated at least one of Vladimirescu's aims; this, for some contemporaries, seemed a happy conclusion to such a bloody period.

Moldavia was in complete disorder after the authorities had taken refuge abroad at the end of March. There is plenty of evidence about the misbehavior of the Etairists who were put in positions of unrestricted power. One of the witnesses records that "Helleno-Greek committees" had existed since the previous year in every residence of the district, "confusion and dissolution began in August and continued till the outbreak of the revolution in January." The same chronicler adds: "The miseries of that time are unimaginable and indescribable; the boyar houses were plundered, Etairists were running desperately from one village to another to pick up arms and food collected by the peasants for their army; the people who found a shelter in the woods and in the mountains felt better protected from the terror of the volunteers" (Drăghici 2017, 215). Such views were tempered by accounts of specific details: "That army did not contain only Greeks—that would be a calumny against that nation—but also

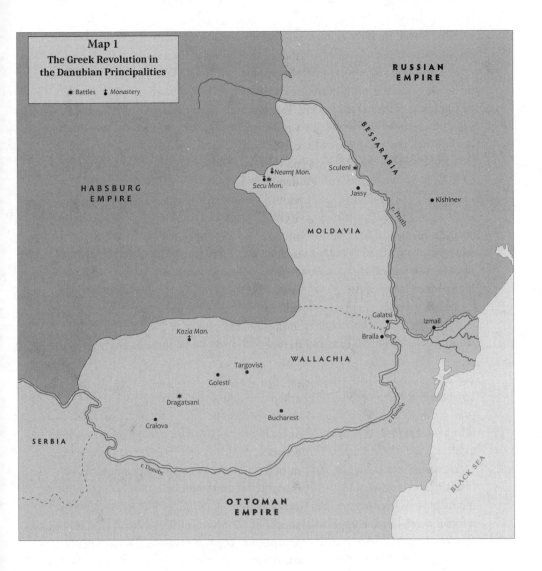

all kind of vagabonds, like servants of the boyars, torch bearers, the worst people from Jassy, Cossacks and Gypsies who, when the Turks came, changed dresses and joined them." The following months, from May to July, during the Ottoman occupation of Moldavia, brought a similar situation: "The ferocious hordes plundered the city of Jassy day and night, innocent people were massacred in the streets, because somebody had denounced them as Greeks. Even country houses of the boyars were attacked" (Drăghici 2017, 221). Some landlords reacted, called three thousand peasants under a red flag and liberated an area of the country from the Greeks (Gorovei 1926, 21–23). A deputy of Ypsilantis, his cousin George Kantakouzinos, like him a Russian colonel, was unable to settle the situation and fled to Bessarabia.

One of the most cultured Moldavian boyars, Ionică Tăutul, manifested his progressive ideas, aiming at political and social emancipation. To clear the way, he criticized the venal and servile representatives of the Phanariot system. This scholar had been deeply affected by the principles of the French Revolution, but his criticism had left unaffected at the top of the boyar class the rich family Rosetti-Roznovanu who continued to beseech Russian tutelage in order to consolidate its own pretentions to found a new dynasty (Georgescu 1970, 102–107, 120–124). The Greek army of Moldavia, weakened and shattered as it was, suffered a great defeat on June 19 at Sculeni. Only its last survivors continued the struggle against the Turks until their self-sacrifice at Secu. By a symbolic coincidence, the battle fought at the gate of Moldavia had as a witness on the left bank of the Pruth General Count Pavel Kiselev who, from 1828 to 1834, was to be the Russian governor of the principalities and patron of the Organic Statutes, the future constitutional organization of the principalities. This legislative reform extended Russian influence over Wallachia and Moldavia but realized the constitutional reforms that Romanians had been demanding for a long time.

Because of his link to the first stage of the war for Greek independence, Theodore, the real name of this Romanian patriot and revolutionary leader, deserves a brief survey of the description of his personality during the three distinct ages of Romanian culture. The rather obscure circumstances of his death have generated a debate about the attitude of the army that could allow its chief to be kidnapped. One explanation is that he had more than once ordered executions to punish disobedience or thefts, so the discontented men abandoned him. However, his memory was cherished in the area of Oltenia, where it became the source of a popular song. In a metaphoric form it was a lament for his murder. In the 1830s "Tudor's Song" sung by gypsies circulated as far as Moldavia. Songs in Romanian celebrated "bimbasha Sava" (Phokianos) or other Etairists, but this kind of peasant lyric has not preserved their names. Among the survivors of 1821, one at least did remember a religious service for the absolution of Tudor's soul, in which people were crying and kissed the cross in the hands of Bishop Hilarion of Argeş who had been Tudor's adviser. Testimonies of Tudor's survival in the memory of the first generation after those dramatic events show that "the 1848 men" drew inspiration from them. Going back in recent history beyond the Organic Statutes, which they condemned, these revolutionaries pointed to 1821 as a glorious moment.

This impetus can be seen in the claim of nationhood in the United Principalities. The romantic evaluation of Tudor is due to a book written by C. D. Aricescu, poet and historian. Its publication predates 1877, the Romanian War of Independence, and the author, who was director of the National Archives, was able to collect massive amounts of documents on 1821.

The negative references to the Phanariot period, like claiming it germinated plagues still present in Romanian society, were disclaimed by Nicolae Iorga, to whom we owe the first rehabilitation of the Phanariots. Iorga's concern with Tudor Vladimirescu, which went as far as making him a hero of a drama he wrote (Iorga 1921a), began in 1914 with the discovery of precious evidence on Tudor's biography and on the economic and social situation of Oltenia. Iorga is the historian who, alone, collected the memoirs of as many of Tudor's companions as possible (Iorga 1914, 1915, 1921). These contemporary impressions, published for the centennial of 1821, were interpreted by Iorga in the political context of a new era of agrarian reform (Iorga 1921b). Thus, elevated as an icon, Tudor, "the defender of the poor," was exploited by the official discourse of interwar Romania, which was inclined toward nationalistic myths. In opposition, Andrei Oțetea, whose vision was already influenced by Marxism, developed a different picture, in which he stressed Tudor's implication in the Etaireia (Oțetea 1945, 1–28 and French summary). Later, Oțetea edited two series of documents from the Romanian and Russian archives, the second being facilitated by Romania's relations with the Soviet Union. New anniversaries have shown that the tradition of commemorations lives on and remains meaningful.

Andrei Pippidi

References

Ardeleanu, Constantin. 2002. "Confruntări militare turco-eteriste în regiunea orașului Galați (1821)" [1821 fights between Turks and Etairists near Galați], *Analele Universității "Dunărea de Jos" Istorie* 1:55–68.

Camariano, Nestor. 1964. "L'activité de Georges Olympios dans les Principautés Roumaines avant la Révolution de 1821." *RESEE* 2, nos. 3–4 : 433–446.

Camariano, Nestor. 1967a. "O prețioasă proclamație a eteriștilor adresată popoarelor balcanice" [A precious proclamation of the Etairists addressed to the Balkan peoples]. *Revista Arhivelor* 10, no. 1: 97–102.

Camariano, Nestor. 1967b. "Planurile revoluționare ale eteriștilor din București și colaborarea lor cu Tudor Vladimirescu" [The revolutionary projects of the Etairist inhabitants of Bucharest and their collaboration with Tudor Vladimirescu]. *Studii* 20, no. 6: 1163–1175.

Camariano-Cioran, Ariadna. 2008. "Un ilustru eterist, Gheorghios Lassanis" [An illustrious Etairist, Georgios Lassanis]. In *Relații româno-elene. Studii istorice și filologice (secolele XIV–XIX)* [Romanian-Hellenic relations: Historical and philological studies, fourteenth to nineteenth centuries], 461–86. Bucharest.

Ciorănescu, Alin. 1934. "O însemnare românească despre Eterie" [A Romanian notice about the Etaireia]. *Revista Istorică* 20, nos. 10–12:308–311.

Clogg, Richard, ed. and trans. 1976. *The Movement for Greek Independence, 1770–1821: A Collection of Documents*. Studies in Russian and East European History. London.

Corfus, Ilie. 1966. "Cronica meşteşugarului Ioan Dobrescu (1802–1830)" [The chronicle of Ioan Dobrescu, craftsman]. *Studii Şi Articole de Istorie* 8:309–403.

Dascalakis, Apostolos. 1974. "Les Phanariotes et la Révolution grecque de 1821." *Symposium: L'époque phanariote*, 71–76. Thessaloniki.

Deletant, Denis. 1981. "Rumanian Society in the Danubian Principalities in the Early 19th Century." *Balkan Society in the Age of Greek Independence*, edited by Richard Clogg, 229–248. New York.

Drăghici, Manolachi. 2017. *Istoria Moldovei pe timp de 500 de ani* [The history of Moldavia through five hundred years]. Edited by Andrei Pippidi. Bucharest.

Elian, Alexandru. 1970. *Clerul ortodox şi răscoala lui Tudor Vladimirescu* [The Orthodox clergy and Tudor Vladimirescu's uprising]. Bucharest.

Filitti, Ioan C. 1932. *Frămîntările politice şi sociale în Principatele române de la 1821 la 1828* [The political and social troubles in the Romanian Principalities]. Bucharest.

Fotino, Ilie. 1874. *Tudor Vladimirescu şi Alexandru Ipsilante în revoluţiunea din anul 1821 supranumită Zavera, tradussă din limba ellenă de P. M.Georgescu, revedută şi editată de Dr. A. I. Fotino* [Tudor Vladimirescu and Alexander Ypsilantis in the 1821 revolution also called Zavera, translated from the Hellenic language, etc.]. Bucharest.

Georgescu, Vlad. 1970. *Mémoires et projets de réforme dans les Principautés Roumaines, 1769–1830*. Bucharest.

Georgescu, Vlad. 1972. *Mémoires et projets de réforme dans les Principautés Roumaines, 1831–1848*. Bucharest.

Gorovei, Artur. 1926. *Monografia oraşului Botoşani* [A monograph of the town of Botoşani]. Botoşani.

Holban, Maria. 1940–1941. "Autour de deux rapports inédits sur Carageà et Callimachy." *RHSEE* 18: 175–241, 19: 1, 75–132.

Holban, Teodor. 1939. *Documente româneşti din arhivele franceze (1801–1812)* [French documents from the French archives]. Bucharest.

Hurmuzaki, Eudoxiu de. 1967. *Documente privind istoria României. Serie nouă, II, Rapoarte consulare austriece (1812–1823)* [Documents concerning the history of Romania. New series, II: Austrian consular reports, 1812–1823]. Revised by I. Nistor and Dan Berindei, under the care of Andrei Oţetea. Bucharest.

Iorga, Nicolae. 1914. *Scrisori inedite ale lui Tudor Vladimirescu din anii 1814–1815* [Unpublished letters by Tudor Vladimirescu]. Bucharest.

Iorga, Nicolae. 1915. *Situaţia agranilorră, economică şi socială a Olteniei în epoca lui Tudor Vladimirescu* [The economic and social situation in agrarian Oltenia in Tudor Vladimirescu's time]. Bucharest.

Iorga, Nicolae. 1921. *Isvoarele contemporane asupra mişcării lui Tudor Vladimirescu* [Contemporary sources on Tudor Vladimirescu's insurrection]. Bucharest.

Iorga, Nicolae. 1921a. *Tudor Vladimirescu*. Sibiu.

Iorga, Nicolae. 1921b, 1926, 1939, *Un apărător al săracilor, "Domnul Tudor" din Vladimiri* [A defender of poor people, "Prince Tudor" from Vladimiri]. Bucharest.

Iorga, Nicolae. 1938. *Istoria Românilor, VIII, Revoluţionarii* [History of the Romanians, The Revolutionaries]. Bucharest.

Iorga, Nicolae. 1939. *"Domnul" Tudor din Vladimiri* ["Prince" Tudor of Vladimiri]. Bucharest.

Lemny, Ştefan. 1986. *Originea şi cristalizarea ideii de patrie în cultura română* [The idea of fatherland in the Romanian culture, its origins and its binding formation]. Bucharest.

Oţetea, Andrei. 1945. "Tudor Vladimirescu şi mişcarea eteristă în ţările româneşti 1821–1822" [Tudor Vladimirescu and the Etairist movements in the Romanian lands]. *Balcania* 4:1–408.

Oţetea, Andrei, ed. 1960. *Documente privind istoria României. Răscoala din 1821* [Documents concerning the history of Romania: The 1821 revolt]. Vol. 4. Bucharest.

Oţetea, Andrei. 1965. "L'Hétairie d'il y a cent cinquante ans." *Balkan Studies* 6:249–264.

Oţetea, Andrei. 1966. "Les grandes puissances et le mouvement hétairiste dans les Principautés Roumaines." *Balkan Studies* 7:379–394.

Oţetea, Andrei. 1967. "Caracterul mişcării conduse de Tudor Vladimirescu: Răscoală sau revoluţie?" [The character of the movement led by Tudor Vladimirescu: Riot or revolution]. *Studii* 20, no. 4: 667–679.

Oţetea, Andrei. 1974. "La désagrégation du régime phanariote." *Symposium: L'époque phanariote*, 439–445. Thessaloniki.

Panaitescu, Petre P. 1933. *Corespondenţa lui Constantin Ypsilanti cu guvernul rusesc 1806–1830. Pregătirea Eteriei şi a Renaşterii politice româneşti* [Constantin Ypsilantis's correspondence with the Russian government to prepare the Etaireia and the Romanian Risorgimento]. Bucharest.

Pappas, Nicholas Charles. 1991. *Greeks in Russian Military Service in the Late Eighteenth and Early Nineteenth Centuries.* Thessaloniki.

Pippidi, Andrei. 1980. "Nicolas Soutzo (1798–1871) et la fin du régime phanariote dans les Principautés Roumaines." In *Hommes et idées du Sud-Est européen à l'aube de l'âge moderne*, 315–330. Paris and Bucharest.

Râmniceanu, Naum. 1987."Izbucnirea şi urmările Zaverei din Valahia" [The outbreak and the consequences of the Zavera in Wallachia]. In *Izvoare narative interne privind Revoluţia de la 1821 condusă de Tudor Vladimirescu* [Internal narrative sources regarding the revolution of 1821 led by Tudor Vladimirescu], edited by G. D. Iscru, 108–128. Craiova.

Românul, Zilot. 1996. *Opere complete* [The Romanian Zealot: Complete works]. Edited by Marcel-Dumitru Ciucă. Bucharest.

Stoica de Haţeg, Nicolae. 1967. *Cronica Banatului* [The chronicle of the Banat]. Edited by Damaschin Mioc. Bucharest.

Todorov, Nikolai. 1975. "Quelques renseignements sur les insurgés grecs dans les Principautés Danubiennes en 1821." In Μελετήματα στη μνήμη Βασιλείου Λαούρδα [Essays in memory of Vasileios Laourdas], 471–477. Thessaloniki.

Vîrtosu, Emil. 1932. *1821. Date şi fapte noi* [1821: New data and facts]. Bucharest.

Vîrtosu, Emil. 1936. *Tudor Vladimirescu. Pagini de revoltă* [Tudor Vladimirescu: Revolutionary pages]. Bucharest.

Vîrtosu, Emil. 1957. "O satiră în versuri din Moldova anului 1821" [A versified label from Moldavia in 1821] in *Studii şi materiale de istorie medie*, II: 521–530.

Vîrtosu, Emil, ed., 1974. Ionică Tăutul 1795–1830, *Scrieri social-politice* [Social and political writings]. Bucharest.

Balkan Hinterlands: The South Slavic Lands

Hellenophone Enlightenment influenced many South Slavs, including the main Serbian advocate of the Enlightenment, Dositey Obradovich. In defining the modern Serbian nation as consisting of Serbian-speaking people, he seems to have been inspired by the Greek Jacobin Rhigas Velestinlis (Kitromilides 2013, 205). The fact that Rhigas was killed at the Belgrade fortress in 1798 inspired many local Christian patriots who became committed to the liberation of the Balkan Christians of the Ottoman Empire, and also to advocating cooperation of different ethnic groups in the Balkans for the same purpose.

The First Serbian Uprising (1804–1813), which Leopold von Ranke called "the Serbian revolution" (Ranke 1829), was originally a revolt against local Ottoman corrupt authorities known as the *dahis*. It was gradually transformed into a rebellion against the central Ottoman authorities. In 1806, an assembly of Serbian insurgents decided to endeavor to attract to their cause other Balkan Christians. This primarily meant encouraging the Christians of western Bulgaria to join the uprising, but it affected ethnic Greeks as well. By that time the Greeks of the diaspora already knew about the Serbian Uprising; there are two prominent contemporary works in Greek related to the uprising.

In 1806, an anonymous Greek published in Italy a book entitled *The Hellenic Nomarchy, or Discourse about Freedom* (Ελληνική Νομαρχία, ήτοι λόγος περί Ελευθερίας), in which he pointed to an example, "a great and a recent one," for which one did not need to quote historians. "It is, O Greeks, the Serbs who give us this example." He was particularly impressed by the leader of the uprising, "admirable George," who has "given many lessons . . . for the behaviour of the Greeks" (Clogg 1976, 116). The next year, Triantaphyllos Doukas, a Greek from Kastoria, who was a successful merchant in the border town of Zemun (Semlin) in Austria, published in Pest in Greek his *Slavic-Serbian History Composed in Political Verses* (Ιστορία των Σλαβενο-Σέρβων συντεθείσα δια στίχων πολιτικών). He dedicated it to Petros Itskos (Petar Icko), a prominent merchant and diplomat of Serbia during the Serbian Uprising, who was himself of Greek-Tsintsar (Vlach) origin. Previously, Doukas had helped in the establishment of a very influential Greek school in Semlin / Zemun (Papadrianos 1979, 279–280).

A major influence of the Serbian Uprising on the Greeks was felt in northern Greece and among Greek-speaking communities in Wallachia and Moldavia. The rebellion of Greek / Romaic *armatoloi* and klephts of April 1808, in the area of Mount Olympus, led by the priest Enthymios Vlachavas, was similar to the Serbian uprising of 1804 (Djordjević and Fischer-Galati 1981, 75; Laskaris 1936: 43). It was organized against corrupt ex-Ottoman official Ali Pasha of Ioannina, but Vlachavas was defeated near Meteora. It was precisely the examples of Rhigas Velestinlis and Vlachavas that Emmanouil Xanthos later quoted as his inspiration to establish the Philiki Etaireia (Clogg 1976, 182–183).

The communication of Serbs and Bulgarians with ethnic Greeks was facilitated through trade networks and by a shared symbolic heritage of "an Orthodox Commonwealth" (Kitromilides 2007). The Orthodox Christian trade network was of a mixed ethnic background (Greek, Vlach, Serbian, Bulgarian, and Albanian), but at the end of the eighteenth century it had been very much hellenized (Stoianovich 1960) and Greek became the trade language of the Balkan Christians between the mid-eighteenth and the mid-nineteenth centuries. At the end of the eighteenth and in the early nineteenth centuries Serbs called all merchants "Greeks" and it became a matter of prestige to be a Greek or a merchant (Dzambazovski 1979, 187). The same was the case in central Europe and the German lands, where all Orthodox merchants from the Balkans were called "Greeks" (Clogg 1973, 10–11; Stoianovich 1960, 290). Bulgarians were fully influenced by this process of hellenization of their merchant class and Serbs to a much lesser degree. However, Serbian merchants also underwent partial hellenization in the late eighteenth century (Stoianovich 1960, 311).

Austro-Hungarian administrator and historian Benjamin von Kallay was the first to claim that the Serbian Uprising was seen by all Christians of European Turkey as their own (Djordjević and Fischer-Galati 1981, 73). Ethnic Greeks and hellenized Vlachs helped the Serbian Uprising in three ways: (1) by participating in the insurrection as volunteers, (2) as merchants who operated in Belgrade and Zemun, and (3) as prominent officials who worked for the Russian and Ottoman empires (Dzambazovski 1989, 187).

After the Serbian Uprising was defeated in 1813, its leader Djordje Petrovich known as Karageorge (the Black George) emigrated to Russia and was attracted there by the Philiki Etaireia. He had been initiated in to that society in June 1817 at Jassy. On that occasion he swore: "ορκισθέντα δι' εαυτόν και δι' όλην την γενεάν εαυτού αιωνίαν έχθραν κατά του τυράννου υπέρ της Ελλάδος δε, της Σερβίας καὶ ὅλων των υπό τους Τούρκους Χριστιανών άνευ διαφοράς εθνικότητος και δόγματος πάσαν αυτού την συνδρομήν προς απόσεισιν του τυραννικού ζυγού" (He took an oath on behalf of himself and of his entire clan to nurture eternal hatred against the tyrant and to support Greece and Serbia and all Christians under the Turks, regardless of nationality and religious confession and offer his total assistance in the cause of overthrowing the tyrannical yoke) (Philimon 1859–1862, 1:7–8). With that in mind, in July 1817, the Etaireia secretly transferred him to Serbia. The then de facto ruler of Serbia Prince Milosh Obrenovich (ruled from 1815 until 1839) could not envisage a general Christian uprising, and rather had Karageorge killed by his own men. In this way, a joint Greek-Serbian uprising was frustrated (Laskaris 1936, 66–70). Karageorge's example was a role model for some Greek insurgents. Ioannis Philimon wrote that with his death "Ήτο άρα φυσική η γενομένη παρ' άπασι τοις Έλλησι κακίστη εντύπωσις διά την απώλειαν ενός τόσω χρησίμου και δυσκόλως αναπληρουμένου προσώπου" (It was therefore natural that the loss of such a useful and almost irreplaceable person caused a very bad impression upon all Greeks) (Philimon 1859–1862, 1:10). Scottish Philhellene Thomas Gordon also noted that the spirit that "Czerni George" had evoked "survived him, and the emancipated Servians gave the unwonted spectacle of a brave and armed Christian nation" (Gordon 1844, 1:27).

A new cooperation between Balkan Christians took place during the uprising in the Danubian Principalities in 1821. In addition to ethnic Greeks and Vlachs, the uprising attracted many Serbs and Bulgarians. Alexandros Ypsilantis, the head of Etaireia since the spring of 1820, staged an uprising in Moldavia after he crossed the river Pruth in February 1821. He had previously endeavored to establish a cooperation with Prince Milosh in 1820 and prepared a letter for him in October of that year announcing a revolt in Constantinople and all of Greece in mid-November. He asked Prince Milosh to send his troops into eastern Serbia. In December 1820, an Etairist named Aristides was caught at Ada Kale and brought to the Pasha of Vidin (Gordon 1844, 1:89). He had letters prepared for Serbian revolutionaries with the plan for a general uprising. Ypsilantis expected that his own action would be joined by troops in Serbia, and rebels in Bulgaria and Macedonia. At that time, Bucharest and Jassy were full of ex-soldiers who had fought in Russian armies or in Karageorge's Serbia (Finlay 1861, 1:145; Gordon 1844, 1:94), and they readily joined either Ypsilantis or Tudor Vladimirescu, who led a local uprising against the notables in Wallachia. Vladimirescu entered Bucharest on March 21, 1821; his troops included a Serbian contingent led by Chadji Prodan (Gordon 1844, 1:98). A prominent part in the revolution was played by the Arnauts, a Turkish name for Albanians, but in Moldowallachia essentially an appellation for mercenaries "though composed of Greeks, Servians and Bulgarians, as well as Albanians" (Finlay 1861, 1:146). They excelled under their chief Karavia already in March, and then at Sculeni on June 17 (1:147).

Ethnic Bulgarians participated in the Greek Revolution in various roles. In the first decades of the nineteenth century, however, protonational identities were much more fluid than national identities in the era of mass nationalism at the end of the same century. A pan-Byzantine or Romaic identity was very present among the Bulgarian upper classes. Education in the Bulgarian language began only in the 1830s (Crampton 2007, 51), after Greece had already gained its independence. So, ethnic Bulgarians who attended schools before the 1830s had been taught in Greek and they easily identified with the pan-Byzantine or even Greek identity.

The same problem applies to ethnic Serbs outside of the frontiers of the autonomous area ruled by Prince Milosh, and particularly to Slavs with a fluid identity throughout Macedonia, who, at the time of the Greek Revolution, were more likely to perceive themselves under the common denominator of Christians (Orthodox Christians) or even as *Romaioi,* rather than under any kind of subsequent Slavic national identity. Enclaves of Romaic identity existed in Bulgaria even at the end of the nineteenth century (Kitromilides 2007, Study IV, 25–28). Therefore, one cannot always definitively establish who was a "Greek," a *Romaios,* a "Serb," or a "Bulgarian" in the Greek Revolution. The same person could easily have had double or triple identities at that time. This is especially the case with the Vlachs in the Ottoman Empire, who were very active participants in the trade networks. One should also have in mind that actors in the Balkan revolutions (1804–1830) may have, and indeed had, changed and complemented their identities during their lifetime.

In the 1970s, a debate on how many Bulgarians took part in the Greek Revolution appeared. Nikolai Todorov and Veselin Traikov (1971) opted for higher figures, while Emmanouil Protopsaltis found their estimations exaggerated (Protopsaltis 1979, 65). Todorov also believed that there had been significant numbers of Bulgarians among the Etairists, but the names that he provided in his study (Todorov 1965, 45–46) could rather be seen as evidence of the high level of hellenization of the Bulgarian upper classes. Having all this in mind, one can only discuss the cases of those South Slavs in the Greek Revolution who were identified by their Greek brethren as "Serbs" (and "Montenegrins") or "Bulgarians."

Protopsaltis identified twelve prominent Serbs and five Montenegrins who fought in the Greek War for Independence but acknowledged that research on

Serbian and Montenegrin fighters "remains yet to be made." Among the Serbs were Chadji Christos Dragović (Dragovits) of Belgrade, Serbian Prince Constantine Nemania, who also fought in the Danubian Principalities, chieftain Athanasios Servos (Mesolonghi), and captain Costas Servos. The Montenegrins include Vasos Mavrovouniotis and General De Wintz (also spelled Ouitz), who distinguished himself at Nafplio (Protopsaltis 1979, 77–81). Among the prominent Bulgarians one should mention Iannis Voulgaris of Philippopolis, Michalis Machairas, Nikolaos Stanof, and Nikolaos Femanlis (Papadrianos 1996, 37–38, 43–44). Todorov and Traikov also insisted that Chadji Christos, who had been born in Belgrade, was a Bulgarian (Todorov 1971).

Spyros Loukatos has compiled the most elaborate lists of Serbs in the Greek War of Independence. He mentions 105 Serbs, who descended to Greece under the Philhellene Anastasi Dmitrevits (Atanasije Dimitrijević), twenty-five Serbs who fought during the siege of Mesolonghi, and a Serbian-Bulgarian detachment under Chadji Christos Dragović that was in the service of Hurşid pasha, but, during the siege of Tripolitsa, joined the forces of Theodoros Kolokotronis. Another notable Serbian chieftain was Stefan Nivica, known as captain Stefou. Bulgarians were often present in Serbian corps and were not infrequently confused with Serbs. Loukatos also lists many volunteers from Monastir and Prilep, who would be Bulgarians for Todorov, and some fighters are mentioned in documents as "Bosnians" and "Slavs." Some Serbs and other South Slavs, who fought in the Greek Revolution, learned Greek, got assimilated with local Greeks, and stayed and died in liberated Greece. Among them were Chadji Christos Dragović and Vasos Mavrovouniotis, Serbian volunteers who took on the Greek cause and considered Greece as their "dearest homeland" (Loukatos 1970, 1979).

Western observers of the Greek Revolution also left some information on Serbian and Bulgarian volunteers. George Finlay mentions that during the Egyptian siege of Navarino in April 1825, the Greek troops included irregular cavalry "consisting in great part of Servians and Bulgarians" led by Chadji Christos (Finlay 1861, 2:66).

The Serbian Revolution inspired some Greek writers and the Greek Revolution encouraged the Serbs. In 1825, Hungarian Serb Jovan Sterija Popović (1806–1856) as a young writer composed his "Sevenfold Flower for the Fighting Greeks." The collection includes his translations of Rhigas Velestinlis, Adamantios Korais and Iakovakis Rizos-Neroulos. A call for subscription was announced but under the conditions of Metternich's authoritarianism in the Habsburg Empire it could not be printed. Yet, Popović's own epic poem on Markos Botsaris was published in 1853 in Novi Sad (Krestić 1979, 45–47).

Leaders of the Greek Revolution tried to form an official alliance with Serbian autonomous areas. They endeavored to attract Prince Milosh of Serbia and the Montenegrin prince-bishop Petar to their side but their efforts failed. Prince Milosh, in spite of his refusal to stage a revolt in Serbia, also helped the Greek cause although not as the Greek insurgents expected. He received many Greek refugees following their defeat during the course of the Greek Revolution, and also got involved in paying ransom for enslaved Greek fighters who were sold by Turks. For this he was decorated in 1839 by Othon, the first king of Greece, with the Order of the Savior. In 1842, he donated 30,000 golden drachmas for the building of the University of Athens (Protopsaltis 1979, 70).

While the number of Western Philhellenes who fought in the Greek War of Independence could be approximately estimated at 1,100 to 1,200 (St Clair 1972, 355), it is very difficult to estimate the number of South Slavs. In the uprising in Moldowallachia Serbs and Bulgarians definitely represented a very large group of fighters; they were the third largest ethnic contingent in the revolution of 1821. The numbers of South Slavs who took part in the Greek War of Independence in mainland Greece still cannot be positively estimated, but it is clear that it attracted numerous Serbian and Bulgarian volunteers.

The Greek Revolution recruited two groups of volunteers, Western Philhellenes and Balkan Christians. The Western Philhellenes fought against what they perceived as Eastern barbarism in favor of European Enlightenment. They viewed the modern Hellenes as an indispensable part of their own civilization. The Christian volunteers took arms against what they saw as Muslim oppression and in favor of a future Christian state of which they had only elementary ideas. The first group had Homer and Pausanias in mind, the second shared a common Christian Orthodox (pan-Byzantine) identity. This common Christian identity should not be understood in a dogmatic sense, but rather in terms of a common mentality of Balkan Orthodoxy that had existed before the rise of Balkan nationalisms (Kitromilides 2007, 1:176–179). Both groups of volunteers lived through revolutionary events in the Balkans (1804–1830), which were indeed closely related to the Age of Revolution.

If the Serbian rebels and Karageorge inspired the Etairists and other Greek and Christian patriots in their endeavors during the Greek Revolution, it was the independence of Greece achieved in 1830 that encouraged Serbs and later Bulgarians in their own strivings to seek full independence. With the emergence of the independent Greek kingdom it became obvious that fully independent Christian Orthodox states in the Balkans were possible. The cooperation of the Balkan Christians from the era of the Serbian and Greek revolutions (1804–1830) paved the way for subsequent efforts to form alliances of Balkan Christians against the Ottoman Empire in the 1860s, the 1890s, and particularly in 1912–1913.

Slobodan G. Marković

References

Clogg, Richard. 1973. "Aspects of the Movement for Greek Independence." In *The Struggle for Greek Indepedence: Essays to Mark the 150th Anniversary of the Greek War of Independence,* edited by Richard Clogg, 1–40. London.

Clogg, Richard, ed. and trans. 1976. *The Movement for Greek Independence, 1770–1821: A Collection of Documents.* Studies in Russian and East European History. London.

Crampton, Richard J. 2007. *Bulgaria.* Oxford.

Djordjević, Dimitrije, and Stephen Fischer-Galati, 1981. *The Balkan Revolutionary Tradition.* New York.

Dzambazovski, Kliment. 1979. "Grci u Prvom Srpskom Ustanku" [Greeks in the First Serbian insurrection]. In *Συνεργασία Ελλήνων και Σέρβων κατά τους απελευθερωτικούς αγώνες 1804–1830* [Cooperation between Greeks and Serbs during their struggles for liberation, 1804–1830], 185–195, 284–285. Thessaloniki.

Finlay, George. 1861. *History of the Greek Revolution.* Edinburgh and London.

Gordon, Thomas. 1844. *History of the Greek Revolution and of the Wars and Campaigns Arising from the Struggles of the Greek Patriots in Emancipating Their Country from the Turkish Yoke.* Edinburgh and London.

Kitromilides, Paschalis M. 2007. *An Orthodox Commonwealth. Symbolic Legacies and Cultural Encounters in Southeastern Europe.* Variorum Series. Aldershot.

Kitromilides, Paschalis M. 2013. "Dositej Obradović and the Greek Enlightenment." *Balcanica* 44:201–207.

Krestic, Vasilije. 1979. "O nekim odjecima grckih ustanka u srpskoj knjizevnosti" [On some echoes of Greek insurrections in Serbian literature]. In *Συνεργασία Ελλήνων και Σέρβων κατά τους απελευθερωτικούς αγώνες 1804–1830* [Cooperation between Greeks and Serbs during their struggles for liberation, 1804–1830], 43–50, 268–269. Thessaloniki.

Laskaris, Mihail. 1936. *Έλληνες και Σέρβοι κατά τους απελευθερωτικούς των αγώνας 1804–1830* [Greeks and Serbs during their struggles for liberation, 1804–1830]. Athens.

Loukatos, Spyros D. 1970. *Σχέσεις Ελλήνων μετά Σέρβων και Μαυροβουνίων κατά την Ελληνικήν Επανάστασιν* [Relations between Greeks, Serbs, and Montenegrins during the Greek Revolution]. Thessaloniki.

Loukatos, Spyros D. 1979. "Σέρβοι, Μαυροβούνιοι και Βόσνιοι μαχητές της ελληνικής ανεξαρτησίας, 1821–1829" [Serb, Montenegrin, and Bosnian fighters for Greek independence, 1821–1829]. In *Συνεργασία Ελλήνων και Σέρβων κατά τους απελευθερωτικούς αγώνες 1804–1830* [Cooperation between Greeks and Serbs during their struggles for liberation 1804–1830], 101–151, 276–277. Thessaloniki.

Papadrianos, Ioannis. 1979. "The 'History of the Slaveno-Serbs' by Triandaphyllos Doukas of Kastoria, and its Significance with Regard to the First Serbian Revolution." In *Συνεργασία Ελλήνων και Σέρβων κατά τους απελευθερωτικούς αγώνες 1804–1830* [Cooperation between Greeks and Serbs during their struggles for liberation, 1804–1830], 279–280. Thessaloniki.

Papadrianos, Ioannis. 1996. *Η ελληνική παλιγγενεσία και η βαλκανική της διάσταση* [The Greek regeneration of 1821 and its Balkan dimension]. Komotini.

Philimon, Ioannis. 1859–1862. *Δοκίμιον ιστορικόν περί της Ελληνικής Επαναστάσεως* [A historical essay on the Greek Revolution]. Athens.

Protopsaltis, Emmanouil. 1979. "Σέρβοι και Μαυροβούνιοι φιλέλληνες κατά την
    Επανάστασιν του 1821" [Serbian and Montenegrin Philhellenes during the Greek
    Revolution, 1821]. In Συνεργασία Ελλήνων και Σέρβων κατά τους απελευθερωτικούς
    αγώνες 1804–1830 [Cooperation between Greeks and Serbs during their struggles for
    liberation, 1804–1830], 65–88. Thessaloniki.
Ranke, Leopold von. 1829. *Die serbische Revolution.* Hamburg.
Ranke, Leopold von. 1847. *A History of Servia and the Servian Revolution.* London.
St Clair, William. 1972. *That Greece Might Still Be Free: The Philhellenes in the War of
    Independence.* London.
Stoianovich, Traian. 1960. "The Conquering Balkan Orthodox Merchant." *Journal of
    Economic History* 20, no. 2: 234–313.
Todorov, Nikolai. 1965. *Filiki Eteria i Blgarite* [The Philiki Etaireia and the Bulgarians]. Sofia.
Todorov, Nikolai, and Veselin Traikov, eds. 1971. *Blgari—uchastnici na borbi za osvobozh-
    denieto na Grtsiya 1821–1828* [Bulgarians: Participants in the struggle for the liberation
    of Greece, 1821–1828]. Sofia.

Diasporas and Homelands

Scholarly discourses on *the* Greek diaspora have long overshadowed the heterogeneity, both in time and space, of social, political, and economic experiences of Greeks scattered across Europe and beyond, from the late Middle Ages to the modern period. In fact, being "Greek" referred to different realities according to the geographical and historical contexts: sixteenth-century Venice, seventeenth-century Amsterdam, eighteenth-century Trieste, or nineteenth-century Tunis. Rather than as a catchword for describing postcolonial hybrid identities, "diaspora" stands here as a general term under which to subsume migratory phenomena of diverse intensity, as well as social and political experiences of different nature, the history of which has long been conceived as radically distinct from that of the formation and development of the Greek state (Harlaftis 2005, 150–151).

In addition to this, only recently have historians started considering diaspora space as one characterized by movement rather than stability, as well as by strong asymmetries and power relations among the different Greek communities (Hassiotis 1989; Seirinidou 2008). For instance, from the second half of the eighteenth century onward, the traditional leadership of the Venetian community had long faded, to be superseded by that of "younger," economically more dynamic Greek communities, such as those in Trieste, Vienna, or Livorno. In turn, this affected what it meant to belong to such "a nation of socially interdependent, but spatially dispersed communities" (Cohen 1971). Almost everywhere, the rise in power of traders, businessmen, and bankers led to a shift in power relations within the Greek communities, as craftsmen, small merchants, seamen, and soldiers were increasingly kept away from positions of community leadership and representation.

The study of homeland-diaspora relations at the time of the Greek Revolution therefore has to be considered in this double context of strong local specificities and of shifting global equilibria. Just as Greek diaspora communities never actually joined in common voice and cause, the political upheavals of the revolution bore different implications to each of them, while at the same time affecting the very nature of diaspora experience as a whole.

Patterns of Politicization

The politicization of diaspora Greeks over the course of the late eighteenth and early nineteenth centuries occurred through different kinds of experiments and practices, to create not *one* political culture and worldview, but several. Hence, a landmark event such as the Orlov revolt of 1770, Lambros Katsonis's harassment of the Ottoman navy in 1778–1790, the French Revolution, or Napoleon's imperial adventure did not bear the same significance, nor did it contribute to shaping a uniform sense of "nationality" among the Greek communities in, say, northern Europe or the Danube, Italy, Egypt, or the Black Sea. At the same time, however, more "centripetal" trends aimed at promoting among diaspora Greeks a distinct, more coherent sense of "Greek-ness" as well as nationhood.

One such effort was undertaken by intellectuals and pedagogues of the "Neohellenic Enlightenment," as they attempted to devise education systems likely to foster social and cultural changes among the Greek people (Kitromilides 1992, 1996). Because most of these reforms mirrored some of the "enlightened" seventeenth- and eighteenth-century Western philosophy on education (Locke, Diderot, Rousseau, etc.), Greek diaspora communities in western Europe were often considered fertile ground for experimentation. As the teaching of the Greek language had taken the front stage in education reforms, the preservation of the "mother tongue" among the children of migrants soon became a matter of pressing concern, both culturally and politically (Katsiardi-Hering 1995). As a result, a number of communities funded their own school, asked for recommendations from the most renowned Greek pedagogues of the time (both in the Ottoman Empire and abroad), and raised funds for the education of poor local Greek boys. Although Greek schools developed successfully in a number of European cities that were home to important diaspora communities (Vienna, Bucharest, Trieste, Venice, etc.), the task was a daunting one. For all the vibrancy of Greek intellectual and cultural life in early nineteenth-century Vienna, students of the local Greek school were still considered "terribly weak in the spoken Greek language," and their parents were accused of "blameworthy negligence and indifference" (Seirinidou 2008, 159). As one of the purposes of education was to foster and strengthen national identity, it comes as no surprise that some of the most active proponents of this pedagogical revival were also vocal supporters of the Greek cause.

Other somewhat more direct evidence of politicization among diaspora Greeks was their participation in secret societies, such as the famous Philiki Etaireia (Society of Friends, founded in Odessa in 1814) and the lesser-known Hôtel Hellénophone (established in Paris in 1809), that specifically aimed at preparing the struggle for Greek independence from Ottoman rule. Recruiting members "from nearly every major social and regional group of the Greek world" (Frangos 1973, 87), the Philiki Etaireia was particularly active among Greeks from southwestern Russia and the Danubian Principalities, as well as among the Phanariots from Constantinople. However, it failed to enroll significant numbers of diaspora Greeks from western Europe (France, Italy, England, the Netherlands) or from the Habsburg Empire. In fact, the society's actual role in the revolution remains largely fantasized, and so is its audience among the upper social strata of Greek diaspora communities. In fact, wealthy businessmen and traders made up only a tiny minority of its members, the bulk of which actually came from middle-class merchant backgrounds. The same holds true for the profile of diaspora Greeks involved in freemasonry, the difference being that most of them apparently avoided membership of openly philhellenic lodges (Grenet 2016, 121–125, 335–341). Although this may sound contradictory, it accounts for the fact that all associations (and even secret societies) were not considered suitable for political activism. It remains true, however, that membership in any of these societies testifies to a broader process of politicization at work among diaspora Greeks.

Eventually, the latter should also be considered in the European political context of the first three decades of the nineteenth century, which, in the wake of the French Revolution, was marked by the spread of liberal and republican ideas. To many foreign observers, the Greek uprising of 1821–1822 was not so much a "national" or "patriotic" movement as one of the many faces of a wider "liberal" nebula, that stretched across the continent to involve radical republicans and secret revolutionary societies, and culminated in riots in Naples (July 1820), Piedmont (March 1821), and Spain (1823). In 1826, a popular *Annuaire historique universel* recalled that the outbreak of the Greek revolution went almost unnoticed: "Although it was an important matter in the general situation of Europe, it was barely noticed amid the heat of religious and financial disputes that created confusion and exacerbated one another" (Lesur 1826, 293). This in turn may have caused some early confusion in understanding what precisely the Greek revolt was about, as well as who exactly was pulling the strings. While it does not really come as a surprise that the pope sought to expose the supposed alliance of Philhellenes with freemasons and Carbonari,

other such instances appear more serious. Hence, the viceroy of Egypt, Mohammed Ali, upon questioning a local Greek trader on the deeds of the Carbonari movement, . . . by which he meant the Philiki Etaireia. At the same time,
the Austrian police in Venice had a hard time navigating the various liberal
groups that gathered in the city's many cafés (Florian, Divina Providenza, etc.),
as "under the cover of philanthropy and assistance to the Greek cause, we shall
fear that there exists a sect, the main goals of which are national independence,
democracy, and the overthrowing of thrones" (police report dated June 6, 1827).

Communities Seized by the Revolution?

While late eighteenth-century political agitation across the Greek world certainly laid the foundations for future uprisings, the outbreak of the 1821 revolution caught most diaspora Greeks off guard. From Ypsilantis's crossing of the
Pruth to rebellions in the Peloponnese, continental Greece, Wallachia, and the
islands, the insurrection spread swiftly (spring to summer 1821), making it exceedingly difficult for contemporaries to take the full measure of the ongoing
movement—and at times just to get the logic of it. Access to fresh, reliable, and
regular information therefore became a key issue, especially as communications
between the eastern Mediterranean and western Europe could take anywhere
from ten days to over a month. This delay often left people frustrated, leading
them to seek additional, and sometimes more informal, sources of information (rumors, doubtful testimonies, and second- or third-hand accounts). The
confused course of events in Greece did not help. As early as in July 1821, the
French *Journal des Débats* reminded its readers of the challenges of covering
this conflict: "We do our best to faithfully and fairly report news from Greece;
but to report news, we need first to understand them, and this is precisely the
challenge with those from Greece." On the following month, the Tuscan journal
Gazzetta di Firenze concluded its "Affari di Turchia" section with the following
statement: "Only time can sort out what to believe in the midst of such incon-
sistency" (*Gazzetta di Firenze*, August 21, 1821).

European newspapers, of course, played a crucial role, all the more since
many (and in some countries, the vast majority) of them adopted pro-Greek
views, at least in the first years of the revolution. As they sought to provide
readers with news of the war, journals faced the double problem of the scarcity
and questionable reliability of their sources, most of which were second-hand
and indirect—we also know of cases of outright forgery, such as with the pro-
Greek *Augsburg Gazette*. Due to their personal and professional ties with the
Levant, Greek sailors, refugees, and traders played an active role in providing
fresh information to local newspapers, which in turn made headlines in the

national press (Dimakis 1968). In many European port cities, all captains sailing from the Levant were summoned to undergo thorough questioning on the places they left or passed by. Although sometimes fanciful, their statements were generally considered reliable sources of information and were quoted as such in newspapers.

Diaspora traders craved for information about the political situation in the Levant, as testified by both their business and their private correspondences. The close-knit structure of Greek trade and family networks made it easier for news to circulate on a large scale, as well as for people to cross-check information from different sources. Meanwhile, a number of diaspora intellectuals (Korais in Paris, Ignatios in Pisa, etc.) spread throughout Europe the information they received from their contacts in the eastern Mediterranean (Kitromilides 2011). This constant flow of announcements, confirmations, and refutations prompted and fueled communication within the diaspora, as well as between Greek merchants in Europe and their friends, partners, and relatives in the Ottoman Empire. However, Greek traders in Livorno and Trieste were often accused of purposefully disseminating across Europe "fake news" about the situation in insurgent Greece.

As the war went on, testimonies from Greek refugees fleeing to western Europe as well as of European volunteers on their way back home also became new, important sources of information. Refugees often provided dramatic (and even sensationalist) narratives filled with realistic details that soon became a fixture among European philhellenic circles. On the contrary, a number of former volunteers had come to bitterly despise the "Greek cause": from 1822 onward, some of them published critical accounts of their adventures that (in spite of attempts by philhellenic committees to prevent their publication) found a growing audience among European readers.

Greek Business and Trade in Time of War

In 1835, German-Russian economist Julius von Hagemeister reported in his *Mémoire sur le commerce des ports de la nouvelle Russie, de la Moldavie et de la Valachie,* that in the Ukrainian city of Mariupol, host of an important Greek community since its foundation in 1779, the wheat trade had been "paralyzed due to the revolution in Greece, only to be revived by the peace of Adrianople [in 1829]." Similar testimonies abound in the historical records, testifying to important "collateral damage" of the revolution, namely the downturn (and occasional interruption) of trade in the eastern Mediterranean, which dealt a heavy blow to the economic activities of Greek diaspora traders. Aside from the consequences of warfare proper, merchants and businessmen were particularly concerned with the upsurge of piracy and privateering in the Aegean (as well as, to a minor extent, in the Adriatic), which threatened ships, cargoes, and crews.

The disruption of commercial activities not only led to a major reconfiguration of trade routes and networks—for instance around the island of Syros, one of the new centers of commercial activities where thousands of Greeks took refuge during the war—it also fueled the distrust among the Greek merchant class toward what many considered as political adventures detrimental to their economic interests. In May 1822, the Austrian police chief in Venice reported that "the Greek families in Venice, with very few exceptions, . . . have so far not displayed great interest in, nor support of, the insurgents, whose rebellion caused them to suffer considerable losses in the Levant; I shall therefore assume that these Greeks are not inclined to assist their compatriots." Three months later, Stephanos Paleologos of Amsterdam bitterly complained about the way warfare had thwarted his plans for reviving Dutch shipping in the Levant: "Thanks to me, this flag was seen in Constantinople again, and had this unfortunate revolution not broken out (may the Lord punish the chiefs and authors of this insurgency, that has caused so much harm), my plan was to direct my ships straight to Constantinople" (quoted in Nanninga 1964, 1074–1075). As businessman and writer Dimitrios Vikelas (born in Syros in 1835) later drily recorded in his autobiography, "I was not born to be a revolutionary" (Moutafidou 2008, 155). More than a mere (conservative) pronouncement on the political outcomes of 1821, cautious statements such as that by Vikelas echo a wider shift, at stake within the upper social strata of the Greek diaspora, toward dissociating patriotic commitment from business ethos.

The Involvement of Diaspora Greeks in the Revolution

Greek national historiography has long taken for granted the participation of diaspora Greeks in the uprising of 1821, just as it has regarded as self-evident their support for Greek independence (Geanakoplos 1976; Tomadakis 1953). As early as the 1820s, however, hosts of pamphlets, brochures, and letters would denounce (or, at best, mock) the supposed indifference of Greek diaspora communities facing the war effort. Under close scrutiny from the Austrian police who accused him of being a Russian agent, historian and philologist Andreas Moustoxydis strongly spoke out against the passiveness of Greek traders in Venice: "The fat cats of Venice sleep peacefully, or rather they are shamefully immersed in lethargy. The image of the homeland does not appear to them even in their dreams" (letter to Capodistrias, May 16, 1828, quoted in Mertzios 1961, 235). How, then, are historians to reconcile these very different views about the involvement of diaspora Greeks in the revolution? Actually, we need to acknowledge once again that there was no such thing as *"the* diaspora," endowed with a unique worldview and agency, but rather several different communities (as well as multiple social strata and factions within each of them), which in turn produced diverse responses to the political agenda of the time. In other words, diaspora Greeks were never unanimous in supporting or opposing the revolution: any attempt at lumping together entire social groups therefore runs the risk of "flattening" out the diversity of their positions, as well as the (often shaky) coexistence of diverging opinions and conflicting stances.

In fact, some communities seem to have been more strongly supportive than others of "the Greek cause." For instance, Greeks in Livorno, Trieste, and Marseilles appeared more active than those in Venice, whose position historians coyly referred to as "lack of enthusiasm," "limited patriotic zeal" (Xanthopoulou-Kyriakou 1978) or "growing inertia" (Enepekides 1965, 134). Yet, while it is sometimes exceedingly difficult to assess exactly *who* did *what,* one also needs to consider the variety of forms of engagement in the conflict: not only were the more vocal patriots not always the most active militarily, but support for the revolution could also translate into more "discreet" types of actions, for instance logistical support to the insurgents or relief of war refugees, in the case of Venice and Sibiu (Karathanassis 1989, 95–96). Eventually, support for the Greek cause could also entail the use of symbols, such as raising the insurgents' flag on Greek vessels touching at European ports (Grenet 2016, 325–326; Karidis 1981, 124–125). Oftentimes, the course of action was predicated upon such prosaic parameters as the economic strength of local communities. Hence, the "Address of the Greeks resident at Trieste on behalf of their suffering countrymen who have taken refuge there and at Ancona," featured in Agnes Strickland's acclaimed novel *Demetrius* (1833): "Owing to the great number of fugitives from all parts who had taken refuge here (in Ancona), and on account of the poverty of the community, [the latter] was no longer able to raise sufficient to support them."

No "Proxy War": Diaspora Assistance to the Philhellenes

In 1824, the Marseilles-based journal *L'Ami des mœurs* published an imaginary dialogue mocking local Greeks' failure to take arms in defense of the homeland: "Young man, your fatherland is in danger, you are tall and strong, why don't you go fight for her and seek to conquer the freedom you seem to value so much?—Ah, I do love her! Let winter pass, and you will hear from me. Now I am cold and frost is biting, but come spring and the Turks will get a chance to see my true colors" (quoted in Guiral 1968, 503). For all its unfairness, this satirical piece was only one of several denouncements of the supposed passiveness of the diaspora Greeks. Needless to say, it hardly reflected their actual involvement in the revolution. In fact, police records of different European port cities testify to the participation of several of the diaspora Greeks in the sending or smuggling of arms, ammunitions, and provisions to the insurgents, as well as in the recruitment of Philhellene fighters and their crossing into Greece. These activities witnessed an early peak in 1821–1822. In September 1821, for instance, Prassakakis, a Chiot trader in Marseilles, shipped 800 rifles onboard a brig bound for Greece, while colleagues in both Marseilles and Livorno (Rodokanakis, Mospiniotis, Patrinos, Pallis) crewed and equipped ships "loaded with a considerable quantity of ammunitions" and other war material (Pouqueville 1825, 235). Meanwhile, Nicolaos Theseus (another of the wealthy Greek traders operating from Marseilles and the nephew of the archbishop of Cyprus) and Costantinos Mavrokordatos (brother of the Phanariot prince-turned-revolutionary leader Alexandros), recruited half-pay soldiers or young liberals who were later sent to the battlefield. At the other edge of Europe, the British consul in Odessa mentioned in a May 1821 letter to Lord Castlereagh "the Greek agents, who at the commencement [of the insurrection], were openly allowed to recruit adventurers, and procure arms and money" (Karidis 1981, 118).

In his memoirs, Italian Philhellene Brengeri recalled the circumstances of his enrollment by Greek traders in Livorno: "The picture of Greece drawn by these gentlemen exceeded those of the most glowing imagination: we were to be received like Gods; and in a year were to march upon Constantinople. . . . I introduced all my friends to the Greek merchants, who told us they envied our happiness, in having such an opportunity of distinguishing ourselves; and that if they had not families, they would go with us" (*London Magazine,* August 1826). Needless to say, the ambiguity of such a position drew heavy criticism on diaspora Greeks, frequently mocked as mouthy patriots who did not dare to expose themselves to the hazards of warfare. This is, to be true, an exaggeration: suffice it to recall that as early as July 1821, Alexandros Mavrokordatos and Andreas Louriotis, along with European Philhellenes and other Greeks living in Italy and France, embarked in Marseilles on an Ydriot brig (*Baron Strogonoff*) to join the rebellion. However exceptional such instances may have been, this notion of a "passive" diaspora in fact calls for a broader assessment of the limitations of historical records. First, the importance of the archival material produced by police control in port cities has led historians to overstate maritime journeys to the Greek lands, at the expense of overland circulation from central and eastern Europe to the southern Balkans (Karathanassis 1989, 91–96; Katsiardi-Hering 2012). Second, the attention drawn by wealthy Greek traders and restless "liberals" has long left in the shadow the participation of lower-profile, and less "glamorous," figures. This is, for instance, the case of Greek sailors and seamen who either joined the insurgents or sabotaged Ottoman vessels in European ports. This was also the case of small-time merchants, such has this Trieste-based "signor Paraschiva," whose story is told by Brengeri: "Having failed, he was obliged to flee from his creditors. Not knowing whither to betake himself, he determined to go to Greece, where Prince Ypsilanti had given him the post of commandant of Kalamata. He was old, short, and very fat. . . . I cannot describe the state of Mr. Paraschiva, who had passed all his life in Trieste, selling sugar and coffee, when he found that he had to provision a hundred and fifty men without funds" (*London Magazine,* August 1826). While this portrait certainly does not resemble the popular imagery of Greek fighters, it sheds light on the hitherto poorly studied trajectories of (diaspora) Greeks of all walks of life who took part in the Revolution (Kitromilides 2017).

A Paper Revolution? The Mobilization of the Greek Diaspora Press

The development of the Greek press is closely linked to the experience of the diaspora, in particular in communities of central Europe such as the one in Vienna. In 1783, the Austrian emperor Joseph II had authorized the free printing of Greek books in his capital city. In June of the following year, the Zantiot George Vendotis published there the first (short-lived) Greek language newspaper; six years later, *Ephimeris* (1790–1797) became the first such journal whose issues have survived to this day; on January 1, 1811, the scholar and priest (and later member of the Philiki Etaireia) Anthimos Gazis published in Vienna the first issue of the famous *Hermes o Logios* (1811–1821), considered the most significant Greek periodical of the prerevolutionary period. Albeit in different directions, these newspapers testify to the politicization of the Greek diaspora between the late eighteenth and the early nineteenth century: while *Ephimeris* published in series the *Declaration of the Rights of Man and of the Citizen* alongside works by Rhigas Velestinlis, *Hermes o Logios* apparently kept its distance from politics to favor the arts and sciences; yet, its editors included several members of the Philiki Etaireia, and the journal was eventually closed down by the Austrian authorities on the eve of the revolution.

The outbreak of the revolution led to a flourishing of Greek newspapers across the diaspora, which echoed the one happening at the same time in insurgent Greece, especially after the drafting of the constitution of 1823 established the freedom of the press (Koumarianou 1971). However, all diaspora communities did not print their own journal: while places such as Paris, Vienna, and Bucharest were instrumental in sending Greek newspapers to communities in southern France, Italy, and Transylvania, diaspora Greeks also received newspapers shipped to them from Greece alongside merchandise of all kind.

In addition to this, Greeks in major European cities of course had access to local journals, in which they sometimes managed to publish articles and petitions. In fact, their familiarity with local media outlets seems to have increased alongside the growing importance that the Greek cause assumed in the European press.

From Backing Insurgents to Building a Nation

While their physical proximity and cultural familiarity with some of the most active centers of the European Enlightenment certainly shaped the political ideas of many diaspora Greeks in the late eighteenth and early nineteenth centuries, it remains difficult to assess the precise role they played in setting the political agenda of the Revolution (Kitromilides 2013). To be sure, some of the most influential political thinkers who championed the cause of Greek independence operated abroad: famous examples include Rhigas Velestinlis (active in Bucharest, Craiova, and Vienna), Adamantios Korais (who spent most of his adult life in Paris), and "Anonymous the Greek" (the author of Ελληνική Νομαρχία [Hellenic Nomarchy] published in Italy in 1806). In turn, the fact that most of them advocated republican and liberal ideas (although of different brands) has long justified the assumption that most diaspora Greeks espoused the same views about freedom and national sovereignty, as well as social justice and equality. Overturning this and similar oversimplified assumptions would require delving into the private correspondence and journals of Greeks settled all over Europe. Daunting as the task may be, it would likely shed interesting light on some hitherto overlooked connections between diaspora Greeks and more conservative brands of patriotism (Ghervas 2004).

For all their (supposed) influence, diaspora Greeks never managed to single-handedly change the course of the revolution. More often than not, they were mere spectators of events that escaped their control. Hence, they witnessed with the rest of the world the gradual splitting of the revolutionary movement into factions, a move that culminated in the infamous "civil wars" of 1823–1824 and 1824–1825. Insurgents themselves had a hard time figuring out the dynamics of power politics, as "National Assemblies" succeeded one another only to be challenged by local governing councils. This came at a heavy political cost, for ever since the First National Assembly at Epidavros, the weakness of the central government as well as the ever-growing distrust between politicians and the military enabled local powerholders to undermine the authority of the new administration. In fact, it soon became clear that the interests of the prerevolutionary elites (such as the primates and the *kapetanaioi*) would eventually thwart early republican ideals and threaten to turn liberated Greece into an "Ottoman society without the Turks" (Dakin 1973, 78).

As they grew increasingly impatient with the conduct of the revolution, diaspora Greeks started criticizing more openly its military and political leadership, as well as addressing the absence of a clear agenda for postwar action. In the midst of this confusion, however, communities did not split along clear "executive" versus "legislative" or "military leaders" versus "central administration" lines. Although, in the early stages of the conflict, a number of diaspora Greeks identified with Mavrokordatos (who had himself experienced exile—albeit a "golden" one—in Padua and Pisa), political factionalism was very much rooted in local family and kin networks. Hence, for instance, the little support received by the "Peloponnesian" notables among diaspora Greeks in western European port cities, most of whom originated from the Ionian Islands and the Aegean, Epirus, Crete, or Asia Minor (Smyrna, Constantinople). Conversely, the bitter feud that arose between Capodistrias and the elite of Greek diaspora trade would later lead to sweeping statements about the unwavering support the governor received from his fellow Ionians.

Eventually, another key factor of political factionalism (which occasionally overlapped with the former) involved the economic interests of the business and trading elite of the diaspora, that largely matched those of the shipowners, at least in the first years of the revolution. As the Greek revolutionary government gained stability, it became clear that the wealthiest elements of the diaspora were to play an increasingly important role. Although Greeks educated in Britain, France, or Russia often identified with the corresponding "party" in the Greek political game, private interests proved more crucial than political ideas in securing their allegiance and support to the new state (Chatziioannou 2016).

Diaspora Greeks and the Birth of the Neohellenic State

Against a dominant narrative that has long considered diaspora Greeks as fully supportive not only of the revolutionary movement, but of the formation of the Greek state, it is worth insisting here on the tensions and ambiguities that actually characterized relations between the homeland and the diaspora by the time the homeland changed not only in name but in nature.

The issue of legal inclusion and political participation of diaspora Greeks in the newborn Greek state was raised as early as during the first national assemblies, when a distinction was drawn between "autochthons" and "heterochthons" (Delivoria 2009). While the first term referred to Greeks native to the insurgent provinces, the latter lumped together three rather different categories of "immigrants," namely Greeks from (1) territories that had remained under Ottoman rule; (2) the Ionian Islands, under British rule since 1815; and

(3) the diaspora communities across Europe, Russia, and northern Africa. Along with the rapid spread of an "antiheterochthon prejudice" among the insurgents (Petropulos 1968, 22), this insistence on the foreign "origins" of the diaspora Greeks regardless of the specificities of their actual experience could only fuel the feeling among them that they were hardly welcome to participate in the power politics of the homeland.

Subsequent reconfigurations of Greek factionalism, for instance, around the so-called English, French, and Russian "parties," only reinforced this sense of political exclusion, which was eventually further complicated by early defini- tions of nationality. While only "indigenous" Christians from the insurgent re- gions were recognized as citizens by the constitution of 1822, the Second Na- tional Assembly (Astros 1823) extended this definition to nonindigenous and Graecophone Christian inhabitants of the same lands, before the Third National Assembly (Troezen 1827) eventually incorporated diaspora Greeks in the name of *jus sanguinis* (Papageorgiou 2005). This ambiguity would culminate in the demarcation of the borders of the new state in 1829–1832: not only were more than two-thirds of the Greeks living outside independent Greece, but a minority of diaspora Greeks originated from the provinces which formed the heart of the country (Peloponnese, central Greece, and the Cyclades). Documents from the diaspora communities testify to the pervasiveness of this ambivalence: in 1835, the Greek consul in Genova informed merchants from Chios of the passing of a new property law, "even though as Chiots they do not belong to the Kingdom of Greece"; five years later, his colleague in Tuscany went even further, as he handed out Greek passports to Chiot traders, who, he thought, had a "right to nationality" because of the massacre that had taken place on the island in 1822 (Grenet 2016, 384; Vogli 2009, 105).

Overall, the difficult legal and political inclusion of diaspora Greeks into the new state left a lasting impression of suspicion about their actual belonging to the national community, as well as about their patriotic commitment. As de- bates raged over the drafting of the 1844 constitution, several representatives backed a resolution banning applications from nonnative subjects of the Greek kingdom to positions in the civil service, a move that was seen as a "*national penalty* for their tardy response to the revolutionary call to arms from the fa- therland" (Vogli 2009, 99). That these parliamentary sessions eventually saw Ioannis Kolettis elaborate, for the first time, the irredentist political project later known as the "Great Idea" (*Megali Idea*), speaks volumes of the strategic role of the diaspora case in articulating notions of ethnicity, nationality, and citi- zenship, as well as in reconciling state sovereignty and the concept of transter- ritorial Hellenism (Kitroeff 1997; Papageorgiou 2005, 420–435).

Capodistrias and the Diaspora

Capodistrias's short tenure as governor of Greece (January 1828 to September 1831) formed a landmark in the complex relationship between diaspora Greeks and "their" homeland. However much historians have disagreed—and still do—about the results of his reformist and modernizing policies as well as his taste for authoritarian leadership (Koulouri and Loukos 1996), little has been said of the role he envisioned for "Greeks abroad" in the young Greek state. Between cooperation and hostility, the nature of this relation however bore heavily on later developments and reformulations of the diaspora-homeland paradigm.

An Ionian aristocrat with strong ties to Russia and only limited familiarity with the Greek political life that emerged during the revolution, Capodistrias had himself had experienced exile (in Padua, St. Petersburg, and Geneva) before he first set foot in Greece in 1828. According to his secretary and occasional biographer, the Swiss Hellenist Élie-Ami Bétant, "three indigenous factions, under foreign influence" opposed the newly appointed governor: the Peloponnesian primates, the Phanariots, and the "half-savants and strong spirits born unto an exotic education." If anything, this testifies to both the multifarious opposition to Capodistrias (Loukos 1988), and the strong contempt he shared for at least a fraction of diaspora Greeks—namely, its economic and business elite epitomized by the figure of the "Chiot merchant." In letters to his friends Alexandru Sturdza and Andreas Moustoxydis, the governor frequently referred to Greeks in Odessa, Vienna, and Venice as "fat cats" (*richards*) and "capitalists," and bluntly expressed his dissatisfaction with "these Greek traders who made colossal fortunes, enjoy them in full security in some foreign countries, yet never ceased being Greeks" (Capodistrias to count de Pahlen in Odessa, 6 / 18 July 1827, quoted in Capodistrias 1839, 156–157). As a diplomat in the service of Russia, he had already stated in his 1811 *Memoir on the Current State of Greece* that "the passion for riches, and especially that for gold, smothers all other passions in one's soul. The lack of patriotism of some of the Greek traders should be understood according to this principle." The only exception he made to this was the involvement of diaspora traders in the funding of schools and other educational institutions both in Greece and abroad, a matter Capodistrias saw as highly political.

This did not prevent Capodistrias from repeatedly calling the same "fat cats" to support the young state's precarious economy. In an 1828 letter to "the Greeks in Ancona, Trieste, Venice, and Livorno," he solemnly reminded them of their moral obligation to the fatherland: "Please do everything you can to assist us. . . . Providence won't let you down. But consider that while she blessed your endeavors and made you enjoy wealth, she did so only for you to fulfill your duties to your homeland" ("Circular letter" dated May 4/16, 1828, in Capodistrias 1839, 85–86). While Greek traders in London, Amsterdam, Livorno, Odessa, or Trieste made hefty donations to the "orphan-box" set up by Capodistrias in Geneva, most of them never supported the governor's policies, which they saw as too authoritarian and subservient to Russian interests. By repeatedly pointing to their egoism and ungratefulness to the homeland, Capodistrias further alienated the economic elite of diaspora communities. By the time of his assassination, many accused him of having made "the people in Greece more miserable than under the Ottoman rule," as well as of "seeding discord among indigenous and exotic Greeks" (*Le Sémaphore de Marseille*, November 17, 1831).

Communities Tried by War

Overall, there is no doubt that the revolution led to a surge in patriotic feelings and national consciousness among diaspora Greeks. At the same time, however, it should be stressed that in virtually all diaspora communities, observation of, and participation in, the events also led to deep strife, conflict, and unrest. If anything, the reception of the revolution among the diaspora thus reshaped community power relations just as it redefined the very notion of "Greek-*ness*."

In June 1821, police chief Francesco Paoli reported that "all the Greeks in Livorno are enthusiastic about things happening in their fatherland; . . . and a community [*nazione*] whose single members used to hate each other until today, now appears all the more united." Yet, such unanimity was short-lived, as discord soon appeared among Greeks and Philhellenes alike. In 1826, a group of self-proclaimed "true philhellenes and Greeks in Livorno" sent Swiss banker Jean-Gabriel Eynard a warning against the local Philhellene Tommaso Petrini, whom they accused of being "a declared and known enemy of the Greeks," a gambler of "an infinity of vicious habits" with a "completely Turkish way of thinking" and connections to local agents of the Egyptian viceroy. Reporting the episode to his friend Gian Pietro Vieusseux, the Greek patriot Spiridon Balbi doubted it was written by his fellow countrymen, "for our Greeks in Livorno care very little about their unfortunate fatherland." Libels such as these are to be found in large numbers among private correspondences, police records, and the press: they testify to the growing discord that had developed within diaspora communities by the mid-1820s, often along the lines of older social and economic divisions. In most cases, trading and business elites were blamed for their lack of patriotism by individuals of lower socioeconomic profile, generally smaller merchants or seamen.

This criticism reached its bitterest expression in Marseilles, when in November 1825, Archimandrite Arsenios, the priest of the local Greek Orthodox church, announced from the pulpit the excommunication of Chiot trader Geor-gios Tzitzinias, whom he accused of building warships in the city's dockyards on behalf of the Egyptian pasha, then the Ottoman sultan's most faithful ally. In a fiery speech, Arsenios called Tzitzinias "Greece's corrupted child" and a "traitor," urging him to "join the Turks, your worthy allies, flee civilized Europe's philan-thropic soil, run and kiss the hands of barbarians, these hands still dripping with your father's blood." Tzitzinias's father had indeed been hanged in Chios in 1822. Factions were soon organized along these lines, which testifies to the visibility of the case. As the incendiary sermon leaked to French and even Italian newspa-pers, Greek pirates sacked French ships in search of goods belonging to Tzitzi-nias, while the Greek business elite in Marseilles organized the boycott of the local Orthodox church, forcing Arsenios to resign—the priest eventually em-barked for Greece the following year and met his death in Mesolonghi.

For all the violence of Arsenios's political anathema, this conflict should not be reduced to an opposition between Greek "patriots," on the one hand, and "collaborators" of the Ottomans, on the other (Petropulos 1976). The broader issue at stake here is that of community leadership, as a new dominant class of wealthy traders from Chios (Chatziioannou 2005; Frangakis-Syrett 1995; Har-laftis 1993) gradually took precedence over older figures of authority. In this per-spective, the revolution led to a reshaping of power relations among different factions within Greek diaspora communities. In Marseilles as in several other diaspora communities, the eventual victory of traders and businessmen came along a series of new regulations that aimed at establishing their authority over local Orthodox clerics (Hatziiossif 1980, 355). Hence the choice of Arsenios's successor, Kallinikos Kreatsoulis, was left to prominent Chiot traders, who con-tacted fellow islanders across Europe to make sure that the candidate (who had formerly taught in Trieste and then Livorno) would remain loyal to their interests. Furthermore, traders also sought to enforce the submission of clerics to their authority by modifying the internal rules of the Greek Orthodox broth-erhoods and church councils of several important communities (Grenet 2016, 112–113, 273).

Celebrating "Heroes," Punishing "Traitors"

By entrusting the fate of Greece to a Bavarian King, the so-called great powers further complicated the already complex legacy of the revolution. As a German newspaper bluntly put it in 1835, Armansperg and his fellow regents "either were not in Greece during the war of Independence, or kept away from the front-stage." In other words, a program of "national regeneration" was to be imposed onto the newly born country by foreign administrators who themselves (and with the notable exception of regent Karl Wilhelm von Heideck) had no direct or personal experience of the revolution. Furthermore, and in spite of the early, often half-hearted support to King Othon of a number of former revolutionary leaders (Mavrokordatos, Kolettis, Metaxas, Makriyannis, Costas Botsaris, Miaoulis), the efforts of the regency to disband irregular fighters as well as the eventual imprisonment and death sentence of Kolokotronis for treason (1834) were widely perceived as a way of overcoming the legacy of the war, even at the cost of cracking down on some of its heroes. In particular, the latter trial resonated deeply within the diaspora, as the consul in Marseilles reported to the ministry of foreign affairs that "people here ask me every day about the fate of Kolokotronis and his accomplices" (Archives of the Greek Ministry of Foreign Affairs 1834). While the "Old Man of the Morea" was certainly a controversial figure during the revolution, his military deeds had gained him respect and legitimacy among most diaspora Greeks, regardless of their political opinions.

Appointments to consulships across Europe exemplify the rising tensions between competing definitions of Greekness in relation to the legacy of the revolution. As early as in 1827, Eynard urged Capodistrias to open consulates abroad as a way to gain the young state international recognition. The governor's premature death however left it to the Bavarian regency to appoint Greek consuls in major Mediterranean port cities. In the fall of 1834, no fewer than fifty-four persons were employed in Greek consulates abroad, most of them located in the western Mediterranean and western Europe. Diaspora traders soon started petitioning for these positions, which they essentially regarded as a means to extend their business activities and gain social respectability. For its part, the Greek state sought every occasion for getting the support of this powerful trading elite. The first wave of nominations (1833–1834), however, mostly rewarded candidates with strong philhellenic credentials and / or good connections with the Greek royal court. In several instances, foreigners of modest pedigree were preferred to their Greek challengers, raising outrage among the diaspora. In 1834, "a deputation of all Greek traders established in London" asked for the replacement of the local consul (the banker Schaetzler) by "a Greek," namely Pandias Rallis, from Chios. The example was soon to be followed in other diaspora communities, eventually leading the regency to prefer Greek candidates over foreigners. In Marseilles, the new consul was none else than Tzitzinias, despite all the doubts still surrounding his attitude during the war, as well as the strong opposition of some local Greeks. While well aware of the embarrassment caused by this nomination, the Greek foreign minister Rizos-Neroulos insisted that he "did not base [his] proposition on the services his family granted to the homeland, but rather on his quality as a Greek, on his wealth, on his credit, and on the obvious stake of the public service in such a

nomination." (Rizos-Neroulos to King Othon, August 21/September 2, 1836, Yp-
ourgeio Exoterikon, 1836, 37/4/Consulate of Greece at Marseilles). While
seeking to secure the economic support to the young state of the trading elite
from Chios, the minister theorized a few lines down the page about his very
own definition of the "patriotism of the expatriates": "The Greeks who had to
stay afar while their fatherland was fighting for its liberation, could contribute
only through loans or donations in money, weapons, ammunitions, etc." Sum-
marizing the patriotic commitment of diaspora Greeks to their economic assistance of the Greek kingdom eventually proved to be a risky bet: not only did it
marginalize those who had opted for more modest and discreet forms of engagement in the conflict, but it also overstated the nature of the link between the
diaspora's economic elite and the young nation. In fact, while support from diaspora bankers and businessmen certainly proved vital to the state's economic and
financial survival over the course of the nineteenth century (Dertilis 2005), only
a few of them eventually moved to settled in the new country. In this respect, as
in others, *the* diaspora never actually "came back *home*": the reconfiguration of
diaspora-homeland relations over the course of the revolution and the early
years of Othon's monarchy by no means led to a "reunification" of two entities of
the same essence, but rather to the articulation of a new grammar of difference,
belonging, and identity that ultimately tied their destinies to one another.

Mathieu Grenet

References

Archives of the Greek Ministry of Foreign Affairs. 1834. "Προξενεία της Ελλάδος εις
    Μασσαλίαν," 37–10.
Capodistrias, Ioannis. 1839. *Correspondance du comte J. Capodistrias, Président de la Grèce*,
    edited by d'Élie-Ami Bétant. 4 vols. Geneva and Paris.
Chatziioannou, Maria Christina. 2005. "Greek Merchant Networks in the Age of Empires,
    1770–1780." In *Diaspora Entrepreneurial Networks: Four Centuries of History*, edited by Ina
    Baghdiantz-McCabe, Gelina Harlaftis, and Ioanna Pepelasis Minoglou, 371–382. Oxford.
Chatziioannou, Maria Christina. 2016. "Merchant-Consuls and Intermediary Service in
    the Nineteenth Century Eastern Mediterranean." In *The Greeks and the British in the
    Levant, 1800–1960s: Between Empires and Nations*, edited by Anastasia Yiangou, George
    Kazamias, and Robert Holland, 159–176. London and New York.
Cohen, Abner. 1971. "Cultural Strategies in the Organization of Trading Diasporas,"
    The Development of Indigenous Trade and Markets in West Africa, edited by Claude
    Meillassoux, 266–281. London.
Dakin, Douglas. 1973. *The Greek Struggle for Independence, 1821–1833*. Berkeley and Los Angeles.
Delivoria, Yanna. 2009. "The Notion of Nation: The Emergence of a National Ideal in the
    Narratives of 'Inside' and 'Outside' Greeks in the Nineteenth Century." In *The Making of*

Modern Greece: Nationalism, Romanticism, and the Uses of the Past (1797–1896), edited by Roderick Beaton and David Ricks, 109–121. Farnham and Burlington, VT.

Dertilis, Georges B. 2005. *Ιστορία του ελληνικού κράτους, 1830–1920* [History of the Greek state, 1830–1920]. Athens.

Dimakis, Jean. 1968. *La guerre de l'indépendance grecque vue par la presse française (période de 1821 à 1824). Contribution à l'étude de l'opinion publique et du mouvement philhellénique en France.* Thessaloniki.

Enepekides, Polychronis K. 1965. *Ρήγας, Υψηλάντης, Καποδίστριας. Έρευναι εις τα αρχεία της Αυστρίας, Γερμανίας, Ιταλίας, Γαλλίας και Ελλάδος.* Athens.

Frangakis-Syrett, Elena. 1995. *Οι Χιώτες έμποροι στις διεθνείς συναλλαγές, 1750–1850* [Chiot traders in international exchanges, 1750–1850]. Athens.

Frangos, George. 1973. "The Philiki Etairia: A Premature National Coalition." In *The Struggle for Greek Independence*, edited by Richard Clogg, 87–103. London and Basingstoke.

Geanakoplos, Deno J. 1976. "The Diaspora Greeks: The Genesis of Modern Greek National Consciousness." In *Hellenism and the First Greek War of Liberation, 1821–1830: Continuity and Change*, edited by Nikiforos P. Diamandouros, Peter W. Topping, and John Peter Anton, 59–77. Thessaloniki.

Ghervas, Stella. 2004. "Le philhellénisme d'inspiration conservatrice en Europe et en Russie." In *Peuples, états et nations dans le Sud-Est de l'Europe*, edited by Elena Siupiur, 98–110. Bucharest.

Grenet, Mathieu. 2016. *La fabrique communautaire: Les grecs à Venise, Livourne et Marseille, 1770–1840*. Rome and Athens. "

Guiral, Pierre. 1968. "Marseille et les Grecs, du XIXe siècle à nos jours" In *Über beziehungen des Griechentums zum Ausland in der Neueren Zeit*, edited by Johannes Irmscher and Marika Mineemi. Berlin.

Hagemeister, Jules de. 1835. *Mémoire sur le commerce des ports de la Nouvelle Russie, de la Moldavie et de la Valachie*. Odessa.

Harlaftis, Gelina. 1993. "Εμπόριο και ναυτιλία τον 19ο αιώνα. Το επιχειρηματικό δίκτυο των Ελλήνων της διασποράς. Η 'χιώτικη' φάση, 1830–1860" [Trade and navigation in the 19th century. The business networks of diaspora Greeks: the "Chiot" phase, 1830–1860]. *Mnimon* 13:69–127.

Harlaftis, Gelina. 2005. "Mapping the Greek Maritime Diaspora from the Early Eighteenth to the Late Twentieth Centuries." In *Diaspora Entrepreneurial Networks: Four Centuries of History*, edited by Ina Baghdiantz-McCabe, Gelina Harlaftis, and Ioanna Pepelasis Minoglou, 147–171. Oxford.

Hassiotis, Ioannis. 1989. "Continuity and Change in the Modern Greek Diaspora." *Journal of Modern Hellenism* 6:9–24.

Hatziiossif, Christos. 1980. "La colonie grecque en Égypte (1833–1856)." PhD diss., Université Paris IV—EPHE IVe Section.

Isabella, Maurizio, and Konstantina Zanou, eds. 2016. *Mediterranean Diasporas: Politics and Ideas in the Long 19th Century*. London.

Karathanassis, Athanasios E. 1989. *L'Hellénisme en Transylvanie. L'activité culturelle, nationale et religieuse des compagnies commerciales helléniques de Sibiu et de Brasov aux XVIIIe-XIXe siècles.* Thessaloniki.

Karidis, Viron. 1981. "A Greek Mercantile 'Paroikia': Odessa, 1774–1829." In *Balkan Society in the Age of Greek Independence,* edited by Richard Clogg, 111–136. London.

Katsiardi-Hering, Olga. 1995. "Εκπαίδευση στη διασπορά. Προς μια παιδεία ελληνική ή προς 'θεραπεία' της πολυγλωσσίας;" [Education in the diaspora: Toward a Greek education, or in service of multilingualism?]. In *Modern Greek Society and Culture,* edited by Dimitris G. Apostolopoulos, 153–177. Athens.

Katsiardi-Hering, Olga. 2012. "Greek Merchant Colonies in Central and South Eastern Europe in the Eighteenth and Early Nineteeenth Centuries." In *Merchant Colonies in the Early Modern Period,* edited by Victor N. Zakharov, Gelina Harlaftis, and Olga Katsiardi-Hering, 127–140. London.

Kitroeff, Alexander. 1997. "The Idea of the Nation and of the Diaspora." In *Greeks in English-Speaking Countries: Culture, Identity, Politics,* edited by Christos P. Ioannides, 277–285. New Rochelle.

Kitromilides, Paschalis M. 1992. *The Enlightenment as Social Criticism: Iosipos Moisiodax and Greek Culture in the Eighteenth Century.* Princeton, NJ.

Kitromilides, Paschalis M. 1996. *Νεοελληνικός Διαφωτισμός. Οι πολιτικές και κοινωνικές ιδέες* [Neohellenic Enlightenment: Political and social ideas]. Athens.

Kitromilides, Paschalis M. 2011. "The Orthodox Church and the Enlightenment: Testimonies from the Correspondence of Ignatius of Ungrowallachia with G. P. Vieusseux," *Egnatia* 15:81–88.

Kitromilides, Paschalis M. 2013. *Enlightenment and Revolution: The Making of Modern Greece.* Cambridge, MA.

Kitromilides, Paschalis M. 2017. "In Search of *Litterae Humaniores:* Presences and Absences in the Readership of the Biblioteca Laurenziana." In *San Lorenzo. A Florentine Church,* edited by Robert W. Gaston and Louis A. Waldman, 679–697. Cambridge, MA.

Koulouri, Christina, and Christos Loukos. 1996. *Τα πρόσωπα του Καποδίστρια. Ο πρώτος Κυβερνήτης της Ελλάδας και η νεοελληνική ιδεολογία, 1831–1996* [Kapodistrias's faces: Greece's first governor and modern Greek ideology, 1831–1996]. Athens.

Koumarianou, Aikaterini. 1971. *Ο Τύπος στον Αγώνα* [The press in the struggle]. Athens.

Lesur, Charles-Louis. 1826. *Annuaire historique universel pour 1825.* Paris.

Loukos, Christos. 1988. *Η αντιπολίτευση κατά του Κυβερνήτη Ιω. Καποδίστρια, 1828–1831* [The opposition to Governor Ioannis Kapodistrias, 1828–1831]. Athens.

Moutafidou, Ariadni. 2008. "Greek Merchant Families Perceiving the World: The Case of Demetrius Vikelas." *Mediterranean Historical Review* 23, no. 2: 143–164.

Nanninga, Jan G. 1964–1966. *Bronnen tot de geschiedenis van den Levantschen handel. 4e deel: 1765–1826.* 2 vols., Den Haag.

Mertzios, Ioannis. 1961. "Ανέκδοτος αλληλογραφία του Ιωάννου Καποδίστρια." *Παρνασσός* 3, no 2: 207–238.

Papageorgiou, Stephanos. 2005. *Από το γένος στο έθνος. Η θεμελίωση του ελληνικού κράτους, 1821–1862* [From genos to ethnos: The foundation of the Greek state, 1821–1862]. Athens.

Petropulos, John Anthony. 1968. *Politics and Statecraft in the Kingdom of Greece, 1833–1843.* Princeton, NJ.

Petropulos, John Anthony. 1976. "Forms of Collaboration with the Enemy During the First Greek War of Liberation." In *Hellenism and the First Greek War of Liberation, 1821–1830:*

Continuity and Change, edited by Nikiforos P. Diamandouros, Peter W. Topping, and John Peter Anton, 131–143. Thessaloniki.

Pouqueville, François.1825. *Histoire de la régénération de la Grèce, comprenant le précis des événements depuis 1740 jusqu'en 1824,* 4 vols. Brussels.

Seirinidou, Vasiliki. 2008. "The 'Old' Diaspora, the 'New' Diaspora, and the Greek Diaspora in the Eighteenth through Nineteenth Centuries Vienna." In *Homelands and Diasporas: Greeks, Jews and Their Migrations,* edited by Minna Rozen, 155–159. London and New York.

Tomadakis, Nikolaos. 1953. *Η συμβολή των ελληνικών κοινοτήτων του εξωτερικού εις τον αγώνα της ελευθερίας* [The contribution of the Greek communities abroad in the War of Liberation]. Athens.

Vogli, Elpida. 2009. "A Greece for Greeks by Descent? Nineteenth-Century Policy on Integrating the Greek Diaspora." In *Greek Diaspora and Migration Since 1700,* edited by Dimitris Tziovas, 99–110. Aldershot.

Xanthopoulou-Kyriakou, Artemi. 1978. "Η Ελληνική Κοινότητα της Βενετίας (1797–1866). Διοικητική και οικονομική οργάνωση, εκπαιδευτική και πολιτική δραστηριότητα." PhD diss., Aristotle University.

Zanou, Konstantina. 2018. *Transnational Patriotism in the Mediterranean, 1800–1850: Stammering the Nation.* Oxford and New York.

Ottoman Context

When one examines the Greek Revolution as an Ottoman experience, several themes revolving around the issue of mobilization stand out as fundamental. This is due to the fact that the forces of the Ottoman *ancien régime* proved untrustworthy and inefficient allies for the Ottoman central state to fight its battles against the Greek insurgents, forcing the Sublime Porte to rethink its system of imperial allegiances and human capital, and recast its military establishment and society in order to prevent collapse (Map 2).

The *Bedeviyet* Project

The first two years of the Greek Revolution witnessed an abrupt change in Ottoman political idiom and culture. Unable to make sense of the "national idea" and the Greek insurgents' unrelenting self-sacrificial activities, Sultan Mahmud II and the Ottoman central state elite turned to Ibn Khaldun, the fourteenth-century Maghrebi scholar and the most remarkable "collapsist" Muslim theoretician of all times, in order to interpret the situation and find a solution to the acute crisis. Official Ottoman documents reveal the Sublime Porte's endeavors to promote a sense of Islamic patriotism and a discourse of peoplehood contesting the Greek national idea through instrumental appeals to a vocabulary of Ibn Khaldunian ancestral imagery. Not only did Ibn Khaldunian concepts and formulations dominate Ottoman administrators' moral and intellectual universe, they were also virtually put to the test for a bizarre social-engineering project as soon as the Greek Revolution broke out.

In his masterpiece, the *Muqaddima,* Ibn Khaldun (1332–1406) determined that dynasties and states have a lifespan and go through five stages similar to those of human beings: they are born, they grow, mature, and eventually die and are replaced by new ones. During the life stages of the dynasty, the society it governs also transforms from "bedouinism" to "urbanism," or, to use his terminology, from *bedeviyet* to *hazariyet,* losing its nomadic vigor to a sedentary lifestyle. In the first stage, the leaders are still organic members of society, visible and accessible to the common folk; the culture is highly warlike; people are motivated, able, can carry out rapid mobilization, and are not plagued by moral and material corruption. The people do not possess conveniences and luxuries beyond the bare necessities. They wear simple clothes, live in tents or modest houses, and eat simple food. Most importantly, they always carry weapons and do not entrust their security to others.

Once people become sedentary, however, they indulge in a life of ease and sink into luxury and plenty. People become lazy and cowardly, and waste and squandering dominate society. People imitate royal habits and "take the greatest pride in the preparation of food and a fine cuisine, in the use of varied splendid clothes of silk and brocade and other fine materials, in the construction of ever higher buildings and towers, in elaborate furnishings for the buildings" (Ibn Khaldun 1967, 249–250). *Hazaris* entrust their security to the state. Behind the secure city walls and with a police system guarding their lives and property, they are carefree and trusting, and cease to carry weapons. Successive generations grow up in this way of life and the energy that motivates people and holds them together (*asabiyet*) weakens to the point that the state and people are no longer able to defend themselves. Eventually, they are swallowed up by other nations.

The rhetoric and terminology used by the Ottoman administrators following the outbreak of the Greek uprising indicate their belief that the Ottoman state was in the fifth and last stage of the Ibn Khaldunian dynastic cycle, namely, the stage of "waste and extravagance," when the people are indifferent and the state is senile and begins to crumble at its extremities. The Ottoman state was in such bad shape that even "the Greeks who had prospered with the benefaction of the Sublime State [i.e. Ottoman Empire] and whom nobody took seriously, rebelled and seized provinces in the Morea and its environs" (Mahmud II's Hatt-ı Hümayun, undated, BOA / HAT 17325). According to the ministers of the Imperial Council, because the Ottomans "all got used to repose and ease, and . . . fell to embellishment and waste, the power and might of the Sublime State and its former awe and dread in the eyes of the enemies had gradually diminished and all enemies felt capable of defeating [the Ottomans]" (Minutes of the Imperial Council, undated, BOA / HAT 40116). Mahmud II's assessment of the crisis also reflected the prevailing Ottoman point of view that the moral decadence of the Ottomans and the weakness of the state were greater causes for insurrection than the conscious political action of the Greeks. The sultan was

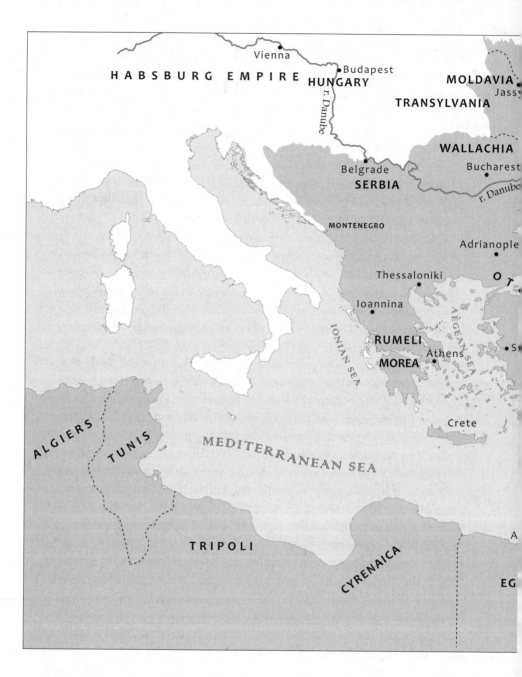

quite vocal about his Ibn Khaldunian apprehensions, deeming that "the infidels [i.e. Greeks] could dare to revolt because they discerned that the Ottoman
dignitaries and officials were engaged in debauchery and indifferent, and did
not have the energy to take action" (Mahmud II's Hatt-ı Hümayun, undated,
BOA / HAT 50174).

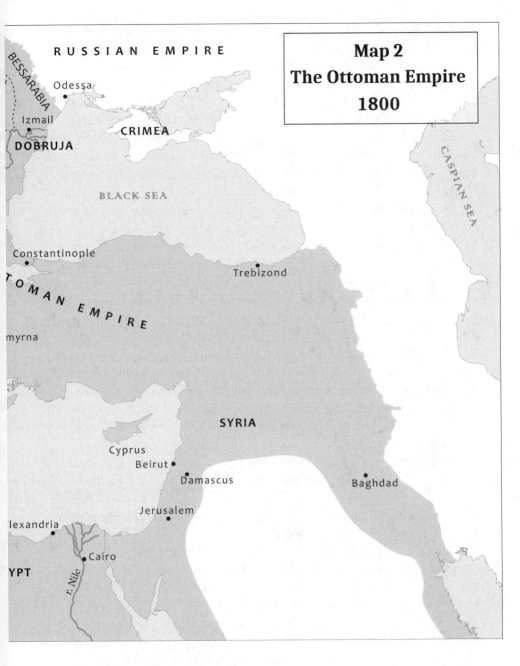

In the face of the Greek uprising, the term used by the Ottoman administrators for the desired condition of the Muslims was *bedeviyet*. The only solution
was to abandon all traits of the *hazari* lifestyle and to adopt *bedeviyet*, in other
words, to revert to the first stage of the Ibn Khaldunian dynastic cycle. The necessity to adopt *bedeviyet* was suggested to the sultan by the Imperial Council

sometime between March 29 and 31, 1821. The council concluded that "*hazariyet* had been, for a long time, a bad habit of human nature almost impossible to give up" and, due to the "commencement of the bandit issue [i.e., Greek Revolution]," it had to be transformed into a state of *seferiyet* (i.e., mobilization, state of war). Incidentally, in the first months of the Greek Revolution, *seferiyet* (mobilization) was used interchangeably with *bedeviyet,* to underline that *bedeviyet* essentially meant mobilization of the people. Furthermore, all Muslims were to "forsake debauchery completely and gradually adapt their manners and actions to [*seferiyet*]" (Minutes of the Imperial Council, undated, BOA / HAT 50174). "As a prelude to the transition from *hazariyet* to *bedeviyet*," the council considered appropriate the acquisition of weapons and horses by those who were as yet unarmed (Minutes of the Imperial Council, undated, BOA / HAT 50174).

Hence, in an effort to regenerate society after the example of the state-forming ancestors, the Sublime Porte carried out compulsory mobilization and compelled the male Muslim inhabitants of major urban centers to mimic the warlike ways of the ancestors as described by Ibn Khaldun. The first public firmans calling for *bedeviyet* were read on March 31 in various neighborhoods of Istanbul and dispatched to every corner of the empire. All Muslims were called upon to "take up arms, acquire horses and abandon all pomp and luxury" (Firman to the Defterdar, March 31, 1821, BOA / C.DH. 6478). In his letter of appointment, the sultan reminded his new grand vizier Benderli Ali Pasha that "the current period was not comparable to any other time" and that "all officials had to abandon *hazariyet,* pomp and ornaments and avoid every sort of waste and debauchery" (Mahmud II's Hatt-ı Hümayun, undated, BOA / HAT 51077).

Consequently, very soon all of Ottoman officialdom, from the grand vizier to the junior scribe at the Sublime Porte, and all male Muslim inhabitants of Istanbul and other major cities were bearing arms. Many inhabitants of Istanbul who received the call rushed to the bazaars to buy weapons. Officers forced even old men and little boys to bear arms.

The galvanizing proclamations of the Sublime Porte and the arming of the Muslim populace, however, paved the way for events unprecedented in Ottoman history. Major Ottoman cities became scenes of indiscriminate public violence against non-Muslims. Although there is no evidence pointing to the Sublime Porte's involvement in organizing the events, apparently, the Muslim city folk perceived the inaction of the state in putting down the riots as a license to kill. The victims were overwhelmingly, but not exclusively, Greek. Other non-Muslim Ottoman nationalities—including Jews—as well as Europeans were also subjected to widespread violence. Greek commercial activities were altogether suspended and non-Muslims were practically placed under curfew. Diplomatic reports and eyewitness accounts mention an armed and licentious population, wandering through the streets of Istanbul and its suburbs, turning loose upon unarmed inhabitants and committing excesses on an everyday basis. There is not much reliable data about the scope of the events that enveloped Istanbul, but British diplomatic documents allow us to trace four waves of collective violence between April and December 1821. According to the only concrete data regarding the extent of the destruction, by the end of the third wave, out of seventy-six Greek churches and chapels in Istanbul and its environs, one was utterly destroyed and thirteen were plundered (Strangford to Castlereagh, July 30, 1821, TNA / FO 78-99 / 36).

In Izmir, the events took the shape of outright janissary riots and continued sporadically for nine months. According to the British consular reports, a general massacre of the Greek population in Izmir was intended at least three times (on June 3 and 15, and November 20), and prevented only by the determined conduct of Hasan Pasha, the castellan of the town. The casualties were in the hundreds. Thessaloniki also witnessed serious crowd action under the supervision of Sirozi Yusuf Pasha, the *ayan* (i.e., provincial magnate) of the region. In Edirne and Kayseri, the janissaries executed dozens of prominent Greeks, not in virtue of orders from Istanbul, but because such was their pleasure.

When the chaos became too much to handle, the Ottoman government endeavored to monopolize the use of violence and issued numerous decrees proclaiming the definition of a true *bedevi* and *bedeviyet*. "Muslims had armed themselves and, to the best of their abilities, acquired horses. Yet, tucking in a *sorani* [i.e., kind of weapon] to one's belt did not mean *bedeviyet*." *Bedeviyet* meant "abandoning whatever ways (of life] people had adopted for themselves" (Salih Pasha [grand vizier] to Mahmud II, undated, BOA / HAT 51338). Carrying weapons was a prerequisite of *bedeviyet* but firing at innocent *rayah* (tax-paying subjects of the Ottoman state) was declared against the sharia. After the third wave of public violence, a *firman* (imperial edict) was issued announcing that inflicting violence on the *rayah* without provocation would be punished with death. Another decree was issued to disarm children. "Little miscreants under seven years of age and armed with daggers and pistols" as the British ambassador called them, "had the privilege of robbing, stabbing and shooting with impunity" (Strangford to Castlereagh, July 10, 1821, TNA / FO 78-99 / 24). Consequently, the shops and markets opened and public order was restored in Istanbul.

Around the same time, a dress code was introduced ordering all officials to abandon flamboyant *hazari* clothes, such as *kaftan* and *dolama* (styles of jackets), and wear unsophisticated, military looking ones, like *şalvar* (baggy trouser) and a headgear called *orta*. The officials were ordered to "acquire horses instead of wasting money on expensive shawls and various items of debauchery" (Edict

Regarding Acquisition of Weapons and Abandoning Paraphernalia of *Haz-ariyet* [June 18, 1821], BOA / HAT 51338-A). Uniformity in clothing—all Ottomans wearing the same military clothes—might call forth a behavioral change and also thwart the most conspicuous expression of class distinction that posed a threat to solidarity among Muslims.

Regulating the daily lives of Muslims was pushed to the extreme with the ban on excessive food consumption. "In the houses of the ulema, dignitaries, officials and Muslims in general, five to seven courses were cooked," and the sultan proclaimed that the ones who exceeded this figure should be condemned and reprimanded (Salih Pasha [grand vizier] to Mahmud II, July 8, 1821, BOA / HAT 49150).

The official historiographers Şanizade and Cevdet narrate this unremarked enterprise of the Sublime Porte in a few passing paragraphs as a mere design of Halet Efendi, Mahmud II's adviser. They mock the venture, condemn the crowd action against non-Muslims, make a scapegoat of Halet Efendi, and absolve the sultan of all responsibility for the sanguinary events. Indeed, the term *bedeviyet* disappears from the documents with the execution of Halet Efendi in November 1822 and the Sublime Porte had stopped urging Muslim folk to carry weapons probably at an earlier date. Yet, official Ottoman documents evince an initiative larger than Halet Efendi's caliber. The *hatt-ı hümayun*s (imperial [re]scripts) demonstrate the sultan's endeavor to unite, mobilize, and eventually transform his Muslim subjects under an identity that would transcend religion and to rally Muslims' loyalties to the state under a constant position of mobilization by homogenizing Muslims and molding them "back" into the militaristic ethos of the state-founding ancestors. With the *bedeviyet* project, the Ottoman central state tested its ability to recast society and paved the way for the second attempt at social engineering during the Greek Revolution, the abolition of the janissary complex.

Ottoman Russophobia

Throughout the revolutionary years, Ottoman administrators, especially Mahmud II, considered that Russia posed a more concrete peril than the Greek insurgents and they expected an eventual Russian war, which finally took place in 1828. The Greek insurgents, for their part, were regarded as mere bandits and easily suppressible if the Muslims united against them. While minimal attention has been devoted to this perception in the historiography of the Greek Revolution, official Ottoman documents reflect the deeply established anxieties about the "Russian threat" in the Ottoman psyche. According to the Sublime Porte, Russia was the power conspiring, provoking, and secretly assisting the

Greek insurgents, and the Greek communal leadership acted as a Russian fifth column. The most immediate result of this perception was the severe punishment administered to the Greek secular and religious leadership. By the second month of the revolution, the number of executed Greek dignitaries passed one hundred. Ottoman documents reveal that a massacre of all the Phanariots was discussed and proposed by the imperial council at least twice, although it never got Mahmud II's final approval. In one instance, the sultan suggested that such a measure would be fit only if Russia declared war, and in another, if the Russian ambassador left Istanbul (Mahmud II's Hatt-ı Hümayun, undated, BOA / HAT 39285; grand vizier to Mahmud II, undated, BOA / HAT 50200). Even the real reason behind the patriarch's execution—according to the information gathered by the British ambassador—was that the patriarch had helped the family of Dimitris Mourouzis, the brother of Constantinos, the executed Russophile dragoman, escape to Russia (Strangford to Castlereagh, April 25, 1821, TNA / FO 78-98 / 25).

From the fifth month of the Greek Revolution onward, more precisely, after the departure of the Russian ambassador Stroganov from Istanbul in protest over the Sublime Porte's treatment of its noncombatant Greek subjects, the Ottoman state not only perceived but actively presented the Greek revolt as a Russian conspiracy. The discourse of the "impending Russian war" became one of the most important tools in the hands of the Sublime Porte to control the janissaries and Muslim public opinion in general, despite the fact that the Ottoman administrators were convinced that Russia would not bring its grievances regarding the Greeks to the point of aggression.

Ottoman administrators' perception of a Russian conspiracy behind the insurgency intensified the violence inflicted by the state. Yet, the Ottoman administrators' reaction toward the Greek subjects of the empire was far from monolithic and was shaped by different variables, such as changes in international politics, different cliques vying to dominate the Sublime Porte, and local administrators' own initiatives. Hence, the Ottoman responses to the Greek insurgency ranged from genocidal massacres and pogrom-like events to offering amnesty to the insurgents and protecting noncombatant Greeks against Muslim looters.

Mahmud II had one constant though: categorical refusal to enter into any kind of negotiations with the insurgents and to accept mediation from other states, especially from Russia. As the sultan reiterated time and again, and imposed upon his ministers in his imperial rescripts, he viewed the Greek uprising as an internal security issue of the Ottoman state. Thus, to the sultan and the Ottoman administrators there was only one kind of solution: a forced peace, for which the Greeks of the insurgent provinces were to (re)accept Ottoman

subjecthood (*raiyyet*). Accepting subjecthood would be verified by Greeks' conceding to take poll-tax tickets, followed by making a "deed of obedience" and
registering it at the local court. In other words, the Greeks' status was to be
placed back into its existing legal infrastructure within Islamic laws and Ottoman customs through a bureaucratic process linking the Greek individual to
the empire. This could be achieved either by force or by policies of accommodation (*istimalet*), namely, coaxing the insurgents and the insurgent provinces
through amnesty and tax exemptions. Both of these policies were tried by the
Sublime Porte during the course of the revolution and in some provinces progressed to a certain extent; while in other provinces they failed to make the
Greek insurgents give up their struggle.

This carrot-and-stick policy toward the Greeks continued as long as Ottoman
policy makers entertained the idea that the Russian court would not breach the
Vienna system for the sake of the Greeks and the Sublime Porte could counterbalance Russia with Great Britain. After 1824, however, already troubled by
the "visionary terrors of the Holy Alliance" and unnerved by the shift in Great
Britain's Greek policy, Ottoman Russophobia resulted in the "deadly closing of
the Ottoman mind." This prompted the Sublime Porte's fear of isolation in international politics, the silencing of the peace party at the Sublime Porte, and the
end of the *istimalet* policy, and it led eventually to the prevention of all means
toward a solution other than the total submission of the insurgent Greeks or the
continuance of violence until either party was consumed.

As late as 1828, just before the Russian declaration of war, the Ottoman foreign minister Pertev Pasha revealed that the Sublime Porte had maintained its
initial view on the Greek Revolution, stating, "it was known to everyone that
the Russians provoked the Greek revolt with the aim to easily seize the possessions of Islam" (Lutfi 1999, 1:290). It is now well established that the Russian
court, especially Tsar Alexander, initially opposed the Greek Revolution and
the foundation of an independent Greek state. However, in the final analysis,
the Russian contribution to the establishment of the independent Greek state
is irrefutable. No matter how fervently the Greek revolutionaries fought, the
revolution had been suppressed in most locations by 1828. The Greek state
would see the light of day only after the Ottoman defeat in the Russian war of
1828–1829, a fact that amplified the Ottoman conviction that a Russian hand
must have been behind the Greek Revolution.

Ottoman Soldiery during the Greek Revolution

A theme that stands out as central in all the documents produced by the Ottoman
state throughout the Greek Revolution is the Sublime Porte's unsuccessful

efforts to mobilize Muslim Albanian magnates-cum-warlords against the Greek insurgents. The multitude of documents is due to the fact that the Ottoman state had essentially no army, nor sufficient means to raise one, and was literally at the mercy of Albanian warlords and mercenaries for the suppression of the Greek uprising until the advent of the Egyptian forces in 1825. To understand what had happened to the Ottoman army and the consequent developments during the Greek Revolution, it is necessary to examine briefly the preceding decade, which constitutes one of the least studied periods of Ottoman history.

The Treaty of Bucharest (May 1812) and Russia's revised nonaggressive imperial agenda in the post-Napoleonic world order brought about the favorable conditions for a certain clique at the Sublime Porte to deal with its internal affairs and eliminate the provincial magnates (*ayans*), without whose support the Ottoman central state could not raise an army or taxes after the Russo-Ottoman war of 1768–1774. The *ayans* had carved out almost autonomous statelets for themselves and, especially during the Russian war of 1806–1812, they became ever more independent and less responsive to the Sublime Porte's demands. Hence, in February 1813, the Sublime Porte officially announced and embarked upon a military and administrative project to reassert itself in the provinces. What followed was, to all intents and purposes, a civil war between the Ottoman central state and a myriad of provincial magnates of varying calibers, religions, and ethnicities, and with varying levels of popular support. Official Ottoman documents and chronicles allow us to trace dozens of urban and rural uprisings led by provincial magnates throughout the empire, from Yemen to Wallachia, from Caucasia to Serbia, against the Sublime Porte's encroachments. The last of these magnates was Tepedelenli Ali Pasha, who led the Tosk, Lap, and Cham Albanians to revolt in 1820. As a result of this "de-*ayan*ization" process, in a decade, large sections of the empire were ruined and the Sublime Porte exhausted its pool of military manpower.

By 1821, the de-*ayan*ization in Anatolia was complete and terminated in Rumelia due to the Greek uprising. Yet, provincial magnates were toppled hastily without their networks and infrastructures having been replaced with effective alternatives. Consequently, the imperial viziers who replaced the magnates found it extremely difficult to recruit and mobilize soldiers.

When the Greek Revolution broke out, the military manpower resources at the Sublime Porte's immediate disposal were extremely limited. Moreover, the Ottoman state engaged in unfamiliar and extremely challenging warfare during the Greek Revolution. Coping with a national uprising required the Sublime Porte to dispatch and maintain troops in a multitude of locations for prolonged periods, even where Greek communities did not participate in the insurgency.

In most of these locations, Muslims were either non-existent or constituted a minority, making local troop recruitment virtually impossible and mobilization extremely costly.

The effectiveness of the janissaries and the *nefir-i amm* soldiers (peasant conscripts), namely the two forces that the Sublime Porte initially managed to mobilize, was tested during the Ypsilantis revolt in Moldowallachia and quickly proved unfeasible for the operations in the Morea. The janissary corps had ceased to be the standing army of the Ottoman central state for more than a century. The Sublime Porte's expectations were lowered to the point that the imperial council considered employing janissaries for putting down the Ypsilantis revolt only as a last resort after figuring out that the governor of Anadolu, Ebubekir Pasha, would need over twenty days to recruit soldiers and reach Moldowallachia. The janissaries constituted the only manpower at the Sublime Porte's immediate disposal; yet, their deployment was a matter of negotiation. After lengthy negotiations for their salary, the janissaries agreed to dispatch five regiments. Many of them deserted their troops and were back in Istanbul by September 1821, wreaking havoc in Moldowallachia and the towns south of the Danube.

The *nefir-i amm* soldiers, on the other hand, were recruited from the non-military people of the areas around the combat zones when emergencies arose. Their provisions were paid for by their own communities or by the people of the locations to which they had been assigned, often to the detriment of local economies. This was a cheaper solution for the state in times of financial difficulty; however, the *nefir-i amm* soldiers were practically useless as fighters. Their most important incentive to join the campaigns was to carry off booty and, when they failed to do so or once they faced hardship, they often deserted their troops despite all precautions taken by their superiors to prevent this. In September 1821, when the commotion in Moldowallachia died down, deserter *nefir-i amm* soldiers swarmed all over Rumelia, causing all sorts of trouble.

Initially, the Sublime Porte tried to quell the revolution in the Morea and Rumelia by mobilizing a variety of resources, including the—mostly Albanian—troops employed by Hurşid Ahmed Pasha, who, at the time, was in charge of putting down the Tepedelenli revolt; the imperial viziers directly under the Sublime Porte; bewildered Albanian warlords trying to find their place in the post-Tepedelenli order; and the *ayans* of Rumelia who had been spared from the Ottoman state's de-*ayan*ization project. Throughout the Greek Revolution, the Sublime Porte could not manage to coordinate these military brokers of different backgrounds and different levels and natures of loyalty to the Ottoman state, and remained unable to centralize the administration of warfare. Officials put in charge of suppressing the insurgency often entered into open conflict with one another.

There are no references to the *nefir-i amm* soldiers in Ottoman documents after mid-1822, which points to the fact that the Sublime Porte gave up early on the common Muslim folk mobilizing their resources for "religion and state." All Ottoman officials writing from the provinces preferred mercenaries over what would become the basis of the postjanissary Ottoman standing army a few years later. According to the officials, mercenaries were more controllable than the *nefir-i amm* because they functioned under a certain chain of command. The Sublime Porte ministers also agreed that "mercenary employment was always and everywhere efficient"; yet, they were initially unwilling to resort to such a measure because of the overwhelming burden on the fisc (Hacı Salih Pasha [grand vizier] to Mahmud II, August 6, 1821, BOA/HAT 45887). By the spring of 1822, however, they came to understand that there was no other option. Under the given circumstances, it was more feasible to outsource the war to military contractors who would operate under the command of imperial viziers: "This would cost some money; however, considering the significance of the matter and the criticality of the situation, it was deemed beneficial to clear up the Moreot issue as soon as possible by spending money instead of leaving the matter in the hands of *nefir-i amm* soldiers" (Hacı Salih Pasha [grand vizier] to Mahmud II, undated, BOA/HAT 39121). For the first planned and somewhat coordinated military expedition of the Sublime Porte in 1823, there was not a single Anatolian *ayan* in the Ottoman army encampment in Larisa (*Yenişehir* in Turkish), and a mere twelve thousand out of fifty thousand soldiers had been recruited by the *ayan*s of Rumelia. The only Anatolians in the encampment comprised freelance mercenary troops, totaling 3,274 soldiers. The rest were mostly Tosk and several Geg Albanian mercenary troops paid by the fisc (Register of the Soldiers Employed in the Morea and its Environs, January 18, 1823, BOA/HAT 39969).

The majority of the imperial viziers dispatched to the insurgent regions had their domains in the de-*ayan*ized provinces of Anatolia. They were cut off from the organic local ties enjoyed by the *ayan*s. As a result, they derived less income and could recruit fewer soldiers from their assigned domains. The imperial viziers arrived in Larisa—the major Ottoman deployment base—with around a hundred men in their retinue and had to recruit mercenaries out of their own pockets before heading to their assigned posts in the Morea. Since the viziers had to confine themselves to the amount sent by the majordomos in charge of their domains, they depended mainly on the Sublime Porte for money. The Sublime Porte often assigned to the viziers a—usually Armenian—banker, who lent them money in advance on their future revenues. There were occasions when the sultan paid the viziers' debt to the bankers following military success but, in general, they were expected to take care of their own finances and were occasionally left to their fate once they were unsuccessful.

In the wake of the Greek insurgency, the Sublime Porte's crumbling prospects for recruitment put the Ottoman state increasingly at the mercy of the
"violence market," whose most important suppliers were first and foremost
tribal Albanian warlords, and only in insignificant numbers, freelance ethnic
Turkish mercenary troops. It is probable that mercenaries were technically a
superior alternative to the *nefir-i amm* soldiers; however, the Sublime Porte
made a serious miscalculation by composing the bulk of the army from an
ethnic group that was not external to the issue. Albanian warlords and mercenaries were at the very heart of the matter and were eager to pursue their survival
instincts. They followed their own agendas to the utmost of their capability and
remained quite unresponsive to the Sublime Porte's demands.

The Albanians followed a peculiar policy throughout the revolution. A strong
party of Tosk Albanian warlords, composed of the loyal supporters of Tepedelenli Ali Pasha, had formed a close alliance with Greek insurgents following
the suppression of the Tepedelenli revolt. Omer Vrioni found himself as the
ostensible yet incapacitated leader of this "Tosk league," which had a special
interest in keeping the Greek uprising alive. The Albanian policy was that of
an armed neutrality, secretly counteracting the Turks when they were likely to
gain the ascendant, and checking the Greeks when they were inclined to en-
croach upon Albanian interests. Hence, despite the Sublime Porte's reiterated
exhortations, Albanian mercenaries were often tardy in taking the field and
obeying orders; even when they followed through, they were reluctant to fight
against the Greeks. Ottoman army encampments and castles in and around the
Morea were in a state of continuous unrest and trouble, especially because of
the Tosk mercenaries.

To the pashas in the field, suppressing the rebellion of a non-Turkish people
depending on the soldiery of another non-Turkish people seemed more and
more unfeasible. Thus, they demanded the Sublime Porte to diversify the ethnic
pool of the soldiery and deploy ethnic Turkish mercenaries (*Türk uşağı*, literally Turkish lads), who, reportedly, were more perseverant than the Albanians.
*Sekban*s from Anatolia, *Evlad-ı Fatihan* (*yörük* troops from northern Rumelia),
and soldiers from the Kırcaali region were among these ethnic Turkish freelance mercenary groups. Nevertheless, they also deserted their troops, demanded higher salaries, and disobeyed orders. The *Evlad-ı Fatihan,* that is the
"Descendants of the Conquerors (of Rumelia)," were "summery soldiers" like
the Albanians and had the habit of retiring to their hometowns in the winter.
They disbanded when they did not receive their salaries and their commanders
were accused of treason by the Sublime Porte.

The Geg Albanians were as disinclined to put down the Greek uprising as
the Tosks. The Sublime Porte had made the most extensive preparations to quell

the Greek uprising in the campaign season of 1823, but the expedition ended in abject failure when Bushati Mustafa Pasha, governor of Shkodër and patriarch of the leading dynasty of the Geg Albanians, lifted the siege of Mesolonghi, the center of Greek resistance, in early December, on the pretext of winter. The consternation and alarm in Istanbul were such that Mahmud II, possibly for the third time in his fifteen-year reign, went around in person from one office to another at the Sublime Porte without any prior notice, "urging, threatening and even imploring his ministers to make some decisive effort to terminate the Greek rebellion" (Strangford to George Canning, December 30, 1823, TNA / FO 78-118 / 21). The most immediate outcome of the failure of the 1823 campaign was the appointment of a new cabinet, whose first initiative was to contract out the suppression of the Greek insurgency to Mohammed Ali Pasha, governor of Egypt.

The number of Ottoman documents bearing opprobrious remarks about Albanians is vast. Ottoman administrators considered and presented the Albanian counteraction, Geg and Tosk alike, as the chief impediment to the suppression of the Greek insurrection. Frustrated by the Albanians' averseness to putting up a united Muslim front against the Greeks, the sultan and "Turkish" viziers accused them of being devoid of religious zeal and faith. Yet, the Sublime Porte was in no state to enforce discipline on the Albanian soldiery and provoke another Albanian uprising, which became a real possibility in 1824. The Ottoman central state's humbling experience with Albanian soldiery further fueled its desire to create a disciplined standing army operating under its direct command and hence, it played a central role in propelling the question of janissary reform to the fore. It still remains somewhat ironic that despite its frustration with and distrust of the Albanian warlords on account of their unreliability, when the Sublime Porte felt the pressing need of assistance to quell the revolution in Crete and in the Morea, it turned to its nominal vassal, the ruler of Egypt Mohammed Ali, who was himself an Albanian, native of the city of Kavala in Macedonia.

Abolition of the Janissary Complex

Arguably, the most important consequence of the Greek Revolution for the Ottoman polity was the abolition of the janissary complex. The Sublime Porte's years of unsuccessful mobilization efforts against unyielding Greek insurgents translated into the need to create a new Muslim man, who would mobilize and sacrifice all his resources, including his life, for "religion and state." The janissary came to be viewed as the antithesis of this imagined protocitizen, and the existence of the janissary complex doomed to failure the prospects for the imposition of a sense of Muslim patriotism and military mobilization.

At the time of the Greek Revolution, the janissaries comprised an autonomous complex of an extremely heterogeneous group of mostly lower urban classes, presenting the characteristics of a political party, part-time urban militia, police force, mercenary band, pension fund, trade union, artisan network, employment office, religious brotherhood, and mafia. It appears that by the time of the Greek Revolution, a certain stratum of the janissaries, the *usta*s, had already established its domination over the corps and become the representative of the common janissary before the state. Viscount Strangford, the British ambassador, defined the *usta*s as "junior officers," who were "the most turbulent and dangerous characters among the chiefs of the janissaries" (Strangford to George Canning, February 28, 1823, TNA / FO 78-114 / 19). They had organic relations with the lower classes of the janissaries and were able to mobilize them. Ottoman documents suggest that it was a body of around thirty *usta*s, rather than the janissary Agha or other senior janissary officers, who conducted negotiations with the Sublime Porte on behalf of the janissary complex.

If we are to believe Strangford's account, in the wake of the Greek Revolution, the sultan and his favorite, Halet Efendi, lived in "continual terror" of the janissaries and the Sublime Porte "was obliged to temporize and to do many things contrary to its judgment and intentions for the sake of keeping them in good humor" (Strangford to Castlereagh, September 25, 1821, TNA / FO 78-101 / 18). The Sublime Porte preferred to content itself with limited and imperfect authority over the janissaries rather than drive them to open insurrection by opposing their wishes.

The *usta*s' direct intervention in Sublime Porte politics began as soon as the Greek Revolution erupted. The Sublime Porte entertained and generated growing apprehensions of an imminent Russian war following the Ypsilantis revolt in Moldowallachia. In the face of the extreme Russophobe atmosphere, the janissary party demanded to participate in the central state's policy-making process in order to keep Halet Efendi's prowar tendencies in check. The disposition of the janissaries against Halet Efendi became evident as soon as they were requested to dispatch troops to Moldowallachia and their opposition to the government turned into uncontrollable demonstrations following the deposition of Grand Vizier Benderli Ali Pasha.

After a train of events and negotiations, for the very first time in Ottoman history, the Janissary Agha and two *usta*s were permitted to be present at the imperial council, launching a two-year period of direct *usta* intervention in Sublime Porte politics. Strangford described this event as "époque making" (Strangford to Castlereagh, May 25, 1821, TNA / FO 78-98 / 41). What was revolutionary about the *usta*s' participation in the imperial council was the fact that for the first time the lower strata of the janissaries had a legal and legitimate venue to negotiate their way through "big politics." The Imperial Council had hitherto been a council of the central state elite and its decisions were imposed on the subjects. The *ustas'* participation, however, was a case of a "meaningful discourse" between the ruler and the subjects, preventing the political crisis of the state from turning into a crisis of legitimacy. In the next two years, the overwhelming human and material cost of the Greek Revolution was legitimized through the inclusion of the most contentious section of society in the state's decision-making process. The confrontations between the janissaries and the state did not reach the point of open revolt and both parties managed to survive this period through minor demonstrations and heated negotiations.

A major turning-point leading to the abolition of the janissary complex took place in June 1822 and was triggered by a janissary conspiracy to instigate a general massacre of the Greeks in Istanbul. Allegedly, "some of the more desperate of the *yamak*s (i.e., auxiliary troops in charge of protecting the Bosporus) in conjunction with the lower order of janissaries" hatched a plot which would secure them the permission of the Sublime Porte to massacre the Greeks in Istanbul and plunder their property. The plan was disclosed and the sultan issued a furious imperial rescript threatening the janissaries with "changing the seat of empire and [retiring] with his sons to some place where he should no longer behold his authority contemned" unless the officers of the corps put a stop to these disgraceful excesses and punished the culprits (Strangford to Castlereagh, June 25, 1822, TNA/FO 78-108/33). As a result, the chief janissary officers, together with those *ustas*, not wishing to be associated with the "riff-raff," launched a massive hunt. The number of those who were executed, imprisoned, and banished reached almost five thousand.

With the disclosure of the conspiracy, the higher echelons of the corps began to separate their interests from those of the lower strata of the janissaries, including the *ustas*. The elderly and the commanders of the corps stood in support of the central state and employed the forces under their direct control to enforce the state's measures. This was a major breaking point within the complex, yet, despite their magnitude and importance, none of these events were mentioned by the official historiographers of the period.

In November 1822, Halet Efendi's miscalculated and bold act in exiling and eventually executing Haydar Baba, a popular Bektashi dervish and a resident of the 99th Janissary Regiment, in whom the janissaries apparently found consolation, gave rise to extreme commotion among them. The strife caused Halet Efendi to lose his head and also precipitated the withdrawal of the *ustas* from the imperial council. The janissaries' attempt at institutionalized political participation had thus terminated.

There are more myths than facts about Halet Efendi, but he was certainly a much-hated figure. Since 1811, he had been the most dominant person in imperial politics and alienated a lot of people. Hence the view that he was the cause of all the empire's problems, including the Greek Revolution, was not a mere discourse of court historians but a widespread perception among the people of Istanbul. With his execution, Ottoman religious, military, and bureaucratic elites coalesced around the sultan, and together they grew into some form of paternalistic autocracy. The sultan was no more the prince in seclusion. He was determined to exercise his sovereign authority by his own personal supervision. As soon as Halet Efendi departed from Istanbul, it was only for the second time since his enthronement that Mahmud II attended a cabinet meeting at the Sublime Porte, at which he urged his ministers to hasten the preparations for the imperial fleet to be dispatched to the Morea in the spring expedition.

The absolution of the dignitaries who had been banished by Halet Efendi responded to both administrative and ideological concerns and fostered the new role the sultan assumed for himself. The benevolent act of the forgiving paternal sultan and the reemployment of dignitaries marked another break with Halet Efendi's regime. By February 1823, dozens of exiled state dignitaries were back in Istanbul. In the years that followed, no important state business could be settled without the approval of the Sultan and "no one beyond the limits of the seraglio was observed to take any lead in the management of affairs" (Strangford to George Canning, December 10, 1822, TNA / FO 78-111 / 27). The ministers refused to act and even hesitated to give an opinion. Nevertheless, the elite's attitude seems more voluntary than enforced. The longer the most detrimental problem of the central state, namely, the Greek Revolution, remained in a deadlock, the more the need for a savior-leader figure was reaffirmed. The legitimacy of the sultan and the state elite increasingly depended on the performance of the state in suppressing the Greek Revolution as the cost of the war on the common folk incessantly escalated.

Public despair had so much increased since the beginning of the Greek Revolution that the common Muslim folk, even the janissaries, also came to tolerate the impositions of a savior-leader, rather than rebel against him. Daily life became ever more difficult because of the protracted instability all around the empire. Commercial life and the provisioning of major cities suffered years of stagnation because of the devastation of Moldowallachia, sluggish Russian Black Sea trade, and Greek piracy in the entire eastern Mediterranean. Consequently, there were often food shortages in Istanbul and apprehensions of famine, which compelled the Sublime Porte to purchase corn from European merchants for exorbitant sums in order to prevent riots. Also, inflation was galloping. Between 1821 and 1826, the Sublime Porte resorted to currency debasement at least four times. The main concern was to pay the salaries of the mercenaries and the janissaries with the debased money and reduce the burden of the state.

In addition to the flagging state of the economy, daily life became intolerable because of occasional fires, epidemics, and various natural disasters, as well as the prolonged drought of 1822, which affected the entire northern hemisphere from China to California. There was at least one serious plague and one smallpox outbreak in Istanbul in December 1824 and the spring of 1825, respectively. One of the most disastrous fires in the history of Istanbul broke out on March 1, 1823, and destroyed fifteen thousand houses. If we are to believe Strangford, the fact that not a single Christian house had been damaged in the fire produced such a strong impression upon the Turks that the populace was loud in declaring this calamity "a visitation of providence in vengeance for the atrocities committed at Chios, and even the ministers of the Porte avowed that they considered it as a mark of divine displeasure" (Strangford to George Canning, March 10, 1823, TNA / FO 78-114 / 23). In short, all these dismal events and ever-increasing popular discontent translated into an apocalyptic mindset and growing expectations of a savior among the Ottoman Turks.

It was only owing to such circumstances that the elimination of the *ustas* from the political scene did not provoke a janissary rebellion. As it became apparent, the Greek Revolution was testing the legitimacy of the janissary corps as much as that of the state. The central state's efforts to curb the influence of the *ustas* culminated with the appointment of Rusçuklu Hüseyin as Janissary Agha. On 28 February 1823, in his second day in office, Hüseyin Agha launched a vigorous hunt of *ustas* and janissaries, which was triggered by the mafia-like intervention of the *seğirdim usta*s in the appointment of a Greek bishop. In the subsequent few months, a great number of the *ustas* were either banished from Istanbul or put to death, and the remaining ones apparently submitted to the Sublime Porte's authority.

In the following three years, there were no negotiations between the state and the janissaries, nor were there any attempts on the part of the state to seek approval from the janissaries for its decisions and actions. By August 1823, the network of the *ustas*, who formed the backbone of the janissary complex, had been silently broken. The lower strata of the janissaries were thus left without leadership. The corps was so humbled that the state was able to publicly execute *ustas*, a hitherto "unprecedented occasion" (Strangford to George Canning, August 11, 1823, TNA / FO 78-116 / 7). In January 1824, Hüseyin Agha began carrying out biweekly European-style military drills supposedly with the most refractory class of the janissaries, the *yamaks*, who quietly gave their consent to this "infidel" innovation. The centuries-old practice of affixing the badges of *ortas* (janissary regiment) to vessels and stores was suppressed altogether in

March 1824. Depoliticization of the corps also brought about some military mobilization. In the 1824 expedition, a janissary force of six thousand men was dispatched to Euboea and the Attica region from Istanbul. However, they proved useless, and lack of coordination and mistrust between the janissaries and the mercenaries caused disorder in the army. During the siege of Athens in the summer of 1824, most of the janissaries fell sick; they lifted the siege and left for Istanbul without asking for permission to do so.

One of the most important consequences of the Greek Revolution for the Ottoman state was the disengagement of the *ulema* (i.e., a body of scholars and jurists with specialist knowledge of Islamic doctrine and law) from the janissary complex and their realignment with the central state. From the very beginning of the Greek uprising, the *ulema* became the promoters of what might be called Islamic or religious patriotism. Only eighteen years previously, in the midst of a Russian war, the ulema-janissary coalition had cost the reforming sultan Selim III his head. This time, in the midst of a war against a *rayah* people (i.e., Greeks) and on the brink of another Russian war, it was the central state that won the competition over the control of the Sharia. The success of the central state lay in gaining the upper hand in determining the index of being a Muslim.

This was achieved by rallying the *ulema* to the state's cause and creating a moral position according to which deeds spoiling the unity of Muslims against the "infidels who were trying to trample upon the Muslims and annihilate the state of Islam" came to mean "giving an opportunity to the enemy" (for example, Mahmud II's Hatt-ı Hümayun, undated, BOA / HAT 25590). This had been one of the mantras invoked by the Sublime Porte throughout the Greek Revolution to allay opposition. Any act of defiance against the authority of the state had become not only illegitimate but also immoral. All legitimacy was given to the state by the "exigency of the time," which allowed for such extraordinary measures.

By the time of the abolition of the complex, the janissaries had already been humbled to the utmost. All sources agree that there was no noteworthy popular support for the defiant janissaries during the so-called Auspicious Incident (i.e., the events of June 15–16, 1826, which led to the abolishment of the janissary complex), probably for the first time in centuries. The dismantling of an almost five-century-old body so deeply seated in society became possible only through the silence of the masses, which indicated apathy more than anything, in an atmosphere of discontent and frustration of apocalyptic proportions. From this perspective, the janissary revolt in June 1826 was the corps' last struggle for survival, rather than the reaction of the monstrous bastion of the Ottoman ancien régime against the forces of modernity.

The unsettling effects of the Greek Revolution paved the way for momentous changes in the dynamics between the Ottoman state and society and created a specific moral universe which enabled the central state elite to stifle social dissent and create, as well as impose, a conformism within Muslim society regarding the downfall of the janissaries. The janissary complex was the guarantor of the "contractual polity" and with its demise, the Ottoman checks and balances system redeemed itself from the sway of the "common folk." It was the abolition of the janissary complex that paved the way for an imposed modernity by creating a homogenized Muslim society with fewer sources of dissent, and also a disciplined standing army composed of ethnic Turkish soldiers.

H. Şükrü Ilıcak

References

Aksan, Virginia. 2002. "Ottoman Military Matters." *Journal of Early Modern History* 6:52–62.

Aksan, Virginia. 2007. *Ottoman Wars, 1700–1870: An Empire Besieged*. London.

Beaton, Roderick, and David Ricks, eds. 2009. *The Making of Modern Greece: Nationalism, Romanticism, and the Uses of the Past (1797–1896)*. Farnham and Burlington, VT.

Bitis, Alexander. 2006. *Russia and the Eastern Question: Army, Government, and Society 1815–1833*. Oxford.

Boyar, Ebru. 2007. *Ottomans, Turks and the Balkans: Empire Lost, Relations Altered*. London and New York.

Erdem, Hakan. 2005. "'Do Not Think of the Greeks as Agricultural Labourers': Ottoman Responses to the Greek War of Independence." In *Citizenship and the Nation State in Greece and Turkey*, edited by Faruk Birtek and Thalia Dragonas, 67–84. London.

Erdem, Hakan. 2007. "Perfidious Albanians and Zealous Governors: Ottomans, Albanians and Turks in the Greek War of Independence." In *Ottoman Rule and the Balkans, 1760–1850: Conflict, Transformation, Adaptation*, edited by Antonis Anastasopoulos and Elias Kolovos, 213–240. Rethymno.

Erdem, Hakan. 2009. "The Greek Revolt and the End of the Old Ottoman Order." In *Η Ελληνική Επανάσταση του 1821: ένα ευρωπαϊκό γεγονός* [The Greek Revolution of 1821: A European event], edited by Petros Pizanias, 213–237. Athens.

Finkel, Caroline. 2005. *Osman's Dream*. New York.

Ibn Khaldun. 1967. *The Muqaddimah: An Introduction to History*. Translated by Franz Rosenthal. Princeton, NJ.

Ilıcak, Şükrü. 2011. "A Radical Rethinking of Empire: Ottoman State and Society During the Greek War of Independence, 1821–1826." PhD diss., Harvard University.

Ilıcak, Şükrü. 2019a. "Greek War of Independence and the Demise of the Janissary Complex: A New Interpretation of the Auspicious Incident." In *Political Thought and Practice in the Ottoman Empire (Halcyon Days in Crete IX Symposium)*, edited by Marinos Sariyannis, 483–493. Rethymno.

Ilicak, Sücrü. 2019b. "Revolutionary Athens through Ottoman Eyes (1821–1828): New Evidence from the Ottoman State Archives," In *Ottoman Athens,* edited by Constantinos Thanasakis and Maria Georgopoulou, 243–259. Athens.

Jelavich, Barbara. 1991. *Russia's Balkan Entanglements, 1806–1914.* Cambridge.

Jewsbury, George F. 1999. "The Greek Question: The View from Odessa, 1815–1822." *Cahiers du Monde Russe* 40, no. 4: 751–762.

Kafadar, Cemal. 2007. "Janissaries and Other Riffraff of Ottoman Istanbul: Rebels without a Cause?" *International Journal of Turkish Studies* 13: 113–134.

Karpat, Kemal. 2001. *The Politicization of Islam: Reconstructing Identity, State, Faith, and Community in the Late Ottoman State.* New York.

Kayapınar, Akif. 2008. "Ibn Khaldun's Concept of Assabiyya: An Alternative Tool for Understanding Long-Term Politics?" *Asian Journal of Social Science* 36:375–407.

Lewis, Bernard. 2001. *Islam in History: Ideas, People, and Events in the Middle East.* 2nd ed. Peterborough.

Lucassen, Jan, and Erik Jan Zürcher. 1999. "Introduction: Conscription and Resistance." In *Arming the State: Military Conscription in the Middle East and Central Asia, 1775–1925,* edited by Erik Jan Zürcher, 1–19. New York.

Lutfi, Ahmed. 1999. *Vak'anüvis Ahmed Lutfi Efendi Tarihi* [Historical chronicle of Ahmed Lutfi Efendi]. Istanbul.

Mardin, Şerif. 1993. "Patriotism and Nationalism in Turkey." In *Nationality, Patriotism, and Nationalism in Liberal Democratic Societies,* edited by Roger Michener, 191–222. St. Paul, MN.

Prevelakis, Eleftherios, and Kallia Kalliataki Merticopoulou, eds. 1996. *Η Ήπειρος, ο Αλή Πασάς και η Ελληνική Επανάσταση. Προξενικές εκθέσεις του William Meyer από την Πρέβεζα* [Epirus, Ali Pasha, and the Greek Revolution: The consular reports of William Meyer from Preveza]. Monuments of Greek History. Athens.

Prousis, Theophilus C. 1994. *Russian Society and the Greek Revolution.* DeKalb.

Quataert, Donald. 1993. "Janissaries, Artisans and the Question of Ottoman Decline." In *Workers, Peasants and Economic Change in the Ottoman Empire 1730–1914,* edited by Donald Quataert, 197–203. Istanbul.

Salzmann, Ariel. 2004. *Tocqueville in the Ottoman Empire: Rival Paths to the Modern State.* Leiden and Boston.

Schmidt, Jan. 2002. "Ottoman Autobiographical Texts the Joys of Philology." In *Studies in Ottoman Literature, History and Orientalism (1500–1923),* edited by Jan Schmidt, 195–201. Istanbul.

St Clair, William. 1972. *That Greece Might Still Be Free: The Philhellenes in the War of Independence.* Oxford.

Sunar, Mehmet Mert. 2006. "Cauldron of Dissent: A Study of the Janissary Corps, 1807–1826." PhD diss., State University of New York at Binghamton.

Zürcher, Erik Jan. 2005. *Turkey: A Modern History.* London and New York.

II

ON THE WAY TO REVOLUTION

Communities

The Greek Revolution established new contexts for the historical study of the experience of Greeks within structures of community. In the history of modern Hellenism under Ottoman rule, communities have been seen as emblematic, studied as institutions as much as they are as economic, social, and cultural formations. Communities have been praised for their role in developing themselves as institutions, providing spaces for promoting leadership groups or as sources of economic development as well as educational and spiritual activity. Regardless of the historiographic viewpoint adopted, the contribution of the phenomenon of community in shaping the terms, ideological and other, defining national identity is considered as more or less given. This approach, however, is limited to the prerevolutionary period. By contrast, in the framework of the historiography of the revolution and of the nineteenth century, communities, perceived as central to the local and traditional framework, are, as a rule, approached as inherently opposed to the state and often regarded as obstacles to attempts to build a unified administration consistent with Western models.

The present essay offers a critical approach to this historiographic "antinomy" by examining various versions of the phenomenon of community in the years prior to the revolution, the changes to the institutional framework organizing the provincial administration which were attempted during the revolution, and the forms of resistance and compliance that were manifested in these changes. Last, by turning attention to the processes that the onset of the struggle set in motion within communities, the essay seeks to highlight their importance as fields of the study of society in revolt and particularly as spaces in which the day-to-day reality of the revolution was played out.

Prerevolutionary Communities

As an intellectual product of the nineteenth century, scholarly interest in communities had at its core the legacies of the dominant ideological currents of its time, nationalism and romanticism. It was first and foremost in the context of romantic national ideology that the community was given substance as the authentic manifestation of emotional cohesion based on a common historical trajectory, and where issues of organization of the rural communities of the past became a subject of political discussion and social deliberation. The context of the scholarly study was not, of course, only Greek, but European and global. Nonetheless, its intellectual effects differed from place to place, depending on the historical experiences and challenges of the period. In the Greek case, the fact of the Ottoman conquest and the centuries-long submission of the Greek populations to the sovereignty of another faith was decisive for hypostasizing communities as hearths of national life and pockets of resistance to the conqueror, while ascribing the origin of the institution to antiquity, via Byzantium, contributed to arguments about the contentious issue of historical continuity. Later, during the twentieth century and in different intellectual milieus and political contexts, the Greek communities in the period of Ottoman rule were acclaimed as epiphenomena of the Greek people's democratic tradition, frequently in counterpoint to the European-inspired centralizing state.

However, we would be doing the practitioners of "traditional" historiography an injustice if we did not acknowledge their undeniable contribution to establishing communities as a research field and mainly to rescuing and bequeathing to us a huge volume of sources. From this material newer research has drawn much, while also tapping into the Ottoman archives. Today, we have available to us a host of studies on prerevolutionary Greek communities. Notwithstanding their different historiographic starting points, these studies converge toward the view that the Greek community phenomenon, as it emerged in the period of Ottoman rule, was the product of the particular historical circumstances of the period, which were inextricably linked with the nature of the Ottoman conquest of Greece (Asdrachas 1986; Kontogiorgis 1982; Koukkou 1980; Liata 2003; Pantazopoulos 1958; Papastamatiou and Kotzagiorgis 2015, 116–128).

Communities were informal collective bodies, based on indigenousness, which provided mechanisms for the transaction of the relations of local populations with Ottoman authorities. Each settlement, village, township, or city, independently of its size, could organize itself in a community. Frequently groups of geographically neighboring communities came together in "federations," known as Koina. Communal authorities were elected on an annual basis—not necessarily democratically—by an assembly of adult male inhabitants and were

charged with a broad range of duties and competences, from the collection of
the taxes of the community and their remittance to the imperial treasury and
the adjudication of disputes and the administration of justice to the provision
of social care and charity within the community. In this sense the communities
can be seen as an informal institution for the administration of the subject
population of the empire with pronounced features of local self-government.
The Ottomans' recognition of the administrative and fiscal particularities of
the regions they conquered was a tactic dictated by reasons of pragmatism and
found its theoretical underpinning in the Koran's proviso for granting administrative autonomy to the monotheistic "peoples of the Book" who had fallen,
without resistance, under the political domination of Islam. Although applied
extensively, the community phenomenon did not receive formal recognition, but
functioned as an informal institution of the provincial administration, whose
primary mission was to secure fiscal good order, in other words, the unimpeded
channeling of the provincial tax revenues into the imperial treasury. Determined
by the sovereign, the fiscal function was at the core of the community institution. So, if the collective taxation obligation lent substance to the notion of the
community as a body and initiated the principle of communal financial responsibility, the autonomous management of the taxation obligation by the community authorities, through the allocation of taxes to the inhabitants and then their
collection and delivery to the state, was the stake of community self-government
and the function through which leadership groups emerged from within the
local population (Asdrachas 1986; Pylia 2001).

However, notwithstanding the fiscal responsibilities shared by all communities, the community phenomenon in Greece was neither unique nor uniform,
nor did all the communities enjoy the same degree of self-government. So, if at
one end of the scale we come across communities with a rudimentary organization, at the other end we find communities that formed federal systems, such
as the Zagorochoria in Epirus and the Mantemochoria in Chalkidiki; if at one
end of the scale are the host of communities in which the presence of representatives of Ottoman power left the inhabitants no leeway for self-management, at
the other end are communities with a high degree of self-government and a
feeble presence of Ottoman authorities, such as the islands of the Cyclades.

Although, on account of the variety of community formations, it is risky to
create a typology of communities, the affinity between the degree of autonomy
of a community and the time and manner of its conquest, its geographic location, population size, economic, or other importance for the state, has been
pointed out in related research (Liata 2003, 311). Without this being a hard and
fast rule, the likelihood of a district developing institutions of self-government
seems to be greater where the direct presence of representatives of Ottoman

power was weak—that is, in mountainous and insular regions, in the zones where the regime of small free landownership held sway, in *vakif* lands, as well as in towns and cities. Even so, it is worth stressing that the degree of autonomy of a community was not fixed but was subject to changes, depending on the disposition of the ruler and internal sociopolitical equilibria (Papastamatiou and Kotzagiorgis 2015, 117–118). Consequently, rather than constituting a common organizational or ideological principle, the system of local self-government in Greece during the centuries of Ottoman rule reflected local particularities and presented different manifestations.

After the outbreak of the Greek Revolution, the regions that made up the Greek space in revolt were called upon to come together under a single administration and to constitute a national territory. Because these were regions with strong but differing community traditions, which critically affected the manner of their inclusion in the national territory, a brief presentation may be useful.

The Aegean Islands

The region with the longest and strongest tradition of community organization was the Cyclades. The island communities, moreover, offer a unique version of the community phenomenon in Greece under Ottoman rule, as their functions went beyond narrow fiscal bounds and were fundamental to the nexus of relations and activities of local societies. Having experienced—some of them at least—forms of community administration from the time of the Latin conquest, the island communities were fortunate, on the one hand, because their administration and taxation were under the jurisdiction of the Capudan Pasha and, on the other, because the Ottomans acknowledged, as early as the late sixteenth century, the possibility of these communities regulating their domestic affairs through recourse to customary law. It was in this environment that, from the seventeenth century, a set of rules was developed to regulate a host of issues, ranging from the operation of community organizations and the dispensation of justice to the terms of practicing trade and industry, transferring properties, urban building, using communal spaces, the moral conduct of the inhabitants, and so on. The written codification, from the mid-seventeenth century on, of the customary statutes in the Aegean islands, with those of Thera (1797) and Naxos (1805–1806) being the most comprehensive, attests, moreover, to the need to secure a framework of rules that was being threatened by intense social and interpersonal conflicts. It is at exactly this point that the community authorities, as the informal (extrajudicial) mechanism of resolving differences acknowledged by the Ottoman power (Anastasopoulos 2013, 281, 283), functioned as fiduciaries of customary law and guarantors of social cohesion.

The functioning in the Aegean islands of community institutions meting out justice, with responsibilities covering all aspects of civil law and extending even to criminal law, which was theoretically under the exclusive jurisdiction of the conqueror, has been commended in the relevant literature as the epitome of community autonomy (Koukkou 1980; Pantazopoulos 1958). In reality, the community system of dispensing justice had to function within the narrow framework defined by the need, on the one hand, to keep internal peace and, on the other, to deter community members from resorting to the justice of the representative of the central power, the *kadi* (Kermeli 2007, 176). His role was primarily arbitrative; through applying the principle of leniency and extensive use of monetary punishments and compensations, he aimed at achieving a compromise (εξισαμό) between the parties.

The Argosaronic islands, and particularly Ydra and Spetses, which were linked more closely with the historical fate of their mainland dependencies in the Peloponnese and central Greece, represent a singular version of the community phenomenon in an insular space. Their administrative system was no different, in its general characteristics, from that of the Cyclades. From 1715, when the Argosaronic islands finally passed to the Ottomans, they were under the direct jurisdiction of the Capudan Pasha, while from 1772 Spetses, from 1778 Ydra, and from 1802 the rest of the islands were granted the privilege of flat-rate collection of taxes by the communities themselves. With the appointment of a local Christian governor of Ydra in 1802, assisted by the island's primates with widened responsibilities for dispensing justice and imposing order, self-government enjoyed remarkable development that was expressed by the adoption in 1818 of the Civil and Mercantile Marine Laws, a code of administrative, procedural, and maritime law that regulated almost all the relations and activities of the islanders (Lignos [1946] 1953). The particular nature of the community organization of Ydra and Spetses in relation to the rest of the Aegean region lies mainly in the way community organization reflected the economic and social processes linked with the growth of Greek merchant shipping during the last quarter of the eighteenth century and until the revolution. As result of the dynamic participation of the Ydriot and Spetsiot fleet in the international trading circuit of the Mediterranean and the Black Sea, and the accumulation of capital in the hands of the merchants-cum-shipowners, social stratification on these islands was more clearly class-based than on islands that were not so heavily involved in the new bourgeois activities. The history of Ydra from the mid-eighteenth century onward is rich in episodes of social conflicts, and the power of the oligarchy of shipowners was tested by both internal strife and popular discontent. The island's community history largely attests to the effort to offset social clashes, which seem to have been exacerbated after the end of the Napoleonic Wars that had been so favorable for Greek maritime trade. After all, one such social conflict triggered Ydra's participation in the Revolution (Lignos [1946] 1953, 180).

The Peloponnese

If in the islands the history of community institutions is linked with phenomena of particular fiscal, administrative, and judicial self-government, in the Peloponnese it is linked with the emergence of the powerful Christian elite of the *kocabaşıs*. Although compiling a genealogy of the Peloponnesian primate elite is hazardous, since powerful Christian families existed in the Morea from the first period of Ottoman rule, the bibliography seems to agree on two basic moments in the constituting of the said group. The first is the period of Venetian rule in the Peloponnese (1685–1715), during which the landowning regime of the peninsula was reorganized, with the Venetians conceding or leasing areas previously belonging to Muslims to Christian community leaders and members of old landowning families who adopted a friendly stance toward the new sovereign power. Thus, the nucleus of a Christian rural oligarchy was formed, which replaced the Ottoman landowners and was strengthened by the settling of refugees from other Greek regions, who were involved in local trade (Sakellariou 1939, 43–45).

The second critical moment for constituting the Christian primate elite, counterbalancing the first, was the recapture of the peninsula by the Turks (1715), which ushered in the second period of Ottoman rule in the Morea. Some Christian community leaders who had not bonded with the Venetian administration opted to join the Ottoman side and help to regain the region, thus securing their participation at all levels of the provincial administration—that is, of the community, the district (*kaza*) and of the Peloponnese as a whole. Specifically, each community elected one or more "elders" (*dimogerontes*), who assembled annually in the seat of the district and elected one Christian and one Muslim representative from their number, as well as a treasurer who, under the supervision of the Ottoman district governor, made up the district council. All the district primates made up the Peloponnesian Senate, from which were elected two members who, together with two representatives of the Muslim primates, made up the council of the Ottoman governor of the Peloponnese (*Mora valisi*) (Photopoulos 2005, 41–57; Sakellariou 1939, 87–96). In parallel, the Christian primates of the Peloponnese enjoyed the right of representation at the Sublime Porte, with the dispatch of accredited assignees (*vekils*) of the senate and the districts to Constantinople (Photopoulos 2005, 59–75).

The formation of a powerful Christian primate elite in the Peloponnese was not, however, exclusively derived from the high degree of autonomy of the region's Christian communities, as earlier historiography has tended to interpret it. On the contrary, recent research tends to place the emergence of the *kocabaşıs* in the context of wider socioeconomic transformations in the Ottoman Empire, which were linked with the abandonment of the *timar* system, the introduction of tax farming (*iltizām*) and the constitution of the provincial *ayan* elite. The participation of the *kocabaşıs* in the *iltizām* system as lessees of tax revenues made them representatives of the state machine in their communities. The strengthening of the said group, rather than indicating a high degree of community autonomy, was a factor in the shrinking of this autonomy, as it subjugated the community functions to the private interests of certain families that monopolized community offices. Indeed, in the (frequent) cases where the *kocabaşıs* were not only tax farmers but also moneylenders to the community, the dependence of the population on them deepened and was expressed at both an economic level, through indebtedness, and a political level, through the induction of the population into the clientage networks of the Christian primates.

The power primacy of the *kocabaşıs* would be felt from the mid-eighteenth century onward, when entire districts of the Peloponnese found themselves under the economic and political control of certain families (e.g., the Notaras family in Corinthia, the Perroukas family in Argos, the Zaimis family in Kalavryta, the Kougias family in Tripolitsa, the Papagiannopoulos family in Karytaina, the Sisinis family in Gastouni and Pyrgos, the Mavromichalis family in Mani, and so on), which had private armies (*kapoi*) and strong connections with representatives of the Ottoman authority. The end of the "good times," as the primates characterized the fifty years after the Ottomans won back the Peloponnese, began in the 1760s, when the upsurge in animosity between rival clans caused the intervention of the Ottoman authorities, which went so far as to cause the execution of important members of the local primate classes, both Christian and Muslim. This development is also indicative of the limits of the "autonomy" of the *kocabaşıs,* who had to act in the space that had been allotted to them by Ottoman power and in the unstable landscape had to strike a balance between the dictates of the Ottoman administration, on one hand, and the needs of the community and their own interests, on the other (Pylia 2001, 94–96).

It was in this climate of constant insecurity which the Ottoman power had created for community notables that some *kocabaşıs* opted to take part in the Russian-inspired Orlov revolt in the Peloponnese (1770), during the Russo-Turkish War (1768–1774). The plan of the high-ranking officer in the Russian army, Gregory Orlov, was to incite the insurrection of Christian Ottoman subjects in the Balkans and the Aegean, assisted by the presence of the Russian navy in the region. Recent research, moving away from the position of traditional historiography on the "perennial resistance" of the Greeks against the Ottomans, has interpreted the Orlov revolt in the context of the period. This new approach views the revolt either as an expression of the encounter between the traditional eschatological notions of the Greeks and modernist ideas about political governance which enlightened despotism had incorporated (Rotzokos 2007) or as a version of the global revolutionary phenomenon of the period, which introduced new political demands and new modes of political action into the Greek experience. Nonetheless, in interpreting the Orlov revolt we should not overlook the dynamics of the antagonism among the primates for the Ottomans' favor, which pushed one group of *kocabaşıs* to attempt to create a new political status quo under their own hegemony and the protection of a foreign power (Alexander 1985, 49).

The repressive measures that followed the crushing of the Orlov revolt in the Peloponnese secured the loyalty of the primate class, which remained unmoved by new Russian calls to insurrection in 1780–1790 (Sakellariou 1939, 233). It is a fact that during the last quarter of the eighteenth century the Christian *kocabaşıs* acquired greater economic and political influence vis-à-vis the corresponding Muslim *ayan* of the Morea (Photopoulos 2005, 251). The burgeoning of trade of agricultural products from the Peloponnese in the Mediterranean, in the early nineteenth century, offered the *kocabaşıs* new fields of economic activity, while their coalition to hound out the klephts from the region (1805–1806) strengthened their primacy (Alexander 1985). What did not change, however, was the inherently precarious status of the Christian primate class. The considerable number of Peloponnesian *kocabaşıs* who joined the Philiki Etaireia (from 1818 onward) and their participation—despite their initial reservations—in the Greek Revolution was not a novel attempt on their part to change the political order; comparable initiatives had been taken in 1715, when some of them allied with the Ottomans against Venetian domination, and in 1770 with the Orlov revolt. Nonetheless, such was the political watershed that the Greek Revolution brought about that it shook the terms of existence and reproduction of the primate class, which fell back on its earlier experience in "community self-government" and tried to adapt and to claim a favorable position in the new, now national, status quo.

Rumeli (Central Greece)

Community organization in the extensive geographical region of Rumeli did not present a uniform picture. In eastern central Greece and specifically in Athens and Livadia, the community phenomenon resembled more that of the Peloponnese, with a powerful Christian primate class with connections to

Ottoman power (Papastamatiou and Kotzagiorgis 2015, 125, 134). In western central Greece, and particularly in the areas of Valtos, Xiromero, Kravara, Karpenisi and Agrafa, community organization tended, during the eighteenth century, to be replaced by the institution of the *armatolik*. The *armatolik* was the geographical area under the jurisdiction of an *armatolos*, who was charged with keeping public order and especially with driving out the klephts. The *armatoloi* themselves came, as a rule, from the ranks of the klephts and were appointed after an agreement between the local pasha and the Christian and Muslim primates of the province, while they were remunerated by the communities (Stathis 2003). Drawing their power from the use of weapons and the exercise of force, some *armatoloi* managed to extend their activities to the levying of community taxes, traditionally the preserve of community representatives; this activity then brought them into opposition with the latter. In the western regions of central Greece, the *armatoloi* succeeded in acquiring primacy, whereas in the eastern part, the power of the primates proved to be more resilient. However, there were also cases of collaboration between primates and *armatoloi*, in order to exterminate rival clans, while occasionally depending on the circumstances, strategies of social mobility led families to alternate between primate and *armatolos* (Tzakis 2014). Nonetheless, as a rule, in the zones where the *armatoloi* were dominant, the leeway for the development of social self-management was extremely limited and the related community structures were rudimentary.

From 1787 onward, the presence of Ali Pasha, initially as keeper of mountain passes and subsequently as governor of a wide geographical area encompassing *pashaliks* of Central Greece, created new circumstances for the Christian *armatoloi*. With the aim of making the *armatoloi* absolutely dependent on him, Ali opted to eradicate or expel the mightiest of them and to promote in their place others of lesser standing. During the decade 1810–1820, the *armatoloi* of Rumeli were to a large degree dependent on Ali Pasha and the special power they enjoyed was due to his support. This explains also the minimal influence of the Philiki Etaireia in the circles of the Rumeliot arms bearers, as well as their reservations about taking part in the revolution of 1821, which abated when, after Ali Pasha's defeat and the restoration of sultanic rule in their regions, their future appeared uncertain.

From Communities to Districts: Organizing a National Territory

In November 1821, Metropolitan Ignatios of Ungrowallachia wrote from Pisa, where he resided, to the insurgent primates and military leaders of the Peloponnese: "If you do not set up an Administration, and a good Administration, however things run along, your fall is certain, and there is no need for me to come and to help you, for you to fall.... Without Administration there is anarchy, polyarchy, tower-building and we shall never be able to work together, nor shall we be able to do good things." The note was accompanied by a plan for a provisional administration, which Ignatios proposed to the recipients with the certainty that "you will gain a great deal in the esteem of your necessary friends" (Protopsaltis 1961, 162). The Peloponnesians who took up arms in March 1821 were not, of course, oblivious to the necessity of the political organization of the struggle. In order to supply the army and to coordinate war operations, they had set up local authorities (ephorates, chancelleries) from the first weeks of the revolution. These were based on the preexisting community schemes, while from late May 1821 the administration of the Peloponnese was temporarily assumed by a committee of primates, known as the Peloponnesian Senate. This inaugurated a system of general ephorates (inspectorates), modeled on the Ottoman administrative division into *kazas,* headed by ephors, who were elected by the people and were accountable to them (Dimakopoulos 1966, 37–50).

However, the spread of the struggle beyond the geographical borders of the Peloponnese, by late spring in 1821, elevated the issue of the political organization from one of practical necessity to one in which the revolution itself was at stake. The transformation of the local communities in revolt into a national territory under a single administration thus became a political priority and a factor in legitimizing the revolution on the international stage. It was in this climate that from the summer of 1821 on, Greek intellectuals living abroad sped to the insurgent homeland, armed with plans for organizing an administration and, needless to say, with political ambitions.

Despite the declaration of a single agency, until the voting of the Provisional Constitution of Greece (January 1822), the organizational scheme of the first Greek administration relied on the previous community organization and kept the form of the discrete local communities, which assumed an institutional status as forms of local government under the regional charters adopted in the course of 1821 (local organizations). With the exception of the geographically circumscribed "Military-Political Organization of Samos" (May 1821) and the "Organizational Encyclical" of Dimitrios Ypsilantis (June 1821), with which the administrative organization of the Aegean islands was attempted unsuccessfully, the first charter that was tried and tested at the level of regional administration was the "Organization of West Mainland Greece" (October 1821), followed by the "Legal Ordinance of Mainland Greece" (November 1821). They were the work of the Phanariots Alexandros Mavrokordatos and Theodoros Negris, respectively. Within the tense climate of conflict between primates and armed chiefs (*oplarchigoi*) who had gathered around Dimitrios Ypsilantis, the "Organ-

ization of the Peloponnesian Senate," modeled on the "Organizations of Rumeli" was voted on in December 1821, while a corresponding regional constitution was voted on in Crete in May 1822 (Daskalakis 1980).

The local polities are a characteristic example of the way in which old and
new leadership groups each appropriated the practices and vocabularies of the
other, to control beforehand the procedures of constituting political power. For
the primates these administrative formations were adaptations of their prerevolutionary administrative autonomy to the new circumstances of the revolution
that allowed them to lay claim to power roles in future structures of statehood.
For the newly arrived Phanariots, who had no local power bases, the founding
of the centralizing state passed through the consolidation of their power at a
regional level, and Rumeli, with its weak community structures, was the most
promising place for this purpose. Their function as institutional backstops for
the uncertain outcome of the conflict for the revolution's political hegemony
is the reason why the local organizations were not abolished after the voting of
the Provisional Constitution of Greece and the formation of the National Provisional Administration, but were placed under the latter's umbrella. However, this function weakened as the creation of institutions of central administration shifted the field of political conflict from the local to the central level.
As a result, at the Second National Assembly (April 1823) the Peloponnesian
primates themselves agreed to abolish the local organizations, particularly as,
in the meantime, control of the Peloponnesian Senate had passed into the hands
of the *oplarchigoi*.

One of the basic changes in the provincial administration that was brought
about by the constitution of a central authority and the abandonment of the
singular federal scheme of the local organizations was the administrative demotion of the community, which had been of such critical importance during
the prerevolutionary years, to the advantage of the district. The demotion had
begun with the Law on the Organization of the Greek Districts (April 1823). The
law made provision for introducing civil administration in the Aegean islands,
which lacked a single regional authority after the model of the local organizations on the mainland. The law also made provision for the division of the
territory into districts and subdistricts, headed respectively by district governors
and subdistrict governors appointed by the administration, and into communities with their heads elected by the population and "elders" (*dimogerontes*), who
were subject to the district authorities. The Law on the Organization was implemented only in the Aegean islands, with the exception of the so-called nautical
islands of Ydra, Spetses, and Psara, which kept the prerevolutionary system of
local self-government and were directly subject to the central administration,
without an intermediary regional authority (Moutzouris 1984, 17–18).

One year after the law was passed (April 1823) and occasioned by the abolition of the local organizations, a new law on regional administration was passed,
which, however, kept the name of the old one. The new Organization of the
Greek Districts divided the country into districts, towns, and villages, the first
headed by district governors appointed by the administration and the second by
elected *dimogerontes*. Although the law concerned the whole territory, excepting
the nautical islands, the administrative scheme that it introduced was not applied wholesale everywhere. In central Greece and the Aegean islands in particular, which bore the brunt of the war, emergency administrative schemes were
also created, in order to cope with the needs (Dimakopoulos 1966, 156–157).

In relation to the previous law, the 1823 Organization of the Greek Districts
went one step further toward weakening the prerevolutionary local powers, as
it introduced localness as an obstacle to the appointment of district governors
(Dimakopoulos 1966, 152–153). Mainly, however, the regional organization introduced by these laws deprived the communities of functions that had been
part and parcel of their existence in the years before the revolution.

The first and most fundamental shift concerned the fiscal function of the
community and the possibility of autonomous management of its tax obligations, which had been of critical importance in the prerevolutionary years. First
of all, the laws on organization of districts made provision for creating a bureaucratic authority with fiscal and auditing responsibilities ("the supervisor
of the economy collects the revenues of the district, keeps exact accounts of the
incomes and expenditures"). The measure was never applied as, for reasons of
necessity, the prerevolutionary system of tax farming through auction to the
highest bidder in the presence of representatives of the ministry of the economy,
was adopted. The auctions concerned initially the revenues from limited geographical sectors, thus giving the communities themselves the opportunity to
undertake the levying and collecting of taxes. This possibility lost ground from
1823 on, when auctioning an area corresponding to a district as one unit was
permitted, thus downgrading the importance of the community as a taxation
unit and favoring the collection of taxes levied by a limited number of persons.
In contrast to the strictly spatially defined localness of the prerevolutionary
community (even in the collective memory), the precise definition of the district boundaries of the national territory was deferred for the future and the
distinction on the basis of the Ottoman division into *kazas* was followed (Dimakopoulos 1966, 110).

The second shift concerned the judicial function of the community. The
Organization of the Greek Districts, and specifically the Law of the Organization
of the Greek Courts, which was issued in May 1822 and revised in October 1825,
entrusted to the *dimogerontes* of each community the duties of conciliatory judge

and remedial judge (arbitrator) for civil disputes not exceeding one hundred piasters. Consequently, the organizations recognized and, in addition, institutionalized the informal judicial responsibility that the community leaders had during the prerevolutionary period, but they greatly limited its scope and demoted its rank in relation to the judiciary authorities. Moreover, it is not accidental that the strongest objections to the introduction of the Organization of the Greek Districts were noted in the Cyclades—that is, the region where the judicial function of the communities was more highly developed before the revolution—the objections targeted the appointment of judges by the commissioners of the administration (Moutzouris 1984, 37–38). In parallel, a blow to the prerevolutionary judicial function of the communities was dealt by the constitutional abolition of the legal validity of local customs and the establishment of Byzantine law as the only one in force (Pantazopoulos 1986, 150).

Even though the provisions of the Organization of the Greek Courts were not activated and the administration itself referred cases for resolution to the district governors and the local *dimogerontes,* and incorporated principles of customary law into official legal practices, as noted already, the resilience of the community system in resolving differences was seriously tested in the course of the revolution. There was a proliferation—in relation to the past—of judicial instruments (executive; parliament; ministries of justice, police, and religion) to which a person could resort, but the abolition of the irrevocability of arbitration decisions (out-of-court compromise) was a blow to the stability of the community system of meting out justice, as its stability was largely due to the irrevocability of arbitration decisions (Pantazopoulos 1986, 153).

Despite the institutional downgrading of the community brought by the new organization of the district administration, the community continued to be the main geographical and social reference space of the local populations, as well as the organizational scheme that corresponded most directly to the practical needs created by the revolution. For example, the communities of the Morea were the basic mechanism for organizing fundraising efforts for the revolution, as well as for dealing with emergency issues regarding the welfare of the civilian population. At the same time, we should not overlook the importance of local institutions of governance for incorporating the populations into the new national political framework, or even the contribution of traditional formations to creating mechanisms of unifying the national territory, as attested by the organization of the first regular postal service in revolutionary Greece by the Peloponnesian Senate.

Given the weak administrative structures of the revolutionary state, the traditional institutions of local self-government functioned as intermediaries between the central Administration and the local populations, and in several cases as channels transferring central politics to the local level. This reality seems to have been recognized even by advocates of state centralization during the Revolution. So, after the Third National Assembly (April 1826), when the administrative commission that undertook the governance of revolutionary Greece and was invested with emergency powers abolished the system of districts introduced by the 1823 organization and attempted to exercise the regional administration, it soon realized its inadequacy. It decided to keep the community councils (*dimogeronties*) and to appoint ephors chosen among the local population, thus abolishing the previous obstacle of localness. The *dimogeronties* of the villages and towns were the only preexisting provincial authority that was kept in the Statute on the Administration of the Greek Territory, which was issued in implementation of the Constitution of Troezen (May 1827) and made provision for the division of the territory into themes or cantons consisting of several districts (something like today's prefectures) and administered by so-called governors. As the statute was not applied, the *dimogeronties* were the only provincial authority that essentially existed until the arrival of Capodistrias.

From "Big" to "Little" History: Social Processes and Everyday Life

In approaching the history of the communities of revolutionary Greece mainly from the perspective of their relation to the central administration, our attention should not be deflected from the diverse processes that caused the outbreak of the struggle within the communities, or from the importance of the latter as exemplary spaces of the everyday life experience during the revolution. We know already from the "civil war" of Samos the armed form that the quarrel between the island's two warring factions took in 1822, occasioned by the application there of the Organization of the Greek Districts (Sevastakis 2005). A corresponding clash between primates of Chora and the leader of the countryside, Michail Makropolitis, took place on Naxos, which ended in the administrative hiving off of the Naxian countryside and the installation of authorities there (Moutzouris 1984, 38–41).

A special chapter in the history of the island communities is the stance of the Catholic inhabitants toward the revolution and their relations with their Orthodox compatriots. The revolutionary constitutions acknowledged the status of Greek citizen for all Christian natives in the Greek territory, among them the Catholics in the Cyclades (Vogli 2007, 71–81). From the perspective of the revolutionary leadership, it seems that there was particular interest in the participation of the Catholics in the revolution and in a separate proclamation that was dispatched in April 1821 to the "Western Christians" they were called "brothers, Christians, and fellow Greeks" and were summoned to struggle "under the same flag in the same spirit." Although there are sporadic testimonies of the participation of individuals in revolutionary assemblies, the response of the Catholic communities to this and to similar invitations that followed was negative; their attitude ranged from indifference and detachment to active expression of pro-Ottoman sentiments and declaration of submission to the Ottoman government (Manikas 2001, 184–216). The incorporation of the Catholic communities into the national framework continued to be an important issue for the revolutionary administration and the application of the Organization of the Greek Districts first and foremost in the Aegean may well have been linked also with the desire to weaken the Catholic *dimogeronties* through their subjection to the appointed district governors. But if elsewhere establishing the single national territory had to deal with local political relationships, in this particular case it had to deal also with the Catholics' refusal to accept Greek nationality, which was granted to them by the Provisional Constitution, and their move, on grounds of religious identity, to seek and to obtain French protection.

The refusal of Greek nationality by the Catholic residents of the Cyclades is perhaps not unconnected to their desire to be exempt from the obligatory taxation imposed on the islanders for the reinforcement of the fleet. However, the tension that accompanied their reaction and characterized their relationship with their Orthodox compatriots, particularly on Tinos and Syros, drew up to the surface the difficulties of cohabitation of the two religious communities and showed that appropriation of the identity of Greek citizen by the local populations was a less obvious procedure than the official constitutional texts took for granted. Indeed, from the end of the second year of the struggle, the mass settlement of refugees in the Cycladic islands, and mainly on Syros with its Roman Catholic majority, altered the demographics to the advantage of the Orthodox Christians and contributed to greater alienation between the two communities.

The clashes between Orthodox and Catholics in the Cyclades did not, of course, have an exclusively religious background. As can be ascertained from Makropolitis's movement on Naxos and the episodes on Tinos, religious discrimination also took the form of opposition between the Orthodox rural population and the Catholic nobles of feudal provenance in the island's main town, Chora. The outbreak of the revolution ignited existing social oppositions also in islands without a Catholic population. The popular uprising against the primates of Ydra, in April 1821, headed by ship captain Antonios Oikonomos is the best-known case, as it signaled the island's participation in the revolution, toward which the attitude of the ruling class of shipowners had been lukewarm, to say the least (Lignos [1946] 1953, 180–202). With the issue of the participation of the individual island communities in the Struggle as a pretext, popular reactions against the unwilling primates were manifested on Kea and Andros, where they took the form of a rural movement with radical egalitarian demands and characteristics of direct democracy (Gaitanou, Kritikou, and Dardanos 1989).

Sometimes ignored to safeguard the national value of the struggle and sometimes trapped in closed interpretive schemes, the study of the social dynamics and the social conflicts that the revolution released is a desideratum of modern research. Generally speaking, emphasis on the military, diplomatic, and political dimension of the revolution has left less space for studying society, the relationships, daily life, and survival strategies of the populace in conditions of military and civil turbulence. Beginning with Apostolos Vakalopoulos's work on the refugees (Vakalopoulos 1939), we now know quite a lot about the population migrations that the revolution caused (Komis 2014), as well as about the strained relations between locals and refugees from regions where the revolution had been put down (Dimitropoulos 2018). The mass advent of refugees, particularly to the Aegean islands, upset existing equilibria where they related to localness and the taxation obligations that arose from being members of the community. The refugees not only came from elsewhere but they were also exempt from taxation, while the presence of armed men among them created serious problems of public order.

The rise in incidents of criminality (theft, violence, murder, rape), especially in the cities of revolutionary Greece, due to the presence of irregular soldiers, proved to be a basic factor in undermining the power of the community authorities, which, unable to cope with the intensity of violence, asked for the help of the administration and the appointment of policemen. The Police Ministry Archive (1822–1826) gives a picture of the troubled daily life during the revolution, which put community cohesion to the test. Apart from acts of violence, the number of accusations between fellow villagers of nonpayment of debts and other obligations (such as those of betrothal) attests to a breakdown, in conditions of generalized unrest, of trust as an element that bound together economic and social relations in the framework of the community. However, these cracks in the community fabric coexisted with manifestations of community solidarity and collective action in confronting the emergency problems of the population's survival, which makes the community a privileged field for studying Greek revolutionary society.

The observed turn of recent historiography to the local level as a context for studying the political and social processes of the revolutionary period has brought the communities to the fore, as exemplary spaces of encounter between the local populations and the "big" history of the revolution—that is, of the formation of the state and of the military and political confrontations. Concurrently, the modern historiographic demand for a social history of the revolution, a history of the "little" and the "everyday," upgrades the community as an object of basic research. Whatever the case, the communities of revolutionary Greece augur an interesting historiographic life.

Vaso Seirinidou

Translated from the Greek by Alexandra Douma

References

Alexander, John Christos. 1985. *Brigandage and Public Order in the Morea, 1685–1806.* Athens.

Anastasopoulos, Antonis. 2013. "Non-Muslims and Ottoman Justice(s?)" In *Law and Empires: Ideas, Practices, Actors,* edited by Jeroen Duindam, Jill Diana Harries, Caroline Humfress, and Hurvitz Nimrod, 275–292. Leiden.

Asdrachas, Spyros. 1986. "Φορολογικές και περιοριστικές λειτουργίες των κοινοτήτων στην τουρκοκρατία" [Taxation and restrictive functions of communities during the Tourkokratia]. *Ta Istorika* 5:45–62.

Daskalakis, Apostolos B. 1980. *Οι τοπικοί οργανισμοί της επαναστάσεως του 1821 και το πολίτευμα της Επιδαύρου* [Local constitutions of the 1821 revolution and the polity of Epidavros]. Athens.

Dimakopoulos, Georgios D. 1966. *Η διοικητική οργάνωσις κατά την ελληνικήν επανάστασιν, 1821–1827: συμβολή εις την ιστορίαν της ελληνικής διοικήσεως* [Administrative organization during the Greek Revolution, 1821–1827: A contribution to the history of Greek administration]. Athens.

Dimitropoulos, Dimitris. 2018. "Πειρατές στη στεριά; Πρόσφυγες, καταδρομείς και καθημερινότητα των παράκτιων οικισμών στα χρόνια του Αγώνα" [Pirates on land? Refugees, privateers and everyday life in the coastal settlements during the struggle]. In *Όψεις της επανάστασης του 1821* [Aspects of the 1821 revolution], 87–105. Athens.

Gaitanou, Eleni, Archontoula Kritikou, and Giorgos Dardanos. 1989. *Το κοινωνικό περιεχόμενο της επανάστασης στην Άνδρο. Η περίπτωση του Δημήτρη Μπαλή* [The social content of the revolution in Andros: The case of Dimitris Balis]. Athens.

Kermeli, Eugenia. 2007. "The Right of Choice: Ottoman Justice vis a vis Ecclesiastical and Communal Justice in the Balkans, Seventeenth–Nineteenth Centuries." *Studies in Islamic Law: A Festschrift for Colin Imber,* edited by Andreas Christmann and Robert Gleave, 160–210. Oxford.

Komis, Kostas. 2014. "Πληθυσμιακές μετακινήσεις στον ελλαδικό χώρο με αφετηρία την επανάσταση του 1821" [Population movements in the Greek lands owing to the 1821 revolution]. In *Πολιτικοστρατιωτικές αναταραχές και πληθυσμιακές μετακινήσεις. Ο ελληνικός 19ος αιώνας και το 1821* [Political and military turmoil and population movements: The Greek nineteenth century and 1821], 49–80. Athens.

Kontogiorgis, Giorgos D. 1982. *Κοινωνική δυναμική και πολιτική αυτοδιοίκηση. Οι ελληνικές κοινότητες της τουρκοκρατίας* [Social dynamic and the politics of self-rule: The Greek communities of the Tourkokratia]. Athens.

Koukkou, Eleni. 1980. *Οι κοινοτικοί θεσμοί στις Κυκλάδες κατά την Τουρκοκρατία. Ανέκδοτα έγγραφα* [The communal institutions in the Cyclades during the Tourkokratia: Unpublished documents]. Athens.

Liata, Eftychia. 2003. "Οι κοινότητες. Ένας θεσμός με πολλές όψεις" [Communities: A multifaceted institution], *INE*, 309–324.

Lignos, Antonios. (1946) 1953. *Ιστορία της νήσου Ύδρας* [History of the island of Ydra]. 2 vols. Athens.

Manikas, Constantinos Ioannis. 2001. *Σχέσεις ορθοδοξίας και ρωμαιοκαθολικισμού στην Ελλάδα κατά τη διάρκεια της επαναστάσεως (1821–1827): συμβολή στην εκκλησιαστική ιστορία της Ελλάδος* [Relations between Orthodoxy and Roman Catholicism in Greece during the revolution, 1821–1827: Contribution to the ecclesiastical history of Greece]. PhD diss., National and Kapodistrian University of Athens.

Moutzouris, Ioannis. 1984. *Η αρμοστεία των νήσων του Αιγαίου Πελάγους στα χρόνια της ελληνικής επαναστάσεως* [The commissariat of the Aegean Islands during the Greek Revolution]. Athens.

Pantazopoulos, Nikolaos. 1958. *Ελλήνων συσσωματώσεις κατά την Τουρκοκρατίαν* [Greek associations during the Tourkokratia]. Athens.

Pantazopoulos, Nikolaos I. 1986. "Η δικαιοδοτική πολιτική κατά την επανάσταση και την καποδιστριακή περίοδο (1821–1832)" [Jurisdiction policy during the revolution and the Capodistrian period, 1821–1832]. In *Αντιχάρισμα στον Ν. Ι. Πανταζόπουλο* [A gift in return to N. I. Pantazopoulos]. *Epistimoniki Epetiris Scholis Nomikon kai Oikonomikon Epistimon* 19:83–222.

Papastamatiou, Dimitrios, and Phokion Kotzagiorgis, 2015. *Ιστορία του νέου ελληνισμού κατά τη διάρκεια της οθωμανικής πολιτικής κυριαρχίας* [History of modern Hellenism during the Ottoman political domination]. Thessaloniki.

Photopoulos, Athanasios. 2005. *Οι κοτζαμπάσηδες της Πελοποννήσου κατά τη Δεύτερη Τουρκοκρατία, 1715–1821* [The primates of the Peloponnese during the second Tourkokratia, 1715–1821]. Athens.

Protopsaltis, Emmanuel G. 1961. *Ιγνάτιος Μητροπολίτης Ουγγροβλαχίας (1766–1828)* [Ignatios Archbishop of Ungrowallachia (1766–1828)]. Athens.

Pylia, Martha. 2001. "Λειτουργίες και αυτονομία των κοινοτήτων της Πελοποννήσου κατά τη δεύτερη τουρκοκρατία (1715–1821)" [Functions and autonomy of the communities of the Peloponnese during the second Tourkokratia, 1715–1821]. *Mnimon* 23:67–98.

Rotzokos, Nikos. 2007. *Εθναφύπνιση και εθνογένεση: Ορλωφικά και ελληνική ιστοριογραφία* [The national awakening and birth of the nation: The Orlov uprising and Greek historiography]. Athens.

Sakellariou, Michail V. 1939. *Η Πελοπόννησος κατά την δευτέραν Τουρκοκρατίαν (1715–1821)* [The Peloponnese during the second Tourkokratia, 1715–1821]. Athens.

Sevastakis, Alexis. 2005. "Το 'Στρατοπολιτικόν Σύστημα' Σάμου και η κεντρική ελληνική διοίκηση" [The "military-civilian" system of Samos and the Greek central administration]. In *Ιστορικά ανάλεκτα* [Historical analects], edited by Alexis Sevastakis, 32–62. Athens.

Stathis, Panagiotis. 2003. "Αρματολισμός: Χριστιανοί ένοπλοι στην υπηρεσία των Οθωμανών" [Armatolism: Armed Christians in the service of the Ottomans]. *INE*, 2:339–360.

Tzakis, Dionysis. 2014. "Οπλαρχηγοί και προεστοί: κοινωνικές κινητικότητες και οικογενειακές στρατηγικές στον ορεινό χώρο" [Armed chiefs and notables: Social mobility and family strategies in the mountain regions]. In *Τοπικές κοινωνίες στον θαλάσσιο και ορεινό χώρο στα νότια Βαλκάνια, 18ος-19ος αιώνας, Πρακτικά συμποσίου στη μνήμη της Εύης Ολυμπίτου* [Local communities in the sea and mountain regions of the southern Balkans, eighteenth to nineteenth centuries: Conference Proceedings in memory of Evi Olympitou], 293–308. Corfu.

Vakalopoulos, Apostolos. 1939. *Πρόσφυγες και προσφυγικόν ζήτημα κατά την επανάστασιν του 1821* [Refugees and refugee question during the Revolution of 1821]. Thessaloniki.

Vogli, Elpida. 2007. *"Έλληνες το γένος": Η ιθαγένεια και η ταυτότητα στο εθνικό κράτος των Ελλήνων (1821–1844)* ["Greeks by birth": Nationality and identity in the Greek nation state, 1821–1844]. Iraklio.

Forms of Resistance

Until the recent antiteleological turn, Greek historiography conceived any form of mass opposition to Ottoman authority as part of a prolonged national resistance to foreign occupation. Yet, between about 1530 and 1821, most violent resistance within the Balkans remained local. Some followed major Ottoman defeats, like the scattered sympathy revolts after the Battle of Lepanto (1571). Others grew from misplaced optimism that rebellion would inspire intervention from Christian powers. The *armatolos* Theodoros Boua-Grivas, for instance, trusted that the Venetians would support the revolt he instigated in Akarnania and Epirus in 1585. Years later, Metropolitan Dionysios—derogatorily named "Skylosophos"—secured funding from the Spanish Empire to launch farmers' revolts in Agrafa (1600) and Ioannina (1611); again, military support did not materialize. A desire to collaborate with Christian powers to free Balkan Christendom from Muslim occupation appears as these disturbances' leitmotif. Many smaller uprisings occurred, most of which resembled spontaneous local riots. Zisis Karadimos's uprising in Naousa (1705), for example, was sparked by local opposition to the *devşirme* (παιδομάζωμα), which led Karadimos, his sons, and fellow *armatoloi* to murder a commissar before retreating to the mountains. Sympathy revolts, naïve rebellions that anticipated foreign support, and many local uprisings occurred in the Ottoman Balkans, as anywhere else in the early modern period; but violent resistance remained localized and generally ineffective, until the eighteenth century.

Resistance can be violent, but often is not. Nonviolent or civil resistance also aims to reconfigure prevailing power relations. Accommodating the Quit India Movement (1942), the Defiance Campaign in South Africa (1952–1953), or the American civil rights movement, resistance refers to a broad range of behaviors, attitudes, and postures. Within Greek historiography, Tom Gallant's work is instructive on subtler modes of resistance, offering "dominion" in place of more constraining terms like hegemony, accommodation, and resistance. For every armed rebel, dozens evaded taxes, migrated, or adopted other strategies to pursue goals that did not align with Ottoman expectations.

Resistance was not the exclusive prerogative of certain factions and constituencies. For many *armatoloi* and other groups commissioned to enforce Ottoman authority, loyalty to the empire was situational. As the use of violence was not regulated by a single authority, armed men offered their services to the highest bidder. Resistance groups were not easily distinguished from state security forces by firm and consistent boundaries. Klephts and *armatoloi* often intermingled within shifting coalitions, neither willing to abide a rigid economy of violence. Economic opportunity trumped imperial loyalty or legal considerations. In eighteenth-century Rumelia, klephts used banditry as a tool to persuade authorities to appoint them as *armatoloi*. A similar tale unfolded on the seas in the seventeenth and eighteenth centuries. Zakyntiot sailors engaged in piracy, while also participating in the *corso,* with legal sanction from Venice or Vienna. Elsewhere, pirates in Syros turned to legal shipping around 1750. On land and at sea, legal boundaries were regularly traversed. Communal boundaries were also frequently ignored, as patronage networks and military alliances incorporated different groups. In the Morea, relations among members of different religions, status groups, localities, and ethnic groups were quite common.

The antiteleological turn valiantly undermined nationalistic myths of a homogeneous Greek community consistently resisting Ottoman authority from 1453, in its place presenting an Ottoman era characterized by shifting allegiances and fluid boundaries. Yet, it has not left many analytical tools for appropriately differentiating anti-Ottoman revolutions from other forms of resistance. The events of 1770, typically referred to as the Morea rebellion or Orlov revolt, are cast by Birol Gündoğdu as products of a serendipitous alignment of interests. Alternatively, 1770 has been portrayed as a rupture, suggesting that a modern capacity and perspective emerged among the *Romioi* at this time (Rotzokos 2007). I would extend this argument: a novel mode of resistance appeared in 1770, one distinguished from previous episodes in scale, heterogeneity, and in its "pathos of novelty" (Arendt 2006, 24). It is appropriate to term these events the 1770 revolution.

Revolutionary Capacities Revealed

The 1770 and 1821 revolutions were fundamentally unlike preceding revolts, rebellions, and uprisings. First, they differed in composition and organization.

These were multiconfessional, multiethnic, and multilingual movements that were organized across empires. Second, they were part of a global crisis in imperial sovereignty (Armitage and Subrahmanyam 2010). These were, partly, efforts by provincial powerbrokers to assert local autonomy. Distinguishing these formations from their antecedents requires careful explication of how disconnected factions with diverse experiences and dissimilar goals *could* be mobilized. It is a truism to say that revolutions require money and military power, and the historiography on the 1821 revolution illustrates quite clearly how commercial elites and Phanariots aligned with *armatoloi*, klephts, and *kocabaşı*s in the Balkans. What has not been highlighted as forcefully are the long-term structural shifts that engendered revolution as a mode of resistance. Specifically, how new mobilities and patterns of exchange produced commercial elites acutely capable of appreciating social alternatives and political possibilities, and how Ottoman military-fiscal reforms spawned a powerful class of provincial elites. Revolution emerged as a possibility in the Balkans only after economic, political, and intellectual elites forged sustained relationships across transimperial networks, and after provincial elites secured substantial independence from Ottoman encroachments.

Throughout the early modern era, the Balkans' rugged topography shaped the political economy of violence on the peninsula. Relying heavily upon *sipahi*s (fief-holding cavalrymen) during its expansion into the region, the Ottoman army found it easier to maintain control over the plains of Thessaly and Western Macedonia than the highlands along the Olympus-Chasia, Pindus-Agrafa, and Vermio-Pieria mountain ranges. Highlanders not only resisted Ottoman incursions but launched raids on communities across the plains, activities that proved quite lucrative for some. The Ottoman conquest of the Balkans thus engendered a new social type: the klepht. To some degree, klephts operated as "social bandits": peasants turned brigands whose violence was often conceived as a prepolitical form of protest. Klephts were familiar with the peasantry, unlike transient raiders (and their role did not preclude engagement with the market—cattle and pig dealers occasionally doubled as bandit leaders and vice versa, as klephts engaged in trade); they organized themselves into highly trained bands of dozens—and occasionally hundreds—of men, rather than operating as individual robbers; and they were leaders who embodied praxis as an alternative to acquiescence, though not activists or ideologues with original ideas or novel political visions. Most importantly, the klepht regarded himself as a free man and prided himself on behaving in accordance with carefully prescribed codes of conduct (Hobsbawm 1969). This self-fashioning received social confirmation through a rich body of klephtic ballads, which cast klephts as symbols of liberty and the collective struggle for freedom. At the same time, the klepht was a self-serving outlaw whose freedom in the mountains depended on his ongoing ability to terrorize peasants and blackmail local potentates.

Establishing order required the empire to ensure open and secure transit routes as well as to suppress brigandage by klephts. To this end, *dervenochoria* (mountain villages located near strategic passes) were assigned collective responsibility for securing these passes in exchange for privileged legal status. Ottoman governors appointed *armatoloi* to maintain order over *armatoliks*—regions heavily affected by brigandage. Numbers fluctuated but, from the fifteenth to the nineteenth centuries, ten to twenty *armatoliks* were typically operational. A *kapetanios* (warband leader) administered each *armatolik*: patrolling the district, collecting taxes from Christian inhabitants to fund security costs, and—if his tenure were long enough—raising flocks and farming. The appointment was often hereditary, such that many *armatoliks* came to be associated with the families who administered them: the Boukovalaioi, the Vlachavaioi, the Stournaraioi, the Kontogiannaioi. In selecting *armatoloi*, Ottoman governors typically appointed powerful klephts who were sympathetic to them; a change in governor would thus often necessitate a change of *armatoloi* as well, leading these former militiamen to revert to brigandage. For peasants, klephts and *armatoloi* were indistinguishable; both were celebrated in Greek folk music as examples of upward mobility and spirited resistance, as well as models of heroism. *Armatoliks* bore some resemblance to the tribal communities of Souli, Mani, and Sfakia, but the latter operated with autonomy and were compelled to pay tribute only on rare occasions. While contacts did exist, there was no sense of solidarity among these communities (Skiotis 1975). Into the eighteenth century, the Balkans' topography ensured that vertical, patron-client relationships between the empire and private armed forces were easier to forge than horizontal bonds among the military classes.

"Transimperial brokers" organized these revolutions by uniting disparate groups and factions across extensive chains of association (Rothman 2011). These networks did not emerge spontaneously. They were cultivated from commercial pathways forged within the Ottoman Empire from the sixteenth century, during an era of increasing monetization, urbanization, and political unification. Imperial integration was an uneven process, but intensifying commercial ties created opportunities for domestic traders and forwarders to accumulate great wealth. Many Phanariot dynasties emerged through such pathways. More importantly for *Romioi,* economic opportunities emerged *across* the frontier as well, especially after the Treaty of Passarowitz (1718), owing to a combination of peace treaties, commercial freedoms, inflation (export competitiveness), and the granting of tax concessions and other privileges by foreign empires. Many Balkan Orthodox merchants exploited the new tariff regime, extending overland trade ties into Austria, Hungary, Moldavia, and Transylvania. Ottoman commercial treaties with the Kingdom of France, Great Britain, and the Dutch Republic around 1750, combined with higher inflation in Europe, spurred grain, cotton, and tobacco exports from Macedonia and Thessaly. Phanariots provided financing to entrepreneurs expanding into markets north of the Black Sea. Ottoman Christian merchants dispersed beyond the empire, establishing colonies and communities of various types. Bonds of trade, credit, and patronage linked homelands to these sites, as did familial and ritual kinship ties (godparentage). Extending circuits of capital, commerce, labor, and migration produced a wealthy class of *Romioi;* one whose ranks swelled with the outbreak of the Seven Years' War and the removal of French competition from eastern Mediterranean trade. These commercial elites were highly affected by their experiences abroad. The cross-fertilization of ideas within mercantile diasporas nurtured alternative allegiances, generated new geographies of belonging, and inspired novel political possibilities, a fact illustrated in the writings of Ioannis Pringos and Adamantios Korais. In prosperity, all remained stable. In crisis, these classes were ideal targets for agitators interested in subverting the sultan's authority, often on behalf of a foreign power or agitators in their own right.

The political relevance of these new elites grew as they cultivated larger webs of association with other reformers. Reformist Phanariots and merchant-financiers spurred a cultural renewal movement, founding new schools and libraries, and staffing them with teachers knowledgeable in languages, modern science, rational philosophy, and natural law. These schools were typically located within regions with established commercial links to international markets and far from imperial power centers and sites of ecclesiastical influence. Among the more notable schools were the Princely Academies of Bucharest (1694) and Jassy (1707), which underwent extensive reorganization during the Phanariot period (1711–1821). Elsewhere, wealthy diaspora families founded schools in their hometowns, most notably in Ioannina (1742), Moschopolis (1743), and Ambelakia (1749). These schools operated alongside institutions in the Ionian Islands like the Academia dei Vigilanti Zacinthi (1625) and Vikentios Damodos's school in Cephalonia (1721). Developments in these three regions initially proceeded independently; but, by the eighteenth century, these institutions were producing new social alignments. Teachers trained abroad were paired with students hungry for modern education, while merchant benefactors forged relationships with intellectuals seeking patronage from less than restrictive sources.

Travel between these sites strengthened and sustained social bonds, as did the advent of subscription publishing. Commercial pathways linking towns in the Balkans with markets abroad soon doubled as circuits of intellectual circu-lation through which formerly threatening—if not blasphemous—works were transmitted to the Greek-reading public. The association of Phanariots, mer-chants, intellectuals, and publishers within voluntary groupings based on in-tellectual curiosity and a vague commitment to renewal was significant. First, it aroused a spirit of inquiry and reflection, inspiring an openness to European scholarship, interest in alternatives to salvation history and sacral geography, and, ultimately, adaptations of existing political models. Second, it gave shape to a nascent public sphere of publishing houses, schools, and libraries—and later newspapers, salons, and masonic lodges—where these alternatives were considered. Third, it expanded these social groups' capacity for political action. These reformers lacked independent military power, and, in most instances, an appetite for violence; yet, their increasing integration created a cleavage between reformers and traditionalists committed to tradition, Aristotelianism, and Or-thodox political theology.

Alongside these increasingly polarized alignments stood provincial elites, more firmly rooted in the Balkans. Their ascendancy owed to fiscal-military reforms connected to the empire's incorporation of gunpowder technology (Ágoston 2005). By the seventeenth century, the increasing use of cannon and muskets in battle had rendered feudal cavalry largely ineffective. Success in major military campaigns in Hungary (1593–1606, 1663–1664), Iraq (1625–1626, 1638), Crete (1645–1669), and Vienna (1683) hinged upon investments in siege and firearms technology. Infantry equipped with modern firearms were needed, and the empire quickly began building more cannon-proof fortifications and provisioning its armies and navies with more artillery. The "largely commis-sioned state army" of janissaries and timariots (benefice-holder cavalrymen) that existed in 1650 evolved into a "federative military system" of "entrepre-neurial ethnic bands" over two centuries (Aksan 2013, 332). Valuing the local knowledge and influence of provincial elites, the empire called upon ayans to assist local military commanders from the early seventeenth century. More gen-erally, they were mentioned within nefir-i amms (general calls to arms) during tumultuous periods and tasked with defending home territory. By 1768, the em-pire demanded their support during conflicts. Local notables and officials evolved into military contractors charged with recruiting levends (temporarily hired troops) and bringing them to the military front, ensuring smooth pas-sage for armies through their kaza, providing lodgings for officials and sol-diers, arranging peksimed (hard biscuits) preparation, and provisioning troops. By the eighteenth century, they served an essential role in imperial defense.

In consolidating their authority, provincial elites unsettled existing power re-lationships. Yet, reform was vital, both to address military deficiencies and to tackle a prolonged economic crisis. The influx of Spanish silver produced inflation in the seventeenth century, which, under a system with fixed tax rates, yielded lower tax revenues for *timar* holders. As a result, many demanded irregular taxes from peasants, who responded by moving to cities or pursuing military careers. Under the pressures of steady inflation and prolonged war, Ottoman finances dwindled. Responding to a sixfold increase in the budget deficit between 1669–1670 and 1690–1691, and desperate for revenue to support the ongoing War of the Holy League (1683–1699), the empire sought new revenue streams. From the early eighteenth century, it appropriated thousands of agricultural estates, reassessed their value, and rented them as *mālikāne-mukātaa* (lifetime tax farms). Additionally, upon the death or dismissal of a *timar* holder, land holdings were not reassigned; rather, vacant lands were outsourced as *iltizām*s (short-term tax farms), ensuring greater imperial revenues. These revenue units were legally designated as "immune enclaves," meaning that the *mālikāne* holder had full administrative authority over these communities. The expectation was that life-term contracts would encourage *mālikāne* holders to develop their estates in order to preserve their investment. In exchange for these revenue units, the central fisc received two forms of payment: a sizeable lump sum amount determined by auction, as well as annual payment, which resembled a property tax. *Mālikāne* lands were "virtually like property" (İnalcik 1983, 112).

Non-Muslims were formally prohibited from acquiring *mālikāne* lands. Yet, in the Morea, managing this system presented myriad opportunities for the majority Christian population as accountants, brokers, financiers, and minor provincial officials. Entrepreneurial individuals seized on the opportunity to subcontract profitable revenue units, typically acquiring financing from Greek, Armenian, and Jewish financiers. Forays into tax farming required a large retinue to ensure security, collect taxes, and combat brigandage. The spread of firearms into the provinces during the seventeenth century ensured plenty of armed mercenaries to meet this demand. As tax-farming fortunes accumulated and personal gangs expanded into small armies, competing factions formed to ensure mutual protection of their members and adherents. By around 1750, a powerful class of Christian elites emerged, the *kocabaşı*s.

This decentralized system worked to affirm sultanic authority, so long as *ayan* and *kocabaşı*s exhibited restraint. Such an expectation, however, ignored the strong incentives to overexploit tax farms, specifically regional factionalism and the absence of local authorities capable of limiting exploitation. Additionally, Muslim entrepreneurs could leverage success in tax farming into state offices and, potentially, inclusion into privileged positions within the central state apparatus. Quite quickly, *ayan* and *kocabaşı*s began issuing *avariz* (extraordinary taxes) and embezzling surpluses, contributing to peasant indebtedness, abandoned villages, intensifying banditry, and rebellions. Unintentionally, "fiscal privatization" spawned powerful regional elites; figures with enough wealth, influence, and temerity to refashion sovereignty.

The emergence of transimperial elites eager for reform and provincial powerbrokers keen to renegotiate sovereignty and territoriality was not unique. In the 1760s, Europe's Old Regime faced its "first crisis," a moment that revealed the deep tensions dividing the traditional order from various factions on the continent's periphery that were pursuing political change (Venturi 1989). American colonies soon experienced their own political unrest, as did West Africa, where *jihād* movements established new states and redefined social relationships. Within the Greek world—admittedly, a politically and culturally fragmented world with amorphous boundaries—the Ottoman Empire's patrimonial system appeared incompatible with the networks that commercial elites inhabited and ineffective to constrain local powerbrokers. Conflicts seemed inevitable.

By the 1760s, the Morea emerged as a likely location. A predominantly Christian province, on the empire's periphery, Moreots maintained extensive maritime ties throughout the Mediterranean. From 1717, the expansion of tax farming concentrated wealth in local notables' hands, while also eroding the checks and balances that operated within the *timar* system. Unchecked elites coalesced into increasingly belligerent factions, the results of which began to be seen around 1750, when forces employed by Halil Bey of Corinth pillaged estates belonging to the province's wealthiest man, Panagiotis Benakis. After bringing the case to the local kadi court, petitioning the sultan to intervene, and receiving a favorable judgment, Benakis sat impotent as Halil seized de facto control over Kalamata. The capital's inability to constrain a provincial notable contributed to a decline in public trust and imperial legitimacy throughout the Morea. Communities began asserting control over their own affairs, often at the expense of imperial officials, notably *sipahi*s, many of whom issued petitions complaining of locals occupying their lands. Ottoman sovereignty became increasingly destabilized. New taxes in Karytaina inspired an attempt by villagers to file a formal complaint, which local *kocabaşı*s tried to stop. Elsewhere, new taxes were similarly met with refusal and—in the case of the island of Sikinos in the Cyclades and Klepa in the highlands of Nafpaktos—organized relocations. Violence erupted in 1770. It was swiftly suppressed by the 11,500 battle-ready militiamen recruited for the task by *ayan* from Rumelia.

Often cast as another localized rebellion, the historiography minimizes the scale of the movement. Georgios Papazolis, a former merchant turned artillery officer, is often credited with the organization of this undertaking although it was being planned for over eight years. Tasked by the quartermaster of the artillery in the Russian army with exploring how receptive Balkan Christians were to revolt, Papazolis and a few collaborators traveled throughout southeastern Europe securing commitments from potential allies in Rumelia and the Morea. The historiography paints Alexei Orlov's arrival in Tuscany in 1768 as a turning point in the conspiracy, after which serious plans for an anti-Ottoman insurrection were initiated (Davies 2016, 154). Yet, this mobilization required careful plotting by many more people than this narrative suggests. The 1770 revolution was the careful work of clerics and clansmen, educators and emissaries, merchants, mercenaries, and officials, who cooperated in pursuit of liberation and a new beginning for the *Romioi*. It required assistance from members of prominent diaspora families who had assumed—or were pursuing—diplomatic posts. Some offered support, covertly, as in the case of Marchese Panos Maroutsis, the Russian consul to Venice. Maroutsis mediated between the Russian court and rebel leaders throughout the Mediterranean, while also securing loans for the leaders of the conspiracy from German lenders. Others, like the Zakyntiot noble Dimitrios Motsenigos, actively supported the Russian navy by repairing ships and sharing maps, while also recruiting five thousand armed men from the eastern side of the Adriatic Sea. Ioannis Palatinos, a young noble from Cephalonia, brokered peace between Georgios Mavromichalis and Athanasios Koumoundouros, rival Maniot *kapetanaioi*. A successful mobilization required provincial powerbrokers like Benakis, who commanded fourteen hundred armed men. Benakis organized a meeting at his Kalamata home in March 1769, where the *voivode*s and *kapetanaioi* in attendance pledged to support an anticipated uprising. Finally, it required the symbolic legitimacy of militant clerics like bishop Anthimos of Methoni, who stirred local populations to revolt. The 1770 revolution was not a local rebellion; it was the product of individuals who had embedded themselves within commercial, diplomatic, mercenary, and social networks that extended from Menorca to Georgia and from St. Petersburg to Damietta. Their efforts produced a fifth column with the reach, legitimacy, and military might to subvert Ottoman sovereignty in the southern Balkans and its surrounding archipelagos. The scale of this endeavor and the heterogeneity of this revolutionary alignment should not be downplayed.

Revolution emerged as a possibility in the Greek world in 1770 when established elites and ascendant powerbrokers mobilized in pursuit of a new beginning. For many observers, the entrance of the Russian navy into the Mediterranean represented the possibility of a forthcoming Greek liberation. It animated figures like Anton Alexianos, who entered the Russian navy as a volunteer when the first squadron of the imperial Russian navy docked in Mahón at Minorca.

Their optimism was fueled by the navy's arrival in Oitylo in February 1770, which sparked not only rebellion in Mani, but a series of independent uprisings in other parts of the Morea, throughout Rumelia, and on islands in the Ionian and Aegean Seas. When news of the insurgency reached Boston, Dimitri Ezop boarded his ship, appropriately named *Liberty*, crossed the Atlantic, and rushed to join the revolution. New institutions were established at Russian instigation, such as the Mizistre assembly that was charged with establishing a system of self-government, and the senate in Paros, which struggled to operate effectively. Others emerged organically, such as the civic governments and independent militias in Mesolonghi, Pyrgos and Gastouni, Vrachori, and Kokolata (Cephalonia). Instability combined with political possibility to encourage novel experiments, including the collective adjudication of criminal cases in Skopelos. Though most uprisings were suppressed before the Russian fleet departed Navarino in June, Russian victories at river Larga in Moldavia (July 7), Chesme (July 7), and Kagul again in Moldavia (August 1) in the coming months aroused hope that an anticipated Russian triumph would lift the Ottoman yoke. Hope inspired political vision, and texts by Antonios Ghikas and Evgenios Voulgaris promoted an image of an independent Greece. Within the Aegean, where Admiral Spiridov, Orlov, and others were already building an independent Greek state, an experimental political vocabulary took root, in an attempt to reconceptualize community and establish legitimacy for a non-Ottoman political entity. The discourse relied heavily upon biological metaphors and emotional terminology, as well as phrases signaling the importance of popular consent. The 1770 revolution questioned the viability of empire, claimed a new place for Greeks in an evolving world, and, in so doing, opened new horizons of political possibility. The revolutionary alignment that emerged in 1821 must be contextualized within this longer history, and the new mode of anti-Ottoman resistance introduced in 1770. Doing so in a manner that avoids determinism and teleology will be challenging.

It is tempting to consider the continuities that bond 1770 to 1821. The klepht Mitropetrovas fought in both conflicts alongside a few others. Numerous families did so as well. Petrobey's father and grandfather, Nikitaras's father, as well as Kolokotronis's father, grandfather, and uncles had all participated in 1770. When Bouboulina was born, her father, Stavrianos Pinotsis, an Ydriot captain, was incarcerated in a Constantinopolitan prison for his role in the revolution. Some like the Prince of Moldavia, Alexandros Mavrokordatos, and Liberakis Benakis, Panagiotis's son, refused to abandon the hope of the moment, bidding the Russians to return in the 1780s. Others, like Stephanos Mavromichalis, commander of the Albanian battalion, travelled to Dulcigno and Mani seeking support for a future Russo-Ottoman war. Some families shifted loyalties over generations. Nikolaos Mavrogenis, a loyalist who served as Dragoman of the Ottoman fleet during the war and Prince of Wallachia after, was great-uncle to Manto Mavrogenous, a heroine of the 1821 revolution. Longer genealogies may be drawn as well. Georgios Motsenigos, whose father was "indispensable in supporting the Russians," according to Spiridov, mentored Ioannis Capodistrias, securing a post in the Russian diplomatic service for the young Corfiot. But 1770 did not produce 1821. Each event was the product of contingent processes and a unique alignment of interests. Yet, the comparison is instructive in illustrating that the revolutionary capacities displayed in 1821 were present decades earlier. It also underscores how the possibility for revolution lay in the structural antagonism between transimperial commercial elites, provincial notables who had consolidated power over vast regions, and an empire transitioning from a patrimonial system. These frictions made conflict likely, but not inevitable.

The Roads to Revolution: 1774–1821

Despite its quick suppression, echoes of the 1770 revolution reverberated for decades. Petros Mengous begins his memoir describing his wet-nurse's account of these brutal events. He vividly describes her recollections of the Tripolitsa massacre, her parents' murder, and her own captivity. Reading Mengous's narrative, one quickly detects that the revolutionary flame had not been extinguished. Grand public proclamations from Catherine II and Orlov, a rough constitution for an Aegean principality, and an evolving political discourse had enlivened the Greek political imagination. At the same time, understandings of "Greekness" were destabilized. The century's last three decades witnessed increasing disputes among Greek- and Serbian-speaking communities, as communal boundaries were being redrawn, and institution sharing grew less common. The post-1774 period saw new liberal and republican visions, with Iosipos Moisiodax presenting a model of popular sovereignty that empowered subjects to enforce limits on imperial authority, and Dimitrios Katartzis promoting a view of the *Romioi* as a distinctive and self-determining political society. It witnessed the rebirth of satire in *Alexandrovodas the Unscrupulous* (1785), a text that lampooned Mavrokordatos, the Phanariots, and, to some degree, proponents of Enlightenment thought.

   And yet, despite its impact, the revolution produced little tangible political change. The Treaty of Küçük Kaynarca (1774) dissolved the Archipelagic Principality. It did not propose any form of local autonomy for the Morea, despite granting semiautonomy to the Crimean Khanate. The peace left Greek observers feeling forsaken by their coreligionists and their God. "Russia should have designated part of the Dodecanese as a refuge for the *Romioi*," Pringos wrote, "however, she only concerned herself with her own interests" (Andriotis 1931, 920). Famed poet Kaisarios Dapontes added: "the empire of the Romans can no longer be resurrected, as prophesied in the oracles" (Sathas 1872, 119). A new conjuncture took shape in 1774.

In the ashes of the revolution, the fight for "faith, fatherland, and freedom" gave way to cultural introspection. Throughout the Balkans, clerics championed intellectual revival and moral renewal. Kosmas of Aetolia, an itinerant monk and evangelist, preached the value of education and Greek learning. His activities quickly aroused the suspicions of Venetian authorities and *kocabaşıs* who feared he was stirring the locals to revolt again. Kosmas was executed in 1779. Elsewhere, the peace inspired an ascetic reaction, captured in the *The Philokalia* (1782). A collection compiled by Athonite monks, Nicodimos the Hagiorite and Macarios of Corinth, the text promoted contemplative prayer and an attention to God's presence within all life. Despite the experiments of the 1770–1774 period, little appetite existed for more radical political experimentation. Many simply sought stability. The Moreots, for instance, suffered endemic violence perpetrated by mercenaries, as well as Dulciniot and Algerian pirates, until order was restored in 1779. Some communities in Rumelia were destroyed for supporting the revolution, most notably Moschopolis.

Armatoloi continued to maintain order in the region's most inaccessible corners, watching over the klephts who inhabited these parts. The extension of horizontal networks of association and exchange continued, unmoved by the turmoil, as did processes of decentralization. While there was little appetite for creating political change, sovereignty was being refashioned, to the benefit of provincial powerbrokers. The sultan had affirmed the authority of these new elites during the war, relying upon *ayan* to suppress the uprisings. Provincial magnates continued consolidating power after 1774. New powerbrokers emerged, figures who wielded greater sway than Halil Bey or Benakis had in their heydays. Among the most influential was Ali Pasha of Ioannina. Having turned success as a bandit leader and *derbendci agha* (guardian of the passes) into extensive landholdings, social rank, and political power, Ali and his sons built a zone of influence along the Adriatic shore that extended from Epirus to southern Albania. In 1799, he was granted administrative oversight over Thessaly, and was later made governor of Rumelia. Yet, he was not content to be regional governor; his ambitions were much larger. Ali was engaged in a state-making project. Documents from the time record agreements within which local communities agreed to pay Ali a fee in exchange for protection from *timar* holders. By 1797, he conducted his own foreign policy, cultivating a diplomatic network that extended throughout Europe. In the years preceding the revolution, Ali constituted the preeminent legal authority of his dominion, and petitioners of all religions appealed to him, rather than the sultan, to resolve grievances. Alongside these efforts, Ali promoted Ioannina as a center of Enlightenment, attracting future leaders of the 1821 revolution, most notably Odysseas Androutsos, Markos Botsaris, and Georgios Karaiskakis. Mohammed Ali of Egypt, Osman Pazvantoğlu, and, to a considerably lesser extent, Tudor Vladimirescu, and many others rose alongside Ali Pasha, acquiring important offices and lucrative contracts, while also negotiating new tax and security arrangements with local communities. This was a new breed of governor, one who interacted with the empire as a *servicer,* not a *servant* (Yaycioglu 2016, 67).

The influence of provincial notables mainly derived from their ability to control large retinues of armed men. William Hamilton, secretary of the British embassy, reported in 1803 that Ali Pasha could raise thirty thousand troops in a matter of days. By this time, Ali Pasha was uninterested in simply recruiting and provisioning armed men during times of imperial crisis. From the 1790s, he was actively working to redefine his relationship with local *aghas, beys*, Christian notables, and especially klephts and *armatoloi,* all of whom prevented him from establishing a monopoly of violence within his zone of influence. More often than not, Ali's interests aligned with the empire's. In 1803, he subjugated the Souliot confederacy, which had maintained an autonomous status for centuries. Ali's interests also aligned with the empire's when it came to curbing banditry. Between 1799 and 1810, Ali adopted the dual strategy of persecuting klephts and *armatoloi* for engaging in brigandage, while recruiting others into his personal army. Sultanic decrees and patriarchal excommunications aided his efforts and helped to curb banditry in the Morea between 1802 and 1806, compelling members of the Zacharias and Kolokotronis families to flee to the Ionian Islands. A similar effort to eliminate bandits took place in Crete beginning in 1812. These attempts notwithstanding, demand for experienced combatants remained high throughout the Napoleonic wars. More than six thousand Greek mercenaries participated in wars in the first decade of the nineteenth century; a significant number, given that the number of armed participants rarely exceeded twenty thousand during the 1821 revolution. Demand declined precipitously with the 1815 peace. As porous frontiers gave way to well-guarded borders between the British Ionian Islands and Ottoman Empire, raiding became increasingly perilous. For many, submission to Ali Pasha or employment within his military became the only option for employment. For others, the 1815 peace inspired a career change. Theodoros Kolokotronis famously worked as a butcher during these years. Sitting idle, desperate for work, or struggling to navigate new careers, former mercenaries were ripe for being instrumentalized by polities pursuing war with the Ottoman Empire, provincial notables with secessionist ambitions, or other groups capable of making enticing appeals.

In Rumeli, the revolution had not disrupted the ascendance of the provincial elites. The peace reshaped power structures in Wallachia and Moldavia, positioning Phanariot rulers as potential leaders of a more robust independence movement. The Phanariots, with their retinues and large networks of clients and affiliates, had risen to prominence in the decades following Dimitrie Cantemir's rebellion (1711). By 1716, they occupied key positions within the fabric of Ottoman governance, combining their influence over the patriarchate with a monopoly over the offices of dragoman and the top administrative positions of Moldavia and Wallachia. Because Christians were formally excluded from the *askeri* (the tax-free ruling elite of the empire), they were well situated to lead a possible Orthodox Christian resistance. The Treaty of Küçük Kaynarca (1774) offered added motivation for pursuing such a role. According to Russian interpretations, articles 7 and 14 granted the tsarina the right to protect all Ottoman Christians, and to intervene in Wallachia and Moldavia in cases of imperial misrule. Despite occupying powerful positions and having legal sanction to cooperate with Russia in refashioning sovereignty in the principalities, Phanariot rulers exhibited little appetite for radical change. Their precarious position between the Russian and Ottoman Empires, as well as between local boyars and rival Phanariot families, provided significant impediments to leading a resistance movement. Retaining power was challenging enough.

The 1774 peace also produced crucibles of revolution within New Russia, the administrative territory formed in the annexed southern regions. The effort to integrate Balkan allies into imperial institutions began during the war, firstly as a means of organizing the over three thousand irregular forces serving in the Russian navy in 1771. Organized originally into five battalions (Albanians, Cephalonians, Maniates, Moreans, and Zantiots), the forces multiplied during the war, to an overall strength of eleven volunteer battalions and 6,413 men. With peace concluded, Russia no longer required irregular military forces; yet, it was important to preserve relationships with allies who could be useful in future conflicts. In a marriage of imperial expansionism and self-serving opportunism, Catherine II appointed influential Balkan Christians to Russian consulships throughout the Adriatic and Ionian Seas. Panos Bitsilis served as consul for Albania and Cheimarra, Captain Gkikas Bitsilis for Cephalonia, and, after requesting assistance for another revolt, Liberakis Benakis became consul general on Corfu. At the same time, the need to populate territories in the Cherson and reward volunteers led to 1,057 officers and men of the "Irregular Albanian Battalions" being settled near Kerch and Yenikal. Russia funded the building of homes and communal buildings, offered settlers exemptions from taxes and conscription for thirty years, and permitted them to appoint their own archbishop. In 1778, the community expanded, as fifty thousand Crimean

Greeks were relocated to New Russia by Metropolitan Ignatius. The community grew with the formal incorporation of the Crimea into the Russian Empire in 1784 and the founding of a Greek military colony in Odessa in 1795. Historians estimate that two hundred and fifty thousand Greeks migrated from the Ottoman Empire to New Russia. Due to provisions of the 1774 treaty that permitted them to sail under the Russian flag, many prospered, creating vast fortunes as shippers. Notable merchant families like the Maraslis, Rallis, and Rodokanakis established great fortunes. Some military volunteers grew rich as well. Ioannis Varvakis, a hero at Chesme, was rewarded with honorary titles and an unlimited and duty-free fishery in the Caspian Sea. Connections were extended in subsequent Russo-Ottoman wars, with members of younger generations like Kolokotronis being recruited as corsairs. Imperial support for allies, volunteers, and settlers produced a prosperous and self-confident diaspora that was deeply loyal to the Romanov dynasty, yet firmly committed to the cause of Greek liberation.

In New Russia, and specifically in Odessa, Greek nationalism took root. To some degree, this owed to a unique alignment of imperial and national interests. Catherine II's "Greek Project," which aimed to extend Russian influence south, required ousting the Ottomans from the Balkans and major Mediterranean islands. In 1782, she proposed to Joseph II that, upon the Ottomans' defeat in a forthcoming war, Venice would retake the Morea, Crete, and Cyprus. In exchange, the empress' grandson—the aptly named Constantine—would oversee a new kingdom comprising northern Greece, Macedonia, Thrace, Bulgaria, and Albania. Ultimately, a European crusade would not come to fruition, but this did not deter Catherine from once again trying to incite the Greeks before the 1787 war. To a greater degree, the rise of Greek nationalism in New Russia owed to Odessa's cosmopolitan and transient character. A port city at the crossroads of various trade-routes and intellectual channels, the convergence of liberalism, carbonarism, and freemasonry produced a unique synthesis. Odessa's political fermentation inspired Nikolaos Skoufas, Athanasios Tsakalov, and Emmanouil Xanthos to found a secret society in 1814, the Philiki Etaireia. It was more self-confidently revolutionary than precursors like the Ellinoglosson Xenodocheion, which educated Greeks as preparation for the independence struggle, or the Philomousos Society, which preserved ancient monuments. The Philiki Etaireia sought to establish an independent Greek state. Despite its ambition, it did not seem destined to lead a revolution in 1816, when it numbered only around twenty. The situation changed rapidly in the coming years, precisely as peace took hold.

The Congress of Vienna destabilized the Greek world, damaging the economic prospects of many merchants. Greek maritime shippers had experienced considerable commercial success in previous decades. From 1774, the ability to sail under the Russian flag had enabled them to profit from Black Sea trade. The Napoleonic Wars offered an additional boon, excluding the French merchant marine from Mediterranean trade from 1803 to 1815. Lucrative opportunities for provisioning armies were quickly exploited. The 1815 peace halted this prosperous period, bankrupting many merchants. Several transferred their attention from economic pursuits to political concerns precisely at this time, with many bankrupt merchants joining the embryonic Philiki Etaireia. Of the 910 identified members who reported their occupations, 489 described themselves as merchants. Some were clearly displaced by the reentry of the French merchant marine into the Mediterranean. Leon Leontidis, who identifies himself as a "ruined merchant" in membership papers, counted on a longer war, a French victory, and the opportunity to supply Napoleon's army in Russia. Skoufas, too, turned to politics only after his trading business failed. 1815 brought many to ruin, driving them into an emerging revolutionary alignment.

The Philiki Etaireia united different powerbrokers into an anti-Ottoman resistance. The organization expanded slowly until 1818, when the base of operations moved to Constantinople, and it began making inroads throughout the Greek world. Anthimos Gazis, founder of the Philomousos Society in Athens and the first Greek philological periodical, Ερμής ο Λόγιος, joined the secret organization during a trip to Odessa. From the Danubian Principalities, leading Phanariots like the Prince of Moldavia, Michael Soutsos were recruited. Alexandros Mavrokordatos, the future prime minister of Greece, was initiated at Pisa. From the Morea, Petrobey Mavromichalis was initiated as a member in 1818, and the following year he brokered a pact among major kapetanaioi in the province to support the forthcoming revolution. Recruits from the United States of the Ionian Islands and the Italian states quickly filled the ranks. In 1820, Alexandros Ypsilantis, the hero of the Great Patriotic War of 1812, was enlisted to lead the organization. Ypsilantis's recruitment lent support to the belief that the tsar supported the liberation movement. Having expanded widely, and with Ali Pasha in open rebellion against the sultan in 1820, the society initiated insurrections in the Danubian Principalities and the Morea. The Etairists initiated the violence of 1821, driving its network of sympathizers to produce the revolution.

"The innovation that the Philiki Etaireia realized among the Greeks," as has been aptly remarked, "was exactly the passage from the open dissemination of ideas to secret and autonomous political action" (Yakovaki 2014, 173). This is correctly considered as an innovation, as never before had a nonimperial entity mobilized Greek communities to rise against the Ottoman Empire. Yet, the conspiratorial network forged by Russian agents in the 1760s also mobilized communities throughout—and around—the Balkan peninsula to rise in revolt. Admittedly, the roughly two dozen Russian agents responsible for organizing the 1770 revolution were dwarfed by the 1,093 known Etairists. Yet, similarities abound. Similar tropes were used to galvanize support. Ypsilantis's proclamation to "fight for faith and fatherland" mirrors Orlov's Navarino speech in May 1770, where he implored his coreligionists to fight for "faith, fatherland, and freedom"—freedom being an implied goal by 1821. Ypsilantis's claim that the liberation struggle was part of a larger effort to foster "happiness," and his blending of political and emotional terminology more generally, resembles political claims advanced by revolutionaries in the 1770s. Androutsos's address to the inhabitants of Galaxidi on March 22, 1821, within which he described the liberation struggle as another revelation of divine providence, reminds one of the language Papazolis uses in his *Didaskalia* (1765). Additionally, both alignments were extremely heterogenous and contained reactionary factions. In 1770, Dimitrios Motsenigos assisted the Russians hoping to leverage this association into a diplomatic post, while in 1821, klephts and *armatoloi* sought to supplant local elites and assume their place within the social structure. In neither case did participation signal a desire to transform the social and political order. Neither revolutionary alignment was united around uniform goals. Moreover, at the onset of both conflicts, it was entirely unclear what sort of polity would emerge from a successful conflict. Forging a coalition with revolutionary capacities required Etairists to belie significant differences differentiating the factions; differences that surfaced in civil wars in 1824 and 1825 that risked tearing the movement apart.

"History doesn't repeat itself, but it often rhymes." The aphorism, often attributed to Mark Twain, is especially poignant when considering the Greek War of Independence. For one, it highlights the continuities and common roots of the 1770 and 1821 revolutions. Both attempted to refashion systems of sovereignty that had been destabilized in the transitions from feudalism to capitalism and from a vertical to a horizontal empire. In each case, new modes of exchange, interaction, and sociability expanded horizons of political possibility. Both movements' architects were transimperial brokers who were incapable of sustaining the unity necessary to function as a "revolutionary vanguard." Both events belong to the global age of revolution; yet, where the Polish fight for religious tolerance was a touchstone in 1770, the Spaniards' desire for freedom and happiness animated the 1821 revolutionaries. And yet, aspirations and expectations differed considerably between these two events. Ypsilantis's and Androutsos's worldviews were informed by successful revolutions in the Americas, France, and Serbia, and the founding of a state on the Ionian Islands.

While Xanthos and others paid occasional lip service to the influence of 1770, the 1821 revolutionaries envisioned their struggle as connected to conflicts in Portugal, Spain, Piedmont, Naples, and Sicily. Divided by a half century, these two events bookend the revolutionary age, a unique era of indeterminacy and possibility in Greek history that sits awkwardly astride the borders marking off the early modern from the modern period, the eighteenth from the nineteenth century, and the Ottoman from the national era.

Vasilis Molos

References

Ágoston, Gábor. 2005. *Guns for the Sultan: Military Power and the Weapons Industry in the Ottoman Empire.* Cambridge.

Aksan, Virginia H. 2013. "Mobilization of Warrior Populations in the Ottoman Context, 1750–1850." *Fighting for a Living: A Comparative Study of Military Labour, 1500–2000,* edited by Erik-Jan Zürcher, 331–352. Amsterdam.

Alexander, John C. 1985. *Brigandage and Public Order in the Morea, 1685–1806.* Athens.

Andriotis, N. 1931. "Το Χρονικό του Άμστερδαμ." [The Amsterdam chronicle]. *Nea Estia* 10: 914–920.

Arendt, Hannah. 2006. *On Revolution.* New York.

Armitage, David, and Sanjay Subrahmanyam, eds. 2010. *The Age of Revolution in Global Context c. 1760–1840.* New York.

Davies, Brian L. 2016. *The Russo-Turkish War, 1768–1774: Catherine II and the Ottoman Empire.* London.

Djordjevic, Dimitrije, and Stephen Fischer-Galati. 1981. *The Balkan Revolutionary Tradition.* New York.

Finlay, George. 1971. *History of the Greek Revolution and the Reign of King Otho.* London.

Fleming, Katherine Elizabeth. 1999. *The Muslim Bonaparte: Diplomacy and Orientalism in Ali Pasha's Greece.* Princeton, NJ.

Frangos, George. 1971. "The Philike Etaireia, 1814–1821: A Social and Historical Analysis." PhD diss., Columbia University, New York.

Gallant, Thomas W. 2002. *Experiencing Dominion: Culture, Identity, and Power in the British Mediterranean.* Notre Dame, IN.

Gündoğdu, Birol. 2012. "Ottoman Constructions of the Morea Rebellion, 1770s: A Comprehensive Study of Ottoman Attitudes to the Greek Uprising." PhD diss., University of Toronto.

Hobsbawm, Eric. 1969. *Bandits.* London.

Ilıcak, Şükrü H. 2011. "A Radical Rethinking of Empire: Ottoman State and Society during the Greek War of Independence, 1821–1826." PhD diss., Harvard University.

İnalcık, Halil. 1983. "The Emergence of Big Farms, Çiftliks: State, Landlords and Tenants." In *Contributions à l'histoire économique et sociale de l'empire Ottoman,* edited by Jean-Louis Bacqué-Grammont and Paul Dumont, 105–126. Leuven.

Katsiardi-Hering, Olga. 2008. "Central and Peripheral Communities in the Greek Diaspora: Interlocal and Local Economic, Political, and Cultural Networks in the Eighteenth and Nineteenth Centuries." *Homelands and Diasporas: Greeks, Jews and Their Migrations,* ed. Minna Rozen, 169–180. London and New York.

Kitromilides, Paschalis M. 2013. *Enlightenment and Revolution: The Making of Modern Greece.* Cambridge, MA.

Koliopoulos, John S. 1987. *Brigands with a Cause: Brigandage and Irredentism in Modern Greece, 1821–1912.* Oxford.

Lovejoy, Paul E. 2016. *Jihād in West Africa during the Age of Revolutions.* Athens, OH.

Mengous, Petros. 1830. *Narrative of a Greek Soldier: Containing Anecdotes and Occurrences Illustrating the Character and Manners of the Greeks and Turks in Asia Minor, and Detailing Events of the Late War in Greece, in Which the Author Was Actively Engaged by Land and Sea, from the Commencement to the Close of the Revolution.* New York.

Mexas, Valerios. 1937. *Οι Φιλικοί: κατάλογος των μελών της Φιλικής Εταιρείας εκ του αρχείου Σέκερη* [The Philikoi: A members' list of the Philiki Etaireia from the Sekeris papers]. Athens.

Molos, Vasilis W. 2014. "Nationness in the Absence of a Nation: Narrating the Prehistory of the Greek National Movement, 1762–1792." PhD diss., New York University.

Nagata, Yūzō. 1995. *Studies on the Social and Economic History of the Ottoman Empire.* Izmir.

Papastamatiou, Demetrios Chrysanthos. 2009. "Οικονομικοί μηχανισμοί και το προυχοντικό φαινόμενο στην οθωμανική Πελοπόννησο του 18ου αιώνα: η περίπτωση του Παναγιώτη Μπενάκη" [Economic mechanisms and the phenomenon of the notables in the Ottoman Peloponnese in the 18th century: the case of Panagiotis Benakis]. PhD diss., Aristotle University of Thessaloniki.

Pappas, Nicholas Charles. 1991. *Greeks in Russian Military Service in the Late Eighteenth and Early Nineteenth Centuries.* Thessaloniki.

Philiou, Christine M. 2011. *Biography of an Empire: Governing Ottomans in an Age of Revolution.* Berkeley and Los Angeles.

Photopoulos, Athanasios Th. 2005. *Οι κοτζαμπάσηδες της Πελοποννήσου κατά τη Δεύτερη Τουρκοκρατία, 1715–1821* [The primates of the Peloponnese during the Second Tourkokratia, 1715–1821]. Athens.

Rothman, E. Natalie. 2011. *Brokering Empire: Trans-Imperial Subjects Between Venice and Istanbul.* Ithaca, NY.

Rotzokos, Nikos. 2007 *Εθναφύπνιση και εθνογένεση: Ορλωφικά και ελληνική ιστοριογραφία* [The awakening and birth of the nation: The Orlof uprising and Greek historiography]. Athens.

Salzmann, Ariel. 1993. "An Ancient Regime Revisited: Privatization and Political Economy in the 18th Century Ottoman Empire." *Politics and Society* 21:393–423.

Sathas, Constantinos N., ed. 1872. *Μεσαιωνική βιβλιοθήκη* [Medieval library]. Vol. 3. Venice.

Sifneos, Evrydiki. 2014. "Preparing the Greek Revolution in Odessa in the 1820s: Tastes, Markets and Political Liberalism." *Historical Review* 11:139–170.

Skiotis, Dennis N. 1975. "Mountain Warriors and the Greek Revolution." In *War, Technology and Society in the Middle East,* edited by Vernon J. Parry and Malcolm E. Yapp, 308–329. Oxford.

Stathis, Panagiotis. 2007. "From *Klephts* and *Armatoloi* to Revolutionaries." In *Ottoman Rule and the Balkans, 1760–1850: Conflict, Transformation, Adaptation,* edited by Antonis Anastasopoulos and Elias Kolovos, 167–179. Rethymno.

Tezcan, Baki. 2010. *The Second Ottoman Empire: Political and Social Transformation in the Early Modern World.* Cambridge.

Venturi, Franco. 1989. *The End of the Old Regime in Europe, 1768–1776: The First Crisis.* Princeton, NJ.

Yakovaki, Nassia. 2014. "The Philiki Etaireia Revisited: In Search of Contexts, National and International." *Historical Review* 11:171–187.

Yaycioglu, Ali. 2016. *Partners of the Empire: The Crisis of the Ottoman Order in the Age of Revolutions.* Stanford.

Secret Societies: The Society of Friends and Its Forerunners

The founding and activity of secret political, cultural, and / or social organizations in Europe throughout the eighteenth century have led historians to dub this period the "century of societies" (Chatzipanagioti-Sangmeister, 2010, 13). Defining factors for the appearance and development of secret organizations were: (1) the dissemination of the liberal and democratic ideas generated and cultivated by the European Enlightenment, (2) the growth of Freemasonry in almost all European countries, (3) the inspiration of the French Revolution and the effort to abolish absolutist regimes throughout Europe, (4) the birth and spread of national-liberationist ideas, and (5) the negative reaction to the new ideas and the vicious persecution of their advocates (Kitromilides 2000, 164–169).

Secret organizations appeared within the fold of Hellenism in the late eighteenth and early nineteenth centuries, but only outside the borders of the Ottoman Empire. This is because the intellectual movement of the Neohellenic Enlightenment was born and flourished either in the communities established by Greek migrants in various cities of Europe (*paroikies*) or in the Romanian Principalities, thanks to the Phanariot princes and the pronounced presence of Greeks in the Danubian lands (Kitromilides 1996, 71–74). By contrast, in the Ottoman East, due on the one hand to the backwardness of the economy and society, and on the other to the attachment to cultural models of Oriental theocracies, by the end of the eighteenth century the overwhelming majority of the sultan's subjects had not yet come into contact with the ideas of the European Enlightenment. For precisely these reasons, the principal purpose of the societies founded by Greeks in Europe was to promote the intellectual development of Hellenism and, in particular, to combat illiteracy and promulgate secular education.

Before presenting the Greek organizations—secret and other—that were founded before the Greek Revolution of 1821, it should be pointed out that an important role in the development of the Greek societal movement was played by the experience gained by expatriate Greeks—mainly merchants—from their initiation into masonic lodges operating in the cities in which they had settled, particularly those in German-speaking countries (Chatzipanagioti-Sangmeister 2010, 61–82).

The first Greek secret society seems to have been founded by Rhigas Velestinlis and was active in Vienna. By the early 1790s, Rhigas had developed considerable activity as an author and publisher, in the framework of the Neohellenic Enlightenment in the Romanian Principalities and Vienna (Kitromilides 1998, 21–53). Then, on the basis of the constitutions of the French Revolution, he went on to draft an exceptionally interesting revolutionary plan aimed at overturning the sultan and establishing in the Balkans and western Asia Minor a unified state, the Hellenic Republic, in which all peoples would live in conditions of "liberty, equality and fraternity" (Manessis 1962). In 1797, Rhigas tried to put his plan into practice. However, he was arrested in Trieste by the Austrian secret police and handed over to the Ottoman authorities. He was executed in Belgrade, together with seven of his comrades, on June 24, 1798 (Vranousis 1963, 123–130).

The existence of the Rhigas society, as it is known in historiography, is referred to in the memoirs of Christophoros Perraivos, one of Rhigas's companions who escaped arrest and later became a member of the Philiki Etaireia and a freedomfighter in the Greek Revolution (Perraivos 1836, viii). However, research to date has been unable to confirm his claim, as well as that of all those who adopted the same view at various times (Vranousis 1963, 82–83). Consequently, all that can be said for certain is that Rhigas had attracted a coterie of companions who shared his ideas and vision, without this necessarily meaning that they constituted an organized conspiratorial network with specific rules, recognition signs, and particular symbols (Botzaris 1962, 30–31).

The second "society" considered here was founded in 1805 by Greeks in the Moldavian city of Jassy and was called the Brotherhood (Αδελφάτον). The statute of this society was drawn up by the Metropolitan of Jassy Veniamin Costache and the Bishop of Roman Gherasim Clipa. According to this statute, the Brotherhood accepted as members not only Greeks but also Romanian boyars (nobles) and wealthy merchants. The ostensible purpose of the society was to collect money for charity, but its real aims were political. Indeed, it seems that tsarist Russia was involved in its founding, since immediately after the declaration of the Russo-Turkish War in 1806 and the Russian invasion of the Romanian Principalities, the Brotherhood in Jassy was dissolved, presumably because the reasons for its existence no longer held (Elian 1962).

During the period of the Russo-Turkish War, in the years 1806–1812, the Romanian Principalities were under Russian domination, and in Bucharest on July 7, 1810, the Graecodacian Literary Society (Γραικοδακική Φιλολογική Εταιρεία) was founded. The initiative was taken by Ignatios, whom the Russians had appointed just two months previously as Metropolitan of Ungrowallachia (Camariano 1968, 39–40). Members of the society included prelates, Romanian boyars, Greek dignitaries in Wallachia, scholars, physicians, and merchants. Its purpose was "to alert" its members "to the progress of learning, and to cultivate the modern Greek language, by elevating it as close as possible to its mother" (*Ερμής ο Λόγιος* 1811, 6). Concurrently, the society totally reformed the Princely Academy of Bucharest, staffing it with excellent Greek teachers and endowing it with the necessary financial resources for its operation. The new educational institution, which was named Lyceum (Λύκειον), was organized on the basis of a very detailed regulation which defined the content of the lessons in the curriculum, the duties of the teachers, and the obligations and the manner of assessment of the pupils, as well as holidays and vacations (*Ερμής ο Λόγιος* 1811, 64–76).

There is a question as to whether the founding of the Graecodacian Literary Society served also a political purpose. Although nothing emerges from the sources on the subject, there are certain indications that it most probably served Russian policy in the Balkans. First, the society was founded while the Romanian Principalities were under Russian occupation; second, it functioned under the patronage of the tsar; third, it was dissolved in 1812, with the withdrawal of the Russians; and fourth, its animating spirit, Metropolitan Ignatios, left Bucharest together with the Russian troops and thereafter lived in Baden in Austria and Pisa in Italy, with a pension granted him by the tsar.

On September 1, 1813, a year or so after the Graecodacian Literary Society was dissolved, the Philomousos Society (Φιλόμουσος Εταιρεία) was founded in Athens, on the initiative of British and Greek intellectuals and antiquarians. According to its statute, the purpose of this society was "the cultivation and enlightenment of the Greek spirit of young people through studying the sciences, publishing books, assisting indigent pupils, discovering antiquities, collecting Inscriptions on stones, Statues and Vessels and whatever else worthy of attention." Whoever agreed to make an annual subscription was eligible for membership. Depending on the size of the subscription they promised to pay, members were named *Synigoros* (advocate) or *Evergetis* (benefactor) and received a bronze or gold ring, respectively, with a representation of the owl and the inscription "Philomouson" (*Ερμής ο Λόγιος* 1814, 98–100). The administration of the society and the management of its finances were undertaken by four ephors(inspectors), who were elected by its members.

Their duties were actually stipulated in a special statute issued on September 27, 1814 (Vellianitis 1993, 52–3).

Around one year after the founding of the society, a new statute was issued "for the Public School and Library in the city." This clarified and amended some of the regulations of the 1813 statute, defined the manner of election and the duties of the ephors, and so on. However, what is noteworthy is that the new statute made provision for part of its monies to be used to equip and run a school in Athens, to engage teachers and award prizes to the top pupils. It also made provision for setting up a library in Athens and equipping it with scientific instruments and books (Vellianitis 1993, 54–60).

The Philomousos Society of Athens operated successfully until the outbreak of the Revolution in 1821. Thanks to its economic support, the old Dekas School was reorganized and renamed the Scientific High School (Επιστημονικόν Γυμνάσιον) of Athens, to which important Greek and foreign educators were invited, teaching with considerable success (Chatzopoulos 1991, 260–263). In addition, the society's ephors collected antiquities and created a small "museum," while at the same time offering their help to foreign travelers who visited Athens to admire its monuments (Vellianitis 1993, 204, 310–311).

The Athenian Philomousos Society appointed Anthimos Gazis as its *Epitropos* (commissioner) in Vienna. When he learned that Englishmen were involved in the founding of the society, Gazis announced to the ephors of the Philomousos Society of Athens that he and others would set up a new "society," the Philomousos Society of Pilion, with the purpose of founding a Philosophical School at his birthplace, Milies on Pilion in Thessaly. He proposed that "the two Societies" "unite in no other way but as two Brothers," in order to support the two schools, the Scientific High School in Athens and the Philosophical School in Pilion (Vellianitis 1993, 80).

He hurried to inform Ioannis Capodistrias, who was a senior official in the Russian delegation at the conference convened by the Great Powers after their victory over Napoleon. Capodistrias, who considered the British involvement in the original society's foundation as suspect, immediately informed the tsar and proposed the founding in Vienna of a new society that would undertake, on the one hand, to set up the new school at Pilion and, on the other, to assist financially the Philomousos Society in Athens (Capodistrias 1976, 23; Koukkou 1958, 38–40). Following the Russo-Turkish Treaty of Küçük Kaynarca in 1774 the tsar had been unofficially acknowledged as protector of the sultan's Orthodox Christian subjects (*Rûm*) (Quataert 2006, 146–147). Thus the founding of the new Philomousos Society of Vienna, the Société des Amis des Muses as historians usually call it, comes under the umbrella of the policy of tsarist Russia in the Balkans.

Discussions about founding the new society seem to have been held between October and December 1814. Participants in these, apart from Capodistrias and Gazis, were Metropolitan Ignatios and some eminent Greeks at that time in Vienna (Laios 1962, 167). Officially the Société des Amis des Muses was founded on January 1, 1815, when Capodistrias submitted its statute, in Greek and French, to the Austrian censorship authority for approval. According to the statute, the society's purpose was purely educational, with the following individual aims: (1) to provide economic support for the development of education in Greece, (2) to publish works by ancient Greek authors, (3) to award scholarships to young Greeks in order to study in Europe, (4) to seek out antiquities, and (5) to fund the school in Athens and to found a *gymnasion* (high school) in Pilion (Laios 1962, 209).

In all other respects, the statute of the Société des Amis des Muses of Vienna barely differed from that of its counterpart in Athens. In this case, too, members were those who agreed to make an annual subscription of at least three Spanish dollars. Depending on the size of the subscription, they were given the title of *Synigoros* or *Evergetis,* while as a sign of recognition they received a bronze or gold ring. The difference was that the rings of members of the Athenian society bore a representation of the owl while those of members of the Viennese society a representation of the Centaur and Achilles. Administration of the new society was entrusted to ephors, who were elected in Athens and Pilion respectively by members who had paid their dues to the treasury. However, responsibility for the management of the money was undertaken by the General Bureau of the society in Vienna (Laios 1962, 206, 210).

Even though the Société des Amis des Muses was not a clandestine organization and its declared purpose was purely educational and while included among its members were the tsar himself and hundreds of aristocrats from various European states, Metternich and the Austrian secret police were convinced that it served political objectives. Indeed, they were certain that its aims were attuned to the political plans of tsarist Russia in the Balkans, which sought the breakup of the Ottoman Empire and the independence of the Greeks. For this reason, they placed members of the society under surveillance and undermined its activities in any way they could (Laios 1962, 177–8, 183, 194, 200).

Notwithstanding its covert pursuit by the Austrian authorities and the gradual decrease in the number of its members, the Société des Amis des Muses of Vienna continued its activity until 1821. Its principal concern was to award scholarships and to monitor the progress of young Greek students attending universities in German-speaking countries (Koukkou 1958, 87–109). Indeed, it should be noted that Capodistrias, farsightedly apprehending the advantages of the monitorial method of teaching in schools, took measures to financially help Greek students in Paris, so that they could be taught this method in the French Société pour l'Enseignement Elémentaire. On completing their studies, these young people were obliged to return to the Ottoman Empire and apply the new method there, in the *Ellinika* (Hellenic, i.e., high) schools (Koukkou 1958, 79).

Although rumors circulated from time to time about underground relations between the Société des Amis des Muses of Vienna and the Philiki Etaireia, despite the fact that some of the members of the former were later initiated into the latter (such as Anthimos Gazis and Alexandros Ypsilantis) and despite the suspicion of the Austrian authorities, the sources show that there was no kind of collaboration or connection between the two societies. This was undoubtedly due to Ioannis Capodistrias's declared opposition to secret organizations and especially to those that had revolutionary aims (Arsh 2015, 224–234).

The last society founded prior to the Philiki Etaireia was the Hôtel Hellénophone (Ελληνόγλωσσον Ξενοδοχείον). From the scant information available, we know that this particular society was founded in Paris in 1809 by Grigorios Zalykis or Zalykoglou and possibly had the appellative Société Hellénique (Ελληνική Εταιρία) (Rousseau 1828, xxi). This was a secret society whose members swore an oath at their induction. Their names were entered in two codices of documents that were called the Bible of Life, they were classed in "grades," they wore rings to identify each other, and they used various symbols and signs of recognition. President of the society was the well-known French Philhellene, diplomat, and antiquarian Choiseul Gouffier, while Greeks and Frenchmen were counted among its members (Sathas 1869, 608). From the scant sources it would appear that the society met with a lukewarm response both from Greeks residing permanently or temporarily in Paris and from French Philhellenes. In fact, the appointment of Zalykis as first secretary of the Ottoman embassy in Paris, in 1816, most probably caused the suspension of its operation. In the following year, the death of the society's president Gouffier must have led to its dissolution (Botzaris 1962, 76).

The ostensible purpose of this secret organization was to support and take care of Greeks living in Paris and, possibly, to provide financial assistance for young Greeks studying at French universities. However, some Greek historians have maintained that these welfare concerns concealed its true purpose, which was to prepare for the revolution that, with the help of France, would lead to the liberation of the Greeks (Philimon 1859–1862, 4:viii–ix). All these are a matter of speculation, since neither the statute of the society nor the correspondence of its members has been found.

What is particularly interesting about the Hôtel Hellénophone is its possible relationship with the Philiki Etaireia. The historian of the latter society Ioannis Philimon has argued that the Parisian secret organization was in some way the "womb" that gave birth to the Philiki Etaireia. His basic contention was that one of its "founders," Athanasios Tsakalov, was a member of the Hôtel Hellénophone. According to this version, when Tsakalov left Paris in 1815, he went to Moscow, where he inducted into the Hôtel Hellénophone the other "founder" of the Philiki Etaireia, Nikolaos Skoufas. Both men, after initiating others, went on to turn the specific society into a clandestine revolutionary organization that became known as the Philiki Etaireia (Philimon 1859–1862, 4:x–xi).

In the last five years before the declaration of the Greek Revolution of 1821, it seems that some Greeks made attempts or at least plans to found in Vienna two further "societies." The first was founded on January 1/13, 1817, seemingly on the initiative of Ioannis Mavrogenis, ambassador of the Ottoman Empire in Vienna, and of certain merchants "φιλογενών και φιλομούσων Γραικών" (Greek patriots and connoisseurs) who were active in the Austrian capital. The statute of this System, as it was called, was published in *Literary Hermes* (Ερμής ο Λόγιος 1817, 8–13). From this it emerges that the sole purpose of the society was the training of young Greeks in the new pedagogical methods being taught in European universities, so that they could go back to the Ottoman Empire and apply these methods there in the so-called *koina* (common, i.e., elementary) schools. For this purpose, the System intended to award scholarships to young Greeks who were either studying in Vienna or had completed their studies in the *Ellinika* high schools of the Ottoman Empire and wished to study in the "Academies of enlightened Europe." The statute also defined the administration of the System, the responsibilities of its *prostatis* (president), ephors, and *epitropoi,* the manner of their election and substitution, the conditions of membership, and the management of the monies contributed. From the sources available, it seems that the Greeks of Vienna showed little interest in the System, which is why it did not have the expected results (Seirinidou 2011, 349–350). This may well have been due to the fact that the System was set up in competition to the Philomousos Society of Vienna, which was under Russian influence.

The second "society" never got off the ground. In 1818, Theodoros Negris, an official in the service of the Prince of Moldavia, in collaboration with two Greek men of letters, Anthimos Gazis and Theoklitos Pharmakidis, planned the founding of yet another society based in Vienna. Indeed, they went so far as to announce their plan to Capodistrias. From its program, it appears that the society's primary purposes were to promote the education of young Greeks in the sciences and to develop education in Greece. However, the fact that the society would be under the protection of Russia allows us to suspect that the plan also had political aims (Seirinidou 2011, 350–351). Even though this attempt proved abortive, the involvement in it of Gazis and the multitasking Negris arouses suspicions. And this is because in the same period the former was, as we shall see, already a member of the *Archi* (supreme authority) of the Philiki Etaireia, while the latter was initiated into the *Archi* on May 15, 1818 (Meletopoulos 1967, 306). Thus, the likelihood that plans to found a new society in Vienna in 1818 were linked with the Philiki Etaireia's endeavor to infiltrate Greek circles in the Austrian capital cannot be ruled out.

The Philiki Etaireia

According to Emmanouil Xanthos, the only one of those accredited with founding the Philiki Etaireia who has left a written account of his activity, the secret revolutionary organization was founded in 1814 in the Russian city of Odessa by three Greeks: Nikolaos Skoufas, a failed tradesman; Athanasios Tsakalov, son of a successful merchant in Moscow and a student in France; and Emmanouil Xanthos himself, a tradesman and shop assistant. Noteworthy is the fact that the founders of the Philiki Etaireia, in contrast to the founders of earlier or contemporary Greek organizations, such as the Philomousos Society, came from the petty bourgeoisie (Panayiotopoulos 2003, 14–15; Xanthos 1939, 30–31).

The exact year of the founding of the Philiki Etaireia is not known. It had formerly been maintained that the secret organization had been founded in the summer of 1814, with September as a *terminus ante quem.* For this reason, it had been claimed that the society's members (*Philikoi*) had established September 14 as the anniversary of its founding, the feast of the Elevation of the Holy Cross in the Orthodox Christian calendar (Vakalopoulos 1952, 70). Today, however, it is known that the three supposed founders were in Odessa from February until the end of April 1814. Consequently, there are good grounds for assuming that the society was founded within this timeframe (Arsh 2011, 490–496).

A second problem concerns the actual founding of the Philiki Etaireia. Given that so far no written document has been found to prove that its supposed founders set up in Odessa a secret revolutionary organization, the question as to whether the society was in fact founded in Odessa in 1814 or whether simply the first discussions between those who took the initiative to set it up took place in that city remains unanswered (Svolopoulos 2010, 76–77).

A third problem linked with the founding of the society and has preoccupied historians concerns its founders. This problem arose just a few years after the Greek Revolution, when the amateur historian and journalist Ioannis Philimon published his work dedicated to the Philiki Etaireia. In this he acknowledged as cofounder of the society Panagiotis Anagnostopoulos but silenced the role of Emmanouil Xanthos (Philimon 1834, 132–134). This sparked off the protracted dispute between the two leading members of the secret organization, who squabbled until the end of their life for "primacy" in founding the Philiki Etaireia (Gritsopoulos 1979, 3–42).

In the absence of documents of the Philiki Etaireia for the period 1814–1816 stating when and by whom it was founded, the only indisputable evidence we have for its existence comes from the three surviving lists of members, which were published by Ioannis Philimon (1859–1862,1:387–416), Valerios Mexas (1937), and Ioannis Meletopoulos (1967, 274–341). From these it is deduced that the Philiki Etaireia began operating on December 13, 1814, when the first member, after the founders, was initiated into it. This was Georgios Sekeris, a young Greek who was studying in Paris but was staying in Moscow at the time (Mexas 1937, 1). A second fact is that the society began its activity in Moscow, where the initiations of its first members took place, and not in Odessa. A third fact relates to its founders: the lists reveal that the members were initiated into the clandestine organization by Nikolaos Skoufas, who was in Moscow from late July into November 1815. Athanasios Tsakalov was also present in the city from April or May 1814 until mid-1817 (Arsh 2011, 490, 496). If to this information we add the fact that Tsakalov and Skoufas are the only members of the sixteen-man *Archi*—the society's "directorate"—who are not referred to as initiates in the secret organization, we reach the conclusion that these two *Philikoi* were indisputably the founders (θεμελιωτές) of the Philiki Etaireia.

This does not, of course, mean that Xanthos did not play a role in the society's founding. To the contrary, it is most probable that, as he himself claims in all the texts he has left us, he met Skoufas and Tsakalov and participated in the discussions that took place in Odessa between February and April 1814, with the aim of founding a "society" whose purpose would be the liberation of the Greeks. Nonetheless, Xanthos had no participation in the society's activity from December 1814, when he left Odessa for Constantinople (Arsh 2011, 492–3), until at least August 1817, when he resumed contact with Tsakalov (Xanthos 1939, 57).

Organization

The organizational structure of the Philiki Etaireia, the initiation procedure, the grades assigned to members, and the documents these received are described in detail in two surviving manuscript "handbooks." The first is entitled Διδασκαλία της μελλούσης Εταιρίας των Φιλικών (Instruction of the future Society of Friends [*Philikoi*]) and is kept in the General State Archives of Greece (Protopsaltis 1964, 135–144, 245–251). The second was found in the State Archives of Romania (*Eteria* 1960, 32–39).

Although these two handbooks are not dated, we have good grounds for assuming that they were written after 1814. And this because, according to Xanthos, the "catechism" of the Philiki Etaireia "was drafted" in Odessa by the three supposed founders of the organization in 1814 but was perfected in Moscow by Skoufas and Tsakalov during their sojourn there from late 1814 until late 1815 (Kampouroglous 1901, 531). If the information published by Ioannis Philimon is correct, namely that after the death of Skoufas at the end of July 1818 "the three, Anagnostopoulos, Tsakalov and Xanthos, took care to perfect the Instruction and to design the Seal of the *Archi*" (Philimon 1834, 197), then the catechism in its final form must have been compiled in the interval between August and September 1818.

Models Followed by the Compilers of the Instruction of the Philiki Etaireia

Some historians have argued that the Greek secret organization displayed great similarities to the Masonic brotherhood. The starting point for the advocates of this view is the claim by Xanthos, who was a freemason, that the supposed founders of the Philiki Etaireia planned it by "borrowing many rules from the society of Freemasons" (Kampouroglous 1901, 531). The "grades," the cryptographic codes, and some of the signs and symbols used by the *Philikoi* were in fact similar to those of the Masons (Kritikos 1965, 128). However, it should be pointed out here that the *Philikoi*, in contrast to Masons, did not have lodges, did not assemble, carried no kind of signs, and had no ceremonies other than their initiation into the society.

As far as the procedure and the stages of initiation are concerned, from a comparison of the Instruction of the *Philikoi* with that of the Carbonari, more numerous and more important similarities emerge than with the Freemasons (Konomos 1973, 23–32).

Last, the likelihood that certain elements of the organizational scheme, the initiation procedure, and the symbols of the Philiki Etaireia derive from the Parisian Hôtel Hellénophone cannot be ruled out. We are led to this hypothesis by the fact that one of the founders of the Philiki Etaireia, Tsakalov, had been a member of the Hôtel Hellénophone while in Paris—probably from 1809 until 1811. So, given that Tsakalov played an important role in "perfecting" the Philiki Etaireia's Instruction, it is very likely that he utilized certain elements from the organizational scheme of the Hôtel Hellénophone (Philimon 1859–1862, 4:x–xi). Unfortunately, however, the very little evidence we have about this particular secret organization prevents us from drawing safe conclusions.

So, in its organizational scheme the Philiki Etaireia presents many similarities to Greek and foreign secret societies of its period, as well as to Freemasonry, but it was neither a faithful copy of some other organization, nor was it an "annex of Freemasonry," as has been argued in the past (Kritikos 1965, 131). It is worth adding that in its Instruction can be detected also elements and ceremonies that stem from Greek folk tradition of that period, such as "fraternization" (Frangos 1975, 427).

Initiation, Grades, *Ephoreies,* and *Kinitirios Archi*

From the Philiki Etaireia's Instruction we know that the procedure followed by the "catechizers" during the initiation of new members lasted seven or eight hours and included the following "stages": the "first oath," sworn by the proselyte "in the ecclesiastical manner" before an Orthodox or a Catholic priest; informing the proselyte of his commitments vis-à-vis the society; the proselyte's "confession," which included answers to a series of questions about himself and his family; his "catechism" in the aims of the society; his initiation, which took place with a simple religious ceremony and the swearing of the "great oath"; and last, his "second confession" and his "dedication" to the society. Two further stages followed, which applied only to the *iereis* (priests). In the first the catechizer informed the proselyte about his duties, as well as about the signs and the ways of recognizing members, while in the second he described the responsibilities of the *iereis* and the basic values of the Philiki Etaireia. The whole procedure concluded with a final "oath" taken by the candidate "*iereus*" (*Eteria* 1960, 32–39) (Figure 1).

From the Instruction as well as from other sources, we know that during the first period of the Society's activity (1814–1817) the initiates were classed in "grades" according to their educational level, profession or status, and the role they were going to play within the secret organization. Classed in the first grade were ordinary men unable to read and write, who were named *adelphopoitoi* (blood brothers) or *vlamides.* The second grade was for "Greeks domiciled abroad of petty class," who were called *systimenoi* (recommended). Classed in the third grade were the "choice and educated," who took the name *iereis* and were responsible for the initiation of new members. One other grade followed, that of the *poimenes* (pastors), to which, so it seems, the *systimenoi* and the *iereis* were promoted, for unspecified reasons (Protopsaltis 1964, 248–249). In some sources a fifth grade appears, that of the *archipoimenes* (chief pastors), but this does not exist in the Philiki Etaireia's Instruction and probably was not used (Philimon 1834, 169–170).

In 1818, when four important chiefs of armed bands (*oplarchigoi*) needed to be initiated into the Society, two other grades were established, of the *aphiero-menoi* (dedicated) and of the *archigoi ton aphieromenon* (leaders of the dedicated), which were apparently assigned only to high-ranking military men (Gritsopoulos 1979, 48, 63).

FIGURE 1   Dionysios Tsokos, *Kolokotronis Puts His Son under Oath,* ca. 1850. Oil on canvas.
National Gallery-Al. Soutzos Museum / E. Koutlides Foundation Collection, Athens.

In 1820, when Alexandros Ypsilantis assumed the leadership (*archigia*) of the
Philiki Etaireia, in the framework of its reorganization, he abolished the grades
of *adelphopoitoi, systimenoi,* and *archipoimenes.* However, "he left the [grade]
of *Aphieromenoi* for the military commanders" (Philimon 1859–1862, 1:36–37)
(Figure 2).

The Instruction specifies that those initiated into the grades of *systimenoi, iereis,*
and *poimenes* should compose a letter addressed typically to a person known
or unknown to them. The initiate wrote down his personal details in this letter
of "recommendation" or "dedication" and accompanied it with the sum of his
contribution to the Philiki Etaireia, which was collected by his catechizer. The
latter gave to the new member a special document called the *ephodiastikon* (letter
of reference), which was written in the society's "coded alphabet" and decorated
with its symbols. This document was tantamount to a confirmation that the
bearer was a *Philikos* and that he held the grade written in it (Protopsaltis 1964,
154–162, 163–173).

FIGURE 2   Dionysios Tsokos, *Portrait of Alexandros Ypsilantis,*
1862. Oil on canvas. National Historical Museum, Athens.

At the pinnacle of the secret organization's hierarchy were the mysterious
Archi, members of which were known only to each other. Initially, these were
the supposed founders of the society—Tsakalov, Skoufas, and Xanthos. However, over time, the first members included some other *Philikoi,* sometimes for
financial or organizational reasons and sometimes under the pressure of emergency situations. Thus, shortly before the leadership was entrusted to Alexandros Ypsilantis, the *Archi* comprised fourteen men (Philimon 1859–1862, 1:34).

The members of the *Archi,* in contrast to other Greek societies founded in
the same period, were, with very few exceptions, "men in the street." Most were
merchants, tradesmen, and shop assistants, two were minor employees in Russian consulates, one was a scholar, one a student, and one a cleric. The exceptions were Ignatios, former Metropolitan of Ungrowallachia, and Alexandros
Mavrokordatos, who had served as senior official in the Romanian Principalities. However, these two men played no role in the society, as they resided in
the Italian city of Pisa—that is, far away from the principal arena of the secret
organization's activity.

The *Archi* members' providence to keep its composition unknown until the end shrouded it in a veil of mystery. To a great degree, this favored the expansion of the Philiki Etaireia and the wonderment of its members. The overwhelming majority believed that hidden behind the enigmatic *Archi* was either Capodistrias, then the minister of foreign affairs of the Russian Empire, or Tsar Alexander I, or both (Vakalopoulos 1980, 71–72).

In the early years of the society's activity, due to the small number of proselytes there was no other organizational "grade" between its base and its apex— that is, the "mysterious *Archi*." However, after 1818, when membership increased significantly, the following problems appeared: (1) phenomena of misappropriation of monies contributed by the new proselytes, (2) an inability to control whatever concerned the initiations of new members, (3) disputes between members living in the same city, and (4) lack of communication and collaboration between *Philikoi* living in different cities (Tzakis 2018, 135).

For all these reasons, an intermediate link was added to the society's organizational scheme. This was the *ephoreies* (inspectorates), which were essentially local councils of the secret organization. The ephors' duties included collecting and managing contributions, controlling the initiations, coordinating the initiated members, corresponding with the *Archi* and between the *ephoreies*, and preparing the revolution (Ypsilantis 1986, 137–145). According to the sources, the first *ephoreia* was set up in Galatsi in February 1819, on the initiative of Panagiotis Anagnostopoulos (Philimon 1834, 235–236). Subsequently, *ephoreies* were set up in almost all the cities of South Russia, the Romanian Principalities, and the Ottoman Empire in which members of the secret organization were active (Kitromilides 2018, 28–32).

It is worth noting here that when Alexandros Ypsilantis assumed the leadership of the Philiki Etaireia in April 1820, acknowledging the effectiveness of the new organizational scheme, he not only kept it intact but also reinforced the role of the *ephoreies*. Indeed, in order to give these local inspectorates greater prestige, he appointed as ephors the most distinguished merchants, primates, and prelates who had been initiated into the society, in each place (Philimon 1859–1862,1:38).

The founding of the *ephoreies* undoubtedly had positive effects on both the organization of the Philiki Etaireia and the preparation of the revolution. However, as Apostolos Vakalopoulos has rightly pointed out, the social provenance of the ephors, particularly after Ypsilantis took over the leadership, caused a "power shift" from "the liberal petty bourgeoisie to the leading conservative merchants and the leading kocabaşıs" (Vakalopoulos 1980, 78). The consequences of this change were immediately apparent after the outbreak of the revolution in the Peloponnese. There the intense conflict over sharing power broke out between the primates and Dimitrios Ypsilantis, around whom the military and the people mustered (Diamandouros 2002, 149–153).

To complete the picture of the society's organizational scheme, mention should be made also of the so-called *apostles*. These were eminent *Philikoi* who were sent to specific regions (e.g., the Peloponnese, the Mani, the Ionian Islands, the Aegean Islands, the Romanian Principalities, and so on) with the following objectives: (1) to recruit new members, (2) to collect as much money as possible in order to cover the society's great needs, and (3) to study the actual state of the regions that would take part in the revolution. The first mission took place in the summer and autumn of 1818, on the order of the *Archi*, after a council held in Constantinople (Kandiloros 1926, 189–190). The second took place in autumn 1820, on the order of Alexandros Ypsilantis, after the secret session of the *Philikoi* in Izmail, Bessarabia, where the final decisions were taken for the declaration of the revolution (Protopsaltis 1964, 72–77). Both these missions had very good results, since the Philiki Etaireia owed its great dissemination between 1818 and 1821 to the *apostles*.

The professionalism shown by most of the *apostles* was striking; they literally devoted themselves to their conspiratorial task, suspending their work commitments and abandoning even their family (Xanthos 1939, 38, 45). In tracking, through the sources, their movements within the Ottoman Empire, tsarist Russia, the Habsburg Empire, and the British-ruled Ionian Islands, the researcher is astonished by their ability to slip through the net of the secret services of the time, to carry out highly dangerous missions with minimal means.

Cryptographic Codes, Symbols, Pseudonyms, Seals

The clandestine character of the Philiki Etaireia imposed, for security reasons, the use of special signs of recognition of members, cryptographic codes for their correspondence, and symbols for promoting their ideas.

Described precisely in the society's Instruction are the signs of recognition of its members, which the catechizer revealed to the proselyte after completion of his initiation. These signs were of course different for each grade, the *adelphopoitoi* or *vlamides,* the *systimenoi,* and the *iereis.* In addition to the signs, the catechizer announced to the new member the passwords that *Philikoi* must exchange in their encounters, in order to confirm that they belonged to the secret organization (Philimon 1834, 145–146, 151, 158, 163, 167–168).

For drafting official documents and the *ephodiastika* in particular, the *Philikoi* created a cryptographic alphabet, in which they combined numbers and letters of the Greek alphabet. They named this alphabet "letters of the *iereis*" because it was known only to members with that grade and those above it (Philimon 1834, 143). *Philikoi* used this alphabet also for their correspondence, but circumstantially and to a very limited degree, obviously to avoid attracting the interest of the secret services if a letter fell into their hands.

For correspondence between themselves, the *Philikoi* used two "lexicons" that they had devised: (1) the metonymic, which contained a total of 112 shibboleths that corresponded to persons, offices, ships, ammunition, abstract concepts, and so on; and (2) the cryptographic, in which the numbers 1 to 115 corresponded to names of cities, regions, and persons (Xodilos 1964, 107–110, 116–117). Furthermore, they used pseudonyms for twenty-seven high-profile *Philikoi,* as well as for the fifteen members of the *Archi* (Philimon 1859–1862,1:137–138). Additionally, the *Archi* members used in their correspondence, as signatures, two capital letters of the Greek alphabet. The first was Alpha (A), which was the same for all, while the second, beginning with Beta (B), they assumed upon joining the *Archi.* Thus, the second letter is, in a way, a clue to the seniority of its members; indicatively, Tsakalov had the letters AlphaBeta (AB), Skoufas AlphaGamma (AΓ) and Xanthos AlphaTheta (AΘ), and so on (Philimon 1859–1862,1:137).

Furthermore, in their official documents, the *Philikoi* used various symbols, such as the cross, anchor, snake, sixteen rods tied with two crisscrossing bands, the letters EtaEpsilonAlpha (HEA) *HEA* (Ἡ Ἐλευθερία, "freedom"), EtaTheta-Sigma (*HΘΣ* (Ἡ Θάνατος, "death"), and so on. It is obvious that these symbols corresponded to specific ideas that the *Philikoi* espoused and wished to propagate (Protopsaltis 1964, 154–162).

Last, the *Archi* had its own seal, with which it endorsed the documents it issued. This seal was circular and at its center were the mysterious number sixteen, a cross, and the letter Epsilon (E), which probably stood for Ellas (Greece). Engraved around its circumference were nine capital letters, which probably corresponded to the initials of the names of the *Philikoi* who made up the *Archi* in 1818, when the seal was made (Philimon 1834, 167; Xanthos 1939, 36).

Philikoi

It is expressly stated in Philiki Etaireia's Instruction that only Greeks were eligible for membership (*Eteria* 1960, 32, 34, 35). Nonetheless, it seems that, in extremely rare cases, some "foreigners" were accepted, obviously for specific emergency needs. Certainly, in these cases, the proselytes were always Orthodox Christians (Philimon 1859–1862, 1:91, 247–248).

Although there is no explicit reference in the Instruction, it should be considered certain that the initiation of women was prohibited. This was due, on the one hand, to the position of women in society at the time and, on the other, to the prejudices that weighed them down. Here too, however, there is mention of one exception: this was the wife of a *Philikos* from Smyrna, whom her husband initiated into the society of necessity when she discovered the documents he was carefully hiding from her (Philimon 1859–1862, 1:170).

The third ban was on "those having major interests close to the Turks." Again, there is no such term in the Instruction, but in the "great oath" the initiate promised, among other things, "to preserve in his heart inexorable hatred of the tyrants of his fatherland, their supporters and like-minded" (*Eteria* 1960, 35). It is very possible that Anagnostopoulos, on the basis of this pledge, reacted against the initiation of the "archons of the Peloponnese," while other *Philikoi* wanted to bar Phanariots and prelates from the society. However, this ban did not obtain in the end, as some Phanariots, such as the Prince of Moldavia, Michail Soutsos, became members of the Philiki Etaireia (Philimon 1859–1862,1:35).

The most important problem that research into the Philiki Etaireia comes up against is the number of its members. This is because the secrecy of the organization, the destruction of documents for security reasons by the *Philikoi* themselves, the loss of documents for many and various reasons, the failure to observe all the terms of the initiation of *Philikoi*, and, mainly, nonuse of documents during initiation into the first grade, of the *adelphopoitoi*, limited to a very large degree the sources that would allow us to reach safe conclusions. For this reason, some historians, obviously influenced by rumors, hypothesized that the members of the Philiki Etaireia ran into hundreds of thousands (Kandiloros 1926, 25, 321).

The only secure information we have on this issue comes from three lists of *Philikoi* that have been published. The first was found in the papers of Panagiotis Sekeris, a high-profile *Philikos* and member of the *Archi*, which are kept in the archives of the Historical and Ethnological Society of Greece. This list includes 520 names of *Philikoi*, the dates of initiation, the names of the catechizers, and "the signs of their dedication" to the cause, and was published in full by Ioannis Meletopoulos in 1967. The second, drafted by Ioannis Philimon, includes 692 names and was published in 1859. The third list, prepared by Valerios Mexas, contains 541 names and was published in 1937. On the basis of these three lists, after crosschecking and removing names that appear twice, the total number of members of the Philiki Etaireia comes to just 1033 (Frangos 1973, 101).

From a careful study of the data in these three lists and from other sources, the following observations may be made:

1. During the first three years of the Philiki Etaireia's existence, from late 1814 until late 1817, only forty-two initiations were made, all in Russia. Indeed, the overwhelming majority of proselytes were living and active in Russia, whereas those living in the Greek provinces of the Ottoman Empire were very few (Mexas 1937, 1–5).

2. Widespread initiations commenced in 1818 and continued at an increasing pace until 1821 (Frangos 1975, 432). During these three years or so, the catechizers extended their activity from South Russia into the Romanian Principalities, Constantinople, the Peloponnese, the Aegean islands, the littoral zone of Asia Minor, the Ionian Islands, and even into Egypt.

3. The Philiki Etaireia had very limited diffusion in Central Greece, Thessaly (except Pilion), Macedonia, and Thrace.

4. The secret organization was unable to infiltrate the Greek communities of central and western Europe. Only in Pisa was there a notable core of *Philikoi* and very few in some other Italian cities (Frangos 1973, 94; Panayotopoulos 1986, 179–180).

5. Most members of the secret organization were merchants (Frangos 1973, 88).

6. Although, in this period, there was a burgeoning of the Neohellenic Enlightenment movement, very few Greek intellectuals became members of the Philiki Etaireia (Frangos 1973, 88).

7. Those Phanariots and prelates who were accepted into the society were initiated mainly after Alexandros Ypsilantis assumed its leadership.

8. Most of the primates and prelates of the Peloponnese were initiated in the last two years before the revolution (Tzakis 2018, 133).

9. The majority of *Philikoi* originated in the Peloponnese (Frangos 1975, 429).

Although we do not know—and in my view will never learn—the exact number of members of the Philiki Etaireia, we have not the slightest doubt that it was they who prepared the Greek Revolution of 1821 and it is to them that we owe its outbreak in the Romanian Principalities, in the Peloponnese, and the islands. It is remarkable indeed that these men in the street, without any previous conspiratorial experience and in very difficult circumstances, succeeded in developing such a wide network of activity for over four years inside the Ottoman Empire without becoming known to the Ottoman authorities, or even to the well-organized secret police of the Habsburg Empire.

Election of the "Leader"

Almost as soon as the Philiki Etaireia was established, its "founders" realized the need to entrust its leadership to some preeminent Greek, who would be, on the one hand, guarantor of the successful outcome of its plans and, on the other, a pole of attraction for the Greeks.

At that period, the person who met all the prerequisites was undoubtedly Ioannis Capodistrias. Apart from his noble birth and splendid career in the diplomatic service of Tsar Alexander I, he had already shown his patriotic sentiments both during his term as secretary of the Septinsular Republic (1803–1807) (Koukkou 1978, 20–29) and as mastermind of the Societé des Amis des Muses of Vienna. For all these reasons, Capodistrias appeared to be ideal for the leadership of the Philiki Etaireia.

The first overtures to Capodistrias were made in 1817. The "founders" of the Philiki Etaireia employed for this purpose Nikolaos Galatis, an ambitious young man from the Ionian island of Ithaka, whom Skoufas had initiated into the society in Odessa, in 1816 and made a member of the *Archi* (Xanthos 1939, 31–32). Galatis went to Saint Petersburg, met with the distinguished Greek diplomat in January 1817, and proposed to him the leadership of the secret organization (Capodistrias 1976, 36–37). This attempt failed for two basic reasons: the first and more important reason was Capodistrias's proclaimed view that the Greeks should first be educated and then claim their independence. The second was his opposition to secret societies that sought the violent overthrow of the regime that had been imposed by the Sacred Alliance (Arsh 2015, 232–235). Consequently, Galatis's effort was doomed to failure.

Even so, nearly two years later, the members of the *Archi* returned to their proposal to Capodistrias. After a secret council held in Constantinople in September 1818, the leaders decided to send Xanthos to Saint Petersburg for this purpose (Xanthos 1939, 37). This time a relevant "joint promise" was drafted, which the members of the *Archi* signed on September 22, 1818. Xanthos did indeed meet with Capodistrias in Saint Petersburg, in January 1820, but the latter refused once again to become involved with the society in any way (Xanthos 37, 39–40, 62–63).

As a way out of this impasse, Xanthos turned to Alexandros Ypsilantis. The son of Constantinos Ypsilantis, and a former Prince of Wallachia, he was hero of the Napoleonic Wars, and held the rank of major general in the Russian army where he served honoris causa in the tsar's bodyguard. Ypsilantis accepted Xanthos's proposal and on April 12, 1820 was named "Ephor General of the Greek Society" (Philimon 1859–1862, 1:31–33).

Entrusting the leadership to Ypsilantis meant neither pushing aside of the members of the *Archi* nor, far less, its abolition. Of course, as ephor general or commissioner general, Ypsilantis was able to take initiatives regarding the organization of the Philiki Etaireia and the preparation of the revolution, but the members of the *Archi* and eminent *Philikoi* continued to play a significant role in the decision-making process of the secret organization. Two characteristic examples are the assembly convened by Ypsilantis in Izmail, Bessarabia, on October 1, 1820, to decide on the declaration of the revolution, and the assembly convened by the ephors of the Peloponnese at Vostitsa (Aigio) in late January 1821 for the same reason (Gritsopoulos 1972–1973, 33–42).

Political Aims of the *Philiki Etaireia*

From the very beginning, the "founders" of the Philiki Etaireia set as its sole goal the liberation of the Greek nation. This is specified in the Instruction, in which it is declared expressly that "aim of [the society's] members is the improvement of the Nation and, God willing, its freedom" (*Eteria* 1960, 34). Xanthos reiterated this in his memoirs. Referring to the founding of the Philiki Etaireia, he noted that its three "founders . . . conceived the idea of setting it up . . . having as immutable aim the freedom of the Fatherland" (Xanthos 1939, 30).

In order to succeed in liberating the Greeks, the *Philikoi* set a series of targets. The first and main one, in my opinion, was the "autonomous struggle"— that is, the revolution of the Greeks against the sultan, without the aid of any foreign power. Once again, Xanthos was the first to emphasize in his memoirs that the "founders" decided to set up the society "in order to carry out alone what vainly and a long time ago they hoped for from the philanthropy of the Christian kings" (Xanthos 1939, 30).

However, the idea of the autonomous struggle was at odds with the entrenched conviction of the sultan's Orthodox Christian subjects, who throughout the eighteenth century believed that they would be liberated by Orthodox Christian Russia. That is why they fatalistically awaited the declaration of a Russo-Turkish war, so that the "blond race" would vanquish the Ottomans and drive them out of the Balkans and the Orthodox Christian "East." This idea was rejected first by Rhigas Velestinlis with his revolutionary project. As we have seen, he asserted the need for the revolution of all the subjects of the Ottoman Empire, in order to overthrow the sultan's tyranny and to create a state based on the ideas and principles of the French Revolution. After Rhigas, other Greek intellectuals too supported the idea of the "autonomous struggle," notable among them the anonymous author of the *Ελληνική Νομαρχία* (Hellenic Nomarchy). Indeed, it is worth noting here that some Greek researchers see in this radical text, which was published in Italy in 1806, the "handbook of the *Philikoi*" (*Ελληνική Νομαρχία* 1982, xxii).

So, the Philiki Etaireia adopted from the outset the idea of the "autonomous struggle" and declared that the Greeks must be freed by relying on their own forces. However, this presupposed the recruitment into the secret organization of as many Greeks as possible, regardless of their social status, economic standing, and educational level. The second goal of the *Philikoi* therefore was the recruitment, if possible, of most Greeks, especially among those living inside the Ottoman Empire, because they had to be persuaded to revolt and they would bear the main burden of the revolution.

The third goal of the *Philikoi* was the common revolt of all the Orthodox Christian Balkan peoples—Serbs, Romanians, and Bulgarians—against the Ottomans. Knowing full well that it was impossible for the Greeks to combat the Ottomans militarily on their own, the *Philikoi* drafted plans for the insurrection of all the Balkan peoples, in order to confront the sultan's forces with success. This goal is described clearly in the so-called General Plan drawn up by the *Philikoi* and approved at the secret assembly convened in Izmail by Ypsilantis on October 1, 1820, in view of the declaration of the revolution (Philimon 1859–1862, 1:47–57).

The *Philikoi* looked for any advantage to attain their primary goal. First was the conflict between Ali Pasha of Ioannina and the sultan (1820–1822), which had caused great upheaval in Epirus, west Central Greece, west Macedonia, and part of Thessaly. The *Philikoi* exploited this conflict to the utmost, so as to gain, first, the return of the battleworthy Souliots to Epirus; second, the reinforcement of the military corps of Greek *armatoloi;* and third, the removal of the Ottoman military forces from southern Greece and mainly from the Peloponnese (Sphyroeras 1952). A second favorable coincidence was the appointment of Michail Soutsos as Prince of Moldavia. By initiating him into the secret organization, the *Philikoi* secured his unconditional support for the imminent revolution (Kamarianos 1964). A third conjuncture was the death in January 1821 of the Prince of Wallachia Alexandros Soutsos. The *Philikoi* exploited the power vacuum created and helped Tudor Vladimirescu to ignite the uprising of the Romanians in Wallachia (Oţetea 1971, 184–202). Auspicious too, in my opinion, was the outbreak in 1820 of the revolution in Italy, because it led the members of the Holy Alliance to decide at Laibach on its quashing by Austrian troops. This set a precedent, because correspondingly Russia could ask permission to send its troops to the Romanian Principalities, ostensibly to restore "order." However, this would have triggered a new Russo-Turkish war, which, of course, would have favored the plans of the Philiki Etaireia.

What the sources do not disclose is whether the *Philikoi* had any definite idea about the kind of state that would be created after the liberation of the Greek nation. From Alexandros Ypsilantis's constant reference to "Greece" and to the "Nation of the Greeks" in proclamations issued after the declaration of the revolution, we come to the conclusion that their aim was to establish a "Greek State"—that is, a Greek nation-state. However, neither the area of this state nor its system of governance was defined. In my view, the most likely reason for this was that the *Philikoi,* having set as their only goal the liberation of the

Greeks and knowing the enormous difficulties they would have to face in order to succeed, deemed premature or even inopportune the formulation of ideas about the state that would come into being after the revolution.

Four basic conclusions can be drawn from the exposition above. First, the Philiki Etaireia was the only Greek secret organization to be founded in the milieu of the expatriate Greek communities (*paroikies*), but it developed and was active mainly inside the Ottoman Empire. Specifically, it was active in the empire's European provinces and the littoral zone of Asia Minor, with Constantinople as the center of its activity. Second, the society was the only Greek organization of its time which was, from its founding, of mass character, with the result that in the end thousands of Greeks of all social classes joined it. Third, this society was the only Greek organization that had from the outset a political character and as its one and only purpose the liberation of the Greeks by revolution. Fourth, the Philiki Etaireia was the only secret organization that succeeded in its goals: it planned and prepared the armed struggle, it organized the Greeks and it declared the Greek Revolution at Jassy in Moldavia on February 22, 1821 (OS), and in Kalamata in the Peloponnese on March 23 of the same year.

Constantinos C. Chatzopoulos

Translated from the Greek by Alexandra Douma

References

Arsh, Gregory L. 2011. *Η Φιλική Εταιρεία στη Ρωσία* [The Philiki Etaireia in Russia]. Athens.

Arsh, Gregory L. 2015. *Ο Καποδίστριας στη Ρωσία* [Capodistrias in Russia]. Athens.

Botzaris, Notis.1962. *Visions balkaniques dans la préparation de la Révolution grecque (1789–1821)*. Paris.

Camariano, Nestor. 1968. "Sur l'activité de la 'Société littéraire greco-dacique.'" *Revue des Études Sud-Est Européennes* 7:39–54.

Capodistrias, Ioannis. 1976. "Επισκόπησις της πολιτικής μου σταδιοδρομίας από του 1798 μέχρι του 1822" [Review of my political career from 1798 until 1822]. In *Αρχείον Ιωάννου Καποδίστρια* [Archive of Ioannis Capodistrias], vol.1. Corfu.

Chatzipanagioti-Sangmeister, Ilia. 2010. *Ο τεκτονισμός στην ελληνική κοινωνία και γραμματεία του 18ου αιώνα. Οι γερμανόφωνες μαρτυρίες* [Freemasonry in eighteenth-century Greek society and literature: The German-language testimonies]. Athens.

Chatzopoulos, Constantinos C. 1991. *Ελληνικά σχολεία στην περίοδο της οθωμανικής κυριαρχίας (1453–1821)* [Greek schools in the period of Ottoman rule, 1452–1821]. Thessaloniki.

Diamandouros, Nikiforos. 2002. *Οι απαρχές της συγκρότησης σύγχρονου κράτους στην Ελλάδα, 1821–1828* [The beginning of modern state-building in Greece, 1821–1828]. Athens.

Elian, Alexandru.1962. "Les écrits politiques de Rhigas en Moldavie." *Revue Roumaine d'Histoire* 1:487–498.

Ελληνική Νομαρχία ήτοι λόγος περί ελευθερίας [Hellenic nomarchy, a discourse on freedom]. 1982. Introduction and comments by Giorgios Valetas. Athens.

Ερμής ο Λόγιος ή φιλολογικαί αγγελίαι [Literary Hermes or philological announcements]. 1811–1821. Vienna.

Eteria în Principatele române [The Etaireia in the Romanian Principalities], 1960. Vol. 4 of *Documente privind istoria României. Răscoală din 1821* [Documents concerning the history of Romania. The 1821 uprising]. Bucharest.

Frangos, George. 1973. "The Philiki Etairia: A Premature National Coalition." In *The Struggle for Greek Independence,* edited by Richard Clogg, 87–103. London and Basingstoke.

Frangos, George. 1975. "Φιλική Εταιρεία" [Philiki Etaireia]. In *IEE* [History of the Greek nation] 12:424–432.

Gritsopoulos, Tasos. 1972–1973. "Η εις Βοστίτζαν μυστική συνέλευσις των Πελοποννησίων ηγετών (26–29 Ιανουαρίου 1821)" [The secret assembly of the leaders of the Peloponnese on January 26–29, 1821 at Vostitsa], *Μνημοσύνη*: 3–48.

Gritsopoulos, Tasos Athanasiou. 1979. "Φιλικά κείμενα. Εμμανουήλ Ξάνθου Απολογία. Παν. Αναγνωστοπούλου Παρατηρήσεις" [Texts of the Philiki Etaireia: Defense of Emmanouil Xanthos; Remarks of Pan. Anagnostopoulos], *Mnimosyni* 7 [offprint].

Kamarianos, Nestor. 1964. "Η συμβολή του ηγεμόνα της Μολδαβίας Μιχαήλ Σούτσου στη Φιλική Εταιρία" [The contribution of the Prince of Moldavia Michail Soutsos to the Philiki Etaireia]. *Nea Hestia* 76:1696–1701.

Kampouroglous, Demetrios Gregoriou. 1901. "Ανέκδοτον υπόμνημα του Φιλικού Ξάνθου" [Unpublished memorandum of the Philikos Xanthos]. *Armonia* 2:529–540.

Kandiloros, Takis. 1926. *Η Φιλική Εταιρία, 1814–1821* [The Philiki Etaireia, 1814–1821]. Athens.

Kitromilides, Paschalis M. 1996. *Νεοελληνικός Διαφωτισμός. Οι πολιτικές και κοινωνικές ιδέες* [Neohellenic Enlightenment: Political and social ideas]. Athens.

Kitromilides, Paschalis M. 1998. *Ρήγας Βελεστινλής. Θεωρία και πράξη* [Rhigas Velestinlis: Theory and practice]. Athens.

Kitromilides, Paschalis M. 2000. *Η Γαλλική Επανάσταση και η Νοτιοανατολική Ευρώπη* [The French Revolution and Southeastern Europe]. Athens.

Kitromilides, Paschalis M. 2018. "Η Φιλική Εταιρεία και η πολιτική γεωγραφία του Διαφωτισμού" [The Philiki Etaireia and the political geography of the Enlightenment]. In *Οι πόλεις των Φιλικών. Οι αστικές διαδρομές ενός επαναστατικού φαινομένου* [The cities of the Philikoi: The urban pathways of a revolutionary phenomenon], 25–35. Athens.

Konomos, Dinos. 1973. *Μυστικές εταιρείες στα χρόνια της Εθνεγερσίας (ανέκδοτα κείμενα)* [Secret societies in the years of the National Uprising (unpublished documents)]. Athens.

Koukkou, Eleni. 1958. *Ο Καποδίστριας και η παιδεία, 1803–1822. Η Φιλόμουσος Εταιρεία της Βιέννης* [Capodistrias and education, 1803–1822: The Philomousos Society of Vienna]. Athens.

Koukkou, Eleni. 1978. *Ιωάννης Καποδίστριας. Ο άνθρωπος- Ο διπλωμάτης, 1800–1828*
[Ioannis Capodistrias: The man, the diplomat, 1800–1828]. Athens.

Kritikos, Panagiotis G. 1965. "Φιλική Εταιρεία και τεκτονισμός. Συμβολή των εις τον
απελευθερωτικόν αγώνα του έθνους" [Philiki Etaireia and Freemasonry: Their
contribution to the liberation struggle of the nation]. *Parnassos* 7:101–134.

Laios, Georgios. 1962. "Η Φιλόμουσος Εταιρεία της Βιέννης 1814–1820" [The Philomousos
Society of Vienna, 1814–1820]. *Epetiris tou Mesaionikou Archeiou* 12:166–223.

Manessis, Aristovoulos J. 1962. "L'activité et les projets politiques d'un patriote grec."
Balkan Studies 2:75–118.

Meletopoulos, Ioannis A. 1967. "Η Φιλική Εταιρεία. Αρχείον Παναγιώτου Δημ. Σέκερη"
[The Philiki Etaireia: The papers of Panagiotis Dim. Sekeris], *DIEEE* 18:181–352.

Mexas, Valerios. 1937. *Οι Φιλικοί: κατάλογος των μελών της Φιλικής Εταιρείας εκ του αρχείου
Σέκερη* [The Philikoi: A members' list of the Philiki Etaireia from the Sekeris papers].
Athens.

Oțetea, Andrei. 1971. *Tudor Vladimirescu și revoluția din 1821* [Tudor Vladimirescu and the
revolution of 1821]. Bucharest.

Panayotopoulos, Vasilis. 1986. "Κάτι έγινε στην Πίζα το 1821" [Something happened in
Piza in 1821] *Historica* 3.5:177–182.

Panayiotopoulos, Vasilis. 2003. "Φιλική Εταιρεία. Οργανωτικές προϋποθέσεις της εθνικής
επανάστασης" [Philiki Etaireia: Organizational preconditions of the national revolu-
tion]. *INE*, 9–32.

Perraivos, Christophoros. 1836. *Απομνημονεύματα πολεμικά* [War memoirs]. Athens.

Philimon, Ioannis. 1834. *Δοκίμιον ιστορικόν περί της Φιλικής Εταιρίας* [A historical essay on
the Philiki Etaireia]. Nafplio.

Philimon, Ioannis. 1859–1862. *Δοκίμιον ιστορικόν περί της Ελληνικής Επαναστάσεως*
[A historical essay on the Greek Revolution]. Athens.

Protopsaltis, Emmanouil. 1964. *Φιλική Εταιρεία* [Philiki Etaireia]. Athens.

Quataert, Donald. 2006. *Η Οθωμανική Αυτοκρατορία. Οι τελευταίοι αιώνες, 1700–1922*
[The Ottoman Empire: The last centuries, 1700–1922]. Translated by Marinos Sarigiannis.
Athens.

Rousseau, Jean-Jacques. 1828. *Περί της κοινωνικής συνθήκης ή Αρχαί του πολιτικού
δικαιώματος* [On the social contract; or, principles of political rights]. Translated by
Grigorios Georgiadou Zalykis, preface by Constantinos Nikolopoulos. Paris.

Sathas, Constantinos N. 1869. *Τουρκοκρατουμένη Ελλάς* [Ottoman-occupied Greece]. Athens.

Seirinidou, Vasiliki. 2011. *Έλληνες στη Βιέννη (18ος-μέσα 19ου αιώνα)* [Greeks in Vienna,
eighteenth to mid-nineteenth century]. Athens.

Sphyroeras, Vasileios. 1952. "Ο Φιλικός Ιωάννης Παπαρρηγόπουλος και ο Αλή-πασάς"
[The Philikos Ioannis Paparrigopoulos and Ali Pasha]. *Ipirotiki Estia* 1:661–672.

Svolopoulos, Constantinos. 2010. "Η σύσταση της Φιλικής Εταιρείας. Μια
επαναπροσέγγιση" [The setting up of the Philiki Etaireia: A new approach]. In
Κατακτώντας την ανεξαρτησία. Δέκα δοκίμια για την Επανάσταση του 1821 [Conquering
independence: Ten essays on the revolution of 1821], 57–81. Athens.

Tzakis, Dionysis. 2018. "Από την Οδησσό στη Βοστίτσα: Η πολιτική ενσωμάτωση των
τοπικών ηγετικών ομάδων στη Φιλική Εταιρεία" [From Odessa to Vostitsa: The

political incorporation of the local leadership groups in the Philiki Etaireia]. In *Οι πόλεις των Φιλικών. Οι αστικές διαδρομές ενός επαναστατικού φαινομένου* [The cities of the Philikoi: The urban pathways of a revolutionary phenomenon], edited by Olga Katsiardi-Hering, 125–148. Athens.

Vakalopoulos, Apostolos 1952. "Συμβολή στην ιστορία και οργάνωση της Φιλικής Εταιρείας" [Contribution to the history and the organization of the Philiki Etaireia]. *Ελληνικά* 12:65–78.

Vakalopoulos. 1980. Vol. V.

Vellianitis, Telemachos. 1993. *Η Φιλόμουσος Εταιρεία των Αθηνών* [The Philomousos Society of Athens]. Athens.

Vranousis, Leandros I. 1963. *Ρήγας Βελεστινλής (1757–1798)* [Rhigas Velestinlis, 1757–1798]. Athens.

Xanthos, Emmanouil. 1939. *Απομνημονεύματα περί της Φιλικής Εταιρίας* [Memoirs concerning Philiki Etaireia]. Athens.

Xodilos, Athanasios. 1964. *Η Εταιρία των Φιλικών και τα Πρώτα Συμβάντα του 1821* [The Society of Friends and the first events of 1821]. Edited by Leandros Vranousis and N. Camarianos. Athens.

Ypsilantis, Nikolaos. 1986. *Απομνημονεύματα του Πρίγκιπος Νικολάου Υψηλάντου* [Memoirs of Prince Nikolaos Ypsilantis]. Translated and edited by Eleutherios Moraitinis-Patriarcheas. Athens.

III

EVENTS AND PLACES

Aegean Islands and the Revolution at Sea

On the eve of the Greek Revolution, Greeks, Ottoman and Ionian subjects, were the most important seafarers of the Levant seas, carrying cargoes from the eastern Mediterranean and the Black Sea to the West. They owned a fleet of 950 merchant vessels of 120,000 tons, fully armed with six thousand canons and eighteen thousand highly experienced seamen armed with weapons. They were based on forty islands and coastal towns in the Aegean and Ionian Seas that were transformed into prosperous maritime communities. The Greeks over the eighteenth century had consolidated a sizeable fleet of mercantile ships manned by able seafarers who sailed across the Mediterranean and the Black Sea, as far as the Atlantic and the Indian Oceans. International shipping and trade brought, along with economic prosperity, revolutionary ideas. It is no wonder that wealth and international communication backfired: the sultan's main seafarers based on the islands of the Aegean Sea, the continental side of the Ionian Sea and the Corinthian Gulf revolted against the Ottoman rule claiming their independence.

Out of the forty maritime islands and towns of the Aegean and Ionian Seas about thirty took part in the revolution, with an estimated fleet of six hundred vessels. Out of these, some of the largest fleets were owned by Ydra (112 ships), Galaxidi (101), Psara (78), Spetses (56) and Kasos (25), followed by Mesolonghi, Santorini, Mykonos, Andros, Skopelos, Skiathos, Ainos, Kydonies, Limnos, Lesvos, Chios, Samos, Rodos, Kastellorizo, and so on. During the eighteenth century, the Greek islands and coastal communities acted as primary sea-carriers for the Ottoman Empire. Lacking other natural resources, they had resorted to maritime activities and were largely deployed as seafarers and traders. They were mostly engaged in the grain trade, hoisting the distinctive Greek-Ottoman flag marking ships of Christian captains, when trading in the western Mediterranean. Furthermore, due to their maritime services the island communities, particularly Ydra, Spetses, and Psara, had the privilege of self-government and by their communal institutions the lives and works of the islanders were regulated. The maritime families of these islands and towns, shipowners and captains, had turned into a dynamic social and economic elite and played an instrumental role in the military and political developments during the War of Independence.

Their active participation in the uprising was crucial for the revolution's economic and military survival. Following the eruption of revolution in the mainland, in March 1821, the islands that spread from the northern end of the Aegean to the Dodecanese and the Cretan archipelago rushed to join the rebels. The maritime communities of Galaxidi (March 26), Spetses (April 3), Psara (April 11), and Ydra (April 16), the fertile island of Samos (April 18), rocky Kasos (April 17), and Crete (June 14) were among the first to hoist the revolutionary flag. By the first two years of the uprising, most of the islands had been drawn into the cause, with the exception of the Cycladic islands of Syros, Tinos, and Naxos, which remained neutral and were placed under papal protection due to their Roman Catholic populations. In addition, in February 1822, the British authorities declared the neutrality of the Ionian Islands and prohibited the belligerents to approach their ports. However, Ionian ships would continue to trade in the Aegean and carry provisions to the belligerents.

It was privately owned ships from the Aegean islands, designated for grain trade and armed with several canons, that acted as warships in the uprising. Their primary aim was to intercept the enemy's transportation of soldiers, supplies, and ammunition from the imperial capital, the coast of Asia Minor, and Egypt toward the theaters of war, in the sieges of the Ottoman fortresses and thus support the operations of the army on the mainland. Another crucial service was the practical unification of the different war fronts in the Peloponnese, Central Greece, and the islands in a combined effort. The islands of Ydra, Spetses, and Psara chartered part of their fleets to the revolutionary government to form the Greek navy, while the remaining vessels were deployed in trade, transport, and privateering. The three-island fleet was complemented by warships, supply vessels, and fireships from the rest of the Aegean islands; it has been estimated that one-third of the Greek revolutionary navy in ships and seamen was provided by the other maritime islands and towns. In effect, Ydra, Spetses, and Psara led the war at sea and acted as instigators and protectors of the islands and coastal towns. On the other side, in the war on land, the Peloponnesians played a leading role among the mainlanders. These two formed the main political and military poles of power juxtaposed in a continuous tug-of-war over political leadership that resulted in recurrent incidents of civil war (1824–1825), which distracted the rebels from their common enemy.

Despite the sea-competence of vessels and crews, the Greek fleet, namely merchant vessels chartered by the revolutionary government, lagged in numbers, arms, discipline, and coordination. Furthermore, the high cost of manning and fitting ships for the expeditions at sea was an insoluble issue over the years that tampered with its effectiveness. The National Navy was formed toward the end of the revolution, in 1827. It was funded by the Greek government, composed of a handful of designated warships such as corvettes and frigates and was placed under the command of a foreign admiral of the fleet, Thomas Cochrane (Figure 3).

For their part, the Ottomans represented a severe threat at sea, especially when they combined forces with the more skillful Egyptian fleet. The Sublime Porte had acknowledged the necessity of an imperial navy to exert its power

FIGURE 3   Robert Cooper, *Portrait of Lord Thomas Cochrane*, 1819. Engraving on paper after the painting by W. Walton (active 1819). Benaki Museum, Athens.

on the seas and made several conscientious efforts to build a sizeable and effective fleet. Although manned by less experienced sailors than the Greek ships, the Ottoman navy was a ferocious adversary due to its size, resources and organization and managed to strike severe blows to the Greek uprising.

The contribution of the Aegean islands and the indirect contribution of the Ionian islands to the rebellion was crucial. Some of the most dramatic events of the war occurred in the Aegean, like the destruction of the islands of Chios, Psara, and Kasos, with the massacre of their populations, which stirred humanitarian feelings among the West European countries. Seminal battles were staged in the Aegean. The most critical naval engagement was the victorious battle of Navarino, that determined the outcome of the war and the fate of the Greek cause (Map 3).

Despite their importance, the role of war at sea and the overall contribution of the islanders remain to date surprisingly underresearched. Traditional his-

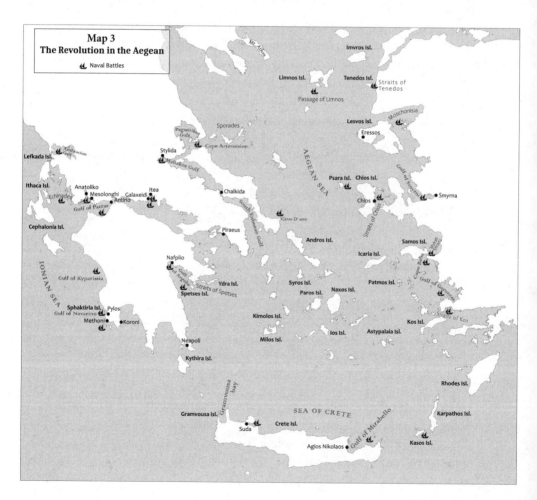

Map 3
The Revolution in the Aegean
⚓ Naval Battles

toriography has taken a rather narrow approach, concentrating mostly on the so-called three-island fleet, that of Ydra, Spetses, and Psara that formed an armada of fifty to sixty vessels. The participation of the remaining merchant fleet of another nine hundred vessels, the role of the other islands that formed an auxiliary navy along with a highly disruptive and continuous *guerre de course* have been to a significant degree neglected.

The Historiography of War at Sea: A Critical Approach

The literature on the history of war at sea during the Greek Revolution is limited to a narrow event-based narrative, focusing on military actions and the three-island fleet. It omits the institutional organization of the navy headed by the ministry of naval affairs and the local branches, that is of the maritime communities; it omits the economics of war at sea and its contribution to the finances of the revolutionary government; it omits the highly significant auxiliary fleet of fireships, transports, and mail vessels provided by a great number of Aegean islands; it omits the supplementary legitimate fleet of Greek privateers that assisted the navy in blockades, attacked the enemy ships, and inflicted economic and commercial damage on Ottoman and foreign merchant vessels carrying supplies; and it omits piracy during the War of Greek Independence. The association of piracy with privateering and war at sea needs to be further examined. Finally, it omits the continuation of trade during the Greek War of Independence in the Black Sea and the eastern and western Mediterranean by the merchant fleet of the Aegean islands that sustained the maritime communities and supported the war. The sole exception to this list of omissions is the seminal book of Despoina Themeli-Katifori published in 1973.

War at sea during the Greek Revolution has been studied in the existing literature through memoirs and books published in the nineteenth century by Greeks and foreigners involved in a direct or indirect way in the revolution. This body of literature brings out accounts of naval operations as well as the involvement of the three islands in the Greek War of Independence, focusing almost exclusively on a war fleet formed of an average of sixty merchant vessels. The largest part of the west European bibliography mainly concentrates on the battle of Navarino while there are very few studies of the Ottoman side of the maritime wars in Turkish.

A strand of literature centered on events was almost exclusively written by amateur historians, predominantly naval officers, who produced numerous books and articles published by the historical department of the navy, the general headquarters of the navy, and the Hellenic Maritime Museum. This literature reproduces a nation-building narrative throughout the history of the modern Greek state and focuses on the military acts and strategies, naval battles and the lives and works of Admirals. It is a history mainly based on secondary literature and nineteenth-century publications and memoirs with minimal or no research in Greek Archives and often lack bibliographical references. However, recent research (Bozikis 2018; Dimitropoulos 2016) and the first research project on Greek merchant shipping and the navy from 1821 to 1831 (Galani and Harlaftis 2021) based on the Greek State Archives has shed light on the commercial, privateering, and piratical activities of Greek islanders and the war at sea during the age of the Greek Revolution.

The Islands and the Formation of the Greek Fleet

The Greek islands and coastal communities had constructed over the years a sizeable fleet armed to counter the perils at sea while trading. However, these grain vessels were not designed for war. The revolutionary fleet comprised approximately two hundred ships that were available on call, ranging between 180 and 400 tons, suitable to serve as warships. The vast majority of these ships originated from the islands of Ydra, Spetses, and Psara; this accounts for the characterization "the fleet of the three islands" that has prevailed in contemporary sources and the secondary literature. The fleet of Galaxidi, a maritime community in the Gulf of Corinth that keenly participated in the uprising, was burnt to ashes by the Ottomans in September 1821, depriving the Greeks of a significant number of ships. In the same way, Kassian ships were either destroyed or seized by the Ottomans after the invasion on Kasos in 1824. Smaller vessels from the rest of the Aegean islands (e.g., Skopelos, Santorini, Mykonos, Milos, and Andros) were deployed for auxiliary services, such as scouting, mail delivery, and transporting men and resources.

Due to the lack of battleships (ships of the line), the Greek fleet relied on the effect of surprise and extensively used fireships, smaller vessels filled with gunpowder that were steered toward the enemy. They were then deliberately set on fire in order to ignite the enemy ships and cause panic that would make the enemy break formation or flee. Fireships were extremely dangerous to maneuver and their effective use relied on the sea-competence of Greek sailors. Small vessels or prizes were transformed and fitted into fireships, and they were constantly in demand, as they were considered the most powerful weapon against the Ottoman navy. Approximately a hundred fireships were used during the years of war, and it was not uncommon for fireships to be destroyed in the course of action without succeeding to inflame the enemy vessels.

Contrary to the notion of a national navy, the Greek revolutionary fleet in practice consisted of independent, private ships that were summoned by the provisional government and were chartered for a specific expedition. Upon its completion, they would return to their home base for repairs and resume their previous activities. Neither the revolutionary government nor the authorities of the islands could commandeer the ships and it remained at the discretion of the shipowner and each individual sailor as to whether they embarked on a mission.

The idiosyncratic nature of the Greek fleet accounts for its weaknesses. First, the fleet lacked coordination. Although a Ministry of Naval Affairs was set up by the provisional government in 1822 to organize warfare at sea, each of the three islands acted as a self-standing admiralty responsible for summoning and preparing their ships to sail. It is evident that overlapping authorities undermined the promptness of strategic planning and the efficiency of the fleet in the course of an engagement. The "fleet of the three naval islands" was in effect three separate fleets with three commanders-in-chief, who were protagonists in the military and political arena. Giakoumakis Tombazis (1782–1829), member of the Philiki Etaireia and representative of Ydra at the national assemblies, was the commander of the Ydriot fleet during the first year of the revolution (Figure 4). However, the most prominent figure of the war at sea was Andreas Miaoulis (1769–1835), commander-in-chief of the Ydriot fleet (Figure 5). During critical moments of the struggle, he was silently acknowledged as admiral of the entire Greek fleet. Miaoulis, along with his deputy, Georgios Sachtouris (1783–1841), was the driving force and the mastermind of the naval operations. Georgios Androutsos (1782–1851) and Nikolis Apostolis (1770–1827) served as commanders-in-chief for the Spetsiot and Psariot fleet, respectively. It is worth noting that they were originally merchant captains of fully armed grain-carrying vessels with an experience of at least thirty years in plowing the turbulent waters of the Mediterranean during the French Revolutionary and Napoleonic wars. They had no experience, however, in disciplined and coordinated naval battles.

Another recurrent issue was the manning of ships and the disobedience of crews. Greek sailors were not trained soldiers and would agree to work onboard out of respect to their captain, inspired by the cause of national independence and / or simply driven by money, especially in anticipation of prizes. Monthly wages were paid in advance and on several occasions the crews refused to embark on a mission at a crucial stage of the war at sea until the settlement of their accounts. The cost of waging war at sea was particularly high. In addition to the operational costs, such as manning and food supplies, one should add fitting and repairs, and ammunition, as well as the cost of transforming a vessel into a fireship; all heavily burdened the provisional government, which was unable to meet these expenses. Regular taxation on the Aegean islands, occasional additional levies, fundraising among Philhellenes, the maritime communities, and wealthy shipowners, and last the income from prizes all proved insufficient.

FIGURE 4   Karl Krazeisen,
*Portrait of Giakoumakis
Tombazis*, 1827. Pencil on
paper. National Gallery-Al.
Soutzos Museum, Athens.

The provisional government, unable to meet the expenses of war, decided in
1823 to seek credit from the London money market. The national loans contributed toward the formation of a professional national navy in 1827 through
the assignment of its command to a British officer, Thomas Cochrane, the purchase of warships (a frigate and two steam-corvettes), and the use of enemy
ships that had been captured as prizes. The small nucleus of battleships was
reinforced by private ships from the three islands.

Military Operations at Sea

The armed grain cargo ships that belonged to the Greek maritime centers of
the Aegean and Ionian seas were transformed into warships, fireships, auxiliary ships, privateering or corsairing ships, and piratical ships. The islands participated fully in the revolution with ships and crews. The rather small size of
the fleet compared to the Ottoman armada and the lack of ships of the line and
heavy armaments did not favor full-fledged naval battles in the open sea. Rather,

FIGURE 5   Karl Krazeisen, *Portrait of Andreas Miaoulis*, 1827. Pencil on paper. National Gallery-Al. Soutzos Museum, Athens.

the Greek ships were mostly engaged in group attacks that aimed to cause the loss of enemy vessels and inflict casualties, and that exploited to the maximum their light and flexible craft and the use of fireships. From the early days, ships were deployed to connect the rebellious regions and convey the declaration of independence to those still hesitant or reluctant, for fear of the sultan's wrath. On a more practical level, they would undertake the transportation of men, provisions, and ammunition to the rebels; the blockade of coastal forts (e.g., Nafplio, Patras, Methoni, Koroni, Pylos) to obstruct the Ottoman fleet from supplying the besieged; occasional skirmishes; and privateering.

According to the law of the sea established by the provisional government, privateers were allowed to attack and seize Ottoman merchantmen and transports, confiscate their cargo, and ransom the vessel, with the intention of undermining the enemy's military operations, destroy its infrastructure, and harm its trade and shipping. The conduct of war required the relocation of thousands of soldiers and sailors to suppress the rebels, along with provisions for the Ottoman army and navy that were transported to the warring sites primarily on merchant ships, and this created a remarkable market for merchantmen. Besides North African ships (e.g., Algerian, Tunisian), British, Austrian, Dutch, French, and even Ionian ships were chartered by the imperial navy and time and again fell prey to Greek privateers. Prizes were particularly enticing for Greek crews, as the loot, following the extraction of 15 percent that was allocated to the central authorities, was divided among the sailors and captain on the spot, adding significantly to their monthly wage. The lure of prizes frequently instigated insubordination of ships that would defy orders while on mission and desert the fleet to pursue privateering. The line between privateering and piracy was frequently blurred, fueling the resentment of the western European countries that questioned the legitimacy of the Greek War of Independence and the intentions of the Greek sea-warriors. To impose law and order, the Greek government tried to regulate privateering by establishing a prize court in Nafplio to adjudicate on the legitimacy of prizes and restitute the seizure of neutral ships.

From the outbreak of the revolution until the cease-fire and the foundation of the Greek state, war at sea went through different stages. From 1821 to 1823, the Greek navy conducted a number of successful, albeit small-scale, operations that spread the revolution and strengthened the confidence of the rebels in their cause. These involved the blockade of ports in mainland Greece, the Peloponnese, the north of Greece (e.g., Chalkidiki), and Crete, the occasional destruction of enemy ships, and some first engagements (e.g., Gulf of Argolis, Suda, Tenedos, Euboean Gulf). A number of raids on the coasts of Asia Minor by Psariots in the north (e.g., Kydonies, Moschonisia) and by Kasians in Syria and Egypt (e.g., Damietta) terrified the Muslim populations. During the first phase of war, a monumental incident that has been exalted in the national historiography was the blasting of the Ottoman flagship in the port of Chios by a Psariot fireship (Captain Constantinos Kanaris), which became a symbol of resistance (Figure 6). In retaliation, the Ottoman forces destroyed Galaxidi (September 21, 1821) along with its entire fleet and in the following year they burned to ashes the island of Chios (March 27 to April 2, 1822), killing or enslaving its entire population, in order to set an example for the rest of the Aegean islands that had revolted against the sultan.

The years from 1824 to 1826 were dramatic for the Greeks and almost led to the defeat of the revolution. After three years of war, contrary to the original estimations of the Porte, the Greek revolt proved resilient and therefore Sultan Mahmud II planned carefully a decisive counterattack to reinstate his rule over the Greeks. One of the first actions was to call for the assistance of Mohamed Ali of Egypt, creating a combined powerful fleet that simultaneously entered the Aegean in 1824 from the north (Constantinople) and the south. The Ottomans

FIGURE 6   Nikiforos Lytras, *Constantinos Kanaris Setting on Fire the Turkish Flagship,* ca. 1873. Oil on canvas. E. Averoff Museum of Modern Greek Art, Metsovo.

aimed to destroy the Greek fleet and islands and then turn to the Peloponnese, where the Greek forts would be easier to take without support from the sea. While the Ottomans designed a major expedition, the Greeks were absorbed in internal conflicts that divided their forces, drained the coffers, and made coordination impossible.

On the south front, the fall of Crete in March 1824 was followed by the destruction of the island of Kasos by the Egyptian armada (May 27–28), in retribution for attacks on coastal villages by Kassian privateers, and led to the submission of the rest of the Dodecanese islands (e.g., Karpathos, Symi, Leros, Kalymnos). On the north front, the Ottoman fleet crossed the Dardanelles and headed to Psara, inflicting what has been described in the national historiography as a holocaust (June 20–24), with the extermination of the Psariot population and ships (Nikodimos 1862, 1438–1475). The tragedy has been immortalized in a deeply moving epigram by Dionysios Solomos. The invasion of these islands deprived the Greeks of two of their most significant naval bases, greatly reduced in size the Greek fleet, and facilitated the access of the Ottoman navy to the Aegean from the north and the south. The next target was the island of Samos, but the Greek fleet reacted timely to engage in a series of battles at the Mycali Straits (August 5), the Straits of Kos (August 24), and the Gulf of Gerontas (August 29) and succeeded in repelling the invasion of the joined Ottoman and Egyptian forces.

Despite naval victories at Methoni (April 30) and Cavo D'Oro (June 4) in 1825 the Greek fleet fell to a standstill, while Ibrahim Pasha reconquered most of the Peloponnese and tightened the siege around the most significant fort in central Greece, Mesolonghi. The siege lasted a year, from April 25, 1825, until April 10, 1826, for as long as Greek ships could supply the city through its lagoon. The mooring of the Ottoman armada in the nearby Gulf of Patras and the Ottoman occupation of the islets in the lagoon of Aitoliko and Mesolonghi made it impossible for the Greeks to approach by sea and condemned the fort to starvation. The resistance and exodus of the besieged and the Ottoman atrocities at Mesolonghi stirred public sympathy in Western Europe and precipitated the interference of European powers in the Greek war (Figure 7).

In 1827, after several years of battling at sea, the number of fit and able ships had dwindled, while the crews were disheartened and exhausted from the ongoing operations. The civil strife over political leadership and the inadequacy of the provisional government's financing of the war at sea had withered the fleet. In the broader picture, the Ottoman forces had reconquered almost the entire Peloponnese, central and northern Greece, Crete, and the vast majority of the Aegean islands, with the exception of Ydra, Spetses, and Samos. Naval operations were in fact limited to a few clashes and ships would turn to piracy (especially in 1826–1827) to ensure the financial survival of the sailors and their islands. Foreign intervention at this point, both on a political and a military level, was crucial for the survival of the Greek cause. The command of the army and navy was handed to British officers, with the intention of coordinating and organizing the armed forces in compliance with European war standards. Furthermore, the presence of the foreign commanders managed to appease tension between the Greek opposing factions at the height of the civil war.

The purchase of warships financed by national loans issued in London, the formation of a national navy, and the assumption of the naval leadership by Thomas Cochrane were meant to remedy the disintegration of the fleet and sus-

FIGURE 7   Constantinos Volanakis, *The Exodus of "Ares,"* 1894. Oil on canvas. National Gallery-Al. Soutzos Museum, Athens.

tain war at sea in anticipation of an intervention from the great powers (Great Britain, Russia, and France). The navy was involved in small-scale, more or less successful operations such as the attempted attack on the Egyptian fleet harbored in Alexandria, the unsuccessful blockade of Chios, and the destruction of several Ottoman ships in the Gulf of Corinth (Itea).

The persistence of the Greeks, after several years of bloodshed, made their uprising finally visible in the courts of Europe and in 1826 the Greek National Assembly officially requested Britain's mediation to a cease-fire and to seek a political solution to the Greek request for independence. The three great powers assumed their role as mediators with the Treaty of London (July 6, 1827) and dispatched naval forces in the Mediterranean to enforce the terms of the treaty on the belligerents. In response to the Ottoman defiance, the commanders-in-chief of the allied Mediterranean fleets entered the Gulf of Navarino (October 20), where the Ottoman armada was moored. Their aim was to proactively obstruct the fleet from leaving the harbor and from undertaking naval operations in the Aegean. In the battle of Navarino, one of the major naval battles in European history, the ships fought at anchor and the Ottoman-Egyptian armada suffered tremendous losses. Although the Greek navy did not intervene, the allied fleet sealed with its victory Greece's independence.

Katerina Galani and Gelina Harlaftis

References

Anderson, Roger Charles. 1952. *Naval Wars in the Levant 1559–1853*. Princeton, NJ.

Bourchier, Jane, ed. 1875. *Memoir of the Life of Admiral Sir Edward Codrington*. London.

Bozikis, Simos. 2018. "Δημόσια οικονομικά και συγκρότηση εθνικού κράτους 1821" [Public finance and the consolidation of a nation state 1821]. PhD diss., Ionian University.

Constantinidis, Tryfon. 1954. *Καράβια, καπετάνιοι και συντροφοναύται (1800–1830)* [Ships, captains and sailors, 1800–1830]. Athens.

Dimitropoulos, Dimitris. 2016. "Pirates during a Revolution: The Many Faces of Piracy and the Reaction of Local Communities." In *Corsairs and Pirates in the Eastern Mediterranean, 15th–19th Centuries*, edited by Gelina Harlaftis, Dimitris Dimitropoulos, and David J. Starkey, 29–40. Athens.

Gordon, Thomas. (1832) 2012. *History of the Greek Revolution*. Cambridge.

Galani, Katerina, and Gelina Harlaftis, eds. 2021. *Greek Shipping during the War of Independence: Naval and Merchant Ships, 1821–1831*. Iraklio.

Harlaftis, Gelina, and Katerina Papakonstantinou. 2013. *Ναυτιλία των Ελλήνων, 1700–1821* [Greek shipping, 1700–1821]. Athens.

Hatzianargyrou, Anargiros Andreou. (1861) 1925–1926. *Τα Σπετσιωτικά* [Spetsiot matters]. Athens.

Katifori-Themeli, Despoina. 1973. *Η δίωξις της πειρατείας και το θαλάσσιον δικαστήριον κατά την πρώτην καποδιστριακήν περίοδον* [The prosecution of piracy and the maritime court during the first Capodistrian period 1828–1829]. Athens.

Konstas, E. Panagiotis. 1971. *Ναυτική εποποιία του 1821* [The naval epopee of 1821]. Athens.

Kurtoğlu, Fevzi. 1944. *Yunan istiklâl harbi and Navarin muharebesi: (Çengeloğlu Tahir Paşa)* [Greek War of Independence and Battle of Navarino: Çengeloğlu Tahir Paşa]. Vol. 1. Ankara.

Leontaritis, Giorgos. 1972. *Ελληνική Εμπορική Ναυτιλία (1453–1850)* [Greek merchant shipping, 1453–1850]. Athens.

Lignos, Antonios, ed. 1921–1923. *Αρχείον της Κοινότητας Ύδρας 1778–1832* [The Archive of the Community of Ydra]. Piraeus.

Mavris, Nikolaos G., ed. 1937. *Ιστορικόν Αρχείον Κάσου* [Historical Archive of Kasos]. Athens.

Metallinos, Constantinos. 2016. *Ο ναυτικός πόλεμος κατά την Ελληνική Επανάσταση, 1821–1829* [Naval war during the Greek Revolution, 1821–1829]. Athens.

Nikodimos, Constantinos. 1862. *Υπόμνημα της Νήσου Ψαρών* [Memoire on the Island of Psara]. Vols. 1–2. Athens. Reprinted 1982.

Sapranidis, Dimitris, ed., 1997. *Γεωργίου Σαχτούρη, Ημερολόγιο του πολεμικού ιστιοφόρου «Αθηνά», 1824–1824* [Georgios Sachtouris, logbook of the war sailing ship Athena, 1824–1827]. Athens.

Simpsas, Marios G. 1974. *Ναβαρίνον. Η ναυμαχία που εθεμελίωσε την ελευθερίαν της Ελλάδος* [Navarino: The naval war that founded Greek independence]. Athens.

Varfis, Costas A. 1994. *Το Ελληνικό Ναυτικό κατά την Καποδιστριακή περίοδο. Τα χρόνια της προσαρμογής* [The Hellenic navy during the period of Capodistrias: The years of adjustment]. Athens.

Woodhouse, Christopher Montague. 1965. *The Battle of Navarino*. London.

Asia Minor

The Philiki Etaireia included in its membership patriotic Orthodox Greeks from Asia Minor, who had been trained in the educational institutions of Smyrna, Kydonies, and Trebizond. Some of its members had been dispatched to cities in Asia Minor to initiate numbers of the Orthodox (*Rûm*) community into the organization. The Greek Orthodox inhabitants of Ionia, Aeolia, and the western coast of Asia Minor demonstrated actively their devotion to the vision of the liberation of the *Genos*. Many of those who were initiated into the Philiki Etaireia and others, who were not even members, offered material assistance for the needs of the struggle. An indicative example is the case of the Smyrniot Georgios Afthonidis, who was probably initiated in Constantinople, where he founded the the Box of Mercy (Κιβώτιον του Ελέους) in 1819 for the cause of the planned revolution. According to some sources, as secretary of Patriarch Grigorios V he played the role of mediator between the Patriarch and the *Philikoi*.

In the existing authoritative lists of the members of the Philiki Etaireia (Meletopoulos 1967, 274–341; Philimon 1859–1862, 1:387–416), one can trace a number of Asia Minor Greeks: twelve from Smyrna, three from Trebizond, two from Kydonies, two from Moudania as well as others from Kyzikos, Koutali island, Prousa, Krini (Çeşme), Caesarea, and so on. These specific data, however, concern only one-fifth or less of the total number of the *Philikoi*, since most of the evidence of the initiated members of the Etaireia has been lost. Some names can be identified in several lists, while most of them mention as places of origin various cities in Asia Minor. Many are listed simply by their first name and instead of a surname they have an adjective signifying a certain place, such as Smyrnaios (Smyrniot), Mavrothalassitis (Pontic), Ayvaliotis, Kusadianos (from Kuşadası), or simply Anatolitis (Oriental).

The military contribution of the Asia Minor Greeks took its most formal shape by the establishment of an independent military unit, the Ionian Column (Ιωνική Φάλαγξ) or Column of the Ionians (Φάλαγξ των Ιώνων), which for approximately two years (1826–1828) fought in the Peloponnese, Central Greece, and Chios (1827). However, there were also many more Asia Minor Greeks who had fought since the beginning of the revolution under the command of various captains or generals or constituted the first soldiers of the regular army.

The creation of a regular army in a Greece in revolt was achieved also due to the participation of Greeks from Asia Minor and especially those from Kydonies. From the beginning of the revolution, there were reports of smaller or larger groupings of irregular fighters from Asia Minor originating mostly from Kydonies and Smyrna. These groups fought as a unit within the military bodies of various captains or generals such as Kolokotronis, Deligiannis, Andreas Lontos, Makrygiannis, Karaiskakis, Gouras, Chatzichristos, and especially Nikitas Stamatelopoulos or Nikitaras. Many of these groups of Asia Minor Greeks fought united at Dervenakia, the siege of Tripolitsa, the battle of Peta, or the second and third sieges of Mesolonghi. It is worth mentioning particularly the Pissas brothers from Kydonies. Nikolaos Pissas fell in battle at Ambelonas or Ambelia near Argos in the battles against Dramali's army. Panagiotis fought in the Peloponnese, in Crete, and finally with the army of the experienced French colonel Charles Fabvier. He fell heroically in 1826 in the battle of Karystos. Efstratios Pissas repeatedly performed brave deeds in Crete, the Peloponnese, Chios, Karystos, Palamidi, Chaidari, and elsewhere. He was even appointed head of one of the three battalions that broke the siege by Kütahı and entered the Acropolis of Athens on December 1, 1826. Other Kydoniates joined the irregular military groups of various chieftains and captains. It should be pointed out that the city of Kydonies itself became also the theater of Turkish reprisals during the revolution, similar to those in Constantinople. Hundreds of inhabitants were massacred and the famous Academy of Kydonies (Ακαδημία Κυδωνιών) was destroyed in June 1821 along with the rest of the city, which was deserted by its population, who fled to mainland Greece as refugees (Argyropoulos and Kitromilides 2007, 59–75).

For the events that took place in Smyrna we have several authentic accounts. One of them is by a leading scholar of the Enlightenment movement, Constantinos Koumas, who, in March 1821 was a professor at the Philological Gymnasium of Smyrna (Φιλολογικόν Γυμνάσιον Σμύρνης). He managed to escape the massacre and the overall terrorism and reach Vienna. From there, he secretly sent a letter on July 11, 1821, to the German classicist and Philhellene Friedrich Thiersch, in which he narrated in a tragic tone and in archaic language what he had experienced as an eyewitness in the panic-stricken and mob-controlled capital of Ionia. Another important source is made up of the reports of the consul of the Levant Company in Smyrna, Francis Werry. He writes that the news of the incipient Greek revolt had profound repercussions in Smyrna with its very substantial Greek population, and most of Consul Werry's reports were concerned with reporting the situation and in particular the severe dislocation of commercial activity which ensued and whose effects were critical for the normal transaction of trade by the Levant Company (Clogg 1972, 313–355).

On the interior of the Asia Minor peninsula, relevant information is limited. There were a few diaspora Cappadocians, who had been initiated in the Philiki Etaireia. Therefore, we know neither the number of Cappadocians who were initiated in the Etaireia nor whether the envoys of the Etaireia (the "apostles") were able to reach Cappadocia. The catalogs of the *Philikoi* published by the historian and secretary of Dimitrios Ypsilantis, Ioannis Philimon, mention a monk from Caesarea named Ioannikios, who was initiated in 1820 in Warsaw by Aristeidis Papas. There is also the testimony by Seraphim N. Rizos that his grandfather Rizos from Sinasos was hanged at Prousa because he was considered a member of the Philiki Etaireia (Rizos 2007, 105–106). The record of the *Philikoi* who served as fighters in the Sacred Battalion held at the state archives of the Odessa prefecture and published by Nikolai Todorov lists men from all the Balkan countries who fought under Alexandros Ypsilantis in Moldavia and Wallachia. Among them are thirty Asia Minor Greeks, who are described as "Greeks holding Turkish citizenship." The catalog mentions three fighters from Caesarea, Vasileios Tourkouletsis, Anastasios Isaak, and Georgios Kaysarlis (Todorov 1982, 193–294).

The names of many Asia Minor Greeks who served as chiefs in groups of their compatriots who fought in the revolution are recorded in surviving sources. Examples include Chadji-Apostolis, who maintained a body of eighty fighters from Kydonies under the general leadership of Panagiotis Giatrakos; Dimitrios Kapandaros, who was the head of about fifty of his Kydoniates compatriots and participated in many battles in the Peloponnese; Constantinos Ayvaliotis, who received an order by Dimitrios Ypsilantis to form a body of fifty Kydoniates, but found himself in an unfavorable position because of the ferocity he showed during the fall of Tripolitsa; Georgios Stavrakoglou from Smyrna; Giannakos Karoglou, also from Smyrna, who headed the Ionian Column; and others.

According to the historian of Kydonies Georgios Sakkaris, during the invasion by Dramali, "three hundred Kydoniates fought as one body at the Argos vineyards" (Sakkaris 1920, 123), whereas a number of other fighters, mainly from Kydonies, fought by participating in small or medium-size military units. Approximately one hundred Asia Minor Greeks fought at the siege of the Acropolis of Athens by Kütahı. During the second siege of Mesolonghi an unspecified but significant number of Asia Minor Greeks fought on the side of the besieged. An existing list of soldiers who fought in Mesolonghi from April 1822 until March 1826 mentions Asia Minor Greeks from Smyrna and Ayvali (General State Archives).

The most important representative of the participation of Pontic Hellenism in the revolution was the Ypsilantis family, while the Neroulos family also originated from Trebizond. Iakovakis Rizos, a member of the latter, initiated into the Etaireia the prince of Wallachia Ioannis Karatzas, while his son Alexandros survived the destruction of the Sacred Battalion.

In 1819, Silvestros Lazaridis, deacon of the Metropolitan of Chaldea Sophronios Lazaridis (1789–1819) and later Metropolitan of Chaldia as Silvestros II Lazarides (1819–1830), joined the Philiki Etaireia. Afterward, Silvestros initiated Metropolitan Sophronios and the chief metallurgist of the mines of Argyroupolis (Gumushane) Iakovos Grigorandis. Ilias Kandilis, principal of the Hellenic High School of Trebizond (Ελληνικόν Φροντιστήριον Τραπεζούντος) and later founder of the Hellenic High School of Cherson (Ελληνικόν Φροντιστήριον της Χερσώνος) was also initiated and supported the Etaireia with the donation of a significant amount of money.

In the above-mentioned catalogue published by Todorov, Odysseas Lampsidis, a prominent authority on Pontic history, managed to identify seventeen Pontic fighters and published their names with full documentation. Their identification was made possible by their toponymic characterization, such as, for example, Trapezanlis, Trapezountios, Mavrothalassitis, Sinaplis, and Kioumouschanelis (Lampsidis 1975–1976, 3–8).

Stavros Th. Anestidis

References

Anastasiadis, Georgios I. 1938, 1940. "Η συμβολή των Μικρασιατών εις την εθνικήν αναγέννησιν" [The contribution of the Asia Minor Greeks in the national regeneration]. *Mikrasiatika Chronika* 1:116–136, 3:213–232.

Argyropoulos, Roxane D., and Paschalis M. Kitromilides. 2007. "Ο Διαφωτισμός στον χώρο της Αιολίδας" [The Enlightenment in the Aeolis region]. In *Μυτιλήνη και Αϊβαλί (Κυδωνίες). Μια αμφίδρομη σχέση στο βορειοανατολικό Αιγαίο* [Mytilini and Ayvali (Kydonies): A bidirectional relationship in the northern Aegean], edited by Paschalis M. Kitromilides and Panagiotis D. Mihailaris, 59–75. Athens.

Athanasiadis, Sotirios. 1982. "Μικρασιάτες Έλληνες εθελοντές στον αγώνα του 1821" [Asia Minor Greek refugees in the struggle of 1821]. *Triphyliaki Estia* 8, no. 47: 416–419.

Clogg, Richard. 1972. "Smyrna in 1821. Documents of the Levant Company Archives in the Public Record Office." *Mikrasiatika Chronika* 15:313–355.

General State Archives, *Αρχείον Αγώνος, Συλλογή Γιάννη Βλαχογιάννη* [Archive of the Struggle. Giannis Vlachogiannis Collection], Catalogue A, ms 72.

Kandilaptis, Georgios. 1962. "Οι Πόντιοι κατά τους αγώνας της Επαναστάσεως" [The Pontic Greeks during the revolutionary struggle]. *Pontiaki Estia* 13:6623–6626.

Kitromilides, Paschalis M. 2018. "Η Φιλική Εταιρεία και η πολιτική γεωγραφία του Διαφωτισμού" [The Philiki Etaireia and the political geography of the Enlightenment]. In *Οι πόλεις των Φιλικών. Οι αστικές διαδρομές ενός επαναστατικού φαινομένου* [The cities of the Philikoi: The urban pathways of a revolutionary phenomenon], 25–35. Athens.

Lampsidis, Odysseas. 1975–1976. "Η συμμετοχή των Ελλήνων Ποντίων εις την εθνεγερσίαν του 1821" [The participation of the Pontic Greeks in the national uprising of 1821]. *Archeion Pontou* 33:3–8.

Meletopoulos, Ioannis A. 1967. "Η Φιλική Εταιρεία. Αρχείον Παναγιώτου Δημ. Σέκερη" [The Philiki Etaireia: The papers of Panagiotis Dim. Sekeris]. Athens.

Mengous, Petros. 1830. *Narrative of a Greek Soldier: Containing Anecdotes and Occurrences Illustrating the Character and Manners of the Greeks and Turks in Asia Minor, and Detailing Events of the Late War in Greece, in which the Author was Actively Engaged by Land and Sea, from the Commencement to the Close of the Revolution.* New York.

Papadopoulou, Archontia V. 2012. *Η συμβολή των Ελλήνων της καθ' ημάς Ανατολής στην Παλιγγενεσία του 1821. Μέσα από τις έγγραφες μαρτυρίες των Αγωνιστών* [The contribution of the Greeks of the Levant in the Regeneration of 1821: Through the documentary evidence of the Fighters]. Athens.

Philimon, Ioannis. 1859–1862. *Δοκίμιον ιστορικόν περί της Ελληνικής Επαναστάσεως* [A historical essay on the Greek Revolution]. Athens.

Pyrgaris, Georgios, ed. 2017. *Στρατηγού Ευστρατίου Πίσσα Απομνημονεύματα 1821* [Memoirs of 1821 by General Efstratios Pissas]. Athens.

Rizos, Serapheim N. 2007. *Η Σινασός* [Sinasos]. Edited by Stavros Th. Anestidis and Mirka Tzevelekis-Kondakis. 2 vols. Athens.

Sakkaris, Georgios. 1920. *Ιστορία των Κυδωνιών* [History of Kydonies]. Athens.

Salkitzoglou, Takis A. 2009. "Καππαδόκες αγωνιστές στην Επανάσταση του 1821" [Cappadocian fighters in the revolution of 1821]. *Mikrasiatika Chronika* 23:123–143.

Salkitzoglou, Takis A. 2010. *Η Μικρά Ασία στην Επανάσταση του 1821. Η συμβολή των Μικρασιατών στον εθνικό αγώνα* [Asia Minor in the revolution of 1821: The contribution of Asia Minor Greeks in the national struggle]. Athens.

Seferiades, Stelios. 1938. "Η Σμύρνη κατά την Επανάστασιν του 1821 (Μία μαύρη σελίς)" [Smyrna in the Revolution of 1821 (A black page)]. *Mikrasiatika Chronika* 1:54–57.

Solomonides, Christos. 1971. "Η συμβολή της Ιωνίας στην Εθνεγερσία" [The contribution of Ionia in the national uprising]. *Parnassos* 13:345–373.

Tenekides, Georgios. 1978. *Η Ιωνία στον πανεθνικό αγώνα της ανεξαρτησίας* [Ionia in the pan-national struggle for independence]. Athens.

Theodoridis, Theodoros. 1980. "Επεισόδιον επαναστατικόν εν Καισαρεία της Καππαδοκίας κατά την Ελληνικήν Επανάστασιν του 1821" [A revolutionary incident in Caesarea of Cappadocia during the Greek Revolution of 1821]. *Mikrasiatika Chronika* 17:216–226.

Todorov, Nikolai. 1982. *Η Βαλκανική διάσταση της επανάστασης του 1821* [The Balkan dimension of the 1821 revolution]. Athens.

Vakalopoulos. Vol. V.

Athens

On his return to England, George Cochrane committed to paper his recollections of what he had lived through in the insurgent Greek regions, when accompanying his uncle, Thomas Cochrane, who in 1827 had been appointed head of the Greek naval forces by the Greeks, in the National Assembly of Troezen. After describing the fateful battle of Phaliron (April 24, 1827) and the loss of Athens for the Greek revolutionaries, he stated: "The very loss of this battle . . . may be deemed the salvation of Greece. Sympathizing Europe found it requisite that she should at last interpose, and wrest this ill-fated country from the hands of her oppressors. Accordingly, England, France and Russia formed a triple alliance, on 6 July 1827, to guarantee to the Greeks their ancient country. . . . I repeat that, however I may deplore those brave men who fell on that unfortunate day, I must still think that the loss of the battle of Athens was the proximate cause of the liberation of Greece. Certain it is that, if the three above-named powers had not interfered, the Sultan would never have made peace with the Greeks, and the War would have been one of extermination on the part of Turkey" (Cochrane 1837, 1:83). He then went on to describe the sea battle of Navarino and the creation of the independent Greek state.

Eight months though prior to the battle in which Mehmed Reşid Pasha, or Kütahı, would be victorious, the Greeks' opponent in the bitter struggle was tense and worried, knowing that the battle for Athens would be like no other. So, in September 1826, Kütahı sent the grand vizier a letter, which, however, fell into Greek hands. In this letter—from which the important Scot Thomas Gordon, who fought alongside the Greeks, quoted in English translation—Mehmed Reşid stated that:

The citadel of Athens ... was built in old times upon a high and steep rock, which defies equally mines and assaults. ... As the said castle is so ancient, and contains many monuments, and many philosophers have gone forth from thence, it fills with admiration the learned men among the Franks; and all the nations of the Infidels ... venerate it as a holy place, and look upon it as their own property. Wherefore they have conspired, promising to assist each other, and to exert themselves to the uttermost, that it may never pass out of the hands of the unbelievers. (Gordon 1832, 2:353, 354)

The significance of Athens for Europe (Tzakis 2015) ominously preoccupied the Ottomans from the time of the first siege of this trading and manufacturing town of some ten thousand inhabitants, in 1821 (Karidis 2014, 46–53). Then, the British ambassador in Constantinople, Viscount Strangford, had, in the name of his king, elicited from the sultan an order addressed to the official responsible for Athens and the Acropolis, Kiose Mehmed Pasha, in which it was emphasized:

as the perfect and sincere affection between the two courts had been increasing day by day; and as the antiquities and ancient monuments in Athens had always deserved the attention of Europe, it befitted the dignity of the Sublime Porte to take the necessary measures to retain these ancient monuments in their current state in order to do something agreeable to His Majesty. Thus, due to the sagacity which characterizes you, you shall order all those concerned to spare and preserve the antiquities and monuments in question, so that there should be no complaint in this regard on the part of anyone. (Ilıcak 2019, 245, 246)

The exhortation could not, in reality, be satisfied. In the course of the Revolution, Athens was besieged twice: the first time by the Greeks, from April 1821 into June 1822, when the beleaguered Turks on the Acropolis surrendered; the second time by the Turks, from June 1826 into May 1827, when the besieged Greeks surrendered (Makrygiannis 1907; Sourmelis 1834; Vakalopoulos) (Figure 8). Naturally, in these two protracted sieges the Acropolis was bombarded relentlessly, suffering enormous damage to its monuments—in August 1826 alone it was hit in the Ottoman bombardments by "2,120 cannon balls and 956 bomb and howitzer shells" (Ilıcak 2019, 254), but this did not mean that the reference to the cultural importance of Athens played no role in the overall unfolding of events. Athens was of cultural importance not only for the

FIGURE 8   Dimitrios Zographos, *The Siege of Athens,* 1836–1839. Watercolor on paper.
The Gennadeion Library, Athens.

Turks, but also for the Greeks, who were well aware that "those Europeans who
come, all have their sights on Athens," and that, therefore, they would help in
many ways (Tzakis 2015, 345, note 14).

The progress of events was complicated. In mid-April 1821, peasants from the
environs of Athens, mainly Menidi, Vilia, Kiphisia, Liopesi, and Chasia—
reached the outskirts of Athens and laid siege to it; their ranks would be swelled
later by armed men from Salamis, Aigina, Kea (Tzia), Megara, and Eleusis. The
Turks in Athens—proportionately few, in a town in which they were always
outnumbered by Christians (Ilıcak 2019, 244)—arrested Greek primates as
hostages, looted Greek shops, set fire to houses, abandoned their homes, and
barricaded themselves on the Acropolis. The Sacred Rock was now besieged
by the Greeks, who already controlled the rest of the town.

Kiose Mehmed Pasha of the Peloponnese sent Omer Bey of Karystos and the
Turk-Albanian Tosk commander Omer Vrioni to assist the beleaguered Turks
of Athens. In June 1821, with infantry and cavalry, they entered an almost empty
town, as the Athenians had, in the meantime, sought refuge on Aigina and
Salamis—the nearby islands which, since antiquity, had been the self-evident
places of escape for them as well as for the inhabitants of Attica. Turks and
Turk-Albanians burned down houses, impaled and butchered captives, and

took control of everything. They retreated, however, in September 1821, when the Greeks won crucial victories in areas not far from Athens. The Greeks came back—this time with the reinforcement of Philhellenes (Dakin 1955, 113–159)— and again laid siege to the Turks, who, once more, had holed up on the Acropolis. Worn out by hardships, the besieged surrendered and left the Acropolis, charitably supported in their helplessness by the victors, in June 1822. Eighteen days later, while events were developing smoothly and those who had surrendered were awaiting their safe conduct to Asia Minor, in accordance with the terms of their capitulation, a menacing rumor reached Athens that the army of Mahmud Pasha Dramali was approaching the city. Panic-stricken, the Greeks launched into a heinous massacre of their captives, from which only one-third of the Muslims who had surrendered survived, and even that was thanks only to the intervention of their saner countrymen and the European consuls in the city. The survivors were later moved to the ships and their salvation.

Athens, devastated by destructions, conflagrations, slaughter, and looting by both sides (Map 4), now functioned under Greek control, successfully confronting the Ottoman forces' attempts to return, in 1823 and 1824. Its population included not only Athenians who had returned, but also refugees from areas beset by battles and massacres, such as wider Attica, Chios, Euboea, and so on. According to estimates of European consuls, in 1824 about thirteen thousand people were living in Athens, three thousand three hundred of whom were in dire poverty and misery (Vakalopoulos 6:734, 735).

Control of the town gradually passed into the hands of the powerful chief of the freedom-fighters in east central Greece, Odysseas Androutsos, a capable, decisive, energetic yet controversial personality, crude and reckless, studious and cunning, power-hungry and ambitious, and of his like-minded collaborator, Giannis Gouras. During the four years between the two sieges of Athens, the town experienced difficult moments, due to the greed, violence, and power lust of these two men and the clashes between them. However, it also experienced cultural achievements, thanks to Androutsos and Gouras, who were open to cultural matters and to the presence of active Philhellenes and consuls of the European powers (particularly the antiquarian Georg Christian Gropius, consul of Austria in Athens, and the important British Philhellene Leicester Stanhope), and, of course, thanks to the existence of a considerable number of Greek men of letters and teachers. The town acquired a fortnightly newspaper, the *Ephimeris Athinon,* with editor-in-chief Georgios Psyllas and its seat initially in Salamis and subsequently in Athens itself; a museum in the Parthenon and later in the Erechtheion; a Philanthropic Society with the parallel revitalizing of the Philomousos Society; six schools of

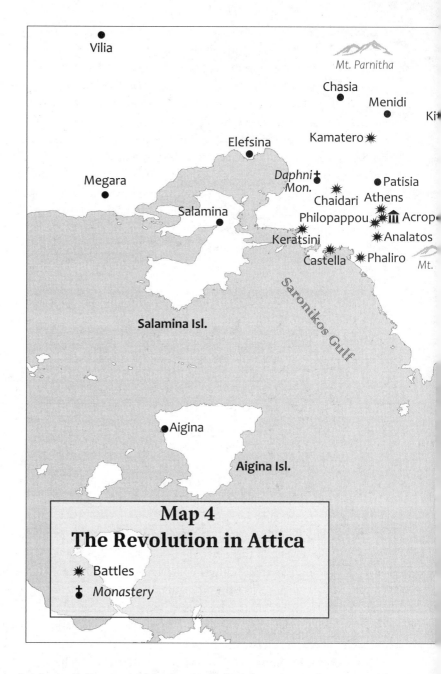

Map 4
The Revolution in Attica

✳ Battles
♱ Monastery

different levels, including a girls' high school (*Parthenagogeion*), monitorial schools, and *Ellinika* (grammar or high) schools that taught ancient Greek; a postal service; a hospital; and other facilities. The central government was also involved in these actions, because it considered that when Greece was liberated, its capital would be Athens and, with this in mind, it adopted a

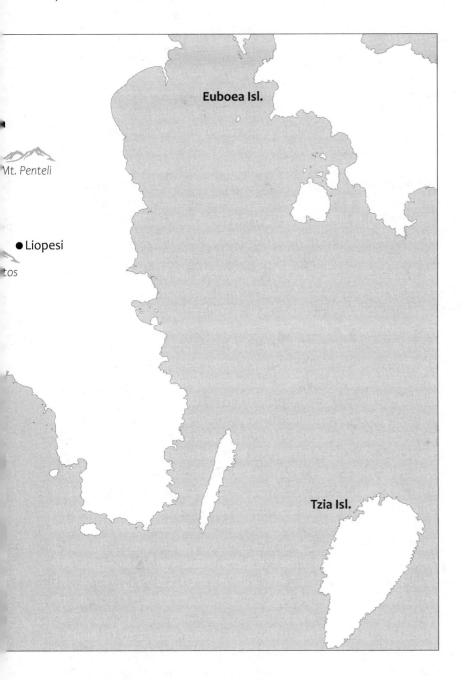

proposal of the Philomousos Society to found a library, a botanical garden, a
school of sciences, an academy of fine arts, and so on.

Concurrently, however, the town was enduring the animosity between Androutsos and Gouras, which was succored by the more general clime of civil war
that shook the revolution in the years 1824 and 1825. In the end, Gouras took over

the administration of Athens and made sure Androutsos was killed—he had been officially accused of siding with the Turks—by hurling him from the Acropolis on June 5, 1825.

When the time of the second siege came, in July 1826, Giannis Gouras was governor of Athens. Circumstances for the Greeks were abysmal; Ibrahim and the Turkish-Egyptian forces were sweeping away the fronts in the Peloponnese and central Greece, at the same time as many *armatoloi* of the region were declaring, after the fall of Mesolonghi, their allegiance to the Ottomans, so as to take back the areas that they used to police (*armatoliks*). Nonetheless, the Athenians were preparing for war, for as Sourmelis noted: "The sad and terrible announcement of the fall of Mesolonghi tore at the very soul of Athens. . . . They see the Nation weak, the affairs of Greece in a wretched state, the enemy strong. With all this, they decide to resist and to fight until their last breath" (Sourmelis 1834, 137). They mustered their final forces, as Thomas Gordon evocatively put it: "Yet, as a taper burns brightly a moment before its extinction, so they summoned up their energies for a last effort, and the result was a vigorous, though unfortunate campaign" (Gordon 1832, 2:375).

The victor of Mesolonghi, Kütahı, did indeed move toward Athens. As he passed through the nearby villages—those that five years earlier had led the way in the revolt—the inhabitants sped to pay obeisance. On July 3, 1826, the blockade of Athens began and the situation was reversed yet again. The civilians fled to Salamis, while the freedom-fighters engaged in fierce battles with the Turks and, in the end, barricaded themselves on the Rock, along with a number of women and children. Gouras and the defenders of the Acropolis turned down Kütahı's overtures for surrender. To the contrary, they steadfastly held out, boosted by daring operations of Greeks and Philhellenes who, crossing the enemy lines, brought supplies of food, men, and ammunition to the besieged.

The government called upon all Greeks to come to assist Athens. Many responded to the appeal: Thracians and Macedonians, Thessalians, Ionian islanders, Souliots, Peloponnesians, inhabitants of central Greece and of Asia Minor, Cretans, Epirots—and the audacious Frenchman Charles Fabvier, at the time head of the regular Greek army which, by force of circumstance, had gained esteem among the Greek freedom-fighters. Gouras lost his life in one of the innumerable skirmishes around the Acropolis, as the Greek forces struck camp mainly on the coast, on the southwest axis of Athens, between Eleusis, Chaidari, Keratsini, and Phaliron. By contrast, Kütahı, who controlled the city, placed his central encampment north of Athens, at Patissia. He unremittingly bombarded the Acropolis from Philopappos hill and held crucial positions toward both the sea and Mount Ymitos.

Europe was following the developments. Concern about the antiquities of the emblematic city mounted. On June 4, 1826, the British ambassador in Constantinople, Stratford Canning, sent a letter to Mehmed Reşid Pasha, whom of all Ottoman dignitaries he considered the one with the soundest appreciation of the war's ideological dimension. In this letter Canning stressed the importance of Athens and its monuments for Europe:

> It is known to everyone that the citadel and suburbs of Athens contain the ruins of several antique edifices, which though of small importance in the eyes of Reason, or of Religion, and wholly unconnected with affairs of state, have justly fixed the admiration as works of consummate beauty and of perfect architectural skill. In the preservation of these buildings, which are so many memorials of the glory and magnanimity of the Turkish sovereigns who spared them for the benefit of posterity, the governments and nations of Europe in friendship with the Sublime Porte are known to take interest regarding them as models in architecture, whence many of the fairest ornaments of the European capitals have been derived. . . . Their preservation through the various events of the war will greatly redound to your Excellency's fame, and I am well convinced that no one will rejoice at it more than the Gracious Monarch, whom I have the honour to serve as my sovereign and master. (Ilıcak 2019, 253, 254)

Equally concerned—not only about the monuments—were those fighting for the Greek cause, as they were well aware that the fate of the entire revolution would be decided here. Many sped to Athens, Greeks and Philhellenes, but the person on whom the Greeks pinned their hopes was Generalissimo Georgios Karaiskakis, "decidedly the best general that modern Greece has produced," in Cochrane's view (Cochrane 1837, 1:41), and "[t]he only and the last Chief of the Forces of Greece," according to Sourmelis (Sourmelis 1834, 212) (Figures 9 and 10). Although suffering from tuberculosis, Karaiskakis had proved his worth in difficult times (Tzakis 2009), leading "the largest and most regular irregular army known to the history of the Revolution" (Vakalopoulos 7:728). He initially gave priority to more general actions in central Greece, so as to take the pressure off Athens, because, as he pointed out, if this city falls, "the whole of Rumeli will be snuffed out like a candle forever" (Vakalopoulos 7:733). At the same time, within and around Athens, frays were an everyday occurrence, with a violence that often recalled previous atrocities. Little wonder that pursued Turks, in order to assuage their position, cried out that "they were not in Mesolonghi" (Vakalopoulos 7:676), meaning that they had played no part in the horrors committed there by their compatriots. Exactly as in the massacre of the

FIGURE 9   Georgios Margaritis, *Karaiskakis mounted, advances on the Acropolis,* 1844. Oil
on canvas. National Gallery-Al. Soutzos Museum, Athens.

Turks who had surrendered during the first siege of Athens, a leading role in
the hostilities was played by Kydonian and Chiot refugees who had experienced
the destruction of their homelands by Ottoman troops in 1821 and 1822,
respectively.

Karaiskakis with his prestige may have been the natural leader of the Greeks,
"but suffering and great misfortune was destined, anyway, to befall them," according to Sourmelis. "The Third Assembly of the Greeks in Troezen appointed
the Englishman Tzourtzin [Church] Commander-in-Chief of all Central
Greece" (Sourmelis 1834, 208, 209) and Lord Cochrane as head of the naval
forces. Modern British ships brought these eminent Britons to Athens, where
they oversaw operations, thus underscoring the special relationship that had
developed since 1823 between rebellious Greece and the paramount global
power of the age, Great Britain (Crawley 1930). Trained to fight head-on battles
of a regular army, these professional military men met with opposition from
the Greek freedom-fighters who had been trained in the tactics of guerrilla warfare, which they trusted implicitly since they had brought them no few victories.
In discussions about the plan of action, a few days before his death, Karais-

FIGURE 10   Johan Georg Christian Perlberg, *Georgios Karaiskakis at the Battle of Athens*, 1835. Oil on canvas. Thanassis and Marina Martinos Collection, Athens.

kakis found himself at loggerheads with Church and Cochrane. Nonetheless, he acquiesced, as these men had been picked to head the Greek armed forces. The divergence of views was clearly described by fellow fighter of the Greeks, Thomas Gordon, who said of Karaiskakis: "[He] was one of the most distinguished Armatolic captains, possessing great acuteness, and uncommon intrepidity. . . . He disliked Franks, looked with an evil eye upon Cochrane and Church, and yet avoided offence; giving them on the contrary, sound advice, which they had done well to listen to. . . . The worst consequence of his death was, that no one remained of sufficient weight to oppose Cochrane's fatal project" (Gordon 1832, 2:394).

The presence of Philhellene volunteers and British soldiers, a contingent of the regular army, as well as of many and motley Greek forces, did indeed harm, instead of benefit, the struggle for control of the Acropolis and the expulsion of the Turks from Athens. Infighting, rivalries, and egoisms; petty jealousies and misunderstandings between the chiefs of the many Greek corps that had come to assist; divergent opinions on strategy between the advocates of regular warfare and guerrilla warfare; deep sorrow at the unexpected loss of Karaiskakis in a minor skirmish on the eve of the major battle; mutual lack of awareness of the differences in mentality between western European and Greek fighters: all brought the strivings of the defenders of Athens to an inglorious end. Following the view of the European staff officers, the final battle was fought in the plain between the Athenian Acropolis and the sea, in places that favored the action of Kütahı's cavalry, which broke up the positions of the Greeks, who were ignorant of war in battle array and were in exposed positions. Kütahı, on the other hand, had his own problems to deal with: shortages of munitions, food, and water; difficulties in the payment of wild and restless soldiers; the attitude of the Albanian fighters as well as divisions and enmities within the Turko-Albanian ranks, with the Tosks being considered as amicably disposed toward the Greeks and, therefore, untrustworthy forces in the battles against them. Even so, as an experienced soldier, he moved calmly and methodically, exploited every weakness of the foe and deployed his troops in such a way that Favier from the Acropolis, watching with binoculars the disposition of the two sides, cried out on seeing the Greeks: "These good men will soon be destroyed" (Vakalopoulos 7:748).

And destroyed they were. On April 24, 1827, in the battle of Analatos at Phaliron, the Greek Revolution suffered its greatest defeat. Within an hour, one thousand freedom-fighters were killed and hundreds of others wounded. The Greeks' defeat was compounded by the fact that, in contrast to the norm until then, where a few Greeks confronted many more Turks, in the battle of Analatos the Greek side fielded its largest-ever force, and instead of winning, it lost. "Whoever heard of nine thousand Greeks, foot-soldiers and horsemen, being taken captive by five hundred Turks?" exclaimed Ioannis Makrygiannis, cursing Cochrane, unable to believe the outcome of the battle in which he himself took part, fighting at critical points on the front line (Makrygiannis 1907, 293).

After the battle, Kütahı executed hundreds of captives and demanded the surrender of those beleaguered on the Acropolis. At first, they refused to comply, but finally surrendered one month later, on May 25, 1827. In accordance with the terms of the treaty of surrender, the defenders of the Acropolis were marched to the sea to board the waiting ships. On their way, they passed amid the corpses of Greeks and Philhellenes, with crows still circling overhead. The Acropolis was to remain under Ottoman control until March 1833—the last of all the fortresses the Turks would surrender, even after the arrival of Othon and the regency in the country. When the Greeks came back, they found the ground still strewn with the skeletons of those who had fought and lost in the battle at Phaliron.

The fall of Athens in May 1827 brought the Greek Revolution to the edge of the precipice. Although the Greeks held out, continuing to clash with the Turks until September 1829, in October 1827, Britain, France, and Russia vanquished the Ottoman navy in the bay of Navarino, and in 1828 they dispatched an expeditionary force of fifteen thousand men to the Peloponnese, under the command of the French general Maison. In 1830, these three great powers cosigned the independence of Greece, the first country in the Balkans to become independent in the nineteenth century, the century of nationalism and of the peoples' national struggles (Gardika 2008). Athens soon after became the capital of this land—the "holy place" of Greeks and Europeans, according to Mehmed Reşid Pasha.

Maria D. Efthymiou

Translated from the Greek by Alexandra Douma

References

Cochrane, George. 1832. *Wanderings in Greece.* London.

Crawley, Charles William. 1930. *The Question of Greek Independence: A Study of British Policy in the Near East, 1821–1833.* Cambridge.

Dakin, Douglas. 1955. *British and American Philhellenes during the War of Greek Independence, 1821–1833.* Thessaloniki.

Gardika, Katerina. 2008. "Η Ελλάδα και το Ανατολικό Ζήτημα (1821–1923)" [Greece and the Eastern Question, 1821–1923]. In *Η συγκρότηση του ελληνικού κράτους. Διεθνές πλαίσιο, εξουσία και πολιτική τον 19ο αιώνα* [The formation of the Greek state: International framework, power, and politics of the nineteenth century], edited by Katerina Gardika, Niki Maroniti, Christos Lyrintzis, Christos Loukos, and Vangelis Kechriotis, 119–145. Athens.

Gordon, Thomas 1832. *History of the Greek Revolution.* 2 vols. Edinburgh.

Ilıcak, Sücrü. 2019. "Revolutionary Athens through Ottoman Eyes (1821–1828): New Evidence from the Ottoman State Archives." In *Ottoman Athens,* edited by Constantinos Thanasakis and Maria Georgopoulou, 243–259. Athens.

Karidis, Dimitris. 2014. *Athens from 1456 to 1920: The Town under Ottoman Rule and the 19th-Century Capital City.* Oxford.

Makrygiannis, Ioannis. 1907. *Αρχείον. Απομνημονεύματα του στρατηγού Ιωάννου Μακρυγιάννη* [Archive: Memoirs of General Ioannis Makrygiannis]. Edited by Ioannis Vlachogiannis. Athens.

Sourmelis, Dionysios. 1834. *Ιστορία των Αθηνών κατά τον υπέρ ελευθερίας αγώνα αρχομένη από της Επαναστάσεως μέχρι της αποκαταστάσεως των πραγμάτων. Διηρημένη εις τρία βιβλία* [History of Athens during the struggle for freedom starting from the revolution until the restoration of things: Divided in three books]. Aigina.

Tzakis, Dionysis. 2009. *Γεώργιος Καραϊσκάκης* [Georgios Karaiskakis] (Athens).

Tzakis, Dionysis. 2015. "Η επίδραση του μύθου της Αθήνας στους στρατιωτικούς προσανατολισμούς της Ελληνικής Επανάστασης" [The influence of the myth of Athens on the military orientations of the Greek Revolution]. In *Μυθοπλασίες. Χρήση και πρόσληψη των αρχαίων μύθων από την αρχαιότητα μέχρι σήμερα* [Fictions: The use and perception of ancient myths from antiquity to the present], edited by Antonis Petridis and Stephanos Efthymiadis, 339–354. Athens.

Vakalopoulos. Vols. 5–7.

Chios

The 1821 revolution on Chios became synonymous with the destruction of a flourishing island in the eastern Aegean. The widespread massacres and captivity of its Christian population by the Ottoman overlords shocked European societies of the time and inspired Eugène Delacroix, who depicted these events in his famous painting entitled *The Massacre of Chios*.

Chios passed into the possession of the Ottoman Empire in 1566 and was incorporated into its administrative system. Its unique product, mastic, and its inhabitants' involvement with trade created favorable conditions for economic growth and prosperity, so that on the eve of the Greek War of Independence Chios was characterized as "blissful isle and wealthiest of all in the Greek sea" (Stamatiadis 1881, 176). Thanks to its geographical location and the special importance of its mastic, Chios enjoyed privileged treatment after the Ottoman conquest and the island's inclusion in the Ottoman system of governance, which permitted a form of self-government. The development of self-government by a council of "aldermen" (*dimogerontia*) gave the local primates status and power. In fact, the people did not experience Ottoman repression as harshly as they did the highhandedness of the local primates, since on Chios the *dimogerontia* was controlled by an economic and social elite. Most primates were descendants of Genoese and Venetian families involved in business and trade. Chiot business activities in the eighteenth and early nineteenth centuries had spread to major urban centers of the empire, particularly Smyrna and Constantinople, but also to great European cities. These activities offered many Chiots the possibility and the opportunities to engage with learning and letters. A characteristic example was Adamantios Korais (Coray), who was born in Smyrna of a Chiot father. Initially, he was involved with trade in Amsterdam but ended up in France, where he studied medicine and rose to prominence as a leading representative of the Greek Enlightenment, publishing exemplary studies on ancient Greek literature.

By the early nineteenth century, Chios was the most economically and culturally advanced island in the eastern Aegean. It was administered by the Turkish district governor (*müsellim*) and judge (*kadı*), who were appointed by the sultan. Estimates of the island's population vary. According to the census carried out on the initiative of Metropolitan Plato, in 1820, shortly before the revolution broke out, 80,000 people were living on the island. The population of the city of Chios numbered about 24,000 and of the countryside 55,000 inhabitants. The majority were Orthodox Christians but there were also about 1,500–2,000 Roman Catholics, 2,500–3,000 Muslims, and a few Jews. Other sources speak of a population of 110,000–120,000 inhabitants. The island's capital had a strong fortress and installations protecting its harbor, schools, churches—Orthodox and Catholic—mosques for the Muslims, a library, a printing press, hospitals, and other social welfare foundations. Its aspect was that of a European city, with much hustle and bustle, due to its proximity to Smyrna. There was, of course, an Ottoman administration, but those who essentially governed the island were the five *dimogerontes* (aldermen), three Orthodox Christians and two Catholics. Economic, political, and cultural circumstances in Chios did not favor social changes, much less revolutionary movements that would overturn the contentment of the upper class and destroy its wealth. This class, from which the *dimogerontes* came, had bourgeois traits, while election to their office was the prerogative of a very limited electoral body. The bourgeoisie of Chios, in contrast to the burghers of other Greek regions, did not adopt changes that might pose a threat to their interests.

The city's *dimogerontia* influenced also the primates of the villages, while the villagers, "humble and harmless," in the words of academician Michail Sakellariou (2014), "were used to buckling under in fear of the primates and to trembling at the Turks." Nevertheless, many young men, intellectuals, and the lower strata of the population were ablaze with the idea of freedom. This general picture meant that at the beginning of the Greek Revolution Chios adopted a different stance from other islands. There were neither the preconditions nor the local powers, specific groups or leaders, that would have brought about Chios's participation in the revolution. Nor had any preparatory processes been set in motion to organize the populace in the common national idea of casting off the Turkish yoke. There was no prerevolutionary foment as in other regions. Although Enlightenment ideas had spread, due to the School of Chios, there was no obvious initiation into the Philiki Etaireia of Chiots living on the island. Those Chiots animated by ideas of liberty were living outside the island. Consequently, it was deemed that Chios's participation in the revolution of 1821 must be achieved through outside intervention and assistance, so as to incite the inhabitants to rebellion against the Turks. There were, however, objective difficulties to be faced for revolutionary plans to succeed. The strong military presence of the Ottomans in the fortress of Chios, the determination of the empire to defend its interests in an area of strategic importance, and the reluctance of the primates to play an active part in revolutionary movements were some visible difficulties that were disincentives to the idea of revolt. Nonetheless, there was some unrest among the popular classes, but it lacked even elementary organization.

The Greeks tried twice to include Chios among the regions in revolt, in 1821 and 1822. In both cases they failed. The second attempt, indeed, had tragic results for the island and is known as the destruction or the massacre of Chios. During the Greek War of Independence one more attempt was made to liberate the island, in 1827, but this too failed.

News of the revolution did not arouse all the island's inhabitants, who preferred to keep the status quo, out of either fear or self-interest. Participation in the revolution came from outside. In April 1821, a Greek fleet made up of Ydriot, Spetsiot, and Psariot ships, under the command of Iakovos Tombazis, skirted the coast of Chios and called upon the inhabitants, with a proclamation, to take part in the revolution. The Ydriots' endeavor was underpinned on the one hand by the encouragement of Chiots resident on Ydra, among them Neophytos Vamvas, and on the other by the Ydriots' conviction that the inclusion of affluent Chios in the insurgent regions would have positive economic and geostrategic results for the War of Independence. The Chiots refused to participate in any way. On the appearance of the Greek fleet, the peasants fled to the mountains for protection, as all islanders had usually done from the time of piracy in the Aegean, while the primates asked Tombazis to leave the area, arguing that he would provoke the wrath as well as the violent reaction of the Turks. Even though Tombazis sailed away, the Ottoman administration of Chios began to take preemptive measures; they demanded guarantees from the primates and strengthened the defenses of the fortress, levying compulsory labor on the population, as well as terrorizing it.

In the second case, the revolution on Chios is linked with the neighboring island of Samos, where not only had the revolution prevailed but it also had successfully repelled the efforts of the mighty Ottoman navy to quash it in July 1821. But Samos did not have a strong Ottoman presence and was fortunate in having many initiates of the Philiki Etaireia, among them the chiefs of its armed bands, its religious leader Archbishop Kyrillos, and its governor Georgios Logothetis Lykourgos, who had organized the islanders politically and militarily in record time. The revolution on Chios was fomented with the intervention of Samiots, who were pressed for this purpose by Chiots and especially by Ioannis Rallis and Chadji Antonios Bournias, a former officer in Napoleon's army. The Samiots' campaign, with its four battalions of a thousand men each, headed by the chiefs of the battalions and its commander Logothetis Lykourgos, but also with Antonios Bournias and his followers, was launched on March 9/21, 1822. It was preceded by exhortations and assurances by fervent Chiots resident in Samos for mass popular participation in the struggle, as well as by reconnaissance visits to the area and sounding out of its inhabitants and some primates, all of which boosted the expectations of a successful operation. It should be noted that the export of the revolution to Chios did not have the explicit approval of the central authorities of the revolution, the executive or the legislative, nor was there any request beforehand for help from the fleet to support operations on land from the sea. Although the Samiot leadership was preparing an expedition against Nea Ephesos aimed at capturing the fortress there, so as to monitor the sea channel between Samos and Asia Minor, it took the decision, in collaboration with the Chiot revolutionaries, to turn the operation's sights to the liberation of Chios. This decision was taken in the light of information about the ever-increasing oppression of the Chiot people, assurances that there would be a great participation of Chiots in the whole enterprise, and that the means, the supplying, and the equipping of the mission had been secured.

The landing on Chios of the expeditionary corps of Samiots under Logothetis Lykourgos and of Chiots under Bournias was successful. At first, the forces easily gained the upper hand in skirmishes with the Turks. They captured the city of Chios and beleaguered the fortress, which was very well fortified and reinforced to withstand a protracted siege. Both the governor, Vahid Pasha, and the Sublime Porte had received timely intelligence of the planned campaign. The first stocked the fortress with supplies of foodstuffs and ammunition, and warned his government about developments, while he imprisoned a large number of primates and the Metropolitan. The sultanic government arrested eminent Chiots in Constantinople, asked for other primates from the island to be sent to it as hostages, while it dispatched post haste the navy and army, intent on putting down the "rebellion" and punishing the inhabitants as an example to all.

For the Samiot and Chiot besiegers of the fortress of Chios, things did not go according to expectations. Lykourgos replaced the *dimogerontia* with ephors, in an effort to apply a system of administration similar to that of Samos, but this proved ineffective for Chios. The insurgent peasants who had flocked to the city lacked weaponry and the necessary discipline, while between the leaders of Chiots and Samiots there was a divergence of views and actions, immediately after the first minor military successes. The lack of a supply chain for the expeditionary corps and the unwillingness of the affluent Chiots to cover its salaries led to a breakdown in discipline with serious negative consequences for the siege of the fortress and the confrontation of enemy attacks. When the Turkish navy under Nuayih Zaade Ali Pasha, also known as Karali, sailed into Chios on March 30 / April 11, 1822, it easily crushed any resistance from the rebels with its artillery and its superior land forces. The expeditionary corps of Samiots and Chiots, despite their brave struggle, was forced to retreat, while the Ottoman forces of both the fleet and the fortress, as well as the irregulars who were attacking from the nearby Asia Minor coast, captured the city and set about an unprecedented massacre of the Greek population of Chios, along with widespread plundering and taking of captives. The biggest mass slaying of Chiots took place in the St. Minas monastery on April 2 / 14, 1822. Metropolitan Plato, the primates who were being held hostage in the fortress, and thousands of civilians all over the island met a tragic death by mass slaughter. In Constantinople, too, distinguished Chiots were executed because of the revolution on their native island. The number of people sold into slavery and of those massacred have not been established precisely. However, it is estimated that two-thirds of the population of Chios were exterminated. If those who escaped as refugees to other islands are added to this number, we realize that Chios was almost deserted.

Those armed Chiots under Bournias who survived sought refuge initially on Psara. The Samiots too, retreating toward the northwest coast of Chios, were rescued on Psara and from there returned home. The looting and killing on Chios continued until early June 1822. The destruction of Chios did not pass without retaliation on behalf of the warring Greeks. On June 6, 1822, Constantinos Kanaris and Andreas Pipinos dealt a severe blow to the Ottoman navy with their fireships, within the harbor of Chios. The Ottoman flagship was blown up by Kanaris's fireship, while Admiral-in-Chief Kara Ali and many officers and crew were killed. The assaults by fireships and the consequent destruction forced the Ottoman navy to cease action and return to Constantinople.

The massacre of Chios evoked emotion throughout Europe and had a negative effect on relations between the legislative authority and the executive in Greece. Almost immediately, those responsible for the tragedy were sought out. Logothetis Lykourgos was held responsible and very serious accusations were made against him. Even though he was acquitted in the end and the charges against him were dropped, some nineteenth-century historians—mainly Chiots—considered that the Samiots were largely responsible for the tragedy of Chios. Lykourgos, however, had undertaken a dangerous operation with a sense of responsibility, patriotism and self-sacrifice. By campaigning on Chios with all his military forces he left Samos undefended and vulnerable to possible attack. His expedition was part of a strategy for wider participation of the islands in the War of Independence, control of fortresses in the eastern Aegean, and protection of the Christian populations of the islands and Asia Minor.

Notwithstanding its catastrophic outcome and horrendous death toll, the uprising on Chios contributed to consolidating the war in the Peloponnese, as it confined the action of the Ottoman navy to the eastern Aegean. The massacre of Chios moved hearts, inspired European artists, and strengthened the philhellenic movement supporting the Greeks' struggle for freedom. Apart from Delacroix, Victor Hugo too was moved by the massacre, composing the poem "L'enfant" (1828): "Les turcs ont passé là. Tout est ruine et deuil. . . . Tout est désert." George Finlay noted in his *History of the Greek Revolution* that "No calamity during the Greek Revolution awakened the sympathy of the civilised world more deservedly than the devastation of Chios" (Finlay 1861, 1:306).

A third attempt to liberate Chios was made between October 1827 and March 1828. The campaign was funded by the Committee of Chiots of Syros, with the approval of the alternate government commission and aimed at including Chios in the Greek state. Colonel Charles Fabvier was appointed head of the operation. However, this campaign too came to naught. The Greek forces retreated, their mission unfulfilled. Chios remained under Ottoman sovereignty throughout the nineteenth century and until 1912, when it was finally liberated during the Balkan wars.

Christos Landros

Translated from the Greek by Alexandra Douma

References

Argentis, Philip Pandely, ed., 1932. *The Massacres of Chios*. Described in contemporary Diplomatic Reports. London.

Argentis, Philip Pandely, ed., 1933. *The Expedition of Colonel Fabvier to Chios*. Described in contemporary Diplomatic Reports. London.

Argentis, Philip Pandely. 1940. *Bibliography of Chios*, Preface by Professsor J. L. Myres. Oxford.

Argentis, Philip Pandely. 1941. *Chius Vincta or the Occupation of Chios by the Turks (1566) and Their Administration of the Island (1566–1912)*. Cambridge.

Belsis, Constantinos. 2014. Από την οθωμανική νομιμότητα στο εθνικό κράτος. Το «άτομο» στο επίκεντρο της Ιστορίας. Λυκούργος Λογοθέτης (1772–1850) Πολιτική βιογραφία [From Ottoman legality to the nation state. The "individual" at the center of history: Lykourgos Logothetis (1772–1850), political biography]. Athens.

Finlay, George. 1861. *History of the Greek Revolution*. 2 volumes. Edinburgh and London.

Giatrakou, Maria "Αναλυτική βιβλιογραφία περί της Επαναστάσεως και καταστροφής της Χίου. Ειδήσεις περί της Επαναστάσεως της Χίου (1822)" [Analytical bibliography on the Revolution and destruction of Chios. News about the Revolution of Chios (1822)], *DIEEE* 22 (1979) 166–180.

Gordon, Thomas. 2015. *Ιστορία της ελληνικής επαναστάσεως* [History of the Greek Revolution]. Translated by Alexandros Papadiamantis. Athens.

Jourdain, Jean Philippe Paul. 1828. *Mémoires historiques et militaires sur les événements de la Grèce: depuis 1822, jusqu'au combat de Navarin.* Paris.

Kastanis, Christophoros P. 1851. *The Greek Exile, or a Narrative of the Captivity and Escape of Christophorus Plato Castanis, During the Massacre on the Island of Scio, by the Turks, Together with Various Adventures in Greece and America.* Philadelphia.

Kokkinos, Dionysios A. 1967. *Ιστορία της ελληνικής επαναστάσεως* [History of the Greek Revolution], Vol. I (Athens).

Makridakis, Giannis, ed. 2005. *Η Χίος κατά την ελληνική Επανάσταση και τη σφαγή: Μαρτυρίες και ιστορικά κείμενα* [Chios during the Greek Revolution and the massacre: Testimonies and historical texts]. Chios.

Moschopoulos, Nikiphoros. 2003. *Ιστορία της Ελληνικής Επαναστάσεως (Τι έγραψαν οι Τούρκοι ιστοριογράφοι εν αντιπαραβολή και προς τους Έλληνας ιστορικούς* [History of the Greek Revolution: What the Turkish historiographers wrote in comparison also to the Greek historians]. Athens.

Perris, Nikos Z. 1974. *Η Χίος στην Εθνεγερσία* [Chios in the national uprising]. Chios.

Sakellariou, Michail V. 2014. *Ένας συνταγματικός δημοκράτης ηγέτης κατά την επανάσταση του '21. Ο Γ. Λογοθέτης Λυκούργος της Σάμου (1772–1850)* [A constitutional democratic leader during the Revolution of '21. G. Logothetis Lykourgos of Samos (1772–1850)]. Iraklio.

Sphyroeras, Vasilis. 1975. "Η Επανάσταση κατά το 1822" [The Greek Revolution during 1822]. *IEE,* 12: 244–249.

Stamatiadis, Epameinondas. 1881. *Σαμιακά ήτοι ιστορία της νήσου Σάμου από των παναρχαίων χρόνων μέχρι των καθ' ημάς* [Samiaka: The history of the island of Samos from most ancient times to our days]. Samos.

Trikoupis, Spyridon. 2007. *Ιστορία της Ελληνικής Επαναστάσεως* [History of the Greek Revolution]. Edited by Vasilis Kremmydas. Athens.

Vahid Pasha. 1861. *Απομνημονεύματα του Βαχίτ πασά πρέσβεως εν Παρισίοις τω 1802, Ρεΐζ εφέντη τω 1808 και Τοποτηρητού της Χίου τω 1822, εξ ανεκδότου Τουρκικού ιδιοχειρογράφου ελευθέρως μεταφρασθέντα και σημειώσεσι συνοδευθέντα υπό Δ. Ε. Δ* [Memoirs of Vahid Pasha ambassador in Paris in 1802, Reiz effendi in 1808 and Locum tenens of Chios in 1822, from an unpublished Turkish manuscript in his hand freely translated and accompanied by notes by D. E. D.]. Ermoupolis.

Viou, Stylianos G. 1987. *Η σφαγή της Χίου εις το στόμα του χιακού λαού* [The massacre of Chios in the mouth of the Chian people]. Chios.

Vlastos, Alexandros M. 1840. *Χιακά ήτοι Ιστορία της νήσου Χίου από των αρχαιοτάτων χρόνων μέχρι της εν έτει 1822 γενομένης καταστροφής αυτής παρά των Τούρκων* [Chiaka that is the History of the island of Chios from most ancient times until its destruction by the Turks in the year 1822]. Ermoupolis.

Constantinople and Thrace

The French Revolution had a substantial impact on the Ottoman Empire's Greek Orthodox population, who were beginning to envisage the foundations of their own liberation. The victorious campaigns of Napoleon and the occupation of the Ionian Islands by the French had already created certain expectations.

The Philiki Etaireia (Society of Friends) founded in Odessa in 1814 by Athanasios Tsakalov, Nikolaos Skoufas, and Emmanouil Xanthos, aimed at organizing a nationwide revolt for the redemption of the *Genos* from Ottoman rule. Apart from the General Plan (Σχέδιον Γενικόν), they prepared another one entitled "Specific Plan about Constantinople" (Μερικόν περί Κωνσταντινουπόλεως Σχέδιον) or Grand Plan (Μέγα Σχέδιον), which was designed by a "patriot," most probably Dionysios Evmorfopoulos. According to this plan, with the outbreak of the revolution, a large number of armed Greeks in Constantinople would instigate a widespread upheaval, set fire to the Ottoman fleet within the Constantinople shipyard, and assassinate the sultan during his approach to the burning naval station. Arson fires in the city would be multiple and parallel, aiming at its seizure. The burden of the project would fall on the Greek sailors of the Ottoman fleet and, in particular, the captain of the Ottoman flagship Constantis Gioustos from Ydra (Philimon 1859, 1:59–72).

The multiple symptoms of decline characterizing the formerly powerful Ottoman Empire created optimism and self-confidence.

After May 1818, the Philiki Etaireia moved its seat to Constantinople and initiated its first members in the capital of the empire. Within a few months, the Etaireia rapidly grew roots at the center of the empire. We know that already since 1818 the fixed meeting places of the *Philikoi* were Xanthos's residence and the Ainian residence at Therapeia, while another reference point became the "office"—rest house—of Panagiotis Sekeris at Pera. A focal point of the activities of the Philiki Etaireia was also the mansion of the Levidis family at Tatavla. In addition, we have evidence which allows us to identify other—even sheltered—outdoor locations of fixed meetings on the insular outskirts, such as for example the island of Chalki in the Princes Islands. Just like Odessa, Constantinople offered a double opportunity to the Philiki Etaireia, which approached both its permanent residents and the several travelers passing through the city. Constantinople thus became a major busy crossroads for the Etaireia.

Following Ypsilantis's appointment as general commissioner of the authority on June 15, 1820, the enthusiasm of the Constantinopolitan Greeks for the expected liberation of the *Genos* reached its climax. The fact of the declaration of the revolution in Moldavia and Wallachia became known to the Sublime Porte on March 1, when Ypsilantis's revolutionary proclamation was delivered to the Ottoman government.

Meanwhile, Ottoman officials became aware of the existence of the Philiki Etaireia as a secret organization aiming at the breakup of their empire. When, together with the news of the massacres of Turks in Moldavia and Wallachia, the authorities found out that some *Philikoi* had escaped, they decided to take harsh measures, turning the *Rûm* community of Constantinople into hostages. Phanariot families settled on the European coast of the Bosporus were ordered to immediately move to the Phanar to prevent their escape. Massacres of Greeks who had relatives in Moldavia and Wallachia began taking place, the metropolitan of Ephesus, Dionysios Kalliarchis, who resided in Constantinople, was arrested, while Greeks who were not residents of Constantinople were ordered to leave the city.

Terrorism against the Greek element was manifested as soon as the first news of the revolution reached Constantinople. Attacks on houses and shops, insults, beatings, stabbings, and rapes were on the daily agenda, obviously instigated by the central authorities. A meeting of local Greek notables and the synod was convened at the patriarchate. At that meeting it was decided to submit a petition to the Sublime Porte, stating that all the notables of the *Genos* would vouch for each other regarding their stay in Constantinople as loyal subjects of the sultan. It was also agreed to state in the petition that the *Genos* had no knowledge of the existence of a revolutionary society, that they condemned the movement of Ypsilantis and that they were ready to join the Reigning Monarchy in suppressing such disastrous movements. The petition was written in Turkish by Skarlatos Kallimachis and was signed by the forty-nine clerics and laymen who took part in the meeting. On Sunday March 13 the petition was presented to the grand vizier by the patriarch himself, who was accompanied by three archbishops.

For his part, Patriarch Grigorios V did not remain passive. As soon as he learned about the rumors regarding a possible general slaughter, together with the patriarch of Jerusalem, who was at that time in Constantinople, as well as three political officials, he visited the Seyhulislam at his residence and assured him that he was not involved in the revolution and appealed for the life of the Greeks in Constantinople. The Seyhulislam Çerkez Halil Efendi followed a delaying tactic for some time and in the end did not issue a *fetwa* condemning the Greeks. He paid this courageous and honest attitude with his life.

Following the election of a new Seyhulislam, a *firman* offering an amnesty was issued with the precondition that the Greeks would reject any revolutionary idea and remain under the status of *rayah*. On March 20 the Porte submitted to the dragoman Constantinos Mourouzis the amnesty ordinance to translate it. At the same time, an imperial decree was issued addressing the *Genos* and the patriarch, in which objections, demands, and threats were formulated (Philimon 1859, 2:103–118).

Under the pressure of this command, an extraordinary new meeting between clerics and lay members was convened with the participation of the patriarchs of Constantinople and Jerusalem, twenty-one prelates, and many laymen. Among those who took part was the former prince of Wallachia Skarlatos Kallimachis, the grand dragoman of the Porte Constantinos Mourouzis, and the dragoman of the Ottoman fleet Nikolaos Mourouzis. The delegates faced the dilemma of either succumbing to extortion or rejecting the sultan's commands and placing the entire Orthodox community of the city in danger of general slaughter.

Thus, it was decided that the laymen would submit a petition renouncing the revolution and a declaration of submission of all the provinces, and the clerics would compose an act of excommunication. On Wednesday March 23 the two patriarchs and twenty-one prelates signed an act excommunicating the revolution, which was addressed to all the prelates and the clergy (Papadopoulos and Angelopoulos 1865, 1:225–241).

The excommunication and the declaration of the complete submission of the Orthodox Greeks of Constantinople temporarily rescued them from the danger of a general slaughter, but when the news of the uprising of the Morea arrived, the sultan proceeded with new measures. Thus, on April 4 the Great Dragoman Constantinos Mourouzis was executed before Sultan Mahmoud, while on the same day many Greeks, especially from the upper class, were killed in Constantinople including members of the prominent families of Chantzeris, Mavrokordatos, Skanavis, and Negris, as well as a large number of Peloponnesians, resident in the city.

Two days earlier, a Turkish mob had plundered and burned the Holy Monastery of Zoodochos Pigi at Baloukli outside the walls. The ecumenical patriarch

Grigorios V was led to the gallows on Easter Sunday, April 10, 1821, in front of the central gate of the patriarchate. The execution was carried out by irregular janissaries, but the execution order posted proves that it was held following a personal order from the sultan. On May 6 Nikolaos Mourouzis, the dragoman of the fleet was executed. Then, the senior metropolitans Dionysios of Ephesus and Evgenios of Anchialos, who had been arrested as hostages in Balık Pazarı, the central market of Pera, and Galata, respectively, were hanged, while Athanasios of Nikomedia died from the hardships of his imprisonment and torture.

The patriarch's martyrdom at the outbreak of the Greek revolution, despite his active opposition to secular values and to any form of liberation initiatives throughout his tenure of the patriarchal throne, transformed him immediately into an icon of Greek nationalism. Throughout the period of the liberation struggle in the 1820s, his name became a symbol and a rallying cry for the fighters of Greek freedom and later, in the independent Greek state, he was ceremoniously incorporated among the protagonists of the liberation of Greece. In the 1870s, his statue was erected outside the University of Athens next to that of Rhigas Velestinlis, whose political ideas he had condemned in 1798 as "full of rottenness."

On the centennial of his martyrdom, in 1921, Patriarch Grigorios V was canonized by the synod of the autocephalous Church of Greece, an initiative regarded with skepticism by ecclesiastical authorities in Constantinople at the time, although subsequently the patriarch as a "hieromartyr" was included in the Great Church's calendar of saints. It is interesting to note that whereas for the Church of Greece Grigorios V is an "ethnomartyr," the Church of Constantinople prefers to refer to him as an "hieromartyr," recalling and connecting him to the tradition of the early church and associating him with such great and popular early saintly bishops like Charalambos and Eleftherios martyred by the Romans.

The story of Patriarch Grigorios V is extremely important and also revealing for understanding the whole nexus between Orthodoxy and nationalism. As should become clear from the brief survey of the patriarch's pastoral activity and ecclesiastical policies above, he remained throughout, with impressive consistency, dedicated to the spiritual, canonical, and pastoral traditions of Orthodoxy, which ipso facto turned him into an opponent of the multiple expressions of secularism, including its foremost political manifestation, nationalism. This in fact was an authentic expression of the Orthodox position, which Grigorios incarnated with a deep sense of responsibility with his life and death. His martyrdom, nevertheless, delivered him to the ideology of Greek nationalism and to the historiography that embodied this ideology, for which Grigorios's antinationalist policies and his skepticism about plans for the liberation of Greece remained a source of profound embarrassment. Throughout the nineteenth and repeatedly during the twentieth century, there have been historiographical attempts to "exonerate" the patriarch from the charge of "collaborationism" with the "foreign and infidel tyrants" of the Greek nation leveled against him by equally ideologically motivated arguments of historians and other commentators with a leftist or "progressive" orientation. Of course, both positions are simply symptomatic of anachronistic thinking, ideological prejudice, and an inability to recover and judge on its own terms, taking into account its religious premises, the ways the Orthodox Church with the ecumenical patriarchate at its head strove against enormous odds to discharge its pastoral duties and to preserve the Orthodox faith within the institutional framework set by the Ottoman state (Kitromilides 2019, 54–56).

The ecumenical patriarch Grigorios V had been aware of the activities of the Philiki Etaireia due to its considerable expansion in Constantinople. Besides, he had been informed originally by the Macedonian chieftain and member of the society Giannis Pharmakis, who had visited him during his exile at Mount Athos in 1818. Among the actions of the Patriarch in favor of the national idea, one should mention the letter of recommendation to the proponent and apostle of the Philiki Etaireia Dimitrios Themelis, which gave him permission to travel and disseminate the principles of the society, and his letter of July 30, 1819, to Petrobey Mavromichalis and the other captains for the establishment of a "common school." One should also appreciate the fact that Georgios Afthonidis, Grigorios's personal secretary and chief secretary of the Holy Synod, was a *Philikos*. Nonetheless, the probative value of these events is not self-evident.

On April 19, mass hangings of laymen took place. On June 3 several bishops were hanged (Ioannikios of Tirnovo on the west coast of the Bosporus, Dorotheos of Adrianople at Mega Revma, Joseph of Thessaloniki at Nichori, Grigorios of Derkoi at Therapia), while Alexandros Soutsos and Skarlatos Kallimachis, who had been successively appointed princes of Wallachia after the eruption of the revolution, were exiled to Asia Minor. Following the news, true or manufactured, arriving from the Morea, a situation of terrorism against the *Rûm* community was created in Constantinople. The victims of that period in the Ottoman capital were estimated at approximately ten thousand (Vakalopoulos 5:494–515).

The tragic events in Constantinople provoked the indignation of fellow Christian Orthodox Russia. Following Capodistrias's intervention, which highlighted the common approach with France regarding the region, Ambassador Stroganov was ordered to deliver an ultimatum to the Sublime Porte. The tsar invoked the right to the protection of the Orthodox subjects of the sultan on the basis of the Treaty of Küçük Kaynarca of 1774 and the treaties of Jassy in 1792 and of Bucharest in 1812 and asked the Sublime Porte to fulfill the following conditions:

1. The Ottoman Empire should undertake to rebuild or repair the churches destroyed by the mob.
2. The Sultan ought to secure the serious protection of the Orthodox Christian Church.
3. The Ottoman government should distinguish between "guilty" and "innocent" Christians, and not harm those who would confirm their submission within a certain timeframe.
4. The Danubian Principalities should return to their previous regime. The Ottoman army that had invaded would have to retreat, according to the privileges established in favor of Russia, under earlier treaties.

Grigorios V has been severely criticized by many historians for his excommunication and the consequences this could have had—but did not—for the outcome of the revolution. If one does not examine the facts in retrospect with a cold-hearted logic, but takes into account that the protagonists of that period experienced an ambiance of terrorism, it will become clear that the patriarch and the leadership of the Orthodox community in Constantinople had to deal with an unrelenting blackmail. The lives of hundreds of thousands of Greek civilians were at imminent risk. The act of excommunication should be judged in this light. The various allegations that the patriarch disapproved of the revolution and reacted accordingly remain unproven, although it is very likely that Grigorios adopted a different approach. The patriarch, just like Capodistrias, believed that the era was not the most appropriate for the attempted movement. He was afraid that the revolution might jeopardize the very survival of the Christian population.

However, the patriarch did not remain inactive throughout the tragic days of March and April. He repeatedly visited the Ottoman authorities, presided over meetings, and seems to have tried, as far as possible, to reduce the impact of the excommunication. With his martyrdom he became a symbol of the nation's uprising, and thus offered the ultimate sacrifice for the revolution.

Throughout the period from the outbreak of the revolution to the formal acceptance by the Sublime Porte of the three London Protocols (January 22 / February 3, 1830) on April 12, 1830, the Greeks of Constantinople were exposed to the atrocities of the mob and the revenge of the sultan through mob action, conditioned by the development of military and diplomatic events. The situation, though not aggravated to the extent of the threatened massacres at the beginning of the revolution, continued to be highly oppressive for the *Rûm* community. The Greeks of the Ottoman Empire began to be encouraged after the naval battle of Navarino in 1827 and Russia's intervention in 1829, when they finally realized that the course of events toward freedom was irreversible.

Eastern and Northern Thrace

The proximity of Thrace to the Danubian Principalities and Russia, as well as the extensive Thracian coast of the Black Sea, had established eastern and northern Thrace as a major blood donor for the struggle for freedom. The fourth initiator of the Philiki Etaireia was Antonios Komizopoulos from Philippoupolis. A large section of the Odessa Greeks was of Thracian origin, such as Grigorios Maraslis from Philippoupolis and Kyriakos Koumbaris from Mesimvria. The seaside cities on today's Bulgarian littoral—Mesimvria, Anchialos, Sozopol, and Varna—contributed significantly to the Philiki Etaireia. One of the most important branches of the society was that of Adrianople.

A revolutionary mobilization was observed throughout the Thracian area in the districts of Philippoupolis, Adrianople, Varna, Anchialos, Sozopol, Mesimvria, Makri, and Kesani, as well as in the Greek villages of Saros bay (an inlet of the northern Aegean Sea). On April 17, 1821, Sozopol rebelled. Metropolitan Paisios Prikaios blessed the rebels at the church of Agios Zosimos. The Greek revolutionaries cooperating with armed Bulgarian groups clashed with the Ottomans. The decisive battle took place near Ropotamos, between Agathoupolis and Sozopol. The numerically superior forces of the Ottomans defeated the disorganized rebels. On April 25 Sozopol was captured by the Ottoman army. The Greek notables together with the metropolitan were hanged in the central square.

In mid-April the Adrianopolitan ex-patriarch Kyrillos VI (1813–1818) as well as twenty-six Greek notables were beheaded in Adrianople. Massacres took place even in small villages in eastern Thrace. In early May 1821 there was a great revolutionary movement at Ainos. The Ainites captured the fortress and arrested the Ottoman garrison. Ainos's contribution to the naval struggle was valuable since its power in 1821 amounted to three hundred ships. Ainitian ships supported the Macedonian rebels in Chalkidiki and Mount Olympus, blocking Ottoman naval forces off the coast of Macedonia. After Ainos was recaptured by the Ottomans, many residents fled to revolutionary Greece.

Young men from Mesimvria and other regions of Thrace had volunteered in the "Sacred Battalion" (Ιερός Λόχος) of Alexandros Ypsilantis. They participated in the revolutionary events in the Danubian Principalities and fought at the battle of Dragatsani. One of the survivors was the national benefactor Constantinos Xenokratis from Samakovo of eastern Thrace. The Adrianopolitan Georgios

Papas, who was wounded and survived, created later an expeditionary corps and led it to southern Greece, where it participated in numerous battles. Other fighters from the Sacred Battalion fled through Trieste to Austria (Vakalopoulos 5:515–544).

Stavros Th. Anestidis

References

Angelopoulos, Georgios I., ed. 1863. Συλλογή εκ των γραφέντων και παραδοθέντων περί του Οικουμενικού Πατριάρχου Γρηγορίου Ε΄ [Collection of texts written and transmitted on Grigorios V, ecumenical patriarch]. Athens.

Kitromilides, Paschalis M. 2018. "Η Φιλική Εταιρεία και η πολιτική γεωγραφία του Διαφωτισμού" [The Philiki Etaireia and the political geography of the Enlightenment]. In Οι πόλεις των Φιλικών. Οι αστικές διαδρομές ενός επαναστατικού φαινομένου [The cities of the Philikoi: The urban pathways of a revolutionary phenomenon], edited by Olga Katsiardi-Hering, 25–35. Athens.

Kitromilides, Paschalis M. 2019. *Religion and Politics in the Orthodox World*. London and New York.

Mavrokordatos, G. Apostolos. 1863. "Ο Μακάριος Γρηγόριος ο Ε΄, Πατριάρχης Κωνσταντινουπόλεως" [The late Grigorios V, patriarch of Constantinople]. In Συλλογή εκ των γραφέντων και παραδοθέντων περί του Οικουμενικού Πατριάρχου Γρηγορίου Ε΄ [Collection of texts written and transmitted on Grigorios V, ecumenical patriarch], 341–376. Athens.

Meletopoulos, Ioannis A. 1967. "Η Φιλική Εταιρεία. Αρχείον Παναγιώτου Δημ. Σέκερη [The Philiki Etaireia: The papers of Panagiotis Dim. Sekeris]. *DIEEE* 18:181–352.

Papadopoulos, Gregorios G., and Georgios P. Angelopoulos, eds. 1865–1866. *Τα κατά τον Πατριάρχην Κωνσταντινουπόλεως Γρηγόριον τον Ε΄* [On Grigorios V, patriarch of Constantinople]. 2 vols. Athens.

Philimon, Ioannis. 1859. Δοκίμιον ιστορικόν περί της Ελληνικής Επαναστάσεως [A historical essay on the Greek Revolution]. Vols. 1–2. Athens.

Crete

It would not be an exaggeration to say that Crete has been a "forgotten chapter" in the history of the "age of revolution." The Great Island between the Aegean and Libyan seas, following five centuries of Venetian rule, since 1669 had been an Ottoman province after a protracted and destructive war of more than twenty years (1645–1669). In the eighteenth century, and especially in the half-century before 1821, Cretan society was marked by many-sided antagonisms, between the local religious communities, Muslim and Orthodox Cretans. The simmering conflict over time stirred up a revolutionary dynamic that ushered in the age of revolution in the eastern Mediterranean. From 1770, when the first abortive revolt against Ottoman rule took place with Russian encouragement, to the end of the nineteenth century, when Crete finally emerged as an autonomous state under the protection of the great powers, Cretan history was marked by revolutionary outbreaks at a remarkable frequency of almost once a decade for most of the period. The main phases of this intermittent revolutionary trajectory were Crete's participation in the Greek Revolution in the 1820s and the Cretan Revolution of 1866–1869.

The century of revolutions from 1770 to 1869 was marked by various forms of social mobilization, primarily movements of refugees seeking to avoid reprisals after every revolutionary initiative; resistance movements opposing oppression, arbitrariness, and inertia on the part of the Ottoman administration; groups resorting to violence against violence emanating from the ruling community especially in the countryside; farmers being involved in multiple conflicts over the exploitation of the agricultural resources of the island, especially olive oil production; intensification of religious conversion and reactions to this phenomenon. If such were the sources of tension between the religious communities, contradictions and divisions within each community, especially within the Christian community, tended also to be complex and explosive: geographical divisions caused by extreme forms of localism, political, social, and even ecclesiastical conflicts created an environment that could easily reach a boiling point and explode given the appropriate stimuli.

Such was the background for the outbreak of the Greek Revolution in Crete in 1821. Although conditions were not particularly propitious given the distance of the island from the main theaters of the revolution on continental Greece and the large proportion of Muslims (in fact Greek-speaking converts to Islam) in the population, the revolution had been prepared in Crete by Cretan members of Philiki Etaireia, who enrolled a number of prominent islanders in the secret society. Revolutionary action broke out in western Crete on June 14, 1821, at the village of Loulos in the hilly Keramia area just to the south of Chania. This is the official date of the initiation of the Greek Revolution in Crete. The decision to join the revolution had been reached slightly earlier at meetings at Sfakia in April 1821.

Reaction to the rising was particularly violent especially in western Crete as local Muslim Cretans joined the Ottoman forces in engaging in reprisals not only against armed fighters but also—and on a large scale—against noncombatants, women, and children. The bishop of Kissamos Melchisedek, in whose diocese the revolution had initially broken out, was hanged on June 19. The bishops of Kydonia Kallinikos and of Rethmymnon Gerasimos were imprisoned and the latter executed. Extreme violence was unleashed in the capital Iraklio (Candia), where upon the reception of the news of the execution of the patriarch of Constantinople the previous April, one of the worst massacres in the history of Crete took place on June 24, 1821. The metropolitan of Crete, Gerasimos Pardalis, and five bishops were executed, the archiepiscopal residence was looted and burned to the ground, and at least eight hundred persons in the city perished in the violence. Similar atrocities took place further east. Monasteries and convents became targets of attack and destruction, and monastic brotherhoods were martyred everywhere. The one surviving bishop in eastern Crete, Ioakeim of Petra, was also martyred by local Turks at the village of Fourni in Merabello.

Despite the violent campaign of suppressing the rising, the revolution in its first year spread all over the island. From its original hearth at Sfakia, it spread to western Crete, in the districts of Apokoronas and Kydonia. On June 15 the Cretan revolutionaries inflicted a crushing defeat on Turkish forces at the highland village of Lakkoi in the White Mountains (Lefka Ori), while their stronghold at Therisso held out successfully against a Turkish assault. Following these victories, the Turkish forces and local aghas retreated and barricaded themselves

inside the fortress of Chania. The revolution seemed to take hold in western
Crete. Similar developments followed in the area of Rethymno, where a Turkish
army attempted to cross through the highlands in order to attack Sfakia overland. The force, which besides Ottoman regular units included some prominent
Turkish-Cretan military chiefs, was defeated and dispersed by Cretan revolutionaries at Rustica on June 17, 1821.

In the central regions of the island (Map 5), in the plains south of the capital
Iraklio, local Turkish-Cretan military men attempted to forestall the coming of
the revolution by engaging preventively in massacres of Christian populations.
The revolution in central Crete eventually broke out in the region of Mesara and
was led by a chief, Michael Kourmoulis, who belonged to a prominent crypto-
Christian clan. This anthropological dimension points to the extremely complex
social and ethnic context of the revolutionary movement in Crete.

By mid-1821, Crete had been swept by the revolution, and the Ottoman military and officials, along with a considerable proportion of the Muslim population of the island, had retreated for protection to the fortified cities on the
northern coast. It was appearing imperative to local Ottoman authorities to attempt to quell the revolution by destroying its hearth at Sfakia. A large-scale
operation was thus set in motion by the general military commander of Crete,
Şerif Pasha of Iraklio, who amassed forces from all other local pashas and started
off against western Crete first. At battles along the way the revolutionaries were
defeated and the noncombatants subjected to massacres. Only Therisso could
hold out on August 19, but one of the leaders of the Cretan revolution, Stephanos Halis, fell in battle. The turn of Sfakia to face the wrath of the Ottoman
rulers was coming up. The Sfakiot chiefs addressed a dramatic appeal to the
notables of the maritime island of Spetses for naval help, but to no avail. In their
appeal they noted that they had received help only from the island of Kasos,
which was to pay dearly in 1824 for its support of the revolution in Crete. On
August 14 Ottoman forces managed to penetrate the formerly inaccessible territory of Sfakia and the entire area was subjected to an atrocious destruction
with countless human victims. The military chiefs tried to evacuate their families onto boats to escape the massacres. For this reason, they were severely criticized by the memorialists of the Cretan revolution and this initiated an interesting historiographical debate that ran through the rest of the nineteenth
century (Kritovoulidis [1859] 2009 vs. Papadopetrakis 1888).

For a moment in the early fall of 1821, the revolution seemed to have been
extinguished in Crete as the Ottoman commanders wrote triumphantly to the
Sublime Porte. By mid-October, however, the revolutionaries in the Chania region managed to regroup their forces and rekindle the movement in the area,
forcing the Turks again to retreat to the fortified city. It was nevertheless,

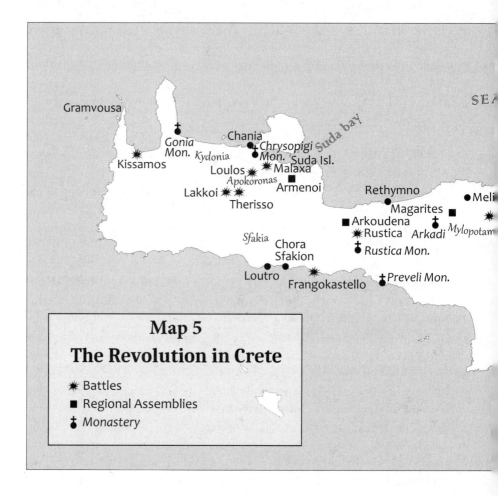

Map 5
The Revolution in Crete

✳ Battles
■ Regional Assemblies
✝ Monastery

becoming evident that for the Cretan revolution to survive it was urgent to introduce order and coordination among the revolutionaries, who fought both the Turks and among themselves. This initiated an appeal to the central authority of the revolution in the mainland to appoint a general commander to lead the liberation effort in Crete. The Cretan appeal was addressed to Dimitrios Ypsilantis, who appointed Michael Komninos Afentoulis or Afentoulief as general eparch and commander-in-chief of Crete.

Afentoulis arrived in Crete in November 1821 and stayed in the island for exactly one year until November 1822. He attempted first of all to introduce an element of political order in the island by laying the foundations of a rudimentary state organization. He called for a general assembly of Cretans, which met at Armenoi in Apokoronas on May 11–21, 1822, with the participation of forty representatives of the various districts of the island. Following the model of the

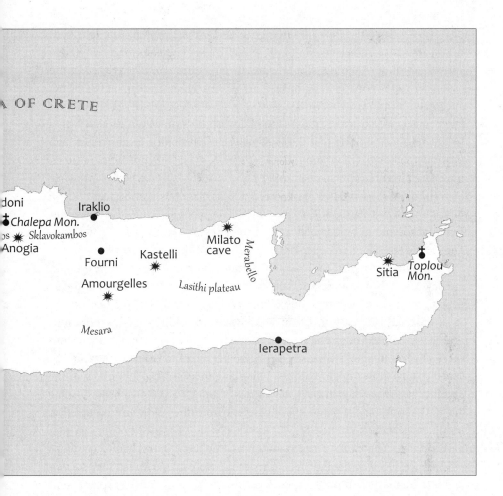

First National Assembly of revolutionary Greece at Epidavros, the Cretan General Assembly issued a Declaration of Liberty and voted a Provisional Constitution of the Island of Crete, and also a Plan of Provisional Administration of the Island of Crete. It was also decided that Crete would be represented in the national parliamentary organs with the election of one representative for every thirty thousand people. A rudimentary administrative structure was also put in place with the introduction of central, regional, and local forms of government.

With this reorganization the revolutionaries, despite continuing factionalism and regional antagonisms, managed to bring the entire island under their control with the Muslims and Ottoman troops shut in the fortresses of the major urban centers. At this point, however, as it was becoming obvious that local Ottoman forces could not reoccupy the island, the Sublime Porte was forced to appeal to the pasha of Egypt, Mohammed Ali, nominally a vassal of the sultan, for help. An Egyptian fleet under Hasan Pasha, the Egyptian toparch's son-in-law, arrived at Suda bay on May 28, 1822. Initially Hasan Pasha attempted to come to an understanding with the Cretan revolutionaries. He released from prison Bishop Kallinikos of Kydonia, the only surviving prelate on the island, and forced him to issue an invitation to the revolutionaries to submit (Tomadakis and Papadaki 1974, 93–95). The Halis brothers, however, replied with a defiant response, noting that the Cretans were determined to die rather than return to the horrors of tyranny (Detorakis 1990, 334). Soon hostilities resumed in western Crete but Cretan resistance was broken at Malaxa in June. Meanwhile the revolutionaries from Anogia inflicted at Sklavokambos a serious defeat upon the forces of Şerif Pasha of Candia, which had penetrated into the highlands. Factionalism and disagreements among the Cretans, nevertheless, made resistance to the superior and better-organized Egyptian forces impossible.

By the end of August, the Egyptian armies, encountering fierce resistance, had destroyed the revolution in the areas of Chania and Rethymno and moved on to eastern Crete, where the revolution was spreading. Hasan's plan was to occupy the highland Lasithi plateau, which was the breadbasket of eastern Crete. On the way, the Egyptian commander set up his headquarters at Chalepa Monastery in Mylopotamos, where on August 30 his forces were fiercely attacked by armed groups from Anogia and Mylopotamos and was forced to move east. The Egyptian forces marched through the regions of Ierapetra and Merabello, burning and massacring on the way, attacked Lasithi from the south and occupied it, bringing destruction everywhere. A terrible atrocity happened in February 1823 at Milato cave, Merabello, where two thousand noncombatants had taken refuge and were besieged by the Egyptian army until, overcome by thirst, they surrendered, to be massacred on the spot. Later the same month, the Egyptian commander died at Kastelli in the Pediada district, after falling from his horse.

The revolution in Crete appeared to be in mortal danger. Afentoulis was blamed by the Cretans for the defeats and was arrested, imprisoned, and eventually deported. The Cretan representatives who were sent to the mainland asked for the appointment of the Ydriot Emmanouil Tombazis as general commissioner of Crete. Tombazis arrived in Crete on May 21, 1823, accompanied by a small naval force and six hundred volunteers. He landed at Kastelli in Kissamos and occupied the local fortress from its Turkish garrison, to whom he offered safe passage to Chania (Figure 11). He proceeded to convoke a new general assembly at Arkoudena (present-day Archontiki) on June 22, 1823. The meeting was attended by delegates from all districts and voted an administrative charter, "Organization of the Annual Local Government of Crete," which followed the model of the Provisional Constitution of Greece of 1822. The new charter provided for a regime based on the rule of law and the division of

FIGURE 11   Dimitrios Zographos, *The Naval Battles of Crete and Samos*, 1836–1839.
Watercolor on paper. The Gennadeion Library, Athens.

powers, with the commissioner at its head as representative of the national government on the mainland (Tomadakis and Papadaki 1974, 247–262).

The new administration did not have much of a chance to bring order to the
affairs of Crete. Military reinforcements and a new commander, Hussein Bey,
arrived from Egypt in June 1823. A well-planned strategy was followed in putting down the revolution in the Great Island. The new commander began with
the eastern provinces and defeated Commissioner Tombazis and his forces at
Amourgelles, south of Iraklio, in August 1823. Mesara was soon also subdued
and the regions around Rethymno followed, with another terrible atrocity committed in January 1824 at Melidoni of Mylopotamos, where a large number of
women and children, who had taken refuge in a cave, were suffocated with
smoke and burned to death. The Egyptian forces moved west unopposed. Tombazis appealed for help to the central government, announcing that "wretched
Crete is at her last gasp," noting also that "if the nation loses Crete, it loses its
right eye and the eventual independence will not be significant" (Tomadakis
and Papadaki 1974, 505–506). It turned out that all this was in vain. The Egyptian army moved fast, looting, burning, and taking captives. The villages in the
region of Apokoronas were violently subdued and then the Egyptian forces

moved into the difficult region of Sfakia. The Sfakiot chiefs capitulated, while thousands of terrified noncombatants crowded at the small local port of Loutro and were evacuated by the Greek navy. A large wave of Cretan refugees had meanwhile left the Great Island for the Cyclades and the mainland. It has been estimated that about sixty thousand refugees were evacuated from Crete in the early months of 1824.

Tombazis issued his last proclamation on April 6, 1824, urging the Cretans to continue fighting and left the island (Tomadakis and Papadaki 1974, 516–517). The revolution in Crete was proclaimed extinct by Hussein Bey, who issued from the port of Suda a general amnesty. Some sporadic guerilla fighting continued, provoking cruel reprisals by local janissaries. Hussein Bey was now free to send reinforcements to his brother-in-law Ibrahim Pasha, who was fighting the Greek Revolution in the Peloponnese. Crete became the major base of support and supply of the Egyptian forces on the mainland.

Two attempts to revive the revolution in Crete followed in the later 1820s. In August 1825, a group of Cretan fighters who had left the island as refugees, returned and occupied the fortress on the island of Gramvousa off the westernmost extremity of the Cretan northern coastline. They also temporarily occupied the fortress of Kissamos but managed to hold onto Gramvousa for three years until 1828. They set up a Cretan council as a nominal revolutionary authority but failed to revive the revolution in the western provinces. From Gramvousa as a base, they engaged in piracy and harassed the Egyptian naval convoys from Crete to the mainland. They were eventually dispersed and the fortress of Gramvousa surrendered to Alexandros Mavrokordatos, who was implementing Capodistrias's antipiracy policy with a British naval force. With these interventions Capodistrias was assisting a broader British and French naval policy to clear the Mediterranean from piracy.

A second attempt to revive the revolution in Crete came in late 1827 and in the early months of 1828. Cretan and other Greek volunteers sailed to eastern Crete and tried, unsuccessfully, to revive the revolution to keep Crete among the Greek territories that were to be considered for inclusion within the frontiers of the new Greek state. Tombazis was writing urging the Cretans to continue fighting in order to keep their claims to liberation viable. Despite various local outbreaks in the areas of Sitia and Merabello the revolution could not be revived on a large scale. Another attempt was connected with a heroic initiative of an Epirot fighter, Chadjimichalis Dalianis, who landed in Crete at the head of a small force in January 1828. He crossed the White Mountains and occupied the fortress at Frangokastello, where he was besieged by hugely superior Turkish forces and eventually, on May 18, 1828, he fell in battle along with almost four hundred select fighters who had accompanied him to Crete.

The last act of the revolutionary drama in Crete was enacted in late 1828 and through 1829 with attempts to mobilize once again resistance to the restoration of joint Turkish-Egyptian rule in order to keep alive Crete's claim for inclusion in the fledgling Greek state. Governor Ioannis Capodistrias sent official emissaries to boost these claims. Initially, the Saxon baron Friedrich Eduard von Rheineck arrived in June 1828 as the governor's representative. Cretan hopes were revived, the Cretan council was reorganized and the revolution flared up in Mesara and in the region of Sitia. The successes of the revolution provoked violent reprisals at the expense of civilians in Iraklio and Rethymno. The new atrocities this time found a sympathetic response on the part of the European powers and the British and French fleets sailed to Suda in October 1828 to protect the island from a new landing of Egyptian forces. Capodistrias sent new emissaries, beginning with the former commissioner Emmanouil Tombazis, who encouraged the Cretans to continue resisting. In February 1829 von Rheineck was replaced by the British Philhellene Captain John Hane and in October of the same year the Cretan Nikolaos Renieris arrived. What is indeed noteworthy is the persistence of Capodistrias's policy to keep the revolution going in order to strengthen his claims for including Crete within the boundaries of the new state-in-the-making.

The revolution was thus kept alive with the Turkish garrisons and a significant part of the Muslim population shut in the fortresses of Iraklio, Rethymno, and Chania. Despite ten years of sacrifices and the unrelenting will to rid Crete from its chains, the Great Island was left outside the boundaries of the Greek state agreed upon by the three allied powers with the London Protocol of February 3, 1830. This signaled the end of the revolution in Crete to the deep disappointment and despair of the Cretans. From Magarites (present day Margarites) of Mylopotamos the Cretan council voiced the general desperation with a proclamation, "To the Greeks," on April 22, 1830, announcing the determination of the Cretans to choose an honorable death instead of submitting anew to tyranny (Detorakis 1990, 349). It was just a premonition that the age of revolution in Crete was bound to continue until the end of the nineteenth century.

Paschalis M. Kitromilides

References

Detorakis, Theocharis. 1990. Ιστορία της Κρήτης [History of Crete]. Iraklio.

Detorakis, Theocharis. 2015. *History of Crete.* Iraklio.

Kitromilides, Paschalis M. 2017. "Κίνηση και στατικότητα στην ιστορία της νεότερης Κρήτης" [Motion and stagnation in the history of modern Crete]. Κρητικά Χρονικά 37:195–215.

Kritovoulidis, Kallinikos. (1859) 2009. Απομνημονεύματα του περί της αυτονομίας της Ελλάδος πολέμου των Κρητών [Memoirs on the war of the Cretans for the autonomy of Greece]. Athens. Partial English edition: Narrative of the Cretan War of Independence. Edited by A. Ioannides. London, 1865.

Manouras, Stergios. 1982. "Η οργάνωση της Φιλικής Εταιρείας στην Κρήτη" [The organization of Philiki Etaireia in Crete]. Προμηθεύς ο Πυρφόρος 32 (November–December): 339–362.

Nikolaidis, Panagiotis. (1824) 1971. Ιστορική και κριτική σύνοψις των εν Κρήτη διατρεξάντων [Historical and critical synopsis of events that have happened in Crete]. Mesolonghi; reprinted Athens.

Papadopetrakis, Gregorios. 1888. Ιστορία των Σφακίων [History of Sfakia]. Athens.

Prevelakis, Eleftherios. 1969. "Το Κρητικόν Ζήτημα 1821–1862" [The Cretan question, 1821–1862]. Κρητικά Χρονικά 21:54–96.

Psillakis, Vasileios. 1909. Ιστορία της Κρήτης [History of Crete]. Chania.

Tomadakis, Nikolaos B. 1959. "Βιβλιογραφία των Κρητικών Επαναστάσεων Α. 1821–1830" [Bibliography of the Cretan Revolutions: 1. 1821–1830]. DIEEE 13:26–32.

Tomadakis, Nikolaos B. 1961. "Τα εν Κρήτη πολιτεύματα (1821–1824)" [Constitutions of Crete, 1821–1824]. DIEEE 15:3–51.

Tomadakis, Nicolaos B., and Anthoula Papadaki, eds. 1974. Κρητικά ιστορικά έγγραφα 1821–1830 [Cretan historical documents, 1821–1830]. Athens.

Cyprus

The island of Cyprus in the early modern period was and still remains the easternmost front of the Hellenic world. It had been a medieval crusader kingdom for three centuries and then passed under Venetian (1489–1571) and Ottoman rule (1571–1878). In the centuries of Ottoman rule, there had been a couple of early abortive revolts in 1606 and 1607 instigated by Western powers that nurtured ambitions in the eastern Mediterranean, the Italian duchies of Savoy and Tuscany, respectively. Oppression and rapacity by Ottoman governors in subsequent periods motivated outbreaks of violence in the form of primitive social protests primarily by the Muslim population of the island (1683, 1765–1766, 1804). The most interesting such primitive rebellion broke out in 1764, when Christians and Muslims joined forces and managed to kill the rapacious Ottoman governor. These sporadic outbreaks of violent social protest cannot be seen as a revolutionary tradition on an island whose population had been reduced to indigence and social malaise by misrule.

In the early nineteenth century, the strivings of the movement of the Neohellenic Enlightenment were felt in the island under the leadership of Archbishop Kyprianos of Cyprus (Figure 12), a prominent representative of the religious Enlightenment observable more broadly in the Orthodox church at the time (Kitromilides 2019, 12–24). This involved the establishment in 1812 of a high school intended to turn young Cypriots into "pious, sensible, civil, upright, just, patriotic, friendly to commerce" men. A second school was founded in 1819 in Limassol, following more closely the model of the Philological Gymnasium of Smyrna, an institution with a more pronounced liberal Enlightenment curriculum. Thus, some social environments in Cyprus were to some

FIGURE 12   Eustacio Altini,
*Kyprianos, Archbishop of
Cyprus, as a young hieromonk
at Jassy*, 1801. Oil on canvas.
Monastery Museum, Holy
and Royal Monastery of
Machairas, Cyprus.

extent receiving the effects of cultural and ideological change in the making
throughout the wider Greek world.

The same period was marked by the apogee of the power of the autocephalous
Orthodox Church of Cyprus in the life of the insular society. A British diplomat,
William Turner, who visited Cyprus in 1815, noted that the island was "in fact governed by the Greek Archbishop" (Cobham [1908] 1969, 447). This of course was a
cause of resentment by both the local Turkish aghas and the Ottoman governors
appointed by the Sublime Porte. This background of antagonism and resentment
was to reach a dramatic climax with the coming of the Greek Revolution.

Archbishop Kyprianos, who had earlier spent a considerable period in Moldavia as representative of his monastery, Machairas, and had developed ties with
liberal and Enlightenment circles there, was approached in October 1818 and
again in June 1820, by one of the emissaries of the Philiki Etaireia, Dimitrios
Ipatros, the society "apostle" to Egypt and Cyprus. The archbishop cautioned
that on account of Cyprus's distance from mainland Greece and its proximity
to the Ottoman provinces of Asia Minor and Syria, no revolutionary outbreak
could hope to survive on the island. He did promise, however, material sup-

port for the society's project. Despite a whole subsequent mythology to the contrary, the archbishop refused to join the society because as a cleric he felt he
could not take the oath required for joining. His willingness to render financial support, nevertheless, was reported to the society's head, Alexandros Ypsilantis, who thanked the archbishop in a warm letter of October 8, 1820, and
charged another emissary, Antonios Pelopidas, to collect the promised aid.
Pelopidas did visit Cyprus probably in early 1821 and collected the promised
funds. The record of this visit created another mythology that Pelopidas massively enrolled Cypriots, clergymen, and lay notables alike, in the society. The
mythology is based on the account of the events of 1821 in Cyprus by Georgios
Kipiadis, who wrote his memoirs many years later and obviously inflated the
involvement of the insular society in revolutionary fervor. In fact, only one Cypriot, Charalambos Malis, is recorded as a member of the Philiki Etaireia in
the authoritative list of Ioannis Philimon. Charalambos Malis remained active
in the politics of the Greek Revolution throughout the 1820s.

Following the outbreak of the revolution, the Sublime Porte's order to disarm
the Christian subjects reached Cyprus and was enforced throughout the island.
On April 22, 1821, Archbishop Kyprianos issued a pastoral encyclical urging his
flock to abide by the order and to remain submissive to their masters and place
their hopes in the hands of God. The climate of alarm in the island, however, was
intensified when it became known that a Cypriot clergyman, Theophilos Theseus,
who was a relative of the archbishop, had arrived in Larnaca in April 1821
and distributed revolutionary pamphlets inciting the people to revolt. This adventurous action was interpreted by the Ottoman governor, Kuchuk Mehmet,
as incriminating evidence of the subversive intentions of the leadership of
Cypriot society. He drafted a list of suspects, comprising 486 names, including the archbishop and all top ecclesiastical dignitaries and lay notables,
and secured the approval of the Porte for their execution.

In the agonizing weeks that followed, the archbishop tried to hearten his flock
by issuing another encyclical, on May 16, counseling calm and hope in God and
urging them to refrain from anything that might cause suspicion or give occasion for trouble. The archbishop's attitude and frame of mind were very mov-
ingly recorded by a British visitor, John Carne, who characterized him as "highly
eminent for his learning and piety, as well as for his unshaken fortitude" (Carne
1826: 2:164–6). Although encouraged by the European consuls to escape to save
his life, Kyprianos appeared determined to tread the road to martyrdom: "I shall
remain here to offer my services to my people till my last breath" (Carne 1826,
2:166; Kitromilides 2020).

Martyrdom indeed came on July 9, 1821. The archbishop, the bishops Chrysanthos of Paphos, Meletios of Kition, and Lavrentios of Kyrenia, along with

all the proscribed ecclesiastical and lay notables on the governor's list, were rounded up and executed on that day in a veritable hecatomb. The slaughter and looting continued in the rest of the island until July 14, reaching deeply into its mountainous hinterland and outlying western regions. The insular society was left metaphorically headless and submerged in deadly fear.

For the rest of the 1820s, Cyprus remained inert, under the terrifying shadow of the hecatomb of July 9. Some Cypriots managed to take refuge in the European consulates at Larnaca and subsequently escaped to Greece or various European cities, especially Trieste, Venice, and Marseilles. A group of dignitaries who survived the slaughter, including the archbishop's suffragan bishop of Tremithus, Spyridon; his exarch Ioannikios, future archbishop of Cyprus (1840–1849); and seven leading laymen, gathered in Rome and proceeded to Marseilles, where on December 6, 1821, they issued a proclamation, calling for military action to liberate Cyprus from its oppressors and incorporate it in free Greece (Peristianis 1910, 779–789).

Among the signatories were the Theseus brothers, Nikolaos and Archimandrite Theophilos, both of whom subsequently played an active role and fought in the War of Independence. Nikolaos Theseus became an aide-de-camp to Dimitrios Ypsilantis and fought at the battle of Peta. The last act of the drama of Cyprus's involvement in the Greek Revolution came with still another appeal signed by Archbishop Panaretos, the prelates and notables of Cyprus to Governor Ioannis Capodistrias on August 28, 1828, asking him to exercise his influence and wisdom so that Cyprus might be included in the fledgling new Greek state.

Many other Cypriots took part as volunteers in the fighting of the War of Independence on land and at sea. Their number is uncertain and various estimates have been suggested on the basis of diverse pieces of evidence, raising the number of up to two or three hundred (Hadjikostis 2008; Philippou 1953). Considering that the population of the island at the time was estimated at only fifty or sixty thousand, their proportionate presence in the Greek Revolution was noteworthy. Some of them are reported in the sources to have taken initiatives for the organization of a campaign to liberate their native island in combination with a contemplated attempt to provoke a rising in Lebanon as a diversion for Ottoman forces in the eastern Mediterranean. This initiative was judged risky and adventurous and was strongly discouraged by authorities in Greece.

The tragedy of July 9, 1821, left the island deeply immersed in the memory of bloodshed but at the same time created a powerful symbolism of Cyprus's sacrifices in the name of freedom. This became a decisive component of the collective conscience of the islanders. This sense of the island's destiny was voiced late in the nineteenth century in a highly evocative and emotive epic, titled "The Ninth of July 1821 in Nicosia Cyprus," in Cypriot Greek by Vassilis Michaelidis (1849–1917), who thus was recognized as the national poet of Cyprus.

Paschalis M. Kitromilides

References

Carne, John. 1826. *Letters from the East.* London.

Cobham, Claude Delaval. (1908) 1969. *Excerpta Cypria.* New York.

Hadjikostis, Giorgos, ed. 2008. *Αρχείον Ροδίωνος Π. Γεωργιάδη* [Archive of Rodion P. Georgiadis]. Vol. 3. Nicosia.

Kipiadis, Georgios I. 1888. *Απομνημονεύματα των κατά το 1821 εν τη Νήσω Κύπρω τραγικών σκηνών* [Memoirs of the tragic scenes on the island of Cyprus in 1821]. Alexandria.

Kitromilides, Paschalis M. 2019. *Religion and Politics in the Orthodox World: The Ecumenical Patriarchate and the Challenges of Modernity.* London and New York.

Kitromilides, Paschalis M. 2020. *Insular Destinies: Perspectives on the History and Politics of Modern Cyprus.* London and New York.

Koumoulides, John. 1974. *Cyprus and the Greek War of Independence, 1821–1829.* London.

Peristianis, Ieronimos K. 1910. *Γενική ιστορία της νήσου Κύπρου* [General history of the island of Cyprus]. Nicosia.

Philippou, Loizos. 1953. *Κύπριοι αγωνισταί* [Cypriot freedom fighters]. Nicosia.

Protopsaltis, Emmanouil. 1971. *Η Κύπρος εις τον αγώνα του 1821* [Cyprus in the struggle of 1821]. Athens.

Sphyroeras, Vasileios. 1995. *Ωδίνες και Οδύνη μιας Επανάστασης. Το 1821 στην Κύπρο* [Birth-pangs and sorrow of a revolution. 1821 in Cyprus]. Nicosia.

Turner, William. 1820. *Journal of a Tour in the Levant.* London.

Epirus

The armed conflict of Ali Pasha of Ioannina with the Sublime Porte, which began in the summer of 1820, created favorable circumstances for the onset and the stabilization of the Greek Revolution in other regions, particularly the Peloponnese. In Epirus, however, these conditions made the revolutionary endeavor especially complex and extremely difficult, due to the amassing there of many Ottoman troops. These forces easily took Arta, Parga, and Preveza, laid siege to the fortress of Ioannina, and maintained garrisons in strongholds and villages that controlled the barely accessible mountainous road network of Epirus (Map 6). To some degree, members of the Philiki Etaireia had been instrumental in Ali Pasha's apostasy, such as the consular official of Russia in Patras, Ioannis Paparrigopoulos, who led Ali to hope that Russia would support him, as well as other *Philikoi* in his close milieu, such as Alexis Noutsos and Manthos Oikonomou.

The Philiki Etaireia was therefore prepared for the conditions prevailing in Epirus and, when Alexandros Ypsilantis planned the start of the revolution in the Peloponnese and its spread to other regions, he anticipated the resistance of Ali Pasha. At the meeting held in Izmail in October 1820, when it was decided to go ahead with the revolution and representatives of Ypsilantis were sent to the regions to prepare for implementing the revolutionary plan, Christophoros Perraivos was chosen to go to Epirus. He was instructed to remain in Mani until the revolution broke out in the Peloponnese. Only then would he depart for Epirus, with the aim of guiding the Souliots to link their effort to win back their homeland with the overall objectives of the Greek Revolution. On January 29, 1821, Ypsilantis sent supplementary orders to Kolokotronis, pointing out that the Greek forces in Epirus should join with those of Ali Pasha, temporarily and ostensibly, until together they defeated the Ottomans. Perraivos's long stay in the Ionian islands and Parga, and his close ties with Souliot chieftains, made the former companion of Rhigas and author of the *History of Parga and Souli* the right person for such a mission.

The Souliots were renowned guerrillas who had been driven out of Souli in 1803–1804, after protracted hostilities with Ali Pasha. They had since been living on the Ionian islands, mainly Corfu, and during the Napoleonic Wars they fought as mercenaries with the European armies. In August 1820, a few hundred Souliots landed on the coasts of Epirus and took part in operations against Ali Pasha, at the invitation of the Ottoman authorities. However, several Muslim aghas in the region, who were suspicious of their combat-fit Christian neighbors resettling in the villages of Souli, objected to their presence. The climate of enmity toward the Souliots, as well as their displeasure with Ismail Pasha, head of the Ottoman campaign, who prevented them from fighting in Souli and driving out the garrisons and the Muslim peasants who had settled there, led them to make an important decision. With the mediation of Alexis Noutsos, they were approached by Ali Pasha and on December 5–6, 1820, they agreed to fight on his side, in return for the handing over of Souli to them, economic backing, and recognition of their privileges in the villages of the wider region. The Souliots immediately clandestinely deserted the Ottoman camp, attacked the Ottoman forces stationed in the village of Variades, expelled them, and entered Souli. By mid-January they had evicted the garrisons and the Muslim newcomers and had fomented insurrection in the villages of northern Souli (Tsangari, Korystiani [currently Phrosyni]).

At the same time the Sublime Porte dismissed Ismail Pasha and replaced him with Hurşid Pasha of the Peloponnese. These developments gave Ali Pasha the opportunity to remobilize his forces centered on Souli, a barely accessible mountainous region located between Parga, Ioannina, Arta, and Preveza. To this end, he dispatched there certain Muslim aghas who had also defected from the Ottoman camp, such as Ago Muhudar and Tahir Ambasi. Thus, at the beginning of 1821 a few thousand armed irregulars, Christians and Muslims, gathered in Souli; on January 15 their leaders ratified the alliance in writing. In the following months, the Souliots consolidated their presence in central Souli, but they were still surrounded by Ottoman garrisons and their position was precarious. Nonetheless, for Hurşid Pasha, who reached Ioannina in late February, the priority was the swift capture of the city's fortress and not the subjugation of the Souliots. That is why, in early March, negotiations with them for their return to the Ottoman camp commenced, but no agreement was reached. On the contrary, the Souliots confirmed their alliance with Ali Pasha, campaigned to the east and, by mid-April, had captured the villages of Lakka Souliou, after battles at Seriziana and Bogortsa (Assos).

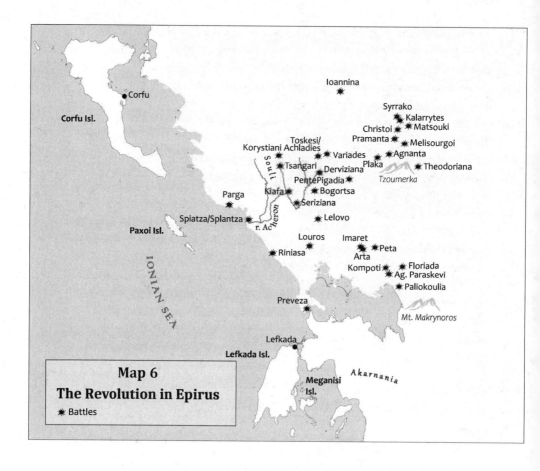

In late March to early April 1821, Perraivos arrived in Souli, bringing the message of the Greek Revolution. Following Ypsilantis's commands, he urged the Souliots to maintain the alliance with Ali Pasha, but to ignore his military priorities and concentrate on operations that would reinforce the spread of the revolution in Epirus. He advised them to turn westward and southward, toward Parga and Preveza, instead of fighting to the east and north of Souli—that is, in the direction of Ioannina. He considered that, by occupying the coastal cities and with Souli as their bastion, a safe territorial nucleus would be created in Epirus, which would communicate by sea with the centers of the Greek Revolution in the Peloponnese and the islands. Furthermore, in collaboration with the ephorate of the Philiki Etaireia in Corfu, he addressed the Pargans who had gone to the island as refugees in 1819 and invited them to fight with him to regain their homeland.

At the end of April 1821, according to Perraivos, or the end of May, according to Ioannis Philimon, the Souliots and their allies advanced southward and expelled the Ottoman garrison from the Louros area. Perraivos proposed that they continue toward Preveza but the Souliots' allies objected and persuaded most of them to turn eastward, on Lelovo (Thesprotiko). Only a small band headed by Perraivos captured the fort of Riniasa, between Preveza and Parga, and in late July, reinforced by Pargans recruited in Corfu, they attacked Parga. Although they captured the town temporarily. they lacked naval support and sufficient forces to hold onto it, and so withdrew. More successful were the battles fought by the Souliots and their Muslim allies in June and July at Lelovo, Variades, Derviziana, Toskesi (Achladies), which enabled them to control Lakka Lelovou and Lakka Souliou and to extend their action as far as the mountain stronghold of Pente Pigadia, which was critical for controlling the main land route between Ioannina and Arta.

After mid-May, a new front was created further south, in the highland provinces of Arta (Radovitsi and Tzoumerka). The armed irregulars (*armatoloi*) of the area (Gogos Bakolas, Koutelidas) whipped up popular support for the Greek Revolution in exactly the same period as Aitolia and Akarnania joined the struggle. From late May, the militia chiefs (*oplarchigoi*) of Arta, together with Akarnanians (Ioannis Rangos, Andreas Iskos, Alexandros Vlachopoulos), fought a succession of battles in the difficult defiles of Makrynoros and staved off the Ottoman army's attempts to move from Arta toward Akarnania, Aitolia, and the western Peloponnese: on May 28–29 at Paliokoulia near Elaiochori, on June 18 in the Agia Paraskevi pass at Marlesi, and a few days later at Floriada. Concurrently, these corps were harassing the garrisons at Kompoti and Peta, starting points for the roads leading to the insurgent highland districts.

In no time, the two centers of rebellion in Epirus were united operationally, as the Souliots and the Artan *oplarchigoi* agreed to coordinate their activity to stir up revolt in the rest of the mountainous districts between Arta and Ioannina. Their aim was to cut off Hurşid Pasha's encampment in Ioannina from the Ottoman forces in Arta, something that Ali Pasha also wanted. In early July, the villages on the north side of Tzoumerka rebelled, with Syrrako and Kalarrytes as centers headed by the primates of the region, among them Ioannis Kolettis. However, in these wealthy head villages in the mountains, where many residents of Ioannina had sought refuge with their possessions after the summer of 1820, there were no local *armatoloi* or armed bands. So, they appealed to the Souliots and the Artans for military support, as did the inhabitants of the adjacent Katsanochoria, who were also in revolt, at the northwest tip of Tzoumerka. The few bands of *armatoloi* that reached Syrrako and Kalarrytes, led by Rangos and Koutelidas, failed to ward off the Ottoman forces that sped there from Ioannina and Arta. They retreated, fighting from village to village (Matsouki, Christoi, Pramanta, Agnanta, Melisourgoi) until the end of July, trying to stem the enemy advance and to facilitate the "exodus" of the inhabitants to Valtos. Similar were the developments in the neighboring Katsanochoria, as well as in the Grammenochoria on the west side of Ioannina, which also revolted at the instigation of the Souliots.

The failure in the northern part of Tzoumerka thwarted the plans of the Greek revolutionaries and Ali Pasha, but it did not diminish their operational capabilities. The Artans, headed by Gogos Bakolas, put up a spirited resistance at Peta on July 15 and averted the invasion of the villages of Radovitsi by the Ottoman forces of Arta. About two weeks later, the same corps were deployed in the mountainous locality of Stavros, close to Theodoriana, and halted the course of the Ottoman troops from northern Tzoumerka to Radovitsi and thence toward Akarnania. In these battles the *oplarchigoi* of Arta succeeded in keeping the revolutionary hearth alight in their region. Furthermore, the victories of the Souliots and their Muslim allies in the same period, at Plaka, Toskesi, and Pente Pigadia, allowed them to keep control of the areas they had captured to the east of Souli.

As a result, communication continued between the Souliots with their "pro–Ali Pasha" allies and the Artan and Akarnanian *oplarchigoi;* their collaboration on the battlefields was rekindled. Their most important representatives gathered at Peta on September 1, 1821, and ratified their alliance by signing an agreement foreseeing military cooperation aimed at supporting Ali Pasha. Once again, Alexis Noutsos played a role in this development and the Greek authorities of the Peloponnese, Aitolia, and Akarnania agreed to it, despite their distrust of Ali Pasha and the skepticism of some about the benefits of this partnership. Their military target was the capture of Arta. In early November about four thousand armed men were amassed. The Artans and the Akarnanians struck camp at Peta, the Souliots and their Muslim allies walled themselves in at Grammenitsa, and a few hundred men headed by Markos Botsaris and Georgios Karaiskakis captured the area of Imaret-Marati, very near Arta but on the opposite bank of the Arachthos river. These advance corps were attacked by the garrison of Arta on November 12, 1821, but stood their ground for as long as it took for the rest of the corps to move closer to the town.

In the following days until the beginning of December, the besiegers gradually captured the greater part of Arta, fighting from neighborhood to neighborhood. However, instead of concentrating on the fall of the fortress they launched into widespread looting, to the detriment of the inhabitants (including the refugees from Ioannina who had fled there). They then left in small groups with the booty they had taken. Moreover, the dispatch of Ottoman troops from the Ioannina camp to the area of Louros and Lamari—that is, close to Souli— as well as to Pente Pigadia, obliged the Souliots to return to their own region. Thus, the siege weakened and essentially ceased. At the same time, the "Greek-Albanian alliance," as it is frequently referred to in the relevant literature dis-

solved, as the Muslim allies of the Souliot and Akarnanian *oplarchigoi* abandoned Ali Pasha and returned to the Sultan's camp. Ali Pasha's resistance had
been broken; the fortress of Ioannina was captured easily in December 1821,
and the apostate was killed while fighting in his last refuge on the islet in Lake
Pamvotis, in mid-January 1822. This significant development put the Souliots
in a particularly difficult position as they were isolated from the other insurgent regions and encircled by Ottoman forces.

The Campaign in Epirus

During the same period in the Peloponnese, close to ancient Epidavros, the business of the First National Assembly was being concluded and the instruments of
the central administration of the rebellious Greeks were being created. Alexandros Mavrokordatos was named president of the executive; it was him that the
Souliots' emissary, Markos Botsaris, addressed when he went to the seat of the
National Administration in Corinth to explain their terrible situation and to ask
for help. Mavrokordatos responded positively to Botsaris's request and one of his
first acts was to organize a campaign to Epirus. The newly formed National Administration then tried for the first time to extend its territory further north,
using troops from regions where the revolution appeared to have been stabilized.
Leading Peloponnesian *oplarchigoi*, such as Kolokotronis (who eventually sent
his son Ioannis, aka Gennaios [= "Brave"]), Giatrakos, members of the Mavromichalis family, and others, were summoned to join the Epirus campaign. This
meant that, for the first time, they would have to fight far away from their home
territory and to collaborate with Akarnanian and Epirot *oplarchigoi*. Equally
important for the military history of the Greek Revolution is the fact that for the
first time the regular army would play an important role in the campaign.

The first small regular corps of two to three hundred men was created by
Dimitrios Ypsilantis in the summer of 1821, in the Peloponnese, and commanded by the Corsican Joseph Baleste or Balestra. This was, however, a
limited and abortive endeavor, as the corps was only used alternatively in some
battles and was disbanded before the year was out. One of Mavrokordatos's chief
concerns as president of the executive was to set up a regular army; the relevant law was passed on April 1, 1822. His military policy was permeated by ideas
and certainties of post-Napoleonic European military thinking about the regular army's superiority over the irregular forces and was directly linked with
his overall political vision of setting up institutions of a modern state in revolutionary Greece. But the transformation of the irregular Peloponnesian and
Rumeliot fighters into regular soldiers was a particularly difficult undertaking,
not only because the war was still in progress but also because of the men's

wariness or even rejection of such a change. Thus, Mavrokordatos set as the government's direct objective the administrative unification of the irregular troops and their subjection to the direct control of the National Administration. At the same time, he created a second military structure, the Greek regular army, because he truly believed that the victories this would bring would help his effort to generalize the new institution. Precisely for this reason, he decided to deploy the regular army in Epirus and indeed assumed command of the campaign, even though he had no military knowledge or experience.

At that time, a regiment (two battalions) of about five hundred Greek soldiers and European officers existed under the command of the Italian Colonel Petro Tarella, as well as two companies with about one hundred European officers, the Battalion of Philhellenes, under the command of another Italian, Colonel Andrea Dania. Last, there were two small corps of Ionian islanders, which were likewise organized along the lines of a regular army. In the second half of May, these forces marched as far as Patras and were transported by ship to Mesolonghi, as were the Peloponnesian troops that took part in the campaign. With the exception of a few hundred Maniots and Mesolonghians, who would move later with ships to the shores of Epirus, as well as the band under Gennaios Kolokotronis, which had gone ahead, the rest of the army set off in early June from Mesolonghi for Karvasaras (Amphilochia) and joined the Akarnanian chiefs who controlled the pass through Makrynoros.

The expeditionary force numbered some three thousand men, considerably fewer than Mavrokordatos's expectations. A quasi-general staff was formed around it, participants in which were the leaders of the regular and irregular corps. Particularly significant was the opinion of the German General Karl Normann, head of the three different regular corps, who drew up the battle plans, ignoring the objections and the alternative proposals of the Greek *oplarchigoi*. On June 9, the army passed through the Makrynoros pass and reached Kompoti, about ten kilometers southeast of Arta. The Ottoman garrison of Arta was aware of their movement and on the following day about five hundred cavalrymen were sent against the force. The Greek bands of irregulars constructed earthworks, where they ensconced themselves. Nonetheless, Normann decided to array his forces in a manner appropriate to a regular army and the spirited militancy they showed forced the attackers to retreat. After all, their primary aim was to test their opponents' fire power. The relatively easy victory at Kompoti instilled optimism in the Greek side, particularly among the ranks of the regular army. Indeed, they proposed an immediate attack on Arta, but the chiefs of the irregulars disagreed on this as they did not want to find themselves exposed on flat ground against the Ottoman cavalry. At the same time, at the meetings held in Kompoti Markos

Botsaris and the Souliots' new emissaries insisted that a section of the army
should move post haste toward Souli.

By now the situation in Souli was difficult in the extreme. Since the beginning of the year it had been encircled by numerous troops under the command
of Omer Vrioni, who preferred to pressure them into capitulation rather than
fight them. So, in February 1822, he proposed that they submit to the Ottoman
power in exchange for an amnesty and the restoration of their former privileges in Souli and the surrounding villages. The Souliots feigned acceptance of
the terms and started negotiations, in the hope that in the meanwhile the Greek
campaign would commence. But in early May, they were forced to give a final
answer, which was negative. A few days later, on May 15, an army of ten thousand or more soldiers captured the village of Variades and on the next day it
entered Souli from three sides. Despite the valiant resistance of the few hundred Souliots, in some cases assisted by civilians, they were forced to cram into
the Kiafa fortress, followed by thousands of civilians, while they placed smaller
corps in Navariko or Avariko and at Chonia, in order to secure their access to
drinking water (Figure 13). In these rugged positions they succeeded in stemming

FIGURE 13   Donato Francesco De Vivo, *Death of Lambros Tzavellas* (at Kiafa, Souli), before
1855. Oil on canvas. National Gallery-Al. Soutzos Museum, Athens.

the enemy advance, just as they did two weeks later, when a second Ottoman attack was launched. In these battles the Souliots confirmed their reputation as formidable fighters, but it was only a matter of time before the Ottoman forces remobilized and attacked again.

For precisely this reason, in the meetings held at Kompoti after the victory of June 10, Markos Botsaris stepped up the pressure for the immediate dispatch of reinforcements to Souli. In the end, it was decided to keep a small garrison at Kompoti, which functioned as a communication node with Akarnania, while a second small corps accompanied Mavrokordatos to the mountain village of Lagada to supervise the provisioning from there. The rest of the forces were divided into two units; on June 21 the first was moved to Peta, where Gogos Bakolas and the *oplarchigoi* of Arta struck camp, while the second marched further north to Plaka. The first unit comprised the regular army and about one thousand five hundred irregulars, and according to the plan they were to lay siege to Arta, while the second unit, with Botsaris, Vlachopoulos, Varnakiotis, and Iskos as commanders of a thousand or more irregulars was to capture Plaka. Botsaris's aim was to breach from there the position of Pente Pigadia, which was held by the Ottoman forces beleaguering Kiafa. Moreover, several hundred Mesolonghians and Maniots under the command of Kyriakoulis Mavromichalis were transported by ship from Mesolonghi to the little harbor of Spiatza or Splantza (Ammoudia), on the Acheron estuary, in order to strike from the west the Ottoman forces besieging the Souliots.

None of these operations went as the Greek side had planned. The Ottoman troops in Arta were reinforced and in late June 1822 they attacked the Greek encampment at Plaka. Despite Botsaris's combative prowess, the Greeks were forced to abandon Plaka and return to Peta on July 1. The landing at Spiatza was also a failure, as Kyriakoulis Mavromichalis was fatally wounded by a bullet on July 4 and his soldiers were forced to abandon the operation. On the same day, the Greek camp at Peta was dispersed rather easily with severe losses by a force of some seven thousand assailants under the command of Mehmed Reşhid Pasha, known in the Greek sources as Kütahı.

The battle at Peta is one of the most controversial in the historiography of the Greek struggle for independence, both older (Spyridon Trikoupis, Nikolaos Spiliadis, Christos Vyzantios, Thomas Gordon, George Finlay, Georg Gottfried Gervinus, and others) and more recent (Douglas Dakin, William St Clair, and others). It owes much of its fame to the presence and sacrifice of the Philhellenes. Several of those who fought in the Battalion of the Philhellenes referred to it in their recollections and memoirs (Daniel-John Elster, Olivier Voutier, Heinrich Treiber, Maxime Raybaud, Brengeri, and others), as did several of the Greeks (Kanellos Deligiannis, Gennaios Kolokotronis, Petros Mengous, and others). In the philhellenic sources in particular, the defeat is attributed mainly to the treachery of Gogos Bakolas (and secondarily to the passive stance of the irregulars). Similar rumors circulated after the battle and were soon adopted by Mavrokordatos and the Greek authorities. Bakolas was accused of intentionally leaving a pass unprotected; as a result, a small enemy force suddenly appeared at the back of the Greek guerilla bands, which had been positioned in the hills behind the village. These abandoned their positions without resistance and retreated into the mountains, leaving the Philhellenes and the Greek regular soldiers fighting in the low hills in front of the village exposed to the main bulk of the Ottoman army. Thus, trapped by the enemy, they were virtually decimated. By contrast, in the Greek sources there is dissension over whether Bakolas left unguarded the place he was supposed to supervise due to carelessness or treachery. The sources are split also as to whether the defeat was due mainly to the militia bands who did not serve the battle plan and abandoned their positions or whether Mavrokordatos and the European officers were primarily responsible, because they had planned the battle on the terms of a regular army. They had therefore entrusted a few hundred regular soldiers to repel the Ottoman assault on relatively even ground, while they had assigned the armed irregulars to supporting roles that canceled out the virtues and skills they showed when they fought in their own way. Discernible in these different accusations are aspects of the wider debate among Greek freedom fighters as to the characteristics that the national army (regular or irregular) should have. The defeat at Peta and the almost simultaneous success of the guerrillas against Dramali in the Peloponnese played a decisive role in the failure of Mavrokordatos's policy of creating European-type troops in revolutionary Greece. The remnants of the regular army were left to their fate and disbanded in the following months.

However, the consequences of the battle at Peta did not concern only or even mainly the issue of the army. They concerned above all the fate of the revolution in Epirus. The ambitious campaign was dropped after the defeat on July 4, as the army was not re-formed; those who survived sought refuge south of the Makrynoros pass. In the following days, the *oplarchigoi* of Arta accepted the proposals of the Ottoman authorities and capitulated, keeping the role they once had as *armatoloi* in Radovitsi and Tzoumerka. The Souliots also negotiated through the mediation of the English consular authorities of Preveza and, in late July, agreed to depart by ship for the Ionian islands. Thus, the two revolutionary nuclei in Epirus ceased to exist. This situation did not change in the ensuing years. The martial turmoil that began in Epirus in the summer of 1820 with the apostasy of Ali Pasha and expanded in the following year with the Greek Revolution came to an end in the summer of 1822. The Ottoman forces could now use Epirus and particularly Arta as launching pads for expeditions to the south, targeting the center of the Greek struggle for independence in western Rumeli, Mesolonghi.

Dionysis Tzakis

Translated from the Greek by Alexandra Douma

References

Ars, Grigori. 1994. *Η Αλβανία και η Ήπειρος στα τέλη του ιή και στις αρχές του ιθ' αιώνα. Τα δυτικοβαλκανικά πασαλίκια της Οθωμανικής Αυτοκρατορίας* [Albania and Epirus at the end of the eighteenth and the beginning of the nineteenth century: The west Balkan pashaliks of the Ottoman Empire]. Athens.

Brewer, David. 2001. *The Flame of Freedom: The Greek War of Independence, 1821–1833.* London.

Dakin, Douglas. 1955. *British and American Philhellenes During the War of Greek Independence, 1821–1833.* Thessaloniki.

Dakin, Douglas. 1973. *The Greek Struggle for Independence, 1821–1833.* Berkeley and Los Angeles.

Kanellopoulos, Nikos, and Nikos Tompros. 2017. "Η στρατιωτική δράση των Φιλελλήνων στη μάχη του Πέτα: Ξαναδιαβάζοντας τον Daniel-Johann Elster και τις άλλες πηγές" [The military action of the Philhellenes in the battle of Peta: Rereading Daniel-John Elster and the other sources]. In *Ο διεθνής περίγυρος και ο Φιλελληνισμός κατά την Ελληνική Επανάσταση* [The international setting and philhellenism during the Greek Revolution], 59–80. Athens.

Nikolaou, Giorgos B. 2015. "Η εκστρατεία στην Ήπειρο και η μάχη του Πέτα μέσα από τα απομνημονεύματα των Φιλελλήνων Olivier Voutier και Maxime Raybaud και Daniel Elster" [The campaign in Epirus and the battle of Peta through the memoirs of the Philhellenes Olivier Voutier and Maxime Raybaud and Daniel Elster]. In *Φιλελληνισμός. Το ενδιαφέρον για την Ελλάδα και τους Έλληνες από το 1821 ως σήμερα* [Philhellenism: The interest in Greece and the Greeks from 1821 to this day], edited by Anna Mandylara, Giorgos Nikolaou, and Lambros Flitouris, 243–271. Athens.

Prevelakis, Eleftherios, and Kallia Kalliataki Merticopoulou, eds. 1996. *Η Ήπειρος, ο Αλή Πασάς και η Ελληνική Επανάσταση. Προξενικές εκθέσεις του William Meyer από την Πρέβεζα* [Epirus, Ali Pasha, and the Greek Revolution: The consular reports of William Meyer from Preveza]. Monuments of Greek History. Athens.

Psimouli, Vaso. 2005. *Σούλι και Σουλιώτες* [Souli and Souliots]. Athens.

Skiotis, Dennis N. 1976 "The Greek Revolution: Ali Pasha's Last Gamble." In *Hellenism and the First Greek War of Liberation, 1821–1830: Continuity and Change,* edited by Nikiforos P. Diamandouros, Peter W. Topping, and John Peter Anton, 98–109. Thessaloniki.

St Clair, William. (1972) 2008. *That Greece Might Still Be Free: The Philhellenes in the War of Independence.* Introduction by Roderick Beaton. Cambridge.

Tzakis, Dionysis. 1997. *Αρματολισμός, συγγενικά δίκτυα και εθνικό κράτος. Οι ορεινές επαρχίες της Άρτας στο πρώτο ήμισυ του 19ου αιώνα* [Armatoloi, kinship networks, and the nation state: The mountainous provinces of Arta in the first half of the nineteenth century]. PhD diss., Panteio University of Social and Political Sciences, Athens.

Ionian Islands

For several centuries the Ionian islands were under Venetian rule, but in 1797 they passed under French rule. Then in 1799, a Turkish-Russian fleet captured them, and in 1800 Russia and the Ottoman Empire established the Septinsular Republic, an autonomous Greek state tributary to the Sublime Porte; this was ceded to the French with the Tilsit Treaty in 1807. The British gradually conquered the Ionian islands (1809–1814), and the Treaty of Paris in 1815 established the United States of the Ionian islands under British protection. These islands were not therefore part of the Ottoman Empire. Nevertheless, the Ionians, the Ionian state, and their British protectors played an important, if not so well known, role in the revolution. Although the Ionians had lived for centuries under various foreign rulers and foreign legal and socioeconomic conditions, they had always been very close to the other Greeks with whom they had a common language and religion.

Their proximity to mainland Greece facilitated their contacts and reciprocal influence. Ionians worked seasonally there, and scholars and physicians from the islands lived and worked in Greece and the Ottoman Empire. The ongoing maritime trade from both sides of the Ionian Sea also encouraged permanent or semipermanent migration on both sides. Finally, the Ionians had actively supported the other Greeks during their previous revolts against the Turks, and they offered them shelter in the islands during those uprisings. Of the non-Ionian Greeks who lived on these islands, some had been previously klephts or *armatoloi* in mainland Greece; there were also Souliot refugees and former inhabitants of Parga, after the town was sold to Ali Pasha by the British. Some of them had formerly served either in a Russian-organized military body at the time of the Septinsular Republic or in the first regiment of the Greek Light

Infantry under the command of Richard Church; Theodoros Kolokotronis was one of them. Hence many Greeks from the Peloponnese and western Greece were permanently or semipermanently living on these islands.

Furthermore, the longstanding association of the Ionians with Venice and other Italian cities, and with other European countries through the currant trade, had helped them establish a wide circle of contacts in western Europe. Upper-class Ionians used to study at the University of Padova or at other Italian universities. Early on, they had been introduced to the Enlightenment, so since the mid-eighteenth century some of the more influential scholars and writers were Ionians. Freemasonry had also made its appearance on these islands and after 1815 there were masonic lodges in Corfu and Zante; other secret societies were not unknown either. (Angelomatis-Tsougarakis 2018, 151–157).

Cephalonia and Ithaki had a large merchant fleet mainly but not exclusively engaged in imports of grain from the Black Sea and in the Danube trade. As a result, they had established a strong network with the Greeks of the Danubian Principalities and Russia, where there was also a very active Ionian community, whose most prominent member was Ioannis Capodistrias. The Ionian islands were therefore geographically and culturally a link between East and West, and their inhabitants were qualified to play the same role between the fighting Greeks and the rest of Europe.

Most of the known Ionian *Philikoi* were from Zante (Zakynthos). A revised calculation of their numbers adds up to 120 names, which list, however, includes some non-Ionians residing permanently in Zante. Cephalonia comes second with sixty-eight members. The known members from the other Ionian islands are significantly fewer: sixteen from Ithaki, thirteen from Corfu, two from Paxoi, three from Kythira. It is noteworthy that Corfu, the capital of the Ionian state, shows a low participation in the Philiki Etaireia (Angelomatis-Tsougarakis 2018, 158–171; Chiotis 1874–1877, 1:308–335; Mexas 1937; Philimon 1859–1862, vol. 1).

Sir Thomas Maitland, the lord high commissioner, had been alerted by William Meyer, the British consul general in Albania, and Ali Pasha of Ioannina to the existence of a Greek secret revolutionary society in Zante led by Kolokotronis. Maitland, suspecting that Capodistrias and the Russians were involved, ordered this matter to be investigated. Kolokotronis, warned by a Greek policeman, managed to hide the incriminating documents; so did other Zantiot *Philikoi,* Count Dionysios Romas among them. Romas was perhaps the most influential of the Ionians after Capodistrias. He was a former member of the senate in Corfu, grand master of masonic lodges in Corfu and Zante and one of the leaders of the Philiki Etaireia in the Ionian islands. He managed to avoid the search by claiming to the British resident Ross, a lower-ranking mason, that these were masonic papers. Further misinformation appeased Maitland's suspicions. In early 1821, Romas moved from Zante to Venice, where he remained until 1824, though still active in the war effort (Chiotis 1874–1877, 1:348–349; Vlachopoulos 2020, 129–132).

The declaration of the revolution by Alexandros Ypsilantis in Moldavia caused great concern in Britain about any possible change to the status quo in the Aegean and the eastern Mediterranean which might affect its trade there and the trade routes to the east. The likelihood of a Russian exit into the Aegean Sea and beyond was a frightening prospect for British diplomacy. The fact that the Corfiot Ioannis Capodistrias had been foreign secretary to the tsar made this scenario look practically imminent. This Russophobia was greatly influenced and encouraged by the two successive lord high commissioners, Sir Thomas Maitland and Sir Frederick Adam, who, against all evidence, believed that Capodistrias was behind whatever movements or events were taking place in the Ionian islands and in Greece in general.

In the meantime, the Ionians abroad, particularly the sailors and merchants from Cephalonia and Ithaki operating in the Danubian Principalities, were close to the leader of the Philiki Etaireia, Alexandros Ypsilantis. A number of them were among those who decided that the revolution should start there and many played an important role in the events in Moldowallachia. Vassileios Karavias from Ithaki was ordered by Ypsilantis to raise the flag of the war in Galați on February 21, 1821. Karavias led a body of about 150 men, most of them from Cephalonia, who killed all the Turks in that town. That was the first battle of the War of Greek Independence (Loukatos 1976, 51–56).

Three days later, Ypsilantis made the declaration of the revolution, which was written by one of his close associates, the Cephalonian doctor Georgios Kozakis-Typaldos. Greek vessels, many of which were from the Ionian islands, were at that time anchored at the river Pruth, a navigable tributary of the Danube. Once the news of the revolution reached them, they put themselves under the orders of Karavias. On March 7, 1821, Greek ships attacked and defeated ten Turkish merchant ships which were seen sailing the Danube. That was the first naval battle of the revolution. For the duration of the war in the principalities and until the final victory of the Ottomans, the Ionians fought in all the battles there (Loukatos 1976, 56–63).

When the revolution started in Greece, there was an influx of refugees, mostly women and children from the Morea and western Greece, into the Ionian islands, mostly Zante. About six thousand women and children had already settled only in Zante by mid-April 1821, and their numbers continued increasing. At the same time, there was a reverse movement from the islands to the Morea and the rest of Greece as Ionians and other Greeks rushed to join the Greek fighting troops across the water. The volunteers were transferred by Ionian vessels, several of which either joined the Greek navy or unofficially helped the revolution by moving people, ammunition, and provisions back and forth. Within a few months, eleven thousand Ionian citizens and expatriates were among those fighting in Greece. In the meantime, the inhabitants of the Ionian islands, excited by the news of the uprising of their compatriots, celebrated in public to the great dismay of the British (Chiotis 1874, vol. 1; Wrigley 1988: 103ff.).

Initially, the British believed that only the Ionians abroad were fighting in the revolution. Thus, on April 9, 1821, the senate proclaimed that it was forbidden to Ionian subjects living in the Ottoman Empire to participate in the hostilities, on pain of losing the protection of the local consuls of the Ionian state. When the massive demonstrations in support of the revolution started on the islands and the extent of the departures to mainland Greece was made clear, a further proclamation, on May 7, 1821, forbade the Ionians from interfering with the Turkish blockade of the Morea. A month later, Sir Frederick Adam, acting lord high commissioner, proclaimed the neutrality of the Ionian state and new and stricter measures: an embargo on the exports of ammunition was ordered, and a special license was required for the defensive armament of the Ionian vessels. All armed Turkish and Greek vessels were prohibited from the Ionian ports, even nonarmed Greek ships flying the Greek flag were included in the prohibition. Any help to the rebels was forbidden, particularly fighting alongside them. Those who took part in the war were to be permanently exiled and their lands and other assets were to be confiscated. The implementation of the measures started immediately with the selling of the properties of several Cephalonian and a few Zantiot fighters. There were attempts to prevent people from Parga and Souli to cross from Corfu to mainland Greece to participate in the war by informing the Turkish fleet of their departure, whereas the people of Parga were expelled from Corfu (Chiotis 1874–1877, 1:409–413; Wrigley 1988, 107–121).

Despite these measures, Ionian neutrality on the seas was frequently violated not only by the Turkish and the Greek fleets but also the British themselves. They usually turned a blind eye to Turkish violations and sometimes actively supported the Turks: they officially accepted the Turkish fleet in Corfu, sent food and ammunition to the Turks in mainland Greece through Corfu and Zante, and accepted their bills of exchange to help them when they needed money. Perhaps the best-known of these cases was the continuous activity of the Turkophile Philip Green, British consul general in Patra, which the British authorities never attempted to put a stop to. Green was running a profitable trade with the Turks through Zante and helped them in many ways. (Prevelakis and Kalliataki-Merticopoulou 1996, vols. 1–2; Wrigley 1988, 107–109, 151–153, 187–189).

The violations of the Ionian neutrality by the two enemy fleets and the obvious partiality of the lord high commissioner to the Turks eventually led to serious troubles and new harsh measures by the British. In early September 1821, when an Algerian ship of the Turkish fleet clashed with Greek vessels and was defeated, it found refuge in a bay in Zante and the British garrison hurried to protect its sailors from the peasants. In the clash that followed, one British soldier was killed and two were wounded. Hence, Zante, Cephalonia, Leukada, and Corfu were placed under martial law, and prominent citizens were imprisoned in Zante and Cephalonia. Those suspected of firing against the soldiers were court-martialed, and four men and one youth were sent to the gallows. The entire Greek population of the Islands was disarmed. Maitland deposed and exiled the acting bishop of Cephalonia Agathangelos Kozakis-Typaldos for his help toward the Cephalonians leaving for Greece to fight in the revolution. A new investigation regarding a possible Russian conspiracy, however, revealed nothing suspicious. In early October 1821, another serious incident happened at Kythira: the British had offered temporary asylum to Turks fleeing the war in the Morea, but some peasants massacred the Turkish refugees (Chiotis 1874–1877, 1:419–431; Wrigley 1988, 108–121).

Since the end of April 1821, at least six corps of mostly Cephalonian and Zantiot men had left the islands and joined the Moreot fighters. They fought alongside other Moreot troops in the battle of Lala, where the Greeks had a very important victory, and at Patras; they also participated in the sieges of Neokastro and Monemvasia and their subsequent surrender (Chiotis 1874–1877, 1:400–419, 435–437; Loukatos 1972–1973, 61–63; Metaxas 1878, 23–43).

Maitland, considering the Greek refugees a potential cause of unrest for the local population, but finding it difficult to deport them as he wished, ordered that women, children, and elderly refugees be transferred to Kalamos, one of the lesser Ionian islands, while young males from mainland Greece were denied entrance to the Ionian state. The transfer of the refugees under bad weather conditions and various other difficulties resulted in the death of many of them (Chiotis 1874–1877, 1:431–432; Wrigley 1988, 135–142).

The Ionian populace collectively reimbursed the cost of sustaining the refugees to the Ionian government in 1821; later, the Colonial Office subsidized the operation of the refugee camp in Kalamos. Until 1828, the cost was £12,594, which was to be reimbursed by the Ionian state. We do not know whether private donations toward the welfare of the refugees were accepted before 1827, but from Capodistrias's presidency onward, any charity offered either by Capodistrias or the Zakynthos Committee was rejected by the high commissioner with the approval of the Colonial Office under the pretext of Ionian neutrality (Chiotis 1874–1877, 1:753; Wrigley 1988, 139–140, 269–271). However, the Zakynthos

Committee and the Ionians in general supported the refugee families who remained on the other Ionian islands.

Turkish refugees were easily offered asylum and were allowed private donations to help them along. British goodwill toward the Turks was made plain in the way they helped in ransoming Hurşid Ahmed Pasha's harem and officials, who had been captured by the Greeks during the fall of Tripolitsa. They appointed the Zantiot doctor Panagiotis Marinos Stephanou as negotiator between the two parties, under the supervision of Sir Frederick Adam. Stephanou eventually managed to conclude the negotiations successfully in 1822 (Chiotis 1874–1877, 1:437–440).

In Britain, the opposition in parliament was against what they considered unnecessarily strict measures adopted by Maitland, particularly the martial law and the compulsory disarming of the Ionians. Criticism against the policy of the Ionian state was also made in the newspapers (*The Times* and the *Morning Chronicle*) under the influence of the philhellenic movement. However, during the first year of the war, neither Maitland nor the British government changed their views toward the Greek Revolution and they still refused to recognize the provisional Greek government (Wrigley 1988, 122–123).

The same year, the Ionians who were fighting with other Greeks, and the Philhellenes at Peta suffered a great defeat. The Cephalonians and Leukadians who survived went afterward to Mesolonghi, which was besieged from October to December 1822. During the siege, the civilian population was sent from Mesolonghi to Zante. Once the Turkish naval blockade of the town was raised, vessels from Zante and Cephalonia brought food and ammunition to the besieged, defying Ionian neutrality, and Mesolonghi successfully resisted that siege. A corps of fifty Cephalonians was also among those besieging the Turks inside the Acropolis of Athens in the first months of 1822 (Chiotis 1874–1877, 1:447–448).

The Ionian government was still unable to enforce neutrality; they could not protect vessels sailing under the Ionian flag and occasionally even British ships. The Greek navy controlled most of the sea routes in the wider region, even as far as Constantinople and Alexandria, and was often able to disrupt Ionian and British trade. It captured and plundered Ionian and British ships, especially those used to transport supplies to the Turks. Missions to recapture Ionian ships held by the Greeks were not always successful. For a while, even the British navy seemed unable to control the situation, until Captain Gawen William Hamilton of HMS *Cambrian* systematically visited the ports of the various squadrons responsible for the attacks on the Ionian vessels and asked for compensation, which he easily received. He also managed to retrieve several of the British ships that had been captured (Wrigley 1988, 149–151).

At the end of 1822 and the first months of 1823, there was an unofficial movement by some Peloponnesian notables to ask for British protection. A secret
communication took place in Zante to sound out Maitland's views on the subject, with the local *protopapas* and future metropolitan of Zante acting as an
intermediary. This scheme, however, was rejected by the Peloponnesian Senate
(Chiotis 1874–1877, 1:464–465).

In the meantime, several Ionians had distinguished themselves in the revolutionary movement. The two most prominent ones were the Cephalonian aristocrats Andreas and Constantinos Metaxas, who had joined the insurrection
from the beginning and had fought at the battle of Lala. In 1822, they were both
appointed to important offices in the Greek administration. Constantinos
Metaxas became minister of justice, subsequently prefect of the Aegean islands,
and army general in 1823. In 1824, he was appointed prefect of western Greece.
He was very successful in the administration of both these regions, under particularly difficult conditions. Andreas Metaxas became a nationalized Greek
citizen and then, minister of the police. He was sent, along with Alexandros
Raftopoulos and the French Philhellene Philip Jourdain, to present the Greek
cause at the Verona Congress. Metaxas was carrying letters of the Greek government to the kings of Europe, but he had to remain in quarantine at Ancona,
so the letters he carried were sent to the recipients with the help of Count Romas
and other expatriate Ionians who came to meet him (Chiotis 1874–1877, 1:477–
494; Vlachopoulos 2020, 165–168; Wrigley 1988, 213–215).

Although diplomatic protection of Ionian citizens in the Ottoman Empire
had been officially removed by the Ionian state, the Sublime Porte was very an-
noyed by the Ionian activities in the revolution. In December 1822, the Porte
demanded that all Ionian residents choose either to become citizens of the
Ottoman Empire or to sell their properties and leave. Soon, the Turks started
confiscating lands belonging to Ionians and even Ionian vessels enrolled in the
British maritime register. Viscount Strangford's repeated complaints and demands
finally resulted in at least the release of those vessels (Wrigley 1989, 170–173).
Maitland was also unable to improve the serious problem of Ionian shipping.
The official recognition by the British government of the belligerent rights of
the Greeks in 1823 helped in solving it. Canning's decision allowed the high
commissioner, in 1824, to proceed to an agreement with the Greek government
about the Morea blockade. In this way, Ionian shipping would be protected from
attacks by the Greek navy, according to Ionian neutrality. The recognition of
the belligerent rights of the Greeks gave them officially the right of asylum,
which included those already residing at Kalamos (Wrigley 1988, 173–179).

In 1824, Dionysios Romas returned to Zante from exile and established the famous Zakynthos Committee (Ἐπιτροπὴ Ζακύνθου), together with Dr. Panagiotis

Marinos Stephanou, member of a banking family, and Constantinos Dragonas, the director of the Zante lazaretto. All three had been members of the Philiki Etaireia, freemasons, and collaborators in the war effort in the Ionian islands and the rest of Greece. The committee's objectives were to help the fighting Greeks: to offer humanitarian aid, equipment, medicines, and ammunition; to charter ships to transport the material; to organize volunteers and ransom captives; and finally to seek the assistance of Britain toward the success of the revolution. Dragonas's position in the lazaretto greatly facilitated the secret correspondence between the Ionians and other Greeks, since all letters passed through quarantine and were opened and read by the British (Kambouloglou 1901–1905, vols. 1–2; Vlachopoulos 2020, 227–244).

The committee played an important role in the so-called Act of Submission, or petition to the British nation for assistance (Αἴτησις τοῦ Ἑλληνικοῦ Ἔθνους πρὸς τὸ Βρετανικόν) delivered in 1825. It took place at a critical juncture of the revolution, when the civil war was still dividing the Greeks and Ibrahim's troops were at the point of conquering the Morea. This imminent danger united most Greeks in this much-discussed controversial act. In the past, it was widely believed, or at least claimed, that Alexandros Mavrokordatos was behind this petition. Today, however, it is considered certain that the Zakynthos Committee had organized it. There must have been some sort of cooperation between the members of the committee and Sir Frederick Adam, all of them freemasons, over a rather vague general strategy, possibly originally organized, or at least endorsed, by British diplomacy (Dakin 1959, 89–94, 105, 125–129, 133–136, 149–150, 152–154; Trikoupis 1860–1862, 3:261–266; Vlachopoulos 2020, 271–282, 350–381).

The petition, written in Italian by Romas in June or July 1825, was sent in several copies translated into Greek to be signed by the main protagonists of the war. The imminent and inevitable danger of failure of the revolution made all important fighters and politicians sign the petition. Those who did not were fewer than ten. On the committee's recommendation, the documents were sent by a Greek ship to London in July to August 1825. Two copies of the petition were also brought to Corfu by Trikoupis, to be given to Adam. The original documents are in the National Archives in London and in Romas's papers in Athens.

The British government rejected the petition, claiming that it might lead to a war between Britain and the Ottoman Empire, but it offered its friendly mediation between the Greek and the Ottoman governments. In the meantime, Adam had reproclaimed Ionian neutrality, and placed an embargo on all Ionian commerce with the insurgents, in order to reduce the tension between London and Constantinople. He also tried to restrict British commerce with the Turks, including, for the first time, Consul Green's activities. Equally, he forbade any commercial transactions with the Greeks, and sequestrated for some time in an Anglo-Ionian bank the first installment of the Greek loan that had arrived in Zante in April 1824. The strict enforcement of neutrality hurt the constantly complaining Turks, who no longer enjoyed preferential treatment (Wrigley 1988, 187–189, 200).

The turn for the worse of the Greek military operations due to the civil war and the invasion of the Egyptian troops further mobilized Ionian fighters. One corps, under Daniil and Spyros Panas, was among those who defended Neokastro when it was besieged by Ibrahim's forces in the spring of 1825. The same year, during the new siege of Mesolonghi, the besieged asked the Zakynthos Committee for ammunition, food, medicines, and money to pay the soldiers, and the Zantiots continued sending the required support, while at the same time all the correspondence of the besieged passed through Zante. Fundraising for the needs of the besieged took place in Greece and in the Ionian islands. The Greek government assigned the task of negotiating another Greek loan of 100,000 Spanish dollars to the Zakynthos Committee, and authorized it to issue two-year bonds corresponding to the above amount on behalf of the Greek nation. Most of the money collected by the committee would immediately be given for the defense of Mesolonghi, but the loan was canceled because Mesolonghi fell on April 10, 1826 (Chiotis 1874–1877, 1:551–571; Vlachopoulos 2020, 444–460).

By that time, the refugee problem on the Ionian islands had serious financial consequences, as people kept arriving after fleeing Ibrahim Pasha's invasion. At first, Adam refused asylum to civilians from Mesolonghi. However, after the fall of the town and the advice of the British ambassador in Constantinople, he was obliged to receive the refugees; so many of the survivors went to Zante and Cephalonia, where the locals maintained them at their own expense, whereas others went to Kalamos, where their sustenance was subsidized by the British government. By September 1827, the refugees in Kalamos numbered about fifteen thousand (Wrigley 1989, 200–203, 206–207).

In 1826, the various small troops of Ionians fighting in Greece decided to unite and form a properly organized, regular corps. Thus, the so-called Eptanisian corps was established in Nafplio. This included most of the formerly Ionian irregular troops, along with the men from Parga. This corps had its own rules, seal, and administration. The men elected a seven-member committee and their own commander, who had to obey the committee's orders. There was also a secretary and a treasurer. The Ithakisian Dionysios Evmorfopoulos was the first elected commander. Soon after, a different Ionian corps was organized, under the influence of Andreas Metaxas and Constantinos Metaxas, who were close to Kolokotronis's faction. It included five hundred men from Zante and Cephalonia. Its structure was similar to that of the other Eptanisian corps, although less democratic. It was funded by two committees on the fighters' respective islands. However, the second corps was dissolved by the end of 1826 and its men were incorporated into the Eptanisian corps (Loukatos 1972–1973, 63–70).

The Eptanisian corps was soon ordered to join the Greek forces in Attica to defend Athens against Kütahı Pasha's army. Other Ionians, under Evmorfo-poulos, were already inside the besieged Acropolis. The newcomers took part in the Chaidari battle in August 1826; more Eptanisians joined them in September. In total, about two hundred and fifty men took part. Along with other fighters, they twice attempted in vain to enter the Acropolis to reinforce its guard. Eventually, they succeeded, and remained there fighting until the capitulation in August 1827 and their exodus from the Acropolis. In the meantime, other Ionians and two hundred men of the Zakyntho-Cephalonian corps had also been fighting in other battles around Athens (Loukatos 1972, 68–79).

The Third National Assembly in April 1827 unanimously elected Ioannis Capodistrias governor, for a seven-year term. Capodistrias's election caused new concerns to the lord high commissioner and the British government. When Capodistrias visited London, he was informed by both the Colonial and the Foreign Office that he should not visit Corfu or the other Ionian islands while the revolution lasted. Adam had cautioned the British government that Capodistrias's visit would incite violence on the islands. Adam firmly believed that Capodistrias aspired to incorporate the Ionian islands within liberated Greece and was suspicious of the governor's recently submitted memoir regarding his views on the future borders of Greece (Chiotis 1874–1877, 1:713–714; Wrigley 1989, 223–227, 255).

Despite the victory of the fleets of Britain, France, and Russia against the Turks in the naval battle of Navarino, Adam still insisted on the strict observance of Ionian neutrality. He was worried about the huge new wave of refugees that reached the Ionian islands after Navarino. He became increasingly suspicious of Capodistrias's intentions as the governor appointed several Ionians, his brothers Viaros and Avgoustinos Capodistrias included, to key positions in the administration of Greece. Being still afraid of Capodistrias's Russophile plans, he refused a loan to the Greek government, and proceeded with costly modifications of the fortresses of Corfu and of the Vido Island (Chiotis 1874–1877, 1:745–746; Wrigley 1988, 275–278).

The Ionian administration had been gathering intelligence throughout the revolution. Sometimes, in order to avoid suspicion, Ionian citizens passed pieces of information and occasional misinformation to the Ionian authorities. In 1827, Adam redoubled his efforts in gathering intelligence through the interception of correspondence, paid informants, or the British residents and Philhellenes.

Several of these last, displeased with Capodistrias's administration, were a major source for information about the events in Greece. Among those was Adam's former aide-de-camp, Major Edward Baynes. One of his salaried agents was George Lee, former secretary of the Greek Committee in London, and afterward of General Church. Lee's Greek connections often fed him information that served their own purposes, as was the case with Andreas Zaimis, a staunch enemy of Capodistrias. Adam's fears were based on rumors rather than actual facts, but his views influenced the policy of the British government (Dakin 1959; Wrigley 1988, 196–199, 258–261).

After the Egyptians' evacuation of the Morea, the refugee camp in Kalamos was closed down, and the Greek government was informed that it was responsible for the refugees' welfare. By December 1828, nearly all the Greek refugees had left Kalamos (Chiotis 1874–1877, 1:753; Wrigley 1988, 269–271).

Another contentious issue was the renewed emigration of Ionians to the Greek state; they went either as volunteers in the reformed Greek army or were otherwise employed by the Greek government in administrative positions. According to British sources, 190 highly qualified Ionians helped Capodistrias reform the Greek administration in 1829. Adam changed the previous punishment for those fighting in Greece to imprisonment and hard labor, but without success (Wrigley 1988, 274–278).

The influx of Ionians and their quick rise in various offices created suspicions and grievances among the local Greeks, who believed themselves marginalized in favor of the Ionians and other educated newcomers from abroad. Among those who served successfully to the end were the cousins Andreas and Constantinos Metaxas. The first was appointed a member of the Panellinion, and as head of the army helped reform it; then he was appointed prefect extraordinary of the Morea. Constantinos Metaxas was made prefect extraordinary of eastern Greece, and negotiated with the local Turks whether the river Spercheios would become the border of the new Greek state in the region.

From the end of 1827 onward, Ionians continued fighting alongside the Greek troops to recover central Greece, in order for it to be officially included within the borders of the Greek state. They participated in military operations in both western and eastern Greece until the last battle of the revolution at Petra, in September 1829. The small Greek state was officially recognized in the London Protocols of 1830, but the Ionian Islands remained a British protectorate. They were united with Greece after thirty-four years, in 1864.

Eleni Angelomatis-Tsougarakis

References

Angelomatis-Tsougarakis, Eleni. 2018. "Ζάκυνθος: η Φιλική Εταιρεία σε μια κοινωνία ανάμεσα σ' Ανατολή και Δύση" [Zakynthos: The Philiki Etaireia in a society between east and west]. *Οι πόλεις των Φιλικών. Οι αστικές διαδρομές ενός επαναστατικού φαινομένου* [The cities of the Philikoi: The urban pathways of a revolutionary phenomenon], edited by Olga Katsiardis-Hering, 149–172. Athens.

Chiotis, Panagiotis. 1874–1877. *Ιστορία του Ιονίου Κράτους από συστάσεως αυτού μέχρι της Ενώσεως (έτη 1815–1864)* [History of the Ionian state from its creation to unification, 1815–1864]. Zakynthos.

Crawley, Charles William. 1930. *The Question of Greek Independence: A Study of British Policy in the Near East, 1821–1833.* Cambridge.

Dakin, Douglas. 1959. "British Intelligence of Events in Greece 1824–1827: A Documentary Collection." *DIEEE* 13:33–217.

Dakin, Douglas. 1973. *The Greek Struggle for Independence, 1821–1833.* Berkeley and Los Angeles.

Frangos, George. 1973. "The Philiki Etairia: A Premature National Coalition." In *The Struggle for Greek Independence,* edited by Richard Clogg, 87–103. London and Basingstoke.

Kambouroglou, Dimitrios, ed. 1901–1905. *Ιστορικόν αρχείον Διονυσίου Ρώμα* [Historical papers of Dionysios Romas]. Athens.

Konomos, Dinos. 1966. *Ζακυνθινοί Φιλικοί* [Zantiot Philikoi]. Athens.

Konomos, Dinos. 1971. *Ιστορικές σελίδες και ανέκδοτα κείμενα. Αφιέρωμα εις τα 150 χρόνια της εθνεγερσίας (1821–1971)* [Historical pages and unpublished texts: Dedicated to the 150 years of the national uprising, 1821–1971]. Athens.

Konomos, Dinos. 1972. *Ο Διονύσιος Ρώμας και η ελληνική εθνεγερσία* [Dionysios Romas and the Greek the national uprising]. Athens.

Loukatos, Spiros. 1972–1973. "Επτανησιακά σώματα και η δράσις των κατά τον αγώνα της Ελληνικής ανεξαρτησίας" [Eptanisian corps and their activities during the struggle for Greek independence]. *Mnemosyne* 4:61–85.

Loukatos, Spiros. 1976. "Κεφαλονίτες και Θιακοί, μαχητικοί πρωτοπόροι κατά την Επανάσταση στη Μολδοβλαχία" [Cephalonians and Ithakisians, belligerent pioneers during the revolution in Moldowallachia]. *Kephalliniaka Chronica* 1:51–63.

Metaxas, Constantinos. 1878. *Ιστορικά απομνημονεύματα εκ της Ελληνικής Επαναστάσεως* [Historical memoirs from the Greek Revolution]. Athens.

Mexas, Valerios G. 1937. *Οι Φιλικοί. Κατάλογος των μελών της Φιλικής Εταιρείας εκ του αρχείου Σέκερη* [The Philikoi. A list of members of the Philiki Etaireia from the Sekeris papers]. Athens.

Philimon, Ioannis. 1859–1862. *Δοκίμιον ιστορικόν περί της Ελληνικής Επαναστάσεως* [A historical essay on the Greek Revolution]. Athens.

Prevelakis, Eleftherios, and Kallia-Kalliataki Merticopoulou, eds. 1996. *Η Ήπειρος, ο Αλή Πασάς και η Ελληνική Επανάσταση. Προξενικές εκθέσεις του William Meyer από την Πρέβεζα* [Epirus, Ali Pasha, and the Greek Revolution: The consular reports of William Meyer from Preveza]. Monuments of Greek History. Athens.

Spiliadis, Nikolaos. 1851–1857. *Απομνημονεύματα δια να χρησιμεύσωσιν εις την Νέαν Ελληνικήν Ιστορίαν (1821–1843)* [Memoirs to be used for modern Greek history, 1821–1843]. Athens.

Trikoupis, Spyridon. 1860–1862. *Ιστορία της Ελληνικής Επαναστάσεως* [History of the Greek Revolution]. 2nd ed. Athens.

Tzouganatos, Nikolaos. 1980–1982. "Η συμβολή των Κεφαλλήνων στην ανάπτυξη της Φιλικής Εταιρείας" [The contribution of the Cephalonians in the development of the Philiki Etaireia]. *Kephalliniaka Chronica* 4:236–265.

Vlachopoulos, Kharalambos Nikolaos. 2020. "Ο Διονύσιος Ρώμας και η Επιτροπή Ζακύνθου στον δρόμο για την εθνική ανασυγκρότηση: στοχεύσεις, υπερβάσεις, επιτεύξεις" [Dionysios Romas and the Zante Committee on the road toward national reconstruction: Purpose, transcendence, achievements]. Athens.

Wrigley, W. David. 1979. "The Ionian Islands and the Advent of the Greek State (1827–1833)." *Balkan Studies* 19, no. 2: 413–426.

Wrigley, W. David. 1987. "The Neutrality of Ionian Shipping and Its Enforcement during the Greek Revolution (1821–1831)." *Mariner's Mirror* 73, no. 3: 245–260.

Wrigley, W. David. 1988. *The Diplomatic Significance of Ionian Neutrality, 1821–1831.* New York.

Macedonia

In the early nineteenth century, Macedonia was not the official name of any Ottoman province; nor was it to become a province until 1913, when the Greek state named its newly annexed northern provinces the Governorate General of Macedonia (Geniki Dioikisis Makedonias). In the 1800s, European travelers, with a sound classical education, discussed the borders of this region in terms of ancient cartography and history; they had to judge themselves whether the northern lands of Paeonia, annexed by Philip II to his kingdom in 354 BCE, were indeed Macedonian or not. Yet they knew that this region was "a celebrated province of Greece," that is of ancient Greece, of course (Leake 1835, 3:440). The question whether it was destined to become part of modern Greece as well demanded an answer from the revolutionary Philiki Etaireia (Society of Friends).

Macedonia was by no means indifferent to the Society members. This brand name was very widely known and treasured by many. Alexander the Great and his glorious achievements had survived in popular culture, not exclusively in Greek-speaking popular culture. The adjective "Macedonian" implied bravery par excellence. In a general uprising, aspiring for the revival of ancient Hellas, Macedonia could not be absent, at least not from the Greek point of view. This region had not been untouched by the Greek Enlightenment but its influence should not be overemphasized outside the monastic society of Mount Athos and a few urban centers in western Macedonia (Kastoria, Kozani, Siatista) (Map 7). These towns were the birthplaces of some "conquering Orthodox merchants," who had earned their impressive fortunes and receptiveness to new ideas in central Europe, Russia, or the Danubian Principalities. A few of them joined the Philiki Etaireia. They were recruited not locally but abroad, together with some educators and men of arms, in the late 1810s. We may assume that they spread the Western ideas back home. However, the actual mission of the Society's delegates inside the Macedonian hinterland was by no means successful, to say the least. From 1819 to 1821 few bishops, monks, and local notables were initiated into the revolutionary cause. The failure to mobilize more Christians was not simply a matter of ill fortune and misunderstanding. Macedonia had a dense Muslim population, rural and urban, while the majority of the rural Christian population was illiterate Slav-speaking farm tenants, working for Albanian and Osmanli beys, a populace least expected to revolt. Hesitation to adopt revolutionary ideas was not just a matter of mentality, temperament, or education; it was not just a matter of mistrust between population groups of different language, culture, and occupation. It was a matter of full awareness that in Macedonia, crisscrossed by the main military arteries of the empire and residence of janissary guards, no revolutionary strategy could guarantee a successful outcome in the long run. Insurgency was a short cut for financial destruction and physical extermination.

Yet some Macedonians took the chance. The most prominent and best known among them was Emmanouil Papas. He was not a man of letters, but the son of a village priest, who made an impressive fortune as a merchant based in Serres, with branch offices in Vienna and Constantinople, and as a moneylender to Ottoman notables and officials, among them the powerful Ismail Bey, the master of eastern Macedonia. After Ismail's death in 1817, unable to extract the full loan from his son Yusuf Bey and fearing for his family security, Emmanouil Papas fled to Constantinople, where he joined the Philiki Etaireia in 1819. It is unknown how he managed to retrieve a good part of his capital from his debtor. What is documented is that he spent it for the purchase of guns and ammunition. After the revolution in the Danubian Principalities, following the orders of Prince Alexandros Ypsilantis, the head of Philiki Etaireia, Emmanouil Papas sailed to Mount Athos in late March 1821 with a full load of war supplies. The choice of the Chalkidiki peninsula in general and of Mount Athos in particular as the base of Greek operations in Macedonia has been explained with mixed arguments. If besieged, the fortress monasteries, built on the rocky slopes of Mount Athos and overlooking steep cliffs, could be easily defended. Monks, some of them already active friends of the Society, were expected to embrace the cause and to assist with their blessings, their treasures, or even with arms. As landlords, the monasteries might also influence their tenants, scattered on the other two pegs (or legs) of Chalkidiki, in favor of the uprising. The monastic peninsula could be easily supplied from the sea and serve as a base for launching naval attacks. The important town of Kavala, a strategic target, was within easy reach by land and sea. The northern narrow pass of Rentina, leading from Chalkidiki to the Strymon (Struma) valley, could be fortified and defended.

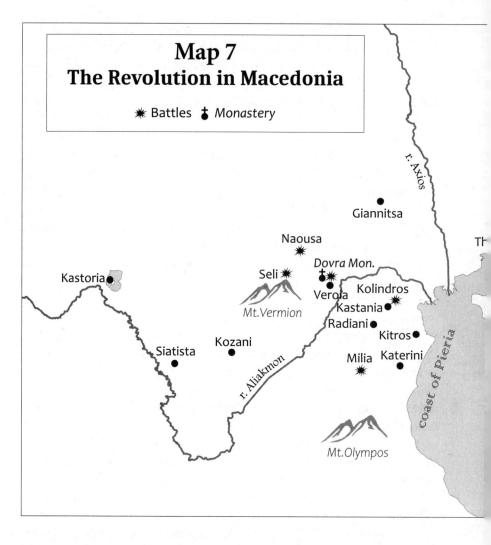

Map 7
The Revolution in Macedonia

✳ Battles ☦ Monastery

Giannitsa

Naousa
✳

Dovra Mon. ☦

Kastoria

Seli ✳

Kolindros
Veroia
Kastania ●
Mt.Vermion
Radiani ●

Kitros ●

Kozani
Siatista   Milia   Katerini
●   ✳

r. Axios

Th

Coast of Pieria

r. Aliakmon

Mt.Olympos

Moreover, dense Greek-speaking populations inhabited central and south-eastern Chalkidiki. In the central part, the well-known mining village communities, the Mademochoria, were in decay. Mine exhaustion and heavy taxation left them with no profit, unable to make ends meet, and therefore more inclined to risk a revolt. In terms of advantages in favor of an uprising, Chalkidiki was the Peloponnese of Macedonia.

At first sight, the choice of Chalkidiki had a serious strategic handicap, which indeed proved fatal: it was easily accessible from Thessaloniki. I believe that Emmanouil Papas's point of view was the opposite. Thessaloniki was close enough to be attacked and captured by the insurgents with naval support from the Aegean islands in the south. Obviously, it was an optimistic plan, disregarding the strong

fortification and the enmity of the demographically dominant Jewish community of Thessaloniki. Yet all available evidence and Emmanouil Papas's actual
maneuvering suggest that this was his master plan. Preconditions for success
were to hold the aforementioned Rentina pass, to muster a force capable of resisting early Ottoman attacks, to attract naval and ground forces from outside
Chalkidiki, and to threaten Thessaloniki sooner than later.

Revolutionaries in Athos kept a low profile until the end of May 1821, anticipating naval support and ammunition from the islands. Both were delayed and
scarce, a clear sign of reluctance and insufficient preparation. The will of the
monasteries to engage was weak. They were not really flourishing financially,
as all contemporaries assumed, and solidarity among them was in short supply.

Meanwhile, the Ottoman authorities, alarmed by the rising in southern Greece, rushed to summon hostages among the Christian notables in almost every single town of Macedonia. A raid launched from the island of Psara toward the mouth of the river Strymon and the subsequent looting of Ottoman merchandise by marine forces mobilized the guard at Serres. The Christians were disarmed, hostages were brought in, and their houses were pillaged in retaliation for Ottoman losses. Whatever weaponry was found in the Iliokali monastery just outside Serres, expected to serve as the headquarters of the rising, was confiscated. Despite Emmanouil Papas's plans and hopes, his homeland could not be mobilized to his assistance. Patrols were also dispatched from Thessaloniki to Chalkidiki. New evidence (Papaoikonomou 2013) suggests that Kassandra, the western peg of Chalkidiki, revolted on May 8, to be followed a week later by Polygyros, a town in central Chalkidiki not far from the coast. The house of the local governor in the latter town was seized and he was murdered with some of his troops. Skirmishes with more casualties followed, as the insurgents in the mountain mining villages engaged with the Ottoman militias and patrols, who were trying to spread and to secure their posts. A forged Ottoman source claimed that there was a massacre of Christians in Thessaloniki in May 1821; however, recently it has been shown that no mass massacre or execution took place (Sariyiannis 2015).

It was only after the bad news from Serres reached Emmanouil Papas, in the last days of May, that revolution was officially proclaimed in Mount Athos. Emmanouil Papas was appointed "Leader and Defender of Macedonia" by the Athonite council. The few villages along Sithonia, the middle peg of Chalkidiki, joined with enthusiasm those of Kassandra and the mining villages of the hinterland. Greek corsairs' patrolling the coast made them all feel secure. Emmanouil Papas put all his effort into securing more support from the islands that had revolted and even started a pourparler with the *armatoloi* of Mount Olympos. In spite of all the enthusiasm, he must have been aware of his weak position. Revolution was spreading toward Thessaloniki but insurgents were more like a mob than an army capable of pursuing strategic goals. Guns and ammunition were almost nonexistent. Experience was missing. As looting and random skirmishes continued throughout Chalkidiki, there was an urgent demand for military leadership. But there were not many men available to rely on. Emmanouil Papas had already turned to Stamos Chapsas, a native of Kassandra and a well-known klepht, who at the time had been hired as *serdar* (armed guard) by the Athos monasteries. Chapsas assisted Emmanouil Papas in recruiting hundreds of volunteers and was placed head of the insurgent forces pushing from central Chalkidiki to Thessaloniki. Emmanouil Papas, for his part, easily expelled the Ottoman guards from the coast of western Chalkidiki and occupied the Rentina pass.

In theory, the revolution throughout the peninsula was proceeding as it had been planned; but soon the tide turned against the Greeks. By early June the aforementioned Yusuf Bey, then deputy governor of Thessaloniki, had mustered, not without difficulty, an army sufficient in numbers and equipment to face the Greek revolutionary irregulars of his excreditor. It numbered eight thousand, followed by five hundred horsemen, and was headed by Ahmed Bey of Giannitsa. This force engaged with and defeated the army of Chapsas on June 9, 1821, at Vasilika, a village some twenty miles to the southeast of Thessaloniki. Chapsas was killed in action. Resistance at Galatista was also broken. Reinforced, the Ottoman army turned to the highlands of central Chalkidiki. It marched toward Polygyros, pillaging and burning the villages one by one, while other units devastated the whole plain of Kalamaria to the southeast of Thessaloniki. Hundreds of women and children were taken captives, brought to Thessaloniki, and sold as slaves. Dozens of heads were presented in triumph. Hundreds of hostages were placed in confinement. The Greek notables of Thessaloniki were arrested and pressed for excessive ransom. Two eminent merchants and the bishop of Kitros were beheaded on July 9, 1821 (OS), followed by a few others a week later (Soulis 1941–1952, 587). Polygyros, abandoned by the revolutionaries, was set on fire.

Meanwhile, the other front, at Rentina, had collapsed in mid-June, overwhelmed by the major forces of *serasker* Chadji Mehmet Bayram Pasha, who was marching on his way from Asia Minor to southern Greece. Crowds of refugees fled to Mount Athos expecting safety behind the trench that once was the Xerxes canal. Emmanouil Papas and most of the surviving fighters sought refuge to the south and barricaded themselves inside the Kassandra peg, protected by a shallow ditch and a wall, built in the early fifteenth century. By the end of June, resistance outside the pegs of Kassandra and Mount Athos had ceased almost entirely. As the army of Bayram Pasha moved to the south, burning the coast of Pieria, in late July, he sent the final account of his deeds to his master. He reported proudly the full destruction of forty-two towns and villages, the slaughter of all the "infidel filthy serpents," the enslavement of their wives and children, and the complete looting of their properties. His force was decimated one month later in the battle of Vasilika, on their way from Lamia to Atalanti.

Emmanouil Papas was trapped and there was no easy way out. He turned once again for assistance to the islanders and the Olympian chieftains. He needed ships to patrol the coast in case there was an Ottoman naval assault, to transport grain for the besieged, and to evacuate the insurgents in case the lines of defense were broken. He needed the gunpower of the Olympos brigands, klephts and *armatoloi* alike, to hold his position and strike back. His advances were met again with reluctance. No one was willing to offer his services for free. Some pressed for profit. They all expected their expenses and salaries to be covered by the monasteries; yet the latter were no less reluctant to invest in a dying cause. Evidence suggests that monks started to flee, carrying away cash and objects of value. The only exception to the rule was the assistance offered by Diamantis Nikolaou, the famous *armatolos* of Katerini, and some other captains, no more than six hundred men in all, some of them coming from Mount Pilion as well. They were enough to launch sudden counterattacks—which they did—but not to reverse the balance of power.

Meanwhile, the Ottomans were regrouping, not without serious impediments. Yusuf Bey assumed the Chalkidiki army leadership in mid-July and kept it for two months, until Mehmed Emin, the fearsome Abulubud, was appointed *serasker* and pasha of Thessaloniki. In mid-October, at the head of a force of three thousand, the new general was ready to launch his offensive against the Greek fortification on the isthmus of Kassandra, defended by fewer than five hundred fighters. The Greeks held their positions for almost two weeks. On October 30, their defense was broken and they were rapidly swept off Kassandra. They were followed by two hundred families who fled to escape slaughter or slavery. They were transported to the north Aegean islands, chiefly to Skopelos and Skyros, some as far as Atalanti. According to *The Times* (January 3, 1822), four thousand female slaves were brought to Thessaloniki and exhibited for sale. Emmanouil Papas crossed to Mount Athos only to realize that it could no longer be defended either. He sailed to Ydra but died on board ship of a heart attack. The monasteries surrendered to Mehmed Pasha peacefully before the end of the year; it has been argued that they even turned against Emmanouil Papas (Kokkinos 1956, 2:420–22). Sithonia and the island of Thasos surrendered too. It was time for compromise and there was hardly any room for negotiation. Mehmed Emin Pasha encouraged the repatriation of the refugees and spared the monasteries but exercised tremendous pressure to extract from the monks as much cash as possible.

It was an irony that the Greek revolutionary government expressed a more serious concern for Macedonia only after the uprising of Chalkidiki had shrunk, sometime in late summer 1821. By that time, the southern insurgents had won many battles and secured a firm grip both in the Morea (Peloponnese) and in Rumeli (central Greece). It was only natural then to see the bigger picture and from their point of view to appreciate any new front in the north which might decelerate the flow of Ottoman forces against them. The middleman was Nikolaos Kasomoulis, member of a merchant family from western Macedonia and a friend of the Society. He had been sent to the south as commissioner for "Southeastern Macedonians" and had tried in vain to coordinate the Olympos *armatoloi* with Emmanouil Papas's forces. His mediation bore fruits only in February 1822 when he returned to Mount Olympos. He was followed by a token expeditionary force which landed at the shores of Pieria, close to Mount Olympos, with two guns, spoils from the Tripolitsa, which had been dragged all the way from the Morea, via the island of Tinos, accompanied by two German gunners. In charge of the force was Grigorios Salas, an ex-officer in the Russian army, appointed by general-in-chief Dimitrios Ypsilantis. Salas was a brave and pompous man, yet unable to convince anyone of his military virtues. Immediately, they dispatched circulars and came into contact with Diamantis and other chieftains. In the eyes of many romantic Greeks and Philhellenes the fighting spirit of the Olympian warlords, their networks of power, and their military abilities had assumed legendary proportions. There could be no proper Greek rising without them.

By early 1822, revolutionary activities had been initiated in western Macedonia, which so far, in spite of the network set by the Philiki Etaireia and the events in Chalkidiki, had remained more or less idle. This must be explained. The western highlands depended a lot on the Olympians and on other renowned *armatoloi* of the interior, like Theodoros Ziakas; Tasos Karatasos, a native of Mount Vermion with an impressive property and six sons; and Angelis Gatsos, a Slav-speaking former klepht. All of them were involved in the war of the Sublime Porte against Ali Pasha Tepedelenli, the Lion of Ioannina, having initially been on his side. In fact, according to Ali's war plan, Karatasos had moved to Rumeli to avert outflanking. During this war Ziakas had suffered severe casualties and was compelled to change sides in order to be reinstated as an *armatolos*. The Olympians, on the other hand, Diamantis included, assisted the Sublime Porte in cleansing from Thessaly Ali's Albanian troops, their longtime adversaries. Karatasos was also involved in this round of fighting, most likely back again on the side of the Porte. By betraying Ali, all of them had managed to protect their posts and titles. Coming out of this civil war, it was not wise to risk a new one on the side of Papas, at least not without a serious reward which the monasteries, as mentioned above, refused to offer. In 1822, as the Olympians were more actively involved in the Greek cause, the *armatoloi* of Mount Vermion, Tasos Karatasos and Angelis Gatsos, were tempted to join. Apparently Greek victories in the south, with the participation of the Rumeli *armatoloi*, encouraged them to risk their *armatolik* offices. They had done so in 1807 and had managed to be pardoned and reinstated. Mass participation made it hard for the Porte to turn them against one another.

The leading notable of Naousa, the impressive and handsome Zafeirakis Theodosiou, and his party, so far reluctant to participate in any warfare which might favor his old enemy Ali Pasha, was convinced to turn against the sultan, after Ali's death in early 1822. His town, situated at the foothills of Mount Vermion had a fighting reputation earned after a decade of strong resistance against the campaigns of Ali Pasha in the years 1795–1804. It would not have been captured by Ali at all without the support from Zafeirakis's opposition party. He then escaped and managed through bribery to have a *firman* issued ordering Ali Pasha to evacuate Naousa. Zafeirakis restored his power and turned his town into a flourishing and fortified commercial center, famous not only for its wines but also for its guild of first-class gun makers. The patriotic letters of Salas, written by the philosopher priest Theophilos Kairis, one of Salas's volunteers, inviting the Macedonians to revolt for freedom, were read by the notables of Naousa in public. Having reconciled with his opposition, Zafeirakis exercised all his power and rhetoric to inspire his flock, until then reluctant to interrupt business. The people of Naousa were mesmerized by the speeches and burst into unnecessary killings, crying "motherland, motherland, freedom!" The much wiser option coined by Kasomoulis, to hit and run in the fashion of the klephts, rather than mobilize the towns and risk civilian lives, was not considered by Zafeirakis (Kasomoulis 1940, 186).

Whatever their plan was, Mehmed Emin Abulubud was waiting for them. The element of surprise had been lost long ago. The pasha was aware of all Greek preparations and secret meetings. As a matter of fact, Kasomoulis and his men, on their voyage to the shores of Katerini, on board two ships from Psara, had convinced the captains to fire some shells against the sea-walls of Thessaloniki. In a way, it was the bell for the second round. From the Ottoman point of view, given the support the *armatoloi* had offered to Ali Pasha and some of them to Papas as well, it was clear that they could no longer trust them.

The insurgents took special care for the control of Pieria, the strategic coastal plain under the shadow of Mount Olympos. Kasomoulis and the Olympians, joined by Salas and his unit, attacked the village of Kolindros in early March. Despite their enthusiasm and the use of artillery, their night operation had no major impact. The Ottoman forces outflanked the Greeks and pushed them deep into their mountain strongholds (Kastania, Radiani), which were successively captured in March. The stamina of the *armatoloi* had been overestimated by contemporary observers. With the exception of Diamantis, most of them opted for retreat and maneuvering, before being pinned down and exterminated. Many more remained neutral. Villagers were not supportive either, foreseeing serious calamities. After the battle of Milia, Diamantis, who had barely escaped, rushed to reinforce the Greeks of Naousa. Salas, Kairis, and a few dozen men, fewer than one hundred altogether, walked all the way back to Corinth.

By the time Diamantis moved to Naousa, the situation there was already desperate. In the last two weeks of March 1822 the offensive initiatives were met at best with moderate success. The insurgents had failed to capture Veroia, a town of considerable importance, but Karatasos and Gatsos had managed to hold back the early counterattacks of the Ottoman army at the monastery of Dovra. The rebels, unable to launch other strategic attacks or to instigate a wider Christian uprising, barricaded themselves in Naousa. Karatasos and Gatsos were placed outside the walls. Abulubud proceeded with an impressive force and artillery, having secured both his flanks and taken numerous hostages. Zafeirakis's political opponents were on his side. The siege most likely started in the last days of March and went on for two weeks. Zafeirakis rejected Ottoman offers for submission in exchange for pardon and from his bastion resisted for a further three days after the Ottoman forces had entered Naousa by assault and with heavy casualties. All the strongholds inside the walls, mostly churches, were conquered in spite of impressive yet little-known acts of bravery and sacrifice. At the top of this list is the suicide of several women with their infants who fell into the waterfall of Arapitsa to escape their destiny in servitude. There followed a general massacre, systematic pillaging, and the large-scale enslavement of women and children. The memory of the mass execution of all male prisoners after the siege outside the town survived in local tradition, supported by some eyewitness testimonies. One by one they were asked to convert and be spared but they all declined the offer (Baker 1877, 93–94). Dozens of captive insurgents and hostages were dragged to Thessaloniki and beheaded. The wives of the protagonists—Zafeirakis, Karatasos, and Gatsos—were tortured in public. Only the last of the three spouses survived, having accepted conversion to Islam. The children of Karatasos and Gatsos were sold as slaves.

Burning and plunder spread in the vicinity. Dozens of villages, perhaps more than one hundred, were raided and leveled. The walls of Naousa were demolished and Zafeirakis's chief opponent, Mamantis, took over the leadership of the Christian community. Siatista, an impressive and flourishing town, also scheduled to revolt, stayed aloof and managed to avoid an Albanian raid directed from Ioannina. Kozani was also spared after a handsome bribe was delivered to the Albanian raiders. In Thessaloniki Mehmed Emin continued to tax arbitrarily, extract money in every possible way, and terrorize. The most notorious example of his tyranny, which went on until his replacement in 1823, was the execution of Emmanouil Kyriakou, the vice-consul of Denmark, in June 1822, on the charge of conspiracy, when he refused the pasha a loan of 100,000 francs.

Surprisingly, Zafeirakis managed to escape from his bastion and to regroup with Karatasos, but they were ambushed and dispersed anew at a mountain pass near Seli. This time Zafeirakis and Giannakis, the son of Karatasos, sought refuge in the vicinity of Veroia but were betrayed, encircled, and killed. Their heads were exhibited at the gates of Thessaloniki. Karatasos, with his other son Dimitrios (Tsamis), Gatsos, and others, continued to raid the region of Mount Vermion for a while, as long as they hoped they could negotiate the release of their next of kin. They failed and left for Rumeli. Warfare in Macedonia was prolonged until mid-August 1822, when the last band of Kostas Malamos and Nasios Kampitis was exterminated after a three-day battle. Malamos was shot dead and Kampitis was hanged from a plane tree at the central square of Veroia. Diamantis and other Olympians with their families sought refuge on the islands of the north Aegean, Skyros, Skiathos, and Skopelos. They had all good reasons to return and extract revenge.

An overall assessment of the 1821–1822 defeat of the revolutionaries in Macedonia must first stress the negative background; not so much the deficit in ideological preparation, but the superiority of Ottoman manpower. Although the janissary system was in disarray, the Sublime Porte could still count not only on the greed of the slave-seeking Albanian mercenaries but also on the Koniars and the Yuruks, hardened agricultural and pastoral Muslim populations, ready to enlist if there were good chances for pillaging. In other words, the Christian army could be easily outnumbered. As mentioned above, it was the full awareness of this reality that maximized the significance of other concerns and cleavages. Even if *armatoloi,* monasteries, notables, villagers, and land tenants wanted to rise, they preferred to do so without exposing themselves too much, without destroying the possibility of negotiating a pardon, without exhausting their assets and manpower. In addition, the master plan of the Philiki Etaireia was not free from serious shortcomings. The war of the Sublime Porte against Ali Pasha indeed favored a revolution in the Peloponnese but not in Macedonia. Preoccupied in various ways with the war of the Porte against Ali Pasha, which seriously endangered their status in 1820, not all the *armatoloi* were prepared to fully commit themselves to a new and extremely risky cause in 1821. Unlike the Peloponnese, where the Maniots had an army of their own, in Macedonia, in the absence of *armatoloi* or if they performed badly, there was no serious substitute to their power and expertise.

This brings us to a more general point: A mass rising of the Christians in all Greek lands was doomed to fail a priori. There were not enough capital assets, war supplies, and manpower, no sufficient communications to organize, coordinate, and sustain a massive revolution and bring it to a successful end. Neither the Aegean islands nor the Athos monasteries could support a front in the distant northern regions under the pressure of major Ottoman armies. For the same reasons, cities in revolt outside a secure military perimeter, like Naousa, could not be defended. Such massacres could be avoided. In this context Macedonia in general might be considered as a necessary and beneficial sacrifice for the overall cause. Although this was not part of the initial plan, it served as a diversion at the time it was greatly needed in the south.

However, for all those Macedonians who fled, the war was not over, nor was hope to liberate their homeland, or at least to return and resume anew their prestigious and remunerative offices. The majority made northern Sporades their home; an archipelago along the east coast of Greece, northeast of the island of Euboea within easy reach of Mount Pilion, the pegs of Chalkidiki, the shore of Pieria, and the island of Psara. In the following months and years, they were joined by more refugee fighters, most likely more than two thousand in all (cf. Hionidis 1977). The local islanders were overwhelmed by the crowd of refugees, their military power and resolution. Soon, the Olympians and some other chieftains from Chalkidiki, like the Doubiotis family, became the true masters of these islands. They suppressed with brutal force any local resistance, assumed all the important offices, and collected and embezzled taxes and port duties. In the absence of food resources sufficient to sustain them, this experienced armed force soon turned to unrestricted piracy against Muslims and Christians alike, without sparing European cargoes, to sustain their families, support and equip their numerous followers, regain their lost property, and assume—even as refugees—a social status of some importance. The booty was crucial for the economy of the Sporades islands and sufficient to bribe the island notables and keep them on a short leash. Their aides-de-camps, petty captains, and other followers had no alternative either. Outlawed in Macedonia, without any steady income or lot of land, with guns as their only tools of trade, it was easy for them to turn into unscrupulous freebooters—especially if their families had perished—yet not always without regrets.

Most of all, this pirate force targeted Mount Athos, the shores of Chalkidiki, Pieria, Thasos, and other accessible and defenseless islands. One of their least-known raids was the night intrusion perpetrated by the Kalamidas brothers, natives of Mount Pilion, into Thessaloniki, in late 1822, through a gutter, to kidnap a Jewish banker for ransom. They failed to arrest the banker but on the same night they killed forty-five Ottomans in a nearby inn and abducted a number of Jewish fishermen. The most impressive raid was that by Constantinos Doubiotis with more than thirty pirate ships on the shore of Ormylia in May 1826. They sacked several villages and the town of Polygyros, several miles away from the coast. The violence exercised on Christian villagers was unspeakable. The governor of Thessaloniki had to dispatch a unit of two thousand men. This force fought against Doubiotis's pirates in the battle of Ormylia but suffered very heavy casualties and failed to expel them. By the time reinforcements arrived, the pirates had withdrawn to their ships and vanished. The most remunerative raid recorded was perhaps the attack on Mount Athos in early

1828 where the same captains managed by torture to collect from the monks around one million piasters.

However, the might of the Macedonian fighters was not invested exclusively in piracy. Relentless war against the Ottomans was their primary task. This rich pool of men, experienced and ready for war, without special concerns for local interests other than their own profit, was indispensable for the conduct of operations in Rumeli, the Morea, and the islands. Homeless and deprived of any steady income other than booty, they depended heavily on the revolutionary governments. Karatasos and Gatsos were allied to Alexandros Mavrokordatos. Soon after their descent to Rumeli, they fought and excelled in the battles of Plaka and Peta (June–July 1822). Gatsos with one hundred men impressed the Moraites in the battle of Dervenakia (July 1822). Diamantis, ambitious and restless, was called on for a more complicated duty. When Areios Pagos, the revolutionary government of eastern Rumeli, and the powerful *armatolos* Odysseas Androutsos drifted apart, the former turned to the Macedonians for military support and invited them to Euboea as mercenaries. Diamantis was appointed chief commander of Euboea, defeated his local adversaries, and spent all his energy to increase his income. Karatasos was also appointed commander of a force of two thousand, mostly of Macedonians, and was stationed at Trikeri, at the very east end of Mount Pilion, supported financially by the Trikeriots. This was the last Greek revolutionary hold in Thessaly.

A few months later, in mid-1823, both faced strong attacks. In April the Ottomans advanced against Trikeri but were checked by Karatasos and other Olympian captains. In one of the side battles Gatsos massacred two hundred and fifty prisoners, a clear sign of his appetite for revenge. In July, Yusuf Berkoftsali Pasha turned to Euboea with a mighty force. Diamantis and his eight hundred men abandoned the Greek camp at Vasilika and fled, but one of his captains, Stavros Vasileiou, and his men resisted but were denied ammunition by Diamantis. It was around that time that Karatasos started to negotiate his retreat from Trikeri, unwilling to engage openly with Mehmed Reşid Pasha, the notorious Kütahı, despite his superior position and better-supplied force. In mid-August, not without complaints from his fellow captains, he accepted the offer of Kütahı (Perraivos 1836, 2:19–20). Among other terms in favor of the Thessalian *armatoloi* and the evacuation of the Ottoman forces from the region of Volos (Magnesia), the pasha provided for the release of Karatasos's and Gatsos's captive children. After the compromise, Karatasos pressed hard and extracted the salaries the villages owed him, some 40,000 piasters. Then, they all together sailed for Skiathos. Their children, however, were never delivered.

In Skiathos, the Macedonian *armatoloi* regrouped and in late August officially appointed Karatasos as their commander. Although their contribution was requested anew fairly soon, they were reluctant to leave the island as their relations with the locals worsened. In fact, the Skiathos notables accepted the Ottoman offer to capitulate on condition that the Macedonians were ousted from their island. In early October 1823, the Ottoman navy landed units on Skiathos, but they were decimated on the beaches. In 1824, Karatasos and his followers returned to action in Euboea, moved to Ydra, where he was assigned the protection of the island, before they ended up in Athens. Meanwhile, another force of Macedonians, one thousand strong, under the leadership of Nannos Tsontzas—a native of Kozani, former klepht in the Mount Olympos region and veteran of the 1822 uprising—had been hired to secure Psara, an island heavily populated by refugees, from an impending Ottoman invasion. The Ottomans managed to land in late June 1824 but then faced the relentless resistance of the Macedonians. As the latter were eventually overrun and the islanders were being massacred, a few dozen of them barricaded themselves in the fortified monastery of St. Nicholas. Desperate but unwilling to surrender, they set the powder keg on fire.

In Athens, Karatasos, Gatsos, and Constantinos Doubiotis were invited by their friend Makrygiannis to join the captains of Rumeli and all together assist, on payment, the revolutionary government of Kountouriotis to suppress the mutiny of Kolokotronis and his party. They consented. Their invasion of the Morea in late 1824, with Gouras on their side, had devastating effects. They committed unspeakable cruelties against civilians, including systematic plundering. By the time the civil war was over, the Arab forces of Ibrahim Pasha of Egypt had landed (January 1825). Unlike other Macedonian captains who evacuated the Peloponnese soon after the looting, Karatasos with three hundred men fought against the Egyptian forces and reinstated his war fame at the battle of Schoinolakkas (May 1825), where he and his men ambushed a mixed force of infantry and cavalry, and captured their lancers. It is hard to follow his less-known meanderings and campaigns in the years 1825–1828 from Ydra, to the Peloponnese, Attica, Skiathos, Thasos, Euboea, Atalanti, Trikeri, Nafpaktos, with or without Gatsos, for freedom and occasionally for tax collection.

Diamantis, for his part, having spent most of his energy in piracy, returned to Thessaly and Olympos, chiefly pursuing his reappointment to his old *armatolik* and from time to time a new uprising. Neither Ypsilantis nor Capodistrias responded to his calls for assistance. When the latter took office as governor of Greece, Admiral Miaoulis was ordered to chase the Olympian pirates from the north Aegean and, in the process, he managed to burn down a considerable part of their flotilla (1828). Capodistrias also provided for a regular army unit consisting of one thousand Macedonians and Thessalians under the command of Tolios Lazos, scion of an illustrious *armatoloi* family, yet a mild and literate man. Naturally, Karatasos and Gatsos, who were too old to assume military offices in the regular army, were displeased. Karatasos died in 1831 and Gatsos in 1839, having achieved the release of his captive son in 1831. Some Macedonian captains returned to their homelands and managed to be reinstated as *armatoloi* for a brief period until 1830, when they experienced another round of hostilities and expatriation. Diamantis Nikolaou was among them.

Macedonian fighters, from Mount Olympos, Chalkidiki, Serres, or from the western highlands can be spotted almost in every single battle of the War of Independence, the sieges of Mesolonghi included. Their services, paid or unpaid, were needed everywhere. They were tough and rough with the enemy, loyal to their captains and to the revolutionary authorities if paid, ruthless freebooters when unpaid. Their leaders were among the most experienced in brigand warfare: cruel with the enemy, ready to capitulate to avoid unnecessary casualties, prepared to die fighting if trapped or ambushed. Most of their followers, however, gradually retreated to their Ottoman-held villages, exhausted from expatriation, poverty, fratricide, and the endless sacrifice of blood. Some settled down in Atalanti, supported financially by their compatriot Baron Constantinos Velios, a wealthy diaspora Macedonian merchant and stockbroker. Others, on both sides of the new border, remained active and participated in the Albanian rebellions of the 1830s, as professional fighters, occasional outlaws, and eternal dreamers of a great idea that would set Macedonia free from the Ottoman Turks.

Basil C. Gounaris

References

Baker, James. 1877. *Turkey in Europe*. London.

Gounaris, Vasilis K. 2017. "Η πειρατική επιδρομή του Κωνσταντίνου Δουμπιώτη στη Χαλκιδική και η άγνωστη μάχη της Ορμύλιας (1826)" [The pirate raid of Constantinos Doubiotis on Chalkidiki and the unknown battle of Ormylia, 1826]. *Makedonika* 42:513–520.

Hionidis, Giorgos. 1977. "Οι Μακεδόνες πρόσφυγες της Σκοπέλου στα 1829" [The Macedonian refugees in Skopelos in 1829]. *Makedonika* 17:124–138.

Hionidis, Giorgos. 1980. "Ανέκδοτα έγγραφα και άγνωστα στοιχεία για κλεφταρματολούς και για την επανάσταση (1821–1822)" [Unpublished documents and unknown data on the *klepht*s and *armatoloi* and the revolution, 1821–1822]. *Makedonika* 20:103–166.

Kasomoulis, Nikolaos. 1940. *Ενθυμήματα στρατιωτικά της Επαναστάσεως των Ελλήνων 1821–1833* [Military reminiscences of the Revolution of the Greeks, 1821–1833]. Vol. 1. Athens.

Kokkinos, Dionysios A. 1956. *Ιστορία της ελληνικής επαναστάσεως* [History of the Greek Revolution]. Athens.

Leake, William Martin. 1835. *Travels in Northern Greece*. London.

Papaoikonomou, Nikolaos. 2013. "Νέα στοιχεία για την επανάσταση της Κασσάνδρας το 1821" [New data on the revolution in Kassandra in 1821]. *Ta Chalkidikiotina Nea* 143 (April–June): 3.

Perraivos, Christophoros. 1836. *Απομνημονεύματα πολεμικά διαφόρων μαχών συγκροτηθεισών μεταξύ Ελλήνων και Οθωμανών κατά τε το Σούλιον και Ανατολικήν Ελλάδα από του 1820 μέχρι του 1829 έτους* [War memoirs of several battles between Greeks and Ottomans both at Souli and in Eastern Greece from 1820 to the year 1829]. Athens.

Sariyannis, Marinos. 2015. "Μια πλαστή πηγή για τις σφαγές του 1821 στη Θεσσαλονίκη: Ο «Χαϊρουλλάχ εφέντης του Αβραάμ Ν. Παπάζογλου»" [A forged source on the 1821 massacres in Thessaloniki: "Hairullah efendi of Abraam N. Papazoglou"]. *Mnimon* 34: 11–36.

Soulis, Georgios Chr. 1941–1952. "Η Θεσσαλονίκη κατά τας αρχάς της Ελληνικής Επαναστάσεως" [Thessaloniki at the beginning of the Greek Revolution]. *Makedonika* 2: 583–589.

Spanos, Kostas. 1980. "Δεκατέσσερα έγγραφα των αγωνιστών Νικολάου-Ολυμπίου" [Fourteen documents of fighters Nikolaou-Olympiou]. *Makedonika* 20:283–306.

Vakalopoulos, Apostolos. 1981. *Εμμανουήλ Παπάς. Η ιστορία και το αρχείο της οικογενείας του* [Emmanouil Papas: History and his family papers]. Thessaloniki.

Vakalopoulos, Apostolos. 1988. *Ιστορία της Μακεδονίας 1354–1833* [History of Macedonia, 1354–1833]. Thessaloniki.

Vasdravellis, Ioannes K. 1940a. "Η Μακεδονική Λεγεών κατά το 1821" [The Macedonian Legion in 1821]. *Makedonika* 1:77–107.

Vasdravellis, Ioannes K. 1940b. *Οι Μακεδόνες εις τους υπέρ της ανεξαρτησίας αγώνας* [The Macedonians in the struggles for freedom]. Thessaloniki.

Xanthopoulou-Kyriakou, Artemis. 1994. "The Revolution of 1821 and Macedonia." In *Modern and Contemporary Macedonia*, edited by Ioannis Koliopoulos and Ioannis Hassiotis. Vol. 1, *Madeconia under Ottoman Rule*, 458–477. Thessaloniki.

Mesolonghi

In the early nineteenth century, Mesolonghi was a small town of 5,500 inhabitants situated at a lagoon in the westernmost part of the Ottoman Empire. According to Edward Dodwell, who had visited there during his travels in Greece, Mesolonghi flourished briefly after 1740, when fifty merchant ships owned by members of its community sailed the Mediterranean. However, ships, profits, and the city itself perished in 1770, when the Ottomans burned down the place while quelling a Greek rebellion that had erupted with Russian instigation during the Russo-Turkish War of 1768–1774. In the aftermath of its destruction, Mesolonghi was rebuilt, recovering its population, if not its previous prosperity; Dodwell recorded merely twelve large merchant ships in 1805 (Dodwell 1819, 1:90–92; Leon 1972, 29–32; Makris 1957, 18–19). This is possibly one of the reasons that delayed the city's commitment to the Greek War of Independence. While an abortive rebellion erupted in the Danubian Principalities (Wallachia and Moldavia) in February 1821 and the Peloponnese and eastern Rumeli followed suit at the end of March, the west was slower to react. Closer to the roads connecting the core Ottoman provinces to Greece, it was easier to reach from the north, where great Ottoman forces were stationed at the time, and destined to bear the brunt of any invading army. It was also an area divided between powerful *armatoloi*, and their own balance of power and power plays held a significant role both before and during the revolution. There was also the matter of the conflict of Ali Pasha of Ioannina with Sultan Mahmud II. What was to consider here was not only whether this would help or hinder the insurgents' cause but also the fact of the existing connection between Ali Pasha and some of the strongest local *armatoloi* (Ioannis Rangos, Andreas Iskos, Georgios Karaiskakis). Most of them, including the foremost among them, Georgios Varnakiotis (1778–1842), initially remained ambivalent.

Politics, Rifts, and Dissension

As a result, Mesolonghi came to the decision to join the revolution on May 20 (June 2, New Style), two full months after the rest of southern Greece and after having at least part of its fleet ferry Ottoman forces to fight against Greeks in the Peloponnese (Efthymiou 2019, 19). In early May, the defeat of the Turkish forces in eastern Rumeli at Gravia and in the Peloponnese at Valtetsi tipped the scales for Varnakiotis. Before his raising the banner of the revolution, though, Mesolonghi had already rebelled when a squadron of ten Greek ships had sailed in the Corinthian Gulf near the town. Local leaders (Athanasios Razikotsikas, Panos Papaloukas, Apostolos Kapsalis, and others) took the initiative receiving at first military help from Dimitrios Makris (1778–1842), another well-known *armatolos*. Almost instantly, the town became the center of gravity of western Rumeli; its position turned it to the northern bastion of the Peloponnese (Spyridon Trikoupis called it "naturally fortified," being defended by marshes and a shallow lagoon [Trikoupis 1888, 2:265], while from quite early on it became the power base of a deft politician, Alexandros Mavrokordatos).

Mavrokordatos, a scion of a prominent Phanariot family, former manager of foreign affairs to his uncle Ioannis Karatzas (who had been ruler of Wallachia under the Ottomans between 1812 and 1818, self-exiled in Italy afterward), arrived in Mesolonghi in July 1821. Skilled negotiator, well versed in intrigue, he charmed or cajoled chieftains and civic leaders alike. He quickly undertook the task of setting up a local administration. In November 1821, an assembly met and voted into existence the Organization of Western Rumeli, a regional constitution written by Mavrokordatos. Brief and clear as to its provisions, it conformed to the pressing need for structures and institutions to wage war. At the same time, Mavrokordatos managed to secure a power base by setting himself up as political and military leader. When the First National Convention convened in Epidavros in December 1821 he could and did play a most significant part as the political power behind western Greece.

Mavrokordatos's conduct highlights the rivalries developed during the revolution. These not merely represented a struggle for power between its constituting elements, former *armatoloi* and klephts, wealthy landowners (*kocabaşıs*), merchant islanders, Phanariots, Western-educated Greeks returned from the diaspora. In Mesolonghi one can detect early on, for example, a social and cultural cleavage between Souliots and natives. Fleeing their villages in Epirus after a successful Ottoman campaign against them in 1822, these warriors, famous for

their military prowess, strengthened the town's garrison but also forcefully demanded money and housing in a way that brought about conflict. At the same
time, a follower of Mavrokordatos noted that "the city's aristocracy" and "a mob
movement" openly denounced a series of his administrative appointees. The
local leader Athanasios Razikotsikas (1798–1826) was mentioned as "disturber-
in-chief" by both Mavrokordatos and Constantinos Metaxas (1793–1870),
prefect of the city in 1823 (Svolopoulos 2007, 66–69). These clashes between
natives and outsiders, former prime movers and new men, well-off and poor,
politicians and military leaders, Peloponnesians and Rumeliots, would develop into two rounds of civil war in 1824–1825.

The first one was already brewing when Lord Byron arrived in Mesolonghi
on December 24, 1823 (January 5, N.S.). Poet and all-round celebrity, supporter
of the Greek cause, in fact, the best-known Philhellene in Europe, he was a
useful symbol and an important financial source (hiring his own personal guard
of five hundred Souliots, he experienced firsthand their ability to polarize people
with their disorderly behavior and was forced to disband it). Cheered by all and
pursued by most factions, Byron chose Mesolonghi as his abode to avoid getting involved in Greek divisions and to work with Mavrokordatos, with whom
he had already exchanged letters (Beaton 2013, 180–189). Although he stood by
his policies throughout his stay in the city until his death on April 19, 1824, on
numerous occasions Byron noted the continuing rifts and spoke of the urgent
need to restore unity among the Greeks through peaceful (or even violent) measures (Beaton 2013, 236–237, 266–267, 277).

Another Philhellene who made his presence felt at Mesolonghi was the Swiss
Johann-Jacob Meyer (1798–1826), who played an active role as one of the founders
of Greek journalism with the publication of the important bi-weekly newspaper
Ελληνικά Χρονικά (1824–1826), one of the most important and influential early
Greek newspapers. The journal promoted the ideas of philosophic radicalism, as
suggested by the extensive extract from Jeremy Bentham's pamphlet on the
freedom of the press, in the prospectus announcing its publication on December 18, 1823 (December 30, N.S.). Bentham's and Byron's associate Colonel
Lester Stanhope supported Meyer's efforts by making available to him a printing
press and typographical font. Meyer died fighting at the exodus on April 10, 1826.
(See further Roxanne D. Argyropoulos, "The Press," in this volume.)

First Siege and Interlude

A war waged under these conditions by political and military elites in a nascent
state, where financial power was a precondition to political and military power,
was bound to suffer from lack of coordination (Kostis 2018, 57–59). This would

hamper repeatedly the defensive capabilities of Mesolonghi, especially in its two long sieges by the Ottomans (October 25 to December 31, 1822, and April 15, 1825, to April 11, 1826). Toward the end of the summer of 1822, after winning a resounding victory in Epirus (battle of Peta, July 4, 1822) Reşid Mehmed Pasha Kütahı (1780–1836) and Omer Vrioni brought an army of ten to twelve thousand into western Rumeli. Before reaching Mesolonghi, they tried to lure Varnakiotis to their side. In order to buy time to prepare the city for a siege, the Greek government authorized him to enter into negotiations. After a protracted give and take, however, he decided to accept the Turkish offer along with Iskos and Georgios Valtinos. This was a blow to the defenders of Mesolonghi, especially since two other major revolutionary leaders in the area, Karaiskakis and Rangos, were feuding over the captaincy of the Agrafa region (Gordon 2015, 2:182–192; Trikoupis 1888, 2:232–235).

According to Thomas Gordon, Mesolonghi at the time could not field more than 380 soldiers with provisions for a month. The city was not adequately fortified: there was a moat only five feet deep and seven feet wide below a short wall four feet high and two and a half feet wide with fourteen cannons; however, the uneven twists and turns of its lines demanded the presence of four thousand for the battlements to be considered fully manned (Gordon 2015, 2:187–188). George Finlay adds that "heavy rain had rendered the bottom of the ditch a soft mass of tenacious clay, which made it impassable to a man on foot" (Finlay 1861, 1:336). Vrioni was reluctant to storm the city and argued to Kütahı and Yusuf Pasha of Patras, who had sent an Ottoman navy squadron to run a sea blockade, that it should be preserved as a prospective base and camp for future campaigns. Negotiating a surrender should be their first priority. Markos Botsaris (ca. 1788–1823), leader of a small detachment of Souliots, became Vrioni's negotiating partner looking again to gain time. On November 11, four Ydriot ships broke the blockade and six hundred soldiers reinforced the guard. At a later date, the added power of Andreas Lontos (1784–1845), Georgios Tsongas (died 1838 / 1839), Dimitrios Makris, and Alexandros Vlachopoulos (1780 / 1787–1865) raised the number of Mesolonghi's defenders to 2,000–3,000 (Gordon 2015, 2:191–193; Trikoupis 1888, 2:268–270). Meanwhile, Ottoman supply lines were being harassed by armed bands of Greeks, and Botsaris broke the negotiations, forcing Vrioni and Kütahı to form a plan of general attack. Set for December 25 to surprise the defenders expected to be at the Christmas mass, it was preceded by artillery barrage, but the guard was informed of it and the charge was repulsed with heavy Turkish casualties. Unable to sustain a working supply line or take the city, Vrioni broke up camp on December 31 and retreated to his base.

The following year proved to be a temporary respite for Mesolonghi. Although Mustai Pasha of Skodra and Omer Vrioni led again an army of fifteen

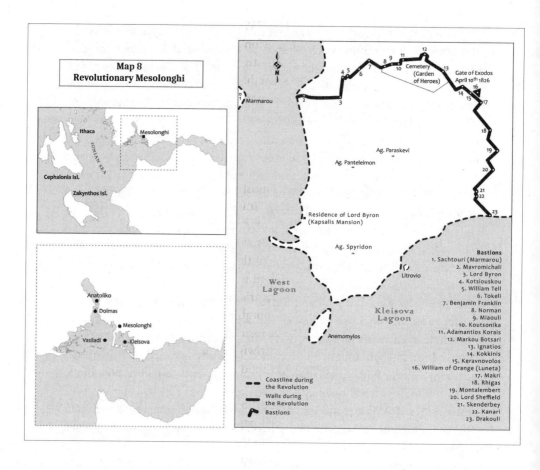

Map 8
Revolutionary Mesolonghi

Marmarou

Cemetery
(Garden
of Heroes)

Gate of Exodos
April 10ᵗʰ 1826

Ithaca

Mesolonghi

IONIAN SEA

Cephalonia Isl.

Zakynthos Isl.

Ag. Paraskevi

Ag. Panteleimon

Residence of Lord Byron
(Kapsalis Mansion)

Ag. Spyridon

Litrovio

West
Lagoon

Kleisova
Lagoon

Anemomylos

Anatoliko

Dolmas

Mesolonghi

Vasiladi   Kleisova

Coastline during
the Revolution
Walls during
the Revolution
Bastions

Bastions
1. Sachtouri (Marmarou)
2. Mavromichali
3. Lord Byron
4. Kotsiouskou
5. William Tell
6. Tokeli
7. Benjamin Franklin
8. Norman
9. Miaouli
10. Koutsonika
11. Adamantios Korais
12. Markou Botsari
13. Ignatios
14. Kokkinis
15. Keravnovolos
16. William of Orange (Luneta)
17. Makri
18. Rhigas
19. Montalembert
20. Lord Sheffield
21. Skenderbey
22. Kanari
23. Drakouli

thousand in western Rumeli, the former's vanguard was stopped at Karpenisi on August 9 and, when the joined armies finally arrived in the Mesolonghi area, they bypassed the city to strike at Anatolikon on the opposite side of the lagoon. They laid siege to it from October 7 to November 18, but its five hundred defenders managed to hold on until heavy rains and sickness discouraged the Ottomans (Gordon 2015, 2:292–300). Meanwhile, as Finlay observed, "Mesolonghi was in a good state of defense" (1861, 2:85). Michael Kokkinis, a Greek engineer who had served in Napoleon Bonaparte's army (Svolopoulos 2007, 97), oversaw the construction of an earthen rampart extending "from the waters of the lagoon across the promontory on which the town was built." Partly faced with masonry, flanked by two bastions near the center, protected by a battery on an islet at the point where it joined the lagoon and endowed with fifty-two guns, it was a definite upgrade from its previous incarnation (Finlay 1861, 2:85). The naming of these fortifications is extremely interesting, showing a mix of influences and perceptions: "Lord Byron," "William Tell," "Benjamin Franklin," "William of Orange," "Kosciuszko," and "Montalebert" lay alongside "Adamantios Korais," "Markos Botsaris," "Constantinos Kanaris," and "Georgios Sachtouris" (Trikoupis 1888, 3:208) (Map 8). At this point, just prior to the renewal of the siege, the city could rely on four thousand soldiers while housing almost twelve thousand noncombatants.

Second Siege and Fall

"The second siege of Mesolonghi is the most glorious operation of the Greek Revolution," according to George Finlay. "It is also one of the most characteristic of the moral and political condition of the nation, for it exhibits the invincible energy of its people in strong contrast with the inefficiency of the military chiefs and the inertness and ignorance of the members of the government" (Finlay 1861, 2:84). Lasting for a year (April 15, 1825, to April 11, 1826), it would indeed test the strength of the revolutionaries at a critical junction; after two civil wars their finances were depleted, morale was low, persons of ability were excluded due to their having backed the losing side in the strife, the insurrection was under mortal threat from a whirlwind campaign the tactical army of Ibrahim Pasha of Egypt (1789–1848) was conducting in the Peloponnese, heartland of the revolution.

Initially, it was Mehmed Reşid Kütahı who returned early in the year before the Greeks had time to man the crucial pass at Makrynoros (Gordon 2015, 3:61) or after they abandoned their positions there (Trikoupis 1888, 3:208). Either way, in mid-April the *wali* of Rumeli was already before the gates of Mesolonghi with a force of more than ten thousand. Bombardment, skirmishes, and sorties began in earnest. During the summer, Yusuf Pasha introduced thirty-six flat-bottomed ships into the shallow lagoon; as a result, Mesolonghi was now completely invested by sea and land. In July, however, the city was provisioned when a squadron led by Andreas Miaoulis managed to chase off the Turkish ships cordoning the city. At the same time, another Greek squadron of small boats slipped into the lagoon undetected and caught Yusuf's flotilla by surprise. After this interlude, however, Kütahı resorted to his most serious attempt so far to build earthen battlements, undermining the Franklin bastion and ordering frontal attacks. The fighting continued unabated until September, at which point the steady desertion of many of the Ottoman diggers and sappers reduced the army's siege capabilities. Casualties also decreased the number of soldiers down to around three thousand, forcing Kütahı to adopt a more defensive stance; he pulled back his remaining force, built a fortified camp to secure his supplies, and prepared to wait out the winter until the time the

Ottoman navy could carry in reinforcements. Meanwhile, Mesolonghi was being regularly provisioned, its guard of four thousand again proved capable of withstanding the relentless pressure of a far superior force; it seemed that the end of the siege was near. Even though the Ottoman artillery kept up the bombardment to harass the besieged, they were planning, along with Georgios Karaiskakis, who was positioned in the rear of the Turkish army, a counterattack of their own to make the enemy retreat (Gordon 2015, 3:67–77).

Ibrahim Pasha intervened at this moment. When he arrived in December 1825 with ten thousand men, after subduing a substantial part of the Peloponnese and preparing stores and provisioning installations in Kryoneri, eighteen kilometers east of Mesolonghi, the two pashas' combined force rose to 22,000–23,000. Not expecting such a development, short of money, preoccupied with the upcoming Third National Assembly, the Greek government had neglected to move ammunition and supplies into the city, another organizational lapse that was partially corrected at the end of November, when a fleet was hastily put together with private subscriptions. Able and methodical, Ibrahim started applying pressure to the besieged. In February Turkish flat-bottomed ships sailed again into the lagoon. Having understood that the key to taking the city was not scaling the land wall but tightening the noose from the sea, the Egyptian pasha managed to seize the islets of Vasiladi and Dolmas between February 25 and 28. On March 1 Anatoliko also surrendered. Kleisova, another islet, managed to withstand the attack; however, Mesolonghi now faced the specter of famine. Repeated attempts by Miaoulis to break the Ottoman blockade kept failing throughout March, and his fleet finally gave up on April 3 (Finlay 1861: 99–105; Gordon 2015, 3:84–101).

"When the Greek fleet departed," wrote George Finlay, "the magazine of Mesolonghi did not contain rations for more than two days." After March 20 there was scarcely any food in the city. Artemios Michos, one of the fighters present in the siege, wrote in his memoirs that soldiers and civilians resorted to eating "horses, donkeys, dogs, cats, mice, crabs, weed . . . and the bodies of their famine-deceased relatives" (Michos 2019, 70). Dead, sick, and wounded lay along the city streets, medicine was nowhere to be found. The only feasible plan was a final sortie: 2,500–3,000 fighters divided into three detachments led by Notis Botsaris (1756–1841), Dimitrios Makris and the local leaders Mitros Deligeorgis (1785/1788–1860), and Athanasios Razikotsikas were to surprise the Ottomans on the night of April 10, clear a path through enemy lines for the civilians to follow and meet in the monastery of St. Symeon, at the foothills of Zygos mountain, about eight kilometers outside the city. To have any chance of success, the besieged arranged for a diversionary attack by the nearby Greek camp at Dervekista. However, confusion ensued during the sortie, something not at all unusual in night operations, and, moreover, Ibrahim and Kütahı's army had already been informed of it. Separated in small groups, the defenders of Mesolonghi fought alone, ambushed and hunted by the enemy. Some of them were forced back into the city, followed by Ottoman and Egyptian forces; others managed to arrive at the Zygos mountain only to find there another enemy detachment waiting (Gordon 2015, 3:101–107; Trikoupis 1888, 3:258–263).

Back in the city the invaders encountered fierce resistance. All those too sick or wounded and thus disabled to join the exodus barricaded themselves in the ammunition magazines, which they set on fire when they could no longer continue to fight. The explosions buried defenders, civilians, and enemies alike under the debris. The emblematic explosion was set off by Christos Kapsalis in his own house, which had been Byron's residence. The last outpost of resistance on the islet of Anemomylos in the lagoon held out for three days and was set ablaze on April 12 by Bishop Iosiph of Rogoi. The two explosions by Kapsalis and Bishop Iosiph became the solemn symbols of heroism and self-sacrifice in the conscience of revolutionary Greece.

Nikolaos Kasomoulis (1795–1872), a survivor of the siege, gave an extremely vivid description of these moments in his memoirs: "the plain boiled in a glaring fire, Mesolonghi was like a candle lighting the whole area from Vasiladi and Kleisova towards the plain, up to where we were. Gunfire flashes all around the city shone like swarms of fireflies. The sound from Mesolonghi's direction was an unclear and terrible noise of women crying out, of shots being fired, of magazines and mines exploding. The city looked like a blazing oven" (Kasomoulis 1941, 2:275). Only thirteen hundred soldiers survived the night, while six thousand women and children were captured and sold as slaves (Figure 14).

Impact and Legacy

Mesolonghi carried a tremendous symbolic weight for revolutionary Greece and its nascent national identity. Its dogged resistance in 1822 and 1823 forged a usable myth combining the elements of heroic conduct in situations of extreme adversity, the favor of divine providence, the defiance of the Ottoman Empire. Indeed, its status for its moral victory was instantly generally affirmed; Thomas Gordon compared its "laurels" to those of Saguntum and Numantia, where desperate (and doomed) defense had stood against the overwhelming Carthaginian and Roman forces, respectively. George Finlay drew a parallel to the destruction of Plataea by the Spartans and Thebans in 427 BCE (Finlay 1861, 2:111; Gordon 2015, 3:109). Militarily devastating to the Greeks—as the road was now fully open to Kütahı to complete the subjugation of Rumeli by taking Athens (May 24, 1827) after another lengthy siege and a tenacious campaign by

FIGURE 14   Theodoros Vryzakis, *The Exodus in Mesolonghi*, 1853.
National Gallery-Al. Soutzos Museum, Athens.

Georgios Karaiskakis, whose death in battle sealed the city's fate—the fall of
Mesolonghi moved again the needle of European philhellenism. Funds flowed
into the coffers of Greek committees, Eugène Delacroix painted *Greece on the
Ruins of Mesolonghi* in 1826 (Plate 18), the German poet Wilhelm Müller published a pamphlet named "Missolonghi" containing four poems inspired by its
defense in the same year, Victor Hugo wrote the poem "Les têtes du sérail" in
1828. During the earlier siege, in Germany the writer Friedrich Bülau and the
future king Ludwig I of Bavaria had produced poems. In London, J. H. Amherst's play *Siege of Mesolonghi* in July 1826 was staged complete with a pyro-

technic display, while in Paris, Gioachino Rossini's opera *Le siège de Corinthe* opened in October 1826 (Hess 2005, 80–97). From Dionysios Solomos's "Eleftheroi Poliorkimenoi" to Kostis Palamas's "Doxa sto Messologgi," it remained a significant topos of Greek literature. Interestingly, its legacy trumps its symbolic and practical value for the Greek Revolution to the point that repeated efforts to recapture it from 1827 on, as well as its surrender by the Ottomans in May 1829, rarely get a mention.

Markos Karasarinis

References

Beaton, Roderick. 2013. *Byron's War: Romantic Rebellion, Greek Revolution*. London.

Dodwell, Edward. 1819. *A Classical and Topographical Tour through Greece during the Years 1801, 1805 and 1806*. London.

Efthymiou, Maria. 2019. "Οι ηρωικές ώρες του Μεσολογγίου και ο Αρτέμιος Μίχος" [The heroic hours of Mesolonghi and Artemios Michos]. In *Αρτέμιος Μίχος, Απομνημονεύματα της δευτέρας πολιορκίας του Μεσολογγίου (1825-1826)* [Memoirs of the second siege of Mesolonghi, 1825–1826], edited by M. Efthymiou and V. Sarafis, 17–37. Athens.

Finlay, George. 1861. *History of the Greek Revolution*. Edinburgh and London.

Gordon, Thomas. 2015. *Ιστορία της ελληνικής επαναστάσεως* [History of the Greek Revolution]. Translated by Alexandros Papadiamantis. Athens.

Hess, Gilbert. 2005. "Missolonghi. Genèse, transformations multimédiales et fonctions d'un lieu identitaire du philhellénisme." *Revue Germanique Internationale* 1–2:77–107.

Kasomoulis, Nikolaos. 1941. *Ενθυμήματα στρατιωτικά της Επαναστάσεως των Ελλήνων 1821-1833* [Military reminiscences of the Revolution of the Greeks, 1821–1833]. Athens.

Kitromilides, Mikis. 1956. *Η δευτέρα πολιορκία του Μεσολογγίου* [The second siege of Mesolonghi]. Nicosia.

Kostis, Kostas. 2018. *History's Spoiled Children: The Formation of the Modern Greek State*. Translated by Jacob Moe. London.

Leon, George B. 1972. "Greek Merchant Marine." In *Greek Merchant Marine, 1453-1850*, edited by Stelios A. Papadopoulos, 13–56. Athens.

Makris, N. D., 1957. *Ιστορία του Μεσολογγίου* [History of Mesolonghi], edited by Emmanouil Protopsaltis. Athens.

Michos, Artemios. 2019. *Απομνημονεύματα της δευτέρας πολιορκίας του Μεσολογγίου (1825-1826)* [Memoirs of the second siege of Mesolonghi, 1825–1826], edited by M. Efthymiou and V. Sarafis. Athens.

Svolopoulos, Constantinos. 2007. *Προμαχώντας στο Μεσολόγγι. Έργα και ημέρες του Θανάση Ραζικότσικα, 1798-1826* [Defending Mesolonghi in battle: Works and days of Thanassis Razikotsikas, 1798–1826]. Athens.

Trikoupis, Spyridon. 1888. *Ιστορία της Ελληνικής Επαναστάσεως* [History of the Greek Revolution]. 3rd edition, Athens.

Morea

At the crucial meeting of the leadership of the Philiki Etaireia (Society of Friends), held at Izmail in October 1820, it was decided that the revolution would start in the Peloponnese, under the leadership of Alexandros Ypsilantis, who would go to Mani clandestinely by ship, via Trieste. Immediately after the meeting, two emissaries left Izmail almost simultaneously, with the Peloponnese as their final destination. The first, Christophoros Perraivos, an old comrade of Rhigas, was one of the Philiki Etaireia's energetic "apostles" and had contributed decisively to reconciling the mutually antagonistic families of Mani, so that they would all serve the revolutionary plan. His task now was to prepare for Ypsilantis's arrival. The second, Archimandrite Grigorios Dikaios, was one of the Philiki Etaireia's leaders, but this role was known only to the other leaders, in accordance with the society's conspiratorial rules. Although "Papaflessas," the nickname by which Dikaios became known, hailed from the Peloponnese, his rich covert action had been carried out in Constantinople and the Danubian Principalities. His mission was to move in all the provinces of the Peloponnese and the islands of Ydra and Spetses, in order to coordinate—as Ypsilantis's representative—preparations, in collaboration with the Philiki Etaireia's local cells.

So, the Peloponnese had a central place in the planning of the revolution. It could contribute its ethnic demography (e.g., the ratio of Christians to Muslims), the geographical isolation of the Morea peninsula from the southern Balkans, its proximity to Ydra and Spetses, the special regime, and the belligerent temperament of the inhabitants of Mani. Furthermore, the Russian-fueled uprising of 1770 and the plans to incorporate the Peloponnese into Napoleonic France, in 1808–1809, showed that the provincial Christian leaderships, the *kocabaşıs* and the prelates, were eager to join in conspiratorial actions aimed at bringing

Ottoman domination to an end. According to data from papers of members of the Philiki Etaireia, which have been processed by George Frangos, about 21 percent of the members were initiated in the Peloponnese, while Peloponnesians constituted the largest group based on the place of their origin (approximately 37 percent), whether they lived in the Peloponnese or elsewhere. Analogous are the percentages among the leaders of the Philiki Etaireia. Equally significant is the fact that *kocabaşıs* and prelates from all provinces of the Peloponnese joined the society. These were economically powerful persons with social and political influence, due to the roles they played in communal administration, agricultural production, trade, and tax farming. They were linked by stable ties of protection and dependence with the people of their province, who treated them as their natural leaders. Their affiliation to the Philiki Etaireia, in combination with the equally great penetration of the society in Ydra and Spetses, created a very favorable environment for the onset of the Greek Revolution in the Peloponnese.

As happened in all regions in which there were numerous nuclei of society members (e.g., the Danubian Principalities), so in the Peloponnese many problems arose, not least rivalries and accusations between members (e.g., for squandering contributions). So, in August 1820, Alexandros Ypsilantis, in the framework of his attempted organizational upgrading of the Etaireia, decided to create the Ephorate of the Peloponnese and placed at its head the Greek consul of Russia in Patras, Ioannis Vlassopoulos. As members he selected prelates, such as the Metropolitan of Old Patras Germanos, and *kocabaşıs*, such as Panoutsos Notaras from Corinth and Asimakis Zaimis from Kalavryta, while as managers of the fund that should be set up he appointed two merchants, Ioannis Papadiamantopoulos from Patras and Panagiotis Arvalis from Tripolitsa. The strategic importance of the Peloponnese in Ypsilantis's plans is apparent also from the order that the monies which would be collected by the ephorate should remain in the Peloponnese—that is, they should not be sent to the Etaireia's central fund. Furthermore, the contributions from other regions, such as Ydra and Spetses, the Ionian Islands, Smyrna, Samos, and elsewhere, were to be directed to the Peloponnese.

Ypsilantis's decisions regarding the ephorate reached the Peloponnese most probably in early October 1820—that is, the time when the leaders of the Philiki Etaireia were meeting in Izmail. The decisions taken at Izmail were made known in the Peloponnese in late December, when Dikaios arrived on Ydra and Spetses and informed the Ephorate of the Peloponnese by letter that Ypsilantis would be coming very soon, to start the revolution. In the three months that had intervened between early October and late December, essentially, the ephorate had not yet operated. This was due mainly to the arrival of the new pasha,

Hurşid, which like every similar administrative change obliged the ecclesiastical and community dignitaries to be present at his seat in Tripolitsa. The members of the Etaireia could, of course, hold meetings but they could not implement practical measures, such as uniting the dispersed local cores of the society and their funds. For these matters they awaited the imminent departure of Hurşid Pasha and a large part of his army, as he had been placed as new *serasker* (commander in chief) in the campaign against Ali Pasha of Ioannina. Hurşid did indeed leave the Peloponnese, in early January, at the same time as Kolokotronis arrived secretly in Mani from Zakynthos.

The ephorate's first important move was the secret meeting of its members and of other Peloponnesian initiates of the Philiki Etaireia with Dikaios at Vostitsa (Aigio), from January 26 to 29, 1821. The subject of the meeting was Ypsilantis's arrival and the final preparations for the revolution, which was scheduled to begin in the coming weeks. A large part of earlier and contemporary historiography considers that at this critical meeting the Peloponnesian members of the Philiki Etaireia clashed with Dikaios, that they rejected the decisions taken at Izmail, and that they tried to curb Dikaios's activity or even to eliminate him. There is no doubt that at Vostitsa strong reservations and intense disagreements were expressed and that proposals were made to postpone the onset of the revolution. However, the altercation with Dikaios, particularly from the side of the Metropolitan of Patras, did not lead to rupture and to the rejection of Ypsilantis's plans. Examination of the letters sent by Dikaios and by the ephorate to Philiki members in Ydra and Spetses immediately after the assembly ended show that at Vostitsa they agreed to begin preparations while awaiting Ypsilantis.

Indeed, in February the preliminary actions were stepped up in many provinces. In some cases, such as at Karytaina, Agios Petros, and Prastos, the local agreements were made on the occasion of the primates' regular assembly for the allocation of taxation obligations. Moreover, on the pretext of the appearance of brigands, the Ottoman authorities were asked to increase the number of chiefs (*kapoi*)—that is, of armed bands that were under the jurisdiction of the *kocabaşı*. In the same period, the central authority of the Philiki Etaireia was sending weapons and ammunition, while many Philiki members sped to the Peloponnese in order to take part in the revolution. Mani, Patras, and the mountain provinces of the central Peloponnese (e.g., Kalavryta, Karytaina) led the field in these actions, on the initiative of the provincial communities and ecclesiastical agents. By contrast, preparations in Corinth were less intensive and did not have the consent of the *kocabaşıs*.

The unusual goings on, preparations for the revolution, did not pass unnoticed by the Ottoman authorities, who met to discuss what they all might mean but without realizing in the end what was actually happening. Around mid-February, they invited once again the *kocabaşıs* and the prelates to Tripolitsa, as they believed that no insurrection could break out without the complicity and participation of these key players. The Peloponnesian Philiki members had discussed at Vostitsa the possibility of such an invitation and had taken decisions about how they would react. However, the decisions were not applied by all, as some disagreed with them and others misinterpreted them. As result, in late February and early March, several *kocabaşıs* and prelates went to Tripolitsa, while others did not, thus heightening the suspicions of the authorities.

The revolutionary turmoil and preparations were not interrupted. Nonetheless, the revolution could not commence because of the absence of Ypsilantis. It is significant that on February 22, the day that Ypsilantis with his army crossed the River Pruth and entered the Danubian Principalities, Dikaios wrote to the heads of the Philiki Etaireia a letter full of despair, in which he puzzled over the delay. As he wrote, everything was ready but the leader to put it in order was missing. That is why he requested the dispatch of some important military man, to organize and direct the war. Given the circumstances at the time, he could not expect an answer for several weeks. In the end, as Vasilis Panagiotopoulos has shown, instead of a reply, in mid-March a ship with letters and the revolutionary declarations of Ypsilantis from Jassy reached Mani (Panagiotopoulos 1957–1958). The Greek Revolution had started, but not from the Peloponnese.

The Revolution as War (1821)

Immediately after the news from the principalities reached Mani, the revolution broke in the Peloponnese, almost simultaneously in all the provinces. Mani, Patras, and the mountain provinces of the central Peloponnese were the combustion points of the "general uprising," which was guided by Dikaios and organized by the *kocabaşıs* and the prelates (those who had not been incarcerated in Tripolitsa). The capture of Kalavryta, Kalamata, and the city of Patras (but not its fortress) between March 21 and 23 was achieved easily and essentially without battle, transmitting the revolutionary flame to the rest of the provinces too. In Kalamata and Patras, the first local revolutionary administrations were set up and declarations to the great powers were published, while gradually revolutionary authorities were created in each province, and these authorities essentially reproduced the organization and hierarchies of the communal system. In the same period, the scattered Muslim populations in the countryside abandoned their homes, in some places unhindered and in others fighting against the insurgent Christians who pursued them. The Muslims were destined for the coastal fortresses (Patras, Nafplio, Monemvasia, Methoni, Koroni, and so on), as well as for walled Tripolitsa. The Lala area in today's Ileia was an exception; there the Muslim inhabitants stayed and fought until early summer, when they too fled to Patras.

Thus, from the first days of the revolution, the rebels became masters of the countryside and began to lay siege to the nearest fortresses. However, until the middle of May the operations were not successful, as the besiegers scattered with each foray from even a small Ottoman force, with the exception of the sieges undertaken by the Maniots in the southern Peloponnese. Furthermore, the local rebels did not follow a common and preconceived plan of action, while the dispersed revolutionary centers that were created were not connected to one another administratively. Consequently, the outcome of the first few weeks was negative for the Greek side, particularly on the main fronts of the war, in Patras and Tripolitsa, where the bulk of the Ottoman forces was concentrated. The Greek corps were scattered twice in Patras, on April 3 and 6, and four times around Tripolitsa, between April 1 and 24. The same happened at Vostitsa, Corinth, and Argos in late April, as well as in the area of Pyrgos and Gastouni.

The insurgence had to spread onto the battlefields. However, in the Peloponnese there were no armed corps similar to those of the *armatoloi* of Rumeli to bear the brunt of the war in its critical initial stages. The majority of those who rebelled did not own arms and had never fought. Therefore, an army had to be organized from scratch and inexperienced civilians turned into battleworthy combatants. These issues, as well as the planning and directing of military operations had not concerned the prelates and *kocabaşıs* who were Philiki members, as they were the responsibility of the society's head; but he had not arrived in the Peloponnese to shoulder this responsibility. Thus, the revolution broke out without a plan of action and a general leader, while the army was formed at the moment of the outbreak, separately in each province (or part of a province), but more or less in the same way.

Generally speaking, the provincial military corps had the characteristics of a militia. They were made up of small bands of kinsmen and covillagers; each one had its own leader and functioned as an organic offshoot of the communities from which it came (and on which it relied for its maintenance), while its primary concern was to protect the people and their property from the Ottoman garrisons in the nearby fortresses. A significant part of the male population of each province abandoned their previous occupations, armed themselves in makeshift fashion, even with agricultural tools, and followed the local leader onto the battlefield. Alongside those who became freedom fighters, we should count as many again, men and women of all ages, who undertook tasks and services to support the camps: preparing gunpowder and food, transporting supplies and munitions, undertaking postal services, tending the wounded, constructing fortifications, building ovens, and the like. This was the new reality for the inhabitants of every province. The unprecedented conditions that the war created were a cause that involved them all and incorporated them in many ways in the revolutionary process.

The army of the Greek Revolution in the Peloponnese took shape as an off-shoot of the rebellious communities; it reproduced their cohesion and confirmed the existing power relations and local hierarchies. Placed as head in each prov-ince were the local leaderships, which directed martial operations with the aid of the *kapoi* and of those who had been klephts and / or mercenaries in the Ionian Islands in the Napoleonic Wars. Thus, the bishop of Vresthena Theodoritos, as-sisted by two other bishops, directed the camp at Vervaina, near Tripolitsa, where corps from several provinces gathered, while the *kocabaşıs* of Kalavryta and Ka-rytaina had first say in the other camps of the central Peloponnese. In the siege of the fortress of Patras, a leading role was played by Metropolitan Germanos, in collaboration with the *kocabaşıs* and prelates of neighboring provinces. Likewise, the bishop of Methoni Grigorios headed the sieges of Methoni and the fortresses of Pylos, while the *kocabaşıs* of Argos headed the siege of Nafplio. All these fig-ures had stirred the inhabitants to revolt and succeeded in gathering them to-gether again, after the defeats of the first weeks. Their persistence was necessary for rekindling the revolution but it was not sufficient to consolidate it.

The consolidation of the revolution in the Peloponnese was due to the dif-ferent way in which the first defeats were handled by the provinces fighting on the Tripolitsa front, in comparison with the other fronts and especially that of Patras. In Patras the prelates and the *kocabaşıs* continued to direct the war even after the defeats of the first weeks. Until the end of the year and the creation of a national administration, no change was noted in the military organization of these provinces and, moreover, no progress was made in the siege. Indeed, the Ottoman garrison made sorties from time to time, scattering the nearby camps, as happened on September 9. By contrast, on the Tripolitsa front, after the first failures, important initiatives were taken that changed the course of the war. New administrative and military institutions were put in place that transformed the old communal structures and differentiated the roles and responsibilities within the province. These initiatives were taken in dramatic circumstances after April 24, when the garrison of Tripolitsa scattered the encampment at Valtetsi, plundering once more the closest villages. On the following days, the garrison was significantly strengthened by the force sent by Hurşid Pasha, which entered Tripolitsa after having in the meantime scattered in its course the Greek encampments at Vostitsa, Corinth and Argos. In the period straight after, the Ottoman forces would attempt initially to control the central Peloponnese and subsequently to move south, to Kalamata.

In these conditions, the *kocabaşıs* and the prelates of the central Peloponnese led the way in agreements and convened provincial assemblies that decided to create new forms of political and military administration: the ephorate and the military head of the province. The ephorate undertook the management of the provincial resources to cover the cost of the war. The military leader had absolute responsibility for the organization of the camps, the composition of the military hierarchies, and the direction of the operations. Stable mechanisms of recruitment were also created. On April 28 Theodoros Kolokotronis was made military leader at Karytaina, while on May 2 Panagiotis Giatrakos was chosen as head in the Vervaina camp, which was maintained by the provinces of Mystras and Agios Petros-Prastos. The power of the military head, however, was given and controlled not by the *kocabaşı* personally but by the assembly of the province. Thus, a relatively autonomous and hierarchical structure was put in place, which strengthened the power of the militia and constituted a mechanism of the local revolutionary power.

These developments proved effective. From the beginning of May, the camps around Tripolitsa were better organized (e.g., recording and training of freedom fighters, ranking, reconnaissance) and were placed in nearby positions that favored mutual support. Also, a network of lookout posts was organized in suitable mountain locations, to monitor the movements of the Ottoman garrison and to send messages with signals. The tactic followed was simple: whatever camp the Ottoman garrison chose to assault was obliged to resist in all ways and not to scatter, until the reinforcements from the neighboring camps surrounded the enemy and forced them to retreat. In other words, each camp functioned as potential bait in a single trap. This happened at Valtetsi on May 12–13, in the first important Greek victory. The battle raged for almost twenty-four hours and the Greeks fought like armed irregulars. In mountainous and almost impenetrable terrain in which the Ottoman cavalry was useless, the Greeks barricaded themselves in "strong" houses and churches or hid behind trenches and rocks, as the Ottoman forces had no artillery. Divided in nearby locations and not gathered together at one point, they exploited their knowledge of the terrain and their ability to march quickly on foot to move rapidly from one place to another along the rugged highland passes, so as to take the enemy by surprise. So great was the surprise of the Ottoman forces when the Greek reinforcements reached Valtetsi that they were routed in panic, leaving behind on the battlefield hundreds of dead and many more weapons and other booty. The same was repeated four days later in the twin battles at Vervaina and Doliana.

In the relevant literature these victories and above all the siege and fall of Tripolitsa have been attributed rightly to Kolokotronis, on account of the experience he had acquired as head of the Greek corps of irregulars which took

part in the operations of the British army of the Ionian Islands during the Napoleonic Wars. However, his tactical skills appeared crucial only after the beginning of May, when he took on the responsibilities of a provincial military leader
and had stable mechanisms of recruitment and logistics at his disposal. These
allowed him to turn the inexperienced villagers into fighting-fit combatants and
to impose his own battle plans, which led to the first Greek victories. The benefits from these were many. The Greeks saw that the foe, their former master,
was not invincible and that by killing him they could accrue not only glory but
also the enemy's weapons and whatever precious things he had with him. At
the same time, the losses made the Ottoman garrison think twice about campaigning again in mountainous regions. Henceforth, it confined itself to short
sorties onto the Tripolitsa plateau, in order to control the harvesting of the
crops. Thus, the most important Ottoman force in the Peloponnese was essentially neutralized and the countryside was controlled by the insurgents. Thanks
to this development, the provincial mechanisms of enlistment and logistics,
which maintained the camps in the central Peloponnese, functioned even more
effectively. Moreover, it enabled the senate of the Peloponnese, which was constituted on May 26 at the monastery of Kaltezon by representatives of all the
provinces and proceeded to establish its seat at Stemnitsa, to exercise true administration in the rebellious Peloponnese (e.g., taxation). From the end of May,
the siege of Tripolitsa began systematically. Of course, the Greeks were not in
a position to attack, since they had neither the skills nor the means to do so.
They kept their camps in highland locations but moved them closer to the
fortification walls. On the fringes of the plateau they constructed improvised
fortifications, ditches, and later trenches, and placed the most battleworthy corps
in these outposts, so as to hold on to them and to push them closer to the city
walls. Their aim was to cut off the beleaguered inhabitants of Tripolitsa from
all source of supplies, so as to force them to surrender.

By early summer, the battle for the harvest was critical not only *extra muros*
of Tripolitsa but also outside the rest of the besieged fortresses, because the besieged lacked the necessary supplies to withstand a months-long siege. Those
in the coastal fortresses awaited help from the sea and indeed the Ottoman fleet
sometimes managed to strengthen them (e.g., in Patras, Methoni, and Koroni),
although, in general, the Greek ships conducted successful blockades which in
the end obliged the fortresses of Monemvasia and Navarino to surrender, in
late July and early August, respectively. These were the first *castra* to pass to
Greek control. In Monemvasia, the terms of the surrender were honored, but
in Navarino the Greeks breached the agreements and the departure of the garrison and the Muslim inhabitants who had sought refuge there were subjected
to looting and slaughter. This was the prelude to what would happen a few weeks

later in Tripolitsa. There, the only hope of the besieged was for new reinforcements to arrive by land. However, the forces sent by Hurşid Pasha remained
grounded in eastern Rumeli after the battle of Gravia (May 8) and never set foot
in the Peloponnese. The same pattern was repeated in a new expedition from
the east, which was confronted at Vasilika (August 26). Unsuccessful too were the
attempts via western Rumeli, since from early summer the Greek revolutionaries
held the Makrynoros defile, stranding the Ottoman forces in Arta. In these
conditions, on the night of August 9–10, a strong detachment of the Tripolitsa
garrison made a foray targeted at the food stocks in nearby villages, without
knowing that the Greeks had constructed a long trench there. The battle of the
Trench (Grana), as it was named, was once again catastrophic for the Ottoman
garrison, which did not attempt a new sortie.

This was the last important battle of the protracted siege. During the month
and a half until the city's fall, optimism and certainty prevailed on the Greek
side. Intra muros the privations hit ever harder the ten thousand and more combatants and at least twice as many civilians—Christians, Muslims, and a few
Jews. From the end of August, the Greek positions reached almost below the
walls and even minor skirmishes ceased, while on September 10 the Ottoman
authorities agreed to negotiate. Nonetheless, the discussions did not end in
agreement. There were disputes over who would cover the cost of transportation and whether the beleaguered would be allowed to withdraw with their
weapons, money, and movable property. Moreover, the multitude from all the
provinces, which had gathered outside the walls of Tripolitsa, thus weakening
the other sieges in the Peloponnese (Map 9), were expecting a solution other
than surrender: the city's fall, so that they could pillage it.

The city's defense had flagged, the bastions were inadequately manned and
the gates were opening frequently, as many desperately sought food in exchange
for jewelry, or someone familiar among the Greeks to protect them. An important part of the garrison, apart from the Ottoman authorities, went ahead with
separate negotiations with Kolokotronis and agreed to be allowed to withdraw
free of harm. Indeed, they began to exit the city on September 23, at the same
moment when, at another point, a small band of Greeks moved of its own voli-
tion, managing to jump onto the walls, to capture a gate and to cause the general and totally unorganized incursion that ended in three days of wholesale
massacre and looting. These events horrified the Philhellenes, who believed in
the idea of the "rebirth of Hellas" and considered the Greek Revolution as a
battle of "civilization" against "barbarity." Furthermore, the plundering deprived
the revolutionary authorities of important income to finance the war. But this
did not deter the thousands of fighters who saw the spoils of Tripolitsa as reward for their months-long war effort and as a means of keeping their families

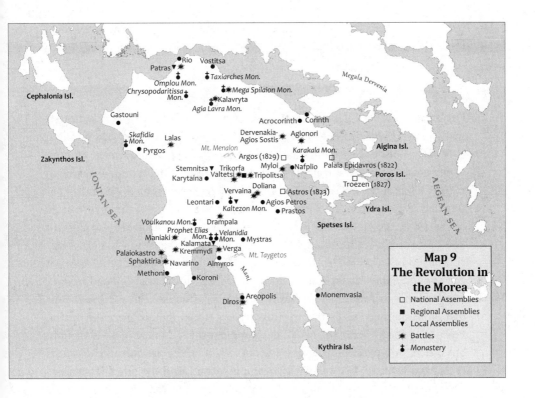

Map 9
The Revolution in
the Morea
□ National Assemblies
■ Regional Assemblies
▼ Local Assemblies
✳ Battles
⚱ Monastery

going. Those who benefited most were the military leaders and especially Kolokotronis, who entered Tripolitsa on the third day of the fall as conqueror,
giving the order for the city to be cleaned up in order to install the revolutionary
authorities there.

The capture of Tripolitsa made a decisive contribution toward consolidating
the revolution, as it neutralized the principal Ottoman force that was headquar-
tered in the heart of the peninsula. There was a mighty garrison in Patras too,
but its operational capabilities were limited to within the city's bounds and the
nearby villages. Consequently, with the fall of Tripolitsa the rebels acquired
a secure territorial core that allowed them to convene the first National Assembly and to establish a common national administration. Concurrently, the
battles that had brought also the booty that the military leaders had acquired,
particularly those of the central Peloponnese (Kolokotronis, Giatrakos, Plapoutas), gave them prestige and cemented their ties with their freedom
fighters—and therefore with the communities from which they came. Thus,
they began to create strong local networks of sociopolitical influence and
to lay claim to a share of the revolutionary power. Indeed, the representatives of the regions of Karytaina and Mystras in the National Assembly were

persons who were supported by the military and not by the established local leaderships of *kocabaşı*s and prelates.

War and Power Relations (1822–1824)

On January 14, 1822, the day when the National Assembly was concluding its work, the revolutionaries gained one more fortress: Acrocorinth. The handing over of the Ottoman garrison was the outcome of a siege lasting several months, which became suffocating after the fall of Tripolitsa. At that point, direction of the siege was taken over by Kolokotronis, who succeeded once again in separate negotiations with the Albanian-speaking contingents of the garrison. As in Tripolitsa, the motive of booty led a large number of men at arms to Corinth and massacres were repeated, but on a smaller scale. However, the other operations were enfeebled by the attraction of looting and especially the sieges of Nafplio and Patras. In fact, in early February the Ottoman fleet landed new reinforcements in Patras. The administration entrusted to Kolokotronis the direction of the siege of Patras, with fighters recruited mainly from the central Peloponnese and Ileia. This was a development that Kolokotronis had sought but which brought him up against the opposition of the prelates and *kocabaşı*s of Achaia. Even so, he organized encampments around the city and successfully fought off the forays of the Ottoman garrison. In May, however, the administration tried to remove him from Patras, as it summoned him to take part in the campaign being organized in Epirus by the president of the executive, Alexandros Mavrokordatos. Kolokotronis did not obey the order. He returned to Corinth from Patras, to the seat of the administration, followed by many soldiers, and managed to have the previous decision revoked. This development not only revealed how politically weak the administration was but also how much sociopolitical influence Kolokotronis had acquired. So, he returned to Patras, but his camp had begun to face problems of supply, as a result of which many men abandoned it. Toward the end of June, the siege of Patras weakened again and was essentially aborted. On the contrary, in Nafplio the beleaguered began discussions regarding their surrender.

At the same time, Hurşid Pasha organized a new campaign to regain the Peloponnese. Appointed as head was Mahmud Pasha of Larisa, nicknamed Dramali, who set off at the end of June from Zitouni (Lamia) with over twenty thousand soldiers, mainly cavalrymen. This was the largest Ottoman army assembled during the Greek Revolution and was accompanied by thousands of pack animals and auxiliary staff. The huge military procession passed through eastern Rumeli, unhindered by Greek forces, captured Thebes and put it to the torch (July 1), and then headed toward the Isthmus, bypassing Athens. At the Der-

venochoria of Megara the force of the inhabitants of Tripolitsa stationed there
abandoned its position and Dramali entered the Peloponnese and captured
Corinth (July 6). In the preceding days, the Greek administration had left the
city and boarded ships. Likewise, Acrocorinth was abandoned by the garrison
and was taken by Dramali without resistance (July 8). Four days later, he entered Argos, unimpeded, and struck camp outside Nafplio.

These developments caused panic among the inhabitants of the northeast
Peloponnese, who sought refuge in safer mountainous regions. The central administration had essentially ceased to operate and only some members of the
senate, which had its seat in Tripolitsa, together with Kolokotronis, Dimitrios
Ypsilantis, Petrobey Mavromichalis and other military men, tried to organize
the defense. They regrouped the troops and positioned them at Myloi outside
Nafplio, and on narrow highland passes between Corinth, Nafplio, and Tripolitsa. Some corps captured the ruined fort of Argos, they repaired it in rough-
and-ready fashion and fought persistently for several days, until July 24, when
they fled to the highlands. The resistance in the fortress of Argos forced Dramali to delay on the Argive plain. The Greeks also organized systematic destruction of the harvest, so as to deprive Dramali and his men of food. This had
indeed been happening since the Ottoman fleet headed toward Patras. The heat-
wave affecting the Peloponnese in those days proved a valuable ally of the
Greek side, as it dried up the wells and streams in the region, creating a water
shortage for Dramali's army.

Of course, all these did not mean that the Ottoman general had been thwarted
or that he lost the initiative of making moves. Having captured Corinth and
Argos, Dramali was able to advance toward Tripolitsa. However, the discontent within his army, due to lack of food and water, militated against taking an
aggressive action that would demand weeks or months to be completed. An
alternative option was to move once more toward Corinth, so that Dramali's
men could rest and he could organize their victualling and plan his next moves.
However, both options necessitated his passing through narrow mountain
passes, which made his large army vulnerable. Confronted with the above possibilities, each of which presupposed a different plan of action, the Greek
leaders were divided. Several considered that Dramali would move toward the
heartland of the Peloponnese and so reinforced their camp at Myloi and at
mountainous points on the road to Tripolitsa. Others headed for the four defiles between Argos and Corinth. At noon on July 26, Dramali's army appeared
at the Dervenakia pass, where the troops of Kolokotronis, Ypsilantis, Nikitaras,
Plapoutas, and other guerrilla chiefs were ensconced (or on their way)
(Figure 15). These corps pushed back Dramali's soldiers, who, assailed from many
sides, tried to escape toward the Agios Sostis defile. The vanguard managed to

FIGURE 15   Dimitrios Zographos, *The Battle at Dervenakia*, 1836–1839. Watercolor on
paper. The Gennadeion Library, Athens.

pass through, but when the freedom fighters of Nikitaras and Papaflessas
reached the pass, the rest of the Ottoman army was trapped and suffered great
losses, retreating in disarray toward Nafplio. From there the Ottoman army
tried, on the following night (July 27 to 28), to escape to Corinth via the Agionori
pass. This move was completely predictable and its losses, inflicted by Nikitaras's
men in particular, were again severe. It is estimated that in these battles Dramali
lost one-fifth of his army, while comparably great were the weapons and booty
seized by the Greek fighters. Dramali escaped to Corinth, where he was besieged
for months. He fell ill and died in October or November 1822.

Kolokotronis's career was very different. His new successes increased his
prestige among the Peloponnesians, who acknowledged him as the defender of
their freedom, life, and property. They saw him too as the leader whose victories
gave his followers the opportunity to gain the booty of their defeated opponents. After the battles at Dervenakia–Agios Sostis and Agionori, he returned
to Tripolitsa, where he was given a triumphal welcome. Characteristic is the
description given by his adjutant Photakos, in his memoirs:

As the news was spread in Tripolitsa that Kolokotronis is coming, straight
away the people, men, women, and children ran as far as Achladokampos,

in order to welcome the generalissimo; they were saluting him and kissing him, and some were laughing and others crying in joy. The priests welcomed him wearing their sacred vestments and with the Gospel and icons in their hands, and the senate accorded him many honors, that is, it too received him with cannon fire, and in the evening there were great fireworks in the generalissimo's house. (1858, 1:238)

Meanwhile, the Greek troops resumed the siege of Acrocorinth, while the siege of Nafplio started once again. Dramali's army had not been foiled and made sorties to seize supplies from nearby villages, while it was also supplied by the Ottoman fleet which was sailing in the Gulf of Corinth. At the same time, Dramali tried to transport supplies to the beleaguered in Nafplio, which he managed to do sometimes. Nonetheless, after October the Greek cordon on land and sea became more effective. In Nafplio in particular the situation was touch and go by November. The garrison and the inhabitants were being decimated by infectious diseases, and there seem to have been cases of cannibalism. In these conditions the new negotiations for the terms of surrender commenced, which continued until November 29–30. Then, totally unexpectedly, as had happened in Tripolitsa, a small band of Greeks breached an almost impregnable gate of the Palamidi and captured this fortress that was so important for the city's defense. This development forced the Nafplio garrison to capitulate immediately and to hand over the city's other fortress Acronafplia.

At the end of 1822, the fortresses of Corinth, Patras, Rion, Methoni, and Koroni, on the north and west coasts, were the only Ottoman enclaves in the Peloponnese. The Acrocorinth was delivered once again to the Greek side on October 26, 1823, since previously, in July, the Ottoman navy had failed to supply the besieged position. In Patras, by contrast, political friction between Kolokotronis and the powerful Achaian politicians once again obstructed the organization of a systematic siege (Figure 16). The fortress was supplied regularly by the Ottoman fleet and from July 1824 onward the garrison endeavored assaults toward the south of the province, taking advantage of the civil strife among Greeks, which monopolized their attention and action that year.

Guerrilla Warfare and European Intervention, 1825–1827

A large part of the troops that the administration had summoned to put down the mutiny remained in the Peloponnese even after early 1825. Although several Peloponnesian soldiers supported the administration in the civil wars or stayed uninvolved, their forces were insufficient to fill the vacuum caused by the arrest of the resistance fighters and the dissolution of their corps. Thus, it

FIGURE 16   Dionysios Tsokos, *The Flight from Patras*, ca. 1850. Oil on canvas. National Gallery-Al. Soutzos Museum / E. Koutlides Foundation Collection, Athens.

was deemed necessary that the Souliots and the Rumeliots remain, and they were entrusted with the siege of Patras. At the same time, a new Ottoman campaign was launched. Its head was Ibrahim Pasha, adopted son of the vassal of the Sublime Porte and ruler of Egypt, Mohammed Ali, who had a strong navy and army trained and commanded by European officers, mainly French and Italian. The Egyptian army resembled European armies, as it had adopted many elements of the uniform, the training, and the conduct of warfare of a regular army. These characteristics proved decisive for the turn of military operations after 1825, as within a few months Ibrahim captured numerous fortresses, including that of Tripolitsa. His army fought differently from the irregular Ottoman corps, which had learnt to confront the irregular Greek freedom fighters, whose way of fighting it shared. As had happened in 1821, so in 1825 the survival of the revolution was destined to be the result of the revolutionaries' adaptation to the new demands of the war. In 1821, the first victories had been based on the restructuring of the provincial revolutionary authorities. In 1825 the problem was not the institutions but the kind of war that they needed to wage in order to hang on to the territorial conquests of the first years. There were two alternative solutions: either the creation of a regular army or systematic guerrilla warfare.

The Greek administration knew of Ibrahim's plans to campaign in the Peloponnese, but it erroneously calculated that the Egyptian fleet would not attempt to transport troops there until winter was over. So, the administration mustered its forces on the Patras front and took no measures to keep its fleet on the alert. As a result, Ibrahim's armada reached Methoni unmolested in mid-February 1825 and landed the first contingent of its expeditionary force, without meeting any resistance. The numerous Greek corps that were besieging Methoni and Koroni were easily scattered and by February 25 Ibrahim had restored overland communication between the two fortresses. Early March saw the arrival of the second contingent of his army, which now exceeded eight thousand men, and soon he moved his forces northward, to Pylos. His target was the fortresses on the north and south sides of the gulf, at Palaiokastro and Neokastro (Navarino), as well as the islet of Sphaktiria at its entrance. His aim was to make this fortified position a safe base for his fleet.

Only then, in early March, did the Greek administration recall its troops from the provinces and direct them to Messinia in southwestern Peloponnese. But its moves were slow, unplanned, and kindled by the optimism born of ignorance of the kind of warfare that the troops were about to face. The general military command was undertaken by the president of the executive, the Ydriot shipowner Georgios Kountouriotis, who appointed as commander-in-chief his fellow Ydriot, the ship's captain Kyriakos Skourtis, sidestepping the military men. He considered that the fleet, which by now had been put in action, and the three to four thousand soldiers who were gathered in the village of Kremmydi in early April, were sufficient to force Ibrahim to retreat to Methoni. However, the site chosen for the battle allowed the enemy's infantry and cavalry free rein. In fact, the center of the Greek camp was virtually undefended and found itself unprotected against the spear-bearing units of the Egyptian infantry, which launched a coordinated attack on April 7 that was not broken up by the Greeks' artillery fire. At the same time, the cavalry attacked the Greek forces from the side, via an almost inaccessible path that had been shown to them by local Muslims. Several Greeks resisted (Karaiskakis, Tzavellas) but most failed to hold their ground and retreated to the neighboring mountain villages, leaving behind hundreds of dead. There was no provision for their remustering or a plan of further action. Indeed, in the following days the greater part of these corps returned to the camps of Rumeli. After the battle, Ibrahim turned his forces to land and sea, in order to capture the fortresses in the Bay of Pylos (Navarino Bay) too. There, for about one month, bitter and bloody battles were fought, the most crucial being that at Sphaktiria, on April 26, in which, among others, the minister of war Anagnostaras and the Italian Philhellene Santa Rosa were killed. Many others, Mavrokordatos among them, escaped by the skin of their teeth in a desperate yet heroic exodus of the small Greek squadron that had been trapped in Navarino Bay. Ibrahim's capture of Sphaktiria obliged the garrisons of Palaiokastro (April 30) and Neokastro (May 6) to capitulate, on the condition of their safe withdrawal.

Throughout this period, the Greek administration was unable to remuster the troops and was without an overall plan of action. Dikaios, who was minister of the interior, organized on his own initiative a new expedition to Messinia in mid-May. However, he gathered no more than fifteen hundred soldiers and of these only five hundred stayed to fight and were killed with him, at Maniaki (May 20), in a battle in which their self-sacrifice embodied and renewed the central rallying cry of the Greek Revolution, "Freedom or Death." The heroism and self-sacrifice of Papaflessas and his freedom fighters at Maniaki, which attracted Ibrahim's admiration, have been immortalized by Michael Mitsakis in a deeply moving story published in 1892, which represents one of the classic topoi of national narrative in modern Greek literature. Two days before the battle, the administration amnestied the Peloponnesian political and military leaders and entrusted to Kolokotronis the direction of operations. After his victory at Maniaki, Ibrahim captured the town of Kalamata and turned his sights toward Tripolitsa. However, in order to approach it he had to pass through the defiles of Leontari, between Messinia and Arcadia. Kolokotronis turned his actions there, having quickly remustered the Peloponnesian troops, organized a network of logistics for their supply, and placed them in mountainous positions, just as he had done in May 1821 around Tripolitsa and in July 1822 at Dervenakia. This time, however, the battles developed differently.

As at Kremmydi, Ibrahim used as scouts local Muslims, who showed him a particularly difficult pass that was undefended. Thus, he found himself at the rearguard of his foes and forced them to fight in positions different from those they had planned. Despite the spirited resistance they put up for two days (June 5–7), in the end they were forced to retreat to the highlands of Karytaina, leaving the villages of the area unprotected. The road to Tripolitsa was now open. This development found the Greek side again unprepared, as it had not taken measures to evacuate the inhabitants and to reinforce the garrison with men, food and ammunition. So, on June 7–8 the inhabitants hastily left the city, while some Greek corps burnt down a part of it, but without demolishing the fortification walls. Ibrahim's army entered Tripolitsa at daybreak on June 11, thus acquiring a mighty base at the center of the Peloponnese, from where it could campaign in all directions.

Its first target was the seat of the Greek administration, Nafplio. Without delay, Ibrahim reached the Argolic plain in the morning of June 13, with some six thousand soldiers, estimating that he would find the Greeks once again unprepared. But, in order to start the siege, he had first to control the coastal site of Myloi, a treacherous area with streams and marshes, about 12 kilometers from Nafplio. Located there were the central warehouses with the supplies for Kolokotronis's army, while there were also water sources and havens for transporting water to Nafplio by ship. Possession of Myloi was crucial for the defenders of Nafplio, so as to withstand a siege from land, but also for Ibrahim, who needed the supplies for his own army, as he had moved a long distance away from his bases in the southwest Peloponnese. In the previous days the Greek administration had sent about five hundred soldiers under the command of Ypsilantis, Mavromichalis, and Makrygiannis, who fortified the warehouses and the yard walls, and undertook to defend Myloi, while many ships came close to the coast in order to assist with their cannons. The battle lasted until the night of June 13, when Ibrahim was forced to abandon the attempt. The militancy of the defenders of Myloi, combined with the choice of position and the appropriate fortifications, gave the victory to the Greek side and made the siege of Nafplio very difficult. Two days later, after an unsuccessful attempt to capture the central aqueduct of the city, Ibrahim withdrew his army and returned to Tripolitsa, after first burning and looting Argos and the villages of the region.

Meanwhile, Kolokotronis gathered two to three thousand men around Tripolitsa, with the aim of cutting off Ibrahim from his supply bases. However, he placed the main part of his forces in the old camp at Trikorfa, on the fringes of Mount Menalon, and not in some more mountainous and fortified position. In the battles fought there on June 23–24, his combatants inflicted great losses on their opponents but in the end they were forced to withdraw to the highlands of Gortynia, leaving behind hundreds of men slain on the battlefield. This was the last large-scale battle that the Greeks fought against the forces of Ibrahim, who strengthened his position in Tripolitsa, organized warehouses and a logistics network, and stationed garrisons to secure communication with his forces in the southern Peloponnese. From that time until December 1825, when he departed with a detachment of his army to take part in the siege of Mesolonghi, he campaigned in Karytaina and later in Mystras, Messinia, and Kalavryta, looting, killing, and taking captive those inhabitants who were unable to seek refuge in almost impenetrable and precipitous mountain locations.

In these campaigns Ibrahim's army did not come up against an ordered Greek force, but even so its losses were significant. After the battle at Trikorfa, Kolokotronis began to work on a new war tactic. Faced with an army that was like a European army and which he had so far failed to deal with in a head-on clash, from the summer of 1825 he began to try out the war tactic that had been applied successfully by the Spanish guerrillas against the French army during the Napoleonic Wars: the tactic of the modern partisan, understood in the political sense of this concept discussed by Carl Schmitt. The Greek irregular freedom fighters were unable to prevent Ibrahim's campaigns. Apart from anything else, this meant that Kolokotronis was unable to maintain large and permanent camps, because this presupposed mechanisms of logistics and central warehouses impenetrable to the enemy. In these circumstances he dispersed his forces in each region in small corps, which were maintained by the inhabitants of the mountain villages, and he had them operate everywhere and all the time, waging a war of attrition, with surprise attacks on detachments of the Egyptian army, on guard-posts, on warehouses, and so on. This tactic suited the militia characteristics of the Greek army in the Peloponnese from the outset of the revolution—that is, the close ties of the irregular fighters of the area with their communities and inhabitants.

At the same time, the Greek authorities were oriented to an entirely different solution: the creation of a regular army. Indeed, it was decided to hire immediately several thousand European and American soldiers, to bear the brunt of the war in the Peloponnese, until the regular Greek army, which the French Colonel Fabvier was commissioned to organize, was enlisted, trained, and had become combat-fit. The materialization of such a plan demanded the clinching of new loans, but this time no willing lenders were found and the plan was scrapped. So, in late 1825 and early 1826, great pressure was put on Kolokotronis and the Peloponnesian military chiefs to accept the immediate transformation of their corps into a regular army. This was something they rejected outright, continuing with guerrilla warfare and counterproposing its systematization. The political crisis that came in the wake of the fall of Mesolonghi (the cessation of the works to build the National Assembly and the temporary assumption of the governance by a politically weak commission) led inevitably to the abandonment of any attempt at the immediate transformation of the irregulars into regular soldiers and allowed Kolokotronis to systematize even further the tactic of guerrilla warfare.

While returning from Mesolonghi, Ibrahim plundered villages in Ileia and Kalavryta, in late April and early May 1826, and then went on to invade Mani. The main part of his army marched from Kalamata toward the narrow Almyros pass, while a second section was transported by ship much further south, to Diros. At Almyros, in the locality of Verga, the Maniots had constructed a stone yard wall about 1,500 meters from the gorge as far as the sea, with battlements, tower, and bastion. After a battle lasting three days (June 22–24), they forced Ibrahim to abandon his effort, leaving hundreds of dead on the battlefield. The landing of the second section of Ibrahim's army, in the area of Diros and Areopolis, was also confronted successfully. His new attempts to invade Mani, in late August 1826, this time from the east side of Mount Taygetos, met with a similar fate. Prior to this, in early August, his army had marched into Agios Petros and Prastos, while in October he campaigned one more time in the province of Kalavryta. In all these operations, with the exception of those in Mani, Ibrahim's army did not fight any critical battle. It destroyed and looted deserted villages, whose inhabitants had taken refuge in fortified mountainous locations and caves, and was subjected to surprise attacks, in the course of systematic guerrilla warfare. This allowed the Greek freedom fighters to keep grinding down his army and to regain part of the supplies and munitions Ibrahim had seized.

The most serious problem Ibrahim faced, after mid-1826, was his inability to keep the upper hand in many of the provinces that were theoretically controlled by his army, because the populace supported the guerrilla warfare. Ibrahim's tactic of destroying, looting, and taking people captive was aimed at breaking the morale of the population, at forcing them to concede in writing their submission to his power, in return for amnesty and the return to a peaceful daily life. In late 1826 and early 1827, several villages, influenced by the capitulation of their neighbors, had begun to submit, particularly in the northwest Peloponnese. The submissions, called *proskynimata* (capitulations) in the Greek sources, inhibited the Greek side from keeping up the war and, consequently, from pressuring the great powers to intervene in order to stop Ibrahim's catastrophic work. In these circumstances the Greek administration branded as traitors those who acknowledged Ibrahim's power as legitimate, while Kolokotronis ordered very harsh reprisals against those who refused to return to the Greek side. "Fire and axe to those who have submitted" (Kolokotrones 1892, 259) was his command, and it was applied without mercy, thus averting further spread of submissions.

More than two years had passed since Ibrahim had arrived in the Peloponnese and he had not managed to quash the Greek Revolution. One of the most dramatic episodes in the Greek resistance to that campaign of destruction was the battle fought at Mega Spilaion monastery, one of the major pilgrimage sites in the Peloponnese and the Orthodox world more generally. Ibrahim camped in the area and invited the monks to surrender and stop supporting the guerilla fighters. The monks, who were sheltering in the monastery hundreds of women and children from surrounding villages, refused. They asked Kolokotronis for help, and he sent to their assistance a few hundred of his soldiers with Photakos, his adjutant, at the head. The monastery was put under siege on June 24, 1827. At the end of a day-long bloody encounter, during which several monks, including young novices aged between fourteen and seventeen, died fighting the invaders, the venerable shrine in its imposing rocky abode, remained impregnable. That was a very important moment in the fortunes of the revolution and Mega Spilaion emerged as a symbol of resistance and hope

for the Greeks. While the mountain communities sustained the guerrilla warfare, Ibrahim stepped up the violence against the inhabitants and strengthened
the Greeks' arguments to the great powers, which they petitioned to intervene.
This is clearly imprinted in the declaration of the Third National Assembly, on
May 5, 1827, in which the phrase "we fight" is repeated many times in the first
paragraphs. It stressed that "the theater of war will not be closed, unless we all
die," and the "mercy and help" of the powerful European states was invoked. A
few weeks later, Britain, Russia, and France declared their decision to stop the
war, with the treaty they signed in London on July 6, 1827. Ibrahim's refusal to
obey the terms of the truce set in the Treaty of London led the naval squadrons of the three great powers to the Bay of Navarino, where on October 8 / 20
they sank the Egyptian and Ottoman fleets. This was a mortal blow to Ibrahim.
In the following months, he was confined to the fortresses of Pylos, Methoni,
and Koroni, after first having destroyed the town and blown up the walls of
Tripolitsa. His forces finally deserted him in the Peloponnese, in September 1828,
when a mighty French expeditionary corps forced him to surrender the fortresses to the Greek side. The Greek War of Independence in the Peloponnese
was now over.

Dionysis Tzakis

Translated from the Greek by Alexandra Douma

References

Dakin, Douglas. 1973. *The Greek Struggle for Independence, 1821–1833.* Berkeley and Los
    Angeles.
Diamandouros, Nikiforos. 1972. "Political Modernization, Social Conflict and Cultural
    Cleavage in the Formation of the Modern Greek State: 1821–1828." PhD diss., Columbia
    University, New York.
Frangos, George. 1971. "The Philike Etairia 1814–21: A Social and Historical Analysis." PhD
    diss., Columbia University, New York.
Frangos, George. 1973. "The Philiki Etairia: A Premature National Coalition." In *The
    Struggle for Greek Independence,* edited by Richard Clogg, 87–103. London and
    Basingstoke.
Kolokotrones. 1892. *The Klepht and the Warrior. Sixty Years or Peril and Daring. An autobiog-
    raphy,* translated and edited by Elizabeth Edmonds, preface by J. Gennadius. London.
Laiou, Sophia. 2011. "The Greek Revolution in the Morea According to the Description of
    an Ottoman Official." In *The Greek Revolution of 1821: A European Event,* edited by
    Petros Pizanias, 241–255. Istanbul.
Lekkas, Padelis. 2005. "The Greek War of Independence from the Perspective of Historical
    Sociology." *Historical Review* 2:161–183.

Panagiotopoulos, Vasilis. 1957–1958. "Η Προκήρυξις της Μεσσηνιακής Γερουσίας προς τας Ευρωπαϊκάς Αυλάς" [The proclamation of the Messenian Senate to the European courts]. *DIEEE* 12:137–150.

Panagiotopoulos, Vasilis. 2001–2002. "Η έναρξη του Αγώνα της Ανεξαρτησίας στην Πελοπόννησο. Μια ημερολογιακή προσέγγιση" [The start of the struggle for independence in the Peloponnese: A calendrical approach]. In *Πρακτικά του ΣΤ Διεθνούς Συνεδρίου Πελοποννησιακών Σπουδών* [Proceedings of the VI International Conference of Peloponnesian Studies], 449–461. Athens.

Panagiotopoulos, Vasilis. 2011. "The Filiki Etaireia (Society of Friends). Organizational Preconditions of the National War of Independence." In *The Greek Revolution of 1821: A European Event,* edited by Petros Pizanias, 101–126. Istanbul.

Panagiotopoulos, Vasilis. 2015. *Δύο πρίγκιπες στην Ελληνική Επανάσταση. Επιστολές αυτόπτη μάρτυρα και ένα υπόμνημα του πρίγκιπα Γεωργίου Καντακουζηνού* [Two princes in the Greek Revolution: Letters from an eye witness and a memorandum written by Prince George Kantakouzinos]. Athens.

Petropulos, John Anthony. 1976. "Forms of Collaboration with the Enemy during the First Greek War of Liberation." In *Hellenism and the First Greek War of Liberation, 1821–1830: Continuity and Change,* edited by Nikiforos P. Diamandouros, Peter W. Topping, and John Peter Anton, 131–143. Thessaloniki.

Photakos [Photios Chrysanthopoulos]. 1858. *Απομνημονεύματα περί της Ελληνικής Επαναστάσεως* [Memoirs of the Greek Revolution]. Athens.

Rotzokos, Nikos. (1997) 2016. *Επανάσταση και εμφύλιος στο Εικοσιένα* [Revolution and civil war in 1821]. Athens.

Rotzokos, Nikos. 2010. "Obéissance traditionnelle et légitimité nationale: Le pouvoir ottoman, l'administration grecque et les actes de soumission pendant la Révolution grecque de 1821." In *La société grecque sous la domination ottomane: Économie, identité, structure sociale et conflits,* edited by Maria Efthymiou, 228–257. Athens.

Sakellariou, Michail. 2012. *Η απόβαση του Ιμπραήμ στην Πελοπόννησο καταλύτης για την αποδιοργάνωση της Ελληνικής Επανάστασης* [Ibrahim's landing in the Peloponnese, as a catalyst in the disorganization of the Greek Revolution]. Iraklio.

Schmitt, Carl. (1963) 2007. *Theory of the Partisan: Intermediate Commentary on the Concept of the Political.* Translated by Gary L. Ulmen. New York.

St Clair, William. 2008. *That Greece Might Still Be Free: The Philhellenes in the War of Independence.* Introduction by Roderick Beaton. Cambridge 2008.

Stites, Richard. 2014. *The Four Horsemen. Riding to Liberty in Post-Napoleonic Europe.* Oxford.

Tzakis, Dionysis. 2010. "Intégration et révolte: élites chrétiennes et musulmanes au Péloponnèse sous la domination ottomane (18e—début du 19e siècle)." In *La société grecque sous la domination ottomane: Économie, identité, structure sociale et conflits,* edited by Maria Efthymiou, 171–200. Athens.

Tzakis, Dionysis. 2018a. "Από την Οδησσό στη Βοστίτσα: Η πολιτική ενσωμάτωση των τοπικών ηγετικών ομάδων στη Φιλική Εταιρεία" [From Odessa to Vostitsa: The political incorporation of the local leadership groups in the Philiki Etaireia]. In *Οι πόλεις των Φιλικών. Οι αστικές διαδρομές ενός επαναστατικού φαινομένου* [The cities of

the Philikoi: The urban pathways of a revolutionary phenomenon], edited by Olga
Katsiardi-Hering, 125–148. Athens.

Tzakis, Dionysis. 2018b. "Πόλεμος και σχέσεις εξουσίας στην επανάσταση του 1821" [War
and power relations in the revolution of 1821]. In Όψεις της Επανάστασης του 1821
[Aspects of the revolution of 1821], edited by Dimitris Dimitropoulos, Christos Loukos,
and Panagiotis Michailaris, 153–174. Athens.

Navarino

The battle of Navarino was fought at the entrance to the Gulf of Pylos in western Greece on October 20, 1827. On that day, a combined British-French-Russian naval force, commanded by the British admiral Sir Edward Codrington, entered the bay harboring the Turkish-Egyptian fleet after several weeks of blockade. Ostensibly, the motive of this sudden movement was to further the pacification of hostilities in Greece by insisting on a process of mediation which European diplomacy had unveiled, though hitherto unavailingly. Though the precise sequence of events in the harbor of Navarin, as it was usually called, remained opaque, a powerful cannonade from Codrington's command was followed by sustained firing on all sides. By the time it had finished most of the Ottoman ships had been sunk. Human losses were significant on both sides, but overwhelmingly so among the sultan's forces.

It has become part of the common understanding that this battle presaged the final emergence of an independent Greek state. John Koliopoulos and Thanos Veremis (2010, 24) state that the naval action at Navarino was "The most decisive event of the Greek war of independence"; while the preeminent account of modern Greek nationhood asserts baldly "Navarino changed everything" (Beaton 2019, 104). Although the generalized truth of this is not to be denied, the underlying nature of the operation pointed to a nuanced morass of competing aims and ambitions, just as the outcome in terms of the future of the Greek state harbored shadows as well as prospects of fulfillment.

It may, anyway, be argued that the most decisive event of the military struggle on the Greek side was harder to pin down but actually more significant than any single battle: the hard-won survival of revolutionary forces against Ottoman military offensives until the European powers themselves felt constrained to intervene.

The ebb and flow of the conflict after the outbreak of rebellion along the Danube in February 1821 are traced in detail elsewhere in this book. After four years of bloody fluctuations, the struggle appeared to have slid into a dismal stalemate, with "free" Greece limited to the islands and a number of pockets of varying size on the mainland.

It was a measure of the Ottoman Porte's own weakness across a range of fronts, internal as well as external, that in seeking to achieve a clean-cut victory Sultan Mahmud II sought the help of his formal subject, the strongman viceroy of Egypt, Mohammed Ali (himself an Albanian Muslim originally from Kavalla). In doing so the sultan took a risk, given Mohammed Ali's own growing ambitions as an Eastern potentate. It was Egyptian ships and troops—commanded by Mohammed's son-in-law Hasan Pasha—who fiercely repressed the challenge to Ottoman rule in Crete. Then during May 1825 Mohammed Ali' s son Ibrahim Pasha led a large expedition crashing into the Morea determined to bring to heel an area which had become a refuge for Greek fighters and their families displaced from surrounding regions.

Up to this point the struggle had often been pitiless in character, involving the massacre of those who had surrendered and the killing of women and children. During the first phases of fighting substantial areas of mainland Greece had been, in today's terms, "cleansed" of its Muslim inhabitants. It became part of the common discourse in Europe about these events that the behavior of Greeks and Turks differed little. Yet it still remained possible to regard such depredations on both sides as occurring amid the fog of a bitter contest. What was new about the Egyptian expedition in the Morea were rumors that it was part of a planned exercise including the bondage of the Greek population at large, their export to slave markets outside Greece, and the importation of Muslim settlers. Solid evidence of such a plan in any systematic sense was never to emerge; indeed, the rumors themselves may have served an Ottoman purpose to break the spirit of their opponents. But the threat of what was described at the time as "a new Barbary state" in Europe (Ward and Gooch 1922, 91) elevated the issue, already a more severe threat to regional political stability than attempted revolutions earlier in the decade in Spain and Naples, onto a higher moral as well as diplomatic plane.

Outside Greece arguably the most telling effect was in Russia. A cultural and religious link between the latter country and the notion of Greek revival went back at least to the 1770s, when Catherine the Great had gone to war with Turkey and sent a small military force to the Peloponnese. Nevertheless, when the revolution broke out in 1821, Tsar Alexander I had, as he put it, remained "pure," by which he meant obedient to the principles of the Holy Alliance in European affairs opposed to any attack on "legitimate" authority (St Clair 1972, 314). But

Russian opinion was increasingly sensitive to any news concerning a war of extermination being conducted against their fellow Orthodox faithful; in his poetry Alexander Pushkin lionized Greek heroes of the ancient past and, by extension, those of the present (Frary 2015, 32). By the time Tsar Alexander died in December 1825 his thoughts were already turning to action; indeed, his final days were spent in the Crimea, the base from which such an initiative might come. For the process we are describing, what mattered was a new sense of crisis in Europe's diplomatic machinery hinging on the likely action of the young new tsar, Nicholas I (Cowles 1990, 705).

At this stage the interaction between Russian and British interests was vital. In London, concerns about Russian reliability in sustaining the handiwork of the Congress of Vienna (1815), as well as keeping France strapped into its current subordinate position, was intense. "You must make up your mind to watch him," Foreign Secretary Castlereagh once said to Prime Minister Liverpool about Tsar Alexander, "and to resist him as another Bonaparte"; certainly the Russians continued to exploit British vulnerability in various parts of the Mediterranean, including its new protectorate in the Ionian islands (Holland 2012, 29). Making sure the tsar's actions were constrained as much as possible within the bounds of congress diplomacy was crucial. But that system was already showing signs of stress when Alexander died, and in early 1826 it seemed all too likely that his successor would exploit the circumstances of the Greek struggle to gain a new freedom of maneuver. For the Russian ambassador in London, Prince Lieven, and for his wife, whose influential contacts among the British elite were celebrated, the allegations of Ibrahim Pasha's alleged brutalities in the Morea offered a useful peg on which to hang implicit threats that unless the British acted in concert with St. Petersburg over Greek affairs, an energetic new tsar might go off at a tangent of his own (Hyde 1938).

In this context, the British foreign secretary, George Canning, became a prime player. The judgment of the Philhellene George Finlay that the British authorities after 1821 had "viewed the outbreak [in Greece] with more aversion than any other Christian government" (Finlay 1861, 161) may have been exaggerated, but is by no means wholly lacking in truth. Castlereagh's first reaction to the insurrection had been that if some kind of political fire blanket could prevent the flames spreading beyond the heartland of Greek resistance, sooner rather than later the Ottomans would snuff it out (Bew 2011, 533). After Canning succeeded as foreign secretary, following Castlereagh's suicide during August 1822, this prospect became increasingly problematical. Canning himself was no Philhellene, though his sometimes scathing remarks about Greeks— "There is no denying," he once said of them, "that they are a rascally set" (Hinde 1973, 384)—are probably best regarded as the prejudicial chatter common at the top of the English greasy pole. But on assuming his office, Canning also set about trying to put a more liberal stamp on a Tory government with a track record of harshness at home and abroad. A more sympathetic stance on the sufferings of Greeks—something that echoed the humanitarian campaign to end slavery in the Caribbean—was a convenient place to do this.

But undoubtedly Canning's most important motives concerned larger diplomatic considerations. He no longer trusted the post-1815 "concert" to work in British interests. France's successful invasion of Spain during 1823 to restore its prime influence had been a warning. Afterward, Canning had skillfully assisted regime changes in Spanish America—the phrase that he had ushered in "the New World to balance the Old" became famous—and in doing so announced a willingness to act outside the present conference system. A similar finesse of the sort that might further boost Canning's reputation as a master of diplomacy seemed possible in relation to the quagmire in Greece.

Hitherto in Britain the assumption had been, as rather caustically summarized by an Austrian diplomat, that the British "were not prepared to see the liberty of Greece bought at the price of Russian supremacy in the Mediterranean" (Holland 2012, 42). Canning now believed, however, that these risks were worth taking and that by linking Britain's emerging claims as the key arbitrator in Greek affairs with Russian influence on Turkey, an apparently intractable issue could be brought to workable resolution; though it seems unlikely that Canning at any point had any clear idea, or indeed cared much, as to what this meant for Greek *political* aspirations (Cowles 1990, 717). The extremity of the Greeks' current situation—the besieged bastion of Mesolonghi came under fresh bombardment after February 1826—made urgent some attempt to quieten things down.

Soon after the accession of Tsar Nicholas, Canning had sent the Duke of Wellington as emissary to St. Petersburg to restrain him from any rash unilateral action. In fact, Wellington discovered that Greece was by no means the main thing on Nicholas's mind—issues surrounding Serbia and the Danubian Principalities were more pressing. Nonetheless, on April 4 Prince Lieven and the Russian foreign minister, Karl Nesselrode for Russia, and the Duke of Wellington on behalf of Great Britain, signed a protocol designed to open a path to end the bloodletting in Greece. This document sketched a solution whereby the Greek lands currently in rebellion would remain part of the Ottoman Empire and pay tribute to the Sublime Porte. The local Christian population would elect their own government and run their administration (Bourchier 1873, 1:359). A significant aspect of this diplomatic instrument was that it was the first to refer to "Greece" as a political entity. But the territorial extent of such a concept, and in particular how in practical terms the armistice called for in the protocol was to be enforced, remained vague and awaited what had inevitably to be a more fully worked-out "European" initiative.

At this stage sympathy for Greece in Europe, and its cultural role as a pivot for romantic soul-searching, was enjoying a fresh surge. Eugene Delacroix's *Greece Expiring on the Ruins of Mesolonghi* was to provide one of the enduring images of the revolution. Yet the position of the French government on these matters remained especially fluid. The restored Bourbon regime was determined to resuscitate its influence in the Mediterranean.

It had to move very carefully not to arouse suspicions of some new Napoleonic spirit of adventure. French policy thereafter incorporated highly contradictory elements. The British ambassador at the Porte, Stratford Canning, cryptically observed that his Gallic counterpart at Constantinople, "Our Frenchman," had "a heart still bleeding for Greece and a hand ever open to the Pasha of Egypt" (Lane-Poole 1890, 445). The latter habit was reflected in the presence of "renegade" French officers in the Egyptian fleet—one of Mohammed Ali's great innovations—that the government in Paris did little to bring to heel (Driault and Lhéritier 1925–1926, 246, 274). The essential goal in Paris was to ensure that France should not be frozen out by Britain—where George Canning had become prime minister in April 1827—and prevent Russia from playing a role in whatever endgame emerged over the struggle. France therefore signed the tripartite Treaty of London in July of that year when the earlier protocol was put on a more formal collective basis. But Austria and Prussia remained aloof, since for Count Metternich in Vienna especially its provisions were a travesty of his belief in allowing no displacement of established authority in Europe.

The acute controversy that later arose stemmed from the failure of the three signatory powers to specify precisely in what circumstances force might be used against any party that now refused to accept the mediation insisted on by the powers. From the outset, the latter really meant Turkey, since the underlying purpose of the mediation itself was to prevent what seemed a looming catastrophe for the Greek insurgents. It was also clear that the force undertaken would be essentially naval, the aim being to intercept the supply and movement of any hostile troops, and so prevent the contending sides from colliding (though Russian land power was to be a constant threat in the background). A natural result of the Treaty of London was that the Levant "stations" of the European navies involved were alerted for possible action. Such action was framed in terms of enforcing an outcome through mediation and hence avoiding any wider war emerging from the present deadlock. The critics of the treaty, however, did not fail to point out that the implicit internationalization of the modalities of the dispute entailed a risk that, far from bringing about peace, they might lead to the very war that it was intended to prevent. The dread of such a new conflict, against the backdrop of the bloody years of war before 1815, was central to European responses as the situation in Greece slid out of control.

In any use of maritime power in the eastern Mediterranean, it was axiomatic that Great Britain's Royal Navy would play the leading role. In December 1826, Sir Edward Codrington had been appointed as commander-in-chief of the British fleet in the Mediterranean, and after spending time in Malta—the strategic role of which in subsequent events was critical—Codrington arrived with his force off the Greek coast in early July 1827. Codrington's part in the ensuing denouement was crucial, not least because the very vagueness of his instructions from the Admiralty at home meant that much hinged on his discretion. Above all, he was determined to assert the place of the Royal Navy in expanding British power overseas after 1815. Suggestively, that place had not been very distinguished in the long interlude since Nelson's triumph at Trafalgar in 1805. It had been the British army that had harvested the gloss from the defeat of Napoleon at Waterloo. The wholesale battering of Algiers in 1816 by an Anglo-Dutch squadron occasioned by the campaign to eradicate so-called white slavery in North Africa began a process in which this could be put to rights. During the early and especially mid-1820s the British Fleet in the Mediterranean had been gradually strengthened and gained a fresh kudos for itself.

For Codrington, therefore, his brief as commander-in-chief to oversee the ending of hostilities in the Greek lands held possibilities to heighten the prestige of the service that was his prime goal. Furthermore, in seeking to secure British naval primacy, the admiral had no doubt who the real enemy might be. It was true that his great predecessor in the Mediterranean, Lord Nelson, had hated the Russians—with their own claims to such places as Malta and Corfu—only slightly less than he did the French (Sokol 1949). But since the Treaty of Tilsit in 1807 the Russians had not had any effective presence in the area. It was the Ottomans who were in a position to frustrate an emerging British order across key parts of the post-Napoleonic Mediterranean, including the freer movement of trade and the ending of both piracy and slavery. For the Greeks themselves, Codrington did not appear to have any particular favor. Writing to his wife from his new posting, he sought to offer her in one letter some description of local circumstances, "as disgusting as the subject is made by the scenes of vice and horror which attend the emergence of a people so debased as the Greeks" (Bourchier 1873, 1:357). A principal aspect of that debasement, in Codrington's mind, was the leading role of Greeks in the hike in piracy across the region that was one of the outstanding effects of the revolution.

Yet there was something deeply personal that told in quite another direction. In 1822 Codrington's son had been drowned off the island of Ydra when serving in the Mediterranean on HMS *Cambrian* (Bourchier 1873, 1:346). Memory of his son's death was never far from Codrington's mind—indeed, another of his sons was to be wounded serving under his command at Navarino. There is at least a suggestion that profoundly personal vibrations affected the admiral's decisions amid all the confused conditions and which underpinned sympathy for Greeks who could be considered victims of Turkish persecution.

If for Codrington "saving the Greeks," whatever their perceived faults, came increasingly to the forefront, the Greek insurgents themselves gradually recognized that they had to be saved by somebody if Ibrahim Pasha was not to go back to Alexandria in triumph, probably taking a lot of captive Greeks with him. Furthermore, their preference was to be saved under British auspices rather than any alternative patron. This would not have been the case earlier in the rebellion. For one thing, there were considerably more Frenchmen, and indeed Germans, than English in the early waves of philhellenic volunteers; the English were distinctly few on the ground. But the fact that the insurgency became so much a maritime phenomenon—so that Aegean islands, above all Ydra, became a potentially final line of defense for the revolution itself—suggested a natural linkage to British agency. This was reinforced by an underlying suspicion of Russian ambitions on land, ambitions that might severely cramp the territorial extent of any future Greek state. By contrast, Codrington encouraged the Greeks—through their Irish commander of land forces, Sir Richard Church—to extend control over as much territory as circumstances allowed at this critical juncture, so that when the time came to draw lines on maps their claims might be maximized.

Meanwhile it was essential for Codrington that the Greeks should be pliable and "moderate" for his own purposes, and also give up their internecine splits. When he went to Nafplio in mid-July 1827, he was confronted by competing local factions tussling for control of the important Palamidi fortress. But before long, these groups ceased their feuding and rallied around the provisional government of Greece, if only because unity had become a precondition of survival. Codrington was therefore enabled in successive dispatches home to depict an obdurate Turkey as the overwhelming barrier to successful mediation. Furthermore, it became a central part of his analysis that in bringing overweening force to bear, not only would a wedge be driven between the Turks and the Egyptians, since the latter were so connected to British commerce in the region, but that eventually Constantinople itself would submit. But even if the Porte did not, he was prepared to go to extremes. "I wish the Sultan would declare war," he wrote at one point to Lady Codrington (Bourchier 1873, 1:359–360), to whom he was franker about his own predilections than when writing to the Admiralty, "as it would simplify matters at once." Ambassador Stratford Canning in Constantinople, responsible for overall control of British involvements in the area, was later to regret not having spotted earlier signs that Codrington might be veering into an unauthorized direction (Lane-Poole 1890, 449).

One event in London had occurred, however, that seemed sure to complicate matters further. On August 8, 1827, George Canning collapsed and died. The Duke of Wellington succeeded him as prime minister. Elements in the Tory cabinet had been unhappy about the Treaty of London from the first. They did not like acting at odds with Austria, whom Castlereagh had previously seen as the true "guardian of the Mediterranean" (Webster 1931, 494). By extension, they saw no sense in allowing Russia to batter its way back into the region over the Ottoman corpse. The duke did not reverse Canning's new policy, but there were intimations that sooner or later he might.

In the interval, the confusion nonetheless meant that Codrington—who was ignorant of the subtle shifts in Westminster affairs (Woodhouse 1965, 161)—had more leeway in pressing on toward a climax, especially once he received his own impatiently awaited copy of the Treaty of London with its apparent authorization, if necessary, to use force. As for any likelihood of Greeks and Turks ceasing their hostilities, Codrington admitted that he harbored "very little hope of claims and pretensions so discordant being ever brought to [any] arrangement" (Bourchier 1873, 1:417). All his actions had that conviction as their premise. This was an important element in the ineluctability of the events that unfolded, a process that on the Ottoman side felt like the shadow of an "unequal armistice" aimed at their own interests and claims (Woodhouse 1965, 82).

Much of Codrington's resulting impatience to bring matters to a conclusion focused on the French, and inevitably on the admiral heading their own Levant "station," Henri de Rigny, a sailor with a distinguished record as a young marine officer in the wars of Napoleon (perhaps one reason for Codrington's unease). The tension between them was political rather than anything strictly naval. For Codrington, the envisaged mediation with Turkey was intended to be one of imposition; de Rigny tended more to negotiation, with all the possible prolongations this implied. Codrington's suspicions were made acute by the way that de Rigny—whom the British admiral described at one point as "quite incomprehensible" (Bourchier 1873, 1:459–460)—sought an understanding with Mohammed Ali in Alexandria. The presence of the French officers in the Turkish-Egyptian fleet continued to be a major cause of irritation to Codrington. Then in early September the Ottoman ships had taken refuge in the harbor of Navarino, frustrating the British admiral's plan to intercept them as the Royal Navy's vessels threw a protective screen around Ydra. The elusiveness of de Rigny's squadron as it crisscrossed the Aegean, its location unknown even to supposed partners (though in this case it had in fact gone off to Kythira), symbolized an unpredictability in French behavior adding considerably to Codrington's impulse to find some way to effect a clean-cut outcome.

On September 20 the British and French ships did nevertheless combine at sea and proceed to the mouth of Navarino Bay (Map 10). Five days later Codrington, de Rigny, and their staffs went ashore. They themselves met on the beach before proceeding to the elevated green tent nearby where Ibrahim Pasha granted them an interview (Woodhouse 1965, 75). Codrington's son, a midshipman on his father's flagship, the *Asia*, immediately afterward wrote an eyewitness account. Notably, after the pipes were smoked and coffee sipped, all the talking on the European side was done by the British admiral; de Rigny maintained a telling silence throughout. Codrington did not mince his words. Pointing to a group of Ottoman naval officers waiting in the wings, he said what a pity it would be to see them destroyed if it came to shooting. That everything said on this occasion had to be translated—from English into French and then into Turkish—meant that on the most sensitive matters misunderstanding was all too easy. As for the pasha, the younger Codrington remarked that he was "surprised by the good sense which Ibrahim showed" throughout the exchanges (Bourchier 1873, 2:6).

The outcome of this meeting was that there should be a stipulated interval in which Ibrahim could seek further instructions from Constantinople. But any chance that this might be the start of a real negotiation shortly imploded. It had been understood that the Turkish-Egyptian ships would remain immobilized in the bay. But with General Church's insurgent Greek forces besieging the port of Patras, Ibrahim Pasha sought permission to send a squadron to relieve Ottoman distress. When he received no answer, the squadron sailed anyway on October 1; its success in gaining the open sea was something Codrington blamed partly on de Rigny, whose ships had again temporarily departed their station. It fell to the British fleet to intercept the Ottoman vessels off Patras and eventually escort them back to Navarino. Christopher Montague Woodhouse's conclusion is that this whole affair resulted from a "genuine misunderstanding" between the European admirals and the Ottomans (Woodhouse 1965, 81). Whatever the rights and wrongs, for Codrington it offered the perfect opportunity to break off all communication with Ibrahim Pasha. "He has forfeited his word of honour," the admiral declared, "and I will not again trust the word of honour of him or of anybody under his command" (Bourchier 1873, 2:32).

With a Russian squadron under Admiral Heiden—a German who, ironically, had once served in the British Navy—arriving off Navarino on October 15, a decision loomed for the Europeans. They could not just stay put and blockade the port. Winter storms made that impossible. The mood among the sailors was sullen and in favor of finishing their task in the region and getting away;

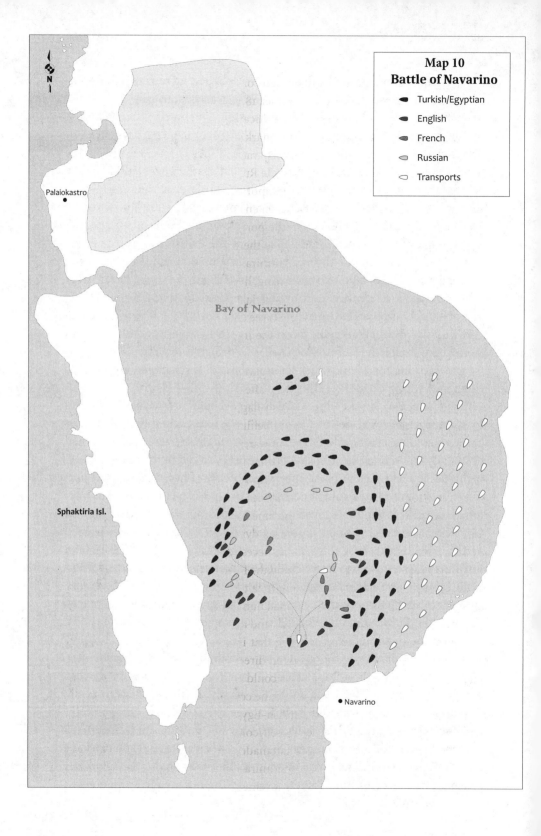

Map 10
Battle of Navarino

- Turkish/Egyptian
- English
- French
- Russian
- Transports

N

Palaiokastro

Bay of Navarino

Sphaktiria Isl.

Navarino

discipline—including violence between ordinary sailors—was especially bad among Codrington's ships (Bourchier 1873, 2:28). Codrington was keenly aware that for the British, this was the critical moment—an exclusively naval moment—if they were to put their own mark on the outcome. But if the European ships were to slink away on their separate tracks, French influence would rise relative to that of Great Britain, while Russian confidence that the British were worth cooperating with would evaporate; a resort by St. Petersburg to crushing land power would certainly then ensue. The alternative for the European force off Navarino was to enter the port itself. But the actual purpose of doing so in terms of effecting a solution to the problem of the ongoing violence in Greece was wrapped in obscurity. Admiral de Rigny nonetheless fully concurred with the decision to enter, knowing, however, that the risks did not fall principally on himself or his country. Crucially, as Woodhouse remarks in his account of the battle, what none of the three allied admirals had any idea of as it approached "was a final decision on the independence of Greece" (Woodhouse 1965, 107).

At 1:30 p.m. on October 20, Codrington gave the order to the European squadrons to "prepare for action," and shortly after they sailed into the horseshoe-shaped bay. Out in front was the British flagship, *Asia,* surrounded by HMS *Genoa, Albion,* and *Dartmouth;* directly behind sailed de Rigny in his flagship *Sirène* with several accompanying men-of-war; and to leeward a Russian flotilla—fewer in number but, strikingly, with greater firepower than either of the other allied components—headed by the flagship *Azov.* At one level this shape embodied the allied unity of the three countries involved; one might say it prefigured the Concert of Europe in what became a classic nineteenth-century form. But at another it indicated more complex dynamics: the British eager to push ahead, blindly if necessary, the French necessarily supportive but sticking to their carefully calculated subsidiarity, and the Russians exercising oversight from the rear, aware that were this operation to falter, they at least had other ways to ultimately secure their aims. Only a small number of Greeks participated, as pilots and interpreters on the allied vessels and as seamen on both sides.

Afterward Codrington was to argue that if his intention had been warlike from the start, he would not have sailed directly into the center of the enemy horseshoe, where the Ottoman vessels could concentrate their fire on his own ships (Bourchier 1873, 2:124). He would, he contended, have sailed around the perimeter of the bay to take the Turkish-Egyptians in the rear. But it was inherent in Codrington's style—with its self-consciously Nelsonian spirit—to go straight to the heart. The Ottomans had made no preparations for a battle. Officers on the flagship of the Turkish admiral, Muharrem Bey, were smoking their pipes when the European ships' movements began (Woodhouse 1965, 112).

By 2 p.m. the Royal Navy warships had anchored right up against the leading Ottoman vessels. What Codrington expected then to happen is hardly knowable for sure. Perhaps, at the mercy of modern firepower, he assumed that Muharrem Bey would promptly surrender. But throughout the preceding period the British admiral, unlike de Rigny, had shown little understanding of Ottoman psychology and, in particular, the religious solidarity that bonded them together (Woodhouse 1965, 96). For Ibrahim Pasha and his viceroy father, as much as for the sultan in Constantinople, the loss of a fleet and many lives was better than caving in to the force majeure of the Christian powers.

Whatever rational anticipations may have been entertained by the protagonists, they promptly disappeared in flames. The phenomenon of the unexpected shot, from a quarter impossible to pin down, but involving fatality and igniting a more general mêlée with huge consequences, represents a distinct category in world history. In the story of British involvement in Greek affairs, the shot that rang out across Syntagma Square on December 4, 1944, that triggered the riots that triggered the civil war is a later example. In this case Codrington, fearing that a Turkish fireship might get in among his leading ships, sent a pinnace with orders if necessary to board one of Muharrem Bey's fireships, as yet not ablaze; when a British coxswain tried to leap aboard the latter, a shot was fired and he fell dead. Much debate later surrounded from where this shot came (for one thing, many stories circulated subsequently of the Europeans firing at each other, mistakenly or not, amid the confusion). Most accounts echo the conclusion that events at this point have "all the hallmarks of miscalculation or accident" (Woodhouse 1965, 116). This may well be true, but, if so, the miscalculations and accidents are logically consistent with a subterranean logic.

The battle that then raged from 2.30 p.m. through to 6.00 p.m. on October 20 was not really a battle as such at all. The firing was point-blank between stationary targets anchored at grappling distance from each other. There was no room for maneuver except for small vessels, which was why losses on the latter were less. Much hinged on the anchoring itself. The Genoa swung stern-first onto its Turkish opponent, limiting the angle of fire. Later one of the criticisms of the whole affair was that the great firepower brought to bear bore no proportion to the damage inflicted.

That damage was still very considerable. Sixty of the Turkish-Egyptian ships were sunk, and some six thousand sailors killed. The Europeans lost no vessels, but fatalities included seventy-five Britons, forty Frenchmen, and fifty-nine Russians, though many more were wounded. Even Codrington admitted that de Rigny's squadron had fought with courage and at points intervened to save the exposed British from more severe punishment. De Rigny's approach to the whole affair was that his force was not to be found wanting when the politics ran out and the firing began. There were to be many allegations that the Russians had kept out of the fray as much as possible, but it is quite likely that this reflected a desire to smear. Certainly, it was not suggested by the losses incurred; and the memorial today to the Russian dead on the island of Sphaktiria is the most impressive among those of the three European allies. Of the unyielding resistance by the Ottoman forces there was no dispute. Lives were still being lost during the night after the fighting ended, with burning wreckage floating across the harbor and stricken ships exploding.

Certainly, if Codrington had hoped that when it was over Ibrahim Pasha would approach him on bended knee, he was disappointed. Tahir Pasha, one of the latter's commanders, came aboard HMS *Asia* on October 22 and, while abjuring any more fighting, said that no commitments could be made about ending those land operations which ultimately were more important than anything that happened afloat. Three days later, the allied fleets could only sail away again, de Rigny as always coy to partners as to wherever it was he was going; testimony to the limited scope of purely naval action in settling matters for good. There was great concern meanwhile that the lives of Europeans were at risk in Ottoman cities, including in Egypt. The British consul in Alexandria rushed to pacify Mohammed Ali, blaming the Turks for firing the first cannonshot at Navarino. Mohammed waved this aside, merely saying "no, no—it was to be; it was to be" (Woodhouse 1965, 149). In its oblique recognition of basic forces this was all that, perhaps, could be said. In Constantinople the mood hardened, and within days the European ambassadors—whose embassies had been surrounded by military guards—had no option but to ask for their passports. The British representative, Stratford Canning and his wife walked to the dockside with their retinue as dawn rose over the city (Lane-Poole 1890, 453–456). It was a humiliating moment.

This explains the quick reaction against what had happened at Navarino in British politics. The strain in Tory sentiment regarding it as madness to use force against Turkey, only to provide new opportunities for the far greater danger of Russia, got an instant boost. On the other hand, Codrington had not only provided, at first sight anyway, vivid testimony of British naval power, but his actions had the legitimacy of striking against the "barbarization" of the Morea. In seeking to go into reverse on its broad policy, the British government therefore had to tread carefully. A series of "Queries" were sent to Codrington, all of which were framed to extract information that might at some point be used against him (Bourchier 1873, 2:124–128). Those queries boiled down to a failure on the admiral's part before the entry into Navarino to conduct substantive discussions on pacification with Ibrahim Pasha. Codrington's answer was that no direct exchanges other than the interview of September 25 had occurred because

Ibrahim was a man who could not be trusted. This was the context of the famous statement in the king's speech in the Westminster Parliament on January 29, 1828, that the "collision" at Navarino—the British government did not dignify it as a battle—had been wholly unexpected and that the "untoward event" should not be repeated.

"Untoward" for whom and in what ways were questions that naturally arose from what had been said. Wellington's subsequent clarification was that what had been "untoward" had been the European fleet's clumsy entry into the harbor precipitating unnecessary and unexpected violence (Bourchier 1873, 2:178–180). English liberals for their part defended Codrington for—in the words of Lord John Russell—having won "as honest a victory as was ever gained by the arms of any Power from the beginning of the world." Still, for British diplomacy the effects thereafter did prove untoward in critical ways. Russia levered open new influence in the Near East and new access to the Mediterranean, before long to climax in the Treaty of Unkiar Skelessi (1833) by which Turkey appeared to recognize a "shadow" Russian protectorate over Christians in Asia Minor. The British were subsequently to expend huge diplomatic and, during the war in Crimea after 1855, military efforts—this time on behalf of Turkey and against Russia—trying to reverse the logic embodied in Navarino. They were never to fully succeed. Meanwhile, however, early in 1828 the Duke of Wellington was to dismiss Codrington from his post in the Mediterranean. Whatever the latter's alleged errors of judgment, Stratford Canning regarded this as a mistake, because it relieved some of the pressure on the sultan to come to an agreement (Lane-Poole 1890, 462). Certainly, British leverage on the overall outcome in Greece was to be rather less than might have been predicted at an earlier stage.

For Greeks in rebellion against Ottoman rule, Navarino did not immediately bring an independent state or indeed relief from the land campaign being waged by Ibrahim Pasha in the Morea. But the odds had turned, and a decision in Constantinople crystallized that Greece was not the best place to devote the resources required to defeat the enemies of the empire. This was confirmed by the Turkish-Russian war after April 1828, with its focus on Wallachia, Danubia, and other territories more vital to the survival of Ottoman power. A French expedition under General Maison intervened to oversee the evacuation of Ibrahim Pasha's forces from the Peloponnese in early October 1828. This supervision ensured that no Greek slaves accompanied the final departure to Smyrna of Muslim civilians shortly afterward. Great Britain had refused to take any part in this military operation. By then a conference of European ambassadors was under way on the island of Poros, drawing up the parameters of an independent Greek state.

But when it came to the critical matter of drawing lines on the map, the dynamics issuing from the "battle" of Navarino were not uniformly favorable to Greek aspirations. The fact that European force had seemingly been instrumental in the liquidation of Ottoman rule meant that a countereffect kicked in, leading to a determination in some capitals that the resulting Greek state should be made as territorially small as possible. This was one thing on which the British and the French in particular did not disagree, since each was concerned to reconstruct its influence at Constantinople that Navarino and its aftermath had severely jeopardized. The "decisive" effects of what had happened therefore cut in various directions.

The exclusion of Crete from the imminent Greek state, insisted on by the Duke of Wellington among others (Holland and Markides 2006, 82), was a key marker in this process. When on February 6, 1833, a fresh European fleet—with seven French, five British, three Russian, and one Austrian warships in attendance— presided over the arrival in Nafplio of the Bavarian Othon in his newly inaugurated Kingdom of Greece, welcomed by boisterous crowds waving the flags of Greece and the European states, the same paradox of superficial unity and mutual suspicion operated as it had in the Bay of Navarino during October 1827. For Greeks within this realm, an independent sovereignty had been won, but what that might actually mean still remained in the balance, just as the territorial limits of the new country were regarded as inherently provisional.

This is in part why, despite its role in shaping the outcome of the struggle after 1821, the event at Navarino has not come to occupy a central place in the Greek memory of the revolution itself. Nevertheless, in the modern town of Pylos—whose main square is named Πλατεία Τριών Ναυάρχων (Plateia Trion Navarchon), after the three admirals Codrington, de Rigny, and Heiden—there is an annual celebration of the battle with participation by local civil and religious figures as well as representatives of Britain, France, and Russia. Paradoxically, it was the often subtle cleavages between powerful European states, inherent in the movements of their fleets before and after Navarino, that in the longer term was to give the independent state of Greece a certain leverage to promote its own distinctive interests (Beaton 2019, 102); this was to continue through the nineteenth and twentieth centuries, and perhaps beyond. Navarino has also assumed significance as a milestone on the way to more modern "humanitarian interventions" of our own times (Bass 2008). If so, it should be said that the battle exemplifies how the humanitarianism of major powers is invariably driven by realpolitik rather than the other way round.

Robert Holland

References

Bass, Garry. 2008. *Freedom's Battle: The Origins of Humanitarian Intervention.* New York.

Beaton, Roderick. 2019. *Greece: Biography of a Modern Nation.* London.

Bew, John. 2011. *Castlereagh, War and Tyranny.* London.

Bourchier, Jane, ed. 1873. *Memoirs of the Life of Admiral Sir Edward Codrington.* London.

Cowles, Loyal. 1990. "The Failure to Restrain Russia: Canning, Nesselrode, and the Greek Question, 1825–1827." *International History Review* 12, no. 4: 688–720.

Crane, David. 2009. *Men of War: Courage under Fire in the Nineteenth Century Navy.* London.

Driault, Edouard, and Michel Lhéritier. 1925–1926. *Histoire diplomatique de la Grèce: Des 1821 à nos jours.* Paris.

Finlay, George. 1861. *History of the Greek Revolution.* Edinburgh and London.

Frary, Lucien. 2015. *Russia and the Making of Modern Greek Identity, 1821–1844.* Oxford.

Hinde, Wendy. 1973. *George Canning.* London.

Holland, Robert. 2012. *Blue-Water Empire: The British in the Mediterranean since 1800.* Oxford.

Holland, Robert, and Diana Markides. 2006. *The British and the Hellenes: Struggles for Mastery in the Eastern Mediterranean, 1850–1960.* Oxford.

Hyde, Harford Montgomery. 1938. *Princess Lieven.* London.

Koliopoulos, John S., and Thanos M. Veremis. 2010. *Modern Greece: A History since 1821.* Chichester.

Lane-Poole, Stanley. 1890. *The Life of Lord Stratford de Redcliffe.* London.

Sokol, A. E. 1949. "Nelson and the Russian Fleet." *Military Affairs* 13, no. 3: 129–137.

St Clair, William. 1972. *That Greece Might Still Be Free: The Philhellenes in the War of Independence.* Oxford.

Ward, Adolphus William, and George Peabody Gooch, eds. 1922. *The Cambridge History of British Foreign Policy, 1783–1919.* Cambridge.

Webster, Charles K. 1931. *The Foreign Policy of Castlereagh.* Vol. 2: *Britain and the European Alliance, 1815–1822.* London.

Woodhouse, Christopher Montague. 1965. *The Battle of Navarino.* London.

Rumeli

The Greek Revolution was a European event. Besides the Philhellenes who advocated its cause, gathered funds, or fought under its banner, there was a broader public interested in its course: one can find regular reports of it in the *Edinburgh Review,* for example. It is interesting indeed to encounter names and locations of distant Rumeli in one of the most influential magazines of nineteenth-century Britain. On the one hand, this shows channels of communication known, but not yet fully explored, running both ways, trading names: of Western figures like William of Orange and Benjamin Franklin adorning the bastions of Mesolonghi, of Rumeliot villages scripted in the pages of an Edinburgh publication. On the other, it reminds us that the War of Independence in Greece, before having been won diplomatically by the great powers, had to be fought tenaciously by the revolutionaries themselves: fought and lost in Epirus, Macedonia, and Crete, come to a standstill in the core provinces of southern Greece, but fought everywhere for time enough to pose a Greek Question and challenge European assumptions about the territorial integrity of the Ottoman Empire. It was boots on the ground in the Peloponnese and increasingly in Rumeli that helped determine the outcome of the Greek Revolution.

Of Purse and Nation

The Greek War of Independence was initially an enterprise of many disparate groups. *Armatoloi* and klephts, traditional professional warriors in the service of the Ottoman state and brigands ambitious to enter the same service, drawing prestige from their military prowess and locked in a seesaw between whichever side of loyalty and lawlessness paid dividends at any given time, formed their own armed bands ranging from a few to a few hundred men (Asdrachas 2019, 147–156). This was a continuation of a premodern ethos into the first stirrings of modernity: military leaders who sought honor, recognition, respect, and remuneration while fighting in the service (and frequently using the language) of a national ideal. Such irregulars expected to be compensated according to their status and on time, becoming "private military entrepreneurs" as John Petropulos put it. As far as logistics go, if a chieftain (*oplarchigos*) could not provide wages, rations, and often bonuses in the form of battle spoils to his troops, he was in dire danger of seeing his men desert him. During the revolution frequently camps were formed and broken up, navy squadrons sailed and returned to port because of money owed. People with the necessary funds, however, whether previously experienced or not, could form their own military force and draw the prestige it provided. An interesting example was Ioannis Makrygiannis (1797–1864), a native of Phokis in western Rumeli, a young up-and-coming merchant who found himself with "a full purse" at the outbreak of the revolution. A member of the Philiki Etaireia, in 1821 he was already on his way to changing his identity from sultan's subject to revolutionary. However, at the beginning of April, in the first days of the insurrection, he was still about his commercial affairs, buying and selling goods in Patras and Mesolonghi while also gathering intelligence on Ottoman military movements. Returning to his base in Arta, he was arrested and jailed by the Ottoman authorities for two months. When he managed to escape and reach the free Greek areas, he joined Georgios "Gogos" Bakolas (1770–1826), a famous *armatolos*, as his own man, leader of a detachment of eighteen, whose wages he was paying from his full purse (Makrygiannis 1947, 1:15–26; Petropulos 1968, 42).

The conduct of Bakolas, an early revolutionary who quickly made an about-turn, reminds us that one should also be careful when delineating the limits of national consciousness. Endless battles have been fought over that question and this is not the place to settle the debate. The scene is replete with Greeks, Albanians, even Turks, who fought on both sides because of common interests and values surmounting what they often professed as the main barrier among them—religion. However, it should be noted that, as far as it concerns the Greek Revolution, the language of the nation was everywhere, permeating proclamations and addresses, constitutional texts, newspaper articles, and everyday speech. That said, adherence to the nation was not a trump card wiping out all other concepts and loyalties once and for all. For example, Thomas Gordon and George Finlay, the most prominent foreign historians of the Greek Revolution, offer many cases where place of origin took primacy; islanders put the interests of their own islands first, the Peloponnesians were reluctant to campaign outside the Peloponnese. There was also the matter of those who capitulated to the Ottomans and worked with them against their fellow Greeks. One should not be quick to always attribute such events to personal or material gains to be had during turbulent times. The *kapakia,* an acceptable arrangement until then, stipulated that under certain conditions negotiations could be opened with an enemy and a truce concluded without blame. Although this practice was widely observed during the Greek Revolution (Georgios Varnakiotis and Odysseas Androutsos used it with the government's permission, but also, significantly enough, without it) it was also questioned because it did not fit with the value system of a nascent nation-state. Gogos Bakolas is again an interesting case. When Alexandros Mavrokordatos (1791–1865), one of the foremost revolutionary politicians, favored another *armatolos,* Ioannis Tsongas, over him and accusations flared of negligence that cost heavy losses in the Greek defeat at Peta in 1822, Bakolas quit the Greek side for the Ottomans. Rather than treason on his part, an act of which he was accused at the time, this could also be attributed to loss of face and fear of losing his honor in the eyes of his peers. Bakolas's adherence to an older ethos could have easily triggered his defection to the Turks, an indication of a flux in ideas, identities, and value systems during the revolutionary years.

Shield of the Peloponnese

Between 1821 and 1829, the years of military engagement in Greece, Rumeli functioned as a fortified outpost protecting the Peloponnese. Geography dictated two ways of reaching the Isthmus of Corinth: from Epirus to western Rumeli through the Makrynoros pass or from Thessaly to eastern Rumeli through Thermopylae and Boeotia (Map 11). In the west, Mesolonghi became a bastion that could not be ignored in the rear of any army marching eastward. In the east, the plain of Boeotia should be secured before marching toward Corinth. Both routes were used by Sultan Mahmud II's lieutenants with mixed results. There was a massive campaign in eastern Rumeli in 1822 by Mahmud Pasha Dramali (ca. 1770–1822) and three attempts to neutralize Mesolonghi in 1822, 1823, and 1825–1826. The former succeeded in passing through Rumeli but petered out in the Peloponnese; Mesolonghi's fall in 1826 threatened the Peloponnese with an invasion from the north at the time it had already been invaded from the south by the forces of Ibrahim Pasha of Egypt. Both cases definitely proved that Rumeli remained difficult to hold and could be defended only as long as guerrilla tactics could apply. The Ottomans could easily take cities such as Salona and Livadia (and in fact did take them almost every year they campaigned) forcing Greek irregulars to their highlands and mountain lairs. However, as long as the Peloponnese could not be pacified and supply lines from the north could not be safeguarded, the Ottomans quit Rumeli in wintertime leaving behind them a few garrisons and permitting the Greeks to regain lost ground. In the meantime, failure to quell the revolt meant the downfall of the Ottoman general in charge: Mahmud II went through Hurşid Pasha, Yussuf Pasha Bercofcali, Aboulaboud Pasha of Salonica, and Dervish Pasha of Vidin

before finally finding in Mehmet Reşid Kütahı an able military governor, a Rumeli *walesi* who seemed poised to end the revolt once and for all. Although this did not come to pass, Rumeli's status as a shield for the Peloponnese bred resentment in many quarters. During the second civil war in 1824, when Rumeliot troops campaigned against Moreot forces and ravaged the Peloponnesian

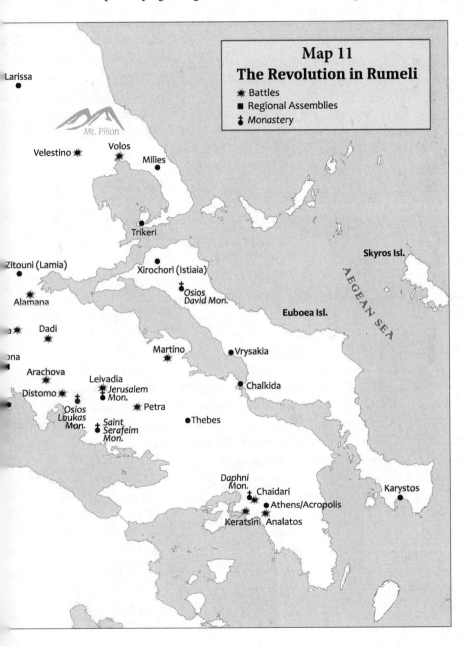

Map 11
The Revolution in Rumeli

✳ Battles
◼ Regional Assemblies
⚜ Monastery

countryside, a chieftain named Efthymios Xydis wrote to his colleague Costas Botsaris that he considered their rough conduct just because, among other things, "the Peloponnesians want to form and bring down a government whenever it suits their own interests . . . and send us to man the Rumeli posts, only to fight and get killed there by the Turks" (Katifori 1975, 359).

In theory, leadership was expected to come from western Rumeli, where the most powerful *armatoliks* were situated. However, the *armatoloi* were biding their time. Significant Ottoman forces still engaged in putting down Ali Pasha's revolt were close to the area but there were other factors as well. Communication with the Peloponnese, where the revolution began, was not easy since Mesolonghi, a maritime city in the eighteenth century, had not recovered from its destruction by the Ottomans during the Greek Revolt of 1770. Tradition and geographical importance, prestige and wealth rendered the western Rumeli *armatoloi* more self-conscious of their position in the Ottoman order and more reluctant to jeopardize it. In order to retain their military status and political capital they had to exercise caution. Simply put, Georgios Varnakiotis, probably the most powerful *armatolos* of his time, had more to lose than his counterparts in eastern Rumeli. Failure to secure Patras and the defeat in Alamana in April gave him pause. Consequently, the west did not rise until May, two months later than the rest of southern Greece. On May 20, 1821, Mesolonghi and Anatoliko rebelled and toward the end of the month the Greeks laid siege to Vrachori, the main city in northwestern Rumeli. Varnakiotis finally moved, helping to take it in early June while the forces of Andreas Iskos (died 1850) and Gogos Bakolas secured the Makrynoros pass, blocking the way south to Ottoman reinforcements from Epirus led by Ismail Pliassa Pasha. The furthest point the revolution reached in western Rumeli was Asporopotamos, a region of sixty-seven villages near the sources of the Acheloos river. In July 1821, Nikolaos Stornaris (1778–1826), the local *armatolos,* secured key positions hoping to march against Trikala. At the end of the month though, two thousand Ottoman troops arrived, forcing them to capitulate (Gordon 2015, 1:375–379; Trikoupis 1888, 1:203–217).

Lesser *armatoloi* in east Rumeli proved more eager to rebel. Dependence on the Ottoman system was not as heavy as in western Rumeli, the prestige of the office being lower than in Agrafa. Open to invasion from the north, east Rumeli was also too close to the Peloponnese to ignore the call to insurrection. When news of the events there reached Livadia, Salona, and Athens, the region quickly produced a small but, for the moment, adequate military force. Already on March 27 Salona fell, to be followed by Livadia, a prosperous city of ten thousand, on March 31. Atalanti surrendered on the same day, Thebes on April 1. Athens revolted later on (April 25), its armed bands laying siege to the Acropolis where the city's Turks sought refuge. Parts of Euboea, where Chalkida was held by a significant Ottoman garrison, rebelled in early May, although an attempt to storm the castle of Karystos failed in July. In all these situations the Ottoman administrators were taken by surprise and had recourse only to local garrisons that, most of the time, were easily overwhelmed by the Greeks. Until early May, the revolution seemed to thrive.

Pitted against weak local forces, the Greeks forced them either to surrender or to retreat into castles and fortified positions to which they then laid siege. This changed when Hurşid Pasha of Ioannina (died 1822) sent eight thousand troops southward under Köse Mehmet and Omer Vrioni, Pasha of Berat. On April 23 they reached Alamana, near ancient Thermopylae and present-day Lamia, defeated a Greek contingent led by Athanasios Diakos (1788–1821), impaled him to terrorize the populace, and moved toward Boeotia (Figure 17). Odysseas Androutsos (1788–1825), arguably the strongest military personality

FIGURE 17   Kozis Dessylas, *Portrait of Athanassios Diakos*, ca. 1870. Oil on canvas. Benaki Museum, Athens.

FIGURE 18   Kozis
Dessylas, *Portrait of
Odysseus Androutsos*,
ca. 1870. Oil on canvas.
Benaki Museum,
Athens.

in east Rumeli until his death, fought a delaying action at Gravia (Figure 18);
however, Vrioni was able to retake Livadia on June 10. The situation in Boeotia
remained fluid because the main Ottoman host left to win back Euboea and
Athens. Indeed, on July 20 he managed to relieve the siege of the Acropolis.
Meanwhile, another host from Larissa under Bayram Pasha, Memis Pasha, and
Sain Ali Pasha marched south with five thousand troops but were met and
stopped by two thousand Greeks in a critical battle at Vassilika (Boeotia) on
August 26.

   In September Tripolitsa, seat of government and wealthiest city in the Peloponnese, fell, and Omer Vrioni realized that his and Köse Mehmet's strategic
goal to relieve the city and snuff out the revolution could not be attained before winter. To avoid being stranded in a hostile area he retreated to Epirus.
At the same time, however, an Ottoman navy squadron, after having resup-
plied a number of besieged cities in the Peloponnese, sailed to Galaxidi on
September 22. Situated on the northern side of the Corinthian Gulf, it was the

only significant maritime center in western Rumeli with forty to sixty ships of various sizes, all at anchorage at the time (Map 11). Defended by two hundred troops, Galaxidi suffered a day-long bombardment that destroyed its batteries and caused its soldiers to scatter. The next day one thousand Ottomans landed killing the few inhabitants who had not fled to safety and carried off thirty-four vessels (thirteen of them battle-ready) while burning the rest and the city. The loss of Galaxidi, a significant point poorly prepared to face the enemy, showed that when the element of surprise faded, logistics did not favor the revolutionaries.

At this point, it was becoming widely accepted that Greece needed to form a central government not merely as a political necessity or a signal to the great powers, but first and foremost as a prerequisite for conducting the war in an effective way. Meanwhile, in November the Greeks laid again siege to Athens, while Livadia had been in their hands once more since the summer. Athens was not to capitulate until June 10, 1822, but a few days later the army of Mahmud Pasha Dramali arrived in Boeotia causing Livadia to change hands (Gordon 2015, 1:257–263, 375–386, 390–393, 400–402, 2:120–129, 184–185; Trikoupis 1888, 1:135–148, 2:1–11, 54–61, 79–81).

Meanwhile, since Euboea remained a thorn in Attica's side, with Ottoman forces ravaging the land and threatening Athens, the Greeks tried on numerous occasions to get a foothold on the island: Chalkida was considered impregnable but Karystos was worth a shot. Results however were meager: most of the time Greeks controlled the mountain areas, Ottomans the plains, each failing to dislodge the other despite constant skirmishing. In January 1822 Elias Mavromichalis (1795–1822) led a detachment of six hundred troops against the castle of Karystos, lost a battle, and committed suicide to avoid captivity. Toward the end of November 1823 Androutsos managed again to invest Karystos with three thousand men but an Ottoman fleet sailed to the island in April 1824 bringing provisions and two thousand janissaries at which point the Greeks retreated. Another attempt was made in February 1826 when Colonel Charles Fabvier, a veteran of the Napoleonic Wars, arrived in Euboea with 1,800 regular troops, 250 cavalry, four cannons, and 700 irregulars. Omer Bey Pasha confronted him with 2,000 of his own men in a battle with no clear winner. Greek guns malfunctioned and Fabvier switched to a defensive stance. Hard pressed by the enemy and under constant bombardment he was only saved by the arrival of twelve ships on March 23. Calmly withdrawing his troops under fire, Fabvier sailed to the mainland two days later. This was the last serious effort to contest Euboea. It would remain in Ottoman hands until the end of the war—and even beyond that: in 1831 it was still under occupation because a solution was yet to be found guaranteeing the local Turks recompense for abandoning their land property (Gordon, 2:108–109, 287–289, 412, 3:137–142; Trikoupis, 2:54–55, 113–116, 3:269–273).

Local Constitutions

Just before the destruction of Galaxidi, in early September, an assembly of primates, chieftains, and clergy prepared to convene in Salona to vote on a local constitution, only to be postponed when news reached the delegates. A similar assembly was to convene in Mesolonghi. Dividing Rumeli in two was a political compromise between early rival forces. Dimitrios Ypsilantis (1793–1832), former officer of the Imperial Russian Army and brother of Alexandros Ypsilantis—who as leader of the Philiki Etaireia had first proclaimed the Greek Revolution in Wallachia and Moldavia in February 1821 and had appointed Dimitrios plenipotentiary in Greece—was a popular figure, albeit with a mere nominal claim to power. Local leaders, primates especially, were reluctant to grant him an elevated position, either political or military. There were other rising political figures whose ambitions clashed with his own, most prominent of which at the time were Alexandros Mavrokordatos and Theodoros Negris (1790–1824). A scion of a prominent Phanariot family, former manager of foreign affairs to his uncle Ioannis Karatzas, who had been ruler of Wallachia under the Ottomans between 1812 and 1818, self-exiled in Italy thereafter, Mavrokordatos arrived in Greece in July 1821 bringing along much-needed ammunition and a printing press. Skilled negotiator, well versed in intrigue, he charmed or cajoled chieftains and civic leaders alike. Negris hailed from a well-known family from Constantinople, had briefly served as Ottoman attaché in Paris, and was considered an active and able politician, if intriguing and unprincipled as a person. Both sought to form a power base of their own, skillfully avoiding, for the time, a conflict between Ypsilantis and the Peloponnesian primates. Ypsilantis assented to their convoking of two assemblies, restricting the scope of their local authority. A general assembly of deputies from all Greece was expected to convene in the Peloponnese at some point in the near future.

The Mesolonghi assembly met on November 4 with only thirty deputies present and Mavrokordatos acting as president. While still in Italy, he had praised a book by Georgios Sekeris that stated the necessary political principles for the restitution of a Greek state. As soon as he arrived in Mesolonghi, he conferred with local chieftains such as Alexios Vlachopoulos (1780 / 1787–1865), Dimitrios Makris (1772–1841), Athanasios Razikotzikas (1798–1826), and others, and on July 27 drew up an agreement stating the need to form an administration. After a five-day deliberation, the assembly voted into existence the Organization of Western Rumeli, a regional constitution written by Mavrokordatos himself.

Rudimentary structures and institutions were installed to provide the necessary administrative, fiscal and military tools to wage war, provide security and justice to the population blending older traditional social hierarchies and new political elements. At the same time, Mavrokordatos set himself up as political and military leader, since the provisions of the organization stipulated that the Senate of Western Continental Greece was the sole responsible body of government in the area. As expected, Mavrokordatos was voted its president (Theodoridis 2012, 246–249, 283–284, 305–312).

A week later, on November 15, seventy-three deputies convened in Salona. Among them were bishops such as Neophytos of Atalanti (1762–1861), later Metropolitan of Athens; known scholars, such as Anthimos Gazis (1758–1828), Grigorios Constantas (1758–1844), and Georgios Ainian (1788–1848); and chieftains such as Odysseas Androutsos, Ioannis Gouras (1791–1826), and Panourgias Xiros (1759 / 1767–1834). Negris drew up an interesting and detailed document guaranteeing civil rights, establishing administrative structures, and introducing practicable arrangements for justice, taxation, and trade. At the time, the Legal Provision of East Rumeli was heavily criticized as unnecessarily complex and long-winded, demonstrating Negris's political views and ambitions. Spyridon Trikoupis, a follower of Mavrokordatos and ally of Negris at the time, noted a number of unsuitable or inappropriate provisions such as those on the freedom of speaking any language and defining the powers of the future national government. However, as in the case of western Rumeli, this constitution should not be taken at face value. Although both texts should be given attention as far as they concerned terms, ideas, and the political language they introduced to Greece, they were simply offering a modicum of local government while functioning as a political springboard; Negris was voted head of the Areopagus just as Mavrokordatos became president of the Senate in order to invest themselves with the aura of an office to rival the power of Ypsilantis and the military chieftains. Both Mavrokordatos and Negris played leading parts the following December in the First National Assembly in Epidavros, where the former presided and then was elected president of the executive (Finlay 1861, 1:290–292; Trikoupis 1888, 2:89–90).

Taking the Western Road

After 1822, it was western Rumeli that became a priority for the Ottomans. They laid siege to Mesolonghi in 1822 and Anatoliko in 1823. Markos Botsaris (1788–1823), leader of the Souliots, sturdy warriors from Epirus, was killed at Karpenisi on August 9, 1823, delaying the progress of Mustai Pasha of Skodra. The main host pressed southward, although their attempt, along with Omer Vrioni's troops, to take Anatoliko (which they besieged for forty days) then move on to Mesolonghi on the other side of the lagoon proved ineffective. They managed to achieve this only in April 1826, after a grinding twelve-month siege with the added help of Ibrahim Pasha of Egypt, who had already dealt a significant blow to the Greeks by landing in the Peloponnese, beating the revolutionaries in many encounters, and ravaging the countryside.

The second siege of Mesolonghi was a textbook struggle with feints and frontal attacks, skirmishes and sorties, bombardments and trench warfare: it was decided by the inability of the Greek fleet to resupply the garrison in late March and early April, falling victim to an organized enemy squadron as well as internal disputes and lack of money. On April 10, 1826, the garrison tried to cut its way through the Ottoman forces, losing more than seventeen hundred out of three thousand troops while six thousand women and children were captured and sold as slaves (Gordon 2015, 3:63–109; Trikoupis 1888, 3:207–266). The loss of the city was a terrible blow to the Greeks as the main bastion and base of operations in western Rumeli was now under enemy control, rendering the whole area inhospitable to chieftains. Accordingly, many capitulated gaining back their old Ottoman positions as *armatoloi;* Andreas Iskos, Ioannis Staikos (died 1861), Georgios Dyovouniotis (1798–1880), Komnenos "Komnas" Trakas (1786–1840), and others followed an acceptable traditional convention that allowed them a temporary respite without sacrificing their honor—an indispensable attribute to a military chieftain. All of them renounced their capitulation later, under more favorable conditions. It should be noted though that these agreements constituted a grey area indeed depending on many factors; personal relations played a significant part, as many *armatoloi* retained connections and back channels to their counterparts on the other side, but also timing and the internal balance of power. The conduct of Odysseas Androutsos, who was branded a traitor, as will be mentioned below, showed what was permitted and what not in such situations.

Treason in Context

Odysseas Androutsos was perhaps the most powerful chieftain in eastern Rumeli. One of many who had distinguished themselves in Ali Pasha's court, he was rewarded by being named as *armatolos* of Livadia, the richest city and most coveted *armatoliki* in the region. After Ali's rebellion against Sultan Mahmud II, Androutsos left Livadia for the Ionian islands, then under British administration, returning in March 1821. Energetic leader, able organizer, respected by the Ottomans for his military qualities, he became a force in his own right in eastern Rumeli. In 1822, however, he was blamed for a string of failures in Patratziki (current Ypati) and Agia Marina by the Areopagus. At the same time, Androutsos felt slighted because he was not awarded the office of general, merely that of chiliarch. He resigned and the government sent two representatives in his place. Androutsos had them killed, whether deliberately or misled by information that they were in fact sent to kill him. Contemporaries also diverge as to whether his troops killed the victims before he could stop them or after he had encouraged them. Stripped from his offices and outlawed, he was later amnestied. Retaining his popularity, he was named commander-in-chief in east Rumeli by a local assembly in September 1822 while, according to some sources, he was now persecuting the members of the Areopagus. In November, he managed to delay the Ottomans by a lengthy negotiation until they retreated north for the winter. In August 1824, though, with the government enmeshed in a civil war and not heeding his warnings of an impending Ottoman threat, Androutsos embarked on another negotiation, far more ambivalent this time. Sources disagree again. Spyridon Trikoupis is adamant on his treason; Nikolaos Spiliadis (1785–1862) states that this was nothing but a feint to put pressure on the government to gain amnesty for past transgressions. Toward the end of March 1825, a former protégé of his, Ioannis Gouras, was sent to campaign in eastern Rumeli, where Androutsos was leading a group of four hundred Turks. He was persuaded to surrender, but then he was jailed in Athens and killed on June 5, 1825 (Trikoupis 1888, 2:172–178, 252–261, 3:175–178; Goudas 1876, 8:124–162; Papadopoulos 1837, 44–58; Spiliadis 1851–1857, 247–250, 411–418).

Androutsos's initiatives, as all similar negotiations, could always be read both ways. After local administrations and then a national government were formed, however, such arrangements were increasingly disapproved of. A local assembly in Salona had explicitly forbidden the *kapakia* in 1824. Awareness of their potentially damaging nature was even earlier: in fact, during the 1822 negotiations Karpos Papadopoulos (1790s–1871), a lieutenant of Androutsos, claims he warned him that a signed document accepting the sultan's sovereignty in Rumeli could have an adverse effect on the Greek Question, if reported to the European powers, at the time in conference at the Congress of Verona. Here it should be noted that Thomas Gordon and George Finlay saw in Androutsos's conduct a continuation of Ali Pasha's methods. Gordon branded him "guilty of barbarous acts," while in Finlay's index he is filed under "Odysseus, a partisan of Ali's," and his character is summed up as "his ambition was to ape the tyranny of Ali in a small sphere." Significantly, Gordon also disapproved of Panourgias, who is depicted as an "ignoble bandit," the worst of a breed of rapacious brigands. Under Western eyes, these primitive rebels or primitive revolutionaries did not fit the model of ideal freedom fighters.

The Siege of Athens and the Battle of Analatos

While Ibrahim returned to the Peloponnese seeking to complete its conquest, Mehmet Reşid Pasha, the other Ottoman general present in Mesolonghi, pressed the advantage, moving swiftly eastward toward Athens, looking to take the city and essentially end the revolution in Rumeli. For the next three years, Rumeli became the main war theater. Indeed, between 1826 and 1829 battles and campaigns followed in quick succession, while the Greek Question increasingly looked like a matter to be determined by great power diplomacy rather than force of arms. It is interesting though to note that the Ottomans mounted a campaign even in late 1828, when it was becoming doubtful whether any gains they made would have any impact in the negotiations. For their part, the Greeks aimed to recapture Mesolonghi for its symbolic value and take back the whole of Rumeli in order to claim the territory for a future independent state.

Athens became the focus of military operations in 1826. Mehmet Reşid besieged the city in August forcing the revolutionaries to concentrate their attention in trying to relieve it. Georgios Karaiskakis, having conducted an energetic and successful campaign in western Rumeli, managed to counter some of the damage the fall of Mesolonghi had caused (Figure 19). Raising the siege of Salona, taking the essential position of Distomo in February 1827 and leaving garrisons in key places, he stabilized the situation, ensuring that the Ottomans were left only with their strongholds in Vonitsa, Nafpaktos, and Mesolonghi.

On February 28, after a quick march, Karaiskakis arrived in Attica with fifteen hundred troops. Reinforcements kept coming, however, and the total number of the Greek army in the environs of Athens reached ten thousand in April. Although a ragtag and unprincipled force, it was one of the strongest the Greeks had ever deployed in the field during the revolution. Karaiskakis, one of the "bravest and most active of the chiefs" according to Finlay (Finlay 1861, 2:148), had in the past clashed with fellow chieftains and Alexandros Mavrokordatos (indeed, the latter put him on trial for treason in 1824) but had moved on from his "unprincipled proceedings" morphing into an able, steadfast, persuasive, and gifted leader of irregulars. At this point, he decided to approach the Acropolis through the great olive grove on the outskirts of Athens in order to avoid being harassed by the Turkish cavalry. Putting his plan into execution, he won the battle of Keratsini on March 4, one of two positions he deemed essential. The other one was the St. Spyridon monastery in Piraeus. There, the Ottoman garrison surrendered on April 13, and despite the pact permitting the guards to leave unmolested, a scuffle ensued and the majority were killed.

A logical next step according to Karaiskakis's plan would be to cut the supply lines of Mehmed Reşid Pasha's army at Oropos, a small port on the northeast

FIGURE 19   Theodoros Vryzakis, *The Camp of Karaiskakis among the Philhellenes*, Theodoros
Vryzakis, 1855. Oil on canvas. National Gallery-Al. Soutzos Museum, Athens.

of Attica, hoping that the Ottomans would then be forced to retreat. However,
since early April the National Assembly had named the Irish officer Richard
Church (1784–1873) commander-in-chief of the Greek armies and Lord Thomas
Cochrane (1775–1860) as admiral of the navy. Church preferred a frontal attack on the Acropolis aiming to disperse the Ottoman armies. Karaiskakis disagreed but hatched a plan for a two-sided attack resting on an operation during
the night of April 22–23. Around noon on April 22 there was a skirmish between Greeks and Turks near Phaliro. Karaiskakis tried to pull the troops back;
however, more arrived, mistaking their leader's presence as a signal to press on.
Mehmet Reşid forwarded cavalry units and a battle ensued in which Karaiskakis was hit. He died the day after. The attack was postponed for April 24, but
low morale and his own absence resulted in defeat with heavy losses; between one and two thousand Greeks were lost in the battle of Analatos. Consequences were dire indeed; the Acropolis surrendered on May 24 meaning that
all eastern Rumeli had practically capitulated. Mehmed Reşid camped in
Thebes, the garrisons Karaiskakis had left in western Rumeli melted into thin

air unable to sustain themselves now that both Mesolonghi and Athens had been captured, and a strong Ottoman army was free to roam the area (Finlay 1861, 2:143–154; Gordon 2015, 3:189–218, 249–284; Trikoupis 1888, 4:68–81, 101–124).

The Final Campaigns

Rumeli remained quiet during the summer and fall of 1827. In the meantime, the National Assembly at Troezen had elected Ioannis Capodistrias (1776–1831), former foreign minister of the Russian Empire, as governor, while on October 20 (N.S.), an Ottoman fleet at Navarino (current Pylos) was destroyed by the combined naval forces of Britain, France and Russia. Along with the treaty that the great powers had signed among themselves on July 6 (N.S.) to mediate between Greece and the Ottoman Empire on the basis of the former becoming an autonomous tributary state of the latter, these were clear indications of a changed diplomatic playfield. Encouraged by these developments, the Greeks under Richard Church returned to the field. In eastern Rumeli Nikolaos Kriezotis (1785–1853), Dimitrios Karatasos (1798–1861), and Vasos Mavrovouniotis (1790–1847) led 2,500 troops, winning a battle at Trikeri on November 15. At the same time, Church landed with a force of fourteen hundred in western Rumeli looking to recapture Mesolonghi and Anatoliko. These moves paid dividends in 1828, when war broke out between Russia and the Ottoman Empire in April and Mehmed Reşid Pasha was hastily recalled. Kyriakos "Kitsos" Tzavellas (1801–1855) campaigned successfully in central Rumeli. In eastern Rumeli it was Dimitrios Ypsilantis's turn to win a battle in Arachova on October 31, and then to speed to Livadia, which surrendered on November 5. Salona followed on November 17. Moving north, Tzavellas recaptured Karpenisi on December 15 while on the same day Richard Church's troops entered Vonitsa. It seemed that Rumeli was on its way to being freed once and for all.

What remained still uncertain, however, was whether the Greeks could hold on to these areas. The relative freedom of movement that the chieftains enjoyed was a cause for concern to Capodistrias, who had taken up his duties as governor of Greece in January 1828. Indeed, on December 24, Mahmud Pasha left Zitouni (current Lamia) with 6,600 troops reaching Livadia without encountering serious resistance. His strategic goal was to join forces with Omer Pasha of Euboea, whose forces held Thebes. When the Greek troops started regrouping, Mahmud tried to force his way through, but was defeated at Martino on January 29, 1829. On February 10 he left for Zitouni leaving a small force of one thousand to garrison three towns. Toward the end of February, they were easily disarmed by Greek detachments, leaving only Athens and Thebes under Ottoman rule. In mid-March, Avgoustinos Capodistrias (1778–1857) campaigned in western Rumeli, where the Greeks had already secured the Makrynoros pass, removing any possible threat of reinforcements from Epirus. Kravasaras surrendered on March 26 and attention turned to Nafpaktos, where a strong force of five thousand Ottomans was placed in a city and fortress that had never been captured since the beginning of the revolution. Nafpaktos surrendered too after a brief siege and was evacuated between April 18 and 25. Mesolonghi also fell on May 3. The sense that only mopping-up operations were left was broken in the summer, when Aslan Bey Muhurdar raided Attica trying to resupply Athens and then lead back to Larissa any remaining troops to assist in the Turkish-Russian war that had erupted in 1828. Dimitrios Ypsilantis massed 2,500 men and met the Ottoman army in Petra on September 12. Although the enemy had almost double their numbers, the Greek forces won the last significant engagement of the War of Greek Independence (Finlay 1861, 2:204–208; Trikoupis 1888, 4:237–245, 258–266, 275–280). On February 3, 1830, the London Protocol between Great Britain, France, and Russia proclaimed Greece an independent state.

Markos Karasarinis

References

Asdrachas, Spyros. 2019. *Πρωτόγονη επανάσταση. Αρματολοί και κλέφτες (18ος-19ος αι.)* [Primitive rebellion: Armatoloi and *klepht*s, eighteenth to nineteenth centuries]. Athens.

Beaton, Roderick, and David Ricks, eds. 2009. *The Making of Modern Greece: Nationalism, Romanticism, and the Uses of the Past (1797–1896)*. Farnham and Burlington, VT.

Dakin, Douglas. 1973. *The Greek Struggle for Independence, 1821–1833*. Berkeley and Los Angeles.

Diamandouros, Nikiforos. 2002. *Οι απαρχές της συγκρότησης σύγχρονου κράτους στην Ελλάδα, 1821–1828* [The beginning of modern state-building in Greece, 1821–1828]. Athens.

Dimitropoulos, Dimitris, Christos Loukos, and Panagiotis Michailaris, eds. 2018. *Όψεις της επανάστασης του 1821* [Aspects of the 1821 revolution], 87–105. Athens.

Finlay, George. 1861. *History of the Greek Revolution*. Edinburgh and London.

Gordon, Thomas. 2015. *Ιστορία της ελληνικής επαναστάσεως* [History of the Greek Revolution]. Translated by Alexandros Papadiamantis. Athens.

Goudas, Anastasios. 1869–1876. *Βίοι παράλληλοι των επί της αναγεννήσεως της Ελλάδος διαπρεψάντων ανδρών* [Parallel lives of distinguished men of the rebirth of Greece]. Athens.

Kasomoulis, Nikolaos. 1941. *Ενθυμήματα στρατιωτικά της Επαναστάσεως των Ελλήνων 1821–1833* [Military reminiscences of the Revolution of the Greeks, 1821–1833]. Athens.

Katifori, Despina. 1975. "Η Επανάσταση κατά το 1824. Τα πολιτικά γεγονότα από τον Ιούλιο ως τον Δεκέμβριο" [The revolution in 1824: Political developments, July to December]. *IEE*, 12:353–361.

Kitromilides, Paschalis M. 2013. *Enlightenment and Revolution: The Making of Modern Greece*. Cambridge, MA.

Kremmydas, Vassilis. 2016. *Η Ελληνική Επανάσταση του 1821. Τεκμήρια, αναψηλαφήσεις, ερμηνείες* [The Greek Revolution of 1821: Documents, re-examinations, interpretations]. Athens.

Makrygiannis, Ioannis. 1947. *Στρατηγού Μακρυγιάννη απομνημονεύματα* [Archive: Memoirs of General Ioannis Makrygiannis]. Edited by Ioannis Vlachogiannis. Athens.

Panagiotopoulos, Vasilis, ed. 2003. *Η Ελληνική Επανάσταση, 1821–1832* [The Greek Revolution, 1821–1832]. *INE*. Vol. 3. Athens.

Papadopoulos, Karpos. 1837. *Ανασκευή των εις την ιστορίαν των Αθηνών αναφερομένων περί του Στρατηγού Οδυσσέως Ανδρούτζου, του ελληνικού τακτικού και του Συνταγματάρχου Καρόλου Φαβιέρου* [Refutation of references to the history of Athens concerning general Odysseus Androutzos, the Greek regular army, and Colonel Charles Fabvier]. Athens.

Petropulos, John Anthony. 1968. *Politics and Statecraft in the Kingdom of Greece, 1833–1843*. Princeton, NJ.

Spiliadis, Nikolaos, 1851–1857. *Απομνημονεύματα δια να χρησιμεύσωσιν εις την Νέαν Ελληνικήν Ιστορίαν (1821–1843)* [Memoirs to be used for modern Greek history, 1821–1843]. Athens.

Theodoridis, Georgios. 2012. *Αλέξανδρος Μαυροκορδάτος. Ένας φιλελεύθερος στα χρόνια του '21* [Alexandros Mavrokordatos: A liberal in the years of 1821]. Athens.

Theotokas, Nikos. 2012. *Ο βίος του στρατηγού Μακρυγιάννη. Απομνημονεύματα και ιστορία* [The life of general Makrygiannis: Memoirs and history]. Athens.

Theotokas, Nikos, and Nikos Kotaridis. 2006. *Η οικονομία της βίας. Παραδοσιακές και νεωτερικές εξουσίες στην Ελλάδα του 19ου αιώνα* [The economy of violence: Traditional and modern authorities in nineteenth-century Greece]. Athens.

Trikoupis, Spyridon. 1888. *Ιστορία της Ελληνικής Επαναστάσεως* [History of the Greek Revolution]. Athens.

Vouli ton Ellinon (Hellenic Parliament). 1971–2012. *Αρχεία ελληνικής παλιγγενεσίας* [Archives of Greek regeneration]. Athens.

Samos

The participation of Samos in the revolution of 1821 was the paramount event in its recent history, since the revolution promoted institutions that affected the island's society throughout the rest of the nineteenth century. The place of Samos in the overall picture of the revolution also presents notable particularities in comparison to other islands of the Archipelago. Located in the east Aegean, it took part in the struggle from the outset and was the Greek territory in which the revolution lasted the longest (1821–1834). On Samos a local system of governance or polity was in force from start to finish, with few brief exceptions; from this, democratic institutions developed that educated citizens. Samos remained free throughout the struggle, successfully repelling attacks by the Ottoman navy and attempts to capture the island.

The Greek Revolution was the outcome of diverse processes over many years, as is the case with major events of history. Among its causes are the development of national consciousness among the Greeks of the Ottoman Empire, the empire's pressing domestic problems—economic, social, and political—the effect of the French Revolution, and the spread of liberal Enlightenment ideas. This general ascertainment holds for Samos too. The ideology of the revolution, summarized in the declaration of Alexandros Ypsilantis and epitomized in the phrase "Fight for faith and fatherland," was embraced by the overwhelming majority of Samiots in 1821, while those who disagreed because they did not believe in the revolution's necessity and success, disappeared from public life as soon as it prevailed.

On Samos, the revolution had national and social characteristics, as mentioned in a document of the period: "Samos took up arms against the Ottoman tyranny and against all forms of sectional oppression." Its herald was the *Karmanioloi*

(Carmagnoles) movement in the early nineteenth century, with the formation on the island of two factions that contested the power of the primates. The *Karmanioloi* included merchants, merchant-mariners, and shipowners, as well as supporters who espoused their progressive ideas, while their rivals, members of the elite, were represented by the old primates, landowners and their followers, who had conservative ideas and identified with the authorities of the Ottoman Empire. These were named *Kalikantzaroi* (Goblins) and exercised power locally as community elders for many decades. The *Karmanioloi* succeeded in assuming community power as primates several times in the years 1805–1812 and promoted notable changes in the internal organization and administration of the island and its economy, introducing a more equitable rendering of taxation to the Sublime Porte and managing the finances in general with transparency and rationalization. During this period, Georgios Ioannou or Paplomatas from Karlovasi was promoted as their leader. Known as Georgios Logothetis, the Samiot man of letters was a dignitary of the patriarchate and the Danubian Principalities. He and the lead group of *Karmanioloi* were protagonists also in the revolution of 1821, during which they applied in conditions of freedom the ideas that they had tried to put into practice before the revolution under the regime of Ottoman domination. The *Karmanioloi* faction lost power in 1813 and its leaders were hounded by their rivals, the elite *Kalikantzaroi*. However, a few years later, members of their lead group were initiated into the Philiki Etaireia and the revolution was supported by the popular movement they headed.

In 1819, Georgios Logothetis, then in Smyrna, was initiated into the Philiki Etaireia by Aristeidis Papas. Logothetis (1772–1850) was given the pseudonym Lykourgos, an allusion to the ancient lawgiver of Sparta (Figure 20). In addition to Logothetis, Papas, now on Samos, initiated Archbishop Kyrillos, Gerasimos Svoronos (vice-consul of Russia), the schoolteacher Ignatios, and other eminent *Karmanioloi* into the Philiki Etaireia. Svoronos then went on to initiate several others into the Philiki Etaireia, among them the subsequent chiefs of the Samiot struggle, Constantis Lachanas, Stamatis Georgiadis, Constantis Kontaxis, and Emmanouil Melachroinis. Consequently, by the eve of 1821, thanks to the social processes of the early nineteenth century and to the contribution of the Philiki Etaireia, there existed on Samos a revolutionary group capable of casting off Ottoman rule when the hour came. It was capable also of handling the new situation, despite the island's unfavorable geographical location, due to its proximity to Asia Minor. To use the expression of the time, Samos was "in the serpent's mouth."

News of the outbreak of the Greek Revolution was brought to Samos around mid-April 1821 by two Spetsiot ships that were operating in the sea between

FIGURE 20   Dionysios
Tsokos, *Lykourgos Logothetis*,
1861–1862. Oil on canvas.
National Historical Museum,
Athens.

Samos and Asia Minor. With the outbreak of the revolution in the Danubian
Principalities and then in the Peloponnese, several of the exiled *Karmanioloi*
leaders began to return to the island. On April 18 / 30, 1821, Kapetan Constantis
Lachanas, in agreement with Gerasimos Svoronos, proclaimed the revolution
at Vathy, surprising the Ottoman officials and replacing the old council of "aldermen" (*dimogerontes*) with a new revolutionary committee. Lachanas's movement was transmitted the next day to Mytilinioi as well. In Chora, capital of
Samos and seat of the Ottoman *voevod* and *kadi,* the leading primates tried to
curb the revolutionary actions and to help the Ottoman authorities slip away.
The primates and the leaders of the prerevolutionary *Kalikantzaroi* were opposed to the prospect of a revolution for fear of losing their power. Their reactionary stance toward the revolution and the *Karmanioloi* took various forms
during the course of the struggle.

On April 24 / May 6, Georgios Logothetis Lykourgos arrived on Samos,
bringing with him his official appointment by the head of the Philiki Etaireia,
Alexandros Ypsilantis, as his locum tenens in the island's revolt. The document
of his appointment had been handed over to him by the member of the Philiki
Etaireia Dimitrios Themelis, when they met on Patmos.

Georgios Logothetis Lykourgos, whose political and diplomatic abilities had been proven by his previous action, was well educated and imbued with the liberal ideas of the Enlightenment, which he combined with Christian principles and, above all, a high sense of duty to the homeland and the people. He quickly showed himself to be the appropriate leader of the Samian revolution, not only because of the status emanating from his official appointment, but also, mainly, for his deeds and the recognition of his abilities by the local assemblies of Samos. At first, Lykourgos founded the National Brotherhood and endeavored to initiate the former great primates into the idea of the revolution, even though they were his fanatical opponents, and to collaborate with them. In this he failed. The leaders of the *Kalikantzaroi* were adamantly against the revolution and in no way cooperative, particularly when they realized that the common people, whom they had been oppressing for years, would have a say in the decisions. Lykourgos spent about two weeks touring all the island's villages, informing, catechizing, and organizing the inhabitants, with respect to the prospects of liberation. When the induction was completed and he considered that he had gained a social base, he officially declared the revolution, first at Mesaio Karlovasi on May 8 / 20, 1821, and then in a festive atmosphere and with the blessing of Archbishop Kyrillos in Chora on May 12 / 24, 1821. At the same time, he drafted the local system of governance, known as the Military-Political Organization of the island of Samos, with the aim of organizing the island politically and militarily. This local system was approved by a local assembly, in which the *Karmanioloi* faction dominated, and had immediate implementation.

The revolutionary polity comprised two sectors: the political and the military. In the political sector the supreme authority was the governor general, who was elected by the General Assembly of representatives of the villages. He exercised the administration, assisted by three political adjudicators who replaced the prerevolutionary leading primates. He personally appointed the subordinate administrative authorities and was answerable to the next assembly for his choices and actions. The political adjudicators were obliged to do the same. The military sector constituted a regulation of the military organization of Samos with the formation of four battalions (*chiliarchies*), at the head of which distinguished chiefs (Kapetan Stamatis Georgiadis, Constantis Lachanas, Constantis Kontaxis, and Emmanouil Melachroinis) were placed. The four battalions corresponded to the four parts of Samos and had a strictly ranked structure, as was appropriate to an organized army. The Samiot battalions were the first regular armed forces of the Greek Revolution and indeed were formed by the local political leadership. Supreme authority in the military system, in time of war, was the political governor general, who then assumed the office of commander-in-chief. In this way the two systems, united under his person, made up the military-political polity of Samos.

The local polity proved to be the salvation of Samos, because administrative and military organization was rapidly established, with those weapons that could be found. Documents of the period state that administrative measures were taken to ensure the supply of the soldiers and the repair of the weapons by armorers, as well as the timely warning of the military command with visual signals and communication with the villages, as well as with boats patrolling around the island.

The revolution on Samos evoked painful reactions in the Sublime Porte, because it was an island whose interior was difficult of access, a military outpost of the Greek Revolution so close to the Asia Minor coast that it could be a launching pad for operations to harass the Ottoman fleet. For this reason, it was a strategic target of the Sublime Porte to quash any revolutionary movement in the east Aegean, so that its fleet could move freely. Samos became the target of the Ottoman navy three times: in 1821, 1824, and 1826.

In the early summer of 1821, the empire's powerful fleet consisting of fifty battleships and many troopships was mobilized, with its main mission the subjugation of Samos. It laid siege to the island on July 3, 1821 (O.S.), and on the following days launched heavy attacks, which were held off successfully by the Samiots, despite their lack of arms. An attempt by the Turks to land at Cavo Tzortzis, although initially successful, in the end failed to create a bridgehead and was reversed in a bloody battle; hence, the headland has been known ever since as Cavo Phonias (Cape Killer). The appearance of the Greek fleet, after notification by Psariots and Samiots, prevented a prolongation of the siege, since it caused serious damage to the Ottoman fleet, which abandoned the effort. The assembly, which convened immediately after, proclaimed Logothetis Lykourgos "benefactor and savior." The first victorious outcome of the Samiots' struggle confirmed Lykourgos's speeches: "Patriots Samiots! This campaign of the enemy first being against the reborn Hellas shall bring immortal glory to the Samiots. . . . The ordained time of our freedom has come. Have no doubt, we will win" (Sakellariou 2014:111). The rest of the year 1821 was taken up in preparing defensive works and in equipping cannon emplacements, as well as in launching assaults into Asia Minor. The assaults aimed initially at protecting fellow Greeks living on the opposite coast, but they soon took on the form of plundering raids, in order to victual the inhabitants of Samos and the refugees who had escaped there, since the war operations had damaged crops and production. To secure the sea lane between Samos and Asia Minor, plans were made—but never implemented—for capturing the fortress of Nea Ephesos.

The military success of 1821 boosted the self-confidence of Logothetis Lyk-ourgos and the morale of the Samiot military chiefs, leading them to plan other operations aimed at consolidating the revolution. However, in the operations of 1822 they failed. The most abysmal failure was the expedition to Chios, in which almost all the Samiot armed forces—that is, the four battalions—took part. This overbold venture was planned and implemented with the aim of get-ting the Chiots to take part in the struggle. Consequence of the failure was the massacre, the taking captive, and the enslavement of a large part of the popu-lation of Chios and the total devastation of the island. Lykourgos was accused by members of the government, his political opponents, and the Chiot elite of being responsible for the catastrophe. He was obliged to defend his actions to the central government, but in the end all charges against him were dropped.

In May 1822, Kyriakos Moralis was appointed district governor (eparch) of Samos and the military-political system of the polity ceased to function. Logo-thetis Lykourgos resigned his office. The appointment of an eparch and the suspension of operation of the local polity caused internal strife on Samos, which verged on civil war. Moralis affiliated the leaders of the *Kalikantzaroi*, neglected the island's defense, and persecuted the *Karmanioloi*. Order was re-stored with the intervention of the three commissioners of the islands in De-cember 1822, the removal of the eparch, and the reinstatement of Logothetis Lykourgos as governor general, as well as the application and function anew of the military-political system, which, despite the abolition of local systems of governance by the Constitution of Epidavros and the Second National As-sembly, continued to hold sway on Samos until 1828, when Capodistrias's system of provincial organization was applied.

Between 1823 and 1828, the local system of governance was applied in full on Samos, with beneficial results for the continuation of the struggle and the consolidation of liberty. Although its preservation would seem to be "mutiny" against the central government, which was the supreme authority of the struggle, this was not the case because, in practice, it was a structure only for the do-mestic organization of the island and did not mobilize against the general sys-tems of governance of the struggle. To the contrary, it reinforced more effec-tively the revolution's aims. The value of the local polity was pointed out from the first year of its implementation, with the following assertions:

> It has been proved by experience that this Military-Political system of Samos, organized since the beginning of May 1821, first year of freedom, dissolved the longstanding revolts and clashes between the Samiots, com-bined into one the dissenting sides and, last, by opposing the first attacks of the Ottoman fleet against Samos, saved with God this homeland, in ex-

treme danger. The most miraculous is that the common good order was kept for one whole year exactly, so that no drop of patriotic blood was spilled. (Landros 2016, 175–176)

Even so, the polity was tantamount to Samos's autonomy vis-à-vis the central government and denoted a different conception of state organization, which resembled a federation under the umbrella of a central authority.

Through the local system of governance democratic institutions were enhanced, the principal ones being the elected governor and the assemblies. The institution of local governor general proved to be stronger than the will of the central government, which in 1823 insisted on appointing a new eparch. This time it appointed Chatzi Andreas Argyris from Psara (with Constantinos Kanaris as temporary eparch). The Samiots did not accept him either, not even when the Psariots attempted to impose him with the power of their fleet. Preserved in a document of the period is the characteristic exchange between Samiots and the council of Psara, with arguments put forward by both sides concerning state organization, promoting the liberal and democratic ideology of the Samiots, which they supported passionately.

The most respected institution in the second period of the polity (1823–1828) was the General Assembly. Speeches, ideas, arguments, decisions, all were animated by the Enlightenment. The General Assembly now had the leading role in the revolution of Samos. It elected the political adjudicators and the governor general, and they were accountable to it for their actions. From 1823 onward, the governor, despite holding the title of commander-in-chief, which had been awarded by Dimitrios Ypsilantis, drew his authority solely from the assembly, since by this he was elected and by this his election was renewed regularly.

After the General Assembly's abolition of the office of the eparch, in December 1822, and the hasty retreat of Moralis, good order was restored on Samos. Logothetis Lykourgos was reelected and set about the internal organization of the island, with emphasis on its best possible defense by building a central stronghold and other fortification works. The new fort with towers and cannon emplacements was constructed very quickly in early 1824, at Tigani, in an area overlooking the most dangerous landing beach, where there were ruins of earlier Byzantine fortifications. Smaller-scale defensive works were made in other parts of the island, while the governor general drafted a detailed plan to push back an enemy threat on all the coasts of Samos by defining the area of responsibility for each village (Map 12).

So, in late July 1824, when the Ottoman fleet, this time mightier and better prepared, set sail to quash the revolution, with three hundred ships under admiral-in-chief Hosref, the Samiots were ready to confront attempted landings on all shores of their island. Indeed, all the attempted landings made on the north coast were dealt with effectively, thanks to an integrated defense plan. Nevertheless, Logothetis Lykourgos was well aware that the entire operation would be decided at sea. For this reason, he forewarned the nautical islands of Ydra and Spetses that an attack by the Ottoman fleet was imminent and requested the assistance of the Greek fleet, undertaking also the costs of its

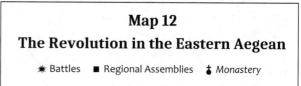

Map 12
The Revolution in the Eastern Aegean

✳ Battles   ■ Regional Assemblies   ⚱ *Monastery*

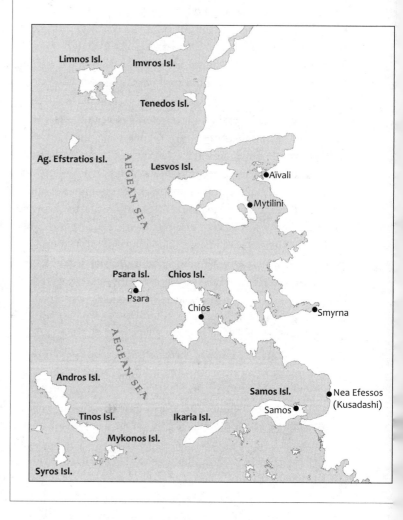

expedition. It should be noted that as the Ottoman fleet sailed away into the eastern Aegean, it razed Psara to the ground (June 21, 1824), while the Egyptian fleet, with which it was to join forces, destroyed Kasos (May 29, 1824).

The Ottoman fleet's next target, after Psara, was Samos. The Greek fleet under Georgios Sachtouris sped to the area in time and engaged with the enemy in

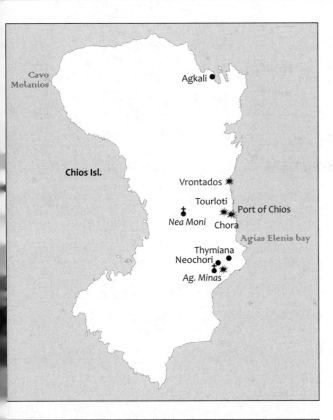

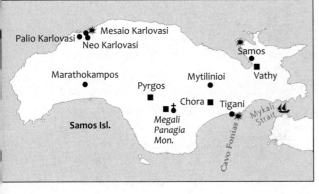

the sea between Samos and Mykali, dealing serious blows to the Ottoman fleet on August 4 and 5, 1824. In the naval battle of Samos, Kanaris was the protagonist, along with the fireship captains Dimitros Tsapelis, Lekkas Matrozos, Antonis Raphalias, Anastasios Robotsis, and Ioannis Vatikiotis. They succeeded in setting alight three large Ottoman ships, while the Ydriot ships with their artillery forced the enemy fleet to break the siege of the island and withdraw from the sea around Samos. The victorious outcome of the sea battle for the Greek fleet was salutary for Samos, and the General Assembly imprinted the event in its official seal, inscribing the phrase "Χριστὸς Σάμον ἔσωσεν τῇ ἕκτῃ Αὐγούστου 1824" (Christ saved Samos on the sixth of August 1824). The importance of the island's salvation was expressed in the years immediately after the revolution by the construction at Tigani, in the Castro area, of the church of the Transfiguration of the Savior, which celebrates its feast day on August 6. In 1888, this anniversary was established as a local holiday of Samos, which is being observed to this day.

The General Assembly and the governor general of Samos were also involved with issues relating to the island's society, with foremost the good management of finances and the organization of education. For the first time a monitorial school was founded officially on Samos, in the capital Chora, and clear instructions were given that the island's inhabitants, rich and poor alike, send their children to it. Parents need not worry about the teachers' salaries or other expenses, their only concern was for their children to become "prudent and educated, moral and polite" (GSA 1824 / Samos / Γ1). In addition to the monitorial school, three *Ellinika* (secondary) schools operated in 1825.

Between 1823 and 1828 there was a regularity in the function of the local polity. The annual General Assembly renewed by decree its trust—and through this the people's trust—in the person of Logothetis Lykourgos as head of the "political system" and general "of the military forces in the fatherland." However, to ensure a more stable stance of the General Assembly and a more resolute body of plenipotentiaries, Lykourgos's lead group founded a secret association known as the Philanthropic Society (Philanthropiki Etaireia). Its purpose was to ensure the selection to the assembly of the most useful representatives of each village, men with the same progressive ideas and between whom there was solidarity. This would safeguard the assembly from the influence of their political opponents, the *Kalikantzaroi*, who at the beginning of the revolution reacted negatively to it as "Turkophiles" and then went on to plot against the central administration, slandering Lykourgos and his followers, as well as Archbishop Kyrillos. The old primates frequently tried to form a strong opposition to Lykourgos and to abolish his system. The activity of the Philanthropic Society was intended to secure the internal unity and the smooth function of the polity.

For about two years after the sea battle of Samos, no expedition of the Ottoman fleet was launched against the island. However, Samiot attacks on Turkish ships and raids into the Asia Minor littoral continued unabated. In July 1826, the Ottoman navy attempted yet again to put down the revolution on Samos. It surrounded the island and tried to land troops in Karlovasi, but the area was very well fortified with ditches and cannons that Samiot divers had brought up from wrecked battleships on the seabed. The landing was successfully averted and the Greek fleet under Admiral Andreas Miaoulis then kept the Turks at bay, putting an end to the enemy fleet's campaigns against Samos.

After the naval battle of Navarino (October 20, 1827) and the international political developments that brought Ioannis Capodistrias to Greece as governor, the liberated regions were organized anew into provinces. Samos together with Ikaria, Patmos, Leros, and Kalymnos made up the eastern Sporades, where Ioannis Kolettis was appointed commissioner extraordinary (governor general) and Dimitrios Christidis as temporary governor during his absence. Logothetis Lykourgos resigned his office and soon after was selected as member of Capodistrias's Panhellenion and appointed commissioner extraordinary of Lower Messenia and Laconia, in a difficult region that also included Mani. On undertaking the administration of Samos, Kolettis did not repeat Moralis's mistake but collaborated with the *Karmanioloi*. Although the military-political system of governance had ceased, he kept two of its basic institutions: the General Assembly, to which, however, the governor was no longer accountable, and the political adjudication, which was named provincial *dimogerontia*.

With the London Protocol of 1830 (January 22 / February 3, 1830)—known as the protocol of independence, although it belonged to the regions of Hellenism that had revolted and had been freed—Samos was not included in the independent Greek state. The same happened to Crete. Logothetis Lykourgos received permission from Capodistrias to go to Samos and continue the struggle, with the aim of canceling the relevant article of the protocol and achieving the island's union with Greece. Henceforth, the Samiots' struggle was to be more at the diplomatic level and to be conducted by them alone, without any outside help. The Greek authorities appointed by Capodistrias were ordered to withdraw from Samos and quit the island in late June 1830.

The General Assembly convened after Lykourgos's arrival on Samos, on June 5 and 6 / 17 and 18, 1830, brought back into force the local system of governance and decided to create an independent petty state with the name "Samian State," headed by a director general of administrative affairs. Logothetis Lykourgos was elected to this post. The revolution on Samos continued for another four years, with the aim of incorporating the island in the Greek state. The Samian state was not recognized as a state entity by any European power, not even by Greece. The diplomatic struggle waged by the Samiots in this period was to no avail. Capodistrias was interested primarily in including in the fledgling state those nonliberated regions closest to it, namely Attica and Euboea, which were still in Ottoman hands, and was little concerned with distant Samos. The Ottoman Empire, which had been defeated at sea (1827) and on land during the Turkish-Russian War (1829), and was involved in its conflict with Mohammed Ali of Egypt (1831–1833), was unable to support its integrity by military means; nonetheless, it was still a power to be reckoned with.

On Samos, power rested completely with the General Assembly of the representatives of the villages, who did not agree with delivering their island to the empire. Their strongest argument was that they had gained their freedom with victory over the Sublime Porte. As director general of administrative affairs in the Samian state, Logothetis Lykourgos became the dispatcher of decisions taken by the General Assembly. The assembly decided and he was obliged to execute. And although he gave account of his actions to the body of plenipotentiaries, he was unable to take initiatives beyond their decisions. The only concession that the European powers made regarding the Samos question was to designate for the island in the London Protocol of 1832 a regime of autonomous principality under the suzerainty of the sultan. The protocol obliged the sultan to issue an organic statute regulating the operation of the new political system to be instituted on Samos. The General Assemblies, both of the villages and of the whole island, did not accept this regime, which foresaw a declaration of submission and a swingeing tribute. They rejected outright and unequivocally every related proposal made either by the great powers or the Ecumenical Patriarchate.

The end of the Samian state and of the revolution on Samos was dramatic. In May 1834, the European powers permitted the Sublime Porte to impose, by military means, the regime of autonomous principality, while the Samian leadership—political, military, and religious—with a host of *Karmanioloi* and other Samiots who had taken part in the revolution, were forced to migrate to free Greece, which meant permanent exile from their native isle. Most of the Samiot migrants settled in areas of Euboea, on lands ceded to them by the Greek government.

To conclude, the singularity of the Samian Revolution of 1821 lay in its duration (1821–1834); the participants' deep conviction that it was a just cause; the unwavering application of the local military-political system of governance, which was strengthened during the Samian state (1830–1834); the Enlightenment ideas that had filtered through to a large part of the island's population, as this manifested itself through general assemblies; and its enlightened leadership, which expressed democratic ideas in theory and in practice. Whatever text on Samos in 1821 one may study, whether letters, encyclicals, commands, speeches, or proceedings of assemblies, one comes across Enlightenment ideas everywhere. This is especially true of the speeches that were delivered in the assemblies over the period 1821–1828, which combine liberal notions with the discourse of the Gospels and the teachings of the Fathers of the Church.

Between 1821 and 1830, Samos enjoyed unprecedented circumstances of freedom and democracy. In these years, an entire generation grew to maturity and could not have remained unaffected, despite the developments that followed. And when Samos was left outside the borders of the independent Greek state (in 1830–1834), the application of democratic and liberal ideas acquired greater intensity and quality. Although the regime of the autonomous principality forced the remaining Samiots to declare allegiance to the sultan, it was unable to dispense with or to diminish established institutions of the revolutionary period, such as the General Assemblies, which it included in its system of governance as an intrinsic element of the island's autonomy. The demand of the Samian state—that is, of the revolution—was satisfied seventy-eight years later with a new revolution in 1912, which abolished the principality and declared the island's union with Greece.

Christos Landros

Translated from the Greek by Alexandra Douma

References

Belsis, Constantinos. 2014. *Από την οθωμανική νομιμότητα στο εθνικό κράτος. Το «άτομο» στο επίκεντρο της Ιστορίας. Λυκούργος Λογοθέτης (1772-1850) Πολιτική βιογραφία* [From Ottoman legality to the nation state. The "individual" at the center of history: Lykourgos Logothetis (1772–1850), political biography]. Athens.

Goudas, Anastasios. 1875. *Βίοι Παράλληλοι των επί της αναγεννήσεως της Ελλάδος διαπρεψάντων ανδρών* [Parallel lives of distinguished men of the rebirth of Greece]. Vol. 7. Athens.

GSA. 1824. Samos Folder Γ1 (January), fols. 61–62.

Laiou, Sophia N. 2002. *Η Σάμος κατά την οθωμανική περίοδο: πτυχές του κοινωνικού και οικονομικού βίου, 16ος-18ος αι.* [Samos during the Ottoman period: Aspects of social and economic life, sixteenth to eighteenth centuries]. Thessaloniki.

Landros, Christos. 2001. *Η μετεπαναστατική Σάμος σε υποτέλεια. Το πρώτο πρωτόκολλο αλληλογραφίας της Ηγεμονίας 1834-1835* [Postrevolutionary Samos in vassalage: The first correspondence protocol of the principality]. Athens.

Landros, Christos. 2010. "Αλληλογραφία του Λογοθέτη Λυκούργου κατά το 1824" [Correspondence of Logothetis Lykourgos during 1824]. *Apoplous* 48:374–406.

Landros, Christos. 2016. "Η δυναμική του στρατοπολιτικού συστήματος Σάμου" [Dynamics of the military-political system of Samos]. *Απόπλους* 70: 173–177.

Matthioudakis, V. 1832. *Σαμίων Πρεσβεία ή Πρακτικά Σάμου* [Embassy of Samiots or proceedings of Samos]. Karlovasi.

Philiou, Christine M. 2011. *Biography of an Empire: Governing Ottomans in an Age of Revolution*. Berkeley and Los Angeles.

Sakellariou, Michail V. 2011. *Θέματα νέας ελληνικής ιστορίας* [Issues in modern Greek history]. Athens.

Sakellariou, Michail V. 2014. *Ένας συνταγματικός δημοκράτης ηγέτης κατά την επανάσταση του '21. Ο Γ. Λογοθέτης Λυκούργος της Σάμου (1772–1850)* [A constitutional democratic leader during the revolution of '21: G. Logothetis Lykourgos of Samos, 1772–1850]. Iraklio.

Sevastakis. Alexis. 1959. *Το δημόσιον δίκαιον εν Σάμω κατά την Τουρκοκρατίαν, την Επανάστασιν και το Ηγεμονικόν καθεστώς* [Public law on Samos during the Ottoman period, the revolution and the principality regime]. Thessaloniki.

Sevastakis, Alexis. 1980. *Οι Καρμανιόλοι στην επανάσταση της Σάμου. Ιωάννης Λεκάτης* [The *Karmanioloi* in the revolution of Samos. *Ioannis Lekatis*]. Athens.

Sevastakis, Alexis. 1985. *Σαμιακή Πολιτεία 1830–1834. Λογοθέτης Λυκούργος* [Samian state, 1830–1834. Logothetis Lykourgos]. Athens.

Sevastakis, Alexis. 1986. *Δίκαιο και δικαστική εξουσία στη Σάμο, 1550–1912: με ανέκδοτα έγγραφα* [Justice and legal authority in Samos, 1550–1912: With unpublished documents]. Athens.

Sevastakis, Alexis. 1995. *Ιστορικά Νέου Καρλοβάσου Σάμου, 1768–1840* [Historical data of Neo Karlovasi, Samos, 1768–1840]. Athens.

Sevastakis, Alexis. 1996. *Το κίνημα των "Καρμανιόλων" στη Σάμο 1805–1812, με ανέκδοτα έγγραφα* [The "Karmanioloi" movement on Samos, 1895–1812, with unpublished document]. Athens.

Sevastakis, Alexis. 2005. *Ιστορικά ανάλεκτα* [Historical analects]. Athens.

Stamatiadis, Epameinondas. 1881. *Σαμιακά ήτοι ιστορία της νήσου Σάμου από των παναρχαίων χρόνων μέχρι των καθ' ημάς* [Samiaka, that is the history of the island of Samos from most ancient times to our days]. Samos.

Stamatiadis, Nikolaos. 1899–1900. *Σαμιακά* [Samiaka]. Vols. 1–2. Samos.

Varvounis, Manolis G. 2008. *Το όραμα της ελευθερίας στη σαμιακή κοινωνία (1800–1912)* [The vision of freedom in Samiot society, 1800–1912]. Athens.

Vourliotis, Manolis. 1990. *Καρμανιόλοι και βιβλίο (1800–1839)* [Karmanioloi and book, 1800–1830]. Athens.

Zafeiris, Giannis. 1977. *Λογοθέτης Λυκούργος. Ο μεγάλος Σαμιώτης αρχηγός του '21* [Logothetis Lykourgos: The great Samiot leader of 1821]. Athens.

Αντιπελάργηση. Τιμητικός τόμος για τον Νικόλαο Α. Δημητρίου [Antipelargisi: Festschrift for Nikolaos A. Dimitriou]. 1992. Athens.

Η Σάμος από τα βυζαντινά χρόνια μέχρι σήμερα [Samos from Byzantine times to today]. 1998. Athens.

Η Σάμος στα νεότερα χρόνια (17ος—20ός αιώνας) [Samos in recent times: Seventeenth to twentieth centuries]. 2002. Athens.

Ο Γ. Κλεάνθης και η εποχή του [G. Kleanthis and his time]. 1991. Samos.

Σάμος και επανάσταση. Ιστορικές προσεγγίσεις [Samos and revolution: Historical approaches]. 2011. Athens.

IV

PERSONS

Clergymen

The attitude of the Orthodox clergy toward the 1821 War of Independence is an issue that arouses, even today, heated and divisive debate in both public and academic discourse. Partial historiographical views are often taken to extremes, constituting an impediment to sober confrontation of the issue and serious debate. Furthermore, the relevant literature is poor compared with that dealing with other leading groups in the struggle.

The view that the Church was opposed to any revolutionary movement and that it was finally dragged into the struggle by the events themselves or even by the people is based on an argument concerning the status of the Church within the Ottoman political system. Its recognition by the sultan as an institution of the empire made the Church ipso facto favorably disposed toward the sultan's power and therefore at odds with anyone who desired the abolition of the Church's status, since any revolution and change of the status quo ante would mean the loss of the Church's privileged position. Further arguments summoned to interpret this standpoint of the Church are its vocal anti-Enlightenment policy, especially during the thirty years prior to the revolution, and its pro-Ottoman stance as soon as the struggle broke out, as became apparent from the Patriarchate's excommunication of Alexandros Ypsilantis and the patriarch's encyclical condemning the revolution.

According to the opposite view, the Church wholeheartedly participated in the struggle or even played a leading role. The supporting arguments are based on the list of clerics who either were put to death or participated in the revolution in different ways. Indeed, some of them had already been members of the Philiki Etaireia before the outbreak of the revolution, proof of their positive attitude toward the likelihood of such an event. Advocates of this view forward as their basic reason for the condemnation of the revolution by the Patriarch of Constantinople and the excommunication of Ypsilantis the suffocating pressure exerted on the Church by the sultanic regime, which also imposed, so they maintain, the specific acts on the patriarch.

In order to understand and study the whole issue, it is essential to sketch the framework (ideological, political, religious) within which the Orthodox clergy was operating before and during the struggle. It is essential to bear in mind that the Orthodox Church should not be approached in terms relating to the Roman Catholic Church. The position of the Roman Catholic Church in prerevolutionary France—and in western Europe generally—was entirely different from that of the Orthodox Church in the prerevolutionary Ottoman world. Even though in both cases the revolutions were modernist, the starting points of the two churches were different.

In the present text, the term "Church" means the administrative institution of the Patriarchate of Constantinople, which was acknowledged by the sultan, under whose jurisdiction were mainly—but not only—the regions of the Ottoman Empire in which there was a Greek population. The administrative structure began from the patriarch and was articulated in a set of metropolitans and bishops, who on the eve of the War of Independence numbered no more than two hundred. These prelates made up the ecclesiastical hierarchy, which was one of the leading groups of Christians within the Ottoman Empire. They did not comprise a closed "caste," because the prelacy was reproduced through society, maintaining networks of clientage though without the character of a nobility of a Western type. At the base of the pyramidal structure were the ordinary priests in the parishes and monks in the monasteries. Despite the strict hierarchical structure, the superiors did not exercise oppressive policy on the inferiors, although the former were economically dependent on the latter, while the latter were politically and ecclesiastically dependent on the former. The principal role of the Church in premodern Christian society was imprinted also in its juridical—in part de jure—and educational responsibilities.

The absence of a closed caste in the Orthodox Church, the full incorporation of the prelates in local societies, and the determinative role of religion (Orthodox Christian faith) in the everyday life and worldview of the people resulted, generally speaking, in breaking down, psychologically and ideologically, whatever social or political distances existed between the ordinary people and the prelates. Thus, apart from the priest or monk, the metropolitan too or the bishop was an organic member of the local society, even if his term of service was not long or if he did not come from the area of his see. Informal social interaction seems to have been stronger than the power relations that developed between the prelates and the people. Such was the position of the clergy not only in the provinces far from the center but also in Christian societies as a whole. Certainly, there was a socioeconomic and, by extension, political differentiation within the clergy, since the prelates were considered a quasi-Ottoman elite and certainly a Christian one. Nonetheless, key for the issue here is the overall interaction between clergy and society.

The Sublime Porte understood the dual role of the Orthodox clergy. On the one hand, the clergy were the spiritual leaders of a large part of the Ottoman Empire's subjects, on the other, they were politically (and fiscally) responsible for these subjects. Just as the sultan took measures to facilitate the collection of taxes on behalf of the prelates, he considered the prelates responsible for solving any problem that arose among the Orthodox Christian subjects of the empire. The sultan was well aware of the leadership role that members of the clergy, from the patriarch to the humblest priest or monk, were playing in local societies. That was why he was always suspicious of them; this distrust was confirmed by prelates participating in—or organizing—uprisings during previous centuries of Ottoman rule. In the years before the War of Independence, an aggravating role in relations between the Church and the Ottoman Empire was played also by the Russophile stance of the former, which was based on the communality of religious doctrine and the Orthodox Christian oracular tradition emanating from it. It should be remembered that Russophobia in the Ottoman court during this period had taken on dimensions of hysteria.

The possibilities of becoming literate in an oral society, since the ecclesiastical vocation was one of the few literate occupations, gave members of the clergy good prospects. Provided the administrative—and political—commitments of a lower-ranking cleric were not pressing, by making the most of his sacerdotal status he could potentially acquire a high level of education, while the natural mobility of the clergy, utilizing the geographically wide ecclesiastical networks, could lead him even beyond the bounds of Ottoman territory. It is not fortuitous that among the first Greek intellectuals of the Enlightenment and until the eve of the revolution there was a notable percentage of clerics, albeit for the most part of low rank. Thus, the clergy was part of the Greek intelligentsia throughout the period of Ottoman rule, even during the Enlightenment period; however, phenomena of illiteracy continued to exist in the ranks of the clergy.

The above *contextus operandi* of the clergy within the Ottoman state, in combination with the earlier Byzantine tradition, shaped the political ideology of the Church. The ruler of the state, although he had not come from the body of the Church as dictated by tradition since the time of Constantine the Great, but whose choice was certainly "from God," secured the peaceful political framework in which the faithful could worship. So, both in the Byzantine and the Ottoman periods, the Church did not exercise politics separately from its spiritual role. Under the Ottomans, however, the different religion of the sovereign not only intensified the spiritual role of the Church toward its flock, but also opened a window for the Church to take political action. The political action walked a tightrope above two contradictory fields: on the one hand, the Church ensured political submission of its flock to the sultan, as it was obliged to do because of its position as an institution of the Ottoman state; on the other, it maintained—if it did not encourage—a spirit of reconstitution of the Christian empire, mainly through the oracular tradition. Sometimes members of the Church, not only low-ranking ones, effected this reconstitution by their participation in—or even organization of—various rebellions; for example, Makarios Melissinos, metropolitan of Monemvasia, in 1572 and Dionysios the Skylosophos (Dog Philosopher), bishop of Larissa, in 1601 and 1611.

The revolutionary ideology pressingly diffused in Greece, with its secular aspirations inspired by the French Revolution, shook to the foundations the existing political-ideological construct of the Church. The rapid military developments during the first twenty years of the nineteenth century drew in their wake corresponding developments at the political-ideological level. Notwithstanding its vacillating stance, the Church was under pressure to adapt to the new conditions. Its reluctance to take action was due not so much to fear of reprisals by the Ottoman side as to the fact that the Church should have understood the modern ideology that members of its flock were introducing impetuously into the Ottoman space. This new ideology, which demanded the undertaking of political action, marginalized the role hitherto played by the Church in both society and politics. The adaptation was difficult, since the Church's role as spiritual leader of its flock, which was part and parcel of its function also as a political institution, was being challenged.

With all the above preconditions in mind, we can sketch the stance and the role of the clergy in the War of Independence. Obscuring the issue are two, apparently contradictory, approaches: one sees the Church as a single political-administrative entity and the other approaches it through the division—to a degree of intense rivalry—into upper and lower clergy. More helpful, however, is the approach through individual persons, within the framework of preconditions outlined above. It should be noted beforehand that the political readiness of the clergy for the revolution can be seen from their participation as members of the Philiki Etaireia. According to the most reliable study (Frangos 1971, 301, table 1), the proportion of clerical members of the Philiki Etaireia (approximately 10 percent) was not much less than that of other population groups, with the exception of merchants, while in one other study of the intellectuals as members of the society (Pizanias 2009, 29, table), clerics involved in teaching or writing formed also a notable percentage.

We should not paint too rosy a picture. When the revolution broke out, there were clerics who fervently supported it and were involved directly as well as clerics who were uncomfortable or hesitant or who even castigated it, or some who simply played no part. We shall focus on those clerics who did take part, since those who were absent do not appear in the sources and for those who desisted we are not well informed. The case, for example, of the monk Evgenios (Papoulakos), who refused to offer the treasure that had accumulated in his monastery for the needs of the struggle and whom Kolokotronis suspected of relations with Ibrahim Pasha, is isolated and poorly documented. The study of the actions of individual clerics leads to the delineation of some types, which emerge from their initial stance toward the revolution as well as their actions during it, and which are correlated with the prerevolutionary realities outlined above.

A first type includes high-ranking clerics (prelates) who were arrested immediately upon the outbreak of the revolution and who were either put to death or were tortured and survived. Two characteristic cases concern Constantinople and the Peloponnese. In the first, the Ottomans arrested, as was expected, Patriarch Gregory V and seven synodic prelates, whom they hanged either right away or a few months later, as legally responsible for the insurgent Greeks. In the second case, the pasha of the Peloponnese had invited the primates, the prelates among them, to the capital Tripoli in order to discuss the rebellion by Ali Pasha of Ioannina. Only eight prelates responded to the invitation and they were imprisoned by the pasha when the revolution broke out, almost immediately after their arrival. Of these, five died in jail, while three survived and were liberated when Tripoli was captured by the Greeks. Two of them, Iosiph, bishop of Androusa, and Kyrillos, bishop of Corinth, also played an active role in the national assemblies of the struggle. As part of the reprisals for the revolution, the archbishop of Cyprus Kyprianos and the prelates of Cyprus were arrested and executed, while the same happened in Crete, as well as in other regions. This first type, then, is characterized by the seniority of the person before the revolution. As mentioned already, the Ottoman Porte considered that the prelates—and above all the patriarch—were responsible for the loyalty of the Christian Ottoman subjects. Any breakdown of order or any action challenging loyalty toward the sultan, especially when this action was accompanied by deaths of Muslims, was blamed on the prelates, who, from the standpoint of Ottoman authority, had failed in their institutional role. The accusations of treacherous behavior, on the basis of which the aforesaid prelates were condemned to death and hanged, emanated from this position.

FIGURE 21   Dionysios Tsokos, *Portrait of Patriarch of Constantinople Gregory V*, 1861. Oil on canvas. National Historical Museum, Athens.

The case of Patriarch Gregory V is characteristic of the stance of all these prelates towards the revolution (Figure 21). Solicitude for his flock, in the midst of rumors of a pogrom against the Greeks of Constantinople, led him to issue the excommunication and the encyclical against the revolutionaries. His execution on Easter Sunday 1821 and the persecutions that followed vindicated his caution and fears.

To a second type belong those clerics who were active participants in the revolution. This category is not only the most numerous, at least with regard to prelates for whom we have numerical data, but also the one that can be divided into subcategories, according to the action of the clerics. This division is not based on some fixed objective criteria but on the personality of each cleric, which led to him taking corresponding action in the revolution. That is why the variations are many, making it difficult to construct a strictly defined typology.

We will start with the most popular ecclesiastical personality of 1821, the metropolitan of Germanos, archbishop of Old Patras, a multitasking prelate, who took part in the front line of the revolution, although at a political level (Figure 22). Born into a farming family in Dimitsana in the Peloponnese, Germanos had a typical clerical career, close to his fellow villager and subsequently thrice patriarch, Gregory V. When the War of Independence broke out, he had been on the metropolitan throne of Patras for fifteen years and a member of the Philiki Etaireia for almost three years. His reputation as a political man with mediating skills and the ability to strike a balance was well founded in revolutionary circles and thus one can explain his active participation in the preparation and conduct of the struggle, for example in the assemblies at Vostitsa and Kaltezon monastery, the Peloponnesian Senate, and the First and Third National Assemblies. The culminating event of his career was his participation in the two-man delegation (together with Georgios Mavromichalis) that was elected by the First National Assembly to go to Italy to negotiate financial and other assistance for the sorely tried revolution, and which was authorized to meet the Pope and western leaders. Germanos's sojourn there for about two years

FIGURE 22 Dionysios Tsokos, *Portrait of Germanos, Archbishop of Old Patras,* 1862. Oil on canvas. National Historical Museum, Athens.

(October 1822 to June 1824) was in the end fruitless, but from it he accrued greater fame when he returned.

Even though Germanos was embroiled in the civil war—which had broken out in the meantime—and was imprisoned, he was elected member of the Third National Assembly and was indeed a member of the committee on home affairs. His health declined and he died in May 1826. Beyond whatever truth or fiction is concealed behind the doxology on the blessing of the revolutionaries' weapons by Germanos in the Agia Lavra monastery at Kalavryta, on March 25, 1821, the Peloponnesian prelate was undoubtedly an energetic member of the insurgent clergy, despite his initial misgivings regarding the revolution, which he had expressed at the assembly of Vostitsa (January 1821).

Other prelates also took political initiatives in the front line of the revolution. Iosiph, bishop of Androusa, from Tripoli, also a member of the Philiki Etaireia, was one of the three who survived from among the eight prelates incarcerated in Tripoli at the beginning of the struggle. After his release from prison, he was appointed by the 1822 executive (*Ektelestikon*) as minister of religion (1822–1825) and for a brief spell also of justice, enjoying general esteem. He was succeeded in the ministry of religion by the likewise energetic Peloponnesian bishop of Damala, Ionas, who in 1821 had taken part in the operation to capture the fortress of Corinth. Theodoritos, bishop of Vresthena and a native of Arcadia, brings us to the type of prelate who was active simultaneously on the battlefield and in politics. He played an energetic role in the first year of the struggle as head of an armed corps (at the battles of Valtetsi and Vervaina), but in the following year he laid down his arms and served in political positions, the most important of which was as vice-president of parliament, elected by the Second National Assembly at Astros (1823). Other prelates who acted politically through participation in national assemblies include the bishop of Corinth Kyrillos and the former bishop of Arta Porphyrios, who took part in the Third National Assembly, and the metropolitan of Athens Dionysios, who took part in the civil organization of east mainland Greece.

There are characteristic examples of another type of prelate, those who were purely freedom fighters. The bishop of Salona Isaias was not only a protagonist, together with Dionysios of Athens and Neophytos of Talantion (Atalanti), in the declaration of the revolution in central Greece, but he also fought in the first battles, losing his young life in the battle of Alamana (April 23, 1821). Similar is the case of the bishop of Rogoi, Iosiph, from Tsaritsani (Thessaly), who, after a brief spell in jail in Arta at the outbreak of the revolution, was active in military operations in western central Greece with the chiefs of armed bands there and led the beleaguered Mesolonghi in its second siege, during which he was killed (April 13, 1826). Last, the Peloponnesian bishop of Methoni Grigorios was another characteristic case of a prelate who played an active role in military operations. He was put in charge of revolutionary forces in the southwest Peloponnese but in the end was incarcerated by the forces of Ibrahim Pasha in 1825 and died in prison.

Apart from the prelates, low-ranking clerics also fought on the battlefields, even though their actions are less well known. Arsenios Krestas was active in the district of Argos, where he lost his life in 1822, while the monks of the Mega Spilaion monastery were involved in the struggle in many ways, as armed freedom fighters on the battlefield but also by tending the wounded or hiding revolutionaries. The Peloponnesian Amvrosios Frantzis, of Mega Spilaio monastery, participated actively in the struggle in the area of Arcadia, served as plenipotentiary in the Third National Assembly at Troezen in 1827, and is known to historiography as author of the first history of the Greek Revolution.

One of the best known and most popular heroes of the revolution was also a member of the lower clergy, a deacon of the Church, Athanasios [Masavetas], known as Athanasios Diakos (1786–1821). He represents a characteristic case of the interpenetration and the blurred limits between the groups of clergymen and men of war. Born in a village in the highlands of Rumeli, he entered the monastery of Saint John the Baptist at Artotina as a novice and was ordained a deacon taking the name Athanasios. In his clerical capacity, he is said to have served at the Church of Saint Dimitrios in the Plaka neighborhood in Athens. Being pursued by an Ottoman official, he took to the mountains and joined the klephts in the highlands of Rumeli. From then on he left his religious functions behind and acted as an oplarchigos, playing an active role in the beginning of the revolution in eastern Rumeli. He proclaimed the revolution at Livadia on March 30, 1821. On April 22–24 he fought against the army of Omer Vrioni at Alamana bridge, near ancient Thermopylai, and was wounded and captured. He was executed at Lamia on April 24 (see also Dimitrios Papastamatiou, "Military Leaders," in this volume). On account of his youth, his sacrifice became a source of inspiration to other fighters and the subject of many revolutionary folk songs. He became an emblematic figure in the symbolism of the war of independence and was celebrated in many sources, including, later on in the nineteenth century, the poetry of Aristotelis Valaoritis and Costis Palamas.

Without doubt, however, the most emblematic figure of all was the Messenian archimandrite Grigorios Dikaios, or Papaflessas (Figure 23). An impulsive character, Papaflessas was initiated as early as 1818 into the Philiki Etaireia and in January 1821 was sent by Alexandros Ypsilantis to the Peloponnese, carrying the message of the revolution. In the assembly convened at Vostitsa, Papaflessas clashed with the local primates and prelates, who were cautious about the likelihood of a revolution. After the outbreak of the struggle, he participated on

FIGURE 23   Alecos Kontopoulos,
Papaflessas, 1941–1944. Chromo-
lithograph. Pechlivanidis
Publishing House Collection,
Athens.

the fronts during the first year of the war and then in the political bodies. He
was appointed minister of the interior by the Second National Assembly.
Ibrahim Pasha's invasion of the Peloponnese mobilized Papaflessas, who, in the
midst of a civil war, tried to set free the imprisoned chiefs of armed bands in
order to launch an effective resistance. In the end, he himself undertook military action, organizing a corps to confront the Egyptian forces. In May 1825 he
was slain in battle at Maniaki, fighting against Ibrahim's army.

The above types are represented not only in the Peloponnese and central
Greece. Both in the islands (Neophytos of Karystos, Ierotheos of Paros-Naxos,
Kyrillos of Samos) and in the northern regions (Ignatios of Ardameri, Constantios of Maroneia, Amvrosios of Stagoi), clerics and preeminently prelates
either took part in the uprisings there or, after the failure of those movements,
moved south to the rebellious regions to offer their services to the struggle.

The monasteries, a special case in the ranks of the clergy, merit special mention. Three elements differentiate them from the rest of the clergy: (1) their notable land property, (2) their usually privileged taxation status, and (3) the
fortress-like character of their buildings. The first two elements were sufficient
to make the monasteries reluctant or even hostile in the face of any revolu-

tionary mobilization. The third, however, allowed them to be actively included in the whole effort. For centuries before the War of Independence, monasteries had been a refuge for Christians hounded by the Ottoman authorities and a hearth for storing and/or circulating artillery and weapons. These factors, in combination with the sacred vessels (church plate), which were potentially liquid assets for the needs of the struggle, as well as the close contact of the monks—although theoretically recluses—with society made the monasteries important units in the entire revolutionary endeavor. Examples of the participation of monks in the revolution, especially in the Peloponnese, abound. Reference has been made to the Mega Spilaio monastery in Achaia. There are cases of individual monks or of hegumens who participated in the vanguard of the revolution as freedom fighters. Their arena of action was mainly the Peloponnese; the hegumens Dionysios of the Avgo monastery in the Argos area, Iosiph of the Voulkano monastery in Messenia, and Nikiphoros of the Nezeroi monastery in Kalavryta may be cited as indicative examples. Of the individual monks, worthy of mention is Theophanis Siatisteas (from Eratyra, Kozani), who took part in the revolution in Chalkidiki and after its failure made his way to southern Greece, where he was active mainly as secretary for various freedom fighters.

Mount Athos is an interesting example. Due to its geographical location and its privileged status, but also to the action of some of its monks, such as the member of the Philiki Etaireia Nikiphoros of Iviron monastery, it was the center of the revolution in Chalkidiki. For all its initial misgivings, the holy community of Mount Athos participated in the movement and when, after it was quashed, the monasteries suffered the reprisals of the Ottoman authorities, most of the Athonite monks left the peninsula and went to the islands and southern Greece.

As mentioned at the beginning of this essay, clerics, basically those of low rank, constituted a significant portion of the Enlightenment intellectuals. Their attitude toward the revolution was by no means unanimous. There were some who considered the whole endeavor excessively rash and did not become actively involved in it (e.g., Daniil Philippidis, Neophytos Doukas, Constantinos Oikonomos), while others, although they made their way to regions in revolt, quickly retreated due to their disagreement with the revolutionaries' actions (e.g., Neophytos Vamvas). There were, however, some who were actively involved. Archimandrite Anthimos Gazis from Pilion (Thessaly), one of the most important personalities of the Greek Enlightenment in the period prior to the struggle, although already of advanced years was initially placed head of the revolution in Pilion and, when this was quelled, he went to southern Greece, where he took part in the national assemblies as plenipotentiary of Thessaly.

In the end, he was appointed scholarch of Tinos and Syros islands, where he died in 1828. Deacon Grigorios Constantas, likewise from Pilion, after participating in the revolution there sought refuge in southern Greece, where he took part in the national assemblies and was elected to the parliaments (*vouleftika*) of the first two. He was active in education, in the post of ephor of education (1824–1828), founding schools, finding teachers and books, and writing reports on education in war-torn Greece. Veniamin Lesvios also went to insurgent Greece and took part in the first two National Assemblies, but died in 1824. Two other intellectual clerics of the younger and the previous generation are known to the historical literature, mainly for their postrevolutionary action. Immediately after the outbreak of the revolution, the deacon from Andros Theophilos Kairis moved from the Asia Minor town of Kydonies (Ayvali), where he was a teacher, to the Greek peninsula, where he offered his services to the cause, mainly representing Andros as member of the national assemblies and Parliament (*Vouleftikon*), and assisting with diverse educational matters. He participated also in the landing of volunteers in Pieria region and in the revolutionary events of Macedonia (1822). Last, the archimandrite Theoklitos Pharmakidis from Larissa also moved to southern Greece immediately after the outbreak of the revolution and was active as ephor of education in the civil organization of east mainland Greece, as member of the first two national assemblies and as editor of the first *Geniki Ephimeris tis Ellados* (Γενική Εφημερίς της Ελλάδος [General newspaper of Greece]), but in the end left for Corfu, where he became a professor in the Ionian Academy.

Another emblematic clerical personality represents a special type, namely Ignatios from Lesvos, metropolitan of Ungrowallachia. Ignatios had served as bishop of Arta (1794–1805), from which position he engaged in intense diplomatic activity between Ali Pasha of Ioannina, various groups of *armatoloi* in the Ottoman territory (primarily the Souliots), and foreign countries with interests in the Ionian region (France and Russia). In addition to honing his diplomatic skills, through this bishopric he made highly placed acquaintances in Russian circles. When Russia captured the Danubian Principalities, during the Russo-Turkish War (1806–1812), he was elected by the synod of the Russian Church as metropolitan of Ungrowallachia, a position he kept until the end of the war and the departure of the Russian troops. Ignatios then settled in Vienna, joining the circles of Greek intellectuals there, but in 1815 he went to Pisa to escape the suffocating political-ideological climate of the Austrian capital. He stayed in the Italian city until his death and it was there that he learnt news of the revolution. Ignatios was held in high esteem among Enlightenment intellectuals and members of the Philiki Etaireia, who approached him repeatedly to initiate him into its fold. He considered any uprising in 1821 premature, because he maintained that it should be preceded by sound spiritual and material preparation. But when the revolution broke out, he strove to aid it in various ways. Tapping into his wide circle of acquaintances among European intellectuals and politicians, he tried to mobilize them into a political campaign supporting the just cause of the revolution. He collected money for the Greek refugees, while he kept up correspondence with the political leaders of the struggle. Moreover, it was he who advised Alexandros Mavrokordatos to go to Greece and recommended him to the insurgents as a highly adept diplomat. Ignatios devised a plan of diplomatic action for the recognition of the struggle by the European states. He was convinced that the Greeks should affiliate with and mobilize Great Britain to the advantage of Greek interests. This view was not at odds with his initial Russophile stance but was the outcome of realistic evaluations, since Great Britain was the major naval power in the east Mediterranean and therefore could reinforce the Greek cause in diverse ways.

The economic dimension of relations between the clergy and the revolution could be summarized as follows. The land property, particularly of the monasteries, was requisitioned and the church plate was confiscated by the revolutionary political instruments, so as to contribute to the financing of the struggle. Clerics, particularly prelates, were called upon to contribute monies also from their personal fortunes and many did so willingly.

A recent question that has been posed concerning the participation of the clergy in the Greek War of Independence is the following: How is the behavior of members of the ecclesiastical hierarchy, such as Germanos of Old Patras, Theodoritos of Vresthena, and other bishops incumbent until 1821, whose revolutionary activism constituted a defiance of the official Church (but not necessarily of the faith), to be interpreted? (Pizanias 2009, 50). Through the prerequisites noted at the beginning of this article, as well as the characteristic examples of clerics, we shall try to contribute some thoughts in answer to this question, as well as clarify the stance in general of the clergy during the War of Independence.

Initially, it should be remembered that, generally speaking, the attitude of the clerics, official Church and prelates, to the revolution was between diffident and negative. This attitude did not necessarily stem from motives of self-interest, namely the loss of their politico-social primacy in local Christian societies, which the Ottoman state had secured for them. Nor did it stem from the expectation of a better position in the postrevolution political landscape through the overturning of the existing one, as was the case with other groups (e.g., chiefs of armed bands). An equally important parameter, which was advanced rather as definitive, was the relationship between the clergy, and indeed the prelates, and the people. Already from the examples cited, it emerges that overwhelmingly the sector of the clergy that played an active role in the revolution originated from the local societies. The characteristic case of the Peloponnese was surely not the only one. Networks of clientage may have secured upward mobility in the ecclesiastical hierarchy, but these networks were geographical and kinship-based in the wider sense and overlapped one another. A prelate's humble origin made him communicant with the hardships and aspirations of the people. Even where prelates came from eminent primate families of the Peloponnese, their contact with society at large was not severed. The clerics who were active on the battlefields belonged neither to the intellectual elite nor to a social elite in the sense known from western European societies of the period. The pre-modern Orthodox prelate—and far more the low-ranking cleric—was not psy-chologically distanced from the people, unlike his Roman Catholic counter-part in the West. He too was brought up—through prophecies and oracles—with the hope of "casting off the infidel dynast" and of founding a Christian state. Possibly, he did not understand in all its depth and breadth the modernist de-mand and what this meant for the position of the Church within this state. Per-haps he considered that the uprising of his flock ought to draw him along with it, since he was its spiritual leader and therefore he considered his participa-tion self-evident. Moreover, any initial uncertainties could be ascribed rather to his spiritual role vis-à-vis his flock—and to the possible reprisals against him. It is interesting, on the other hand, that while there were different approaches to the revolutionary phenomenon by intellectual clerics—as by intellectuals generally—this was not the case with the clerics who did not belong to the in-tellectual elite. In short, the political action taken by clerics in the War of Inde-pendence was determined by their more general spiritual-social role.

This argument is supported by observations on the role of the clergy in the regions in revolt. And it is apparent from the examples that in the Peloponnese and to a lesser extent in central Greece and the islands there was great mobiliza-tion of the clergy in support of the revolution. From the stance of clerics in all the rebellious regions, we see that the participation of the clergy was directly proportional to the momentum of the revolution and the likelihood of its suc-cess. Initially hesitant, as clerics saw the local revolutionary movement swelling or subsiding, they regulated their stance accordingly. Whether because of fear of reprisals or consciously and purposefully, several of them moved to southern Greece, when movements in their regions were suppressed. This was the case of several monks from Mount Athos, but also of some individual prelates.

Approaching the Church as a unified administrative and political institution should be done with great care by the historian of the Greek Revolution. As an institution, albeit premodern, it had a head, the Patriarch of Constantinople, who theoretically expressed it. The paradox and apparent contradiction between words and actions of the Church during the Ottoman period and especially in the period leading up to the Greek Revolution have been discussed. This factor is critical also for understanding that the clergy's stance toward the revolution was of the nature of personal choices and was not shackled by some imposed canonical frame of action. Even though overall the struggle was the outcome of personal paths, in the ranks of the clergy this phenomenon acquires special dimensions, due to its institutional—and therefore theoretically constituted—character in relation to other population groups (merchants, intellectuals, primates, guerrilla chiefs, and so on), who were not under the umbrella of some institution. Thus, the issuing of the patriarchal excommunication or the patriarchal encyclical on the revolution was not comprehended by the members of the ecclesiastical hierarchy or the lower clergy in the same way, nor even in the literality of their texts. This is the perspective in which the different attitudes of the clerics, many prelates included, toward the revolution can be interpreted.

Ideological differences should be dealt with in the same framework. The condemnation of "philosophical lessons" and in general of Enlightenment ideas was, on the eve of the revolution, the official line of the Church, as expressed by the Patriarchate. Nevertheless, this too should not be overemphasized. Over and above any political ramifications this official condemnation might entail (e.g., the support of the revolution by advocates of the Enlightenment) and without taking into account the existence of only important prominent Enlightenment clerical intellectuals, another parameter is significant. The ideological conflict was not perceived with the same intensity by nonintellectuals. So the ordinary prelate, especially if he was living far away from the important centers of the Enlightenment—which, incidentally, were mainly outside Ottoman territory—did not grasp the conflict in all its dimensions. Furthermore, it was not easy to make the connection between modern ideas and political developments and particularly the revolution. For example, we do not know what role the ideological conflict between Enlighteners and anti-Enlighteners played in the thinking of bishop Isaias of Salona, and therefore whether this defined to a degree his stance. This argument is reinforced when we bear in mind cases of Enlightenment clerical intellectuals with traditional roots, who adapted their ideological equipment during the progress of the struggle. Ignatios of Ungrowallachia is a case in point. Consequently, the clergy should not be treated en bloc either at the political or the ideological level. Although an institution—certainly premodern—perhaps because it was also a body of people, the clergy were not a monolithic group but adaptive in character.

Moreover, it should be borne in mind that the modern sense of liberation was imbued with the idea of the glorious Greek origin and emerged as a revolutionary program, creating a new collective identity which accommodated all traditional groups, among them the clerics—prelates and others. The traditional oracular ideas about the "resurrection of the nation" were grafted onto modern ideas about liberation through revolution, thanks to the promotion—in the imagined community—of the Greek origin as a value of religious character. Therefore, the response of the clergy to the revolutionary summons was included in the new national ideology, which took on religious overtones and was occasionally understood as the will of God.

The Greek Revolution, as a modern event par excellence, was unable to preserve the prerevolutionary—that is, premodern—role of the Church. So, even before the constitution approved by the Third National Assembly at Troezen prohibited clerics from holding political and military offices, the role of clerics in the revolution had diminished considerably. The course of divergence seemed inevitable. Moreover, what already concerned the clergy, among others, were the ecclesiastical problems that had arisen from the revolution, principally the relationship with the Patriarchate, but also the issue of the ordination of bishops, so that political participation seemed a secondary matter. The loss of important ecclesiastical figures in the early years of the struggle and the establishment of a secular political tradition during its course were the basic causes of supplanting the Church, not only in political matters but also theretofore in its privileged sectors of pastoral activity, namely family law and education. Furthermore, the capital issue of the manner of incorporation of the Church within a modern state in the postrevolutionary period remained open.

Phokion Kotzageorgis

Translated from the Greek by Alexandra Douma

References

Frangos, George. 1971. "The Philike Etaireia, 1814–1821: A Social and Historical Analysis." PhD diss., Columbia University, New York.

Frazee, Charles. 1969. *The Orthodox Church and Independent Greece, 1821–1852*. Cambridge.

Gazi, Efi. 2009. "Revisiting Religion and Nationalism in Nineteenth-Century Greece." In *The Making of Modern Greece: Nationalism, Romanticism, and the Uses of the Past (1797–1896)*, edited by Roderick Beaton and David Ricks, 95–106. Farnham and Burlington, VT.

Georgantzis, Petros. 1985. *Οι αρχιερείς και το Εικοσιένα (αντίδραση ή προσφορά;)* [The prelates and 1821: Reaction or contribution?]. Xanthi.

Goudas, Anastasios. 1869. *Βίοι Παράλληλοι των επί της αναγεννήσεως της Ελλάδος διαπρεψάντων ανδρών* [Parallel lives of distinguished men of the rebirth of Greece]. Vol. 1, *Κλήρος* [Clergy]. Athens.

Hatzopoulos, Marios. 2009. "From Resurrection to Insurrection: 'Sacred' Myths, Motifs, and Symbols in the Greek War of Independence." In *The Making of Modern Greece: Nationalism, Romanticism, and the Uses of the Past (1797–1896)*, edited by Roderick Beaton and David Ricks, 81–93. Farnham and Burlington, VT.

Kitromilides, Paschalis M. 1989. "'Imagined Communities' and the Origins of the National Question in the Balkans." *European History Quarterly* 19: 149–192.

Kitromilides, Paschalis. 2006. "Orthodoxy and the West: Reformation to Enlightenment." *The Cambridge History of Christianity*, Vol. V: *Eastern Christianity*, edited by Michael Angold, 187–209. Cambridge.

Kitromilides, Paschalis M. 2011. "The Orthodox Church and the Enlightenment: Testimonies from the Correspondence of Ignatius of Ungrowallachia with G. P. Vieusseux." *Egnatia* 15:81–88.

Kitromilides, Paschalis. 2013. *Enlightenment and Revolution: The Making of Modern Greece*. Cambridge, MA, and London.

Kitromilides, Paschalis. 2019. *Religion and Politics in the Orthodox World: The Ecumenical Patriarchate and the Challenges of Modernity*. London and New York.

Michailaris, Panagiotis, and Vasilis Panagiotopoulos. 2010. *Κληρικοί στον Αγώνα. Παλαιών Πατρών Γερμανός- Ιγνάτιος Ουγγροβλαχίας-Νεόφυτος Βάμβας* [Clerics in the struggle: Germanos of Old Patras—Ignatios of Ungro-Wallachia—Neophytos Vamvas]. Athens.

Pizanias, Petros. 2009. "Από ραγιάς Έλληνας πολίτης. Διαφωτισμός και επανάσταση 1750–1832" [From reya to Greek citizen. Enlightenment and revolution, 1750–1832]. In *Η Ελληνική Επανάσταση του 1821: ένα ευρωπαϊκό γεγονός* [The Greek Revolution of 1821: A European event], edited by Petros Pizanias, 13–77. Athens.

Sherrard, Philip. 1968. "The Orthodox Church in Greece." In *Modern Greece*, edited by John Campbell and Philip Sherrard, 189–213. New York and Washington.

Sherrard, Philip. 1973. "Church, State and the Greek War of Independence." In *The Struggle for Greek Independence: Essays to Mark the 150th Anniversary of the Greek War of Independence*, edited by Richard Clogg, 182–199. London.

Simopoulos, Theophilos. 1971–1972. *Μάρτυρες και αγωνισταί ιεράρχαι της ελληνικής εθνεγερσίας, 1821–1829* [Martyrs and fighting prelates of the Greek national uprising, 1821–1829]. Athens.

Zacharopoulos, Nikolaos G. 1974. *Γρηγόριος Ε'. Σαφής έκφρασις της εκκλησιαστικής πολιτικής επί Τουρκοκρατίας* [Grigorios V: Explicit expression of ecclesiastical policy during the Tourkokratia]. Thessaloniki.

Civilian Leaders and the Beginnings
of the Modern State

Politics, like nature, the old adage goes, abhors a vacuum. The revolution of 1821 was no exception, as the rebels strove immediately after the outbreak of the revolt in the Morea (Peloponnese) in March 1821 to create political and administrative structures that would support and sustain it. In fact, a crucial factor for the successful beginning of the revolution, apart from the inability of the Ottomans to crush it at its birth, was that the Greeks managed to build political institutions that prevented its degeneration into a rudderless rising and gave it a sense (however tentative) of direction, leadership, and unity of purpose. All those elements, however, were intensely contested at the time, for views on what should replace the crumbling Ottoman system diverged widely. However, the consolidation of a unified political leadership in the lands that eventually became the first Greek state, consisting of the Morea, Rumeli (central Greece), and some Aegean islands, was an extremely daunting task, for it had to be accomplished over a society that was deeply fragmented along regional, social, cultural, and political fault-lines. In addition, another deep cleavage, a "cultural rift," separated the *autochthon* Greeks (those born in revolutionary Greece), who were largely cut off from the European world and its ideas, from the *heterochthons* (those who came from other lands), many of whom lived or were educated there.

It should be emphasized that political leadership was not the exclusive preserve of civilians, given that members of four distinct groups entered the political scene of the struggle. The majority of political leaders were indeed civilians and came from the Moreot notables and the shipowners of the islands, the traditional political elite of the Greek world, as well as from the *heterochthons*, who were also called "newcomers." The latter group included a handful of

Phanariots and a larger number of mostly Western-trained intellectuals, who went to Greece after the outbreak of the revolt. There were also clerics, especially in the Morea, and military men (*armatoloi* in Rumeli, and *kapoi* in the Peloponnese), who exercised political control of varying significance. Many civilian leaders were also involved in military operations and therefore the distinction between political, religious, and military leaders was often purely theoretical.

Before the outbreak of the revolution, the configuration of political power in the Greek lands was shaped by the highly variated Ottoman system of regional self-government, a kind of indirect rule that met two pressing Ottoman needs: taxation and governance of local communities. That system was crystalized (although never formalized officially by the Ottomans) in the *eyalet* of the Morea in the eighteenth century and allowed for an elaborate power structure of which Greek notables were an integral part. The one or two village notables (*dimogerontes*), elected for one year but with the right to be reelected, ran the local affairs of their community, managed its budget, and looked after public order. They met once a year in the provincial capital and elected the district notables (the *morayan vilaetlides* or *kocabaşıs*), whose duties were wider and included apportioning the burden of taxation, as well as some judicial authority over Christians. They, in turn, elected two notables (the *morayanides*), who sat on the pasha's council, together with two Muslim notables (*ayans*) and the *dragoman* (also a Christian, but appointed by the Ottomans). The notables also sent envoys to Constantinople (*vekils*) to consult directly with the Ottomans on Moreot affairs.

Firmly locked into the Ottoman system, the political power of the primates was thus quite considerable as they played a decisive role in the government of the Morea. They were tax farmers, engaged in trade and usury, and acquired substantial land holdings, roughly 30 percent of the arable (but not the best-quality) land. Although most notables shared common social and political characteristics, they were not a politically unified class, although occasionally they acted as such, when threatened by other groups such as the military men at the beginning of the revolt. They were constantly in competition for acquiring or keeping office, prestige, and fortune, but their political power was intensely personal in character, local in scope, and centered on the extended family, the most fundamental political and economic unit in the Ottoman Greek lands. Although in theory they were elected, in practice powerful notables secured their positions for years, passed them on to their family, becoming in effect "self-elected." Giannis Deligiannis (Papagiannopoulos) of Karytaina, for instance, himself the son of a *morayianni*, was *morayan-vilaetlis* for thirty-two years, *morayianis* for sixteen, and *vekils* for three. The primates had to possess certain qualities; they had to be prudent, judicious, and cautious. Some of them took this to the extreme, such as Asimakis Zaimis of Kalavryta, "the silent primate," who spent hours in meetings smoking his pipe without uttering a word.

Before the revolution, their political control over the peasantry was assured, leading to an acute consciousness of being the only legitimate men of affairs. Importantly, keeping their political position intact was absolutely crucial for their financial security; participation in politics guaranteed access to resources. The primates adopted the dress and occasionally the manners of their Ottoman masters and most of them had not much education, although they employed men who had. The regional character of their rule meant that, with the exception of some leading families, they were not much interested in affairs beyond their community, and certainly not beyond the Morea, in so far as developments elsewhere did not impinge directly on it. They had connections with the consuls of foreign powers, and some were legally "protected" by them, but that did not denote any political or ideological allegiance. Their "fatherland" was the Morea, when not their native community, and their loyalty was reserved primarily for their family. The maxim "all politics is local politics" aptly epitomized their political attitude.

The preservation and enhancement of their privileged position led them to form alliances (always shifting) both with the Muslim notables and with other prominent Greek primates. Those bonds were, in the latter case, reinforced by intermarriages, and supported by patron-client relationships with lesser notables. Such arrangements led to the proliferation of clientelistic networks, or "factions" (*phatries*), led by, and frequently named after, the most powerful families. Most of these were purely local, but there were also two rival factions, formed in the eighteenth century, which were alliances of family factions and percolated through the whole of the Morea: the so-called Achaean faction and the Karytinomessinean faction. The former was led by Sotirakis Lontos (Vostitsa) and consisted of the families of Zaimis (Kalavryta), Sisinis (Gastouni), Dareiotis (Messini), Kopanitsas (Mistras), and Meletopoulos (Vostitsa); the latter, led by Giannis Deligiannis (Karytaina), included the families of Palamidis (Tripolitsa), Charalambis (Kalavryta), Christakopoulos (Tripolitsa), Kanellopoulos (Andritsaina), Poniropoulos (Arcadia), and Notaras (Corinth).

Many members of these powerful families played a major role in the political leadership of the struggle, on a local or a national level, and it is precisely their participation that ensured that the revolution would have enough of a political backbone not to die a natural death. The primates' participation was also determined by the need to safeguard the dominant political position they enjoyed under Ottoman rule, while others participated only when they realized that, after the outbreak of the revolt, they had no other viable option, and opting out would be costlier than joining in. Their aim, at least initially, was to preserve the local, decentralized and personal kind of politics that characterized the pre-modern Ottoman structure.

The equivalent of the Moreot notables in the islands of Ydra, Spetses, and Psara, that provided the bulk of the revolutionary navy, were the *oikokyraioi*. These were shipowners who had made their fortunes, some of them very substantial, from trade and not from land ownership. As in the Morea, important families emerged, and formed factions competing for power. Most of these factions, however, were local, with the notable exception of the Ydriot Koundouriotis family. Their faction, led by the brothers Lazaros and Georgios, established connections and alliances beyond the island and played a prominent role in the political leadership of the revolt; Lazaros kept himself in the background, while Georgios, a man of no particular qualities, moved to center stage. In Rumeli, the situation was different. The communal system there was weak, and the notables never attained the power of the Moreots, due to the existence of a powerful military class, the *armatoloi*, who, apart from military power, held considerable political leverage over their communities.

The other important group that participated in the civilian leadership of the struggle was the "newcomers," who broadly represented the modernizing (that is: Westernizing) wing in Greek politics. That group included three Phanariots, Dimitrios Ypsilantis, Theodoros Negris, and Alexandros Mavrokordatos, who left their mark on the political scene, although only the last retained his prominent political position throughout the revolutionary period, and indeed long after that. They themselves, however, did not form a unified group, due to personal ambitions and diverging political considerations.

Mavrokordatos, the scion of a very distinguished Phanariot family, highly educated and polyglot, is widely (and rightly) considered a prime westernizing force (Figure 24). He was at home in foreign policy and when drafting constitutional texts, but he pursued his considerable political ambitions with verve, and did not hesitate to align himself with traditional notables and powerful *armatoloi* to build initially a local and later a national power base. Negris, who had acquired political experience in the Danubian Principalities, had been appointed deputy ambassador of the Porte to Paris, but rushed to Greece when the revolt broke out. His political star shone brightly but for a short time. By the time he died, in 1824, he was already a spent political force. Ypsilantis, the brother of the leader of the revolutionary Philiki Etaireia (Society of Friends), Alexandros Ypsilantis, can also be counted among the modernizing elite of the struggle, at least in the sense that he wanted to impose a centralized government against the control of the notables; but he wanted its leadership for himself. A man of noble intentions and character, he commanded substantial popular support, partly because he came to Greece as official representative of

FIGURE 24   Karl Krazeisen,
*Portrait of Alexandros
Mavrokordatos,* 1827. Pencil
on paper. National
Gallery-Al. Soutzos
Museum, Athens.

his brother and partly because he pitted himself against the notables. But he
failed to capitalize on these assets and was quickly sidestepped.

Ioannis Kolettis, a Vlach from Syrako in Epirus, whose political career also
survived the revolution when he became the first elected prime minister of
Greece, in 1844, was also a prominent member of the *heterochthons*. His political
outlook was a blend of traditional and modernizing elements. He had studied in
Italy but learned much of his politics in the court of Ali Pasha of Tepeleni, where
he served as physician. He had many contradictory attributes; his scheming
went with a genuine political acumen and a ruthless determination to establish
a commanding position. He emerged as a man of power in the middle of the
revolutionary period and retained a prominent political presence thereafter.
Apart from those newcomers, the modernizers also contained a wider circle of
well-educated men, including Georgios Glarakis, Ioannis Theotokis, Anastasios
Polyzoidis, Drosos Mansolas, and Spyridon Trikoupis. Although they played a
rather secondary political role, they also left a westernizing imprint on Greek
politics, despite developing diverging political orientations.

Overall, the Phanariots and the other newcomers, unlike the indigenous Greek elite, had no local power base when they entered the Greek political scene, no established clientelist networks, and therefore no vested interest in the preservation of the old configuration of political power. Consequently, they had nothing to lose from the western political ideas that they sought to advance: a centralized government free from local particularisms, supported by a modern bureaucracy and guided by a liberal constitution. They were young, many of them educated in German, French, and Italian universities; they quickly staffed the emerging bureaucratic institutions and ministries, and played a prominent role in the national assemblies and the drafting of the revolutionary constitutions. It has been suggested (Diamandouros 2002, 130) that there were two reasons they managed to rise to positions of influence. First, the primates underestimated the significance of the bureaucratic structures that the modernizers wished to build, and the threat that these bodies represented for their own political position. Seeing the world through Ottoman eyes, they were more interested in controlling persons than institutions. Provided they kept a firm hold over their local power base, which would allow them to undermine, or ignore, any decision made from above, they saw no immediate threat in letting the newcomers occupy important administrative, ministerial, and political positions. Second, their endemic infighting not only prevented them from forming and sustaining a unified camp against the westernizers but also led them to form alliances with the newcomers, to strengthen their position against other primates. Furthermore, the education of the *heterochthons* made them obvious choices for positions, though in some cases they were also perceived (wrongly) as "representatives" of foreign powers, something that added to their prestige.

In March and April 1821, there was a flurry of political activity as a great number of provincial institutions were set up in almost all places that had taken up arms, in order to attend to the pressing needs of the war and offer the rudiments of a civilian government. All of these, in keeping with the prerevolutionary traditions, were local in scope, and were led by the traditional political elites. The most important of these were the Messinian Senate and the Achaian Directory. The former was established in Kalamata on March 23 by Petros Mavromichalis, the prerevolutionary *bey* of Mani. Both a military and a political leader, Petrobey, as he was commonly known, was head of a substantial family faction with considerable power that extended beyond Mani, due to his alliance with Panagiotis Benakis, a prominent Messinian notable, which was sealed by the marriage of Benakis's sister to a brother of Mavromichalis. He occupied important political positions during the revolt but retaining the control of his native Mani remained uppermost in his mind.

The Achaian Directory, which was formed three days after the Messinian Senate, was based initially in Patras and later in Kalavryta. It included many powerful primate families, such as those of Andreas Zaimis (of Kalavryta), Andreas Lontos (of Vostitsa), Benizelos Roufos (of Patras), Sotirios Theocharopoulos (of Kalavryta), and Ioannis Papadiamantopoulos (Patras). Two bishops who commanded considerable political presence, Germanos of Old Patras and Prokopios of Kernitsa, were also members. Other important notables, such as Kanellos Deligiannis (of Karytaina) controlled the Ephorate of Karytaina (*Ephoria Karytainis*), while Georgios Sisinis, the primate of Gastouni, set up the Commune of Ilis (*Koinotis Ilidos*). These institutions attempted to fill the vacuum created by the rapid disintegration of the Ottoman system, organized and provisioned the armed bands, restored some semblance of public order in their regions, and made an effort to alleviate the hardship that the war was causing to the peasantry. Much of the necessary funding for all these activities came directly from the primates.

Importantly, by establishing these institutions, the notables reaffirmed their role as the only legitimate political leaders. Before the revolution, that was an indisputable fact, but the outbreak of the revolt ushered in new contenders for political power. The first was the Philiki Etaireia, which considered itself the prime source of political leadership. The fiery cleric and envoy of Alexandros Ypsilantis, Grigorios Dikaios (known as Papaflessas), had already clashed with Bishop Germanos, and cautious notables, including Andreas Lontos, Asimakis and Andreas Zaimis, Sotiris Charalambis, and others, at a meeting in Vostitsa (Aigio) in late January 1821, in attempting to persuade them that the revolt should begin immediately. But the issue of its leadership was also raised by notables who were deeply suspicious of outside political control. Although many primates were members of the Etaireia, they loathed surrendering their political power. Shortly afterward, Papaflessas suffered an even more forceful rebuke by the Deligiannis family, who told him bluntly that they would not allow outsiders, who "did not even own a tree on which to be hanged," to lead men like them, who had "large families, fortune, large properties," and consequently they were not prepared to listen to their "stupidities" (Deligiannis 1957, 112). Those who had (and therefore risked) everything, the primates felt, should not be subordinated to those who had nothing.

Military men of every description, with their power augmented by the fact that they undertook the revolutionary struggle, comprised another group that posed a threat to the notables, although they were never unified, with the partial exception of the Morea under the leadership of Theodoros Kolokotronis. Many of them viewed the emissaries of the Etaireia as a useful ally against the primates and were willing to support them. To compound the difficulties of the primates, the Moreot peasantry, which had long felt oppressed by the notables, started seeing the leadership of military men as the only way to break away from the primates' rule and as an opportunity to acquire land.

In order to reinforce their political position before the expected arrival in Greece of Dimitrios Ypsilantis as official plenipotentiary of his brother, the primates established in May the Peloponnesian Senate, a body controlled by prominent notables, including Sotiris Charalambis, Athanasios Kanakaris, Anagnostis Deligiannis (Papagiannopoulos), and Asimakis Zaimis, which assumed the political and military leadership of the revolt in the whole of the Morea. Although Ypsilantis was enthusiastically received by political, military, and religious leaders when he arrived in Greece in June, partly because it was still widely believed that behind the Etaireia stood Russia and not least because he brought with him an impressive chest thought to contain money, a clash soon ensued between him and the Moreot primates.

Ypsilantis demanded nothing less than the abolition of the Senate and the concentration of power in his own hands, as president of a "parliament," which would combine executive, legislative, and judiciary powers. That conflict, which erupted during meetings in Vervena and Zarakova, led to a deadlock as the notables, although prepared to offer a prominent role to Ypsilantis, refused to relinquish their political power. Seeing the deadlock, the military men, who saw in Ypsilantis not only their "lord" (*afentis*), but also an enemy of the notables, attempted to attack the primates in Vervena, something that was prevented only with the intervention of Kolokotronis. Interestingly, in order to neutralize Ypsilantis the primates insisted on wide suffrage, which they could easily control, and suggested that the "prince" should not act without the consent of an assembly thus elected. Ypsilantis, for his part, favored the limitation of suffrage, precisely in order to curtail their power. He aimed to introduce a centralized government, perceived as "democratic," for it was directed against the "aristocratic" or "oligarchic" power of the notables, but he meant to achieve it by concentrating power largely to himself. After those meetings, Ypsilantis set up his headquarters in Trikorfa, was given the position of the leader of the Greek forces besieging Tripolitsa by his military allies, and continued his feud with the Peloponnesian Senate. His failure to assert decisively his leadership over the primates, despite his popular and military support, meant that his political power gradually started to wane, especially when it was realized that Russia had nothing to do with the Etaireia and that his brother Alexandros had suffered defeat in Dragatsani in June.

The conflict between Ypsilantis and the notables led the other two Phanariots, Mavrokordatos and Negris, to search for a local base outside of the Morea, in order to set up their own regional institutions. Both understood all too well that without a local power base and a personal political faction it would have been impossible to play a wider role in Greek politics. Westernizers they were, but such an inclination did not prevent them from playing the traditional political game, which was, after all, "the only game in town." After consultations, they divided between themselves the region of Rumeli: Mavrokordatos, with the authorization of Ypislantis, established his political base in west Rumeli and Negris in the eastern part. Both wrote elaborate constitutional texts (that few read and even fewer understood), which were approved in November by regional assemblies, established senates—Negris the Areopagus, in Salona (Amfissa), and Mavrokordatos the Senate of Western Continental Greece, in Mesolonghi—and the rudiments of a bureaucracy, and they attempted to impose some sort of centralized government, albeit with limited success. In Rumeli, as has already been noted, it was the *armatoloi*, not the primates, who were the most important source of local power, and they were determined to keep it. Mavrokordatos, however, both acknowledged and benefited from that reality, and by displaying consummate political skills managed to secure his position by approaching both camps. He institutionalized the position of many powerful captains by appointing them regional military leaders, while at the same time assuring the primates of protection from the excesses of the military men. In east Rumeli, Negris was not that fortunate, for the beneficiary of the local power struggles was not himself but the most powerful *armatolos* of the region, Odysseas Androutsos. In the face of his opposition, Negris attempted to forge alliances with both the primates and the *armatoloi*, but his leadership was never assured and it came to an end a year later.

By December 1821, when fifty-nine delegates from Rumeli, the Morea, and the Aegean islands convened in the village of Piada, close to ancient Epidavros, to form the First National Assembly, the cleavage between the civilian leaders and the military men was all too evident, and had led to the emergence of two distinct factions, which contemporary observers called "parties": the "political" and the "military." The former camp was a heterogeneous and loose coalition that included the political elites of the Morea and the islands, as well as Mavrokordatos and Negris, with the former emerging as its leader. That coalition was based on expediency, not choice, for its members had no connecting bond other than their opposition to the military captains and to Ypsilantis's attempt to assume the leadership of the struggle. The military party consisted mainly of the Moreot captains, who still favored Ypsilantis. The latter, however, did not participate in the assembly, nor did Kolokotronis, the leader of the Moreot military men. Mavrokordatos was elected president of the assembly, the presence of the Moreot deputies was overwhelming, and consequently the domination of the political party was complete. The assembly, which solemnly proclaimed the independence of the Greek nation, voted the first constitution of the country, the Provisional Constitution of Greece. The constitution, which was the work of Mavrokordatos, Negris, and the Italian radical Vincenzo Gallina, followed broadly the French revolutionary constitutions, and was rightly perceived as a triumph of the modernizing forces; it proclaimed the "natural rights" of the nation, and attempted to establish the rule of law and the separation between the executive, legislative, and judicial powers.

That triumph, however, was mostly on paper rather than in substance, and the establishment of a strong centralized government did not materialize. First, the three existing regional entities, in the Peloponnese and in eastern and western Rumeli, were not abolished and continued to run local affairs, acting in many respects as the real source of political power. Second, the constitution established a five-strong executive body, the *Ektelestikon*, which would also appoint the eight ministers of the government, and a legislature, the *Vouleftikon*, but it was stipulated that the two bodies should cooperate on legislation, and consequently the separation of powers remained a dead letter. Furthermore, each body had the right to veto the decisions of the other, leaving each with little real power. Importantly, the constitution accommodated the notables' demand that the members of both bodies would serve a one-year term and would be appointed after elections, for they firmly believed that their control of the peasantry would safeguard a favorable outcome.

The balance of power between modernizers and traditional elites, as well as between the regional centers, was aptly demonstrated in the apportioning of offices. Mavrokordatos was elected president of the executive, the *Ektelestikon*, which in theory had substantial powers, and did not contain any representatives of the military. Negris was appointed foreign minister, secretary-general of the state (*Archigrammatefs tis Epikrateias*), and president of the council of ministers, while Ioannis Kolettis was appointed minister of the interior. The Moreot primates were represented in the *Ektelestikon* by the leading notables Anagnostis Deligiannis and Athanasios Kanakaris, and the islanders by Ioannis Orlandos, whose main asset was that he had married the sister of Lazaros and Georgios Kountouriotis. Three islanders became also ministers of marine affairs. All these offices, however, despite their impressive titles, meant very little in terms of actual political power and, recognizing that reality, Mavrokordatos and Negris returned shortly afterward to their regional centers. In an attempt to placate him, the primates offered Ypsilantis the presidency of the *Vouleftikon*, with Petrobey as vice-president, but the latter understood that the position was of no consequence, and certainly beneath his expectations, and resigned shortly afterward.

The political domination of the civilian leaders that marked the First National Assembly was reaffirmed in the Second National Assembly, which was held in Astros on March 29, 1823, and revised the Constitution of Epidavros. This time, the military party participated in the assembly under its leader, Kolokotronis, who had now eclipsed Ypislantis and whose power was at its peak after the crushing defeat he had inflicted on the Ottoman forces in July 1822. But their deputies and armed followers were both heavily outnumbered by those of the notables. The rift became immediately and emphatically visible, as the rival parties camped in different areas. During the meetings of the Assembly, two cleavages were observed: between the military and the politicians, and, within the political camp, between the Moreot notables and the modernizing Phanariots. Mavrokordatos and Negris, as well as other Westernizers, were again involved in the constitutional revision, but the outcome was a compromise. The revised constitution abolished the three regional entities, and it was also decided that Greece should be divided into sixty districts, to be led by governors who should not be locals and would be appointed by the government. Those decisions aimed at strengthening the position of the central government and enhancing the institutional unification of the country, a key aim of the Westernizers. The ever-present localism, however, immediately asserted itself as Ydra, Spetses, and Psara refused to integrate themselves into the new scheme. The notables in the assembly moreover managed to counterbalance the imposition of centralism by substantially weakening the powers of the executive; the latter would now be appointed by the *Vouleftikon*, and could only delay, but no longer veto, the decisions of the legislature. The military party suffered a defeat, when the position of the commander-in-chief, which had been given to Kolokotronis by the Peloponnesian Senate, was abolished, but it managed to thwart the decision of the politicians to sell the so-called national lands, the lands previously owned by Muslims, fearing that those properties would be eventually appropriated by the primates.

The politicians, and especially the Moreot notables, dominated both the newly strengthened legislature and the executive. Orlandos, who belonged to the Kountouriotis faction, became president of the *Vouleftikon*, while the executive's presidency went to Petrobey, with the notables Andreas Zaimis and Sotiris Charalambis as members, together with Andreas Metaxas, a politician from Cephalonia. Ypsilantis and Negris were offered no position in either body. Mavrkordatos, however, was appointed secretary general of the executive, but when Orlandos resigned, he was also made president of the legislature. He resigned, however, shortly afterward. At that time, the cleavage between the military and the political party was becoming even more acute, as Kolokotronis refused to recognize the new configuration of power, but in May he accepted

the position of the vice-presidency of the executive, a clear attempt by the notables to restrain him. That move, however, backfired on another front, for it
was perceived by the Moreot military men as a capitulation of their leader to
the primates, and Kolokotronis resigned in October.

The executive and the legislature were now at loggerheads, and the situation
was rapidly disintegrating into open conflict. In November, the legislature dismissed Metaxas, a supporter of Kolokotronis, from the executive, and appointed
Kolettis, and at the end of the month Kolokotronis sent his son, Panos, to attack the legislature in Argos. Most of the legislature's members fled to Kranidi,
where they dismissed Charalambis and Petrobey, who sided with Kolokotronis,
and appointed a new executive, with Georgios Kountouriotis as president, the
Spetsiot Panagiotis Botasis as vice-president, and Andreas Zaimis, Nikolaos
Lontos, and Kolettis as members.

By the end of 1823, there were two opposing political camps that broadly
represented the rift between the politicians and the military, although each
side included elements of the other. On the one hand, there was the old executive, which was supported by the military strength of Kolokotronis. The
government at Kranidi, on the other hand, which claimed, not without justi-
fication, that it was the legitimate one and was negotiating a loan in London,
was backed by an alliance consisting of the islanders, Mavrokordatos, Kolettis, and a number of Moreot notables, including the powerful allied factions of Andreas Lontos and Andreas Zaimis. The civil war that ensued ended
in June 1824, when Kolokotronis surrendered his last bastion, the fortress of
Nafplio, to the government.

The end of the hostilities, however, brought immediately to the forefront in
high relief another, ever-present, cleavage, based on regional loyalties, that pitted
the political and military men of the Morea, the warring camps of the first civil
war, against the islanders and the Rumeliot captains. Moreots, Rumeliots, and
islanders felt little affinity with one another, as attachment to their region was
a much more powerful force than an abstract sense of nationhood. The over-
bearing presence of the islanders, as demonstrated by Kountouriotis's government, was noted with dismay by the Moreots, and was confirmed when a new
government was formed in October: Kountouriotis and Botasis were both re-
appointed as president and vice-president, respectively, of the executive, as was
Kolettis. Mavrokordatos was later appointed secretary-general and wielded considerable influence, due to his alliance with Georgios Kountouriotis, whom he
effectively controlled (Figure 25). He was also in charge of foreign policy, a field
in which he had neither equal nor rival. The factions of Zaimis and Lontos were
excluded from the new executive, and although two Moreots were appointed
to it, one of them, Asimakis Fotilas, soon resigned.

FIGURE 25   Karl Krazeisen,
*Portrait of Georgios
Kountouriotis,* 1827. Pencil
on paper. National
Gallery-Al. Soutzos
Museum, Athens.

At that juncture, the hand of the government was decisively strengthened
by the arrival of the first installment of a loan from Britain, thus allowing it to
dispense funds for the recruitment of loyal military men. This was undertaken
by Kolettis, who was now emerging as the political patron of Rumeliot captains
and was building his own personal faction. His moment had come, and he
seized it without hesitation. The need to counter the influence of the islanders
and Kolettis, and secure their political leadership in the Morea, brought together
the Moreot primates, including Zaimis, Lontos, Georgios Sisinis, and Kanellos
Deligiannis, and the Moreot military men led by Kolokotronis. As the Moreots
defied openly the government and refused to pay taxes, the situation came to
a head in November 1824, when the government sent a large contingent of Rumeliots to Arcadia. This marked the beginning of a second civil war, much more
brutal than the first. Scores of ill-disciplined Rumeliot irregulars, paid hand-
somely by Kolettis and encouraged by the prospect of plunder, descended on the
Morea and by December they had put down the Moreot forces with extreme ferocity. The defeated leaders ended up prisoners in Ydra, with the exception of

Zaimis and Lontos, who found protection by Mavrokordatos in west Rumeli. However, the invasion of the Morea, led by Ibrahim Pasha, forced the government to grant a general amnesty to its opponents in May 1825, which they followed up by appointing Kolokotronis as commander-in-chief of the Greek forces.

The perilous state of the revolution in the Morea, due to Ibrahim's successes, and in Rumeli, meant that the Third National Assembly was not able to convene until April 6, 1826, in Epidavros. The assembly, which elected the primate Panoutsos Notaras as president, soon heard the devastating news of the fall of Mesolonghi and decided to postpone its sessions, but not before taking two important decisions. The first was to suspend the legislature and the executive for a year and, given the gravity of the situation, to concentrate all political power in a newly formed Administrative Committee of Greece. Comprising eleven members and representative of all regions, the committee marked the return to power of those defeated in the civil war: Andreas Zaimis (who was elected president), Georgios Sisinis, and Anagnostis Deligiannis were included in it, as was Petrobey. Lazaros Kountouriotis was also elected, but he did not accept the position due to ill health and was substituted by his fellow Ydriot Dimitrios Tsamados. The assembly's second decision was to appoint another committee, called Committee of the Assembly, which, in a secret resolution, was given the mandate to conclude peace with the Ottomans, using as intermediary the British ambassador to the Ottoman Empire, Stratford Canning. Ypsilantis attacked this decision forcefully but was sharply rebuked by the assembly, which moreover excluded him from all political and military positions.

During that period, a new and significant factor entered the calculations of the Greek political leaders: Britain, Russia, and France had started making their presence felt, as they attempted to settle the "Greek question" diplomatically. Thus, a number of political alliances emerged, which sought the support of the powers, and were named after them: the English, Russian, and French "parties." These parties, which would be crystallized during the Capodistrian and Othonian periods, have been perceived as little more than the sum of personal and family factions of individual leaders. True, each party was based on preexisting factions: the English party coalesced around Mavrokordatos's faction, which consisted of military and political leaders of west Rumeli, but also included the factions of Zaimis and Lontos, as well as those of Miaoulis and Tompazis; the Russian party had its base in the Morea, around Kolokotronis; while the French party was led by Kolettis and his faction of Rumeliot military men.

That notwithstanding, careful research (Hering 2008, 105–109) has pointed out that all parties gradually widened their base and gained allies that had not previously been members of those factions: Moreot primates joined the French party, for example, while others approached Kolokotronis, although they did not belong to his personal faction. Mavrokordatos's English party also included many supporters who were not his direct political clients. Personal and local power struggles played a major part in those decisions; if a faction joined a particular party, then their local competitors were forced to ally themselves with another. That said, wider cultural, ideological, and political considerations were not absent; the Russian party was fed by the strong Orthodox attachment to Russia, while modernizing and Western-trained intellectuals joined the English party due to their Anglophile political sentiments.

The combination of personal and political (or party) rivalries, continued to divide the Greek political leaders, delaying the reconvening of the Third National Assembly. By the end of 1826, Zaimis and the deputies who followed him had camped on the island of Aigina, and Kolokotronis with his own followers on Ermioni. After pressure on both sides from Thomas Cochrane and Richard Church (two Britons, a naval officer and a general, who had close connections with the Greeks) it was agreed that they should convene in Troezen, where the Third National Assembly was eventually held on March 19, 1827. The assembly voted a new constitution, the Political Constitution of Greece, which had a liberal and democratic orientation, following not only the French revolutionary constitutions but also the American one. It was also decided to offer the position of governor of Greece to Ioannis Capodistrias, for seven years. His name had been put forward by the Russian faction of Kolokotronis but faced the opposition of the English faction of Mavrokordatos, as well as that of Kountouriotis. Capodistrias's election was eventually agreed upon, but only after the English had party succeeded in installing Cochrane and Church as chiefs of the Greek navy and army, respectively. Until the arrival of Capodistrias, the assembly appointed a three-member Vice-Presidential Committee to act as the executive power. Three nonentities were appointed: Georgios Mavromichalis, a son of Petrobey; Ioannis Markis Milaitis, from Psara; and the Rumeliot Ioannis Nakos. The equal representation of the three regions was the only positive feature of the committee, which soon became the stuff of ridicule; the committee, it was said, consisted of "a boy, a sailor, and a cuckold" (Dakin, 1973, 204).

Overall, the civilian leadership of the revolution was shaped by the multiple cleavages that divided the Greek world: between *autochthons* and *heterochthons*; Moreots, islanders, and Rumeliots; military men and local primates; the Moreot peasantry and the notables; and between those who looked to Russia, France, or Britain. The revolt also witnessed a confrontation between forces of tradition, which sought to preserve the substance of the Ottoman structure of power, and those of modernity, seeking to establish a nation-state, based on European political ideas. In addition to those cleavages, the major upheavals brought about by the revolution profoundly affected the traditional family factions and allowed the emergence of new (and personal) ones, led by newcomers, such as

Mavrokordatos and Kolettis. The role of politics was also transformed: from the running of local affairs under premodern imperial rule to state building. That transformation, however, was not radical, for the perception of politics as a means of personal and family advancement survived the revolution.

As has rightly been observed (Petropulos 1968, 106), sometimes a certain cleavage acquired prominence and overshadowed others (although never extinguished), as happened with the clash of the politicians with the military in the early stages of the revolt, with localism in the second civil war, and with the attachment to foreign powers at the end of the revolutionary period. The existence of such rifts, however, although of fundamental importance, should not imply that the political camps and factions that emerged during the revolution were homogeneous or a direct reflection of those rifts. Consequently, the political leadership of the struggle contained representatives of all sides of those cleavages, in shifting alliances. Arguably, that fact gave to the struggles for political domination an almost existential quality, given that their outcome determined nothing less than the overall character and orientation of the nascent state.

Dimitris Livanios

References

Dakin, Douglas. 1973. *The Greek Struggle for Independence, 1821–1833*. Berkeley and Los Angeles.

Deligiannis, Kanellos. 1957. *Απομνημονεύματα* [Memoirs]. Vol. 1. Athens.

Diamandouros, Nikiforos. 1972. "Political Modernization, Social Conflict and Cultural Cleavage in the Formation of the Modern Greek State, 1821–1828." PhD diss., Columbia University, New York.

Diamandouros, Nikiforos. 2002. *Οι απαρχές της συγκρότησης σύγχρονου κράτους στην Ελλάδα, 1821–1828* [The beginning of modern state-building in Greece, 1821–1828]. Athens.

Hering, Gunnar. 1992. *Die politischen Parteien in Griechenland, 1821–1936*. Munich.

Hering, Gunnar. 2008. *Τα πολιτικά κόμματα στην Ελλάδα*. Vol. 1. Athens.

Kitromilides, Paschalis M. 2013. *Enlightenment and Revolution: The Making of Modern Greece*. Cambridge, MA.

Kostis, Kostas. 2018. *History's Spoiled Children: The Formation of the Modern Greek State*. London.

Papageorgiou, Stefanos. 2005. *Από το γένος στο έθνος. Η θεμελίωση του ελληνικού κράτους, 1821–1862* [From genos to ethnos: The foundation of the Greek state, 1821–1862]. Athens.

Petropulos, John Anthony. 1968. *Politics and Statecraft in the Kingdom of Greece, 1833–1843*. Princeton, NJ.

Veremis, Thanos M., and John S. Koliopoulos. 2002. *Greece: The Modern Sequel, from 1831 to the Present*. London.

Diplomats and Diplomacy

When the Greek War of Independence began, the international environment could hardly have been less promising. An uprising on the basis of the principle of nationalities was something "almost unheard of" (Heraclides and Dialla 2015, 106) and equally damnable from the point of view of the great powers dominating the European state system as reconstituted in 1815 by the Congress of Vienna. Moreover, these powers, minus Britain, still subscribed to the principles of the Holy Alliance, which dictated the suppression of any activity that threatened the stability of the post-Napoleonic order. Preciously few Greek revolutionaries had an understanding of this context. These men were either diaspora people or Phanariots, like Alexandros Mavrokordatos, who would manage Greek foreign affairs during much of the war period. Their cause might have been better served had they secured a leader recognizable abroad. Ideal for this role would have been Count Ioannis Antonios Capodistrias, joint foreign minister of Russia and arguably the most eminent Greek of his time.

Capodistrias (1776–1831) was born into a noble family of Corfu with ancestry from Istria, then a dependency of Venice (Figure 26). After studying medicine, philosophy, and law in Padua, he served as minister and later chief minister of the short-lived Septinsular Republic (1799–1807). His talents were appreciated by the Ionian-born Russian envoy Count George Mocenigo, who facilitated Capodistrias's entry into the diplomatic service of Tsar Alexander I. He brilliantly succeeded in his first mission of securing the unity, stability, and independence of Switzerland, before taking part in the Congress of Vienna, where his reservations toward absolutist restoration earned him Prince Klemens von Metternich's life-long enmity. He was then appointed foreign minister of Russia, jointly with Count Karl von Nesselrode. When he was approached by

FIGURE 26   Sir Thomas Lawrence, *John, Count Capo d'Istria*
(1776–1831), 1818–1819. Oil on canvas. Royal Collection Trust.

Mavrokordatos and leading members of the Philiki Etaireia, the secret society
which had undertaken to prepare the ground for a national uprising, Capodistrias declined both the leadership and an intercession to his sovereign, Tsar Alexander I, on behalf of the Greek cause. For one thing, he was not alone in
judging the whole project ill-conceived and untimely; and he would never attempt to cause his adopted country to be at odds with the rest of the great
powers.

Undeterred by Capodistrias's reaction, the Etaireia self-servingly clung to the
myth of Russian support even after the tsar's opposition became clear. The uprisings in the Danubian Principalities and the Peloponnese, in February and
March 1821, broke out during the Congress of Laibach (Ljubljana), where representatives of the great powers, including the emperors of Austria and Russia,
were considering steps against revolutionary movements in Spain, Portugal, and

Naples. The news that a rebel army headed by his former aide-de-camp Prince Alexandros Ypsilantis had crossed into Ottoman territory from Russia shook the tsar. The Austrian foreign minister, Prince Metternich, played upon Alexander's worst fears, presenting the uprising as part of a pan-European revolutionary conspiracy. True to his fame as the founding spirit behind the Holy Alliance, the tsar publicly condemned the uprising and decommissioned Ypsilantis from the ranks of the Russian army. No further action was deemed necessary, as Alexander consented to the intervention of an Ottoman army against the rebel forces in the principalities.

The Russian denunciation was a major blow for the Greek revolutionaries, who were seeking to enlist the support of local chiefs across the Balkans for their cause. More importantly, Ypsilantis and the Etaireia failed to take advantage of two rebellions against the Ottoman authority that had preceded the Greek uprising. One was Tudor Vladimirescu's revolt, which primarily aimed to rid the peasants of Wallachia of landlord exploitation. When he refused to join Ypsilantis's campaign, the latter's men, suspicious of Vladimirescu's contacts with the Ottomans, seized him and put him to death. In Greece proper, the Etaireia failed to promote even a tactical alliance with Ali Pasha, the insubordinate satrap of Epirus and southern Albania, who had been fighting for survival against the sultan's forces since the summer of 1820. Distrustful of Ali's intentions, Mavrokordatos, from his position of influence in central Greece, discouraged military cooperation with the pasha. The latter was eventually defeated and killed in January 1822. His rebellion, however, benefited the Greek cause to the extent that it tied down large Ottoman forces during the crucial first year of the uprising.

Despite these odds, the Greek revolutionaries could still benefit from the lack of unanimity between the powers on the Greek and other questions, as manifested during the lengthy congress at Laibach. Faced with the counterrevolutionary zeal of Austria and Russia, Britain and France rejected intervention. The British premier, Lord Liverpool, and his "Europhobic" foreign secretary, Viscount Castlereagh, opposed collective action on behalf of embattled European crowns, in whose fate Britain had little stake. As a venerable Greek diplomatic historian, Michail T. Lascaris, has noted, it was not so much the Greek uprising but the prospect of a Russo-Ottoman conflict that really upset the great powers (Lascaris 2006, 82). Fearing that it would use the Greeks as a pretext for expansion, Castlereagh's policy was to avoid giving Russia "any just or even plausible motive for war" (Bass 2008, 62).

It was the sultan's harsh reprisals, involving the execution of numerous Phanariots and prelates, and widespread atrocities against the Christian Orthodox of the empire that shocked Europe and raised the prospect of intervention. After the hanging of Patriarch Grigorios V, on Easter Day 1821, his excommunication of the revolutionaries notwithstanding, Capodistrias convinced the tsar to approve an ultimatum demanding an end to the indiscriminate persecution of Christians, the protection of their religious practice, and the withdrawal of Ottoman forces from the Danubian Principalities. The Ottoman Reis Efendi (foreign minister) denied that the Porte had declared an all-out war against the Christians and implicitly rejected the ultimatum. In response, Russia withdrew its ambassador.

Though Alexander reckoned "a war with Turkey inviting and popular" (Bass 2008, 62), he would not provoke the reaction of Austria and Britain. Capodistrias was stressing to him the merits of intervention by conservative powers, such as Russia, which would prevent Greece from becoming a hotbed of liberal revolutionaries. His efforts, however, were undercut by Metternich, who did his utmost to destroy the tsar's confidence in Capodistrias, and Castlereagh, who raised the specter of general conflagration. "Humanity shudders at the scenes" unfolding in Greece, Castlereagh admitted to Alexander in mid-July 1821; yet, Ottoman savagery notwithstanding, European peace and stability were at stake and should not be endangered for the sake of a "moral duty under loose notions of humanity and amendment" (Bass 2008, 63).

Under pressure from the ambassadors of Britain and Austria, the Porte eventually agreed to withdraw its troops from north of the Danube and offered guarantees to its Christian subjects, including an amnesty to the Greek rebels who laid down their arms. Himself under pressure from Castlereagh and Metternich, Alexander I considered the terms of the ultimatum satisfied and desisted from further escalation. As he wrote to Capodistrias, who still advocated intervention, a declaration of war against the Ottomans would play into the hands of "the Paris directing committee" of revolutionaries and "no government will be left standing." He had concluded that a war with Turkey should be avoided "at all costs." (Heraclides and Dialla 2015, 109) Defeated, Capodistrias took an indefinite leave of absence in August 1822, possibly on the same day that his rival, Castlereagh, took his own life with a penknife.

As the rulers of Europe shunned intervention, the Greek revolutionaries pinned their hopes on public opinion. Their declarations and constitutions, drafted mostly by diaspora Greeks, versed in the teachings of the European Enlightenment, aimed not so much to transform a premodern institutional landscape as to attract the sympathies of Europe. The problem was that their democratic outlook, however appealing to liberal circles, was bound to upset the conservative ruling elites, steeped in the principle of legitimacy. Heeding Capodistrias's advice, Greek assemblies and representatives abroad strove to disclaim any association with contemporary revolutionary stirrings elsewhere. Instead, they presented their undertaking as a "legitimate" struggle of national self-preservation against an oriental despot whose rule, resting on violent subjugation, was fundamentally alien to the principles of European civilization. That civilization, the Greeks were careful to stress, owed much to their glorious ancestors. As proof of their intention to conform to the norms of conservative Europe, the revolutionary authorities underlined the provisional character of their institutions, in anticipation of a monarchy under a member of a European royal family. It was an option that, ideally, might stir the interest of one or more powerful states in the fate of the Greek struggle. Yet this quest for respectability and recognition was an uphill task, as demonstrated by the refusal of the great powers meeting at Verona to admit a Greek delegation, in October 1822.

At Verona, the powers minus Britain adopted a resolution which invited the Porte to pacify Greece. Coming in the wake of the wholesale ransacking of the prosperous island of Chios and the slaughter or enslavement of its Greek population, this statement seemed both ironic and hopelessly out of step with public sentiment in Europe. The cruelty of Ottoman reactions appeared to confirm the stereotype of "Turkish barbarity" at a time when the educated public on both sides of the Atlantic, under the spell of classicism and romanticism, was warming up to the Greek cause. Across Europe and in the United States, the sympathizers of the Greek struggle formed numerous philhellenic societies. In Russia, co-religionism guaranteed the sympathy of the Orthodox Church and even the illiterate peasant communities. However, only in Britain would elitist bodies, such as the London Greek Committee and its regional offshoots, influence the similarly elitist policymakers to some effect.

The tangible impact of the philhellenic movement was the arrival of some one thousand volunteers to Greece and its contribution to the finances of the provisional Greek authorities. Although most private donations came from the United States, members of the London committee played a decisive role in negotiating and managing the first Greek loan, which was floated in the London money market in March 1824. After the deduction of a high-risk interest rate and various expenses, out of a nominal £800,000 the Greeks would receive considerably less than half that amount. As a result of this and a second loan contracted in early 1825, the London money market and, at least indirectly, the British government acquired a vested interest in the survival of their Greek debtor. The first installment of these loans reached Greece shortly after the death of the most celebrated Philhellene, Lord Byron, who was supposed to supervise its disbursement. Yet the poet's death at Mesolonghi proved a publicity windfall for the philhellenic movement and helped to further swing public opinion in favor of the Greek cause. These developments and pressure from the press, Christian groups such as the parliamentary faction of evangelical Christians led by William Wilberforce, and high-profile intellectuals, like Jeremy Bentham, were a significant factor in rendering the policy of nonintervention hard to defend (see Roderick Beaton, "Philhellenism," in this volume).

The power most decidedly hostile to the Greek uprising was Austria. For its chancellor, Metternich, the great powers had a right and duty to take counter-revolutionary measures and intervene across the board to suppress uprisings against legitimate rule. He also considered the entire philhellenic movement part of "that very villainous game which takes religion and humanity for a pretext in order to upset all regular order of things" (Bass 2008, 132). His views were shared among conservative circles in Europe. In Britain, the victor at Waterloo and aspiring Tory leader, the Duke of Wellington, could envisage great power intervention only "with a view to restore the power of a legitimate government" (Bass 2008, 122).

Quite misplaced proved the Greek expectations of recognition from across the Atlantic. Having received a Greek appeal dated March 25, 1822, Secretary of State John Quincy Adams used an Independence Day address to articulate what could be termed a liberal doctrine of nonintervention: while wishing well to those fighting under "the standard of freedom and independence," the United States should "not go abroad, in search of monsters to destroy." (Bass 2008, 89) In December 1822, President James Monroe also refrained from extending recognition to revolutionary Greece. While expressing hope that the Greek nation would gain its independence, he offered nothing but the "great example" of the United States as a supporter of "the cause of liberty and humanity." Monroe resisted domestic pressure to include Greece in his famous doctrine enunciated a year later, whereby the US government sought to deter European intervention against the newly independent former Spanish and Portuguese colonies in the Americas. However, he expressed his "most ardent wishes" that "Greece will become again an independent nation" (Bass 2008, 93, 95). In summer 1825, newly elected president Adams sent a secret envoy to Greece with a view to revising the US position. The attempt proved abortive when the envoy, William C. Somerville, fell ill and died before reaching his destination. Washington would not recognize Greece until 1833 (see Ioannis Evrigenis, "American Philhellenism," in this volume).

Last but not least, the Ottoman government steadfastly rejected the prospect of outside intervention in a conflict that it considered a strictly domestic matter (see further H. Şükrü Ilıcak, "Ottoman Context," in this volume). "Why do not Christian Sovereigns interfere to prevent the Emperor of Russia from sending his subjects to Siberia?" Reis Efendi asked the British ambassador, on the occasion of the latter's demarche over the Chios massacre. "Because they know very well what answer they would receive! Thus there is one law of humanity for Turkey and another for Russia!" (Bass 2008, 68) In Ottoman eyes, European double standards were further confirmed by the selective projection of atrocity stories from the war zone. Indeed, the Philhellenes proved adept at excusing Greek excesses, citing precedents of European atrocities or the human impulse to avenge "centuries of galling and intolerable oppression" (Heraclides and Dialla 2015, 109).

The Road to Navarino

The noninterventionist bloc of European powers appeared to crack by the time of the Congress of Verona, which was to prove the last of its kind. This opposition was manifested when the Liverpool government withdrew its representative from the congress, on the initiative of Castlereagh's successor, George Canning (1770–1827) (Figure 27). The new foreign secretary had read Classics and

FIGURE 27   Frank Moss Bennett, after Sir Thomas Lawrence, *Portrait of George Canning,* early twentieth century. Oil on canvas. Oxford and Cambridge Club, London.

Law at Oxford before entering parliament, aged twenty-three. A charismatic orator, he served in various Tory cabinets, twice as foreign secretary (1807–1809 and 1822–27). He succeeded the incapacitated Lord Liverpool as prime minister in April 1827 but he died a mere 119 days later. His policy ensured that the Greek War of Independence would be treated as a European problem rather than a domestic matter of the Ottoman Empire.

Like his prime minister, Canning was opposed to Britain's joining the continental powers in "policing action," be that in Italy, Spain, or Latin America. Canning, in particular, sympathized with the cause of Greek liberty. Yet, in line with his predecessor and former rival, Castlereagh, he was eager to avoid a war between Russia and the Ottoman Empire. For the time being, he was in favor of keeping the latter as a bulwark against Russian expansion and feared that "if war occurred, Russia would gobble Greece at one mouthful and Turkey at the next" (Heraclides and Dialla 2015, 111). In order to prevent the unilateral intervention of the Russians, he would later engage them in seeking a joint settlement of the Greek crisis.

An important development occurred in March 1823 when, though reaffirming British neutrality, Canning formally recognized the Greek revolutionaries as belligerents, giving them the protection of the laws and customs of war. He presented this move as intended to bring the hostilities in Greece "within the regulated limits of civilised" warfare (Bass 2008, 114) and, above all, to protect British shipping interests. Indeed, recognition of belligerency did not imply diplomatic support for the insurgents but it would not fail to be received as an unfriendly act by the Porte.

The tide was turning in St. Petersburg, too. In addition to the shuddering impact of Ottoman atrocities, Russian elites were upset by the decrease of wheat exports from southern Russia through the Turkish Straits by more than half between 1819 and 1822, as a result of Ottoman restrictions related to the Greek emergency. In January 1824, Russia invited the other great powers to consider a pacification plan for Greece on the basis of a joint mediation that would lead to the establishment of three autonomous Greek principalities. Both the Ottomans and the Greeks rejected the plan, which Metternich also disliked as bound to establish a dangerous precedent. Canning, who had always been averse to Russia's collective diplomacy, withdrew British participation from the conference, which would sit at St. Petersburg for nearly a year. Mavrokordatos, the Greek foreign secretary who considered Britain Greece's best hope, wrote to Canning protesting that the Russians actually aimed to bring the proposed statelets under their influence and asked for British mediation. Replying to the Greek appeal in December 1824, Canning stated that Britain would mediate only if invited by both belligerents, but significantly added that it would not be party to an agreement unacceptable to the Greeks. Incensed by what he saw as British obstructionism, Tsar Alexander vowed not to talk to the British on the Greek question ever again.

On April 7, 1825, the summit of the European Concert minus Britain in the Russian capital agreed on the principle of intervention in the Greek crisis and demanded that the Porte agree to it. With Metternich distracted by his wife's serious illness, even the Austrian delegation agreed to try threatening the Ottomans with possible recognition of an independent Greek state in the Peloponnese. Meanwhile, swallowing his pride, Sultan Mahmud II had asked his nominal vassal Mohammed Ali Pasha of Egypt to help him put down the Greek uprising in return for concessions over Crete and the Peloponnese. Counting on Ali's French-organized forces for a swift solution of the Greek impasse, the sultan was in no mood to countenance European intervention.

Weakened by their endless internal feuds, the overwhelmingly irregular Greek fighters proved no match for the Egyptian army commanded by Ali's son, Ibrahim Pasha. In July 1825, desperate for outside intervention, Greek leaders petitioned Liverpool's government, offering to place their nation under British protection. This so-called Act of Submission was subsequently repeated to France and Russia by antagonistic Greek factions, which were by then commonly identified as "French" and "Russian" parties, in addition to the "English" one (Koliopoulos 2002, 48). In early October 1825, Dimitrios Miaoulis on behalf of the provisional Greek government submitted the "act" to the Foreign Office, in London. Although Canning rejected the protectorate offer, he did not exclude the prospect of British mediation aimed at "a fair and safe compromise." (Heraclides and Dialla 2015, 113) The British foreign secretary wanted the Porte to accept some kind of autonomous Greece—it hoped short of full independence. His rival within the Tory hierarchy, Wellington, considered that great power intervention would only serve Russian interests. Instead, he preferred Britain to align itself with Austria and, if possible, France, in order to deter Russian meddling in the affairs of the Ottoman Empire. However, even he had come to realize that "the Turkish government is so oppressive and odious to all mankind that we could scarcely expect to carry the country with us" in helping the Ottomans (Bass 2008, 122).

In October 1825, the Russian ambassador in London told Canning that his government had "positive information" of an Ottoman-Egyptian scheme, once Ibrahim had conquered Greece, "to remove the whole Greek population, carrying them off into slavery in Egypt or elsewhere," and repopulate the country with Egyptians and other Muslims (Bass 2008, 124–125). The news from Greece seemed to lend credence to the "barbarization project," which, however, was denied by both Ibrahim and the Ottoman Reis Efendi. Canning, however, could not dismiss it out of hand. "I begin to think that the time approaches when *something must be done*," he wrote to the British ambassador in Paris (Heraclides and Dialla 2015, 114). Apparently, he was thinking in terms of great power intervention that would revise the existing order in the Levant. Yet Canning's sympathy for the Greek cause always had to be weighed against his fear of a Russo-Turkish war that, in his view, "would spread throughout Europe" (Richmond 2014, 142).

"I hope to save Greece through the agency of the Russian name upon the fears of Turkey without war," was how George Canning summarized his policy to his cousin Stratford, the new British ambassador in Constantinople, in late April 1826. However, exceptional diplomatic acumen was needed to overcome the mutual suspicion arising from diverging interests in the Levant: Britain's interest in keeping its imperial route to India free from great power interference was running against Russia's desire to gain access to the Mediterranean via the sultan's shaky realm. Matters were further complicated by Alexander's death in December 1825, just as the tsar had almost resolved on war with the Ottoman Empire.

Significantly, Canning entrusted the coordination with Russia to Wellington, who visited St. Petersburg as royal envoy to Alexander's successor, Nicholas I, in March 1826. Wellington found the new tsar unwilling to commit Russia to supporting the Greeks. He told his guest that his "quarrel with the Porte was not about the Greeks, but for his own just rights under treaties which the Porte had violated" (Bass 2008, 129), namely, the treaty of Bucharest of 1812 and especially its terms regarding the status of the Danubian Principalities and Russian acquisitions in the Caucasus. Although the tsar considered himself entitled to settle these issues with the Sultan alone, he agreed that the Greek question should be dealt with in concert with the other Powers.

The first step toward collective action was taken on April 4, 1826, when Wellington, the tsar's foreign minister, Count Nesselrode, and the Russian ambassador to London, Prince Lieven, signed a secret protocol at St. Petersburg, which, for the first time, recognized the prospect of Greek secession in the form of an autonomous state tributary to the sultan. If the Porte disagreed, mediation and autonomy were to remain on the table. A self-denying clause was inserted, renouncing any "augmentation of territory, any exclusive influence," or commercial advantage on the part of the signatories. If mediation failed, the two powers could intervene jointly or separately between the warring parties. It was this latter clause, which could lead to unilateral Russian intervention, that produced much criticism of Wellington's handling in London and which British diplomacy sought to rectify in the subsequent, tripartite treaty with France, more than a year later.

By the St. Petersburg Protocol, Britain and Russia invited the other three powers of the European Concert to accede to its terms and join Russia (but not

Britain) in guaranteeing "the final transaction which shall reconcile Turkey and Greece" (Crawley 2014, 62). As Vienna and Berlin rejected the proposal outright, Canning personally tried to draw in the French. He needed their participation in order to keep the Russians in check. Until then, Paris had displayed a very limited interest in the fate of Greece. French caution was partly due to the association with the khedive of Egypt, whose armed forces were being organized by French officers. At the same time, philhellenic feeling was growing strong, bringing together personalities from across the political spectrum as well as the arts. Last but not least, a Greek faction, in concert with the Comité grec de Paris, had canvassed the candidacy of an Orleanist prince for the Greek throne. Yet this was not an end in itself but a move designed to frustrate the appointment of Capodistrias, who was quite erroneously considered a tool of Russia.

According to a French memorandum from January 1826, the Greeks faced certain annihilation, if France did not listen to "the voice of religion and humanity as well as that of policy" (Bass 2008, 135). In view of its talks with Britain, France suspended its assistance to Egypt. Yet, as a condition for joining the alliance of the willing that Canning was promoting, Paris proposed the signing of a formal treaty between the three powers. In Constantinople, Sultan Mahmud showed no signs of complying with the Anglo-Russian initiative. He felt his grip on power strengthened after crushing the rebellious janissaries in June 1826, thus removing a major stumbling block to reform; and as a result of Ibrahim's campaign, which had resulted in the capture of Mesolonghi earlier in that year, only pockets of resistance remained in mainland Greece. It seemed reasonable to expect that, before long, outside mediation would become meaningless.

The way to a tripartite intervention in Greece was cleared in the spring of 1827, after Russia accepted the signing of a formal treaty. Canning agreed, over Wellington's strong objections. Having succeeded Liverpool as prime minister, Canning convened a conference in London, which would intermittently meet until the final settlement of the Greek question, five years later. There, the representatives of Britain, France, and Russia signed a treaty on July 6, 1827, asking for an immediate armistice as a precondition for negotiations on the basis of the St. Petersburg Protocol. The Treaty of London was probably the first instance when "sentiments of humanity" as well as "the interests of the repose of Europe" were invoked in order to justify intervention against a sovereign state. Oddly enough, the terms of the treaty were to be imposed without the use of force against any of the two contending parties, which, after the Greek government accepted an armistice, meant the Ottomans and the Egyptians. Indeed, Mahmud once again rejected any foreign interference in his relations with his own subjects. As a defiant gesture, two large fleets, one Ottoman, the other

Egyptian, set sail for the Peloponnese. Consequently, the three governments assigned the commanders of their squadrons "in the seas of the Levant" a near impossible mission: to practically blockade the Ottoman-Egyptian forces operating against revolutionary Greece but, at the same time, to avoid hostilities "unless the Turks persist in forcing" the blockade (Richmond 2014, 165).

Although the three signatories to the London Treaty were committed to act in concert, their individual considerations varied widely. Britain sought to restrain Russia from going to war with the Ottomans and disrupt the imperial route to India, Russia wished to consolidate its recent gains and increase its influence in the Balkan peninsula, and France wished to keep both Britain and Russia in check. As Crawley (2014, 77) put it, "the mutual suspicion of the Powers was the Greeks' best security."

Domestic developments would also enable the Greek side to take advantage of the shifting diplomatic context. Faced with mortal danger, the exhausted warring factions were persuaded to invite Capodistrias, whom the Third National Assembly had nominated governor of Greece in March 1827. As a diplomatic figure of international standing and untarnished by the preceding civil strife, Capodistrias appeared ideally suited to try and capitalize on the momentum created by the incipient three-power mediation. Although Mavrokordatos had also attempted to exploit the rivalries among the European powers to Greece's advantage, Capodistrias's diplomatic acumen and foreign connections were unparalleled. Besides, Mavrokordatos had compromised himself by his involvement in partisan feuds and would later oppose the new governor.

In mid-September 1827, the Ottoman and Egyptian fleets assembled in the Bay of Navarino, on the southwest coast of the Peloponnese. The Allied commanders were ordered not to allow this force, which greatly outnumbered their squadrons combined, to exit the bay. All three commanders sought clarification regarding their mandate and terms of engagement, in case friendly persuasion proved ineffective. Under the circumstances it was not realistic to expect instructions from their capitals, thus the burden of sorting out the contradictory terms of the treaty fell on the ambassadors in Constantinople. In an oft-quoted dispatch dated September 1, Stratford Canning (1786–1880) conveyed to the British admiral, Edward Codrington, what he assumed to be the common view of his colleagues:

> Although it is clearly the intention of the Allied Governments to avoid, if possible, anything that may bring on war, yet the prevention of supplies, as stated in your instructions, is ultimately to be enforced, if necessary, and when all other means are exhausted, by cannon shot. (Bass 2009, 139; Richmond 2014, 170–171)

Stratford Canning's contribution to the course of events can hardly be exaggerated. Having entered the Foreign Office in 1807, he served four terms in Constantinople, first as minister plenipotentiary (1810–1812) and then as British ambassador (1825–1828, 1831–1832, and 1841–1858). He had been closely involved in diplomatic deliberations on the Greek question ever since he represented Britain at the abortive St. Petersburg conference of 1824. He was instrumental in interpreting the London Treaty of 1827 in a way that facilitated the subsequent forceful intervention of the three-power fleet at Navarino. Admiral Codrington immediately sent out Canning's dispatch of September 1 as a general order to his fleet.

Over the following weeks, Stratford Canning and his French and Russian colleagues, Armand-Charles Guilleminot and Alexandre Ribeaupierre, vainly tried to break through the diplomatic stalemate with the Porte. At the end of the month, Codrington and his French counterpart, Rear Admiral Henri de Rigny, met with Ibrahim and informed him of their orders not to let his ships depart from Navarino. After protesting, Ibrahim pledged to suspend operations and await fresh instructions from Constantinople. Sensing a showdown, Metternich offered mediation to save the Ottomans from their predicament. The Ottoman's acceptance on October 23 came too late to have an effect on the turn of events.

Faced with breaches of Egyptian good faith, the commanders of the Allied fleet, which had recently been reinforced by the Russian squadron under Admiral Lodewijk van Heyden, warned Ibrahim to desist from his devastating campaign or else face "the immediate consequences of a refusal or evasion" (Bass 2008, 142). In order to bring their determination home, the Allied commanders led their fleet into Navarino Bay. Tension mounted and in the ensuing naval battle, on October 20, the Ottoman-Egyptian fleet was destroyed. (See Robert Holland, "Navarino," in this volume.)

As a result of this battle, the last major engagement of the sailing-ship era, the Ottoman Empire lost its ability to reassert its control over southern Greece. Navarino also marked a point of no return for the Greek policy of the three powers: it made it all but impossible for them to go back on the emancipation of Greece, even if they wanted to, as was the case with Wellington, who assumed the premiership in January 1828. Last but not least, as an omen of things to come, several official documents from the late 1820s would describe the naval battle at Navarino as a humanitarian operation, the first of its kind in history.

Toward the Diplomatic Settlement of the Greek Question

The news of the battle stunned Europe. At one extreme, the Russians relished the fact that Ottoman sea power was severely crippled, while their own now extended to the eastern Mediterranean. The event was enthusiastically received by the French public, though less so by its government. For Metternich, however, it was nothing short of a "frightful catastrophe" (Heraclides and Dialla 2015, 118). In Britain, the successors of George Canning, who had died in August, appeared genuinely embarrassed. In the king's speech to Parliament on the occasion of the formation of his government, Wellington lamented the destruction of the fleet of a "friendly power" at Navarino as an "untoward event," not to be repeated (Woodhouse 1978, 348).

The Ottoman government angrily demanded condemnation of the "tragic episode" as unintended, and compensation and recognition of its right to treat its subjects as it saw fit; pending satisfaction, the Porte imposed an embargo on all European ships calling on Ottoman ports. In their reply, the Allied ambassadors admitted that the battle had indeed been unintended but insisted that the Ottomans had opened fire first, and reaffirmed the commitment of their governments to an armistice and mediation on the basis of the London Treaty. In reply, the Porte denied the powers' right to concern themselves with the fate of dominions "held by conquest under the sanction of God" (Richmond 2014, 175). In December 1827, the three ambassadors left Constantinople. Shortly afterward, the sultan repudiated the Convention of Akkerman of October 1826, which had satisfied the Russian demands in the Danubian Principalities and the Caucasus. Moreover, in his capacity as caliph, he reminded all Muslims of their duty to defend their religion against an as yet unidentified enemy. Significantly, the sultan's only ally, Mohammed Ali, far from sharing his suzerain's bellicosity, was now inclined to negotiate the withdrawal of his troops from the Peloponnese.

At last, Russia had a valid pretext to go to war, while France was putting pressure on its two allies to allow the dispatch of a French expeditionary force to expel Ibrahim. Rather than try to wield influence in a new Greece, Britain lapsed into inaction and then, under Wellington's premiership, would vainly try to reverse the consequences of the London Treaty and Navarino. Wellington's hostility was based on his conviction that Greece was destined to fall under the influence of France or Russia, or both, and, therefore, become essentially hostile to Britain. Against the advice of Ambassador Canning, Wellington and his foreign secretary, Lord Aberdeen, would insist on Ottoman suzerainty over Greece as a lesser evil, and they opposed further collective action as proposed by France and Russia. As a result, for more than two critical years, Britain would helplessly watch as the other two powers, backed by armed force, appeared to seize the initiative in the Greek question.

On April 25, 1828, the long-awaited Russo-Turkish war broke out, though, as Anderson noted, the Greek question played only a secondary part. The limited objectives of the Russian government, that is the reaffirmation of the terms of the Akkerman Convention, owed much to the realization, corroborated by a special study commissioned by Tsar Nicholas, that "the advantages of the preservation of the Ottoman Empire outweigh its disadvantages" (Anderson 1978, 71). The same study had examined and rejected a plan by Capodistrias providing for the reorganization of the Balkan peninsula as a confederation of five new independent states (Dacia, Serbia, Macedonia, Epirus, and Greece). Unaware of Russian moderation, Metternich unsuccessfully tried to convene a great power conference on the fate of the Near East as a whole.

Meanwhile, Capodistrias had arrived in Greece in January, after touring the capitals of the three signatories of the London Treaty. While in London, he welcomed the treaty as delivering his people from "the calamities which would have inevitably ended up by annihilating the Hellenes" (Bass 2008, 135). Unfortunately, Canning had died on the eve of his visit and the new government did nothing to help him secure one of his main tasks, namely, the raising of yet another loan for his de facto state. Subsequently, Capodistrias would concentrate on securing full independence, rather than autonomy, for Greece, and the greatest possible extension of its boundaries. He intended to further Greek territorial claims through the steady nibbling of Ottoman strongholds south of the Arta-Volos line. To that end, he sought to attract foreign organizers and even troops. However, stiff British opposition frustrated his persistent attempt to have General Nicolas Joseph Maison, commander of the French force which had landed in the Peloponnese on the heels of the departing Egyptian army, extend his operations to the north of the isthmus of Corinth.

The French expedition to the Morea in 1828–1829 under one of the great veterans of Napoleon's armies, General Maison, was an important operation in terms of supervising the evacuation of the Egyptian forces from the peninsula and ensuring the release of thousands of civilian hostages. The presence of the French force in liberated Greece was due largely to the mutual distrust between Britain and Russia and made France appear as an honest broker in the Greek question. King Charles X had been a supporter of the Greek cause and the early stages of Greek state building had benefited from his generous economic aid to the country. The mission of General Maison was part of his policy in support of Greek independence. Charles's overthrow by the July 1830 revolution in France brought French philhellenic policy to an end.

General Maison's French mission, however, left an important legacy beyond its military mandate. The military mission was accompanied by an *Expédition Scientifique de Morée* under the supervision of the three academies of the Institut de France, whose aim was to collect and compile "material of all kinds in the peninsula of the Peloponnese with the purpose of publishing a work like the one produced by the Mission to Egypt" (Papadopoulos 1971, 9).

Setting up the *Mission Scientifique en Egypte* as its model meant a very ambitious standard for the work of the new mission to the Morea, but the result of about eight months of research, from March 1829 to January 1830, proved to be up to the challenge. The mission's main work focused on three subjects: archeology, geography, and natural science (botany, zoology, geology). In all these disciplines invaluable data were recorded through archeological topographic surveys, excavations, and recordings at major sites; geographical surveys using the triangulation system which for the first time produced maps of great accuracy; and detailed demographic data and population censuses, which proved invaluable to the administration of the new state. The imposing volumes of the work of the *Expédition Scientifique de Morée* laid in fact the foundations for serious academic work in liberated Greece.

In October 1828, under instructions from the London conference, the ambassadors of the three allied powers proceeded to the Greek island of Poros to work out a blueprint for the status of Greece, on the basis of an autonomous and tributary entity under a hereditary prince. With regard to its territory, the future state was to include "a fair proportion of the Greek population" who had taken up arms against the sultan. Steadily lobbied by Capodistrias and led by a Stratford Canning loyal to the spirit of his cousin's policy, the ambassadors gave a decidedly pro-Greek interpretation to their mandate. In their report, submitted in mid-December, the ambassadors concluded in favor of a line drawn from the Gulf of Volos in the east to the Gulf of Arta in the west, including the large island of Euboea. They also suggested the inclusion of the islands of Samos and Crete.

Paris and St. Petersburg accepted the Arta-Volos line but London objected, considering the report only as a basis for renewed and, as it turned out, dilatory negotiations. The British government had already attempted to prejudice the territorial settlement through a protocol, signed in November, which offered a provisional tripartite guarantee only to the Peloponnese and the Cyclades. Capodistrias's demarches to France and Russia, and, more decisively, the resumption of the Russian offensive against the Ottomans led to Britain's acceptance of the Arta-Volos line in a new tripartite protocol signed in London on March 22, 1829. Still, on British insistence, Samos and Crete were excluded. Unhappy with his government's maneuvering, Ambassador Canning submitted his resignation. He would return to the Ottoman capital nearly three years later, in January 1832, with the question of Greece's frontiers still pending.

Capodistrias indicated acceptance of the 1829 London Protocol, though not without protesting its territorial provisions as well as the exclusion of the Greeks from the selection of their future hereditary ruler. The sultan, still locked in war with Russia, rejected European mediation for a few more months. Although it took them more than a year to overpower Ottoman resistance, by August 20, 1829, the Russians had captured Adrianople. With a Russian advance on Constantinople looking imminent, Mahmud had little choice but to come to terms. In addition to territorial and other concessions, the Treaty of Adrianople of September 14, 1829, forced the Porte to accept the London Treaty and Protocol and thus recognize Greek autonomy under Ottoman suzerainty. It was Capodistrias's turn to reject the tributary status. His policy benefited from the fact that, as a result of the Russo-Turkish war, Austria and Britain no longer looked upon the Ottoman Empire as an effective barrier to Russian expansion. Metternich and Wellington feared that it would be easier for Russia to gain sway over a tributary Greek state, both directly and by bullying its suzerain, the sultan. As a lesser evil, they were prepared to accept a completely independent but miniscule state (Map 13).

On February 3, 1830, the three-power conference in London signed three protocols confirming the independence of Greece, though without the provinces of Aitolia-Akarnania, across from the British-held Ionian islands. Capodistrias tried to delay his response invoking requirements of the Greek constitution. He also tried to gain leverage from the selection of Prince Leopold of Saxe-Coburg by the three powers as Greece's future sovereign. Leopold, with whom Capodistrias had been in contact for some time, had been related to the Hanoverians through his deceased wife, though this hardly made Wellington and Aberdeen more forthcoming, especially on Greek territorial aspirations.

Progressively, Capodistrias's standing with France and Britain, in particular, suffered on account of reports from their diplomatic representatives ("residents") to Greece, who had arrived in autumn 1828. Based on misinformation from disgruntled Philhellenes but also from the Greek governor's domestic enemies, reports to London and Paris portrayed him as a Russian surrogate. It was an unjust picture. As Lord Aberdeen would later confess, Capodistrias "loved Greece" and "he never conceived the idea of sacrificing her to Russia" (Woodhouse 1978, 510). Rather, British and French suspicions and hostility toward him often worked as a self-fulfilling prophecy. This was amply demonstrated during the last summer of Capodistrias's presidency and life, when Anglo-French inaction helped to prolong a rebellion centered on the island of Ydra, while the Greek governor vainly waited for concerted three-power action. Eventually, he had to resort to the aid of the Russian squadron.

Meanwhile, events beyond the Greeks' control delayed the settlement of their fate for nearly three years. The powers did not hurry to respond to Leopold's conditions for accepting the throne of Greece—territorial, financial, and

Vienna

Budapest

RUSSIAN
EMPIRE

BESSARABIA
1812 to Russia

Jassy   Kishinev

MOLDAVIA
1829

HABSBURG EMPIRE

WALLACHIA
1829

Belgrade   Dragatsani   Bucharest

PRINCIPALITY
OF SERBIA
1830

DALMATIA

BLACK
SEA

MONTENEGRO
1852

OTTOMAN
EMPIRE

ADRIATIC
SEA

Constantinople

ITALY

Thessaloniki

Ioannina

Corfu Isl.

AEGEAN
SEA

OTTOMAN
EMPIRE

IONIAN ISLANDS
BRITISH
PROTECTORATE
1815-1864   Lefkada Isl.

Smyrna

Chios Isl.

Cephalonia Isl.

Athens

1834
Samos Isl.

IONIAN
SEA

Nafplio

Zakynthos Isl.

KINGDOM
OF GREECE
1830

Kythira Isl.

Crete Isl.
1830-1840 to Egypt

Map 13
The Balkan Peninsula at the time
of Greek independence c.1830

Ottoman Domains 1830
1830 Date of independence
1829 Date of autonomy

constitutional—and the prince renounced his candidacy, in May 1830. Capodistrias was unjustly blamed for this development, which, nonetheless, reinforced his argument that a reduced Greek state was not viable. However, for more than a year, the attention of Europe's great powers was diverted to the successive crises triggered by revolts in France, Italy, Russian Poland, and, particularly, the Low Countries, where the Belgians successfully seceded from the Dutch crown. The fate of the new state crossed with that of Greece, as Leopold was offered the Belgian crown and was duly enthroned in July 1831.

Four factors facilitated the extension of Greece's frontiers back to the Arta-Volos line when, after a fourteen-month hiatus, the London conference reconvened in September 1831: first, the need to improve the offer to the country's prospective sovereign; second, the death of King George IV, Wellington's downfall, and the pro-Greek outlook of the new Whig government, especially its foreign secretary, Lord Palmerston; third, the fact that the powers had never appointed representatives on the commission which was supposed to delineate the Greek-Ottoman frontier, according to the February 1830 protocols; and fourth, the appointment of Charles Maurice de Talleyrand-Perigord, the inveterate French diplomat, as ambassador to London by the new "citizen-king" Louis Philippe with a mandate to negotiate the revision of the 1830 protocols. However, before he was able to receive the good news from London, Capodistrias was assassinated by disaffected members of a Maniot clan, on September 27, 1831. There followed a period of renewed anarchy, which necessitated another round of multilateral diplomacy on Greece.

Having abandoned Wellington's obstructionism, Palmerston entrusted Stratford Canning with the mission of persuading the Porte to accept the independent status and the frontiers of Greece. Back in Constantinople, the British ambassador coordinated his demarches to the Porte with his French and Russian colleagues. Their task was considerably eased by the fact that the sultan would find himself in desperate need of European help against a new threat, the expansionism of his vassal and former ally, Mohammed Ali of Egypt.

The search among the lesser royal houses of Europe produced the underage prince Otto of Wittelsbach as future king of Greece. This selection was sanctioned by the Convention of May 7, 1832, which Palmerston, Lieven, and Talleyrand signed with the special envoy of the king of Bavaria. The protocol also finalized the Greek-Ottoman frontier along the Arta-Volos line and the powers guaranteed a loan of £2,400,000 to the new state, partly intended to cover the indemnity to the Porte for its loss of territory and the expenses of a Bavarian force which was to form the nucleus of the Greek regular army. Although Britain, France, and Russia would subsequently be labeled "guarantor" or even "protecting" powers of Greece, such designations had no foundation in the letter of the treaties, with the partial exception of the loan guarantee. In the early hours of July 22, 1832, the negotiations between the ambassadors and the Porte resulted in the Treaty of Constantinople. Stratford Canning had played no small part in this outcome, having gained the confidence of both Ottomans and Greeks as an honest broker. Under the terms of the treaty, the Porte finally recognized the independence and the frontiers of Greece, in return for support in its war with Mohammed Ali. On the basis of yet another London protocol, signed on August 30, 1832, a five-member committee undertook to fix the new frontiers on the ground. Its work would be completed by the end of 1835.

Despite its inauspicious beginning, the Greek struggle for independence lasted long enough to secure the diplomatic and, crucially, the military intervention of key European powers. That intervention came at a critical moment and ensured that at least part of Greece would not revert to servitude. Subsequently, national liberation movements across the Balkans and beyond would try to follow the Greek path from uprising to statehood through the agency of one or more great powers of Europe. This pattern seems to justify Anderson's exaltation of Greek independence as "an event of European, not merely of Near Eastern significance," which not only manifested the decline of the Ottoman Empire but also "showed that the territorial and ideological *status quo* of 1815 in Europe could be successfully challenged" (Anderson 1978, 76–77).

Ioannis D. Stefanidis

References

Anderson, Matthew Smith. 1978. *The Eastern Question, 1774–1923: A Study in International Relations.* London and Basingstoke.

Bass, Garry. 2008. *Freedom's Battle: The Origins of Humanitarian Intervention.* New York.

Bouvier-Bron, Michelle. 1984. *La mission de Capodistrias en Suisse (1813–1814).* Corfu.

Crawley, Charles William. 2014. *The Question of Greek Independence: A Study of British Policy in the Near East, 1821–1833.* Cambridge.

Dakin, Douglas. 1973. *The Greek Struggle for Independence, 1821–1833.* Berkeley and Los Angeles.

Divani, Lena. 2000. *Η εδαφική ολοκλήρωση της Ελλάδας, 1830–1947* [The territorial integration of Greece, 1830–1947]. Athens.

Driault, Edouard, and Michel Lhéritier.1925–1926. *Histoire diplomatique de la Grèce: De 1821 à nos jours.*Paris.

Heraclides, Alexis, and Ada Dialla. 2015. *Humanitarian Intervention in the Long Nineteenth Century.* Manchester.

Kennedy, Patricia Grimstead. 1969. *The Foreign Ministers of Alexander I: Political Attitudes and the conduct of Russian Diplomacy, 1801–1825.* Berkeley.

Kissinger, Henry. 1957. *A World Restored: Metternich, Castlereagh and the Problems of Peace 1812–22.* Boston.

Koliopoulos, Ioannis. 2002. *Ιστορία της Ελλάδος από το 1800* [History of Greece after 1800]. Vol. 2, *Η διαμόρφωση και η άσκη σητησεθνικ ής πολιτικής* [The development and practice of national policy]. Thessaloniki.

Lascaris, Michail T. 2006. *Το Ανατολικόν Ζήτημα, 1800–1923* [The eastern question, 1800–1923]. Vol. 1, *1800–1878.* Thessaloniki.

Papadopoulos, Stelios A., ed.1971. *Liberated Greece and the Morea Scientific Expedition: The Peytier Album.* Athens.

Papageorgiou, Stefanos. 2005. *Από το γένος στο έθνος. Η θεμελίωση του ελληνικού κράτους, 1821–1862* [From genos to ethnos: The foundation of the Greek state, 1821–1862]. Athens.

Richmond, Steven. 2014. *The Voice of England in the East: Stratford Canning and Diplomacy with the Ottoman Empire.* London.

Rodogno, Davide. 2012. *Against Massacre. Humanitarian Intervention in the Ottoman Empire, 1815–1914: The Emergence of a European Concept and International Practice.* Princeton, NJ.

Šedivý, Miroslav. 2013. *Metternich, the Great Powers and the Eastern Question.* Pilsen.

Skiotis, Dennis N. 1976. "The Greek Revolution: Ali Pasha's Last Gamble." In *Hellenism and the First Greek War of Liberation (1821–1830): Continuity and Change,* edited by Nikiforos P. Diamandouros, Peter W. Topping, and John Peter Anton, 98–109. Thessaloniki.

Woodhouse, Christopher Montague. 1973. *Capodistria: The Founder of Greek Independence.* London and New York.

Intellectuals

The number of intellectuals during the War of Independence was undoubtedly smaller compared to the mass of illiterate people. Though the number of scholars could hardly have exceeded 2 percent of the population, their multi-faceted influence was disproportionate. In becoming a dynamic elite, they intensified their influence on many levels, as educators, spiritual leaders, warriors on the battlefields, administrators appointed to various official positions, even as poets of war songs with contemporary significance. It is evident that for them the revolution was a transformational experience that brought out in them new public abilities beyond their specializations and engaged them directly in social issues. For them this challenge was abrupt because they transmuted scholarship into politics. Through newspaper articles and pamphlets, these liberal Westernized intellectuals generated public debate in support of the insurrection and during the first years, they took on the important task of informing European countries of the real aims of the Greek cause and its international dimensions.

Adamantios Korais (born Smyrna 1748, died Paris 1833), the most influential figure and leading spokesman in the last phase of the Greek Enlightenment, insisted on the political morality that ought to guide his nation's liberation. As a liberal theorist for republicanism, he issued exhortations on how the legal system should function that were close to the ideas of Condorcet and Benjamin Constant. Although he never set foot in Greece, Korais did not agree on the outbreak of the insurrection. He considered it premature, advocating for a slower tempo: had it happened later, the nation would have had a better-educated leadership and would have pursued its liberation with greater caution. In his declining years, he ascribed the misfortunes of the revolution to the lack of education of those who had become involved. The whole endeavor was considered excessively rash by some intellectuals who did not become actively involved, though they had adopted a positive attitude toward the possibility of Greece's liberation. The highly educated teacher Constantinos Koumas (born Larissa 1777, died Trieste 1836), never returned to Greece and had to stay in Trieste for health reasons. Daniel Philippidis (ca. 1750–1832) and Stephanos Doungas (ca. 1760–1830), representative thinkers of the Neohellenic Enlightenment, who, in collaboration with Benjamin of Lesbos and Theodoros Negris, undertook the organization of the Philiki Etaireia in Jassy, remained in Moldavia for the rest of their lives. Others who went to the regions in revolt finally adopted a critical distance toward it because of their disagreement with the actions of the revolutionaries.

Within this context, those who strongly argued for the liberal vision of an uprising had no illusions about the excesses into which a revolution could descend. They shouldered the responsibility of shaping the ideological basis of the new Greek state. From the first year of the events, their vital project was to found the state's administration and institutions, and also to draft its new constitution in the assemblies. Employing the language of reason, they played a conciliatory role in overcoming the increasing dissensions between the different factions that arose soon after the beginning of the liberation struggle. Having studied in Western centers of learning, these men of letters were imbued with the democratic values of national patriotism, spreading them even among the military leaders. Such was the case of Odysseas Androutsos (born Ithaka 1788, died Athens 1825) who, at the peak of the revolt in April 1823, with true patriotic spirit, wrote a letter to Korais inviting him to join the revolution. He expressed his deep concern over the general deterioration due to the conflicts between the revolutionaries with these significant words: "Greece needs you as well as all our educated compatriots. Bring with you all those that you can and come to participate together with your brothers in the fairest and most legitimate fight all over the world. Our struggle is for Christian faith and human rights" (Korais 1983, 117–119). On the complex correlation between the cultural authorities and other groups of fighters, Nikolaos Dragoumis (born Constantinople 1809, died Athens 1879), in his Ιστορικαί Αναμνήσεις (Historical recollections) (Dragoumis [1874] 1973), shows his literary awareness, saying: "These intellectual leaders either surrounded the central power, or perambulated in the provinces or crossed the seas, preaching in the camps or representing the people in the assemblies and the parliaments, striving to strengthen their enthusiasm, to guide the struggle and give a form of order and decency to government" (Dragoumis 1973, 1, 28). The scholars spontaneously gave their support to Alexandros Mavrokordatos (born Constantinople 1791, died Aigina 1865) and Dim-

itrios Ypsilantis (born Constantinople 1793, died Nafplio 1832), the two rival
political leaders whose Western-oriented education was in accordance with
theirs. Mavrokordatos, who dominated directly or indirectly the various assemblies, had the support of a number of intellectuals, some of whom, like Georgios Praidis (born Moudania 1791, died Athens 1873) and Constantinos Polychroniadis (died 1826), had previously belonged to Korais's circle in Paris,
whereas Dimitrios Ypsilantis was mostly surrounded by those who had taken
part in the battle of Dragatsani, such as Georgios Kozakis-Typaldos (born Cephalonia 1790, died Athens 1867) and Georgios Lassanis (born Kozani 1793, died
1870).

In spite of the strong emphasis given on action, during this period cultural
activity continued to be a significant element in everyday life. It is worth noting
that, even in those desperate times, an educational program was set up with
the foundation of schools and of an academy in the Peloponnese. Dragoumis
once more in his *Historical recollections* managed to add, in a few lines, a description of the broad range of the scholars' attitudes in those difficult moments:
"Among those who dispensed education, either oral or written, either for free
or for money, some were crowned with martyrdom. Others dispersed, suffering
famine, or even perishing from their ordeals. Among the scholars, some were
reduced to silence, others, breaking their pens, sought refuge in a Greece that
had arisen and undertook to preach freedom, harmony, and public order"
(Dragoumis 1973, 1, 160). Meanwhile, the conflict over the Greek language had
never ceased. In his literary work, Spyridon Trikoupis (born Mesolonghi 1788,
died Athens 1873), as a moderate purist, attacked the proponents of archaic
Greek and promoted Korais's middle way. He even expresses the hope that the
spoken and written language would become one and the same through their
mutual influence. In his poem called *Ο Δήμος: Ποίημα κλέφτικον* (Dimos: A klephtic poem), one of the earliest literary imitations of Greek folk songs praising
the courage of the klephts, he used the meter and language of the people.

The manpower of the revolution was enriched by human resources drawn from
the Balkan hinterlands. The fact that Greek was the lingua franca in the Ottoman
Empire acted as a channel for the broader cultural assimilation of groups whose
collective identity had not yet been articulated. The Hellenic cultural and linguistic universe with its Enlightenment ideas and aspirations for liberty was
an attractive milieu for all the peoples under Ottoman rule. Strongly associated
with the Greek national struggle was Nikolaos Savas Piccolos, a man of letters
and a doctor, born in Bulgaria (born Veliko Tyrnavo 1792, died Paris 1865) to
Greek parents and educated at the Greek Academy of Bucharest. Known for his
various translations and a tragedy called *Ο θάνατος του Δημοσθένους* (The death
of Demosthenes), his early activities had a clearly Greek national dimension.

The uprising of the revolution found him studying in Paris. He was acquainted with French Philhellenes and worked with Claude Fauriel on his collection of Greek folk songs. As one of Korais's closest collaborators, he was involved in different patriotic activities along with his friend Athanasios Vogoridis (born Kotel, Bulgaria ca. 1788, died Paris 1826). In August 1821, together with Constantinos Polychroniadis, he contacted Albert Gallatin, the US ambassador in Paris, regarding the Greek issue. For the same purpose, he also approached Jeremy Bentham and other liberals in London in order to request their support. Back in Paris, he decided to leave for Greece along with the poet Stephanos Kanellos (born Constantinople 1792, died Crete 1823), a member of the Philiki Etaireia, who previously had taught natural sciences and mathematics at the Greek Academy of Bucharest and became Alexandros Ypsilantis's follower at the battle of Dragatsani. On reaching regions in revolt, Piccolos was registered in July 1822 as a citizen of Ydra. He was selected as a member of the diplomatic mission at the 1822 Congress of the Holy Alliance in Verona to advise about the Greek revolt. To his deep disappointment, he did not participate in the congress because he did not agree with the Ydriots about who ought to be the head of the mission.

It is clear that the picture of the revolutionary intelligentsia is more nuanced and should not be construed as a single entity. First, there was a group of thinkers of acknowledged prestige. Some had taken minor orders in the Church and had acquired renown during the Neohellenic Enlightenment with their complex role as professional teachers and pioneers of modernity. With a high level of education, they not only paved the way for independence but fought heroically for it. At that time, most of them, at a relatively advanced age, had lived more than half their life in the previous century. As encyclopedists, their curriculum included, beside classical studies and religious education, experimental physics, modern philosophy, and advanced mathematics. A prominent figure was Grigorios Constantas (1758–1844), who, of humble origins from the village of Milies on Mount Pilion, had attended courses in the ecclesiastical schools of Mount Athos and Constantinople. He studied abroad and, in 1784, began his teaching activity at the Greek Academy of Bucharest. Together with his cousin Daniel Philippidis, he had written in 1791 the Γεωγραφία Νεωτερική (Novel geography), considered one of the most remarkable works of the Greek Enlightenment. When the war broke out, he joined the revolutionary forces and became one of the delegates at the Argos Fourth National Assembly. As ephor for education (1824–1828), he played an active role in education. In 1829, he worked as a teacher in the orphanage of Aigina founded by Ioannis Capodistrias.

One of the most distinguished scholars whom one can credit with an extraordinary involvement in the Revolution's military affairs was the archimandrite

Anthimos Gazis (born Milies 1758, died Ermoupolis, Syros 1828), primarily known as the director of the famous periodical *Hermes o Logios* in Vienna. On May 11, 1821, he officially declared the beginning of the insurrection to the representatives of the twenty-four villages surrounding Mount Pilion, calling them to rise against the Ottomans. Gazis represented Magnesia at the Aeropagus of eastern central Greece and at the National Assemblies of Epidavros and Astros, and worked in commissions of military affairs and education. He provided support to the insurgents of Euboea and obstructed Ottoman efforts to send supplies to their garrisons in Morea. During that time he presented with Constantas a draft proposing the creation of an academy in Argos named Protypon Didaktirion.

Benjamin of Lesbos (born Plomari Lesbos 1759, died Nafplio 1824), a cleric with a passion for learning, who had received a scholarship from the community of Kydonies, was an influential thinker and an ardent supporter of the revolution. During a long period of studies in Paris, he came to comprehend the potential of the new political ideas, though he witnessed at first hand the violent events of the French Revolution. A follower of liberalism, Benjamin rejected despotism and oligarchy, and defended democratic principles. During his teaching years in Kydonies and Bucharest, he cultivated in his students' young hearts the ideals of the Enlightenment and the seed of love for freedom. A member of the Philiki Etaireia, he was one of the first to fight for his nation and also took part in drafting the earliest plans for a Greek constitution. Appointed as commissioner (Armostis) of the Aegean Sea, he had the difficult task of encouraging the national awakening of the islanders who had been reluctant to join the Greek revolt. In December 1821, he became one of the Peloponnesian deputies at the Epidavros National Assembly and a member of the committee appointed in 1822 to draw up a provisional penal code. His death was caused by a typhus epidemic which devastated Nafplio in 1824. At that time new conflicts and rivalries between the local chieftains were impairing the progress of the war and his absence as a mediator was notably felt in those difficult moments.

It is also worth mentioning that an important number of Benjamin's former disciples at Kydonies promoted the revolution. Apart from Georgios Kozakis-Typaldos (see below), there was Theophilos Kairis, who succeeded Benjamin at the Academy of Kydonies; Dionysios Pyrros the Thessalian (1774–1853), a polymath, priest, teacher, scholar, and doctor; and Nikiphoros Pamboukis (born Chalkiana of the district of Kalavryta 1784), brother of the head teacher in Nafplio, Charalambos Pamboukis, who was also involved in the revolution. Nikiphoros Pamboukis was among the first to join the Philiki Etaireia and to spread the revolutionary ideas to the primates and clergymen in the Peloponnese. He went to study at the university of Pisa but, as soon as the revolution began, he returned to Greece and took part in the assemblies and the battle of Dervenakia. Physician and philosopher George Kalaras (1782–1824) from Agionori in Corinthia, member of the Philiki Etaireia, who had studied at Pisa, also participated in the same battle. He became a member of the Second National Assembly in March 1823, as one of the representatives of his region. He has been discussed as the possible anonymous author of the Ελληνική Νομαρχία (Hellenic Nomarchy) (Kitromilides 2013, 404).

Neophytos Vamvas (born Chios 1776, died Athens 1855) and Theophilos Kairis (born Andros 1784, died Syros 1853) were considerably younger than Constantas, Gazis, and Benjamin of Lesbos. While in Paris for his studies, Vamvas became Korais's follower. As an assistant to Dimitrios Ypsilantis, he passed to Ydra, where he encouraged the Ydriots to campaign against the Ottomans in his home island, for the wealth of Chios could help the revolution. The failure of the expedition undermined his prestige. Later, he became professor and dean of the faculty of Philosophy at the newly founded University of Athens. Theophilos Kairis bore the legacy of Benjamin of Lesbos in Kydonies and held the same liberal approach. He was born into a distinguished family of Andros. On May 10, 1821, he declared the War of Independence by raising the Greek flag at the cliffside church of St. George of the island. At the same time, with a famous speech he inspired shipowners and merchants to contribute funds and ships to build a Greek navy. He also fought bravely in the Olympus campaign, where he was severely wounded; his emotional enthusiasm is described by Nikolaos Kasomoulis in his Ενθυμήματα στρατιωτικά (Military reminiscences of the Revolution of the Greeks, 1821–1833). In his homeland, he created the Orphanotropheion for orphans, especially from the massacre on the island of Psara. But when Otto of Bavaria was installed on the throne of Greece, Theophilos Kairis was not ready to integrate himself into the new system. Moreover, his unorthodox views on Christianity made him a controversial figure and brought him into conflict with the Orthodox Church.

Furthermore, noted politicians gained their own place in the history of Greek letters. One of them was the Phanariot Theodoros Negris (born Constantinople 1790, died Nafplio 1824), who was influenced by French revolutionary values and the Declaration of the Rights of Man and Citizen. Press freedom interested him in particular, and he therefore corresponded on this subject with Jeremy Bentham and published in the Ephimeris Athinon his critical comments on Article 8 of the Law of Epidavros. An active member the Philiki Etaireia, he arrived at the outbreak of the war secretly on the island of Spetses and joined Alexandros Mavrokordatos. He participated in November 1821 in the establishment of the Areopagus of eastern central Greece, becoming its first president. After taking part in the First National Assembly

VOYAGE PITTORESQUE

DE LA

GRECE

TOME PREMIER.

A PARIS,

M. DCC. LXXXII.

PLATE 1 *Exoriare Aliquis.* Lithograph, frontispiece in volume I of *Voyage Pittoresque de la Grèce*, Le Comte Choiseul-Gouffier, 3 vols, Paris, 1782-1802.

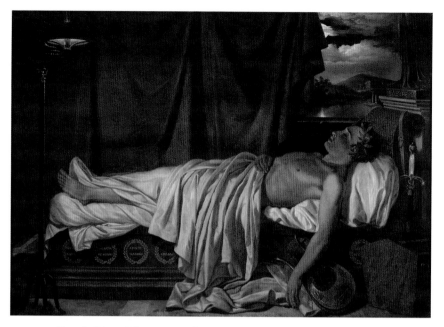

PLATE 2   Joseph-Denis Odevaere, *Lord Byron on His Deathbed*, 1826. Oil on canvas.
Groeningenmuseum, Bruges (Inv. no. 350)

PLATE 3   Peter von Hess, *A Greek Commander and His Pallikars in the Fight*, 1829. Oil on canvas, after the lithograph by Karl Krazeisen. Thanassis and Marina Martinos Collection, Athens.

PLATE 4   Louis-Léopold Robert, *A Young Greek Warrior Whetting his Knife on Ancient Marble*, ca. 1830. Oil on canvas. Private collection, Athens.

PLATE 5   Vincent-Nicole Raverat, *The Death of a Young Deacon*, 1824. Oil on canvas.
Musée de l'Hôtel Sandelin, Saint Omer.

PLATE 6   Cesare Mussini, *"Saremo Liberi"* (We will be free), 1849. Oil on canvas. Palazzo Reale, Turin.

PLATE 7   Miche Philibert Genod, *The Oath of the Young Freedom Fighter*, c. 1829. Oil on canvas. Thanassis and Marina Martinos Collection, Athens.

PLATE 8 Ary Scheffer, *A Young Greek Defending His Father*, 1827. Oil on canvas. Benaki Museum, Athens.

PLATE 9   Horace Vernet, *The Defeat*, 1827. Oil on canvas. Benaki Museum, Athens.

PLATE 10
Henri Auguste
Serrur, *The Wounded
Greek Warrior,* 1825.
Oil on canvas. Musée
de la Chartreuse,
Douai.

PLATE 11 Unknown
artist, *A Greek Mother
Lamenting her Dead
Child,* French School,
mid-19th century.
Oil on canvas. The
Michael and Demetra
Varkarakis Collection,
Athens.

PLATE 12 Jean-Baptiste Vinchon, *Modern Greek Subject, after the Battle of Samothrace,* 1827. Oil on canvas. Musée du Louvre, Paris.

PLATE 13 Stanislas-Henri-Benoit Darondeau, *Greek Women in the Slave Market,* 1835. Oil on canvas. The Michael and Demetra Varkarakis Collection, Athens.

PLATE 14   François-Emile de Lansac, *Episode from the Siege of Mesolonghi*, 1828.
Municipal Gallery, Mesolonghi.

PLATE 15   Theodoros Vryzakis, *Hellas in Gratitude,* 1858. Oil on canvas. National Gallery, Athens.

PLATE 16   Baron Carl Wilhelm von Heideck (or Heidegger), *A Scene in the City of Nafplio*, 1831. Oil on Canvas. Thanassis and Marina Martinos Collection, Athens.

PLATE 17   Eugène Delacroix, *Scenes of the Massacres of Chios: Greek Families Awaiting Death or Slavery*, 1824. Oil on canvas. Musée du Louvre, Paris.

PLATE 18   Eugène Delacroix, *Greece on the Ruins of Mesolonghi,* also known as *Greece in Mesolonghi,* 1826. Oil on canvas. Musée des Beaux Arts, Bordeaux.

PLATE 19   George-Philip Reinagle, *The Naval Battle of Navarino*, 1827. Inscribed on verso: "The Battle of Navarin 20th October 1827, representing the explosion of a Turkish 56 Gun Frigate which happened about five minutes after she was clear of the 'Albion' alongside which Ship she had been burning for an hour. Exhibited at The R. A." Oil on canvas. Thanassis and Marina Martinos Collection, Athens.

PLATE 20
Thomas Phillips, *Portrait of George Gordon, Byron in Greek Dress,* 1813. Oil on canvas. British Embassy in Athens.

'Tis living Greece no more

PLATE 21 Joseph Mallord William Turner, *'Tis Living Greece No More*, 1822. Watercolor on paper. Museum of the City of Athens.

PLATE 22 Denis Dighton, *Defeat of the Turks under the Command of Ali Pasha by the Souliots*, 1823. Oil on canvas. Private Collection, Athens.

PLATE 23 Sir Charles-Lock Eastlake, *Greek Fugitives: An English Ship Sending Its Boats to Rescue Them*, 1833. Oil on canvas. Benaki Museum, Athens.

PLATE 24   Francesco Hayez, *The Refugees of Parga*, 1831. Oil on canvas. Pinacoteca Tosio Martinengo, Brescia.

PLATE 25   Filippo Marsigli, *The Death of Markos Botsaris*, 1850. Oil on canvas. Benaki Museum, Athens.

PLATE 26 Ludovico Lipparini, *The Oath of Lord Byron on the Tomb of Markos Botsaris,* 1850. Oil on canvas. Museo Civico, Treviso.

PLATE 27 Peter von Hess, *The Reception of King Otho of Greece in Athens,* 1839. Oil on canvas. Bayerische Staatsgemäldesammlungen, Neue Pinakothek, Münich.

PLATE 28   Carl Rottmann, *View of the Bay of Poros,* 1838. Oil on canvas. Private Collection, Athens.

PLATE 29   Christian Perlberg, *A Festival in Athens (Koulouma), by the Temple of Olympian Zeus*, 1838. Oil on canvas. National Historical Museum, Athens.

PLATE 30   Albert Riegel, *Portrait of Dimitrios Botsaris,* 1829. Oil on canvas. Benaki Museum, Athens.

at Epidavros and the Second National Assembly at Astros, he succumbed to typhus on November 22, 1824, in Nafplio.

In mid-March 1821, Alexandros Ypsilantis formed in Wallachia the Sacred Battalion, the first organized military unit of the revolution composed of volunteers, who were students from the Greek communities in Moldavia, Wallachia, and Odessa. He thought that these young intellectuals could become the soul of his army. In June 1821, the Sacred Battalion was ultimately defeated by the Ottomans at the battle of Dragatsani. The devotion to the cause of liberating Greece of those young men was viewed as a heroic prelude to the War of Independence. Most former students at the Lyceum of Bucharest were captured, including the architect Stamatios Kleanthis (born Velventos near Kozani 1802, died Athens 1862). After the defeat, their professor Georgios Gennadios (born Silyvria of Thrace 1786, died Athens 1854), who was a great influence thanks to his patriotic discourses and his liberal activity, went to Greece in 1826 and took part in the unfortunate expedition of Karystos. Gennadios had begun studying philology at the University of Leipzig and returned to Bucharest in 1815, where he became an assistant to Neophytos Doukas, then head at the Lyceum. During the period from 1817 to 1820, he helped found and direct the Greek School of Commerce in Odessa.

Numerous rescued members of the Sacred Battalion were able to join the exodus of many other Greeks from the country. Among them was the scholar and playwright Iakovos Rizos-Neroulos (born Constantinople 1778, died 1849), who had served as prime minister of the Hospodars of Wallachia during the period from 1812 to 1818 and had dedicated himself to the preparation of the revolution in Moldavia. With the intention of going to Greece, he traveled across Europe. In 1823, he first reached Geneva and then Pisa, where the exiled Metropolitan Ignatios of Ungrowallachia held great influence over Greek political and military dignitaries. In 1826, back in Geneva he gave lectures on contemporary Greek history and literature, which were highly appreciated. In 1827, Capodistrias appointed him commissioner for the Cyclades islands, and later minister of foreign affairs. Another surviving member of the Sacred Battalion was Georgios Kozakis-Typaldos, who lived as a physician in Kishinev, Bessarabia, after having studied medicine in Padua and Paris. There, he developed a close relationship with the Ypsilantis family and Alexandros Kantakouzinos. Thus, belonging to Alexandros Ypsilantis's entourage, he fought at the battle of Dragatsani and it was he who wrote the famous revolutionary manifesto of Ypsilantis entitled *Μάχου υπέρ πίστεως και πατρίδος* (Fight for faith and homeland). After the defeat at Dragatsani, he followed Dimitrios Ypsilantis to the Morea and fought at the siege of Neokastro. Wounded, he left for Italy. In the postwar years, he wrote in 1839 the *Φιλοσοφικόν δοκίμιον περί της προόδου* και της πτώσεως της παλαιάς Ελλάδος (Philosophical essay on the progress and fall of ancient Greece) and later became the first director of the National Library and the editor of the seven volumes of one of Europe's earliest Indologists, Dimitrios Galanos. Another adjutant of Alexandros Ypsilantis was Georgios Lasanis, who had studied literature and philosophy in Leipzig. Along with Ypsilantis, he was arrested by the Austrian authorities. They were both kept in close confinement for seven years in the military fortress of Terezín near Prague. Immediately after Ypsilantis's death, Lasanis returned to Greece, where he collaborated with Dimitrios Ypsilantis. Kyrillos Liverios or Liverios Liveropoulos (born Vrachori of the district of Nafpaktos 1785?, died Mesolonghi 1853) also joined Dimitrios Ypsilantis. One of the first to benefit from a scholarship from the Philomousos Etaireia, he studied physical sciences at the universities of Wurzburg, Leipzig, Vienna, and Göttingen. Upon the outbreak of the insurrection in Wallachia, he followed a wave of students heading for Jassy, but the difficulties they encountered in Prague forced them to move to Trieste. There, in mid-June 1821, he joined Dimitrios Ypsilantis, who was just leaving for the Morea and who appointed him head of the siege of Athens. Also participating in the battle of Dragatsani was the scholar Nikolaos Skoufos who, born in Smyrna at the end of the eighteenth century, studied with a scholarship from the Philomousos Etaireia at the military schools of Munich and Vienna. After the defeat, he had to resort first to Sibiu and afterward, in May 1825, he went to Greece through Bessarabia and Italy. He worked on the island of Ydra as secretary of the community and wrote articles for the newspaper Ο Φίλος του Νόμου (Friend of the Law). He led the Ionian Phalanx (Ιωνική φάλαγξ) with 350 men under the general command of Nikitaras. Involved in the assembly at Troezen, he became a member of the committee for the revision of the constitution.

Meanwhile, upon hearing about the revolution, a stream of volunteer Greek students from around Europe interrupted their studies, as did the Thessalian Drosos Mansolas (1779 / 1789–1860). Some of them had been members of the Philomousos Etairia or were studying at Lord Guilford's expenses. At the call of the revolution they interrupted their studies and rushed back to their homeland to fight for liberty. Those from Pisa took the boat from Livorno and via Marseilles moved to the Peloponnese and Ydra. From Jena, Göttingen, and Berlin, centers of liberal ideas, a group of Greek students reached Trieste after a series of adventures under the surveillance of the Austrian authorities. With them was the archimandrite Theoklitos Pharmakidis (1784–1860), one of the best-educated Greek clergymen of the Enlightenment era and former editor of Ερμής ο Λόγιος, who was studying Protestant theology at the University of Göttingen. This group included much younger scholars than Pharmakidis, such as Georgios Psyllas, Alexandros Glarakis, Kyrillos Liverios, Anastasios Polyzoidis, and Frangiskos Mavros. On their way to Greece, they met in Leipzig Wilhelm Traugott Krug, the renowned professor of philosophy at the university. He was a warm advocate for liberalism, and his goal was to stimulate German Philhellenism with his speech entitled *Griechenlands Wiedergeburt* delivered in the presence of the Greek students in Leipzig.

Georgios Psyllas (born Athens 1794, died Athens 1878) developed a significant activity as a representative in the Epidavros and Astros National Assemblies and for a short period (January–February 1822) served as second secretary of the legislature. In 1824, his position as editor of the *Ephimeris Athinon* gave him the opportunity to express his liberal and humanitarian ideas. He was elected member of the ephorate of Athens and, when Ömer Vrioni's troops entered Attica, he fled along with other Athenians to Salamis. During the siege of the Acropolis, the Ottoman troops, desperate for ammunition, began to dismantle sections of the temples in order to recover the lead clamps which they intended to use for bullets. In the hope that the Acropolis would be spared such destruction, an Athenian patriot, the pioneer self-taught archaeologist Kyriakos S. Pittakis (1798–1863) took the initiative to send bullets to the besieged enemy.

Anastasios Polyzoidis (born Melnik 1802, died Athens 1873), who later became a politician and judge, studied Law and History in Vienna, Göttingen, and Berlin. From Trieste, he passed to Mesolonghi along with some Philhellenes. He cooperated with Alexandros Mavrokordatos, was appointed to several gubernatorial positions in the provisional administration and took part in the Epidavros National Assembly. There, almost on his own, he wrote the new state's constitution and the declaration of January 1, 1822, which informed the European powers that the insurrection was a national movement. In 1823, he was in charge of the committee which was sent to London for the negotiation of a public loan. In 1827, he was elected representative to the National Assembly at Troezen. In order to continue his studies, he went to Paris in October of the same year. Upon his return, he joined the opposition against Ioannis Capodistrias, publishing in Ydra the newspaper *Απόλλων* (Apollo). In 1832, he was nominated by the Bavarian regency to be the president of the law court of Nafplio, which had to judge Theodoros Kolokotronis, Dimitrios Plapoutas, and other former leaders of the War of Independence on trumped-up charges of treason. Along with Georgios Tertsetis, he refused to countersign their conviction.

Upon the establishment of the Greek state, the mission of the intellectuals regarding what they had lived through did not stop; it raised a keen interest in recent history. Fully aware that they had participated in a great work, they felt the need to relate and describe from their own points of view their various experiences. The historiography of that period is provided not only by professional historians but also by those who, eager to describe them, had acquired their knowledge through participation in the events. Although these first accounts contribute to our better understanding, they suffer from several deficiencies concerning impartiality and objectivity. The writers treated history as a chronicle of facts that they had experienced, giving their narrations both a personal and an ideological angle. This led inevitably to conflicts between different historical reconstructions. This pluralism was fundamentally due to the fact that their authors belonged to opposing and antagonistic political factions. In this sense, their perception of the past was marked by a defensive character which tended to justify or exalt their exploits. For example, Kanellos Deligiannis (1780–1862), son of the prominent notable Ioannis Deligiannis, wrote memoirs portraying the rivalries of the various groups and leading families of the Morea before and during the revolution. Nevertheless, Deligiannis's *Memoirs* are considered controversial, as they seek to justify his father's pro-Turkish stance as being beneficial for the Greeks. What remains true is that a strong feeling of national solidarity emerges from those writings, but the time of their writing was too early for a comprehensive study of the various experiences.

The earliest narration on the revolution's first two years are the *Memoirs* of Germanos, archbishop of Old Patras (1771–1826), an invaluable testimony for students of Greek history. In 1828, Georgios Gazis (born Delvinaki 1795, died 1855), a pupil of Neophytos Doukas in Bucharest and a member of the Philiki Etaireia, who also fought at Dragatsani and Mesolonghi, and later became Georgios Karaiskakis's secretary, edited in Aigina the *Βιογραφία των ηρώων Μάρκου Μπότσαρη και Καραϊσκάκη* (A biography of the heroes Markos Botzaris and Karaiskakis) with first-hand information. In 1829, Alexandros Soutsos published his *Histoire de la Révolution grecque* in memory of his brother Dimitrios, one of the four commanders who perished at Dragatsani. Next, we have Ioannis Philimon's *Δοκίμιον ιστορικόν περί της Φιλικής Εταιρίας* (A Historical Essay on the Philiki Etaireia) published in 1834 in Nafplio and his four-volume *Historical essay on the Greek Revolution*, published in Athens (1859–1862). As secretary of Dimitrios Ypsilantis, Ioannis Philimon (born Constantinople 1798/1799, died Athens 1874), attended the unsuccessful siege of Nafplio, the surrender of Acrocorinth by the Turks, and the battle of Dervenakia, where he risked his life. A meticulous chronicler, he used abundant documentation and attempted to neglect no detail of the events he related, though he did not succeed in providing a synthesis. The statesman Spyridon Trikoupis (born Mesolonghi 1788, died Athens 1873), the first prime minister of Greece, who during the war served in high administrative and diplomatic posts, added weight to his narrative with political criticism in his four-volume *Ιστορία της Ελληνικής Επαναστάσεως* (History of the Greek Revolution), published in London (1853–1857). In the introduction, which constitutes a balanced composition and one

of the most mature monuments of the language of the time, he agreed that historians were shaped by their era and the cultural environment in which they
studied the past. Nikolaos Spiliadis (born Tripoli 1785, died Nafplio 1862), secretary of State in 1829 under the authority of Ioannis Capodistrias, in his three-
volume *Απομνημονεύματα διά να χρησιμεύσωσιν εις την νέαν Ελληνικήν
Ιστορίαν (1821–1843)* (*Memoirs to be used for modern Greek history, 1821–1843*),
shed light on even obscure facets of the revolutionary events. He had previously
worked as a clerk in a Greek trading firm in Constantinople and Odessa. A
member of the Philiki Etaireia, upon the outbreak of the war he went to the
Morea and, after the siege of Tripoli, he served as secretary of the Peloponnesian
Senate and as a member of most of the national assemblies. The poet, jurist,
and scholar Georgios Tertsetis (born Zante 1800, died Athens 1874) was a totally different case; he was fascinated by the fighters' heroic spirit and took on
the difficult task of writing down the accounts that were dictated to him. Mostly
known as one of the judges who refused to condemn Theodoros Kolokotronis
and Dimitrios Plapoutas to death, he never wrote his own memoirs. On the contrary, he systematically attempted to convince fighters such as Nikitaras to
write theirs (see Konomos 1953). His most famous work is a narrative biography
of Theodoros Kolokotronis under the title *Διήγησις συμβάντων της ελληνικής
φυλής από τα 1770 έως τα 1836* (A narration of the events of the Greek race
from 1770 to 1836), published in Athens in 1846.

At the same time, there exists another kind of testimony based on the firsthand
experience of uneducated fighters who came from the illiterate peasantry and the
klephts. With no literary pretension, they took up the pen to record their reminiscences about the heroic deeds and self-sacrifices they had witnessed. For instance,
General Makrygiannis and Photios Chrysanthopoulos, better known as Fotakos,
the aide-de-camp of Theodoros Kolokotronis, appeared unwilling to break with
the past. Makrygiannis learned to write only enough to compose his celebrated
memoirs in a style that constitutes a synthesis of folk linguistic elements. According to Constantinos Th. Dimaras, he revived the memory of the still un-
changed Greek culture in its ultimate phase. As for Fotakos, using simple terms,
he narrated without exaltation and passion, and attempted to correct the inaccuracies of other historians. The charm of the spoken language is found in the historical accounts of the Athenians Panagis Skouzes and Angelos Gerontas. Details
of the military operations in central Greece and the siege of Mesolonghi are given
by General Spyromilios in his memoirs. In August 1825 he was fighting in the
second siege of Mesolonghi at the head of a group of 250 armed Chimariots. In
September he was sent as member of a committee to Nafplio to ask the government for more effective aid for the besieged city. Similarly, with admirable clarity
but negligible education, the Macedonian Nikolaos Kasomoulis (1795–1871), in

his long three-volume memoirs under the title of *Military reminiscences of the Revolution of the Greeks 1821–1833,* sought to tell everything he had seen.

During the ideological ferment in the aftermath of the War of Independence, fighters born around 1800, who were merely adolescents during the revolution, in their later life acted as bridges with postrevolutionary Greece as they became important citizens in building the new state. In 1822, under the leadership of the newspaper publisher Emmanouil Antoniadis (born Chalepa, Chania 1791, died Athens 1863), the Greeks had decisively defeated an Ottoman-Egyptian army of some ten thousand men at the battle in the village of Malaxa in Crete. When Ibrahim Pasha and his army invaded the Morea, Emmanouil Antoniadis with numerous Cretans at the victorious battle at Myloi, near Argos, forced the Egyptian troops to retreat to Tripoli. Among the younger fighters of the last phase of the revolution was the distinguished playwright Michail Chourmouzis (1804–1882), a native of Constantinople, known for his comedies, in which he expressed social criticism in situations that followed the War of Independence. With a vivid, everyday language he explored mentalities of the urban class of the time. Likewise, young Nikolaos Dragoumis held many public offices in the newly established Greek state. In addition to his governmental positions, he worked as a journalist for the newspaper *Aion* and was one of the editors of the periodicals *Pandora* and *Le Spectateur de l'Orient.* Two future prominent professors of philosophy at the University of Athens, Philippos Ioannou (born Zagora, Andros 1796, died Athens 1880) and Nikolaos Kotzias (born Psara 1814, died Athens 1885), had fought in battles. Ioannou, who served as secretary of Andreas Miaoulis, had fought in the region of his homeland, Zagora, while Kotzias, a member of a shipowning family of the island of Psara, had been wounded in a naval operation. The different types of persons that are presented in this essay were portrayed with the vivacity of his spirit by playwright Dimitrios Vyzantios (born Constantinople 1790, died Patras 1853), who had also been involved in the revolution in his early youth. In his popular play *Βαβυλωνία* (Babylonia) he described Greek society of 1827, bringing together persons with totally different backgrounds and dialects, a feature which undoubtedly left an imprint on the making of modern Greece.

Roxane D. Argyropoulos

References

Angelou, Alkis. 1971. *Οι λόγιοι και ο Αγώνας* [The intellectuals and the struggle]. Athens.
Antoniadi, Sophia A. 1971. *Εμμανουήλ Αντωνιάδης. Ο αγωνιστής. Ο δημοσιογράφος 1791–1863* [Emmanuel Antoniadis: The fighter, the journalist, 1791–1863]. Athens.

Argyropoulos, Roxane D. 1972–1973. "Ο W. T. Krug και οι Έλληνες. Η ελληνική μετάφραση του *Griechenlands Wiedergeburt*" [W. T. Krug and the Greeks: The Greek translation of *Griechenlands Wiedergeburt*]. *O Eranistis* 10: 268–273.

Chryssathopoulos, Photios. 1888. *Βίοι Πελοποννησίων ανδρών και των έξωθεν εις την Πελοπόννησον ελθόντων κληρικών, στρατιωτικών και πολιτικών των αγωνισαμένων τον αγώνα της Επαναστάσεως* [Lives of Peloponnesians and of those clerics, military, and politicians who came to fight for the struggle]. Athens.

Clogg, Richard. 2013. *A Concise History of Greece*. Cambridge.

Dakin, Douglas. 1973. *The Greek Struggle for Independence, 1821–1833*. Berkeley and Los Angeles.

Deligiannis, Kanellos. 2005. *Απομνημονεύματα* [Memoirs]. Athens.

Dimaras, Constantintos Th. 1972. *History of Modern Greek Literature*. Translated by Mary P. Gianos. Albany, NY.

Dragoumis, Nikolaos. (1874) 1973. *Ιστορικαί αναμνήσεις* [Historical recollections]. Edited by Alkis Angelou. Athens.

Enepekidis, Polychronis C. 1965. *Ρήγας-Υψηλάντης-Καποδίστριας. Έρευναι εις τα αρχεία της Αυστρίας, Γερμανίας, Ιταλίας, Γαλλίας και Ελλάδος* [Rhigas-Ypsilantis-Capodistrias: Research in the archives of Austria, Germany, Italy, France, and Greece]. Athens.

Gardika, Katerina. 1971. "Ο Αναστάσιος Πολυζωΐδης και η Ελληνική Επανάσταση" [Anastasios Polyzoidis and the Greek Revolution]. *Mnimon* 1:23–52.

Gazis, Georgios. 1971. *Λεξικόν της Επαναστάσεως και άλλα έργα* [A dictionary of the Revolution and other works]. Edited by Leandros Vranoussis. Ioannina.

Goudas, Anastasios N. 1869. *Βίοι Παράλληλοι των επί της αναγεννήσεως της Ελλάδος διαπρεψάντων ανδρών* [Parallel lives of distinguished men of the rebirth of Greece]. Vol. 2. Athens.

Gritsopoulos, Tasos Ath. 1970–1971. *Ιστοριογραφία του Αγώνος* [The historiography of the struggle]. *Mnimosyni* 3:33–253.

Henderson, George Patrick. 1970. *The Revival of Greek Thought, 1620–1830*. Albany, NY.

Kasomoulis, Nikolaos. 1940. *Ενθυμήματα στρατιωτικά της Επαναστάσεως των Ελλήνων 1821–1833* [Military reminiscences of the Revolution of the Greeks, 1821–1833]. Vol. 2. Athens.

Katifori, Despoina. 1990. "Νικόλαος Σκούφος. Σχεδίασμα βιογραφίας" [Nikolaos Skoufos: A biographical sketch]. *Mnimon*, vol. 4, Supplement. Athens.

Kitromilides, Paschalis M. 2010. *Adamantios Korais and the European Enlightenment*. Oxford.

Kitromilides, Paschalis M. 2013. *Enlightenment and Revolution: The Making of Modern Greece*. Cambridge, MA.

Konomos, Dinos. 1953. *Βίος Νικήτα Σταματελόπουλου ή Νικηταρά. Καταγραφή Γεωργίου Τερτσέτη εκ τεσσάρων νέων χειρογράφων* [The Life of Nikitas Stamatelopoulos or Nikitaras written by Georgios Tertsetis from four new manuscripts]. Athens.

Korais, Adamantios. 1983. *Αλληλογραφία* [Correspondence]. Edited by Constantinos Th. Dimaras. Athens.

Koumarianou, Catherine. 1973. "The Contribution of the Intelligentsia towards the Greek Independence Movement, 1798–1821." In *The Struggle for Greek Independence: Essays to*

Mark the 150th Anniversary of the Greek War of Independence, edited by Richard Clogg, 67–86. London and Basingstoke.

Mackridge, Peter. 1981. "The Greek Intellitgentsia, 1780–1830: A Balkan Perspective." In Balkan Society in the Age of Greek Independence, edited by Richard Clogg, 70–77. Totowa, NJ.

Mattheou, Sophia. 2018. "Κύριλλος Λιβέριος: Ένας «πεπαιδευμένος» στην υπηρεσία της Ελληνικής Επανάστασης" [Kyrillos Liverios: An educated man at the service of the Greek Revolution]. In Όψεις της Επανάστασης του 1821 [Aspects of the revolution of 1821], edited by Dimitris Dimitropoulos, Christos Loukos, and Panagiotis Michailaris, 271–306. Athens.

Mayers, David. 2007. Dissenting Voices in America's Rise to Power. Cambridge.

Panagiotopoulos, Vasilis. 2015. Δύο πρίγκιπες στην Ελληνική Επανάσταση. Επιστολές αυτόπτη μάρτυρα και ένα υπόμνημα του πρίγκιπα Γεωργίου Καντακουζηνού [Two princes in the Greek Revolution: Letters from an eye witness and a memorandum written by Prince George Kantakouzinos]. Athens.

Philimon, Ioannis. 1834. Δοκίμιον ιστορικόν περί της Φιλικής Εταιρίας [A Historical Essay on the Philiki Etaireia]. Nafplio.

Philimon, Ioannis. 1859–1862. Δοκίμιον ιστορικόν περί της Ελληνικής Επαναστάσεως [A Historical Essay on the Greek Revolution]. Athens.

Protopsaltis, Emmanouil, ed. 1968. Απομνημονεύματα Αγωνιστών του '21 [Memoirs of the fighters of 1821]. Athens.

Sathas, Constantinos N. 1868. Βιογραφίαι των εν τοις γράμμασι διαλαμψάντων Ελλήνων από της καταλύσεως της Βυζαντινής Αυτοκρατορίας μέχρι της Ελληνικής Εθνεγερσίας 1453–1821 [Biographies of prominent Greek men of letters from the fall of the Byzantine Empire to the Greek national uprising, 1453–1821]. Athens.

Sideri, Aloi. 1989. Έλληνες φοιτητές στο πανεπιστήμιο της Πίζας (1806–1861) [Greek students at the university of Pisa, 1806–1861]. Athens.

Vakalopoulos, Apostolos. 1978. Οι Έλληνες σπουδαστές στα 1821 [Greek students in 1821]. Thessaloniki.

Military Leaders

A distinction between the military and the political leadership of the Greek Revolution is highly problematic, though in the pertinent romantic literature this demarcation is a commonplace. Yet, reality was more complex, for all political—and even ecclesiastical—elites partook in the military operations, energetically commanding military units. Hence, a distinction between the political and military upper crust is to be understood mainly in terms of social descent rather than as an expression of differentiated revolutionary action. In other words, the issue of who the real military leaders of the Greek Revolution were is somewhat irrelevant, as all social strata and factions along with their heads participated in the war and contributed, in varying degrees, to the final military victory.

Keeping this in mind, the military leaders of the revolution may be classified into five distinct groups in accordance with their social and professional background, namely, chieftains of irregular bands, notables (*kocabaşıs*), foreigners (Philhellenes), clergymen, and members of the Philiki Etaireia (Society of Friends). This distinction remains somewhat ambiguous, since military commanders who do not fit into this schema can always be found. Indeed, there are two instances of members of small professional groups or politicians who conducted occasional military operations. Panagiotis Giatrakos was a doctor from Mystra, who is invariably regarded as a warlord because he partook in battles and was affiliated with the Peloponnesian military fraction. Alexandros Mavrokordatos, the most emblematic politician of the revolution, did not hesitate to embark on military ventures, such as the catastrophic campaign of 1822 in Epirus and the successful defense of Mesolonghi at the end of the same year. Still, these military enterprises were only auxiliary for Mavrokordatos's career—he would never consider himself a professional of war. Despite these reservations, a description of the military leadership in terms of the aforementioned distinction retains its value, as it allows a rather accurate delineation of the major characteristics of these groups.

Despite the engagement of all social elites in the war, the real professional warlords were the chieftains of irregulars, the major conductors and designers of a particular type of guerrilla warfare that consolidated the revolutionary authority in the Greek lands. These irregulars belonged to five groups: they were the *armatoloi* of Rumeli, the *kapoi* of the Peloponnese, the Souliots, the Maniots, and the groups of Macedonian refugees and other volunteers from assorted Balkan provinces. As the Philiki Etaireia had not elaborated any feasible plan of operations before the insurrection, the armed irregulars that had already been active in the Greek lands were to play an indispensable role in the revolutionary venture. The founders of the society and the other members of its supreme authority were obliged to count on the irregulars, despite the fact that little was known about these would-be freedom fighters outside the confines of their homeland.

Rumeli and *Armatoloi*

The protagonists of the revolution in Rumeli were the commanders, or *kapetanaioi*, of *armatoloi*, that is to say, armed bands of local Christians with duties and authorities of a gendarmerie working for the Ottoman state. A *kapetanaios* commanded a group of around fifty men or *pallikaria*, and his area of jurisdiction was called *armatolik*. These men-at-arms were considered *askeri*, and thus enjoyed tax exemption. In principle, they were selected from among the locals, but in reality they came from the ranks of Christian brigands, or klephts, who typically demanded their integration into the Ottoman power system and administration order in return for their abstinence from violence and uprisings against regional authorities. The outlawed gendarme, in turn, would transform into an unruly brigand seeking to resume his position in the administrative cadre and reinstate his negotiating power. This general pattern varied according to regional and temporal idiosyncrasies, yet these armed irregulars were entangled in a continuous circle of violence in pursuit of political power.

In the eighteenth century, the leadership of these bands had acquired a familial and hereditary character, thus contributing to the consolidation of a Christian elite of professional warriors. These aristocratic men-at-arms were loyal to their Ottoman employers and were engrossed in bitter conflicts with their usual enemies, the bandits, but with *kapetanaioi* of adjoining *armatoliks* as well, concerning the borders of their areas of jurisdiction. Intricate networks of kinship, marital and spiritual relations established strong and enduring alliances between different *kapetanaioi* and their families so that any private wars against common enemies would be conducted successfully. Around twenty-three Christian *armatoliks* covered Rumeli.

On the eve of the revolution, the Rumeliot *kapetanaioi* had been put under the administrative control of Ali Pasha of Ioannina, who had eradicated the most recalcitrant armed clans and replaced them with loyal ones. Many *armatoloi* fled to the Ionian islands, where they served in the English, Russian, and French armies until 1815. The end of the Napoleonic Wars left them unemployed, and so many conceded to their submission to Ali's rule and returned home, where they resumed their *armatoliks*. This was a new reality of restricted independence for the intractable warriors, for now they obtained their legitimization, salaries, and offices from a powerful lord to whom they were utterly liable.

Those who remained in the Ionian islands, under British suzerainty from 1815 onward, had to face poverty, unemployment, and misery. They awaited the first opportunity to return to their homeland aspiring to a better future—and this was an adequate motive for them to participate in an uprising that promised new offices, roles, and, of course, loot.

The clash between Ali Pasha and the Sublime Porte left the Rumeliot chieftains in a very precarious position. Although they were obliged to fight for their lord, most abandoned him, understanding the futility of Ali's mutiny. Still, the chieftains remained reserved toward the new rule, not unjustifiably, since the maintenance of *armatoliks* was not among the desiderata of Greek revolutionary plans. Revolution was a risky venture with uncertain prospects for the chieftains; thus, they had to find a way to retain their social and economic position against all perils entailed in both alternative objectives that lay before them, namely revolutionary rule or unconditional submission to the Ottomans. Opportunism was inevitably the only sensible strategy. Furthermore, adventurers without landed power took advantage of the revolutionary conjuncture to lay claim to *armatoliks*. Ioannis Rangos and Georgios Karaiskakis were examples of would-be commanders, whose activity in the first years of the revolution caused only trouble.

The *armatoloi* were particularly powerful in western Rumeli, and their private armies were highly organized and disciplined. Thus, they felt no need for additional recruits from the ranks of untrained peasants. The widespread weakness of local notables rendered the dominance of the *armatoloi* even more unequivocal. Their omnipotence was systematically undermined only by the national revolutionary center administered by Mavrokordatos and located in the picturesque town of Mesolonghi.

Georgios Varnakiotis was the most prominent *kapetianios* before and during the first two years of the revolution, as well as the major instigator of the uprising in western Rumeli. He beat the Ottomans in the famous battle of Aetos in 1822, but a few months later, quite inexplicably, he joined the Ottomans for keeps—it is highly probable that he was trapped into this by Mavrokordatos, who wished to rid himself of a dangerous opponent. Although Varnakiotis attempted many times to contact the revolutionary authorities, he failed definitely to link himself with the Greek camp.

Varnakiotis's position at the leadership of the rebel forces in the area was gradually taken over by Karaiskakis, though his military activity until 1824 was restricted to a bitter clash with Mavrokordatos's adherent Rangos over the vacant *armatolik* of Agrafa. He succeeded in having the office granted to him, but his erratic and controversial political stance and military activity, usually neutral or occasionally aggressive toward the Greeks, convinced the revolutionary government to have him sentenced for treason by a court martial. After 1824, Karaiskakis abandoned his opportunistic intrigues and opted to support the Greek government. After fighting with excessive zeal in the second civil war on the side of the central government, in 1826 he was appointed field marshal of Rumeli and engaged himself in the long siege of Athens by Mehmed Reşid Pasha. He launched a masterful three-month campaign in central and eastern Rumeli beating the Ottomans many times in historic battles and restoring the revolutionary authority. In 1827, he returned to Attica, conducted a series of hard and bloody battles, but was killed in a skirmish.

A good many other chieftains stood out as liberty fighters but also retained their landed autonomy with great zeal. Gogos Bakolas, Andreas Iskos, Nikolaos Stornaris were influential *kapetanaioi,* who readily joined the Ottomans whenever the latter advanced and returned to the revolutionary camp when the course of operations was favorable for the Greeks. These chieftains displayed an excessively unreliable behavior and acted in accordance to their own personal vested interests. The maintenance of their *armatoliki* was a crucial objective of theirs, and accordingly they would join the rebels only when the military conjecture favored their own commitments.

Armatoliks prevailed in eastern Rumeli also, yet their number was smaller and the assorted *kapetanaioi* were more willing to follow a distinguished chieftain. Moreover, opportunities for *kapetanaioi* from other Greek lands to deploy their power, influence and activity were abundant; for instance, Ioannis Makrygiannis from western Rumeli, Dimitrios Ypsilantis from Russia, Ilias and Kyriakoulis Mavromichalis from Mani, Nikitaras from the Peloponnese. Military leaders also included westerners like the French Colonel Charles Fabvier and the British Thomas Cochrane and Richard Church (Figure 28), who stood

FIGURE 28   Spyridon
Prosalentis, *Portrait of Sir
Richard Church*, 1873. Oil
on canvas. National
Historical Museum, Athens.

out as commanders in the area. The manpower of the guerrilla bands was rather limited and less disciplined than those in western Rumeli, and, thus, the chieftains were obliged to recruit and train common villagers.

The revolution was organized and instigated by a quartet of *kapetanaioi*. Dimitrios Panourgias from Salona (Amfissa), Dimos Skaltsas from Lidoriki, Athanasios Diakos from Levadia, and Ioannis Diovouniotis from Boudanitsa formed a sort of revolutionary directorate. Among the members of this company, all of whom came from the milieu of Ali Pasha, Diakos was the most prominent and was elected commander-in-chief of all rebel forces in eastern Rumeli. Yet, this young upstart did not enjoy many days of glory. A few days after his appointment he was defeated by Omer Vrioni at the battle of Alamana (April 22, 1821), was captured, and executed in Lamia.

Diakos's office was taken over by Odysseas Androutsos, his former superintendent and one of the most distinguished leaders of the revolution. Androutsos had also served Ali Pasha, by whose political attitudes and behavior he was heavily influenced. He was particularly notorious for his brutality, suspiciousness, and personal ambition. After the assumption of the military leadership of eastern Rumeli, Androutsos won the significant battle of Gravia. During the years 1822–1825 his military career deteriorated and a series of failed ventures followed; two sieges of Chalkis and the battle of Agia Marina were all unsuccessful but also strongly undermined by the regional government. His energy was utterly consumed by the exigencies of the internal strife, though he retained his high profile as a warrior and his strong influence on the peasants. He was twice accused of treachery owing to his negotiating with his Albanian enemies as a means of effective distraction when he could not repel them. Although Androutsos got hold of Athens in the summer of 1822, his political power dwindled, until his career came to a miserable end. Deprived of political allies and friends, he joined the Ottomans in 1824, was arrested by his adjutant Ioannis Gouras, imprisoned, and executed on the Acropolis the following year.

In Euboea, the revolution was inhibited by a bitter conflict between local would-be warlords and chieftains sent to the island by the revolutionary government to take over the leadership of the war. Among the locals, the most prominent was Angelis Govginas, a close friend of Androutsos, and winner for the famous battle of Vrisakia. He was killed in action on March 22, 1822. Nikolaos Kriezotis headed the rebels in the region of Karystos, and later on was distinguished in Athens.

Likewise, in Attica a good number of aspirant military men were attracted by the prospects offered by the absence of *armatoloi,* but the progress of the revolution was slow and uncertain. The aforementioned Ioannis Gouras stood as guardian commander of Athens but was killed in action in 1826 during the siege of the Acropolis. Ioannis Makrygiannis excelled in the retinue of Androutsos before launching this own career. He is known as the winner of the battle of Myloi against Ibrahim, and was an important general in the battles of Attica in 1826–1827.

The Peloponnese and *Kapoi*

The military leadership of the Peloponnese came from the class of *kapoi,* that is bodyguards or military men at the service of the powerful *kocabaşı* families. Each significant notable maintained a retinue of armed men, responsible for his physical protection and the safety of his landed estate and edifices, as well as the consolidation of public order in his lands. In contrast with *armatoloi, kapoi* were not considered *askeri* and their decision-making autonomy was restricted. Extended families linked with banditry networks of the countryside were employed and attended the notables faithfully until the outbreak of the revolution. In this way, they tied their fate with that of the *kocabaşıs,* and their participation in the revolution was preempted by the notables' decision to start it. The groups of *kapoi* were structured in a similar manner to that of the *armatoloi,* yet the number of men was rather small, and thus the bands had to be reinforced with recruited and untrained peasants.

The chiefs of the *kapoi* regarded the upheaval as an excellent opportunity for their social rise and their release from the ties with the *kocabaşı* families, a means of political and social glorification as well as economic independence. Evidently, the military operations were to be conducted by *kapoi,* and their successes increased their political autonomy, self-confidence, and influence over the grass roots. These new self-righteous heroes of the Greek world rejected the political hegemony of the notables and were highly reluctant to return to their former inferior social position. In effect, they demanded an equal portion of power—if not the exclusive right to supremacy.

This controversy determined the course of the war and the strategic priorities of the chieftains. Unlike their *armatoloi* counterparts, the *kapoi* were not inclined to use negotiations with the Ottomans as a means of political pressure, yet they were fully determined to clash violently in open civil wars initially with the notables and then with the central government. At the same time, they remained closely affiliated with their former employers, so they would easily shift political alliances or seek aid from the notables when in need. This means that their political agenda differed from that of the notables only in terms of personal aspirations and not in ideology or social prospects. Theodoros Kolokotronis, continually fluctuating between overt enmity and alliance with his former employers, the Deligiannis family, is a typical case. In search of political affiliations and alliances, his essential means were kinship, marriages, blood brotherhoods and baptisms.

Likewise, the relations of the *kapoi* with the newly formed revolutionary authority after 1822 were inimical from the beginning. Despite the absence of *armatolikia* and landed interests, the *kapoi* defended fiercely their administrative autonomy, their rights to loots, their freedom to recruit men from the provinces, and their ability to determine their position in the Peloponnesian power balance.

The incontestable military leader of the rebels in the Peloponnese and the most influential personality of the revolution was Kolokotronis, an undeniable folk hero, with a fame spreading far beyond the Peloponnese (Figure 29). He was the only chieftain of irregulars with essential knowledge of the contemporary European art of war, as he had served as a major in the English army of the Ionian islands. Moreover, he was a leader who had a rather clear conception of the aims of the revolution. Although not a representative of modernity, he was able to comprehend the new realities emerging from the birth of the nation-state. Kolokotronis was also an excellent morale booster, succeeding in instilling

FIGURE 29   Peter von Hess, *An old Commander and his Warriors,* 1869. Oil on canvas.
The Thanassis and Marina Martinos Collection, Athens.

military ethos, discipline, and courage in bands of untrained farmers who soon
turned into his personal, highly effective army.

His effectiveness, eloquence, strategic mind, cleverness, and political flexibility
imposed Kolokotronis as the commander-in-chief of the Peloponnese. His military career was boosted by three crucial operations of the revolution, all conceived, planned, organized, and conducted by him: the fall of Tripolitsa, the administrative capital of the Peloponnese, in September 1821; the crush of the
invading army of Dramali in June 1822; and the fierce resistance he organized
against Ibrahim from 1826 onward were all Kolokotronis's feats. He was additionally glorified when he seized Nafplio and Corinth in 1822 and 1823, respectively.

Kolokotronis was heavily involved in the politics of the revolution, though
his interests were seemingly limited to the power balance of the Peloponnese.
Initially, he clashed with the notables of the peninsula as the head of the military party. Later, he became the leader of the alliance against the central government in the two civil wars of 1825 and was imprisoned at the end of the same
year, but changed parties and allied with the government in 1827. In general,

he adopted a compromising stance between the conflicting fractions, and always retained contact even with his enemies, whether the *kocabaşıs* or the central government.

Kolokotronis was assisted and followed by a circle of close friends and loyal commanders. Among them stood out his two sons, Panos, who was killed in the second civil war, and Gennaios; his nephew Nikitas Stamatelopoulos (or Nikitaras), who embarked on a good many military expeditions in Rumeli and made a good name as an honest and exemplary patriot; Albanian-speaking Dimitrios Plapoutas, *kapos* of the Deligiannis family and scion of a large family of bandits; and various members of Petimezas family from Achaia. Lastly, Anagnostis Papageorgiou (or Anagnostaras), who initiated Kolokotronis into the Philiki Etaireia, was also a renowned warlord, who was killed in the battle of Sphaktiria (April 26, 1825).

Maniots

Mani was a secluded primitive war society in the peninsula of Taigetos, which was organized in clans and extended families and was scourged by ferocious vendettas. After 1780, Maniot society was transformed into a web of a constantly changing number of *kapetanies,* a type of small landownership based on personal principalities administered by extended families, like those of Mavromichalis, Kapetanakis, Koumoundourakis, Mourtzinou-Troupakis, Dourakis, Venetsanakis, and Grigorakis.

The inhabitants of this utterly dry, barren, and densely populated peninsula suffered serious problems of survival; they became famous warriors specialized in plundering and piracy. It is noteworthy that the Orlov uprising in 1770 started from Mani, and accordingly the Philiki Etaireia counted heavily on these ruthless and bold warriors (Figure 30). Moreover, the administrative autonomy that Mani had enjoyed since around 1780 under the command of an elected *kapetanios* or *başbuğ* (chief governor) gave the Maniots additional political and military flexibility.

The Maniots participated in all major military events in the Peloponnese and some important expeditions in Rumeli. They were excellent guerrilla warriors, loyal exclusively to their commanders, yet with a strong inclination to plundering. It was not rare for them to desert the revolutionary camp and return to Mani after a victory that secured considerable loot. Yet they fought fiercely and more reliably when they defended their homeland, as when they repelled two Egyptian attempts to enter Mani in 1826.

Petros Mavromichalis (Petrobey), one of the most emblematic Greek rebels, was the Maniot military and political leader throughout the entire revolutionary

FIGURE 30   Eugène Delacroix, *Mounted Greek Warrior,* or *Episode from the Greek War of Independence,* 1856. Oil on canvas. National Gallery-Al. Soutzos Museum, Athens.

period. He had been the *başbuğ* of Mani since 1815, and was the first appointed commander-in-chief in the Peloponnese in May 1821. Though Kolokotronis superseded him, Petrobey participated in significant battles under his command, and stood by Kolokotronis even during the civil wars.

The Mavromichalis family provided a good number of military men willing to risk their careers and lives far from the Peloponnese in search of opportunities for glory, wealth, and political power. Petrobey's son Ilias fought in Euboea where he was killed in action in 1822, while Petrobey's brother Kyriakoulis moved to Epirus, where he was also killed in the same year.

Souliots

Souli was a similar patriarchic war society in southern Epirus. The Albanian-speaking Christian Souliots settled in four villages and lived on animal husbandry, raids, and armed protection of the neighboring villages and *ayan*s. Their long fierce war with Ali Pasha during the period 1789–1804 led to their expulsion from their homeland to the Ionian islands, where they were employed by the Russian, French, and British authorities as auxiliary armed forces. Their poverty, unemployment, and lack of prospects after 1815 made them willing to return to the Ottoman lands at any cost. The conflict between Ali Pasha and the Sublime Porte offered them the desired opportunity. In 1820 they accepted the invitation of the sultan to fight on his side, but soon they changed sides and joined their former persecutor. The fall of Ali Pasha produced for the Souliots the same dead-ends as for the chieftains or officers of his army and drove them inevitably to the revolutionary camp.

Initially, they were systematically used by Mavrokordatos as a militia of the regional government of western Rumeli causing distress, suspicion, and enmity among the local chieftains. The most prominent Souliot clans, those of Botsaris and Tzavelas, were clashing with one another, and offered their armed services for money to those interested. As they were, also, in search of permanent residence, they were perceived as invaders by the local chieftains and population. Their irksome persistence toward uninterrupted payroll was their major obsession, creating the impression among the other Greeks that the Souliots were fighting only for their salaries.

Markos Botsaris was the most distinguished commander-in-chief of the Souliots, and one of the most renowned Greek warlords. He became adjutant and close partner of Mavrokordatos but was killed in 1823 during a night battle. He was succeeded by Kitsos Tzavelas, a chief of the adversary clan.

Macedonians and Other Refugees

Small bands of volunteers and refugees from other Greek as well as Balkan lands joined the revolutionary forces of the Peloponnese and Rumeli. For example, Nikolaos Kasomoulis, a leader of the unsuccessful revolution in Macedonia, became secretary of Stornaris, *kapetanios* of Aspropotamos in western Rumeli. Others formed their own bands, rambling around without a stable base, offering their armed services to the revolutionary governments or conducting raids and looting the countryside. Anastasios Karatassos, major leader of the revolution in Olympus and Naousa, his son Tsamis Karatassos, and his adjutant Angelis Gatsos formed such a unit of Macedonians, who like the Souliots, were employed by Mavrokordatos and the central government during the two sieges of Mesolonghi and the invasion of the Rumeliot army in the Peloponnese in the second civil war.

More controversial was the role of another major Macedonian rebel chief, Diamantis Nikolaou, who, along with a force of around 250 Macedonians, was employed by the regional government of eastern Rumeli in its struggle against Androutsos. He was also involved in a bloody civil war in Euboea against the local military leader Kriezotis. Later on, he and his men settled on Skopelos and Skiathos, where they turned to piracy, provoking a good deal of complaints from the local populations for their misbehavior.

Little is known about volunteer military units from other parts of the Balkans. Andreas Metaxas from the Ionian island of Cephalonia was the commander of a small, but well-trained and disciplined group of Ionian volunteers who dispersed the Albanian Lala settlements in Ilia in May 1821. Interestingly enough, this corps fought in an almost tactical manner and wore uniforms. Spyridon Spyromilios was the leader of a unit of 250 Greeks from Epirus during the second siege of Mesolonghi. Vasos Mavrovouniotis was a Montenegrin volunteer, who led a small band of Slavs in the battles of Euboea and the struggle against Ibrahim. Likewise, Bulgarian Chatzichristos, head of a small cavalry army of Bulgarians and Serbs, fought for the Greek cause in the Peloponnese.

Kocabaşıs, Clergymen, Philiki Etaireia Members, Philhellenes

A good many Peloponnesian notables put together their own groups of warriors, financed them, and conducted operations under their own leadership. Andreas Londos, Andreas Zaimis, Georgios Sisinis, Sotiris Charalambis, and others engaged energetically in military activities. The fear that the chieftains would acquire political influence through their military feats rendered the notables extremely suspicious and soon inimical to the military caste. Their military inexperience did not prevent the notables from undertaking initiatives, organizing their own corps, assuming the role of commander, and conducting military operations. A typical example was Charalambis, who commanded his corps by himself, demoting his military subordinates, the Petimezas family, to the position of simple officers. Of course, these impromptu generals were not successful. For instance, the siege of Patras undertaken by Andreas Zaimis and Andreas Londos ended in a stalemate for the rebels.

In the same vein, some metropolis sustained their own bands of guerillas and participated in military operations. The most prominent example was bishop of Karystos Neophytos, who organized two failed campaigns to Euboea with his own private army. Likewise, Germanos, the renowned metropolitan of Patras, took part in the sieges of Patras and Tripolitsa as a leader of the rebels and head of a camp.

No member of the first supreme authority of the Philiki Etaireia was a professional man of arms. When in 1820 Alexandros Ypsilantis became the supreme head of the society, this situation changed, though not radically. The serious difficulty in finding Greeks acquainted with the modern state of the art in warfare rendered the Greek Revolution a venture based on fleeting Balkan allies and recalcitrant irregulars, both with little or no comprehension of the objectives of the society. This handicap explains the absence of concrete and feasible military plans for the upcoming revolt.

The Greek Revolution started in Moldavia and Wallachia, where Alexandros Ypsilantis, at the head of an uncertain alliance of varied Balkan troops, led a hapless and badly organized campaign. He was supported by Tudor Vladimirescu, a celebrated Vlach bandit, or *pandur,* and his army made of experienced Balkan irregulars, as well as Vlach peasants of little fighting value. Moreover, Ypsilantis's staff comprised the small Moldavian and Vlach armies and their commanders, the experienced Greek officers Savvas Fokianos, Giannis Farmakis, and Georgios Olympios. Despite the desertion of Fokianos, the other two proved to be the most reliable and worthy commanders. Olympios was killed in action, while Farmakis was captured and executed in Constantinople. Finally, Ypsilantis had formed a small regular army of around sixteen hundred Balkan and Russian fighters. The core of this corps was a special unit, called the Sacred Battalion and composed of young Greek students of European schools. Apparently, Ypsilantis did not trust irregular warfare and planned to conduct conventional warfare, yet in such an inconsistent manner that disaster became inevitable.

Dimitrios Ypsilantis, Alexandros's younger brother, was sent by the Philiki Etaireia to the Peloponnese to take over the general command of operations (Figure 31). Yet, his claim to the general leadership was rejected by the local notables, while Kolokotronis's influence was too strong to be superseded. As a result, Ypsilantis was used by the Peloponnesian military party only for the legitimization of their political aspirations. He was an honest and brave officer with a limited vocation for military leadership and thus his role soon became symbolic, an expression of the supposed Russian support.

The society produced a good number of men-at-arms, such as Georgios Lassanis and Christophoros Perraivos who, despite their lack of military education, stood out as officers and advisers. Special mention should be made of Grigorios Dikaios, known as Papaflessas, a versatile politician and member of the supreme authority of the society, formally a priest and occasionally a warrior. He died in action at the battle of Maniaki in May 1825 against the invading Egyptian forces.

European volunteers, the Philhellenes, went to Greece to fight for its freedom or in search of adventure, glory, and offices. Among renowned men of letters, such as British Lord Byron, and politicians, such as Italian Santore di Santa Rosa, there were a good many professional men-at-arms, former officers of

FIGURE 31 Dionysios Tsokos, *Portrait of Dimitrios Ypsilantis*, 1887. Oil on canvas. National Historical Museum, Athens.

European armies and veterans of the Napoleonic Wars. All got involved in battles, and many, like British Frank Hastings or German Karl von Normann-Ehrenfels, died either in action or because of the hardships they had suffered. They were critical of the way the Greeks fought, and thus formed their own company fighting according to the rules of modern warfare. Most, like British Thomas Gordon and George Finlay, fought as high officers in assorted posts and many battles; others, such as Corsican Joseph Baleste, Italian Pietro Tarella, Gubernatis, and Frenchman Charles Fabvier took over the hard task of organizing a small Greek regular army, while the Irishman Richard Church assumed the office of commander-in-chief of the Greek army and Thomas Cochrane that of fleet admiral in April 1826 (Figure 32).

Some Major Characteristics of Irregular Warfare

The insurrection was conducted by the rebels without any long-term plan or coordination and was based almost entirely on irregulars. The military units consisted exclusively of infantry men, with scanty cavalry and no artillery. Their

FIGURE 32   Karl Krazeisen, *Portrait of Major Thomas Gordon*, 1827. Pencil on paper. National Gallery-Al. Soutzos Museum, Athens.

military effectiveness was based on a careful selection of the battlefield, ambush strikes, raids behind the enemy lines, clashes at close quarters, and defense behind natural fortifications (rocks, fallen tree trunks, ditches) or trenches (*tambouria*). The Greeks avoided battles in the open field, and refrained from decisive confrontations. Maximal Ottoman casualties and the pillage of their supplies, ammunition and weapons were the major objectives of the Greek ir-regulars' operations. The Greeks took excellent advantage of their exceptional shooting capacities and the mountainous landscape, moving with formidable alertness through steep slopes and gorges, and withstanding extreme weather conditions (either heavy cold or intense heat) and lack of food and water for long periods.

This style of warfare rendered sieges undesirable. Yet, as the Ottomans took refuge in the nearest fort or castle from the early days of the revolution, sieges became unavoidable. The Greeks' inexperience in this kind of operations, their lack of artillery, internal strife over the command of the besieging troops, and the easy supply of the besieged by the Ottoman fleet rendered most of these fortresses (Patras, Methoni, Koroni, Rio in the Peloponnese, Antirio, Chalkis, Karababa, Karystos in Rumeli) impregnable. Few were seized (Monemvasia, Tripolitsa, Neokatro, Corinth in the Peloponnese, Athens in Rumeli), mainly when they were effectively blockaded and their defenders were threatened with starvation. The seizure of a fortress offered unprecedented glory to the lucky chieftain and a fortified base for his headquarters.

The most distinctive idiosyncrasy of the Greek irregulars was the exclusive affiliation of each band with its commander. The men remained loyal only to him and would refuse to take orders even by the central administration if not ratified by him. As a consequence, rebel groups retained a remarkable administrative autonomy and acted on the battlefield as independently as possible. Coordination among the chieftains was extremely hard. It was vital for the dignity of each commander to act on his own initiative, and when this autonomy was relinquished for the sake of a joint large-scale operation, the condition was only provisional, to be abandoned after the end of the common cause. Only the aegis of an influential and widely favored military leader, such as Kolokotronis, Karaiskakis, or Androutsos, would enable a more lasting coalition. This operational discord was often the cause of major Greek defeats, and made the revolution seem in the Ottoman eyes as a series of local mutinies. This parceled picture led Omer Vrioni, the Ottoman field marshal from 1821 to 1824, to believe that he had to quench a series of local unrelated uprisings.

Autonomy offered the guerilla bands a significant degree of operational flexibility, which enabled them to survive even after major defeats. They would retreat, move, or counterattack impressively swiftly without being hindered by any decision making from the central headquarters or being entangled in any military bureaucratic procedures. In this way, they would defeat the Ottomans who continually confronted Greek guerilla bands, even when the Ottomans had crushed some of them. This is why Omer Vrioni began negotiations with the Greek chieftains to bring about their voluntary submission to Ottoman rule as more sensible tactics than open war with them.

The energetic participation of the chieftains in the battle was the rule. In contrast with regular senior officers, these *kapetanaioi* did not abstain from the dangers of the battle and fought like common soldiers in the first line, usually trying to prove themselves braver than their men. For this reason, a good number of them died, usually during insignificant skirmishes. The list is long: Karaiskakis, Markos Botsaris, Diakos, Ilias and Kyriakoulis Mavromichalis, Govginas, Gouras, and many other less renowned men met their death on the battlefield, while a good many others were seriously wounded (e.g., Makrygiannis). This bravado was not unreasonable but an integral prerequisite for the legitimization of the chieftain's superiority. It underlined the military merit of the chieftain in the eyes of his men and reinforced his reputation among the leaders of other bands. Only Kolokotronis, who had studied the tactics of contemporary modern armies escaped from this pattern and commanded the battle from a safe standpoint.

The logistics and payroll of the band were an exclusive (and onerous) burden of the commander. The autonomy of a warlord was contingent on his right to levy regional taxes and to recruit soldiers from among the local population. These two possibilities defined the authority of a chieftain, were vital for the financial maintenance of the band and the replacement of casualties or desertions, and consequently became the principal bone of contention between rival chiefs or military commanders and notables. It is not surprising that the cohesion of the irregular groups was extremely loose. Men-at-arms were invariably locals, the chieftain's compatriots or emissaries from other localities, and any delay in salaries or better offers from other warlords readily entailed the disbanding of the corps.

Apart from western Rumeli, where professional armies monopolized the military operations of the revolution, in all the other Greek lands, chieftains had to concede to the recruitment of conscripts invariably from the peasantry. The companies formed by these villagers initially did not correspond to any form of military unit. The soldiers, very often residents of the same village and/or relatives, brought their families to the camp, or would come and go on their own initiative. No court marshals existed and men regulated the relations between them according to local customary law. Few had any idea why they were there, while many joined the revolution only for the loot. They were susceptible to rumor spreading and enemy propaganda, which they tended to intensify and diffuse. Thus, the transformation into real warriors of these naïve, cowardly, and poorly equipped makeshift rebels would prove to be one of the hardest tasks for the Peloponnesian military leaders, but which was nevertheless accomplished. Kolokotronis invested a lot of energy and innovation in keeping up some elementary discipline and convincing his men to follow him.

Because of their strong localism, the chieftains refused to campaign far from their homeland. Thus, it was hard for the central government to find Peloponnesian troops to fight in western Rumeli in 1822, while Rumeliots rapidly abandoned the Peloponnese after their defeat by the Egyptians in the battle of Drambala in 1825.

Greek Rumeliots and Albanian chieftains had made acquaintances in Ali Pasha's army as brothers in arms. This relationship lasted throughout the Revolution. The longstanding friendship of Varnakiotis and Androutsos with Omer

Vrioni is the best-known case. This acquaintance paved the way for easy negotiations between the Rumeliot chieftains and the Ottoman authorities, the
so-called *kapakia*. Likewise, the Peloponnesian chieftains were well acquainted
with the Albanian population of the peninsula, the blood brotherhood of Kolokotronis with Ali Farmaki of Lala being the best-known case. This relationship
facilitated negotiations between Rumeliot and Albanian warlords as well as the
surrender of Ottoman fortresses to Kolokotronis.

It is not surprising that relationships between these irregular teams were not
always amicable. On the contrary, the struggle against the Ottomans was seriously affected by rivalries between diverse chieftains, which, a good number of
times, took the form of civil microwars within the broader context of the national revolution, regardless of its aims.

The Irregulars and the Challenge of Organizing a Regular Army

As soon as Ioannis Capodistrias assumed his position as governor of Greece,
he attempted to reorganize the irregulars and gradually transform them into a
regular army. His immediate objectives were dictated by the need for a reliable
force able to recapture Rumeli, and the abrogation of the *armatoliks*. This project
was carried out in two stages. Initially, in January 1828, Capodistrias dismissed
all Peloponnesian irregular bands and assigned Ypsilantis the task of organizing
the Rumeliots. Ypsilantis formed ten *chiliarchies,* one thousand-man units, and
a significant number of smaller companies. The old *kapetanaioi* either had to
concede to their relegation to the office of *chiliarchos* or retire. This phase lasted
for a year and was characterized by the successful recapture of Rumeli by the
Rumeliot forces, a good many problems with provisions and salaries, the controversial appointment of Avgoustinos Capodistrias, the governor's brother,
as general inspector of Rumeli, discontent and complaints of the irregulars, and
mutiny of units at Thebes in August of 1829. Then, in October 1829, these *chiliarchies* were converted to twenty light battalions, a development that further
downgraded the former *kapetanaioi* who had joined them as officers.

The formation of a modern European-like regular army by the rebels proved
to be a hard venture, envisaged since the early days of the Revolution but in-
completely carried out in practice. Irregular chieftains perceived these attempts
as a serious threat to their military and political hegemony, while the grass roots,
completely unacquainted with European warfare, derided all pertinent endeavors. Dimitrios Ypsilantis was the first to plan and organize some small
regular units, but it was Mavrokordatos who officially enacted the formation
of a company of regular infantry under the command of Pietro Tarella. The

FIGURE 33   Karl Krazeisen,
*Portrait of Colonel Charles
Fabvier,* 1827. Pencil on
paper. National Gallery-Al.
Soutzos Museum, Athens.

company was annihilated in its first serious operation at Peta of Epirus (June 4,
1822). In 1824, a battalion was re-formed under the command of Panagiotis Ra-
dios, replaced by Charles Fabvier the following year (Figure 33). This army
launched two unsuccessful campaigns in Euboea and Chios, and had a difficult collaboration with the irregulars in the operations around the besieged
Acropolis during 1826–1827. After Fabvier's return to France, Capodistrias appointed Bavarian colonel Carl Wilhelm Freiherr von Heideck, and later on
French general Camille-Alphonse Trézel, head of the regular corps. The latter
strove to introduce the regulations of the French army. Until the assassination
of Capodistrias the organization of the regular army had not advanced
significantly.

   As becomes apparent, the Greek Revolution was the monopoly of irregulars,
who fought in accordance with their own archaic modes. Although they did
not constitute a homogeneous group spreading throughout the Greek lands,

their leaders, vested interests, and types of warfare had enough commonalities for them to be considered a distinct revolutionary elite.

Dimitrios Papastamatiou

References

Dakin, Douglas. 1972. *The Unification of Greece, 1770–1923*. London.

Dakin, Douglas. 1978. *The Greek Struggle for Independence, 1821–1833*. London.

Diamandouros, Nikiforos. 2002. *Οι απαρχές της συγκρότησης σύγχρονου κράτους στην Ελλάδα, 1821–1828* [The beginning of modern state-building in Greece, 1821–1828]. Athens.

Ιστορία του Ελληνικού Έθνους [History of the Greek nation]. 1975. Vol. 12. Athens.

Ιστορία των οργανώσεων του ελληνικού στρατού, 1821–1954 [History of the organizations of the Greek army, 1821–1954]. 1955. Athens.

Kokkinos, Dionysios A. 1974. *Η Ελληνική Επανάστασις* [The Greek Revolution]. Athens.

Kotaridis, Nikos G. 1993. *Παραδοσιακή επανάσταση και Εικοσιένα* [Traditional revolution and 1821]. Athens.

Papageorgiou, Stephanos. 1986. *Η στρατιωτική πολιτική του Καποδίστρια. Δομή, οργάνωση και λειτουργία του στρατού ξηράς της καποδιστριακής περιόδου* [The military policy of Capodistrias: Structure, organization and function of the army of the Capodistrian period]. Athens.

Rotzokos, Nikos. 1997. *Επανάσταση και εμφύλιος στο Εικοσιένα* [Revolution and civil war in 1821]. Athens.

Stathis, Panagiotis. 2007. "From Klephts and *Armatoloi* to Revolutionaries." In *Ottoman Rule and the Balkans, 1760–1850: Conflict, Transformation, Adaptation*, edited by Antonis Anastasopoulos and Elias Kolovos, 167–179. Rethymno.

Theotokas, Nikos. 2012. *Ο βίος του στρατηγού Μακρυγιάννη. Απομνημονεύματα και ιστορία* [The life of general Makrygiannis: Memoirs and history]. Athens.

Theotokas, Nikos, and Nikos Kotaridis. 2006. *Η οικονομία της βίας. Παραδοσιακές και νεωτερικές εξουσίες στην Ελλάδα του 19ου αιώνα* [The economy of violence: Traditional and modern authorities in nineteenth-century Greece]. Athens.

Tsiamalos, Demetrios. 2007. "Κοινωνική και επαναστατική συνείδηση των ενόπλων της Ρούμελης στην επανάσταση του 1821" [Social and revolutionary conceptions of the armed men of Rumeli during the revolution of 1821]. PhD diss., Panteio University of Social and Political Sciences.

Tzakis, Dionysios. 1997. "Αρματολισμός, συγγενικά δίκτυα και εθνικό κράτος. Οι ορεινές επαρχίες της Άρτας στο πρώτο ήμισυ του 19ου αιώνα" [Armaloloi, kinship networks, and the nation state: The mountainous provinces of Arta in the first half of the nineteenth century]. PhD diss., Panteio University of Social and Political Sciences.

Vakalopoulos, Apostolos. 1991. *Τα ελληνικά στρατεύματα του 1821. Οργάνωση, ηγεσία, τακτική, ήθη, ψυχολογία* [The Greek armies of 1821: Organization, tactics, morals, psychology].Thessaloniki.

Veremis, Thanos. 1997. *The Military in Greek Politics: From Independence to Democracy.* London.

Vyzantios, Christos. 1837. *Ιστορία του τακτικού στρατού από της πρώτης συστάσεως κατά το 1821 μέχρι του 1833* [History of the regular army since its formation in 1821 to 1833]. Athens.

Vyzantios, Christos. 1956. *Ιστορία των κατά την Ελληνικήν Επανάστασιν εκστρατειών και μαχών ων συμμετέσχεν ο τακτικός στρατός από του 1821 μέχρι του 1833* [History of the campaigns and battles during the Greek Revolution in which the regular army participated from 1821 to 1833]. Athens.

Women

Wars have a direct and tragic effect on the civilian population, but they also act as a catalyst for shaping their future. This is exactly what happened to Greek women in the revolution of 1821.

Class, social status, and the economic situation of the families to which women belonged usually affected their chances for survival, and advantages often allowed them to continue their lives in some safety and in the traditional way. The situation of poor, lower-class women was dismal.

Most sources refer to women only in connection with certain events, like long-lasting sieges or the hard conditions the refugees had to face, but mainly focus on their sufferings from massacre, rape, and enslavement. Whenever they are reported, the numbers of women actually killed are often approximations or pure conjecture. Ordinarily, however, the number of women captured must have been higher than those killed, as both the Turks and the Egyptians were much more interested in selling young women and children as slaves for a large profit. The possibility of prisoners being ransomed or exchanged was also something that was taken into consideration by the enemies for both sides. Older women were often slaughtered by the Turks and the Egyptians because they did not have any market value.

From the first days of the outbreak of the revolution, the higher social classes tried to move their families—women, children, and elderly parents—to safer regions. Town and village authorities attempted sometimes, but not always successfully, to move all the civilian population away from areas near which battles were taking place.

Wherever there were foreign consulates, it was common for women and children to seek shelter there. Pierre David, the French consul general at Smyrna,

bravely helped many residents of the city, both European and Greek, during
the months of persecution that followed the outbreak of the war in the Principalities. However, the Russian consul, Spyridon Destounis, a Greek from Cephalonia, himself and his family being in danger, could do little to help the
Greeks. The French consul at Patras, Hugues Jean Louis Pouqueville, brother
of the better-known traveler, consul at Ioannina and writer François Pouqueville,
saved many women and children, offering them shelter in the consulate. Quite
the opposite happened with the British consul in the same city, Philip James
Green, a notorious friend of the Turks, who sent away the women and their
children who asked for his protection. In the island of Psara, however, the Turks
broke down the door of the Russian consulate and killed both the consul and
the women he was protecting there (Germanos 1837, 23–25; Massé 2017, 105–
106, 112–117; Nikodimos 1862, 451–452; Prousis 1992; Raffenel 1822, 243–272).

Soon after the news of the revolution reached Constantinople, the lives of
the noble ladies of Fanari were directly and drastically affected. Those who remained in the city saw their high-ranking husbands and relatives being executed, and were themselves often exiled to faraway towns of Asia Minor.

Massacres and destruction took place in Thessaloniki, where a considerable
number of women were also sold as slaves. Extended and indiscriminate massacres took place at Naousa in western Macedonia. In Smyrna and the nearby
villages, the massacres lasted over two months. Even European merchants and
their families were in danger. Early on, some Greek families managed to flee to
neighboring Aegean islands. Later, there was a general prohibition on leaving
the city and even the European ships were searched in order to stop the exodus of the Greek population. The French consul, David, with his undaunted
attitude hid many Greek families in the consulate. We have no information on
the number of the victims. At Kydonies it was the male population that was
massacred, whereas women and children were captured to be sold as slaves
according to the information given to Stratford Canning, the British ambassador in Constantinople (Prousis 2011, 196–197). Perhaps the worst and best-
known massacres took place in Chios. According to the estimate of the British
consul general at Smyrna, Francis Werry, forty-five thousand women and
children were taken alive and then sold as slaves. Some of them were later
ransomed.

At the end of May 1824, forty-five Egyptian ships arrived at the island of
Kassos in the Dodecanese. The subsequent pillage, massacre, and enslavement
of women left the island desolate. It is said that the Egyptian ships took two
thousand women to Alexandria, where they were sold. Only a few of them were
eventually ransomed. The inhabitants who survived were moved to other islands, mainly to Paros and Naxos.

Less than a month later, the total destruction of the small, but important for its fleet, island of Psara took place. About half of the seven thousand population escaped in their own ships, but most of the women of the island were lost. Some fell with their children into the sea and drowned to avoid capture, others died when the defenders detonated the ammunition depot as soon as the Turks entered the town's fortress. Some women who tried to escape in rowing boats were killed. Others were captured. The population that survived was settled first at Monemvasia and later in Euboea.

An estimated four thousand women and children were captured by the army of Ibrahim Pasha and his Egyptian troops in 1826, when they conquered the town of Aitoliko in western Greece. Soon after, the besieged Mesolonghi fell. Much has been written about the women of this heroic town, mainly surrounding the events of its second siege. A great deal of publicity was given to its fate all over Europe, because Lord Byron had died there.

We do not know the exact number of the women who died or were captured in Mesolonghi, as several estimates were given by both Greek and foreign sources, the latter in fact giving a much greater number of captives, five to six thousand. The fate of those captured has been described by various authors. It is said that the women were first examined by doctors to establish whether they were virgins and whether they had some disease. Then Ibrahim chose the prettiest, kept the ones he liked himself and the rest were given as gifts to his officials. Those men, women, or children who were sold in the slave market of Methoni, a town of the southeastern Morea, had a much worse fate. Charles Deval (1830, 185–187, 192–194) describes the horrible conditions he saw there. He met a group of about twenty older women from Mesolonghi, who were carrying wood from the mountains and were beaten when they slowed down. He saw an old woman killed because she was considered useless since older women sold at extremely low prices. On the contrary, a young virgin could fetch 1,500 piastres. Some women and children of distinguished Greek families were ransomed, but we do not know the details.

Most sources repeatedly refer to the panic-stricken flight of women to the mountains; their hiding in remote caves and inaccessible places to avoid their pursuers was quite common. When they found themselves in a desperate situation, they fought by throwing stones and rocks at their enemies. These bids for escape usually had a tragic end: the women killed themselves by falling off cliffs, often with their children. Sometimes they managed to drag their enemies down to death with them. Alternatively, they fell into a lake, a river, or the sea to drown, or set themselves on fire. Similar tragedies were also mentioned in the press, as for example that the Turks of Patras pillaged neighboring villages, killed four hundred women and children, and captured even more. Generally, women chose to die rather than be taken as slaves, a much worse fate. Women successfully fighting off their pursuers were also given publicity; on June 8, 1825, in eastern Rumeli, women who were hiding in a cave managed to kill six men by throwing stones at them and obliging the rest to withdraw. In the fight two women were killed.

Although there must have often been exchanges of women and children with captive Turks, we know little about them. They usually belonged to prominent families, as was the case with Kitsos Tzavellas's son. In Crete, as well, women of high-ranking Ottoman families were exchanged with simple captive Cretan women. We know a little more about the families who ransomed their womenfolk and children, or their attempts to do that in the early years of the revolution. To ransom a captive was complicated and required a long time and large sums of money, usually several times more than the money paid to buy a slave. Years later families were still trying to find their captive relatives, as we know from their petitions and official lists.

It was almost impossible for poorer people to find the money to ransom their families. On July 29, 1824, the men of Psara petitioned the Greek Parliament (*Vouleftikon*) for the money to ransom their womenfolk and send it with their representative on a European ship to buy them off from Smyrna, Chios, Mytilini, and Koussandassi, where they were at that time. Their petition was endorsed. Then the government (*Ektelestikon*) asked for a name list of the women and children, and the places where each was held. Finally, only 10,000 piastres were given to be shared proportionately for ransoming the captives. The money was entirely inadequate since 10,000 piastres were demanded just for captain Constantinos Karatzas's wife and child. The people of Psara were assisted, however, by their rich compatriot Ioannis Varvakis, a member of Philiki Etaireia (Nikodimos 1862, 1:537–544, 554).

During the civil wars and particularly the invasion of the Morea by troops from Rumeli, women also suffered, this time by the Greeks. The attacks against them and the destruction of the crops that deprived them of any means of subsistence were not much different to those made by the Turks. The sources do not agree whether there were actually rapes by irregular soldiers. Some claim that rapes were rare, since they were morally condemned. There was also a widespread superstition that anyone responsible for such a crime would be killed in the war. But in the prevailing chaos, people's behavior was changing radically.

Before the war, it would have been extremely rare to see a group of young Greek men attempting to rape a young girl. Makrygiannis, however, describes seeing and stopping such a crime in Athens. Similar phenomena appeared even in the Aegean islands. So the sexual abuse of women became a matter of public concern, but usually the guilty parties could be punished only in places where conditions were reasonably normal. In fact, the violation of a virgin was sometimes punished even more strictly than what Byzantine laws or the newly introduced criminal law required. Often, however, the culprit had to pay a considerable fine, but usually he was obliged to marry the girl.

Apart from the violence, women faced a decreasing amount of food for themselves and their children. Agricultural production had greatly declined during the revolution and it was often insufficient for the local populations, the troops, and the refugees. If there was any production somewhere, it was not certain who was going to benefit from it, because often the enemy might either collect or destroy it in order not to leave it for the Greeks. Trade was also at its lowest in most places. For lack of proper housing many families lived in caves or improvised huts. Basic, decent clothing was also scarce, and women and children were in rags.

In 1823–1824, George Waddington (1825, 85–95) tried to collect valid information about the long-suffering residents of Athens, Aigina, Salamis, Syros, Tinos, and Mykonos, and the respective refugees from various regions at the same places. Information was collected through the clergy, in cooperation with Gropius, the old consul of Austria in Athens. In Athens there were 3,350 women and children and 433 men in dire need, 672 of them were refugees. In Salamis, apart from the Athenians, there were refugees from various towns and villages of Boeotia, Euboea, and Kydonies. From the 11,477 people living in Salamis, the local population was only 192 people. In the above-mentioned six places, out of the 20,851 people who lived there in extreme poverty, four-fifths were women.

During the second siege of Athens, the living conditions of women and children was so bad that the bishop Neophytos of Talanti, as acting bishop of Athens, along with the abbot of Penteli monastery and Georgios Psyllas, asked the inhabitants of Aigina to help them. The news became widely known and fund raising began for the Athenian women and children. A moving article presented their tragic situation in the *Geniki Ephimeris tis Ellados* on March 16, 1827, and listed the names of those who had already contributed to the fund raising and the amount each of them had offered; the sum amounted to three thousand sixty-two piastres.

In Nafplio, where the population had greatly increased through internal migration and by an influx, most people lived in desperate conditions. It was not only the prevailing poverty, but also the recurring epidemics due to the unhealthy living conditions. The widows of fighters, and other women who had been set free from their captivity and had no relatives and means of subsistence, were begging in the streets and filed petitions asking for a small pension (Doxiadis 2012, 172–175). The government tried to help, but the economy was so bad

that there was nothing much to be done. The first systematic attempts to ame-
liorate somewhat the living conditions of the refugees were introduced by Capodistrias, but even in 1830 refugee women and children continued coming
from Crete (Archeia Ellinikis Palingenesias 1971–2012 [1821–1832] 14, 257–258).
Women were employed along with a smaller number of men to build the pier
and the Orphanage in Aigina (1827–1828). That at least provided them with
some minimal means of sustenance.

In 1822, after the defeat of the Greeks and the Philhellenes at Peta, a second
wave of refugees followed, but these were denied asylum in the Ionian islands.
A couple of years later, when British policy started to change and the Greeks
were considered belligerents and not rebels, more refugees were accepted.
During the second siege of Mesolonghi, women from this town went not only
to Kalamos, but to Zante as well. There they begged in order to collect contributions for the fighting men of Mesolonghi. There is a shattering prose draft
by Dionysios Solomos, partly repeated in "I gynaika tis Zakythos" ('Η γυναίκα
τῆς Ζάκυθος; The woman of Zakythos), describing the drama of those women
who begged while listening at the same time to the sound of the cannon-fire
from Mesolonghi, which could be heard even in Zante. When Mesolonghi fell
in 1826, the British felt obliged to accept surviving civilians from the town, and
other women fleeing Ibrahim Pasha's invasion.

Apart from those women who occasionally fought against their pursuers,
there were others who took part in the war proper. Two of these women have
been celebrated and admired ever since: Laskarina Pinotsi (1781–1825), called
Bouboulina from her second marriage to Dimitrios Bouboulis; and Manto Mavrogeni (1796 / 1797–1840), daughter of the merchant Nikolaos Mavrogenis,
member of an important family of the Cyclades, which included Nikolaos Mavrogenis (1735–1790), former great dragoman of the Ottoman fleet, and prince
of Wallachia and Moldavia. Their contemporary Philhellenes and foreign travelers were fascinated by these women and devoted long passages to them in
their books. Their portraits and illustrations, not always realistic, also appeared
at that time. In France, a costume like the one Bouboulina used to wear came
into fashion and was named after her: *robes de dame à la Bobeline*. To the present day the memory of these women is vibrant and alive in the collective sub-
conscious of the Greeks, wrapped in a rather romantic aura created mostly by
older semiacademic writings. Proof of the official acclaim of Bouboulina today
is the fact that on March 30, 2018, a presidential decree posthumously conferred
on her the honorary rank of rear admiral, the Medal of Exceptional Acts and
the First Class War Cross.

Bouboulina came from the island of Ydra, but through her two marriages
became connected to distinguished nautical families of Spetses (Figure 34). In

FIGURE 34 Unknown artist, *Laskarina Bouboulina*. Second half of the nineteenth century. Oil on canvas. National Historical Museum, Athens.

1821, she was already a widow from both of her marriages to wealthy shipowners and she had managed to increase her family wealth even further. She had six children, and three of her sons were killed during the war. Philimon (1860, 3:155) describes her as "a phenomenon" and "an exceptional natural being." Although it is often said that she had been a member of the Philiki Etaireia, this assumption is not corroborated by the existing lists of its members.

At the beginning of the war, she took part in the blockade of Nafplio onboard *Agamemnon*, her newly built eighteen-cannon ship, and three smaller ships of her own. She was at the siege of Tripolitsa, where it is said that she procured a very large sum of money from the women in the pasha's harem by promising them her protection. She participated in several other naval operations, such as the blockade of Monemvasia. In the first years of the revolution, she spent nearly all her assets on her small personal fleet. During the civil war, she was on the side of Kolokotronis and the military, so she ended up being herself persecuted. In 1825 she was killed during a family dispute with another Spetsiot family, whose daughter one of her sons had abducted in order to marry her.

Manto (Magdalini) Mavrogeni was a different personality. She was young and pretty, rich and dressed in the European fashion (Figure 35). She was also well educated and spoke Italian and French. Through surviving private documents we know a great deal about her personal problems, but the details of her participation in the war are less well documented. She made considerable financial contributions to the revolution, which eventually ruined her completely. It was said that she was also a member of the Philiki Etaireia, but her name is not found on the lists either. It has not been confirmed that Capodistrias conferred on her the honorary rank of lieutenant general. Incidentally, it should be made clear that only one woman's name is included in the lists of members of the Philiki Etaireia, that of Kyriaki, wife of the physician Michail Naftis. They lived in Smyrna, and since Kyriaki found some secret documents that her husband held, with the consent of other members of the Philiki Etaireia the husband initiated Kyriaki, who gave the prescribed oath and contributed 3,000 piastres.

In Mykonos, Manto armed 150 men to go and fight in the Morea, but only fifty of them, under Antonis Rakas, took part in an expedition to prevent the

FIGURE 35   Fausto Zonaro, *Manto Mavrogenous,* 1901. Oil on canvas. National Historical Museum, Athens.

Turks from landing in Samos in July 1821. Manto mentions that, to avoid troubles with her family, she had secretly funded another expedition to Chios under the name of her cousin Dimitrios Valetas. In October 1822, leading a band of men, she helped repel an attack of Algerian pirates on Mykonos. Some Philhellenes write that she participated with ships in the expedition to Karystos, but the only certainty is that she offered 2,000 piastres for that cause. An official letter from Dimitrios Ypsilantis certifies that during the first two years of the war she financed two hundred men to fight in the Morea. During the war she also started, in vain, a futile legal battle for breach of promise against Ypsilantis, to whom she had once been engaged.

Manto spent her considerable dowry and she even borrowed money in order to finance the revolution. Her relationship with her family deteriorated, and in the end she depended on occasional small state allowances for her living. Her many attempts to recover money that she had lent, and several stolen valuable objects of hers, proved fruitless. Capodistrias, and later King Othon, gave her a more permanent small pension. She died in extreme poverty in Paros in 1840.

Manto wrote two letters on the subject of the revolution, one to the women of England and the other to the women of France. Blaquiere claims that the first was written at his suggestion. It is said that she sent the letter to the French women with two French officers who gave it to Jean-François Ginouvier, and it was published at the end of his book *Mavrogénie ou l'héroïne de la Grèce* (Paris 1825). Eugène de Villeneuve also included a French version of a text in which Manto described the character of Greek men (Blancard 1909, 651 ff.; Tasoulas 1997).

Another widow also participated in naval operations: Domna Visvizi (1783–1850) was from Chios but married in Ainos in Thrace. Domna and her five children were aboard the ship *Kalomoira,* owned and commanded by her husband, Chatzi Antonis Visvizis, during the war. When Visvizis was killed in a naval operation in Euboea in July 1822, Domna took over the command of the ship with her crew of seventy-five men and continued fighting. By the end of 1823, she had no means of maintaining the ship any longer. She asked for financial help from the government, but it was not given, so in 1824, she conceded the boat to the fleet of Ydra. The family lived in penury, petitioning the state for a small allowance. One of her sons, Themistocles, among a handful of other boys, was sent by the French Philhellenic Committee in Paris to study in France.

A young woman who led a small group of men is mentioned mainly by Blaquiere and François Pouqueville. The former met her at Gastouni and he claims that the local notable Georgios Sisinis confirmed everything she had told him. She was Constantina Zacharias, one of the daughters of a famous klepht killed in the early nineteenth century. In the winter 1822 she was wounded and retired to Gastouni to recover; later she fought at Patras, where she was again wounded and at that time she was still recovering. Blaquiere writes that he persuaded her to give up fighting and promised to secure for her a small allowance through the London Greek Committee. Pouqueville's account of Constantina does not seem reliable, as it reads like a romantic novel.

Another woman from Mani, a middle-aged mother of five children, Stavrianna Savvaina, fought with Kyriakoulis Mavromichalis's corps in Morea and in Rumeli. In 1829, at the Argos National Assembly, she submitted a petition asking for a small pension for her participation in several battles, confirmed by the signed certificates of a number of chieftains. The assembly recommended to the government the acceptance of her petition.

In general, it was common for the women of Mani and Souli and occasionally in Crete to participate in fighting. The former took part in the siege of Tripolitsa and its subsequent looting. They showed exceptional bravery when Ibrahim Pasha invaded Mani, fighting to push back the Egyptian troops. They successfully faced down sieges in their towers and fought in the battles of Verga and Polyaravos. They did not bear arms, but went into battle carrying all kinds of domestic or farm tools or clubs, iron rods, and stones. The most famous participation of the Souliot women in battle was at Navariko.

An educated lady, Evanthia Kairi (1799–1866), became more widely known at the time through a letter to philhellene ladies that received great publicity and emotionally moved the ladies abroad. Evanthia, sister of Theophilos Kairis, an enlightened teacher and fighter, corresponded with Korais and on his suggestion she had translated into Greek François Fénelon's *Traité de l'éducation des filles*, which, however, was never published. In 1820, her Greek translation of Jean Nicolas Bouilly's *Conseils à ma fille* was printed at Kydonies, and in 1826 her tragedy *Nikiratos*— inspired by the events of Mesolonghi—was printed at Nafplio. Her letter to philhellene ladies was printed anonymously at the printing house in Ydra in 1825, under the title: "A Letter by Some Greek Women to the Philhellene Ladies: Composed by One of the Most Important Greek Ladies. E. N." Thirty-one Greek women signed the letter. Most probably Evanthia wrote one more letter, published anonymously in the *Geniki Ephimeris tis Ellados* on December 24, 1827. She discussed the problem of the refugees from Kydonies and Moschonisia, who, years after of the destruction of their home towns, had not been given a specific place to settle. Evanthia cared about them because she had lived in Kydonies with her brother, who had taught at its famous school, since 1812 (Kitromilides 1983).

With the exception of Bouboulina, women were not normally involved in politics, but it seems that they did occasionally influence certain developments. Perhaps the best-known case is that of Asimina Goura, wife of the general

Giannis Gouras, who, according to Anastasios Goudas, had received some education. It is said that through her influence, Gouras signed the petition for British protection. When Gouras became commandant of the Acropolis of Athens, she lived with him there. Her friction with Odysseas Androutsos's mother affected the relationship between Gouras and Androutsos, and the Athenian notables as well. When Gouras was killed, at his funeral Asimina encouraged his troops and declared herself their leader. Subsequently, she became a member of the acting committee of the Acropolis (Figure 36). She was killed on January 12 / 13, 1827, when part of the Erechtheion collapsed after bombing by the Turks. Another literate woman, Vasos Mavrovouniotis's wife,

FIGURE 36   Nicolas-Louis-François Gosse, *A Greek Heroine,* *aka The Battle of the Acropolis,* 1827. Oil on canvas. National Gallery-Al. Soutzos Museum, Athens.

Eleni, was said to have acted as his advisor and secretary who carried out his correspondence with Kütahı (Mehmed Reşid) Pasha.

During the civil war, Georgios Kountouriotis, then president of the executive, attempted to use Angelina, the wife of Nikitas Stamatelopoulos, or Nikitaras, as an intermediary with Kolokotronis's faction. Angelina was one of the daughters of the klepht Zacharias. On March 1, 1824, she wrote a diplomatic letter to Kountouriotis detailing the tragedies caused by the civil war; she did not take sides but made it clear that she would not get involved in these affairs. Only one woman attended the workings of one of the national assemblies: it was Manto, but her presence there was not due to her interest in public affairs but rather to her hope of having her appeal against Dimitrios Ypsilantis on the matter of the breach of promise read and discussed.

At the beginning of August 1826, a protest was organized at Salamis by Athenian women refugees, supposedly instigated by the Athenian notable Zacharitsas. The women demonstrated in front of the house where Colonel Charles Fabvier, commander of the regular army, resided, demanding that he should not leave Salamis but stay and fight with the Greeks who were besieged in the Acropolis of Athens.

Despite the exceptional circumstances, people's private lives went on as before, and were often connected to politics and public affairs. It was claimed that marriages never stopped, regardless of the enemy presence and the burned villages, which made the Greeks refugees in their own country, because they wanted to increase their population. Class and wealth were still fundamental considerations of marriages, as were the establishment or consolidation of alliances between influential families or the need for reconciliation with old enemies and the securing of mutual trust. All these were of paramount importance among the Greek chieftains and politicians, and marriage became a very useful tool, since kinship by law was considered to be the same as kinship by blood in Greek society. There are several examples which show how connections established through marriages could influence politics. Theodoros Kolokotronis arranged his elder son Panos's marriage to Eleni, Bouboulina's daughter. Through this he secured not only a very considerable dowry, but he also linked his own family to another influential shipowning family of the islands. Bouboulina, on the other hand, extended her influence into the Morea. When Panos was killed, Kolokotronis attempted to keep his widow with her dowry in his household, but Bouboulina took her secretly away, leaving her dowry behind. Eventually, either through love or for political purposes, Eleni married the general Theodorakis Grivas, establishing thus a bond with the Rumeliot warlords (Angelomatis-Tsougarakis 2008, 47–51).

Similar unions were very common: the notable of Rumeli Anastasios Lidor-ikis, gave his four daughters to four chieftains; one of them, Asimina, became Gouras's wife. General Nikolaos Makris wedded the daughter of Athanasios Razi-Kotsikas, a local notable of Mesolonghi, during the siege of the town. Alexandros Mavrokordatos gave his sister Aikaterini in marriage to Spyridon Trikoupis, Lord Guilford's former secretary, politician, and historian of the Greek Revolution. Papaflessas managed to marry his niece to Constantinos Mavromichalis. As far as we know, it was exceptional for a future bride to refuse to wed the man chosen by her family.

Love and politics combined with financial considerations made the option of marriage even by violent means desirable. This is demonstrated by a couple of well-documented cases. Gennaios Kolokotronis, in love with Diamantoula Notara, wanted to abduct her with the help of his soldiers. Makrygiannis, however, dissuaded him by pointing out that, if he abducted her, she would never receive her very considerable dowry. On the other hand, Diamantoula's brother Ioannis Notaras and his men entered into a fight with his relative Panagiotis Notaras and his followers because both wanted to marry Sophia Rentis, daughter of Theocharis Rentis, another very rich *kocabaşıs* of Corinth. Their fight resulted in the destruction of the best part of Sofiko, a village near Corinth. In both cases the rivalry was of course not just for the woman, but also for her dowry: a part of the revenue from the Corinthian currant. This must have been the principal motive in both of these supposed love stories. Sophia was eventually married to Dimitrios Kallergis (Angelomatis-Tsougarakis 2008, 51)

Marriages of Greek men with Muslim women, after they converted and were christened, were not unknown either. Greek women regarded this with displeasure and disdain. At least two well-known Greek fighters, Constantinos Metaxas and Panagiotis Rodios, are said to have married converted Muslim girls. This was also the case with Chatzichristos Dragović, who was of Serbian descent.

Occasionally, Greek women also married non-Greek men, European Philhellenes or travelers, who often give us the relevant information themselves. We have already briefly mentioned Eugène de Villeneuve who was married to a Greek, Angelina Katsaiti, while he was in Smyrna. Johann Jacob Meyer married Altani Inglezou in Mesolonghi.

During the revolution, the role of the Church in marital affairs was partly restricted and marriage took on a civil character as the legal procedure changed and the adjudication of divorces was entrusted to state courts. The Church remained responsible for the spiritual dissolution of the marriage, according to Byzantine laws which remained state laws, and its mediation in an attempt to reconcile the couples was a prerequisite. An abundance of still unpublished documents of divorces in the Greek Public Archives show that it was usually women who filed for a divorce, mostly on grounds of abandonment, maltreatment and abuse, drunkness, and / or unsocial habits and behavior. Illegal marriages were also dissolved.

A case of a divorce granted is very strange, if true; a woman of the island of Psara, Angeliki Tsakali, was granted a divorce from her husband, Papadimitrakis, because he had shown cowardice during the expedition to Chios and had deserted Kanaris's fireship. (Angelomatis-Tsougarakis 2008, 53; 2016, 70; Doxiadis 2012, 217; Tsoukala 2010, 893–894).

It has been shown that the legal changes and their intricacies introduced during the revolution made the previously easy personal recourse of women to justice more difficult, but they did not affect their rights, which were considerable in comparison with the legal rights most European women enjoyed (Doxiadis 2007, 75–80; 2012, 217).

However, in Public Archives of Greece in Athens there are many documents of the revolutionary years showing that women actively petitioned the Ministry of Religion, either themselves, or through a representative, claiming their rights according to the family law, when they believed they were wronged.

Social mores were also changing, and previously unacceptable liberties made an appearance. The relaxation of the very strict prewar morals was regarded with disapproval by contemporaries. Even though innocent European customs were frowned upon, much more loose practices were introduced. Concubinage was one of them. Although it had used to be rather common in the Ionian islands during the Venetian rule, it was rarely encountered in the rest of Greece. During the revolution, however, warlords often kept their lovers or concubines openly, and occasionally took them along in their camps or their expeditions.

The less scandalous case, which is seldom referred to, is that of Theodoros Kolokotronis, whose wife Aikaterini died in 1820. Five years later, in Ydra he met Margarita Velissari, who became his partner until the end of his life. In 1836 they had a son, Panagiotis, whom Kolokotronis acknowledged in this will. Panagiotis became a distinguished officer of the Greek army himself.

Professional female dancers and musicians made their appearance at that time, too. A dancer called Anastasia was popular and made quite an impression on Édouard Grasset, who describes her performance in detail. Much stranger is the information that Papaflessas, on his way to fight Ibrahim Pasha, took with him a woman who played the tambourine and a male violinist.

Organized prostitution, common only in the big cities of the Ottoman Empire, was unknown in the largest part of Greece. In small, local Greek communities there may have been some women of loose morals, but this was socially unacceptable, and those accused of an indecent lifestyle were punished to exile

by both the Greeks and the Turks. One such seems to have been the anonymous woman with whom Panagiotis Monastiriotis and Dimitrios Christidis
had some sexual encounters, as the former mentions cryptically in his diary
recording his stay in Athens (February 6 to March 14, 1826) (Angelomatis-
Tsougarakis 1992, 349–350; 2008, 63–64; 2016, 72). However, in 1828, we have
an account of more or less organized prostitution at the outskirts of Patras
(Mangeart 1830, 191–194).

On the positive side, the place of women in society was changing in the field
of education. The revolution brought the first sign of change on April 27, 1822,
when the Peloponnesian Senate recommended to all parents to take care of the
education of the children of both sexes.

Two years later, four of the largest monasteries of Athens decided to establish and fund schools for boys and girls, using the Lancasterian system. Their
actual establishment was undertaken by the Philomousos Etaireia ton Athinon.
The girls' school was housed on the Acropolis and appropriately enough was
called Parthenon, not only after its location, but because it was a school for girls,
or *parthenoi*. The school was attended by fifty-two girls of the best Athenian
families, and an equal number of young boys. The head teacher was Neophytos
Nikitoplos (Evangelidis 1936, 1:244–247; Sourmelis 1834, 71–72, 126–131).

On the island of Syros, the most important Greek commercial center in the
Aegean, there was a school for both boys and girls, before 1829. It was directed
by a German doctor, Christian Ludwig Korck, member of the American missionary society. This school used the Lancasterian system. A committee of eight
women was officially appointed to supervise the school and the girls. Kyriak-
oula Nafti, the only woman member of the Philiki Etaireia, was a member of
this committee. A fund-raising drive began and contributions toward the
building of the school came from sixty-one women and sixty-seven men (Evangelidis 1936, 2:81–84).

Greek women's painful path during the War of Independence led through
narrow and difficult passages to the new reality of the small but free Greek state.
Gradually, this state and its women citizens joined the rest of the European countries, accepting most of their values and ways of life, but keeping alive the central
core of their old traditional world of family and social values. In the *longue durée*,
however, as a result of the Greek Revolution, this traditional world and its values
as far as women were concerned was bound to enter a course of change.

Eleni Angelomatis-Tsougarakis

References

Primary sources

Vouli ton Ellinon [Hellenic Parliament]. 1971–2012. *Αρχεία ελληνικής παλιγγενεσίας* [Archives of Greek regeneration]. Athens.

Γενική Εφημερίς της Ελλάδος [General Newspaper of Greece]. 1825–1832.

Γενικά Αρχεία του Κράτους, Κεντρική Υπηρεσία, Μινιστέριον της Θρησκείας [General State Archives, Central Service, Ministry of Religion]. Athens.

Protopsaltis, Emmanouil, ed. 1974. *Ιστορικόν Αρχείον Μαυροκορδάτου* [Mavrokordatos historical archive]. Vol. 4, *Έγγραφα του Αγώνος 1824* [Documents of the Struggle 1824]. *Μνημεία Ελληνικής Ιστορίας* [Monuments of Greek History]. Athens.

Secondary sources

Angelomatis-Tsougarakis, Helen. 1992 "Greek Women, 16th–19th century: The Travellers' view." *Μεσαιωνικά και Νέα Ελληνικά* [Medieval and Modern Greek], 4:321–403.

Angelomatis-Tsougarakis, Helen. 2008. "Women in the Greek War of Independence." In *Networks of Power: Essays in Honour of John Campbell,* edited by Mark Mazower, 45–67. London.

Angelomatis-Tsougarakis, Helen. 2016. "Maidens and Matrons, Ladies and Labourers: Tradition and Innovation in Greek Women's Lives in the *Longue Durée.*" In *The Greeks and the British in the Levant, 1800–1960s: Between Empires and Nations,* edited by Anastasia Yiangou, George Kazamias, and Robert Holland, 63–79. London.

Argenti, Philip Pandely, ed. 1932. *The Massacres of Chios Described in Contemporary Diplomatic Reports.* London.

Blancard, Théodore. 1909. *Les Mauroyéni. Essai d'étude additionelle à l'histoire moderne de la Grèce, de la Turquie et de la Roumanie.* Paris.

Deval, Charles. 1828. *Deux années à Constantinople et en Morée, 1825–1826; ou Esquisses historiques sur Mahmoud, les janissaires, les nouvelles troupes, Ibrahim- Pacha, Solyman-Bey, etc.* London and Paris.

Doxiadis, Evdoxios. 2007. "Standing in Their Place: The Exclusion of Women from the Judicial System in the First Decade of the Modern Greek State, 1821–1850." *Journal of Modern Greek Studies* 25:75–97.

Doxiadis, Evdoxios. 2012. *The Shackles of Modernity: Women, Property and the Transition from Ottoman to Independent Greece, 1750–1850.* Cambridge, MA.

Evangelidis, Tryfon. 1936. *Η παιδεία επί Τουρκοκρατίας: ελληνικά σχολεία από της αλώσεως μέχρι Καποδιστρίου* [Education during the Tourkokratia: Greek schools from the fall of the Constantinople to Capodistrias]. Athens.

Germanos, Palaion Patron. 1837. *Υπομνήματα περί της Επαναστάσεως της Ελλάδος από το 1820 μέχρι του 1823* [Memoranda on the Greek Revolution from 1820 to 1823]. Edited by Kallinikos Kastorchis. Athens.

Kitromilides, Paschalis M. 1983. "The Enlightenment and Womanhood: Cultural Change and the Politics of Exclusion." *Journal of Modern Greek Studies* 1:39–61.

Mangeart, Jacques. 1830. *Souvenirs de la Morée recueillis pendant le séjour des Français dans le Péloponnèse*. Paris.

Massé, Alexandre. 2017. "French Consuls and Philhellenism in the 1820s: Official Positions and Personal Sentiments." *Byzantine and Modern Greek Studies* 41, no. 1: 103–18.

Maurer, Georg Ludwig von. 1835. *Das griechische Volk in offentlicher, kirchlischer und privat- rechtlicher Beziehung vor und nach dem Freiheitskampfe bis zum 31 Juli 1834*. Heidelberg.

Nikodimos, Constantinos. 1862. *Υπόμνημα της Νήσου Ψαρών* [Memorandum of the island of Psara]. Athens.

Philimon, Ioannis. 1859–1862. *Δοκίμιον ιστορικόν περί της Ελληνικής Επαναστάσεως* [A Historical Essay on the Greek Revolution]. Vols. 1–4. Athens.

Prousis, Theophilus C. 1992. "Smyrna in 1821: A Russian View." *History Faculty Publications* 16:145–168.

Prousis, Theophilus C. 2011. "British Embassy Reports on the Greek Uprising in 1821–1822: War of Independence, or War of Religion?" *History Faculty Publications* 21:171–222.

Raffenel, Claude Denis. 1822. *Histoire des événemens de la Grèce, depuis les premiers troubles jusqu'à ce jour, avec de notes critiques et topographiques sur le Péloponnèse et la Turquie, et suivie d'une notice sur Constantinople*. Paris.

Sourmelis, Dionysios. 1834. *Ιστορία των Αθηνών κατά τον υπέρ ελευθερίας αγώνα αρχομένη από της Επαναστάσεως μέχρι της αποκαταστάσεως των πραγμάτων. Διηρημένη εις τρία βιβλία* [History of Athens during the struggle for freedom starting from the revolution until the restoration of things: Divided in three books]. Aigina.

Tasoulas, Manouel. 1997. *Μαντώ Μαυρογένη. Ιστορικό αρχείο* [Manto Mavrogeni: Historical archive]. Mykonos.

Tsoukala, Philomila. 2010. "Marrying to the Nation." *American Journal of Comparative Law* 58: 873–910.

Waddington, George. 1825. *A Visit to Greece in 1823–1824*. London.

Walsh, Robert. 1836. *A Residence to Constantinople at Constantinople, during a Period Including the Commencement, Progress and Termination of the Greek and Turkish Revolutions*. London.

V

INSTITUTIONS

Assemblies and Constitutions

You are not cursed by Kings.
You are not cursed with Nobles.
Your minds are not under the tyranny of Priests.
Your minds are not under the tyranny of Lawyers.

These widely cited words from Jeremy Bentham's 1823 letter to the "Regenerative Legislators" of Greece (Bentham 1990) show better than a multitude of other documents, accounts, and testimonies the idealized picture of a reborn Greece that progressive intellectuals were anticipating in the West at the time. Heirs of an ancient civilization, they were above all perceived as "innocent" and free from the evils that tormented old nations. As such, the newly liberated motherland of the insurgents was seen as the ideal place to experiment with new forms of government. Did modern Greeks meet the challenge?

Long before it was endowed with a king, in 1832, Greece experimented with various forms of republican government, from the very first months of its War of Independence. Throughout the years that followed the outbreak of the Greek Revolution in 1821, even at the most difficult moments of their fight, when they were faced with the imminent danger of a total military defeat, the insurgents kept electing delegates and debating their future government. Although the real stake of the constitutions adopted by the three national assemblies from 1821 to 1827 was the formation of a strong central government capable of running the war, the issues raised throughout those years were much more complex and reflected different approaches to how the new country should be governed. What kind of regime was better fit for a country whose geography favored local traditions and family dominance rather than a centralized state? And, technically speaking, how could the constitution attain effectiveness in state building along with democracy and the respect of minorities and regional particularities?

Prelude

In January 1822, less than a year after the outbreak of the Greek Revolution, the liberated lands of the insurgents found themselves with no fewer than four "constitutions," three local and, above them, a national constitution. They were all voted by assemblies which, in spite of the irregularities that had marked their election, were hardly contested as representing genuinely the populations concerned, especially their elites.

First in chronological order came the Statute of the Senate (*Organismos tis Gerousias*) of western central Greece (Rumeli), which was written by a thirty-year-old intellectual, Alexandros Mavrokordatos (1791–1865) and voted by an assembly of thirty-three primates, convened in the city of Mesolonghi in November 1821. Of Phanariot origin, multilingual, and educated in Italy, Alexandros Mavrokordatos was to become the most important diplomat of the insurgents until the accession of Ioannis Capodistrias in 1828; he corresponded with, among others, Jeremy Bentham, whose advice he sought on constitutional matters, and later became the leader of the so-called British party.

A week later that same November of 1821, the second local constitution was voted in the city of Amphissa (at the time called Salona) in the eastern part of central Greece, by an assembly of seventy notables, clerics, and chieftains of armed irregulars (*armatoloi*). It bore the title of Legal Charter (*Nomiki Diataxis*). The members of that assembly had been convoked by another young intellectual, Theodoros Negris (1790–1824), who had studied law in France and whose contribution to the institutional organization of the insurgents during the first months of the Revolution was also decisive.

The third local constitution, entitled Statute of the Peloponnesian Senate (*Organismos Peloponnisiakis Gerousias*), was designed to regulate the government of the Peloponnese, the cradle of the revolution; it was voted at Epidavros in December 1821 by an assembly of twenty-four leading local notables presided over by prince Dimitrios Ypsilantis (1793–1832). Ypsilantis had served in the Russian army during the Napoleonic wars and was acting as plenipotentiary of his brother, Alexandros Ypsilantis (1792–1828). The latter, a former general of the Russian army, was the leader (supreme authority) of the Philiki Etaireia, the clandestine organization created by prominent members of the Greek diaspora in Russia, who had prepared the ground for the insurrection; at the time, he was leading the ill-fated Greek insurrection in the Danubian Principalities.

Finally, a national assembly, which later adopted the first national constitution of the newly born state, met at the village of Piada, near ancient Epidavros, on the eastern coast of the Peloponnese, on December 20, 1821. Its sixty members came from all liberated regions, including the islands. Due to various acute discords, neither Ypsilantis, who had initially taken the initiative to convoke the assembly, nor Theodoros Kolokotronis and Odysseas Androutsos, the most important military leaders in the Peloponnese and Rumeli, respectively, were present. In spite of these significant absences, the First National Assembly convened and deliberated for almost ten days under the chairmanship of Mavrokordatos. On January 1, 1822, it adopted the first modern constitution in southeastern Europe; its framers though avoided calling it a "constitution" to avoid being blamed for usurping governmental powers. An English translation of the Epidavros Constitution was printed in London as early as 1823 in a bilingual edition, by John Murray, Lord Byron's publisher.

The coexistence of the above four documents reveals the complexity of the situation that had prevailed in the ranks of the insurgents following the outbreak of the revolution. First, it should be stressed that, besides Orthodox Christianity and language, no strong feeling of belonging to the same community existed in Greece before 1821. As subsequently observed by a British historian, George Finlay,

> the attachment of the inhabitants, whether of the Greek or the Albanian race, to their native district is the element of patriotism in Greece. The associations of family and tribe are strong; but unless Orthodoxy coincides with nationality, the feelings of genuine patriotism are weak. (Finlay 1861, 1:282–283)

Owing, however, to the failure of Ypsilantis and of the supreme authority of the Etaireia to be recognized as their uncontested military and political leaders, the insurgents turned toward the only other available source of legitimacy to sustain their fight: the traditional leaders of the local population. The latter, thanks to the competence of the Western-educated Phanariots who had joined the revolution from its very beginnings, agreed to envisage a common future beyond the limits of their respective local strongholds and to participate in an endeavor which extended beyond local community and age-old habits. In doing so, however, they could not ignore, let alone forget, their vested interests.

In deciding to transfer a substantial part of their power to a central government that was to be formed for the conduct of military operations and, subsequently, for running the affairs of the new state, the local elites, including notables, clerics, and armed leaders, did not, however, renounce their traditional

interests. They preferred to reserve as much power as they could in their respective local communities. That was reflected in the very wording of the local
constitutions.

It is no surprise therefore that *distrust toward central government* was the
most salient common characteristic of the three local constitutions. It was expressed first by the granting of all substantial powers, including the conduct of
military operations, to the local assemblies; and, second, through the invocation in very vague and broad terms of the role of the National Assembly (*Eth-
niki Vouli*), to be elected. The term of the local assemblies was yearly, no details though were provided for the modalities of their election. Therefore, in
spite of democratic appearances, the local constitutions tended to confirm the
supremacy of local primates, who thus retained the essence of their previous
privileges. As late as 1823, a foreign observer noted that local rural populations
regarded the national government "as alien in sentiment and unworthy of the
nation's confidence" (Finlay 1861, 1:285).

The only notable exception was the constitution of eastern central Greece,
an extensive document which, contrary to the other local constitutions, contained a Bill of Rights, inspired by the French Declaration of the Rights of Man
of 1789. Under the influence of Theodore Negris, another correspondent of
Jeremy Bentham, that constitution proclaimed among other things, that all
Greeks "have the same rights," taking into consideration though their "personal
ability" (*ekastou i axiotis*). Interestingly enough, the same constitution was the
only one stipulating that the National Assembly, whenever elected, would be
"the center of Greece" and, at the same time, the "caretaker" (*topotiritis*) of the
future king, whom Greece would request from "Christian Europe" and whom,
"after placing him under her National Laws," she would recognize as her "monarch," provided he agreed to abide by them. Under the circumstances, no
better reference to a forthcoming national constitution could be made.

The Epidavros Constitution

Would the first national constitution of Greece, the Epidavros Provisional Constitution (*Prosorinon Politevma*) as it was officially named, cope with that situation? Or would it yield to the ambitions of the local elites?

Mavrokordatos and Negris were the principal drafters of that document; they
were assisted by an Italian philellene, Vicenzo Gallina (1795–1842), a lawyer
from Ravenna, former Carbonaro and personal friend of Lord Byron, who had
been invited to join the First National Assembly as an expert. He is said to have
submitted to the delegates and explained the logic of all known constitutions
at the time. They were either monarchical and inspired by the French Consti-

tution of 1791 or republican, which included the American Constitution of 1787 and, in particular, the French constitutions of 1793 and 1795. The monarchical models included the Swedish Instrument of Government of 1809, the Spanish Constitution of Cádiz of 1812 (which, however, was repealed as early as 1814), the Dutch Constitution of 1815, and the French Charter of 1815. The fundamental provisions of the two French republican constitutions had been popularized in Greece by Rhigas Velestinlis, the most important Greek intellectual and activist of the prerevolutionary period and author of a charter—the *New Polity of the People of Rumeli, Asia Minor, the Mediterranean Islands, and Wallacho-Moldavia.* This document was designed to encompass the Balkan peoples in a single multinational republic (Velestinlis 2000, 31–71).

At first glance, the new constitution was marked by French influence. Both the terms used and the division of its content into "titles" and "sections" imitated the Jacobin constitution of 1793 and the moderate constitution of 1795. However, as far as its content is concerned, it was to a great extent original, in the sense that it reflected the complex realities of the local situation.

With the exception of equal protection by the law, which as a constitutional right was provided for in no fewer than four different articles (paragraphs), and some other rights, the Epidavros Constitution, as it has since then been called, did not contain a comprehensive declaration of human rights.

Article 1, qualified Orthodoxy as the "prevailing religion" (*epikratousa thriskeia*) of the country; although it proclaimed, immediately afterward, that the government would "tolerate" all other religions, that clause, which all subsequent Greek constitutions have reiterated, has since been criticized for privileging the Greek Orthodox Church at the expense of other denominations and religions. Adamantios Korais (1748–1833), the other emblematic Greek intellectual of that period, as early as the 1820s was wondering what was the precise meaning of the word "prevailing." Since, as he wrote in his famous *Notes* on the 1822 constitution, "we do not run any risk of becoming Turks or Jews," why use that dubious term?" (Korais 2018). And he was right, to the extent that up to the present day the "prevailing religion" clause has been used systematically by Greek courts for justifying discriminatory practices against religious minorities (Alivizatos 1999).

Article 7 placed "under the protection of the laws" private property, and the honor and security not of every resident of Greece but of *Greek* citizens only, and Article 99 "abolished forever" torture and the confiscation of properties. At the same time, Article 3 proclaimed the principle of equality before the law of all Greek citizens, Article 4 the equality between those Greeks born in Greece (*autochthones*) and those coming from the diaspora (*heterochthones*). Article 6 proclaimed the principle of meritocracy (*axiokratia*) and Article 8 the rule that all "classes" and "sections" of the population with no exception should pay taxes.

The distinct treatment of equality compared to the other human rights, was praised at the time by prominent philosophers such as Jeremy Bentham (Papageorgiou 2012); it has become since then a steadfast characteristic of all Greek constitutions. It reflected the undisputed supremacy of equality over liberty in the hierarchy of values of the Greek people, to whom the egalitarian theories of Rousseau have always appealed much more than the liberal thought of philosophers like Montesquieu and Voltaire.

The remaining one hundred short articles of the Epidavros Constitution referred to the government (*Dioikisis*) of Greece, which comprised two bodies, the legislature (*Vouleftikon*) and the executive (*Ektelestikon*), which were deemed equal and whose "mutual assistance" was judged necessary for the enactment of laws. The legislature comprised a single chamber, composed of delegates elected annually. However, neither their number nor the precise method of their election was clarified. It could deliberate only if two-thirds of its members were present. It was supposed to vote for the laws, which, nevertheless, could not be enacted without the consent of the executive. It approved the budget and the state's annual account, and its consent was necessary for the promotions of high-ranked military personnel. The executive comprised five members, who could not be members of the legislative body and were elected every year as well "by an Assembly convened for that purpose." It appointed the chief-secretary of state (*archigrammatefs tis Epikrateias*), that is the prime minister, who was also the minister of foreign affairs, as well as the remaining seven ministers. It further appointed public servants and ambassadors and had the command of the armed forces. Finally, the judiciary (*Dikastikon*) was independent from the other two branches and was composed of eleven members, who were to be elected by the legislature and the executive branch. The courts (*kritiria*) would adjudicate civil and criminal cases, in accordance with a law, yet to be adopted.

Neither the five-member executive nor the brevity of its term were haphazard choices; they reflected the mutual distrust of the delegates of the National Assembly, who refused to sacrifice old-time habits and privileges. For instance, the five-member executive, which, at first sight recalled the five-member *directoire* of the French Constitution of 1795, was intended to guarantee the representation of the three principal regions of the new state (that is, the Peloponnese, central Greece, and the islands), as well as of the military leaders and primates. Needless to say that in case of disagreement between the executive and the legislative branches on a new piece of legislation, the legislation would be rejected and the government paralyzed. No doubt, ultimately, the legislative branch would prevail, since it could impeach the executive as well as the ministers. However, the confusion was important since, for a series of very significant acts that fell, by their nature, under the jurisdiction of the executive— such as the declaration of war, the conclusion of peace agreements, and the approval of international treaties—it was provided that the legislative should give its consent.

The Constitution of Epidavros sacrificed effectiveness, efficiency, and simplicity to the very complex realities of local politics. By tolerating the existence of the local constitutions, it institutionalized a situation that a very keen constitutional historian, Nicholas Kaltchas, qualified as *dual sovereignty*. That was true as regards, in particular, the Peloponnese, whose senate had managed to retain extensive powers; it thus "sowed the seeds of civil war" (Kaltchas 1940, 45).

However, regardless of the flaws of the specific document, the adoption of the Constitution of Epidavros as such should not be underestimated. In the intervals of hard fighting, it soon appeared to serve a threefold function. First, it established legality, in the sense that it ascribed legitimacy to those elected to the offices it provided for. What is more, that legitimacy was unprecedented, to the extent that it aspired to overcome local patriotisms to the benefit of the nation. Seen from that angle, in spite of the conflicts it generated, the new constitution had, in the last resort, a unifying effect. That was the second function of the Epidavros Constitution. The third was its didactic function; by setting, albeit in vague terms, the basic rules of the game, the new constitution encouraged legal argumentation, starting from the use of technical terms, that were until then unknown. To the extent that stakeholders could not from then on ignore those rules, the constitution could not but motivate them to compete for power with ballots and not with bullets. From that point of view, Finlay's cynical conclusion that a "good deal was done by the Greeks at Epidaurus to deceive Europe; very little to organize Greece" (Finlay 1861, 1:299), was a rather partial reflection of what was happening.

On January 15, 1822, the Constitution of Epidavros was complemented by a Declaration of Independence, which was voted by the First National Assembly the day it was dissolved. Modeled on the American Declaration of 1776 and the French Declaration of 1789, the document was addressed to Greeks, wherever they lived (*Panellinion*), as well to Europeans. Symbolically, it was undoubtedly the most important text of the Greek Revolution, because it enunciated in a very concise and emotional way the aims pursued by the insurgents:

The war we are waging against the Turk, far from being founded on principles of demagoguery, sectarianism, or the selfish interests of any one part of the Greek nation, is a national and holy war, the object of which is to reconquer our rights to individual liberty, property, and honor, rights enjoyed by all the civilized neighboring peoples of Europe and which from us alone the cruel and unprecedented tyranny of the Ottomans has tried to violently remove and within our very chests to crush. (Alivizatos 2011, 66)

The Astros Constitution

On November 9, 1822, that is less than a year after the adoption of the Epidavros Constitution, a Second National Assembly convened. It ultimately met at Astros, a small mountain town in east central Peloponnese, in March 1823. Its avowed aim was to cope with the problems posed by the enforcement of the Epidavros Constitution, namely the conflict between the legislative and the executive branches of government, which reflected a deeper dispute between, on the one hand, the Peloponnesians and, on the other, the islanders, who were joined at the time by the Rumeliots. Behind the first camp was Kolokotronis and the strong local military chiefs and primates of the Peloponnese, while behind the second were the more Western-oriented leaders of Ydra and their principal ally, Mavrokordatos.

Although the latter had managed to control the majority of the 230 delegates, the military chiefs, whose troops had camped around Astros, weighed in significantly over the proceedings of the National Assembly. While initially, with the suppression of the office of the commander-in-chief, the Peloponnesians suffered an important defeat, the final outcome was not as negative for them as initially expected, since the military had had a substantial number of leaders from their faction elected in various offices. For instance, Kolokotronis, the former commander-in-chief, was elected vice-president of the executive in May 1823.

Parallel to the above, another conflict, which was to deeply affect Greek politics in the following decades, made its first appearance at Astros: the clash between Greeks born in the newly liberated areas and those coming from the outside. Although in theory the Epidavros Constitution provided that both groups should be treated equally before the law, it soon appeared that the *autochthones* were very reluctant to give up old privileges in favor of the *heterochthones*. The "outsiders," however, had a significant advantage over the representatives of old Greece; they shared a common vision of a modern, centralized nation-state—hence their qualification as "modernizers" (Diamandouros 2002), while their opponents lacked a project, as to the characteristics that should shape Greece after independence. In the long run, the *heterochthones* would win the "war," though not without losing some significant battles.

The suppression of the three local constitutions was no doubt the most important achievement of the Astros National Assembly, which voted the new constitution on April 13, 1823. It contained ninety-nine separate paragraphs, worded in a more succinct and legally precise way than the Constitution of Epidavros. While it confirmed the basic rules of the latter, the new constitution introduced some significant changes. The status of the legislative branch was reinforced, first, through the limitation of the executive's veto power in the law-making process and, second, with the provision that the chamber should approve the nomination of an important number of officials. The list of protected human rights was extended to provide for the express abolition of slavery, for freedom of speech, and for the guarantee of the basic rights of aliens as well. Another innovation was the precocious proclamation of some basic social rights, such as the right to education through the establishment of schools throughout the national territory and the provision of pensions for the widows and children "of the soldiers who died in combat." Finally, the Astros assembly adopted a new electoral law which extended the right to vote to all "respectable men" (*evipoliptous andras*), while the law voted a year earlier in Epidavros had limited the same right to the "elders" (*gerontes*) only.

The Astros constitution had no better fate than the Constitution of Epidavros. Two open civil wars led to its being sidestepped by the conflicting parties, who established two antagonistic governments, one in Tripoli and the other in Kranidi, each with its own "elected" legislative and executive branches. The civil wars ended in December 1824. Less than two months later, the landing of Turkish and Egyptian troops under the leadership of an Egyptian prince, Ibrahim Pasha, led to the capture of the main cities of the Peloponnese and to the almost complete devastation of its countryside. Under those circumstances, in September 1825, the proclamation of new elections for a Third National Assembly was clearly not the most efficient way for facing the most tragic turn of the revolution.

The Troezen Constitution

The Third National Assembly first met in the village of Piada in April 1826. Soon its proceedings were interrupted due to another civil conflict, in which, this time, the Anglophiles led by Kolokotronis opposed the Francophiles led by Kolettis. Later, the assembly itself split into two separate assemblies, each under the leadership of the respective chief, the first meeting on the island of Aigina and the second in the town of Ermioni. A third faction, the Russophiles, joined the latter. It took a few more months for the disputes to be overcome and, finally, the Third National Assembly met in the town of Trizina, ancient Troezen, on the northeastern coast of the Peloponnese, on March 19, 1827.

The military defeat of the revolution could not but weigh decisively on the proceedings of the assembly. Before embarking on one more discussion about how to combine national government with local privileges, the assembly made a cardinal preliminary decision that was to anticipate decisively the drafting of the new constitution. The dramatic turn of the events on the military front, combined with the need for an experienced negotiator in the diplomatic domain, led to the abandonment of the idea of a collegiate body—that is, the five-member executive of the Epidavros and Astros constitutions—in favor of a one-man executive. And that man could be no other than the most experienced Greek statesman at the time, Count Ioannis Capodistrias (1776–1831).

It is difficult to say whether that decision was made *ratione materiae* or *ratione personae;* whether, in other words, the institutional decision to provide for an efficient one-man executive, disposing of a collegiate body which would allow for the participation of local political and military elites, was made before the election of the specific person. It was one of the rare moments that the two conflicting sides converged. At any event, it soon became clear that the delegates of the Third National Assembly were almost unanimous upon securing strong checks and balances, that would limit the powers of the one-man head of state.

The third constitution of the newly born state was voted by the Troezen National Assembly on May 1, 1827, almost a month after Capodistrias's election as governor of Greece (*Kyvernitis tis Ellados*) for a seven-year term. It was by far the most complete and, technically speaking, the most elaborate text voted after the outbreak of the revolution, and its fundamental characteristics may be summarized as follows. The executive power was assigned to the governor. Inspired by the model of the president of the United States, the governor would be at the same time head of state and prime minister. As such, he would appoint the six ministers who would be accountable for his acts. Qualified "inviolable" (*aparaviastos*), the governor was to be elected for a seven-year term; the constitution, though, did not specify who were to be the electors. Article 120 merely referred to a law, which would be voted by the assembly after the enactment of the constitution. In relation to Parliament, the governor had no power to dissolve it and he could not veto a law of which he did not approve (Article 73). The legislative power belonged to a unique elected chamber, whose composition would be renewed by one-third every year. No one could be elected for more than two continuous terms and the members of parliament had the right to be informed by the ministers on all current issues. The Troezen Constitution, moreover, apart from the principle of equality, which was guaranteed by no fewer than five different articles, proclaimed all major human rights, including the freedom of the press, the right to property, and the nonretroactivity of criminal laws.

The reason nevertheless why the third Greek revolutionary Constitution, the first to be called by that name, has since then been unanimously praised by historians and politicians does not lie in the original way in which it sought to combine efficiency and representation but in the symbolic significance of a single provision. Article 5 was indeed the first to expressly provide that "sovereignty" (*kyriarchia*) "belongs to the Nation. All powers derive from the latter and exist for it." With a similar wording, that phrase has since then been included in all Greek constitutions, starting with the constitution of 1864, and it is rightfully praised as the cornerstone of the democratic form of government.

Aftermath

Ioannis Capodistrias arrived in Greece on January 8, 1828. His first act, though, was to suspend the Constitution in view of the "hard" circumstances faced by the nation, which in his view did not permit its full enforcement. It was at least in these words that the Third National Assembly, which in the meanwhile continued to function, endorsed the governor's decision. It moreover referred to the principle *salus patriae suprema lex esto* and transferred all powers to the governor (Resolution of January 18, 1828). Next to the governor, it established a consultative body, the Panellinion, ultimately composed of twenty-seven members, chosen and appointed by him. Divided into three separate nine-member sections, the Panellinion had no legislative powers; each section was expected to give nonbinding opinions to the governor on financial, administrative, and military issues, respectively.

Neither the promise of the call for a Fourth National Assembly, nor the functioning of the Panellinion as a consultative assembly could hide the real nature of Capodistrias's regime as a one-man dictatorship. It remained so even after the election of the Fourth National Assembly, which met at the ancient theater of the city of Argos, on July 11, 1829. In his message to the 236 delegates, Capodistrias did not hide his intentions; Greece could not be governed "under constitutional and stable rules" as long as its fate had not been decided. The assembly abided by this and, instead of a constitution, adopted several resolutions, by way of which it replaced the Panellinion by another twenty-seven-member consultative body, the Senate (*Gerousia*), whose members would be appointed by Capodistrias either directly or out of a list of sixty-three persons that the National Assembly would approve. Up until his assassination in Nafplio, on September 27, 1831, by a member of the prominent Mavromichalis family, who opposed him because they considered that he was curtailing their longstanding privileges in the Mani area to the benefit of the central government, Capodistrias had avoided adopting any rules that would curtail his powers.

This is not the right place for an overall assessment of Capodistrias's record. While he led the negotiations for the recognition of the new state by the great European powers, his action in terms of domestic policies laid the foundations of the new Greece. Neither his devotion to that noble cause nor his efficiency has ever been contested. Capodistrias, therefore, deserves his characterization as the founder of the modern Greek state. The question, though, remains whether he could have achieved the same results without suspending a Constitution that had been drafted with his presence as the head of state in view. On that subtle issue, historians remain divided. What remains true is that Capodistrias was fully aware of the realities of Restoration Europe, when governments throughout the old continent sought stability and the respect of the status quo, while by contrast peoples were increasingly attracted by the ideas of national emancipation combined with constitutional government. Judging from his eagerness to accept the idea of appointing prince Leopold of Saxe-Coburg as head of state of the kingdom of Greece, an idea that ultimately was rejected by the future king of Belgium himself, one can draw the conclusion that, for him, the ideal regime for Greece would have been a constitutional monarchy modeled on the French charters of 1815, if not of 1830, and the Belgian Constitution of 1831. In that regime it is clear that he would have felt more comfortable as prime minister than as head of state.

After the assassination of Capodistrias, a Fifth National Assembly was called; it met at Argos on December 5, 1831, and voted a draft constitution, which was to be submitted for the approval of the future king of Greece. That constitution was named "hegemonic" (*hegemonikon*) or "royal" (*vasilikon*) to the extent that it established a constitutional monarchy, which imitated the French Restoration model. As, however, the faction of the National Assembly that had adopted it on March 15, 1832, was subsequently defeated, and Prince Otto, the future king of Greece, would not endorse it, that draft constitution, the fourth after the outbreak of the revolution, was never enacted in practice.

How may the first experience of Greece in modern constitutionalism be assessed? I would draw the reader's attention to the following conclusions. First, as far as the way the constitutions of the revolutionary period were adopted is concerned, it is important to note that none of them was imposed; they were *all adopted after unhindered deliberation, in a democratic way,* that is by elected assemblies, whose legitimacy, in spite of the objections that were raised from time to time as regard the fairness and the transparency of their election, has never been seriously contested. An important precedent was thus created that, since then, no one but the colonels' dictatorship from 1967 to 1974 dared to ignore.

Second, as regards the content of the revolutionary constitutions, they were all marked by *the latent conflict between local elites and central government.* The five-member executive of the constitutions of Epidavros and Astros reflected the strength of the first, while the office of governor in the third constitution marked the transition to a stronger, more disciplined, and more efficient executive. In both cases, however, strong checks and balances were provided for, in order to prevent authoritarian deviations. Seen from that angle, and taking into consideration that both the executive and the legislative powers were entrusted to elected bodies, whose legitimacy had to be renewed every year through open elections, it would not have been inaccurate to claim that the four constitutions of the revolutionary period were all democratic in their essence. To the extent, moreover, that they proclaimed the full range of basic human rights, the same constitutions possessed a strong liberal character as well.

Finally, that being said, although they were never properly enforced, *the four constitutions of the period 1822–1832 formed an acquis* that was to weigh decisively in both the proceedings and the major choices of the national assemblies that were to meet after Greece's accession to independence. Along with the holding of general elections at regular intervals, that democratic and liberal acquis was almost unanimously accepted as one of the fundamental characteristics of the constitutional identity of modern Greece, thanks to which the country was ultimately able to successfully overcome the authoritarian challenges of the twentieth century.

Nicos C. Alivizatos

References

Alivizatos, Nikos C. 1999. "A New Role for the Greek Church?" *Journal of Modern Greek Studies* 17, no. 1: 23–40.

Alivizatos, Nikos C. 2011. *Το Σύνταγμα και οι εχθροί του στη νεοελληνική ιστορία 1800–2010* [The Constitution and its enemies in Modern Greek History 1800–2010]. Athens.

Bentham, Jeremy. 1990. "Jeremy Bentham to Greek Legislators (1823)." In *Securities against Misrule and Other Constitutional Writings for Tripoli and Greece,* edited by Philip Scholfield, 193–205. Oxford.

Diamandouros, Nikiforos. 1972. "Political Modernization, Social Conflict and Cultural Cleavage in the Formation of the Modern Greek State: 1821–1828," PhD diss., Columbia University, New York.

Diamandouros, Nikiforos. 2002. *Οι απαρχές της συγκρότησης σύγχρονου κράτους στην Ελλάδα, 1821–1828* [The beginning of modern state-building in Greece, 1821–1828]. Athens.

Finlay, George. 1861. *History of the Greek Revolution.* Edinburgh and London.

"Greek Declaration of Independence (1822)." https://en.wikisource.org/wiki/Greek
_Declaration_of_Independence.

Kaltchas, Nicholas. 1940. *Introduction to the Constitutional History of Modern Greece*. New
York.

Kitromilides, Paschalis M. 2004. "*Οι καταβολές του ελληνικού συνταγματισμού* (179–1827)"
[The origins of Greek constitutionalism, 1797–1827]. In *30 χρόνια από το σύνταγμα του
1975* [Thirty years from the constitution of 1975], 15–24. Athens.

Korais, Adamantios. 2018. *Σημειώσεις εις το Προσωρινόν Πολίτευμα της Ελλάδος* [Notes on
the provisional constitution of Greece]. Edited by Paschalis M. Kitromilides. Athens.

Kyriakopoulos, Elias, ed. 1950. *Τα Συντάγματα της Ελλάδος* [The constitutions of Greece].
Athens.

Papageorgiou, Constantinos, ed. 2012. *Ο Ιερεμίας Μπένθαμ και η ελληνική επανάσταση*
[Jeremy Bentham and the Greek Revolution]. Athens.

Phillips, Walter Alison. 1897. *The War of Greek Independence, 1821 to 1833*. London.

Velestinlis, Rhigas. 2000. *Άπαντα τα σωζόμενα* [Complete surviving works]. Vol. 5. Edited
by Paschalis M. Kitromilides. Athens.

The Economics of the Revolution

Thucydides's aphorism that "war is a matter not so much of arms as of money" (1.83.2) holds true for every war, and the protracted Greek War of Independence is no exception. Merely skimming through the sources on the struggle is sufficient to convince even the most skeptical among us of the importance that financing had for the success or failure of the martial operations, as well as for the outcome of the social conflicts played out in the framework of the war. After all, it would be difficult to claim that the islanders' side prevailing in the second civil war and the formation of a central authority were not due to the economic superiority given to them by the so-called independence loans, or that the fall of Mesolonghi was unrelated to the government's failure to find the necessary resources for supplying the town. Finally, the Greeks' military stagnation before Navarino was not unrelated to their inability to find even the smallest capital sums to mobilize the army and navy. The Egyptians' economic superiority was clear.

Initially, funding of the Philiki Etaireia's activity in preparation for the war, as well as the first operations in the Danubian Principalities, were supported exclusively by monetary contributions made by private individuals, members of the Etaireia. This was the funding that underpinned the organization of Alexandros Ypsilantis's campaign, as well as the preparation of the struggle in the Peloponnese. It was thanks to such funding that Dimitrios Ypsilantis reached Greece, having loaded weapons and other supplies on a ship he had chartered for this purpose, while Alexandros Mavrokordatos did the same.

Finding the necessary funds was neither easy nor self-evident for the leadership of the Philiki Etaireia. Alexandros Ypsilantis tried to collect money through fundraising activity among the Greeks of the cities of south Russia, without great success, as he himself admitted, which is why he attempted to conclude loans on his own for the common purpose. As he writes in a letter addressed to Emmanouil Xanthos, dated August 25, 1820: "My only hope is in the loans, which I am struggling to find. All the merchants here are tight-fisted (that is parsimonious to the point of disgust), even though they could contribute five hundred thousand, if they had principles" (Philimon 1859–1861, 1:210).

From the moment the war broke out, however, circumstances changed. The way in which operations against the Ottomans were conducted determined also to a large degree the way in which they were financed. An organized army did not exist and the armed bands of Christian freedom fighters were formed at first from former klephts and *armatoloi* with plenty of combative experience, but also from military corps secured by primates and *oplarchigoi,* who paid the corresponding remunerations. Whoever had the economic power organized and maintained their own military corps, without which it would have been impossible to fight the enemy troops and—equally importantly—to keep control of their districts.

Thus, the acquisition of economic power was an essential prerequisite for maintaining military and, by extension, political power. The need to acquire economic resources, by any means, frequently explains the behavior of the leadership groups, as well as the dynamic of the military operations. It explains too the often ruthless and merciless exploitation of the Christian populations by the insurgents, when they were not on home ground.

Thus, the Greeks' army was made up of freedom fighters who, as the war progressed, were turned more and more into professional soldiers, but without being organized into a regular army. It is not fortuitous that the first timid attempts to organize military operations were made only after the arrival of the monies from the foreign loans, which led also to the temporary superiority of the central government, as will be seen in due course.

For many peasants, payments from their leaders, booty, and hope of economic and social advancement were the incentives for taking part in the War of Independence. The gathering of a host of peasants outside beleaguered Tripolitsa expressed not so much a disposition to fight as an expectation of plunder after the town's capture, which is indeed what happened. However, from the moment that amassing loot lost its importance, as it did when the capture of fortresses ended—that is, from the beginnings of the struggle—the leeway for recruitment was limited. As a result, violence was often used to mobilize villagers, particularly in extremely dangerous situations for the development of the war. Whatever the case, the successful sieges of strongholds and forts also played a very significant role in equipping the rebellious Greeks:

The capture of Tripolitsa armed all the Peloponnesians, because they took the Turks' weapons, since as we said most of them had been armed with knives made by gypsy blacksmiths, and skewers. Before Tripolitsa fell, the Greeks had no weapons, and they should not write that they had many thousands; there are those who forget apparently so quickly that two or three Greeks went to serve with just one rifle . . . but we became double when we took the weapons of Tripolitsa and of the other fortresses. (Chrysanthopoulos 1899, 1:260–261)

The organization of the Greeks' fleet faced similar economic problems. The ships that took part in war operations until the last years of the struggle, when warships were purchased by the central government, were privately owned merchant vessels. With the necessary interventions these were made battleworthy, but the basic problem that had to be confronted, and which in reality was never resolved during the revolution, was the financing of naval-military operations. The cost was high, while wages had to be paid to the sailors too, to ensure that they would continue to offer their services. According to some calculations, the monthly cost for the upkeep of the fleet was one and a half million kuruş, a sum that exceeded the total revenues of the central administration in these years. In the early days of the war, the skippers-cum-shipowners themselves and the primates of the islands bore a large part of the cost of martial operations, while piracy and privateering also made a not inconsiderable contribution to funding the war at sea, as did the booty from the capture of enemy ships. But as time passed, the captains and the primates demanded money from the government, although it was rarely in a position to meet their claims. This was frequently the main reason for the inertia of the Greek fleet, while bouts of piracy increased, to the great displeasure of the great powers, who continued to press claims for compensation from the Greek administration. The piracy issue was not resolved until the period of Capodistrias, only to resurge after his assassination.

However, if the possibilities of drawing resources by capturing fortresses were nullified from the second year of the war, emergency resources would continue to be a basic source of revenue for the Greeks. Emergency monetary contributions had already played a very important role in covering expenses from the beginning of the struggle and many of the primates paid out significant sums for the upkeep of armed corps and warships or to cover other needs of the revolutionaries, such as taking care of the refugees.

Of course, in most cases these monetary contributions seemed to represent loans to the nascent Greek state, which is also the reason why the contributors usually received a bond for the sums they had expended. It goes without saying that this money was never paid back.

In tandem with monetary contributions of this type, various fundraising efforts were made, as in 1823, when Parliament voted Law no. 26 of January 2, 1823, which made provision for raising one million kuruş, which was allotted to the various provinces according to their potential (the Peloponnese undertook to raise 500,000 kuruş, Crete 100,000, Euboea 40,000, the three nautical islands 37,500, the Aegean islands 160,000, eastern Greece 100,000 and western Greece 62,000).

The size of the individual inputs in the form of monetary contributions, fundraising activities, or even undertaking expenses is apparent, albeit indicatively, from the claims made by the three nautical islands—Ydra, Spetses, and Psara: to illustrate, out of a total of ten million kuruş Ydriot claims the contribution of Lazaros and Georgios Kountouriotis exceeded one and a half million kuruş. Psara for its part claimed four million kuruş and Spetses five million kuruş. In these two islands no persons could even come close to the claims or the contributions of the Kountouriotis family.

Revenues of the same order came from the Philhellenes and the various philhellenic committees. The outstanding figure in this sector was none other than Lord Byron, who in several cases boosted war operations from his own purse, while he paid for the upkeep of an armed band of Souliots at his own expenses, as indeed did the other British philhellene Frank Abney Hastings, who maintained a corps of 150 men. The aid sent by the American government, consequent on a decision of Congress, should perhaps also be included in this category. Nonetheless, it is very difficult to estimate the sums that all these reinforcements for the struggle represented, as well as their relative importance in the total costs of the Greeks in revolt. Andreas Andreadis speaks about the millions of kuruş that philhellenic aid represented, yet he himself points out that no more than a few hundred thousand were entered in the national books.

Finally, one further source of income mentioned in the relevant literature was that from church plate, gold and silver, collected from monasteries on the basis of the executive's statute issued on February 1, 1822. The president of the executive Alexandros Mavrokordatos estimated that 140,000 kuruş were gathered in this way, a somewhat trivial sum.

However, a critical role in the development of the struggle was played by the conclusion of the two so-called independence loans from private lenders in London. Reams have been written about them, namely that they were the start of the Greek state's dependence on the great powers and therefore a basic cause of the Greek state's malaise, or even that the country's economic backwardness was due precisely to these loans and to the stringent terms on which they were concluded, or finally, that on account of these loans the Greek freedom fighters began to demand money to wage war. The two independence loans certainly played a significant role in the development of the revolution, but not for the reasons mentioned.

The first loan was concluded in 1824 and was for £800,000. The issue rate was 59 percent. The Greek government provided the national properties as collateral for repayment of the loan, while for the payment of the interest the country's public revenues would serve as collateral. The second loan, which was issued in 1825, was for two million pounds with a real value of £1,100,000— that is, it was issued at 55.5 percent of its nominal value. Of these loans, from the first £308,000 reached the hands of the Greek government and from the second £233,000.

The governments, into whose hands this money came, used it to impose their authority on their rivals and detractors through the recruitment and payment of armed men, the majority of them from central Greece. Consequently, the accusations that this money was used for the civil wars become meaningful, if it is taken into account that with it was created a central power that was as stable as possible, by the standards of the time. Beyond this, the fact alone that the City of London agreed to issue loans in the name of the Greek government was a success, since in reality neither a legally recognized state nor a government existed. Consequently, the rigorous terms on which the two loans were issued are not inexplicable. In today's terms we would say that the risk was not merely great but essentially incalculable.

The rest of the money was used for the advance payment of annual installments of the loans, for payment of commissions, and so on, and for military equipment from the United States and the United Kingdom. Of the last, that which was perhaps significant was the building of the frigate *Hellas,* which reached Nafplio in 1826. Concurrently, the intention in Britain was to build steamships that would reinforce the Greek national fleet; of these only one proved functional and participated in the war, the *Karteria.* From then on, there were some minor expenditures for weapons as well as for the expenses of the committees that traveled to London in order to conclude the loans.

In addition to the emergency expenses which covered an important part of the financial needs of the war, from the second year structures were created that allowed the governments of the revolution to procure also ordinary revenue. The ministry of finance was one of the ministries set up upon the formation of the first government and which theoretically undertook the organization of the economic affairs of the nascent Greek state. How effective this was can be seen from the report of the National Accounts Committee to the Third National

Assembly, dated August 11, 1827, in which it is mentioned that "the national registers were adulterated and full of abuses, falsifications, shortcomings, errors, and inconsistencies" (Andreadis 1925, 4). Consequently, the official data that are given should be used with circumspection and only indicatively. Well known in this respect is the example of the claims made by the various *oplar-chigoi* for the remuneration of the freedom fighters who followed them; the sums demanded were far in excess of those corresponding to the actual number of men.

Of course, the setting up of the first government instruments aimed at determining the sources of income of the Greek state, as well as at monitoring and controlling its expenditures. As far as income is concerned, the Greek governments abolished those taxes that represented the Ottoman regime and primarily the head tax (*haraç*), but they kept all the other taxes, such as the tithe on produce of the land, the 12 percent duty on imports and exports, various tariffs, and the tobacco monopoly. The mechanism for collecting tax revenues followed in the prewar footsteps of tax farming. This was a mechanism that by its very nature was open to abuses and which the governments—including that of Capodistrias—exploited in order to support their own coteries.

At the same time, a serious part of the governments' and the national assemblies' work had to do with clarifying the status of the "national properties," an issue critical for the social constitution of the new state. So, with the outbreak of the War of Independence, an issue of first priority was dealing with the problem of the national lands—that is, of the lands that before 1821 belonged in full or bare ownership to the Ottoman state, to Islamic charitable foundations (*vakufs*), and to Muslims, and which were now on Greek territory, or at least claimed their inclusion in it.

The solution given already at the beginning of the war was simple and natural: "by right of war" all properties of this category came to the ownership of the Greek state, with the ultimate aim of allocating them to farmers, but also to any Greek or foreigner interested in putting them to good use. But things did not go according to plan and the complications that arose in utilizing the national land, until its formal distribution in 1871, were many and had a decisive effect on the development of agriculture, and social and political relations in the Greek state.

As hinted at above, the issue of the national lands did not concern exclusively land but the whole of Ottoman properties, which is why the term "national properties" (εθνικά κτήματα) is encountered more often. These were differentiated into perishable, which for the most part included buildings (houses, mills, oil-presses, etc.), and imperishable, which included rural areas, cultivated lands, pasturages, and also fallow lands. During the struggle, it was permitted to sell perishable properties and to use them generally to cover the economic needs of the war, in contrast to imperishable properties, sale of which had been prohibited by the national assemblies. Moreover, as noted already, these properties were pledged as surety for the conclusion of national loans during the struggle or even as coverage for the issue of a banknote by the National Finance Bank that was founded by Ioannis Capodistrias. In several cases important tracts of land came into the possession of *oplarchigoi* and primates, as recompense for their services, or were simply trespassed upon. As one researcher into this issue states: "We were not able to find out of what area or what value were the sold estates. But as far as can be seen, the value of the lands was considerable and the amount collected was small" (Kolyvas 1917, 27).

We have no measurement of the extent of the national lands. The most reasonable estimates, which were made after the War of Independence, converge on that the arable lands ranged between 400,000 and 456,000 hectares (988,421–1,126,800 acres), while national lands as a whole approached one million hectares (2,471,054 acres). Any estimate is risky, however, since no attempt was ever made to measure the national lands. But the vagueness as to their exact extent should not detract from their importance, which was catalytic for forming the regime of land ownership in Greece during the nineteenth century and therefore for the social makeup of the country.

The first official position on the national lands from the side of the warring Greeks came from the Peloponnesian Senate, which with the Encyclical of Stemnitsa defined the levies that should hold henceforth for the lands that had belonged to Ottomans before the onset of the struggle and which would be used to cover the needs of martial operations. Similar decisions were taken by the first assemblies of west and east central Greece. In other words, the local authorities that were formed directly after the outbreak of the War of Independence sought immediately to take over the property rights of the Ottoman state as well as of the Muslim landowners.

Next, the First National Assembly of Epidavros allowed the sale of part of the national lands, on condition that Parliament give its consent, while not long after, the same body adopted the decision of the Peloponnesian Senate for the villagers to pay the *tritodekato* tax in the case of cultivation of national lands, while at the same time generalizing this levy. To put it differently, the cultivator of national lands was obliged to pay the tenth as tax due to the state—the tithe—while the remaining 20 percent was the usufruct—that is, rent paid to the state for the cultivation of national land.

During the Second National Assembly at Astros in 1823, a regulation was voted empowering Parliament to decide on the sale of all the national lands, depending on the needs that might arise. However, because opposition was expressed to this regulation it was amended immediately. In the end, decree number XXXII was adopted, according to which only perishable properties— that is, workshops, houses, mills, mosques, hostelries, oil presses, and so on could be sold. The major sales of national lands were made on the basis of the law of June 15, 1823, which permitted the sale of one-quarter of the perishable properties of each district.

Not surprisingly, the absence of revenue of the governments, particularly after the siege of Mesolonghi, led in the end to law LI of February 6, 1826, which allowed, on the basis of decree XXXII of the Second National Assembly, the sale of national properties of every kind in order to collect money to assist the besieged. It is argued that on the basis of this law important areas of national lands were sold off. This was followed by law XIV of August 16, 1826, which annulled all sales in contravention of decree XXXII and banned other sales. However, it is debatable to what extent the properties that had been sold were returned.

In parallel, the authorities of the struggle tried to use the national lands to attract and reward those who had taken part in military operations. Already with the law of May 7, 1822, Parliament had adopted as remuneration to every soldier one stremma (0.1 ha, 0.25 acres) of land for each month of service. Following this, decrees XI of May 5, 1827, and July 29, 1829, made provision for the distribution of land to the freedom fighters, while decree X of February 8, 1832, enabled the government to concede national lands not only to freedom fighters but also to their widows and orphans, as well as to others who suffered during the struggle. However, none of these legal provisions was put into practice.

Be that as it may, the importance of the national lands in the formation of alliances and rivalries, not only at home but also abroad, should not be downplayed. Ioannis Capodistrias, for example, who expected to utilize the national lands in order to boost his government's finances, met with the vehement opposition of the great powers to the prospective allocation of these lands, as they had been pledged as collateral for the independence loans. But on the home front too, the fate of the national lands would determine the land-ownership regime of the country and consequently its social structures.

The issue of the national lands was only one of the many problems that Capodistrias had to cope with on his arrival in Greece, because the situation he found was far from pleasant. The Ottomans occupied almost the whole of central Greece, which was thus in danger of finding itself outside the regulations for the borders of the Greek state. In the Peloponnese, Ibrahim was in a position to rule, directly or indirectly, over a very large part of it: the fortresses of the west coast were under his control, while with the garrisons he had placed at various fortified sites he could control a large part of the hinterland. In addition, the remaining regions were not under the control of the central government, whose role was rather virtual, but under the thumb of various local dynasts, while brigandry and piracy were rife.

Consequently, the first matter with which the governor dealt was organizing the army and navy, so that they could drive out the Ottomans from as much territory as possible, in order for the Greeks to claim it, an effort that demanded significant expenditures.

At the same time, other issues that apparently preoccupied Capodistrias, at least as emerges from the frequency with which he mentions them in his correspondence, were what to do with the refugees and how to feed the populations facing starvation. Both these problems were vital and urgent, and Capodistrias tried to resolve them within the framework of the possibilities offered him by the economic reality of the country. His confrontation of the food-supply problem was more original, as it was combined with an innovation, the introduction and dissemination of potato cultivation in Greece. This innovation had two important benefits: the employment of many workhands for cultivating this crop and the anticipated high yields per acre, which would help to cope with the problem of feeding the refugee populations.

Capodistrias also tackled the problem of settling the Greek countryside. The depletion of the population due to the wars, as well as Capodistrias's intention of introducing new farming techniques, showed that the problem could be dealt with by settling incomers from Italy or France or, last, Switzerland, who would offer their experience and skills, not only of farming the land but also of putting the country's destroyed cottage industries back on their feet. Capodistrias was soon forced to abandon these efforts, on learning of the hostility of the local populations to any settlement of incomers, even of refugees, in lands they considered their own. The attempt to settle refugees, under the guidance of the American philhellene physician Samuel Gridley Howe, is a case in point. The governor responded with much reservation to such proposals made by the French general Schneider, realizing that it was not possible to grant national lands to foreign incomers, while the problem of the distribution of lands to the native populations remained unresolved.

Among the first measures Capodistrias took in his endeavor to put down some foundations for rebuilding the economy were the efforts to grow potatoes, first by the Irishman William Bennet Stevenson and then by his Greek successors; the attempts to settle the country and to plant trees in various areas that had been ravaged by the invading Egyptian troops; and the construction of a road on Aigina, which gave employment to the refugees, to the benefit of themselves and the government. Even so, during a tour in the spring of 1829, he saw at firsthand that despite the restoration of public safety the land continued to lie fallow and the problems of the populace remained unresolved. The piecemeal measures he had taken until then clearly had no more to give, the problems of financing the economy—in other words, lack of capital—appear to have become even more acute.

Of course, at the base of the problems Capodistrias faced was his inability to amass the essential revenues to finance the military operations and the war on piracy, not to mention the peaceful projects too. He was not in a position to conclude a loan, as has been proven post hoc, but instead relied on aid that reached him from abroad, as well as on advances of the future loan that was granted him by the philhellene Swiss banker Jean-Gabriel Eynard, as well as the government of Russia, and of France until the July revolution.

Capodistrias sought to improve the collection of revenues at home and in 1829 he tried to reform the taxation system. Although his intentions were good, the results of the new taxation system, whose implementation began in early 1830, were pitiful, provoking indeed the forceful reaction of those it adversely affected. The introduction of taxation in money, in a period when this was difficult to come by, resulted in the rural populations having to resort to usury. At the same time, in an attempt to increase the income from taxation, Capodistrias proceeded to levy taxes on pasturage and increase the tax on livestock, measures he soon had to revoke, in the face of the economic impasse his policy caused. So, Capodistrias found himself obliged to return to the old taxation system, of which he had been so vocally critical.

If Capodistrias failed in his attempt to improve the taxation system, his work in the sector of security and combatting brigandry was crowned with success. Unlike his Bavarian successors, he was well aware of the relationship between the military organization and brigandry, and by keeping the bands of Rumeliot armed irregulars he succeeded, albeit temporarily, in wiping out one of the major scourges of the countryside.

In Capodistrias's view, the disbanding of the Rumeliot bands could be achieved only with the concurrent distribution of land and some monetary input that would allow the restoration of Rumeliot agriculture on a firm basis. The only related measure taken during his governance, though it was not enforced, was the provision for distributing lands to the men of Karaiskakis's corps and to the Mesolonghians, with the proviso that: "These lands shall not be given as property to those entitled to take them, before the fate of Greece is decided and before the national lands are released from the mortgages to which they are subject" (Vouli ton Ellinon 1973, 172]. Capodistrias was effective in dealing with piracy too, as the government fleet under the command of Andreas Miaoulis succeeded in suppressing it.

The creation of the Greek state brought to the forefront the need to solve the country's monetary problem, which required the adoption of a national unit of currency, perhaps the most representative symbol of national sovereignty.

Beyond the symbolic aspect of such a move, state intervention in monetary affairs was more than essential to reinstate regular transactions. By the end of the struggle even the copper coins—that is the petty money for everyday dealings—were hard to come by: this was even more true about gold and silver coins, which had been smuggled out or hoarded. All this made even rudimentary transactions difficult.

The situation was exacerbated by the diversity of coinage: every kind of coin was accepted in transactions—particularly Spanish or Mexican dollars, but above all Turkish kuruş and paras, which were the basic currency for petty dealings.

Finally, all the available evidence converges on the fact that most of the paras used in daily dealings were underweight, often even counterfeit coins, which made every transaction even more complicated.

Capodistrias tried from the outset to put the monetary sector in order, by defining the rates on the basis of which the various coins would be exchanged. The French franc was taken as the basis for calculating the exchange rates, but efforts to evaluate the relevant prices of the coins were not always successful, resulting in necessary readjustments of the rates.

Under these conditions, the monetary situation in Greece was at the whim of foreign influences and mainly of the choices of the Ottoman state to devalue its unit of currency in order to increase revenues. So, about the middle of 1829, the governor proceeded to the adoption of the first national monetary system. The unit of currency was the phoenix and the monetary base was silver.

Thus, Capodistrias adopted a silver weight standard, an inevitable consequence of the fact that Greece belonged to a silver zone that encompassed the whole of the east Mediterranean. The weight of the phoenix was fixed at 4.163 grams and its silver content or title, as it is commonly called, was 900/1000.

Very few silver coins were struck by the first National Mint, which operated on Aigina in rather primitive conditions, on the one hand because silver was extremely difficult to obtain, and on the other because the technique of producing the coins was soon found to be problematical, or, in other words, the domestic value of the phoenix was less than its face or nominal value.

The bulk of the coins struck were copper and Turkish howitzers that had come into the hands of Greek troops as booty were used for their issue (Dimakopoulos 1971). As has rightly been pointed out, in the system that Capodistrias introduced, copper coins played the main role and were not petty cash,

Minting of Coins on the Basis of the Phoenix

	Quantity	Value in phoenixes
Silver coins	11,978	11,978.0
1 lepto	1,312,400	13,124.0
5 lepta	642,074	32,103.7
10 lepta	2,884,905	288,490.5
20 lepta	1,305,848	261,169.6
TOTAL		606,864.8

Source: National Bank of Greece 1929.

since no ceiling had been placed on their issue and the main aim was to replace the paras.

The phoenix system was doomed to failure and as Nicolaos Kougeas has ap-
positely argued, the basic reason for this was the limited issue of silver coins.
As a consequence, the copper coins, which circulated in considerable quanti-
ties, could not be exchanged for the reference coin, which was the phoenix.
Therefore, because these coins contained no precious metal and their value was
determined by the exchange ratio of 1:100 with the numismatic unit, they soon
followed the fate of the paras, with whose value the unit had been identified
already in 1829.

Certainly, the fixed aim of minting coins is to increase public incomes, since
the coins are put in circulation at a rate higher than the cost of their production, and Capodistrias by no means overlooked this aspect of coinage.

For the same reason, as early as February 1828 he decided to set up a rather
curious credit foundation, the National Finance Bank. This bank had no capital of its own and its resources consisted of various sums that were deposited
in it for at least one year at 8 percent interest. When the deposit time limit ex-
pired, the bonds could be used for the payment of taxes or for the purchase of
national land, should the National Assembly decided to sell the bonds. Moreover, apart from money, exportable merchandise could be deposited as capital
in the bank and a receipt given for the value that emerged from the sale of the
merchandise. There is no doubt that this endeavor attests to Capodistrias's fiscal
despair and could not create propitious expectations for the future.

After all, the political environment was not conducive to monetary stability,
or to the survival of the National Finance Bank. Capodistrias soon found himself obliged to exercise even force in order to secure new resources for the bank,
and the whole enterprise soon turned into a compulsory loan. And the fact that
the bank's board was made up of the minister of the economy, the public trea-

surer, and the director of the mint could not but lead to a gridlock. The course to collapse was accelerated in 1830 by Capodistrias's decision to issue a banknote, in a desperate attempt to meet the state's pressing needs. The assassination of Capodistrias led to total disintegration of the whole venture and the bank formally terminated its activities in 1834.

The assassination of Capodistrias brought total disarray in the, albeit rudimentary, state organization and of course made economic development very difficult. When Othon arrived in Greece he was able to say, addressing his subjects:

> Your fields are devastated, your industry moribund, your once so flourishing trade is in decline. Vainly, under the aegis of peace, the arts and the sciences awaited the hour that each would be allowed to return to their ancient homeland. The place of despotism has been taken by anarchy, which hits you on the back inhumanely with its bloody whip, and whatever good the love of the fatherland brought you, with the most noble enthusiasm, the internal discord of the most loathsome egoism makes it disappear. (Pantelis, Koutsobinas, and Gerozinis 1993, 158)

Kostas Kostis

Translated from the Greek by Alexandra Douma

References

Andreadis, Andreas M. 1925. *Μαθήματα δημοσίας οικονομίας (σχολικόν έτος 1924–1925).* *Μέρος Α΄: Από της Επαναστάσεως μέχρι της πτωχεύσεως* [Lessons in public economy, school year 1924-1925. Part I: From the revolution to bankruptcy]. Athens.

Chrysanthopoulos, Photios. 1899. *Απομνημονεύματα περί της Ελληνικής Επαναστάσεως* [Memoirs on the Greek Revolution]. Edited by Stavros Andropoulos. Athens.

Dimakopoulos, Georgios D. 1971. *Το Εθνικόν Νομισματοκοπείον της Ελλάδος, 1828–1833* [The National Mint of Greece, 1828-1833]. Athens.

Kolyvas, Nikolaos. 1917. *Ιστορικόν σημείωμα επί της νομοθεσίας των εθνικών κτημάτων κατά την ελληνικήν επανάστασιν* [Historical note on the legislation of the national properties during the Greek Revolution]. Athens.

Kougeas, Nicolaos. 1992. *Η τιμή του συναλλάγματος και η νομισματική πολιτική στην Ελλάδα (1843–1879)* [Exchange Rates and monetary policy in Greece (1843–1879)]. Athens.

Loules, Dimitris. 1985. *The Financial and Economic Policies of President Ioannis Kapodistrias.* Ioannina.

MacGrew, William W. 1986. *Land and Revolution in Modern Greece, 1800–1881.* Kent, OH.

National Bank of Greece. 1929. *Στατιστικαί τινές πληροφορίαι και σημειώσεις περί ελληνικών νομισμάτων (1828–1928)* [Some statistical information and notes on the Greek currency, 1828-1928]. Athens.

Pantelis, Antonios, Stephanos I. Koutsobinas, and Triantaphyllos Gerozinis, eds. 1993. *Κείμενα συνταγματικής ιστορίας* [Texts on constitutional history]. Vol. 1, *1821–1923*. Athens.

Philimon, Ioannis. 1859–1861. *Δοκίμιον ιστορικόν περί της Ελληνικής Επαναστάσεως* [A Historical Essay on the Greek Revolution]. Vols 1–4. Athens.

Tsangaris, Ioannis S. 1917. *Συμβολή εις την δημοσιονομικήν ιστορίαν της Επαναστάσεως* [Contribution to the fiscal history of the revolution]. Athens.

Vouli ton Ellinon (Hellenic Parliament). 1973. *Αρχεία ελληνικής παλιγγενεσίας, 1821–1832* [Archives of Greek regeneration, 1821–1832]. Vol. 2, *Αι Εθνικαί Συνελεύσεις. Δ΄ εν Άργει Εθνική Συνέλευσις* [The National Assemblies, IV National Assembly in Argos]. Athens.

Education

Almost as soon as the struggle for independence broke out, the insurgent Greeks pressed the case for the "enlightenment" and the education of the people, declaring their catalytic role in winning and maintaining their freedom, the rebirth of Hellenism, the progress and moral cultivation of society, the prosperity of citizens, and the espousal of the European exemplar (Antoniou 2002).

These views gave rise to the sense of continuity between the peak period of the Neohellenic Enlightenment (1780 onward) and the period of the revolution. However, during the years of the latter, certain ideological shifts are observable, such as the idea of justice losing ground to ideas of duty and loyalty toward authority, or the placing of emphasis on the moral orientation of education at the expense of the practical, ideas and values obviously dictated by exigencies of the struggle and the requirements of state building (Skopetea 1988, 31–33). Concurrently, the assertive presence of Western-educated scholars alongside traditional ones compounded the ideological vagueness and the tendency toward a syncretism of ideas, a process from which the fusion of neohumanist—most of the Western-educated scholars came from German universities—and traditional ideals emerged reinforced (Mavroskoufis 1996, 705–706).

This was the framework in which the ideological trends, which were to be eventually established as the basic traits of the subsequent state educational system, were shaped. The philosophy that guided relevant decisions during the Greek Revolution first and foremost considered that the establishment of an educational system was a fundamental obligation of the state. It was further held that education should be democratic and free of institutional barriers. The educational system should be marked by centralization and uniformity. It was believed that this administrative organization would combat localism and factionalism. The strengthening of central authority was expected to contribute to the cultivation of national ties and a shared national identity. This philosophy of course accepted a priori the superiority of European models, which Greek education should aspire to emulate. Finally, it propounded as a fundamental goal an expanding interest in education, even among the lower strata of society.

Needless to say, the emergency circumstances of the time were largely responsible for impeding or even annulling many of the efforts made to implement the theoretical concepts and the official decisions on education. There were other problems too, the most serious among them being the lack of stable resources for funding education. Characteristic of the magnitude of the problem was the fact that the only schools founded on the initiative of the revolutionary administration—that is, those of Tripolitsa and of Argos—faced serious economic difficulties. In other cases, although the administration had decided to allocate local resources for founding and operating schools, practically it was not in a position to impose this decision on local interests (Daskalakis 1968, vol. 1, passim; Mavroskoufis 1996, 96–98, 103–112).

A second serious problem was the scarcity of capable teachers even for elementary education. This hindered the pace of dissemination and application of the monitorial or Lancasterian system, as well as the preponderance of "old dough" teachers—to use Adamantios Korais's phrase (Korais 1979, 3:514–515)—which inhibited the teaching of "advanced lessons" (mathematics, physical sciences, economics, philosophy, and so on) in the Ellinika (that is, secondary) schools.

Finally, a third difficulty was caused by the dearth of teaching material, both for the monitorial and the Ellinika schools. Indeed, most of the available textbooks were at odds with modernist views on education, coming as they did from different periods and different ideological currents. So, very rarely is there any mention of teaching "rudiments of philosophy" and foreign languages, and even more rarely of teaching mathematics, history, geography, and, especially, the natural sciences.

It can be argued that attempts to set up a machinery of education were subject to a rough and ready practice running through the organization of schools, curricula, textbooks, and other teaching media, as well as the quality of the teachers and of teaching.

Plans and Measures for Education during the War of Independence

Following the outbreak of the revolution the first official expression of interest in education came from the Assembly of East Central Greece, based at Salona

(Amphissa) which, with its statutory text of November 15, 1821, the Legal Ordinance of East Central Greece, conferred responsibility for setting up and supervising schools on local administration and proclaimed education in schools part of social welfare, indeed combining it with inculcating the notion of citizenship and improving economic conditions.

The Peloponnesian Senate, based at Kalamata, was moving in the same direction. As it can be ascertained from two of its Proclamations (March 16, 1822, and April 27, 1822), it considered that basic obligations of "every enlightened Administration" were to set up and to supervise schools, as well as to instruct the young. Furthermore, it adopted as a teaching method the monitorial system and summoned the young people of the Peloponnese to make haste to be taught for free, while at the same time it reminded parents of their duty to educate their sons and daughters (Mavroskoufis 1996, 15–18).

Given the early expression of official interest in education, it is puzzling that the Provisional Constitution of Greece, voted by the First National Assembly at Epidavros on January 1, 1822, not only did not include a ministry of education in its list of eight ministries but also omitted any article on education.

These omissions appear even stranger when it is borne in mind that important men of letters with European education took part in the First National Assembly. Possibly these shortcomings were due to the political circumstances in which the National Assembly met and which led to a hurried imitation of the French constitutions, in which too there are no such regulations.

The significance of the previous omissions was mitigated by the fact that provision for education was made in the statutes for the organization and operation of the provisional administration (February 27, 1822). With these statutes the following were defined:

1. Responsibility for formulating an educational machinery was conferred on the minister of the interior (at the time Archimandrite Grigorios Dikaios);
2. Educational foundations would be included in the already known three-tier scheme;
3. Measures should be taken to found a naval and a military school;
4. At the elementary level the monitorial method was introduced, by which children of all social classes would be taught the elements of basic literacy.

It should be noted here that, in parallel with the ministry of the interior, the ministry of religion also dealt with educational issues, at least until the end of 1825, as becomes evident from a series of files deposited at the General State

Archives. Although most of the related documents refer to economic matters or contain moral exhortations on the smooth running of schools and the value of education, there are also documents confirming the more general interest of the ministry, which, continuing the widespread practice of the church during the Ottoman period, considered that "schools are attendant branches of the ministry of religion" (Mavroskoufis 1996, 20–22).

In the revised constitution that was voted in by the Second National Assembly (April 1823), the defects of the first constitution on educational issues were partly remedied. There were now two articles pertaining to education: with the first, Parliament was charged with overseeing public education (Article 37), while with the second, it was stipulated that the administration must make provision for the systematic organization of education and the introduction of the monitorial method (Article 87).

Shortly after the voting in of the Constitution, the scholar Theoklitos Pharmakidis was appointed as "ephor [inspector] of the education and the moral upbringing of children" (July 1823). However, on account of the political disputes of the day, he declined to take up his duties and instead went to Corfu, where, at the invitation of Frederick North, Fifth Earl of Guilford, he was to teach theology in the Ionian Academy. One year later, hierodeacon Grigorios Constantas, a leading Enlightenment thinker, was appointed as his replacement.

The task entrusted to Constantas was nothing if not ambitious. In practice, however, very little was achieved. Due to the Turkish-Egyptian campaign and the threat of piracy, the "ephor of education" limited his tours of inspection to islands of the Cyclades, where he led the way, together with the monitorialist Georgios Kleovoulos, in founding schools and appointing teachers. During the same period, he sent to Count Giuseppe Pecchio, representative of the British lenders to Greece, a report presenting a rosy picture of the current state of education and government intentions.

In April 1824, a "Plan for Some Kind of Academic Foundation" (Σχέδιον περί Ακαδημαϊκού τινος Καταστήματος) was submitted to Parliament. This was to be placed under the auspices of the administration, it was to be called "Prytaneion or Diataktirion (Institut), very closely similar to that of Wise France," and would aim "at the moral improvement of the Greek Nation, and the improvement of Sciences and Arts." The plan was signed by thirty well-known members of the intelligentsia. Heart and soul of the movement was the Francophile freemason Petros Omiridis Skylitzis, whose deeper motive was to boost the French presence in Greece. Perhaps that is why the anglicizing parliament let the matter drop.

Not long after the aforesaid plan was tabled, the assembly decided (May 1824) to set up a five-member committee, chaired by Anthimos Gazis and with mem-

bers the scholar and statesman Spyridon Trikoupis, the physician Michail Ka-
vvas, the former scholarship holder of the Philomousos Etaireia of Vienna Kyrillos Liverios, and the Corinthian primate Panoutsos Notaras. It should be
noted here that Gazis, Trikoupis, and Liverios enjoyed close relations with Lord
Guilford. The committee's mandate was to draft a plan for the structure and
organization of education. In July 1824, the committee submitted its proposals,
according to which the following educational institutions should be founded:

1. "schools for preparatory and vernacular education,"
2. *lykeia* (lycées / high schools) in the capitals of the provinces,
3. at least one university with four faculties: of Theology, Philosophy, Law,
   and Medicine.

However, the committee deemed that circumstances were inimical to the full
implementation of its plan and proposed to the administration that it limit itself, for the time being, to implementing the monitorial method and to founding
a Central School of Monitorialism in Argos for the training of teachers.

In October 1824, Parliament decided to set up a new committee, composed
of Grigorios Constantas, the head teacher of the Central School Georgios Gennadios, and the deputies Theophilos Kairis, Georgios Kalaras, and Anagnostis
Didaskalos, in order to revise the plan of the Gazis committee. The lack of specific information on the work of the new committee suggests that it probably
never got off the ground.

In January 1825, the assembly set up still another committee, participants in
which were deputies Lykourgos Krestenitis from Pyrgos, who had studied at
the Ionian Academy; Nikolaos Milianis, a scholar and political friend of Ioannis
Kolettis; Spyridon Trikoupis; Theophilos Kairis; and Ioannis Dimitriou, a military chief (*oplarchigos*) from Aitoliko. Its job was to draft the organizational
plan for provincial schools. In the course of the committee's existence, Kairis
was replaced by Nikolaos Chrysogelos, subsequently a close collaborator of
Capodistrias.

In March, the committee submitted the "Plan for the Establishment of
Schools," according to which the spread of elementary education using the
monitorial method of instruction was acknowledged as being of prime importance, while special mention was made of the Gazis committee's recommendation of setting up a Central School of Monitorialism. Due to the rarity of competent monitorial teachers, the committee proposed the training in the aforesaid
school, at public expense, of ten young persons who would be placed afterwards
in provincial schools and would, in their turn, train others. It was judged essential that in at least the largest provinces, two teachers should be appointed,

to teach ancient and modern Greek, French, history, and geography. For the time being it was judged that just one *lykeion* was sufficient, which would be incorporated in the Central School. Finally, the committee recommended free access of all Greeks and foreigners living in Greece to the provincial schools.

Educational Initiatives of the Third National Assembly

The Third National Assembly, which during its first phase (April 6 to 16, 1826) met at Epidavros within a heavy climate due to political disagreements and adverse developments in the struggle, appointed a new five-member committee "for the Organization of Schools." However, this produced nothing, and not only because of circumstances then prevailing. With the exception of the physician Agamemnon Avgerinos, scion of a merchant family from Ileia with studies in Italy, none of the other members of the committee had anything to do with education. In fact, some of them were totally uneducated: Nikolaos Velissarios was a sailor from Psara, Constantinos Zotos a sea captain from Ydra, Ioannis Vasileiou an *oplarchigos* from Attica, and Ioannis Lasiou a primate from Corinth, kinsman of Panoutsos Notaras.

The Third National Assembly, after interrupting its activities because of the fall of Mesolonghi and the exit of a new Turkish fleet from the Bosporus, resumed activities at Troezen one year later and voted in the Political Constitution of Greece. In matters of education the new constitution provided for freedom of education and protection and supervision of "public education" by Parliament. It also established the post of minister "for Justice and Education" (Article 126).

The above measures were consistent with the views of Adamantios Korais, of liberal circles, and of agents of Greek and foreign educational and missionary societies active in the country.

The National Assembly of Troezen entrusted the provisional executive authority to a three-member acting government commission, which was assisted by six secretaries (ministers). The first minister of education was the former officer in the Russian navy and member of the Philiki Etaireia Gerasimos Kopas (May–October 1827), even though he had no expertise in educational matters. In November 1827, Parliament approved, but without follow up, the proposal of deputy Anagnostis Didaskalos to found in Aigina, the provisional seat of the administration, three schools: monitorial, *Ellinikon,* and a school of music. It even appointed a seven-member committee of deputies and of members of the Philanthropic Society of Nafplio, with the aim of submitting proposals for founding schools, again without follow up. In December 1827, the acting government commission recommended to Parliament setting up a "standing council," made up of the minister of education, deputies, and members of the

Philanthropic Society in order to found, organize, and supervise schools, as well as to find funding for their operation. The recommendation was referred to the seven-member education committee, but this essentially took no action.

The Educational Philosophy and Policy of Capodistrias

The educational philosophy of the first governor of Greece, Ioannis Capodistrias, was guided by the following principles. It assigned top priority to the moral and Christian edification of children and to the national education and gradual Europeanization of Greek society.

These principles were not at variance with the desire of Capodistrias and his collaborators to provide the young with an education such as would make them "as good as the now enlightened peoples of Europe" and "equal to the refined nations." The only proviso was that the approach to European models should be gradual and cautious, adapted to the conditions and needs of Greek society. Otherwise, it would lead to false Europeanization, which would characterize mainly the upper classes, without leading to the improvement of the mores "of the middle and lowest class of the people," which mainly made up the nation.

The governor's educational philosophy was also concerned with the political socialization and social education of youth. This was an exceptionally important chapter in the thinking of Capodistrias and his collaborators. Indeed, the pedagogue and political theorist Ioannis Kokkonis undertook to disseminate the government's relevant ideas, writing series of articles in the press, in which he argued in favor of "political instruction," "learned teaching," and "basic education," which would comprise the entire range of basic knowledge "necessary to the welfare of the nation."

A fourth principle of the governor's educational philosophy referred to the social usefulness of education. Capodistrias was well aware that education alone, without property and employment opportunities, was not enough for social and economic progress. That is why he was interested also in technical and professional training, expressing the intention of sending young Greeks abroad to be instructed in crafts and to introduce the teaching of technical and professional courses in the public educational establishments. At the same time, a basic concern of the government remained the production of capable state officials and civil servants, a task also entrusted to education. As to the content of education, Capodistrias frequently expressed his mistrust of the practitioners of traditional grammatical teaching but also of bookish men educated abroad who were unable to agree with one another and to offer anything practically useful to their fatherland. He maintained characteristically: "grammar is one thing, society is another, the state another" (Trikoupis 1862, 4:278).

The application of Capodistrias's educational philosophy was predicated on, among other things, the diffusion of education to all social classes and geographical departments of the country, the enhancement of the public character of schools, and the achievement of uniformity in the educative process. In the governor's mind, the diffusion of elementary education to the lower classes was linked with their social and political emancipation from local primates.

Government interest in the generalization of elementary education included, with the necessary modifications, the education of girls. Indeed, Capodistrias expressed his personal interest also in orphan and indigent Greek girls living as refugees abroad and in their repatriation (see Eleni Angelomatis-Tsougarakis, "Women," in this volume).

Capodistrias upheld freedom of education as a general principle. However, this principle should not be understood as unconditional. The government line vis-à-vis educational activities emanating from private initiative and from special interest groups was clear: it tolerated these activities, since the funding of education entirely from public resources was impossible, but at the same time the activities had to submit to government control. From a series of documents, it is ascertained that the government aimed at limiting or at least controlling private schools and sought to have a say in the selection of inspectors and teachers, the approval of curricula, and so on (Mavroskoufis 1996, 252–257).

Thus, Capodistrias occasionally clashed with special interest groups and sometimes adopted a cautionary stance. Examples of clashes with sectional interests included government opposition to the intention of the Roman Catholics of Santorini to found a "special school," and to the actions of the merchants of Ermoupolis on Syros in proceeding to collect money to set up a private commercial school. More ambivalent was Capodistrias's position regarding Protestant missionaries. Although he was worried about their covert proselytizing and political intentions, and sought to control their educational activities—as happened for example with J. Brewer, Christian Ludwig Korck, R. Anderson, and others—at the same time, he praised their work and accepted their contribution. The serious lack of resources and teaching means, the security situation in the eastern Mediterranean, external pressures, and the need for Capodistrias to maintain his influence abroad dictated a tolerant stance toward the Protestant missionary societies. At the same time this tactical stand was combined with an indirect discouragement of the expansion of their activities.

Public Educational Foundations in the Period of Capodistrias (1828–1831)

Schools that were founded on the initiative of the government and operated under its direct control by means funding were understood as public educational foundations. On the basis of these terms, the following can be listed as the main public educational foundations set up under Capodistrias.

The first concern of Capodistrias was the gathering, care, education, and instruction of orphans of the struggle and pauper children. The orphans were gathered first on the island of Poros, at the monastery of Zoodochos Pigi, under the supervision of Andreas Papadopoulos-Vretos, while Georgios Kleovoulos was appointed their teacher. After his death he was succeeded by Petros Vouas. Several orphans were gathered in Nafplio, too, with the priest Neophytos Nikitoplos as their teacher.

Capodistrias was instrumental in building, mainly with donations from Philhellenes, suitable premises in Aigina, which from March 1829 began to take in gradually some five hundred orphans. This was his major educational establishment, the Orphanage. Supervision of the Orphanage was entrusted to a committee, whose president was the commissioner extraordinary Viaros Capodistrias. Two clergymen scholars, Grigorios Constantas and Leontios Kampanis, were members of the committee; Nikitoplos and Ioannis Venthylos, who drafted the rules and regulations, were appointed assistants. In October 1829, Andreas Moustoxydis, Corfiot scholar and personal friend of Capodistrias, was appointed president of the Orphanage Committee. He took measures for instructing the children and training some of them in crafts. Also annexed to the Orphanage were a monitorial school and classes of Greek lessons, meaning the teaching of ancient Greek.

The Protypon, a model monitorial school, operated in connection with the Orphanage. Its aim was the basic training and refresher training of monitorial teachers, which was necessary because those who claimed to be monitorial teachers were of little learning and without method. The first teacher of this method was Nikitoplos, who withdrew after the system of the Frenchman Louis Charles Sarazin was introduced. Georgios Mamakidis was appointed in his stead, but although he had studied in Paris, he was considered inadequate by Moustoxydis.

The refresher training of the candidate monitorial teachers lasted three months and there were four terms a year. Candidates were examined by a special committee and those approved as suitable entered the Protypon as government bursary holders. Those who passed the examinations, on completing their retraining, were appointed to a monitorial school somewhere in Greece. It is estimated that no more than forty successful candidates graduated from the Protypon.

At the end of 1829, the Kentrikon (Central) school was founded, whose aim was to prepare future head teachers of secondary schools, to provide the essential knowledge to those who wanted to become monitorial teachers, and to educate future civil servants. Moustoxydis was appointed ephor of the school, while Gennadios and Venthylos were appointed head teachers, whose duties included teaching ancient Greek language and literature, history, geography, and French. Over time, other teachers were engaged: Athanasios Avramiadis for music, Petros Chalikiopoulos for drawing, Anastasios Erkoulidis for French and Georgios Zochios or Zochos for mathematics (he was replaced by Nikolaos Chortakis, former pupil at the Philological Gymnasium of Smyrna, with studies in Germany), and for physical education Georgios Pagonis, pupil of the gymnast in the Military Academy of Munich Hans Ferdinand Maasmann.

The Prokatarktikon (preparatory) school operated from late 1830, with two classes, as continuation of the preparatory classes that existed already from the beginning of the year, with assistant teachers Iosiph Distomitis and Constantinos Oikonomidis.

The military school known initially as the School of Cadets and Artillery (Σχολείον των Ευελπίδων και της Πυροβολικής) began operating in Nafplio in 1828, with director the Italian lieutenant Saltelli. However, due to Saltelli's failure to carry out the task, the French lieutenant Pauzier took over from him. The school was renamed as the Central Military School (Kentrikon Polemikon Scholeion) and its senior superintendent was the commander of the regular army corps Colonel Carl Wilhelm Freiherr von Heideck. It operated with three classes and towards the end of 1830 had sixty students and ten teachers.

At the beginning of 1830, the monastery of the Life-Giving Source (Ζωοδόχος Πηγή) on Poros was chosen to host an Ecclesiastical School, and archimandrites Venediktos Rosos and Prokopios Dendrinos were appointed as teachers. However, the school's inauguration was slow in coming (October 1830) and its work did not prove particularly consequential. The competence of the teachers and the standard of the courses were criticized, while the number of seminary students remained extremely small.

Motivated by the example of the Swiss pedagogue Philipp Emanuel von Fellenberg, in late 1829 Capodistrias founded the Protypon Agrokipion (Model Field Garden) at Tiryns. Its director was Grigorios Palaiologos, who had studied at the School of Agronomy in Roville at the expenses of the Comité grec de Paris. Palaiologos presented an ambitious agrarian program, while Capodistrias planned to turn the Agrokipion into a model productive and educational unit.

By the end of 1830, the school's premises were almost ready, and the first students reached thirty in number. However, the work carried out in the school was mediocre, due to economic difficulties and the inability to find specialist technicians. Furthermore, the director was accused of financial misconduct and exploiting farmers, which led to his dismissal.

Capodistrias's realization that laying the foundations of educational institutions demanded serious planning, in combination with his view that education is a "public service," necessitated the establishment of a bureaucracy capable of undertaking the organization, administration, and supervision of education. So, by the autumn of 1830 a pyramidal bureaucracy for the management of education had taken shape; at its apex were the governor and the secretary for ecclesiastical affairs and public education, and at its base local school ephors (inspectors).

The Monitorial Method and Its Systematic Application

As far as education is concerned, the dilemma of centralization or decentralization of political responsibility has basis only if systematic educational institutions already exist, if the penetration of the school network in the provinces and the percentage of pupils are at satisfactory levels, and if there are appropriate teaching materials and a sufficient number of well-educated teachers. In Greece at the time, the number of monitorial teachers was not large, monitorial schools were few and they operated with flaws and serious deficiencies, while in some regions of the Peloponnese and the greater part of central Greece no such schools existed at all. Furthermore, the exact application of the method demanded strict codification, something that came up against the lack of uniformity of monitorial systems being implemented in the existing schools.

At this time, the following monitorial systems, with or without variations, were applied in Greece.

1. The system of Georgios Kleovoulos, who had studied the monitorial method in Paris. Although his system was the most widely disseminated (it was applied by about one-third of monitorial teachers) it presented imperfections and gaps.
2. The system of Athanasios Politis, who introduced monitorialism and was ephor of the monitorial schools in the Septinsular Republic. His system was considered better than Kleovoulos's and was applied by about 10 percent of monitorial teachers, mainly in the south Peloponnese. However, the interpretation of the method was summary and drew on a hotchpotch of views.
3. The system of Synesios Kyriakidis, who had been a teacher in the monitorial boys' school of the Philomousos Etaireia during the struggle. His system was basically a copy of that of Politis, with fuller interpretation of arithmetic.
4. The English or Lancasterian system, which was known in Greece from 1827 and was a translation of the English work by the missionary Daniel Temple. The system was judged as incomplete and without method, and

its translation was unsuccessful; it was found suitable, nevertheless, for the education of girls.

5. The system of the missionary Christian Ludwig Korck, member of the American Church Missionary Society. It was followed by about 5 percent of monitorial schools, mainly in the Cyclades, and was rather a fusion of Kleovoulos's and the Lancasterian system.

So, with the aim of achieving the necessary uniformity in monitorialism, in October 1829 Capodistrias formed the committee on the *Propaideia*, with Henri Dutrône, Ioannis Kokkonis, and Neophytos Nikitoplos. Its task was to prepare a regulation for monitorial schools (method, organization, operation, examinations, and so on) and to select the appropriate monitorial system.

The committee ended up presenting two plans (of Kokkonis and of Nikitoplos) for public examinations, which were the basis of the related regulation that was approved by the government. Decrees followed concerning the public holidays, vacations, organization, and operation of the monitorial schools, while at the beginning of 1830 Kokkonis's proposal was submitted for the selection of the manual by the Frenchman Louis Charles Sarazin, *Manuel des écoles élémentaires ou Exposé de la méthode d'enseignement mutuel* (Paris 1829), which was translated as Οδηγός της Αλληλοδιδακτικής Μεθόδου (Guide to the monitorial method). The manual was translated by Kokkonis himself and published by the National Printing Press in July 1830.

The Οδηγός, stipulated that it should be applied in all monitorial schools. Monitorial teachers would either study at the Protypon on Aigina, which was reformed in accordance with Sarazin's system, or be examined by the committee and receive a certificate for their studies. At the same time, Kokkonis was appointed inspector of the teaching establishments in the Peloponnese, in order to collect information on the schools and to oversee the application of the system.

However, the choice of this system and the reform of the Protypon were to have a side effect; although Nikitoplos accepted the superiority of Sarazin's manual, he disagreed with Kokkonis's and Moustoxydis's manipulations and resigned, and thus the school lost the services of one of the most accomplished Greek educators and pedagogues of the time (Dimaras 1974).

Secondary and Higher Education

Several documents bear witness to the government's measures to strengthen the *Ellinika* schools and to organize secondary education, as well as to Capodistrias's displeasure over the lack of uniformity in their operation and their paltry contribution to the education of pupils. The governor, having personal experience from his service as inspector of public education in the Ionian islands, set up a committee with Constantas, Gennadios, and Venthylos as members, and instructed it to prepare a "plan of courses"—a curriculum—and to write, translate, and select textbooks. He also founded the Kentrikon (Central) school on Aigina, where future secondary school teachers were trained and information was collected on the state of the *Ellinika* schools from reports of the Commissioners Extraordinary and the administrators, and the reports of teachers, inspectors, and Kokkonis. Last, the committee was concerned with the uniform organization of secondary education. For this last issue, several plans and proposals were submitted to the government, the most important of which were the following:

1. The Kokkonis plan, "Πίναξ παραστήνων τὸν διοργανισμόν τῆς κοινῆς Ἐκπαιδεύσεως κατὰ τούς τρεῖς Βαθμοὺς τῆς Παιδείας" (Table presenting the organization of common education according to the three levels of education) (1829), whose variation was published later in the newspaper *Η Αιγιναία* (The Aiginetan) (1831). This plan, which was based on the theoretical views of Descartes and of the philosopher and statesman Victor Cousin, was the most complete scheme of the time. It proposed for secondary education the establishing of "intermediate or *Ellinika* schools," with three-year attendance, and of "high schools" (*lykeia*), with five-year attendance (the first three years coinciding with the *Elliniko* school), as well as the teaching of a broad spectrum of subjects (e.g., ancient Greek language and literature, mathematics, geography, history, physics and natural history, philosophy, Latin, and so on).
2. The plan of the *Propaideia* committee, "On Public Education" (1830), proposed the founding of preparatory or *Ellinika* schools with three-year attendance, as middle schools between the monitorial and the Kentrikon school, and their uniform organization.

However, despite the government's strengthening of the *Ellinika* schools, no decisive measures were taken for their uniform organization. Capodistrias's vacillations about the content of secondary education, his view on the gradual systematization of education, the lack of an adequate number of educated teachers, and the country's dire economic straits must have been the main reasons for this. These reasons, along with the insufficiency of pupils and teachers, played a significant role also in shelving thoughts about founding a university until more favorable times.

Aspects of Education

The Teachers

As ascertained from reports by local figures and by Kokkonis, the monitorial teachers were often unsuitable (due to bad behavior, young age, low level of knowledge, ignorance, or a mechanical application of the method). Nonetheless, the situation began to improve from the end of 1830, when the government appointed graduates of the Protypon of Aigina.

As regards the provenance of the teachers, over half the monitorialists were Greeks, mainly islanders from the Cyclades and the Sporades, while about three-quarters of the teachers in the *Ellinika* schools were Greek. Of the candidates for the Protypon, most were paupers or refugees, while the number of teachers who were clerics was also relatively large: about 12 percent of monitorial teachers and 50 percent of *Ellinika* school teachers.

School Buildings and Teaching Means

Among the most serious problems confronting the government was the building of new schools, the repair of older ones, or the conversion of buildings intended for other uses. In many cases, old churches or mosques, small monasteries, and monastery cells were used as schools. In several cases, schools were installed in privately owned or rented houses and workshops, or even in buildings that were without roof or half-ruined. Indeed, sometimes pupils were taught in the open air. The situation gradually improved, especially for the monitorial schools, which were given priority, with the application of Sarazin's plans outlined in his *Manuel* and the employment of government architects and members of the French mission.

Many problems arose from the lack of tables (teaching aids) of the monitorial method for the basic lessons, as well as of alphabet books and reading primers. The deficiencies in the *Ellinika* schools were greater; as a result curricula were often adapted to the available material and the teaching tradition of the Ottoman period still dominated. The shortages in the monitorial schools began to be dealt with from early 1831, with government care and foreign assistance.

Curriculum and Teaching Methods

In most monitorial schools, writing, reading, arithmetic (usually only the four operations), Christian catechism, and drawing were taught, and only in a very few the principles of grammar and music. From the end of 1830, the teaching method began to be systematized on the basis of Sarazin's *Manuel*.

There was no uniformity in the *Ellinika* schools, which lacked regulations of operation and books. This meant that the curricula were dependent mainly on the level of the teachers and pupils. However, since most of the teachers were of "old dough," as Korais called them, they were limited to teaching ancient Greek, using basically texts of the older didactic tradition such as the widely distributed anthology of ancient Greek and patristic literature entitled *Philological Encyclopaedia,* by Ioannis Patousas, or a similar work by Stephanos Kommitas, as well as grammar "in the old way." Use of the modernist work Στοιχεῖα τῆς Ἑλληνικῆς γλώσσης (Elements of the Greek language) by Theoklitos Pharmakidis (Corfu 1829–1830) was rare, while the interpretation of ancient Greek texts in accordance with Korais's recommendations (careful translation into the spoken language, rendering of and critical approach to the meaning, thematic repertoire, etc.) was just as marginal. Last, encountered sporadically in *Ellinika* schools was the teaching of elements of mathematics, catechism, and sacred history, while much more rarely of history, geography, physics, and natural sciences, French or Italian, and so on.

The School Network and the School Population

The general picture of the school network, as this emerges from the official reports of the period, shows an increasing trend in the number of both schools and pupils:

Year	Schools	Pupils
1830	111	7,824
1831	123	9,737
Increase %	10.8	24.45

Source: Reports by Nikolaos Chrysogelos, February 26, 1830, and January 25, 1831 (Mavroskoufis 1996, 688).

The state of education was clearly better in the islands, mainly in the Cyclades, where there were more schools and pupils than on the mainland. Also, more balanced in the islands was the ratio between *Ellinika* and monitorial schools, on the one hand, and of the pupils attending them, on the other (approximately one to three, whereas in the Peloponnese it was one to four). The situation was worst in central Greece, which in early 1831 had only nine schools (two *Ellinika* and seven monitorial). The penetration of the school network into individual provinces was uneven, with some, such as Ileia, Arcadia, Achaia, Messinia, Argolid (except Argos), Corinthia, Ydra, Spetses, and central Greece, presenting marked backwardness.

It is significant for the *Ellinika* schools that in several cases these were established prior to the monitorial ones. They were favored by the primates and wealthier members of society, and mainly the children of the most prominent families studied there.

Last, there were great age imbalances in the school population, mainly in the monitorial schools, which were attended by pupils from four to forty-five years old. The coeducation of boys and girls was not forbidden, but seems to have been a more widespread phenomenon in the islands. As for the geographical provenance of the pupils, incomers frequently attended school alongside the locals.

Epilogue

Between the period of the revolution and the governorship of Capodistrias, a notable consensus was established regarding the moral-practical orientation of education, its socializing functions, and the social usefulness of knowledge, as well as the need for formulating and diffusing a uniform educational machinery aimed at the progress and Europeanization of Greek society. Of course, between the two periods some shifts are observed too, such as the priority accorded to the moral cultivation of society and, consequently, to elementary or technical and professional education.

Nonetheless, the differentiations were due less to the personality of Capodistrias and more to international circumstance and historical happenstance. The widespread view that Capodistrias showed no interest in secondary and higher education or that his policy on educational matters was completely contrary to the visions of the period of the struggle (Dimaras 1973, xxvii–xxix) is due either to the recycling of criticisms voiced by anti-Capodistrian circles or to an idealistic overestimation of the effectiveness of the Neohellenic Enlightenment. Historically speaking, the appraisal of the two subperiods of the revolutionary decade as absolutely distinct as far as educational policy is concerned is not supported by available evidence.

Dimitris C. Mavroskoufis

Translated from the Greek by Alexandra Douma

References

Antoniou, David, ed. 2002. *Η εκπαίδευση κατά την Ελληνική Επανάσταση 1821–1827.*
Τεκμηριωτικά κείμενα [Education during the Greek Revolution, 1821–1827: Documentary texts]. Athens.

Daskalakis, Apostolos B., ed. 1968. *Κείμενα—Πηγαί της ιστορίας της Ελληνικής Επαναστάσεως.*
Τα περί παιδείας [Texts—Sources on the history of the Greek Revolution: Education]. Athens.

Dimaras, Alexis, ed. 1973. *Η μεταρρύθμιση που δεν έγινε. Τεκμήρια ιστορίας (1821–1894)* [The reform that never happened: Documents of history, 1821–1894]. Athens.

Dimaras, Alexis. 1974. "Νεόφυτος Νικητόπλος (1795–1846). Για ένα αλλιώτικο ελληνικό σχολείο" [Neophytos Nikitoplos, 1795–1846: For a different Greek school]. *Ο Ερανιστής* 11: 323–332.

Evangelidis, Tryphon. 1936. *Η παιδεία επί Τουρκοκρατίας* [Education during the Turkokratia]. 2 vols. Athens.

Korais, Adamantios. 1979. *Αλληλογραφία (1810–1816)* [Correspondence, 1810–1816]. General editor Constantinos Th. Dimaras. Athens.

Mavroskoufis, Dimitris K. 1996. *Εκπαίδευση και εκπαιδευτική πολιτική στην Ελλάδα 1821–1832* [Education and educational policy in Greece, 1821–1832]. Thessaloniki.

Skopetea, Ellie. 1988. *Το "Πρότυπο Βασίλειο" και η Μεγάλη Ιδέα. Όψεις του εθνικού προβλήματος στην Ελλάδα (1830–1880)* [The "Model Kingdom" and the Great Idea: Aspects of the national problem in Greece, 1830–1880]. Athens.

Trikoupis, Spyridon. 1968. *Ιστορία της Ελληνικής Επαναστάσεως* [History of the Greek Revolution]. Reprint. Athens.

The Orthodox Church

Nineteenth-century patriotic Greek historians notwithstanding, the Eastern Orthodox Church was not the spearhead of a precocious national project, although religion was at the core of the tragic cycle of retaliation and reprisal that characterized the War of Independence. Under the Ottomans, people were classified for purposes of taxation and status strictly along religious lines. Religious consciousness did not necessarily entail ethnicity or nationality in the twenty-first-century sense. Ottoman subjects were Muslims, Christians, and Jews, not Greeks or Bulgarians or Albanians. In the post-Byzantine Greek peninsula, the locus of Christian identity was the local church, where social networks formed around clergymen, monks, and parishioners. Once the Greek-Ottoman collision commenced in 1821, the early subscribers of the revolution, including the bishops and parish priests, understood well that the Orthodox Church and mass participation went hand in hand on the road toward independence. The formation of the Greek kingdom (the first political core) and the founding of the independent Greek Orthodox Church are two intertwined historical problems. Once Greece at last became a sovereign kingdom in 1830, the new leadership put the idea of autocephaly into practice, and the Greek case became the paradigm for the breakup of the Orthodox ecumene into national churches.

For a sharper understanding of the role of the Orthodox Church in the Greek emergency, it is essential to understand the special institution of the Orthodox patriarchate of Constantinople under Ottoman rule. After 1453, in exchange for a steady stream of income, the sultan's government issued for each new patriarch *berat*s (licenses), which assigned the patriarch certain administrative and judicial functions over the metropolitan sees under his jurisdiction. In the first post-Byzantine century, the patriarch wielded religious and judicial authority in Thrace, Macedonia, central and southern Greece, the islands of the Aegean, and the coastlines of the Black Sea and Asia Minor. Gradually, over the following three hundred years, the patriarchate began to expand its authority, and by the second half of the eighteen century the patriarch had become the leader of the entire Orthodox community of the empire, with privileges to delegate authority to the ecclesiastical hierarchy from the archbishop down to the village priest. This was colloquially known as the *millet* (autonomous self-governing religious community) model of the empire. Now largely contested by scholars, the construct of the *millet* system is still used in general histories. Part of the critical view is that the main features of the *millet* changed over time and the breath of its scope was not uniform, at least before the nineteenth century (Papademetriou 2015; Zachariadou 1996).

After 1453, it is clear that the Sublime Porte sanctioned the Christian faith by deciding clerical appointments and issuing *berats* to the religious leadership, which enabled the clergymen, who transacted their functions among the "people of the book" or the "protected people" (*dhimmi*) to supervise and guide their flocks. Ambitious churchmen, including members of the post-Byzantine elite, attempted to outbid each other for episcopal appointments, and the Ottoman leadership encouraged the competition as a method of amplifying their influence. The incorporation of the patriarchate into the Ottoman administration was lucrative for the elite of each confession. The level of secular authority possessed by the Church hierarchy evolved over time and strengthened the allegiance of the religious elite to the sultan's government.

During the late eighteenth century, following the panic caused by the French Revolution, admonitions urging obedience to the sultan, addressed by the Orthodox hierarchy to the Christian populations of the empire, became frequent. In Constantinople, the patriarchate organized heresy trials and book-burning protests against the idea of liberty and the newfound emphasis on natural science. The booklet entitled *Paternal Instruction,* published in Constantinople in 1798 under the name of Patriarch Anthimos of Jerusalem, counseled passive submission to God's gift of the Ottoman monarchy, which protected Orthodoxy from heresy. The author asserted that the Ottoman conquest came about by God in order to preserve Orthodoxy as the true faith. Arguments along these lines help explain the conservative reaction of the Orthodox hierarchy during the opening salvos of the Greek struggle.

For the enlightened visionaries of Greek independence, religion constituted an essential component of their writings. Jacobin politics aside, the leaders of the Greek Enlightenment considered the religious establishment as a source of legitimacy and expertise. Atheism, as such, was a rare phenomenon in preindependence Greece. The famed political theorist of the Enlightenment

Adamantios Korais framed his polemic against Ottoman despotism entitled *Fraternal Instruction* to avoid the risk of appearing antireligious. The Philiki Etaireia (Society of Friends), the secret organization that played a leading role in the Greek national movement, adopted initiation rituals whereby new recruits were sworn in before candles, Orthodox icons, and the Gospel. "Fight for Faith and the Motherland!" was the slogan behind the uprising in the Danubian Principalities launched by Alexandros Ypsilantis in February 1821. Finding themselves in the crucible of revolution, many Orthodox clergymen became engulfed in the drama and often unwittingly piloted the transition of the Eastern Orthodox Church into a new era of church-state relations. Several clergymen gained the status of ethnomartyrs on account of their sacrifices on the battlefield. Many religious elites joined the Greek national project with little if any enthusiasm under the belief that their social position would be protected in the new state, as it once was under the Ottomans. The perception of the eternal and essential connection between Greek nationhood and the institution of the Church emerged in consequence of the cooperation between the religious and political elites during the fight for independence and the decade of reconstruction and reform that followed.

In the Peloponnese, the Greek insurrection caught fire in important towns and villages under the leadership of the Orthodox hierarchy. According to classic accounts, in March 1821, the Ottoman pasha of the Morea summoned eight bishops to Tripolitsa, where they were held hostage and imprisoned, and five of them died in jail. Another group of clergymen, led by Archbishop Germanos of Old Patras, met at Kalavryta in violation of the pasha's order. According to later reports, on the feast of the Annunciation, Archbishop Germanos raised a banner with the cross on it at the monastery of Agia Lavra and led a group of armed rebels to Patras, singing psalms and promising salvation to those would fall in battle against the Muslims (Finlay 1877, 4:145; Frazee 1969, 19). In the following weeks, Patras became the center of the Greek rebellion with its bishop in charge.

The cooperation of the religious leaders in the Greek national cause and the linking of religious and national identity characterized the 1820s. Orthodox clergymen were at the forefront of the fighting from the beginning. Contemporary records indicate that priests were responsible for the escalation of violence. According to Philip James Green, the brother of the British consul in Patras, when the Ottoman garrison at Nafplio capitulated in August 1821, the bishop of Modon insisted that everyone inside, including women and children, be put to death. The Scottish historian George Finlay wrote that in April 1821, in the Morea, twenty thousand Muslims were murdered without mercy or remorse. (Finlay 1877, 4:147–148) In Kalamata, two dozen priests conducted a liturgy before five thousand armed Greek Christians, who then laid waste to Muslim farms and dwellings.

When news of the February uprising in the Danubian Principalities reached the Ottoman capital, and again when reports of the massacres of Muslims in the Morea arrived, a general belief in an empire-wide uprising led by the Greek Christians pervaded. Patriarch Grigorios V (1818–1821) had obligations of submission toward the sultan, and he needed to ensure that the clerics below him continued to turn over revenues and maintain order. He immediately denounced the rebellion in an encyclical, endorsed by twenty-one other prelates, that exhorted Orthodox Christians to remain loyal to the sultan. Then, on Palm Sunday the patriarch released a letter of excommunication and anathema that solemnly referred to the insurgents as ungrateful traitors, "who were rising against their common protector and lawful sovereign, and against Christ" (Walsh 1836, 1:311).

Nevertheless, the sultan's advisors became convinced that the patriarch was complicit. On the evening of Easter Sunday, the patriarch was seized in church and hanged on the central gate of the patriarchate at Phanar, where his body, still in the robes of office, remained for three days with a placard charging him with supporting the rebellion. Metropolitans Dionysios of Ephesus, Athanasios of Nikomedia, Grigorios of Derkoi, and Evgenios of Anchialos (Pomorie) were executed at the same time in different quarters of the city. By the end of April, reports that Muslims were being massacred by Greeks in Galatsi and Jassy caused the arrest of seven more Orthodox bishops. Still more bishops were arrested in June, together with clergymen of lesser rank, and publicly hanged in Thessaloniki, Tirnovo, and Adrianople. Public executions became a daily occurrence in Constantinople and groups of janissaries plundered and destroyed churches. The European and Russian press began reporting of a war of extermination in the Ottoman Near East (Rodogno 2012, 88).

The lack of reliable reports caused the Sublime Porte to magnify the extent of the uprising and amplify the call for reprisals. Lord Strangford, Britain's ambassador in Constantinople, referred to "the spirit of relentless fanaticism" among the Muslims and a "reign of terror" in Constantinople (Prousis 2010, 77). Random attacks on Christians followed in Smyrna, Thessaloniki, Adrianople, and Crete, as Muslim mobs destroyed, plundered, and looted Greek churches. On Cyprus, Archbishop Kyprianos, Bishop Chrysanthos of Paphos, Bishop Meletios of Kition, and Bishop Lavrentios of Kyrenia were executed along with more than thirty clergymen. Strangford reported that the Orthodox ecclesiastical leadership in Constantinople begged the Sublime Porte to be merciful to the churches and the Christians.

Ottoman policy toward the Orthodox Church was not arbitrary or lawless, but based on centuries of agreements between the sultan and the patriarch. The

Ottoman response is not surprising for the leading members of the Church hierarchy appeared to have failed to fulfil their primary obligation to guarantee the loyalty and obedience of the Orthodox flock. Despite excesses, the Ottomans did not kill priests and monks out of wanton religious hatred, but because they judged that the warrior-priests were guilty of crimes against the state. Nevertheless, the execution of Patriarch Grigorios V was a turning point in the Greek Revolution, for it helped unite the European monarchs against the sultan.

In Constantinople, the Mother Church responded with discipline. On the day of the execution, the Holy Synod elected Evgenios II (1821–1822) to the patriarchal throne. In the following months the Sublime Porte demanded that the patriarch distribute additional condemnations against the rebels. On May 24, Evgenios II presented a solemn decree, in Turkish, craving the sultan's clemency toward his religion and compatriots, and referring to the Ottoman government as an affectionate mother and the perennial source of kindness and mercy. The statement failed to achieve the intended effect, and most of the Greek rebels disregarded the condemnation, as well as those of the succeeding patriarchs. In the Peloponnese and central Greece (Sterea Ellada), bishops ceased commemorating the Ecumenical Patriarch in prayer, a critical act symbolizing separation. A combination of pragmatism and prudence convinced many of the Orthodox clergymen to strengthen their ascendency in the districts they inhabited by adopting the national mantel, and by girding for war. The prelates of the Peloponnese went so far as to anathematize Patriarch Evgenios II, describing him as a Judas and a wolf in sheep's clothing (Frazee 1969, 35).

The organization of the Church, as a political body, was an ideal tool for spreading the uprising. In the critical early days of the rebellion, Archbishop Germanos emerged as the leader in the Peloponnese. He was assisted by Archimandrite Grigorios Dikaios (Papaflessas), the firebrand clergyman-soldier of the war. The personas of Germanos and Papaflessas embodied the priest as central actor in the movement for liberation. Undeniably, the names of bishops and clergy lent legitimacy and prestige to many revolutionary declarations and decrees. The outstanding prelates included Ioseph of Androusa, Kyrillos of Corinth, Daniel of Tripolitsa, Dionysios of Rheon and Praestos, and Neophytos of Karystos. The monk Athanasios Diakos was the hero of the Greeks in eastern Rumeli. During a legendary incident in April 1821, Diakos and the bishop of Salona led a rebel detachment under a banner with a depiction of Saint George and inscribed with the motto "freedom or death." Outmatched by the Ottomans at Alamana bridge, near Thermopylae, the Greek force was destroyed. The bishop was killed, and Diakos was taken prisoner and was impaled at nearby Lamia. A popular poem of the era accords him the respect of an ethnomartyr.

Later action on the mainland proved successful for the rebels, and in June 1822, the Greeks took the Acropolis of Athens, and rededicated the Parthenon to the Virgin Mother of God (Frazee 1969, 52; Gordon 1832, 2:13).

On the eve of the revolt, a network of powerful monastic institutions, embracing thousands of monks, controlled vast properties throughout the Greek peninsula. During the opening phase of the war, the monasteries sheltered refugees who flocked in droves. The fighting led to the destruction of many monastic buildings and hundreds of monks were killed in action. In the Peloponnese and the mainland, all of the monasteries were active in support of the revolution. The Mega Spilaio community appointed their monks to lead armed operations. It supplied gunpowder, and the lead of the monastery was melted down for bullets. In view of the prominent role which monasteries played in political and military affairs, it is no surprise that the Ottomans attacked and burned many of them.

Amply provisioned and stocked with muskets and artillery, the thousands of monks on Mount Athos at first delayed. When no relief from Russia arrived, the abbots worked with the Ottoman authorities to secure amnesty for those who had revolted, while attending to the growing number of refugees. In December 1821, an Ottoman garrison established itself in Karyes (the administrative capital of Athos), where it remained for years and extracted a payment. In the neighboring region, dozens of Christian villages were destroyed. Baron Grigorii Stroganov, Russia's ambassador at the Sublime Porte, reported impalements and other gruesome tortures of Christians in the district of Thessaloniki, where holy Christian treasures and artifacts, once housed in the churches and monasteries, were being plundered by Ottoman soldiers.

In the Aegean, the Greek Orthodox clergy were highly active in the islands of Spetses, Poros, and Ydra. Kyrillos, bishop of Aigina, called upon the clergy of the three islands to lead the fight against the Muslims, promising salvation to those who fell in the sacred struggle. Symbolic ceremonies took place where the higher clergy made sermons and blessed vessels before the captains and their crew departed on missions. The Latin Catholic population of the Greek islands Syros, Tinos, Thira, and Naxos were more reluctant to join the rebellion. On the British-ruled Ionian islands, the Orthodox clergy were involved in the rebellion nearby. Filling vacant ecclesiastical posts became important tests of allegiance. In early 1823, the clergy petitioned the Ecumenical Patriarch to approve the newly elected bishops for vacated dioceses. The patriarch granted the request under the condition that his name would be commemorated during the liturgy and that the canons would be observed. The new bishops were instructed to separate themselves from the revolutionary contagion and not get involved in politics (Prousis 2014, 55–56, 92–96).

Although the revolution made gains in 1821, 1822, and 1823, a profound change resulted in the institution of the Orthodox Church, which lost much of its financial, political, and administrative power. The intensity of violence meant an early death for many priests. When the uprising began there were forty-one metropolitans, archbishops, and bishops in the territory that would become Greece. Sixteen were in the Peloponnese, fourteen in central Greece, and eleven on the islands. Over two thousand priests in the Peloponnese, who took part in the fighting, were killed, exiled, or otherwise left or died in the first years of the war. The immediate impact caused profound disorder in the religious life of ordinary people, due to the absence or death of so many clergy.

The delineation of the religious authority and the revolutionary state's civil authority became blurred during the war. The leading clergymen, who decided to support the Revolution, took part in the various political discussions that occurred in the first years of fighting. Prelates became members of the National Assembly at Epidavros in December 1821. The Ministry of Religion, which oversaw all churches and monasteries, was formed under the leadership of Bishop Iosiph of Androusa, a leading member of the Philiki Etaireia. Decisions of the ministry included the administration of weddings, baptisms, funerals, and the appointment of new bishops to sees that had fallen vacant. As the relations between the episcopates in the territories under revolt and the Ecumenical Patriarchate reached their nadir, the active cooperation of men like Iosiph of Androusa provided legitimacy for the architects of the revolutionary Greek state.

As the sectarian violence persisted, the prevailing attitude was to maintain the orderly regulation of ecclesiastical administration and the canons of faith in the liberated areas. The revolutionary governments' constitutional charters, recognizing Orthodox Christianity as the official religion, were intended to address concerns over uncanonical practices. The Constitution of 1822 stated that "all those indigenous inhabitants of the state of Greece who believe in Christ are Greeks (*Hellines*)." In reality, however, the members of the clergy in the liberated regions no longer maintained the dominant position in the life of the individual and the community that they had once enjoyed under the Ottomans.

As far as the patriarch in Constantinople was concerned, the episcopates in the regions of revolt were no longer answering missives and sending funds. Although Grigorios V was revered as a martyr, the same attitude during the years of fighting was not accorded the other appointees to higher Church positions by the Ottoman government. Most Orthodox clergymen, including bishops, in the regions of unrest treated the patriarchate as vacant, and deliberately omitted the patriarch's name during the liturgy. The subsequent terms of Patriarchs Anthimos III (1822–1824), Chrysanthos I (1824–1826), Agathangelos I (1826–1830), and Constantios I (1830–1834) were beset by trials and vexations.

Hospitals, orphanages, schools, and public services suffered as a result of the dislocation of the economy during the war and the lost tax revenue. The patriarchs were forced to reorganize the church treasury to raise money to pay off debts and fulfill vital social functions. Despite the major disruptions, regulations and reforms dealing with diocesan administration, monasteries, and family life continued to emanate from the patriarchal offices. Once the political fight was over in 1830, the patriarchs aimed to restore their rights and privileges lost during the turmoil. Due to this manifold activity, the patriarchate eventually regained some of its authority in the postrevolutionary decades.

From the start of the insurrection, the maintenance of canonical ties with the ecclesiastical hierarchy in Constantinople was in doubt. Contemporary observers foresaw the potential for a rupture. As the guidance from Constantinople, whose leadership had been decapitated and whose ranks were in disarray, vanished during the 1820s, the clergy took on new responsibilities. Prelates and religious functionaries played important roles during the national assemblies at Astros (1823) and Troezen (1827), where delegates discussed measures to put Church administration onto a firmer footing. As head of the Ministry of Religion, Iosiph of Androusa struggled to uphold canonicity and respect for the patriarch. Episcopal appointments and transfers of clergy were particularly difficult. The Ministry of Religion also dealt with daily problems, such as church repairs and inheritance petitions. Since the state legal system was in its infancy, religious involvement in legal issues was explicitly supported by the fledgling Greek governments. The general chaos of the war introduced unforeseen and seminal changes into the roles of local clergy, including the problem of sharing power with the political leaders and the generals who led the armies in the field.

As the fighting continued, the clergy continued to support the struggle and provide it with legitimacy. During the invasion of the Peloponnese by Ibrahim Pasha in 1825, the monastery of Mega Spilaio, with ten thousand refugees crowded behind its walls, stood strong. In the months preceding the battle of Navarino (1827), the major prelates of the Morea were planning to establish a synod to govern the new Church of Greece (Frazee 1969, 67; Oikonomos 1862–1866, 2:44–47). Its constitution would follow the apostolic and council canons, and it would be charged with filling vacancies, creating schools, supervising the moral conditions of monasteries, and providing spiritual guidance and divine service to the laity. The prelates professed their unity with the spiritual and ecclesiastical community, without causing any schism or division.

The Constitution voted by the Troezen National Assembly (1827), which banned the clergy from civil or military functions, marks a significant step in the decline of Church power in Greece. Five leading prelates addressed the assembly and requested a general convocation of bishops. Further plans were prepared for the formation of a synod of prelates to govern an independent Church of Greece, which would work in conjunction with the government in conformity with doctrine and canons, but which would avoid political issues. Although the Constitution of the Troezen Assembly eventually was not enacted, it attests to the enduring significance of religion in the conflict, and to the decline of the religious leaders' prerevolutionary status.

A more focused religious policy began to take shape during the government of Ioannis Capodistrias (1828–1831), who was elected governor by the Troezen National Assembly. Not long after his arrival in Greece, he assigned a committee of hierarchs to investigate Church affairs in the Morea and the islands. Capodistrias desired lists of Church and monastic properties, the maintenance of proper records, and reports on the condition of buildings. He recognized the need to establish a judicial system that would replace the old courts, and wrote many letters settling disputes and complaints between clergymen and parishioners. The governor also worked to improve the social activities, such as orphanages and schools, and pledged to pay special attention to raising the clergy of Greece through education. He planned for a seminary and requested that the renowned prelate, Constantinos Oikonomos, and several of his assistants be sent from Russia to lead it. He also received liturgical books, collections of sermons, catechisms, and other religious works from Russia, where he had been well acquainted with the administrative system of the Church, which was governed by a Holy Synod and in essence formed part of the state administration.

A deeply pious individual, Capodistrias took Church affairs seriously and intervened frequently. In May 1828, Patriarch Agathangelos I sent a mission of four senior prelates to Greece asking the clergy and notables of the Peloponnese and the Aegean islands to recognize the sultan as their legitimate ruler. In a written response, Capodistrias requested Agathangelos's blessing and claimed that it was impossible to ask the people of Greece to surrender their newly won freedom. Yet, complete ecclesiastical independence was not the only option for the new nation. One alternative was the creation of a relationship similar to the one existing between the patriarch and the Church in the Danubian Principalities, which retained local autonomy under Ottoman sovereignty. Another plan, proposed by the Russia foreign ministry, would have made the patriarch the head of the Greek state.

By requiring candidates to take an oath on the Gospels priests were coopted into the voting process for a Fourth National Assembly at Argos in 1829. The assembly at Argos approved measures to help improve Church affairs and established an official post for public education and ecclesiastical affairs. The majority of the Orthodox clergymen objected to state control over Church affairs, but their general poverty and weariness diminished their influence during the assembly. In the sphere of education, the ecclesiastical hierarchy was called on to prepare curriculum and select and edit school textbooks, prayer books, and catechisms. Part of the involvement of the clergy in early state efforts at public education stemmed from the threat posed by foreign missionaries, who began establishing schools in the country in the late 1820s.

In 1830, the patriarchal election in Constantinople led to the ascension of Constantios I, who, soon after his investiture, sent good wishes and blessings to the Greek state and its people. Capodistrias expressed his gratitude and firm intention to end the progressive degradation of the Orthodox Church and to remain alert to heretical teachings. In such an atmosphere of renewal, optimism spread about the governor's plan to secure episcopal nominations in accordance with canonical practices, while providing destitute clergy with pensions and instituting a special ecclesiastical committee to search for solutions. Capodistrias recognized the advantages of direct negotiations with the patriarch, especially concerning the status of dioceses and the renewal of investitures. He claimed that the government shared the wishes of the patriarch and ardently desired to cement the unity of Orthodoxy. In the meantime, the governor's detractors claimed that he aimed to fully subject the Greek Church to his jurisdiction.

According to the international treaties that established Greek independence, Capodistrias's term in office was to end when the protecting powers (England, France, and Russia) agreed upon a sovereign for the new kingdom. Capodistrias argued repeatedly that the ruler must profess the Orthodox faith, and he expressed deep frustration that the London Protocol (1830) remained silent about the religion of the state and its people. Unfortunately, the innovative spirit that he applied to the religious institution earned him the resentment of clergy and parishioner alike. His assassination on September 27, 1831, as he stepped out of the church of Agios Spyridon in Nafplio, was a major setback for relations between Greece and the Patriarchate of Constantinople.

The increase in respect, affection, and authority that many clergymen enjoyed during the revolutionary period transformed the Orthodox Church from an agent of canonical conscience into a national institution. Overlap between religion and sovereign civil authority became increasingly apparent in the fields of law and education. Even before the initiation of armed conflict, some leaders of the national movement considered the Ecumenical Patriarchate to be an instrument of tyranny. Dreams of political freedom naturally inspired the desire for an independent church. The opponents of autocephaly typically considered the idea of foreign origin, although the first to pose the question of ecclesiastical independence was Adamantios Korais. In his commentary on Aristotle's *Politics,* published in 1821, Korais forwarded his idea of a Greek Church independent of the patriarch of Constantinople. Convinced that the old institution was contaminated by the sultan's tyranny, Korais preferred a freely elected synod to direct Church affairs. He was the first writer to articulate a clear vision on ecclesiastical independence, and his arguments inspired both admiration and dissent. Ultimately, in an act of August 4, 1833, the clergymen Theoklitos Pharmakidis and Neophytos Vamvas, the civil servants Iakovakis Rizos-Neroulos and Spyridon Trikoupis, and the Protestant members of the Bavarian regency made Korais's vision a reality by unilaterally declaring the Orthodox Church in Greece autocephalous (independent).

The Greek Revolution had a profound impact on the Eastern Orthodox Church. Religion became an essential factor in the national struggle, and it contributed greatly to the intensity of the fighting during the war. After the creation of the Hellenic kingdom, the independent Greek Orthodox Church lent power and depth to the development of a sense of nationhood. It took the deeply rooted values, symbols, myths, and traditions embedded in Eastern Orthodoxy, in addition to the efforts of the new state, focused on the creation of a secular, centralized, and modern public institutions to make a modern nation. As part of this process, the ecumenical concept of Eastern Orthodoxy was called into question and a separate national Church of Greece emerged. In this fashion, the Balkan Orthodox world began to fragment into national parts.

Lucien Frary

References

Clogg, Richard. 1976. "Anti-Clericalism in Pre-Independence Greece c. 1750–1821." In *The Orthodox Churches and the West,* edited by Derek Baker, 13:257–276. Oxford.

Fabbe, Kristin. 2019. *Disciples of State? Religion and State-Building in the Former Ottoman World.* Cambridge.

Finlay, George. 1877. *A History of Greece from Its Conquest by the Romans to the Present Time.* Edited and revised by Henry Fanshawe Tozer. Oxford.

Frary, Lucien. 2015. *Russia and the Making of Modern Greek Identity, 1821–1844.* Oxford.

Frazee, Charles. 1969. *The Orthodox Church and Independent Greece, 1821–1852.* Cambridge.

Frazee, Charles. 1977. "Church and State in Greece." In *Greece in Transition: Essays in the History of Modern Greece, 1821–1974,* edited by John T. A. Koumoulides, 133–152. London.

Gazi, Efi. 2009. "Revisiting Religion and Nationalism in Nineteenth-Century Greece," *The Making of Modern Greece: Nationalism, Romanticism, and the Uses of the Past (1797–1896),* eds. Roderick Beaton and David Ricks, 95–106. Surrey.

Gordon, Thomas. 1832. *History of the Greek Revolution*. Edinburgh.

Kitromilides, Paschalis M. 2006a. "The Legacy of the French Revolution: Orthodoxy and Nationalism." In *The Cambridge History of Christianity*, Vol. 5: *Eastern Christianity*, edited by Michael Angold, 229–249. Cambridge.

Kitromilides, Paschalis M. 2006b. "Orthodoxy and the West: Reformation to Enlightenment." In *The Cambridge History of Christianity*, Vol. 5: *Eastern Christianity*, edited by Michael Angold, 187–209. Cambridge.

Kitromilides, Paschalis M. 2013. *Enlightenment and Revolution: The Making of Modern Greece*. Cambridge, MA.

Kokkinis, Spyridon. 1976. *Τα μοναστήρια της Ελλάδας* [The monasteries of Greece]. Athens.

Konstantinidis, Emmanouil I. 2001. *Ιωάννης Καποδίστριας και η εκκλησιαστική του πολιτική* [Ioannis Capodistrias and his ecclesiastical policy]. Athens.

Maurer, Georg Ludwig von. (1835) 1968. *Das griechische Volk in offentlicher, kirchlischer und privat- rechtlicher Beziehung vor und nach dem Freiheitskampfe bis zum 31 Juli 1834.* Reprint. Osnabrück.

Oikonomos, Constantinos. 1862–1866. *Τα σωζόμενα εκκλησιαστικά συγγράμματα Κωνσταντίνου Πρεσβυτέρου και Οικονόμου του εξ Οικονόμων* [The surviving ecclesiastical writings of reverend Constantinos Oikonomos the elder]. Athens.

Palmieri, Aurelio. 1902. "La Chiesa ellenica nel secolo XIX." *Bessarione* 2nd series, 3, no. 69: 281–286; 4, no. 70: 70–87; no. 71: 205–216; no. 72: 347–354.

Papademetriou, Tom. 2015. *Rendering unto the Sultan: Power, Authority, and the Greek Orthodox Church in the Early Ottoman Centuries*. Oxford.

Papadopoulos, Chrysostomos. 1920. *Ιστορία της Εκκλησίας της Ελλάδος* [History of the Church of Greece]. Athens.

Petrovich, Michael B. 1982. "The Role of the Serbian Orthodox Church in the First Serbian Uprising, 1804–1813" In *The First Serbian Uprising, 1804–1813*, edited by Wayne S. Vucinich, 250–302. New York.

Prousis, Theophilus. 2010. *Lord Strangford at the Sublime Porte: The Eastern Crisis (1821)*. Istanbul.

Prousis, Theophilus. 2014. *Lord Strangford at the Sublime Porte: The Eastern Crisis (1823)*. Istanbul.

Rodogno, Davide. 2012. *Against Massacre: Humanitarian Intervention in the Ottoman Empire, 1815–1914: The Emergence of a European Concept and International Practice*. Princeton, NJ.

Sherrard, Philip. 1973. "Church, State and the Greek War of Independence." *The Struggle for Greek Independence*, edited by Richard Clogg, 182–199. London.

Sokolov, Ivan I. 2012. *The Church of Constantinople in the Nineteenth Century: An Essay in Historical Research*. New York.

Walsh, Robert. 1836. *A Residence at Constantinople, during a Period Including the Commencement, Progress and Termination of the Greek and Turkish Revolutions*. London.

Zachariadou, Elizabeth A. 1996. *Δέκα τουρκικά έγγραφα για την Μεγάλη Εκκλησία (1483–1567)* [Ten Turkish documents on the Great Church, 1483–1567]. Athens.

The Press

With the outbreak of the Greek War of Independence the need for reliable information about developments on the front became imperative. The newspapers that circulated were published in key towns, because on account of the military operations, the geographical ambit of their circulation was limited, due also to the lack of an organized postal network. Apart from news relating to the war, commentaries, and some reports from abroad, they included articles reflecting the expectations of Greek society in the planning of a modern state. Issues relating to legislation, system of governance, constitutional institutions, freedom of the press, and the vocation of the newspaper writer (*ephimeridographos*) were analyzed, while interest was shown too in literature and poetry. Reading newspapers was undoubtedly a privilege of the literate in a period when illiteracy was a serious obstacle to disseminating information by the printed word.

It is interesting that writings reflecting the oppositions and rivalries that had broken out between the various social and ideological groups of freedom fighters as well as articles urging concord and conciliation, were published in the newspapers of the period. It should be borne in mind that the broad social strata were by no means indifferent to the press and in fact looked forward to learning about the political unrest and the world-shattering events of the war that suddenly shook the whole of Greece. Even the unschooled fighters were quick to realize the power of the press and were eager for their names to appear in newspaper columns.

It is characteristic that, as a whole, the newspapers of this period were permeated by the radical humanist values of the Enlightenment, as their editors were moving politically in the sphere of liberalism. Freedom of speech as an inextricable part of the political liberty of the individual was recognized by the groundbreaking—for their time—revolutionary constitutions though they were out of sync with the then conservative political situation in the rest of Europe. Every Greek citizen had the right to express his views through the press, provided these views did not offend Christian beliefs and morality, and did not insult third parties. There were copious articles dealing with the sensitive subject of freedom of the press, which was a constant preoccupation of publishers. Although preventive censorship was prohibited, this issue frequently sparked clashes between the political leadership and responsible publishers. This was due largely to two factors, the semiofficial character of the press, since newspapers received financial support from the local authorities, and the fact that printing presses had not been offered by their foreign donors to private individuals but to the warring Greek nation.

Handwritten Newspapers

During the first critical years of the revolution, three short-lived handwritten newspapers circulated in west central Greece: the newspaper *Εφημερίς Αιτωλική* (Aitolian newspaper) (August–September 1821), and the *Αχελώος* (Acheloos) (February 24 and 25, 1822). They represent the only known copies of these Rumeliot broadsheets, which were written initially by the editor and then copied by the readers in order to distribute them more widely. They also confirm that there was a need for rudimentary information concerning the revolution given the uncertainty about the outcome of this risky venture. The existence of another newspaper published at Galaxidi, on March 27 1821, was brought to light in 1869, in an article in *Pandora* by Constantinos N. Sathas, who came from Galaxidi, though he did not mention anything specific about the publisher, the format, or the number of pages. The news items published in the newspaper are indicative of the prevailing unstable psychological climate. They are mainly rumors—encouraging yet misleading—reiterated with the intention of boosting the morale of the people and helping them to overcome their misgivings. Sathas justified this ploy, which was the brainchild of the Galaxidi revolutionary committee and was designed to rouse other provinces from their inertia. The most impressive news item concerned a declaration of war between Russia and Turkey, as well as the arrival of Russian reserves for the revolutionaries. These are elaborations of the narratives and prophecies that during the Ottoman period fed the imagination of the enslaved Greeks loyal to the Russophile Orthodox religious traditions of the Christian Greek nation. This is why this Galaxidi broadsheet is known in history as a pseudonewspaper. Because the outcome of events in the Danubian Principalities had not yet been known, another fiction circulated concerning Alexandros Ypsilantis's arrival in Greece. Indeed, as we learn from Ioannis Philimon, if anyone dared dispute this, they risked the accusation of being a Turk worshipper (*tourkolatris*) (Philimon 1860, 3: xxi).

In his study in *Neos Ellinomnimon* (*Νέος Ελληνομνήμων*) in 1904, Spyridon Lampros presented two issues of the *Acheloos* dated February 24 and 25, 1822. The *Acheloos* was produced in Vrachori (Agrinion) and was the official newspaper of the provisional administration of west central Greece; its character is revealed by its header, above which is the seal of the Senate and below the signature of the chief secretary, Nikolaos Louriotis (born Ioannina 1783, died Kalamata 1833), close collaborator of Alexandros Mavrokordatos and subsequent chief secretary of the territory of western Greece. Louriotis, who as the newspaper's editor wrote the first issue, was concerned about publishing the acts and statutes of the Senate, as well as news items relating to government business, appointments, the activities and movements of the Senate's president, Mavrokordatos.

In the same article, Lampros also discusses the third manuscript newspaper, entitled *Ephimeris Aitoliki*, which came out in Mesolonghi on August 10, 1821— that is, before the assembly of west central Greece. The next two issues, which circulated on August 15 and September 10 of the same year, are known too. According to Lampros, to whom we owe the reference and the description of the texts, its editor was once again Nikolaos Louriotis. His sources were letters and oral announcements and the newspaper was useful for accounts of military events in Aitolia and Akarnania. For that summer of 1821, there is a rich flow of valuable news about operations in Epirus and central Greece; the sacrifice of Athanasios Diakos is extolled and information is given on the joint action of Greeks and Albanians. However, there are also items that do not correspond to reality, such as news about a war between Russia and the Ottoman Porte and the tsar's alliance with the Greeks. Ioannis Philimon (born Constantinople 1798/1799, died Athens 1874), himself a freedom fighter and publisher of two newspapers, singles out, in his "Historical examination of the political newspapers of Greece," the *Ephimeris Aitoliki* as a notable source about events in west central Greece, characterizing it as "innocent in its time of any spirit of partiality whatsoever" (Philimon 1833, issue 2, 6).

Printed Newspapers

In all, eight printed newspapers were published in the period 1821–1828, six in Greek and two in foreign languages. The first group comprises: *Σάλπιγξ Ελληνική* (Greek clarion), *Ελληνικά Χρονικά* (Greek Chronicles), *Εφημερίς Αθηνών* (Newspaper of Athens), *Ο φίλος του Νόμου* (The friend of the law), *Γενική*

Εφημερίς της Ελλάδος (General newspaper of Greece), and Ανεξάρτητος Εφημερίς της Ελλάδος (Independent newspaper of Greece). The foreign-language newspapers were the *Telegrafo Greco* (Italian) and *L'Abeille Grecque* (French). The arrival of the first portable manually operated printing presses was due to the parallel initiatives of Alexandros Mavrokordatos and Dimitrios Ypsilantis. When Mavrokordatos came to Greece from Pisa in 1821, he brought not only munitions but also a small printing press of French manufacture, which ended up in Mesolonghi, while the wooden printing press that Ypsilantis obtained in Trieste was installed in a mosque in Kalamata, provisional headquarters of the commanders of the freedom fighters. The dispatch of other printing presses, by diaspora Greeks and Philhellenes, was to follow, in order to meet the needs of the press and the provisional administration.

Salpinx Elliniki

Publication of the first printed newspaper of the fighting Greeks, *Salpinx Elliniki*, commenced in Kalamata on August 1, 1821. Its editor was the cleric and scholar Theoklitos Pharmakidis (1784–1860), formerly editor of Ερμής ο Λόγιος in Vienna, and its printer was Constantinos Tompras from Kydonies, who had learnt his craft in the famous printing house of the Parisian publisher and philhellene Ambroise Firmin-Didot. Each in his own way embodied the type of Greek whose personality had been forged within the spirit of the Enlightenment and who immediately responded to the call of the revolution. In the announcement of the newspaper, in late July, Pharmakidis presented both its aims and his thoughts on the decisive role of the press in briefing the Greek nation and generating public debate:

> The entire nation fighting in the struggle for freedom wants to see that through the press its struggles are reported, the virtues of the good are publicly praised, and the evils of the bad are checked, so as to avoid imitation; it wants to learn what is happening in each and every province, and in this way through the newspaper all sides [of the struggle] should be represented. Furthermore, the foreign nations have become curious about our affairs and very frequently write about us, they judge and criticize, praise and accuse; and all these things declared through their newspapers the nation wants to learn about, translated from those [countries], in its own newspaper.

Only three issues of *Salpinx Elliniki* circulated (August 1, 5, and 20, 1821). Its publication was cut short because of its disagreement with the preventive censorship that Dimitrios Ypsilantis tried to enforce in his effort to impose himself as envoy of his brother Alexandros. As the person responsible for preparing the revolution in the Peloponnese, he demanded to monitor the newspaper's content. Published in the first issue were his proclamation, an appeal to the inhabitants of Livadia, in which he summoned them to take up arms, and the famed declaration "Fight for Faith and Fatherland," which Alexandros Ypsilantis had circulated in Jassy in February 1821. Published in the third issue was the very important "Forewarning to the European Courts" of the Messenian Senate to the European powers (March 23, 1821), which tried to attract the attention of European diplomacy by officially making known the uprising of the Greeks and asking for European support with money and arms. It was signed by Petros Mavromichalis, senior general of the Spartan and Messenian army, but it is believed to have come from the headquarters of the Philiki Etaireia in Wallachia and to have been sent to the Peloponnese. Particularly interesting are Pharmakidis's texts in which he advised freedom fighters to be merciful toward the unarmed Turks and toward those who handed over their weapons. The aim of the revolution, he said, was to strike at tyranny and not at weak opponents.

Ellinika Chronika

After the closure of the Kalamata newspaper, there was a hiatus in publishing in the years 1823 and 1824, due to internal organizational shortcomings. In the meantime, there was an appreciable boosting of philhellenic associations, which became agents of European public opinion particularly favorable to the Greek cause. The philhellenic movement, with the impetus it gave and with the printing equipment it offered, contributed decisively to establishing the press and typography in warring Greece. Letters and diaries of Philhellenes who visited the land not only provide notable testimonies about various events but also sketch the personalities of emblematic figures of the struggle. The Philhellenes came to Greece at a difficult period of successive internal calamities which, after the three manuscript newspapers and the *Salpinx Elliniki*, left every publishing endeavor ineffective. "And yet in the midst of such terrible circumstances, there began from 1824 the *Ellinika Chronika*," Ioannis Philimon remarks (Philimon 1833, issue 2, 5). The inspiration of this publication came from Colonel Leicester Stanhope, Earl of Harrington (1784–1862), who went to Mesolonghi as representative of the London Greek Committee. At the printing press of Alexandros Mavrokordatos he made the acquaintance of the young physician from Zurich, Johann-Jacob Meyer in whom he perceived straight away the Swiss virtues that he so admired. Together they conceived the title of the newspaper and Meyer drafted the prospectus, despite Mavrokordatos's objections, as he wanted to print his own text. Because the Swiss Philhellene's command of Greek was deficient, he wrote his articles in French and they were translated by Dimitrios Pavlidis, a schoolteacher from Siatista. The newspaper's linguistic choices were criticized by Athanasios Psalidas, as he believed that they altered the linguistic style of the texts (readers' letters and descriptions of battles), whereas according to Philimon, who had been brought up in a Phanariot milieu and had attended the Great School of the Nation (*Megali tou Genous Scholi*), they were "written in good and easily understood language."

Before long, Leicester Stanhope was acting as a conscientious advocate of the utilitarian ideas of the eminent philosopher Jeremy Bentham, of whom he was a close friend. He was involved with setting up a school and with the health-care of the Greeks, and he organized a postal service at his own expense. Since his ardent wish was to promote freedom of the press, he managed to publish in the first issue of *Ellinika Chronika* an excerpt from the political pamphlet *On the Liberty of the Press, and Public Discussion,* which Bentham had published in London in 1821. On December 18, 1823, the newspaper announced that it would circulate on New Year's Day. However, on December 24, it was preceded by the Πρόδρομος των Ελληνικών Χρονικών (Forerunner of the Greek chronicles), a two-page paper in quarto format that was put out in order to give explanations about the protest of the Lord High Commissioner of the Ionian islands, Thomas Maitland, concerning the violation of the neutrality of Ithaka and Lefkada by Greek ships on December 10 and 12, 1823; Mavrokordatos was considered responsible for the case of Ithaka. The *Ellinika Chronika,* for whose installation Byron paid the sum of two hundred and fifty dollars, operated as the unofficial instrument of the administration, which funded the newspaper by purchasing a number of copies. The system of subscribers was introduced and the newspaper circulated widely also in the Ionian islands. It was a four-page publication that appeared twice a week. The first issue, with the motto "The Greatest Good of the Greatest Number," which was the fundamental axiom of utilitarianism, circulated with news of the war, as well as with a letter from Lord Byron, whose central theme was conciliation between men; in this way Byron wanted to castigate the factionalism of the governors and the difficulty of communicating with them. After all, such was the pressure put upon Meyer to project specific freedom fighters that he kept in parallel a diary, in which he wrote down the events as they occurred in reality. There were also more clear-headed participants who, as we learn from Kasomoulis (1941), supported him and counseled him always to write the truth: "When you are going to print, ask us to give you strength, and write whatever you know freely, without inhibition, the good and the bad about us."

The *Ellinika Chronika,* like the other newspapers, aimed at the ideological publicizing of the struggle, as Philimon notes that "they made an effort to silence foreign negative criticism caused by the backbiting over several years, and to keep vigorous the sometimes universal enthusiasm on behalf of Greece" (Philimon 1833, issue 2, 5). Concurrently with relaying information from operations in west central Greece and the siege of Mesolonghi, the newspaper republished articles from European newspapers with texts on political theory infused with the spirit of liberalism. The literary column hosted poems by Iakovos Rizos-Neroulos, as well as Spyridon Trikoupis's Greek translation of the last poem written by Byron in Mesolonghi. Issues 1–31 were printed at the press of Mavrokordatos, while from issue 32 (April 20, 1824), the newspaper was printed on the English press that had arrived in the meantime. In 1824 we have 106 issues, in 1825 105, and in the third year fifteen issues; the last issue appeared on February 20, 1826, a few weeks before the Exodos from Mesolonghi, in which Meyer and the typesetter Dimitrios Mesthenefs were killed fighting heroically.

Telegrafo Greco

At first Stanhope aspired to publish the *Ellinika Chronika* in both Greek and Italian, but limited himself to the Greek publication because Mavrokordatos's printing press had only Greek type. When the English printing press arrived it was decided, with the good offices of Byron, to publish a foreign-language newspaper with texts in Italian, French, English, and German. Appointed editor-in-chief of the *Telegrafo Greco,* as the new newspaper was named, was the exiled Carbonaro Count Pietro Gamba (1801–1827) from Ravenna, Byron's secretary. Byron and Meyer collaborated in writing the newspaper's prospectus and chose its motto, a maxim from the *Odyssey* with its Italian translation: "Giove toglie metà d'ogni virtute all'uom nel dì che il lega in servitute" (Zeus takes from man half his virtue when he binds him in servitude). Their basic concern was to brief the foreign public about the course of the struggle, without commentary, as Byron wanted to avoid the reactions of certain European circles which were negatively inclined toward the Greek insurrection and therefore would misinterpret the newspaper's mission and brand it as subversive. It was impossible to avoid linking the *Telegrafo* with democratic views. We come across letters from British Philhellenes then in Greece, such as Edward Trelawny and Edward Blaquiere, enthusiastic supporters of the expectations and demands of the Greek fighters. The *Telegrafo* was a purely philhellenic publication, which had ambitions to be sent abroad, even to the United States. On March 12 the upcoming publication of the *Telegrafo* was announced. However, it was short-lived, and in all thirty-nine issues circulated between March 20, 1824, and December 11, 1824. A contributing factor to the newspaper's demise was the untimely death of Lord Byron and the hasty departure of Stanhope and Gamba, who accompanied the poet's body to his birthplace. Gamba soon returned to Greece and continued to serve the Greek cause until his death of typhus at the age of twenty-six.

Ephimeris Athinon

Rightly, 1824 was dubbed the year of Greek journalism because, in addition to the *Ellinika Chronika* and the *Telegrafo Greco,* that year saw the publication of the *Ephimeris Athinon* in Athens and *O Philos tou Nomou* on Ydra. A committed supporter of the social mission of the press, Stanhope was planning to found a newspaper at Kranidi, seat of the administration, which endorsed the proposal, suggesting as a suitable editor Theoklitos Pharmakidis, who, however, had meanwhile withdrawn to Corfu, where he taught at the Ionian Academy until 1825. Stanhope, in his letter to the administration, stated that he had already approached Georgios Psyllas (1794–1878) who, as a member at the Second National Assembly at Astros, in 1823 had played a leading role with intelligence and quick-wittedness in the discussion on the institutional protection of freedom of speech and the press. As a scholarship holder of the Philomousos Etaireia, this Athenian had resided in Jena and Berlin, centers of liberal ideas; this experience was decisive for his subsequent ideological orientation. Stanhope, for his part, headed for Athens and offered the council of elders (*dimogerontia*) the second printing press he had brought with him, determined to entrust the publication of the newspaper to Psyllas. His choice was due also to the general high regard in which this promising young man was held by his fellow citizens, who were particularly interested in education and culture. The pervasive view about his integrity is attested by the following words of General Makrygiannis in his *Memoirs:* "Georgios Psyllas is always the pure son of the fatherland, who speaks prudently and patriotically in fairness and says his opinion freely" (Makrygiannis 2003, 506).

Moreover, another candidate had proposed himself, Panagiotis Sophianopoulos from Sopoto near Kalavryta, who was practicing medicine in Athens. Inconsistent in his political choices, he had made an unfavorable impression on Stanhope. The British philhellene William Henry Humphreys had formed a similar impression of Sophianopoulos, whom he described as a "villainous character." However, this did not prevent Sophianopoulos from writing articles for the *Ephimeris Athinon* and indeed from addressing a censorious letter to Adamantios Korais, criticizing him for not having come to Greece to instruct the inexperienced Greeks in political science.

The "announcement" of the newspaper's publication was written by Stanhope and Psyllas and circulated on July 18, 1824, while the first issue was printed on August 20 in Salamis, where the elders (*dimogerontes*) of Athens had sent the printing press, for fear of an enemy assault. From the second issue, on September 6, the newspaper, which appeared twice a week, was printed in Athens. In the first year there were 103 issues, until October 30, 1825, and in the second year just thirty-seven issues, the last appearing on April 15, 1826, when the publication suddenly ceased. The *Ephimeris Athinon* was the only newspaper that was not the mouthpiece of the administration and its publication was identified with Psyllas, who was, in Philimon's view, an opponent of the aristocratic system and was frequently at loggerheads with the administration. A friend of Spyridon Trikoupis, Psyllas did not hide his sympathies for Britain in the sphere of foreign policy. An Enlightenment man, he strove to give a pluralistic presentation of the events and his intention was to shape public opinion accordingly. During these very critical years, Psyllas showed his interest in the everyday life of Athens and its problems. He published news about the war on land and sea, about the movements of Ioannis Gouras and Odysseas Androutsos, government documents, news about the Philomousos Etaireia, thoughts and opinions on freedom of the press, criticisms of the administration and of the behavior of some millitary leaders. Psyllas used simple language, in keeping with his ideological preferences. Later, Georgios Tertsetis projected Psyllas as a model of the "natural voice of the nation," comparing him with the efforts of two towering figures, Dionysios Solomos and Spyridon Trikoupis, to make the most of the vernacular (demotic) tongue.

The newspaper's motto was the phrase "Publicity is the Soul of Justice," as proposed by Stanhope, who had also proposed its title. According to Psyllas, without publicity and forthright reports, the people would be kept in the dark about what their representatives said and did. With regard to the highly controversial issue of freedom of the press, he published the interpretive comments of Theodoros Negris, his main collaborator, on Article 8 of the 1823 Constitution. With his characteristic broadmindedness, Negris declared "Never is a nation free if it is not permitted by the laws to say, to present, to write and to print publicly whatever he has in his mind." The newspaper stopped in April 1826, when the troops of Mehmed Reşid Pasha, also known as Kütahı, were threatening Athens and its inhabitants sought refuge on Salamis. However, in issue number 60 of the *Geniki Ephimeris tis Ellados*, May 26, 1826, there is the news item that it was publicized and approved that the elders of Athens ordered not to publish in the newspaper anything against what was adopted by the Third National Assembly, nor anything personal or private, which may stir the passions, or trigger pointless disputes.

From this news item we can draw the conclusion that the administration must have considered the closure of the newspaper as temporary, due to the Ottoman attack on Athens.

O Philos tou Nomou

Ο Φίλος του Νόμου, Εφημερίς της Νήσου Ύδρας circulated concurrently with the Εφημερίς Αθηνών from March 10, 1824, until May 27, 1827, with a total of 296 issues, two a week. This was the longest-lived revolutionary newspaper, with editor-in-chief the philhellene Giuseppe N. Chiappe, an Italian exile who sought refuge first in the Ionian islands and then on Ydra. A teacher of foreign languages by profession, he was also a doctor of laws. Chiappe took part in many nautical operations and was registered as a citizen of Ydra. Secretary to Anastassios Tsamados and confidant of Lazaros Kountouriotis, he served also as secretary of the community for the duration of the War of Independence. Alerino Palma, a fellow exile on Ydra, where he got to know Chiappe well, describes him as an "intelligent and well-informed man, and very useful." (Palma 1826, 13). The maxim adopted for the newspaper was a phrase from Aristotle's *Politics* (book 1, chap. 1): "At his best, man is the noblest of all animals; separated from law and justice he is the worst."

Ο Φίλος του Νόμου received from the administration, as did the Ελληνικά Χρονικά, an annual subvention of 100 talers. Initially, it was printed on a makeshift press and had no official status. From issue 15 (May 5, 1824) until October 12, 1825 (issue 150), its title was changed to Ο Φίλος του Νόμου, Εφημερίς της Διοικήσεως και της Νήσου Ύδρας (The Friend of the Law, Newspaper of the Administration and of the island of Ydra). Under Article 44 of the 1823 Constitution, the institution of "Newspaper writer" of the administration was established and concurrently the printing of the paper improved as it was printed on the new press sent from Paris by Ambroise Firmin-Didot. As Giuseppe Pecchio informs us relating to the circulation of the newspapers, around 1825—an important year for Greek revolutionary journalism—the subscribers of the Ydra newspaper were no more than two hundred and of the Athens newspaper even fewer (Pecchio 1825, 309).

From issue 150 (October 12, 1825), *O Philos tou Nomou* ceased to be the official instrument of the administration, because on October 7 the *Geniki Ephimeris tis Ellados* circulated in Nafplio. *O Philos tou Nomou* then started to be harshly critical of official policy, defending the constitutional institutions. It published numerous articles relating to the freedom of the press, occasioned mainly by the persecution of Theoklitos Pharmakidis when, as we shall see, the administration decided to dismiss him from the post of editor of the *Geniki*

Ephimeris. O Philos tou Nomou attached much importance to naval history and had a special column headed: *Naftika* (naval or maritime matters). Its circulation was terminated on May 27, 1827, and the following year Chiappe moved to Aigina, where he continued his publishing activity with the weekly French-language newspaper *L'Abeille Grecque: Feuille périodique hebdomadaire.*

L'Abeille Grecque

The reasons why Chiappe decided to go ahead with publishing a newspaper in French were that from the moment the *Geniki Ephimeris* appeared on the scene, *O Philos tou Nomou* ceased to have exclusive rights to government news and, furthermore, he wished to turn toward the foreign-language public, as his newspaper had readers also in philhellenic circles abroad. He opted for French because it was the lingua franca in the wider Mediterranean region and because of the significant presence of French philhellene officers in Greece at that time.

With "Dieu et la liberté" as its motto, the newspaper was published initially on Ydra; when Capodistrias installed the seat of government on Aigina, Chiappe moved his printing press there and continued publishing the *Abeille*. Its first issue is dated March 31, 1827. The issues that circulated on Aigina were 45–137 (March 19, 1828, to March 28, 1829). From issue number 55 on, the format changed, becoming larger, and while the newspaper was weekly at first, it then became biweekly. The *Abeille* met the more general need of informing an international readership. Numerous letters from Colonel Philippe Jourdain narrating events in Greece were published and its columns frequently featured the names of French philhellene officers, such as Admiral de Rigny and Baron Higonet.

Alongside the *Abeille,* between 1828 and 1829, first in Patras and then in Aigina, the weekly newspaper *Le Courrier d'Orient* was circulated by the French Colonel Maxime Raybaud. This was followed in Nafplio by the *Moniteur Grec,* published by the legal expert C. D. Schinas, a purely Francophone newspaper that appeared weekly from July 1832 until January 1833, serving as an official state organ. Bilingual newspapers also circulated, such as the *Ελληνικός Καθρέπτης / Le Miroir Grec, O Σωτήρ / Le Sauveur, Η Εποχή / L'Époque,* and *Η Εθνική / Le National.*

Geniki Ephimeris tis Ellados

In the session of October 7, 1825, the provisional administration, based in Nafplio, decided to publish a newspaper entitled *Γενική Εφημερίς της Ελλάδος* (General newspaper of Greece) and appointed as *ephimeridographos* Theoklitos

Pharmakidis, who was also director of the administration's printing house, which comprised three presses. According to decree 13563 on October 19, 1825, civil servants with a salary of 200 piastres and above became subscribers, the sum being deducted from their pay. The first official organ of the administration, the *Geniki Ephimeris tis Ellados* published over seven consecutive years (1825–1832) the laws, edicts, decrees, and other acts of legislative content of the administration. It circulated biweekly, on Wednesday and Saturday, and was a political paper that published domestic and foreign news. It showcased philhellenic support for the War of Independence; it referred continuously to the philhellenic committees of Germany, France, Holland, and Belgium. The *Geniki Ephimeris tis Ellados* had rich news reporting, which the editor drew from foreign newspapers, and for this reason it often circulated supplements. The paper was continually changing headquarters, following the administration in its movements. The first issue appeared on October 7, 1825, in Nafplio, where the newspaper was printed for one year with a total of fifty-two issues. From issue 6 of the second year, November 24, 1826, until March 16, 1827, it was published on Aigina, moving subsequently to Poros (March 30, 1827, to June 4, 1827), Nafplio (June 22, 1827, to August 10, 1827), Aigina (August 24, 1827, to June 15, 1829), Argos (July 3, 1829, to August 13, 1829), again Aigina (from August 14, 1829), and finally in Nafplio from October 18, 1830, until March 23, 1832.

In many cases, Pharmakidis opposed government policy, at the risk of losing his job. On February 24, 1827, he included an anonymous letter criticizing the debate of the Third Assembly over the election of Ioannis Capodistrias as governor of Greece. Since the publication of antigovernment texts was not acceptable, the letter provoked the inevitable reaction and the decision was made to dismiss Pharmakidis. The written protest of three deputies, headed by Spyridon Trikoupis, in which they maintained that the publication was neither insulting to religion nor slanderous or illegal, advocated the revocation of the decision. The sequel of this controversial letter was published in full by *O Philos tou Nomou,* which in this way showed its support of Pharmakidis. Meanwhile, on April 2, 1827, the newspaper published the declaration of the president of the Third National Assembly on the election of Ioannis Capodistrias as governor of Greece. However, Pharmakidis disagreed with the assumption of authority by Capodistrias, whom he considered an instrument of Russian policy. On June 4 he tendered his resignation, in which he expressed his sentiments:

Desiring always to serve the Fatherland with all my strength and to be useful to the Nation I accepted the editorship of the newspaper, even though I knew, from experience, how demanding, how hard, how vexing and thankless a task I was taking on and for three semesters I bore this burden.

Pharmakidis then went to Ydra, where he joined with the anti-Capodistrian faction, putting an end to his career as a journalist.

The Macedonian scholar and politician Georgios Chrysidis was appointed to the helm of the now weakened *Geniki Ephimeris,* serving from June 22, 1827, until December 31, 1831. During his term he went along with government policy. In his views about the freedom of the press he pointed out the dangers of its abuse. On April 18, 1832, the newspaper changed its title to *Εθνική Εφημερίς* (National newspaper), and on February 1, 1833, it was renamed finally *Εφημερίς της Κυβερνήσεως* (Government gazette), the title it keeps to this day.

Anexartitos Ephimeris tis Ellados

The *Ανεξάρτητος Εφημερίς της Ελλάδος* (Independent Newspaper of Greece) was published initially on Ydra by Pantelis C. Pantelis, an Ydriot seaman with little education and cultivation. The journalist Marinos Papadopoulos-Vretos, who worked closely with Pantelis, notes in the *Ethnikon Imerologion* (1871) characteristically that "he was uneducated, almost illiterate, but was passionate about newspaper writing" (Papadopoulos-Vretos 1871, 482). The newspaper circulated weekly in 1827 and 1828, with no dependence on the wielders of political power. It covered the need to keep the public informed, in a period during which other newspapers had ceased publication, with the sole exception the *Geniki Ephimeris.* In his announcement of July 20, 1827, Pantelis mentioned, in his own vivid way:

> So, the Greeks have newspapers, but do they all shine like a mirror? Do they all speak the sacred truth? Do they all recount the acts of the head, and of all the parts, with the same precision as the patient represents the symptoms of his illness to the doctor? Of course not, and that is generally admitted.

The newspaper's motto was a maxim from Aristotle's *Nicomachean Ethics:* "Όσιον προτιμᾶν τὴν Ἀλήθειαν" (it is holy to prefer the Truth). Champion of democratic institutions, Pantelis commented caustically on the upper echelons of the revolutionary hierarchy. In his articles he had no qualms about turning against the *kocabaşıs* and the Phanariots, even publishing anecdotes satirizing them. With vehement assaults on the *Geniki Ephimeris,* which he considered their mouthpiece, from the end of July 1827 until the end of May 1828, the *Anexartitos* was the second biggest-selling Greek-language newspaper. Due to its critical stance toward authority, it was threatened with closure many times, and in issue 7 (September 17, 1827) it published an order of the *dimoge-rontia* of Ydra, in accordance with a decision of the government, that the newspaper should be shut down. From issue 32 of April 10, 1828, the *Anexartitos* moved to Aigina, became biweekly, and supported Capodistrias, without reservations. Its circulation ended on March 18, 1829. The impression it gave with its excesses was not to its advantage and according to the testimony of Philimon in his *Historical examination of the political newspapers of Greece*, "despite the boundlessness of a democratic spirit and its continuous, but pointless, insults against the aristocratic system nothing else distinguishes this newspaper written for the most part in an unpolished language" (Philimon 1833, issue 5, 17).

The new era ushered in by the emergence of independent Greece was marked by the effort to build a modern state, and as a result the administration became increasingly centralized. The press, after its liberal beginnings, followed a persistent road through its never-ending clashes with the power system that put obstacles in the way of its freedom. Even though, over time, the need for printed matter grew and the increase in the number of schools facilitated this development, the situation for the press deteriorated. The interventions of the Capodistrian authority and later of Othonian absolutism placed their own onerous terms on the operation of independent journalism, and the newspapers, on their part, waged a merciless polemic. Reflecting the mores of the time, we have still the well-known adage of Alexandros Soutsos: "The press is free, so long as you don't write."

Roxane D. Argyropoulos

Translated from the Greek by Alexandra Douma

References

Antoniadi, Sophia. 1971. "Ο τύπος κατά την Επανάστασιν και κατά την βασιλείαν του Όθωνος" [The press during the Revolution and during the reign of Othon]. *Parnassos* 13:403–418.

Argyropoulos, Roxane D. 1970. "Ο ελληνικός τύπος στον Αγώνα του 1821" [The Greek press in the struggle of 1821]. *Nea Estia* (Christmas): 304–305.

Dascalakis, Apostolos. 1930. *La presse néo-hellénique*. Paris.

Droulia, Loukia, and Gioula Koutsopangou, eds. 2008. *Εγκυκλοπαίδεια του ελληνικού τύπου 1784–1974* [Encyclopedia of the Greek press 1784–1974]. 4 vols. Athens.

Droulia-Mitrakou, Elli, and Triantaphyllos E. Sklavenitis. 2000. "Η συμβολή της τυπογραφίας στη στήριξη της Επανάστασης του 1821" [The contribution of printing to the support of the Revolution of 1821]. In *Πεντακόσια χρόνια έντυπης παράδοσης του Νέου*

Ελληνισμού (1499-1999) [Five hundred years of printing tradition of modern Hellenism, 1499-1999], 173-191. Athens.

Hatzis, Aristides N. 2020. "Establishing a Revolutionary Newspaper: Transplanting Liberalism in a Pre-Modern Society." In *Human Rights in Times of Illiberal Democracies (Liber Amicorum in Memoriam of Stavros Tsakyrakis),* edited by Lucy Kiousopoulou, Marialena Tsirli, and Panayotis Voyatzis, 293-317. Athens.

Kasomoulis, Nikolaos. 1941. *Ενθυμήματα στρατιωτικά της Επαναστάσεως των Ελλήνων 1821-1833* [Military reminiscences of the Revolution of the Greeks, 1821-1833]. Vol. 2. Athens.

Koumarianou, Aikaterini. 1971. *Ο Τύπος στον Αγώνα* [The press in the struggle]. 3 vols. Athens.

Koumarianou, Aikaterini. 1994. "British Philhellenism and the Greek Press (1824)." In *Europäischer Philhellenismus. Die europäische philhellenische Presse bis zur 1. Hälfte des 19. Jahrhunderts,* edited by Evangelos Konstantinou, 115-123. Philhellenische Studien 3. Frankfurt.

Koumarianou, Aikaterini. 2010. *Ιστορία του ελληνικού τύπου (18ος-19ος αιώνας)* [History of the Greek press, eighteenth to nineteenth centuries]. Edited by Alexis Malliaris. Athens.

Laios, Georgios. 1960. "Die griechischen Zeitungen und Zeitschriften (1784-1821). Quellenmaterial hauptsächlich aus der Österreichischen Staatsarchiven gesammelt und zusammengestellt." *Berliner Byzantinische Arbeiten* 15:110-195.

Lampros, Spyridon. 1904, 1909. "Χειρόγραφες εφημερίδες του Αγώνος" [Handwritten journals of the struggle]. *Neos Ellinomnimon* 1:450-474; 5:481.

Leonidis, Grigorios. 1992. *Die griechische Presse unter König Otto: 1832-1843.* Munich.

Loukatos, Spyros D. 1996. *Ο ιταλικός φιλελληνισμός κατά τον Αγώνα της ελληνικής ανεξαρτησίας, 1821-1833* [Italian Philhellenism during the struggle for Greek independence, 1821-1833]. Athens.

Makrygiannis, Ioannis. (1907) 2003. *Αρχείον. Απομνημονεύματα του στρατηγού Ιωάννου Μακρυγιάννη* [Archive: Memoirs of General Ioannis Makrygiannis]. Edited by Iannis Vlachogiannis. Reprint. Athens.

Mazarakis-Ainian, C. Ioannis. 1987. *Το τυπογραφείο των Αθηνών. "Εφημερίς Αθηνών" 1824-1826. Ευρετήριο* [The Athens printing house: The *Newspaper of Athens,* 1824-1826. Index]. Athens.

Mazarakis-Ainian, C. Ioannis. 2007. *Τα ελληνικά τυπογραφεία του Αγώνα 1821-1827* [The Greek printing presses of the struggle, 1821-1827]. Athens.

Moschopoulos, Nicéphore. 1931. *La presse dans la renaissance balkanique: Étude historique.* Athens.

Palma, Alerino. 1826. *Greece Vindicated in Two Letters.* London.

Papadopoulos-Vretos, Marinos. 1871. "Πως μουντζουρόνουν το χαρτί ήτοι περί εφημεριδογραφίας" [How to smear the paper or on journalism]. *Ethnikon Imerologion,* 475-489.

Pecchio, Giuseppe. 1825. "Greece in the Spring of 1825." *New Monthly Magazine* 14:291-320, 409-427.

Philimon, Ioannis. 1833. "Ιστορική εξέτασις των πολιτικών εφημερίδων της Ελλάδος" [A historical examination of the political newspapers of Greece]. *Chronos* 1-6 (May 1-18).

Philimon, Ioannis. 1859–1861. *Δοκίμιον ιστορικόν περί της Ελληνικής Επαναστάσεως* [A Historical Essay on the Greek Revolution]. Vol. 3. Athens.

Psyllas, Georgios. 1974. *Απομνημονεύματα του βίου μου* [Memoirs of my life]. Edited by Eleutherios Prevelakis. Introduction by Nikolaos Louros. Athens.

Queux de Saint-Hilaire, Auguste de. 1871. "La presse dans la Grèce moderne depuis l'indépendance jusqu'en 1871." *Annuaire pour l'encouragement des Études Grecques* 5:47–178.

Rosen, Frederick. 1992. *Bentham, Byron and Greece: Constitutionalism, Nationalism and Early Liberal Political Thought.* Oxford.

Sathas, Constantinos N. 1868–1869. "Επιστολή" [Letter]. *Pandora* 19:214–216.

St Clair, William. (1972) 2008. *That Greece Might still Be Free: The Philhellenes in the War of Independence.* Introduction by Roderick Beaton. Cambridge.

Stanhope, Leicester. 1824. *Greece in 1823 and 1824: Being a Series of Letters, and Other Documents on the Greek Revolution, Written during a Visit to That Country.* London.

Vakalopoulos, Apostolos E. 1950. "Φήμες και διαδόσεις κατά την Ελληνική Επανάσταση του 1821. (Συμβολή στην ψυχολογία των ελληνικών επαναστατικών όχλων)" [Rumors and reports during the Greek Revolution of 1821: Contribution to the psychology of the Greek revolutionary mobs]. *Epistimoniki Epetiris tis Philosophikis Scholis tou Panepistimiou Thessalonikis* 6:209–229.

Vranousis, Leandros I. 2008. *Αθανάσιος Ψαλίδας, ο διδάσκαλος του γένους* [Athanasios Psalidas, teacher of the nation]. Ioannina.

VI

IDEAS AND CREATIVE EXPRESSION

Enlightenment

The Enlightenment in Greek culture and its broader southeast European context had been a protracted and rather slow but nevertheless sustained process of intellectual change which eventually, over the *longue durée,* proved to have revolutionary effects.

Considered through the prism of the periodization of the Enlightenment as a whole, its expressions in the Greek intellectual tradition can be seen to follow the standard pattern recognizable in the development of pertinent phenomena on the larger scale of European culture. From the early Enlightenment in the opening decades of the eighteenth century, we can witness a move to a more affirmative phase articulating the claims of intellectual change, criticism, and rationalism up to about 1770, and then onward to a period of mature Enlightenment from the 1780s to the early nineteenth century. During the first two decades of the nineteenth century, especially following the occupation of the Ionian islands by revolutionary France in 1797 and Napoleon's campaign to Egypt (1798), Greek culture appears immersed in the Age of Revolution and the Greek Enlightenment can be clearly perceived to reach its radical democratic apex. That was also a period of ideological conflict that set Greek society on the road to revolution that eventually came in 1821.

Although conventional periodizations of the Enlightenment in the western European heartlands would see the movement ending with the coming of the French Revolution, which in turn can be considered to have inaugurated a new era in the intellectual history of the Western world, it would still be legitimate, on the basis of a broad range of historical evidence, to consider the Enlightenment, in its democratic phase, as living on the periphery, in central and southeastern Europe and in the Hispano-Iberian world. In all these regions, with the

Greek world as a prominent case among them, we can witness a strong continuity in ideological and intellectual developments from the 1780s, and certainly from the 1790s through the 1820s. The foremost exponent of democratic Enlightenment thought in the Greek tradition, Adamantios Korais, embodied this movement and gave the Greek Enlightenment a belated dynamism that was quite exceptional.

On the basis of the periodization outlined above, we can witness the growth of the Greek Enlightenment as an expanding horizon throughout the Greek Mediterranean. That expanding horizon delineating cultural change was reflected in a remarkable geographical polycentrism, with many hearths of intellectual and educational activity in many regions, including major urban centers like Constantinople, Ioannina and Smyrna, medium-size commercial cities on the road of overland trade with central Europe and even highland communities and of course the main communities of the Greek diaspora in Italy, and central and western Europe. These expressions of intellectual activity were increasingly, over the decades, marked by a deepening sense of the need for change, reorientation, and reform, not only of intellectual life but also of the moral culture of modern Hellenism, in an effort to bring about a new order in collective life. It was this aspiration that was gradually politicized and after 1789 could be articulated as a vision of freedom.

The initial expressions of intellectual change associated with the early Enlightenment took the form of asserting the superiority of the Moderns in the Quarrel of Ancients and Moderns and affirming the value of modern science, as stated by Nicolaos Mavrokordatos in his novel *Φιλοθέου Πάρεργα* (The leisure hours of Philotheos; 1720). Mavrokordatos was a model of the cosmopolitanism of the early Enlightenment as he found himself at the center of a broad network of correspondence and exchange of books and ideas in the "republic of letters" of his time. His correspondents included Jean Le Clerc, editor of the leading early Enlightenment journal, *Nouvelles de la république des lettres,* and the Archbishop of Canterbury William Wake (Bouchard 1974).

This cosmopolitan foundation shaped the spirit of the Greek Enlightenment. In the generation after Mavrokordatos, two clergymen, both born in Corfu, Evgenios Voulgaris and Nikiphoros Theotokis, emerged as towering figures in the movement of intellectual renewal, facing up to the challenge of demarcating the domains of faith and reason, so that philosophy and scientific knowledge could be pursued without impediments from the direction of religion and the church. Both remained strictly within the boundaries of Orthodox doctrine and produced important theological works. At the same time, nevertheless, they argued that as long as the principles of faith and the teachings of the Church and of Orthodox tradition were unquestioningly respected, the human mind could pursue the quest of truth in other domains according to the dictates of reason. Thus, Voulgaris in his imposing philosophical treatise, *Logic* (1766), introduced to Greek readers the philosophical systems of the Moderns, stressing the significance of the philosophy of Descartes, Leibniz, and John Locke (Kitromilides 1990, 222–225). He also coined the Greek term for religious toleration, ἀνεξιθρησκία, claiming that his own Orthodox perspective was truer to the ideal than the arguments of Voltaire. In his turn, Nikiphoros Theotokis introduced Newtonian physics to Greek readers in a treatise on *Elements of Physics*, published in the same year, 1766, and at the same printing establishment in Leipzig as Voulgaris's *Logic*.

With these imposing spokesmen and their work, the Enlightenment became a recognizable force in the Greek intellectual universe and the religious loyalty of the two great pioneers protected the fledgling movement from possible reactions by the official Church. As a matter of fact, at a time when the Inquisition and the *Index* were still in operation in the Western Church, the Orthodox Church appeared predisposed, in the middle decades of the eighteenth century and later, to enlist the human resources of the Enlightenment in upgrading its own pastoral work in the field of education. Thus Voulgaris, in 1753, was charged by the patriarchate of Constantinople with improving the curriculum of the leading Orthodox educational institution at the time, the Athonite Academy, "through changes and reforms" (Kitromilides 2007, Study VII).

From the ranks of Voulgaris's students emerged some of the most articulate representatives of the mature and fully self-aware Enlightenment in Greek intellectual life. Most notable among them was Iosipos Moisiodax, a model of the committed intellectual, who argued for the need of moral reform as a necessary precondition for the improvement of Greek society and education. To this end, he translated in 1761–1762 Lodovico Antonio Muratori's *Moral Philosophy*, to which he prefixed long prolegomena, which amounted to a manifesto for cultural and social change. Moisiodax's courage and commitment to change, which included drastic educational and language reform, gained him many enemies. In response to the calumnies against him he published in 1780 his *Apology*, which is one of the emblematic texts of the Greek Enlightenment. In its pages Moisiodax argued for the use of the vernacular as the language of Greek education, he supported the introduction of modern philosophy, Newtonian science, and mathematics against neo-Aristotelian commentaries as the appropriate content of instruction in higher schools, and in a long footnote introduced for the first time in modern Greek political thought the idea of a non-monarchical republican regime on the model of the Swiss confederation as a constitution of justice (Kitromilides 1992, 167–182).

Iosipos Moisiodax could be considered a genuine exponent of the radical Enlightenment writing in the Greek language. His exact contemporary Dimitrios Katartzis, a high official at the court of the principality of Wallachia, wrote extensively on cultural change, language, and politics. He went further than Moisiodax in supporting the spoken vernacular as the appropriate language of learning and literature, if Greek society sincerely wished to break free from its backwardness. He did not, however, dare to commit his views to print. Like Moisiodax, he was a fervent supporter of French Encyclopedism and he elaborated a theory of the Greek people, although still subject to the Ottomans, as a political community defined by its language and institutions. The conceptualization of the Greeks as a political community on the basis of Aristotle's definition of citizenship made them recognizable among the other modern European nations as a nation in their own right (Katartzis 1970, 44). What remained unstated in this definition, but could be inferred without much difficulty from it, was the prospect of freedom, to which the Greek nation could aspire in the future.

That prospect appeared on the horizon in the year 1789. The French Revolution had a profound impact on Greek culture and society, and contributed to the politicization of Greek thought with the explicit articulation of the vision of freedom. The 1790s were a decade of enthusiasm and hope but also of reaction and ideological conflict (Kitromilides 2013, 175–199). In fact, it could be stated that 1789 provided the threshold for the entry of Greek society on the road to revolution.

The most articulate exponents of the debate provoked by the French Revolution were the younger associates of Moisiodax and Katartzis in the Danubian Principalities, Gregorios Constantas, Daniel Philippidis, and Rhigas Velestinlis. The two clergymen from the village of Milies on Mount Pilion, Constantas and Philippidis, also known under the shared name Dimitrieis, from Dimitrias, the major ancient Greek city in the area, coauthored one of the major sources of Greek Enlightenment literature, the treatise *Novel Geography* (Γεωγραφία Νεωτερική). The work was published in Vienna in 1791, just in time to comment on the "great conflagration" that had been lit in France, but the authors remained uncertain whether it was going to burn or illuminate humanity (Philippidis and Constantas 1988, 425). Despite the suspended judgment on the revolution, *Novel Geography* was informed genuinely and authentically by the spirit of the democratic Enlightenment. It surveyed and appraised the achievements and prospects of cultural and political change in Europe, thus projecting models to be emulated in the effort of reconstructing Greek society. The detailed survey of the geography of Greece formed the main part of the work and amounted in fact to a historical sociology whose obvious aim was to ex-

plain the decline and enslavement of Greece, to appraise the record of her revival in the period of the Enlightenment and to discern in the distant horizon
the dawn of freedom. This attitude transpires in their address to their fellow
countrymen, the inhabitants of Milies, upon whom they urge the love of
country, the eros of the motherland, as the recipe that would cure the social
ills in their community. This impassioned appeal is clearly informed by republican patriotism inspired by Enlightenment radicalism to which the two authors
felt themselves heirs and devotees (Philippidis and Constantas 1988, 184–185).

The republican vision in the culture of the Greek Enlightenment culminated
and found its clearest expression in the political and social thought and the revolutionary activism of Rhigas Velestinlis (Figure 37). Rhigas's historical presence and activity remain elusive and haunted by legend but his ideas and visions are bracketed by his publications within a short period of seven years, 1790
to 1797, and can be clearly understood and appraised. Since the writings of R. R.
Palmer and Jacques Godechot, Rhigas has been established as the emblematic

FIGURE 37   Dionysios Tsokos, *Portrait of Rhigas Velestinlis*, 1862.
Oil on canvas. National Historical Museum, Athens.

Greek presence in the Age of Revolution primarily on the evidence of his pamphlets of 1797 that announced his initiative to start a revolution in southeastern Europe to overthrow Ottoman despotism and to establish a sovereign Hellenic Republic modeled on the Jacobin constitution of 1793. The new republic was meant as a state not just for Greeks, but for all nationalities, ethnic and religious groups in the Ottoman Empire, including Muslims and Turks, on the basis of equal citizenship and recognition, and political and social rights for all, men and women, privileged and underprivileged (Velestinlis 2002).

This was certainly a revolutionary vision, especially in the context for which it was enunciated. It could be said, however, that Rhigas's most substantial revolutionary contribution came with an earlier work, in fact his first published work in 1790, his selection and translation of six love stories from Restif de la Bretonne's *Contemporaines mêlées,* under the title *School of Delicate Lovers* (Σχολεῖον τῶν ντελικάτων ἐραστῶν). Through the medium of the literary narrative of the passion, pain, and emotional suffering caused to the tender and innocent "delicate lovers" by the inequality and multifarious social prejudices prevailing in a rigidly stratified society, Rhigas was in fact appealing for a liberation of social sentiments, an emancipation of feeling and the passions of the heart as part of a broader social transformation that might secure genuine human rather than just formal political liberation (Velestinlis 2001).

Such was the source of the movement of Greek republican radicalism that emanated from Rhigas's ideas and was morally fortified by his martyrdom in 1798. The movement ran through the first two decades of the nineteenth century and culminated in 1821. The most prominent intellectual monument of Greek republican radicalism was the treatise *Hellenic Nomarchy or a Discourse on Freedom,* published by an anonymous patriot in Italy, probably in Livorno, in 1806. The identity of the author has never been revealed and it is still contested in Greek historical scholarship (see Roxane Argyropoulos, "Intellectuals," in this volume). It would not be an exaggeration to claim that this was the most important work of political and social theory in Greek Enlightenment literature. Although the anonymous author placed himself in the radical tradition inaugurated by Rhigas, to whose memory he dedicated his work, he did not use Rhigas's own political vocabulary. He coined instead his own evocative term, *nomarchy,* obviously an inversion of the term *monarchy,* to denote the regime of the rule of law, freedom, and equality that was expected to replace despotism after the coming revolution. The Anonymous Hellene, the pseudonym he gave himself, put forward a clear conception of the political subject that was looking forward to its accession to freedom and independence: it was the nation of the Hellenes, a community defined by an unequivocal historical identity that connected it with the ancient inhabitants of Hellas, their own cherished homeland. The al-

ternative names Greeks derived from the ancient Latin denomination—
Romaioi, Romaics, *Rûm,* as the Church and the Ottoman rulers called the Orthodox Christian subjects—were now definitely abandoned. Thus, a clearly
defined modern nation emerged and entered the foreground of history claiming
its rights and its place in the world of free nations.

The visualization of freedom and a clear-cut modern national identity in the
pages of *Hellenic Nomarchy* was combined with sharp social criticism of all
those "agents of tyranny," that is a host of corrupt elements in Greek society
who appeared as willing collaborators of Ottoman despotism and wished
through this means to perpetuate the enslavement of the Hellenic nation and
their own privileged status within it. The denunciation of the collaborators of
despotism—landed primates, Phanariot officials, ecclesiastical dignitaries,
above all obscurantist monasticism, but also self-serving merchants and other
professionals in the diaspora whose avarice left them indifferent to the plight
of their homeland—sets the tone of the whole treatise. The anonymous author
attached a complete sociology of captivity to his republican theory in order to
leave no reasonable doubt as to the magnitude of the challenge involved in the
struggle for liberation. Thus, republican theory and social criticism, especially
in the form of anticlericalism, appear as the defining characteristics of the radical democratic vision marking the apex of the Greek Enlightenment on the
eve of the revolution (Kitromilides 2006).

Another author who flirted with radical republicanism at the turn of the eighteenth to the nineteenth century was Adamantios Korais (Figure 38). A medical doctor trained at the University of Montpellier, Korais had made his first
appearance in Greek letters with the publication of two works of Christian catechism in the early 1780s. He spent the 1790s in revolutionary Paris and in his
voluminous correspondence recorded as an eyewitness his impressions and
judgment of the drama and pathos of events. Although his commitment to the
democratic Enlightenment was not shaken, he came out of the revolution hating
Jacobinism and firmly convinced that freedom should be joined with justice
and that the rule of law should be respected at all costs (Kitromilides 2013, 176–
189). Napoleon's campaigns to the Mediterranean, however, rekindled his enthusiasm. For a moment he hoped that the liberation of Greece might come
through the French intervention in the East and in a revolutionary song, entitled Ἄσμα Πολεμιστήριον (War song) published in 1800, he proclaimed that
the common cause of freedom had made the two peoples, French and Greeks,
one nation, "la nation Gallo-grecque." His support for the French plans gained
Korais the reputation of a French agent in conservative circles, but in fact after
Napoleon's autocratic turn following the campaign to Egypt, he resolutely took
his distance from the new regime and the empire.

FIGURE 38   Augusto Picarelli,
Portrait of Adamantios Korais,
second half nineteenth century.
Oil on canvas. Athens
University History Museum
Collection, National and
Kapodistrian University of
Athens.

Like the anonymous author of *Hellenic Nomarchy,* Korais was deeply moved
by Rhigas's martyrdom, which he recorded in a pamphlet entitled *Fraternal Instruction.* The pamphlet was published in 1798 as a response to the call for
willing submission to Ottoman rule and for resistance to the deceptive new
ideas of liberty and equality, contained in the pamphlet *Paternal Instruction,*
which was issued earlier that year under the name of the ailing patriarch of Jerusalem. Obviously, the publication of *Paternal Instruction* was instigated by
Ottoman pressure on the Church in the climate of panic caused by Napoleon's
campaign in Egypt. This gave the opportunity for Korais to publish his first political work, calling for the overthrow of despotism and proclaiming the
struggle for freedom as a duty incumbent on all true Christians. In this climate
of revolutionary expectancy, Korais felt that he should contribute to the preparation of his countrymen for the duties of free citizenship by translating a
work of politics and legislation, and as such he chose Cesare Beccaria's *Of Crimes
and Punishments,* which was duly published in 1802. In a note in this work Korais announced his intention to further serve the political reeducation of his
fellow Greeks with a translation of Jean-Jacques Rousseau's *Social Contract.*

   That translation project, which could be taken as a characteristic expression
of Korais's flirtation with republican radicalism at the dawn of the nineteenth
century, never materialized. After the collapse of the hopes for an imminent
liberation through the expansion of revolutionary France in the world, a hope

shared by many liberal nationalists around Europe at the time, Korais developed a more reflective long-term perspective on the prospects of Greek freedom. Liberation could not and in fact should not be actively pursued, according to Korais, before the Greek national community, which had been gaining awareness of itself as a collective historical subject, was ready by means of education and cultural development first to undertake responsibly the overthrow of the yoke of despotism and second to govern itself under the rule of law.

That was a daunting task in Korais's judgment and it would require decades to accomplish. He therefore felt that he should dedicate his efforts to the reeducation of his compatriots through systematically exposing them first to the substance of classical learning, their ancestral heritage, and second to the philosophical, scientific, and political ideas of modern Western civilization, the culture of the Enlightenment. Part of the project of Greek reeducation was also the improvement of the spoken modern version of Greek. This was Korais's main contribution to the major cultural debate in the Greek Enlightenment, the "Language Question" (Mackridge 2009, 102–125).

According to Korais, it was pointless to try to revive ancient Greek, as the archaists in the Language Question were arguing, as the language of learning and education in modern Greek society. Instead the modern language, which was a direct descendant from ancient Greek, should be purified from foreign lexical accretions, which over the centuries has adulterated its linguistic character, and grammatically corrected so as to make plain its affinities with classical Greek. This was what Korais described as the "middle road," an intermediate position between the archaists and the extreme vernacularists, who supported the use of the spoken language as the medium of education and literature. Korais was accused by later supporters of demoticism for introducing an artificial linguistic medium, *katharevousa,* that later in the nineteenth century went to extremes of which without doubt Korais would have disapproved. Korais knew that language, its cultivation and improvement as the medium defining the nation, and education as the means for the production of civility and a civil society capable of governing itself, were components of the broader political problem of the liberation of Greece. Hence his dedication to the causes of language and education through his monumental project of publishing modern editions of key ancient Greek texts, selected for their relevance to civic education. This project produced his Hellenic Library, his major editorial achievement. It comprised sixteen main volumes and nine supplementary editions (*Parerga*) of Greek classics. The broad educational purposes of this editorial project are clearly documented by the extensive prolegomena Korais wrote for each volume. In these long and reflective essays of cultural criticism and advice, Korais over the years leading up to 1821 took up and discussed all the major issues he considered critical for the preparation of Greek society to claim its liberation: education, language, science, and morality, while after the outbreak of revolution he turned his attention to politics and state building.

With his presence in the classical tradition, Korais emerged as the leading personality of the Greek Enlightenment and he became internationally known and respected. From his Parisian base he could play a leading role in convincing European public opinion that Greece had revived as a social and cultural entity and that the Greek nation was getting ready to assume its appropriate mission in the world of nations as the heir and guardian of a unique ancient heritage. This role, as the intellectual "ambassador" of his nation, Korais had consistently discharged since 1803, when he read his famous address "On the Present State of Civilization in Greece" at the pioneering anthropological society Société des Observateurs de l'Homme, in which he announced the return of civilization to Greece (Kedourie 1970, 153–188).

He continued to play this role throughout his life, especially during the revolutionary decade of the 1820s, through his contacts with leading French liberals, German classicists, British Utilitarians, including Jeremy Bentham, and even President Thomas Jefferson (see Ioannis Evrigenis, "American Philhellenism," in this volume).

The Enlightenment as a movement of ideological change exercised a broader influence on Greek society and culture beyond the debates over language, education, and politics. Its impact was felt in literature, with the emergence of works of creative expression both in poetry and in prose. Literary expression in modern Greek was greatly enriched thanks to translations of major works of European literature: Rhigas's translation of Restif de la Bretonne has been noted above, but he also translated Metastasio, Marmontel, and Montesquieu as part of his political strategy. Molière and Voltaire were repeatedly translated and included versions of Molière's L'avare and Voltaires's Zadig on the eve of the Greek Revolution. Translation was particularly important for the emergence of a distinct Enlightenment theatrical literature, which contributed decisively to the cultivation of the national sentiments of Greek audiences attending the staging of these works on the eve and during the years of the Greek Revolution (Tabaki 2003).

In the revolutionary decade of the 1820s the Enlightenment heritage continued to make itself felt in Greek life in multiple ways. The liberation struggle was understood by those fighting on the battlefield in terms of the ideals of freedom that had been voiced by the democratic Enlightenment in the previous decades. The hopes for the future of Greek society were shaped by those ideals and the expectation of securing for Greece the rule of law and civic order enjoyed by the civilized nations of the West, the nations that had been projected by the Enlightenment as the models to be emulated by the Greek nation. The active presence of Enlightenment ideology, especially its radical residues, in Greek culture and politics at the time of the revolution is recorded in the print culture of the period, which can be followed in detail in the imposing bibliographical compendia covering the 1820s (Iliou and Polemi 2011). On the basis of this documentation we can observe the impact of Enlightenment ideals on the birth of free Greece.

What strikes the observer's attention in surveying the print culture of the years of the Greek Revolution is the incontrovertible impression that the main part of book production comprised religious works, primarily publications destined for liturgical use in Orthodox churches. Next to this characteristically traditional output, another species of religious literature increasingly made its presence quite palpable, books and pamphlets serving the work of Protestant missionaries, mostly published by missionary presses in Malta. The coexistence of these two kinds of religious literature forms a regularity dominating Greek print culture throughout the 1820s.

Amid this dominant regularity, some offshoots of the Enlightenment continued making their appearance, amidst the drama of revolutionary action. Just on the eve of the revolution, the year 1820 witnessed a noteworthy output of theatrical literature: Voltaire's *Brutus* and Vittorio Alfieri's *Orestes* were translated and printed in Bucharest, perhaps as reminders of the duty of tyrannicide. Rhigas's translation of Pietro Metastasio's *Olimpiade,* of more than twenty years earlier, was anonymously reprinted and thus the hymn of liberty it contained was again made accessible to the Greek readership.

The entire corpus of Sophoclean tragic poetry was published in Paris, edited by Constantinos Nikolopoulos, a disciple of Korais, known for his republican ideas. In the year 1820 Nikolopoulos, a book collector and librarian in Paris, also edited seven of Plutarch's *Parallel Lives,* an edition whose selectivity bespoke the political intentions of the editor: from the Plutarchian biographical pairs, only the Greek life was republished, omitting the Roman parallel life, with the exception of Julius Caesar. The Greek models of republican virtue and patriotism were all present: Themistocles, Theseus, Pericles, Pelopidas, Timoleon, Phocion, Philopoemen.

Alongside this Plutarchian school of civic virtue, an essay on the virtues and actions of Demosthenes by Spyridon Kafirefs was published at the public press of Corfu. The same year witnessed the anonymous publication in Paris of one of Korais's most outspoken works of religious criticism, *Counsel of Three Bishops.* The stage for the revolution appeared to be set.

The coming of the revolution was registered in Greek bibliography and print culture not massively or in a manner that completely overturned the regularities noted above, but, nevertheless, in some characteristic ways that reflected the transition to a new age that Greek society was dramatically making. The Enlightenment was asserted as the agent of that transition with two monumental editions by the movement's doyen, Adamantios Korais, who judged that the moment dictated the need for education in free citizenship. Accordingly, in the years 1821 and 1822 he published Aristotle's *Politics* and *Nicomachean Ethics,* with long prolegomena trying to provide a blueprint for the moral and political culture of the new state. His reflective prolegomena made a strong impression on his contemporaries and were twice translated into German. One of the translators, the Swiss Johan Kaspar von Orelli, compared Korais to Fichte, describing both thinkers as "literary architects" of their nations.

A new edition of his old translation of Beccaria with up-to-date prolegomena was added in 1823 to these works of political pedagogy. In the same spirit, Korais published also Plutarch's *Politics* in 1824 and his only edition of a work by Plato, *Gorgias,* in 1825. With indomitable energy, despite his advanced age, the Enlightenment sage of Paris produced also works to hearten the fighting Greeks by extolling military prowess and virtue. Thus, Onesander and Tyrtaeus were published in a volume in 1822.

In these early years of the revolution, and specifically during the year 1823, Korais had also been at work on what turned out to be his most important political work, his detailed commentary, article by article, on the Provisional Constitution of Greece voted by the First National Assembly at Epidavros on January 1, 1822. The commentary was a remarkable work of liberal democratic political thought that touched on all the fundamental issues of modern politics: toleration and the place of religion in a liberal state, state organization, representation, civil liberties, economic freedom, public education, and freedom of the press. This text could be considered the most complete and mature expression of Korais's political thought, but it remained unpublished in his lifetime and did not appear in print until 1933 (Korais 2018).

The year of the outbreak of the revolution was marked by the publication of militant pamphlets urging the Greeks to join the revolutionary action. The most remarkable of these pamphlets was a collection of patriotic poetry edited by the Cretan scholar Manuel Vernardos and published in Jassy. The editor characterized the collection as "the pamphlet of the songs of freedom." It included revolutionary songs by Rhigas and by the editor and other anonymous patriots calling the Greeks to arms. A good indication of the revolutionary character of the pamphlet is the fact that it has survived in only three known copies (Iliou and Polemi 2011, 123–124). Three other pamphlets appealing to the patriotism of the Greeks and inciting them to revolt were published in Paris (138–139).

Besides the venerable dean of Greek letters, a group of younger scholars, inspired by his ideas, made substantial contributions to the implantation of a liberal tradition of political thought in fighting Greece. Thus, Anastasios Polyzoidis in 1824 produced translations of the foremost liberal constitutions of the time, the constitution and declaration of independence of the United States and a constitutional text entitled "Political Constitution of Britain." These texts were appended to a new edition by Polyzoidis of the *Provisional Constitution of Greece*. The following year the young jurist produced his most important political work, which could be considered one of the foundations of political science in Modern Greece, *A General Theory of Various Systems of Administration and Especially of Parliamentary Government* (Polyzoidis 2011). The work was published in the besieged city of Mesolonghi, a major bastion of the Greek struggle until the heroic exodus of its defenders a year later.

The same year as Polyzoidis's *General Theory,* another important work of liberal political theory made its appearance, the Greek edition of François Daunou's *Essai sur les garanties individuelles,* translated by Philippos Fournarakis, a close associate of Korais, who had taken an active interest in the project (Iliou 1978). By such means the aging Korais was persisting in his life-long struggle to teach his compatriots the values of liberty and respect for individual rights.

Inscribed in the same logic of civic education was also the publication in 1828–1829 of another major work of political science, a two-volume treatise *Of Republics* (Περὶ πολιτειῶν) by Ioannis Kokkonis, another one of Korais's younger associates in France. The work was a survey of forms of government in antiquity and in the modern period that attempted to establish a connection between the "progress of the human spirit" and the emergence of constitutional and republican forms of government. The second volume is a treatise on the "constitution of states" and concluded with a discussion of "which form of government is appropriate for reborn Greece." Kokkonis' s recommendations are remarkable: he judged that neither a sovereign constitutional monarchy nor an autonomous principality under Ottoman suzerainty could be appropriate forms of government for Greece and he outlined in detail his arguments in support for these views. He judged most appropriate for the historical experiences and the prevailing conditions in Greece a form of decentralized republic on the model of the Swiss confederation and appealed to the leadership of Greek society to abandon their endemic factionalism and pursue concord instead in order to serve the public interest and the Greek nation.

Next to the works by Polyzoidis and Kokkonis, liberal political thought in the revolutionary period produced the pamphlet *On the Utility and Extent of the Political Sciences* by George Athanasiou, published in Aigina in 1828 (Iliou

2011, 344). The author discussed the utility, in fact the necessity, of the knowledge of law, economics, politics, and political history for civil society.

The Enlightenment tradition in the Greek Revolution was not limited to the expressions of liberal political thought we have surveyed. The print culture of the revolution also documents the survival of another constituent of the Enlightenment heritage, radicalism, which had found outlets in sharp social criticism and anticlericalism. This current of radical social thought harkens back to *Hellenic Nomarchy* and the anonymous critics of religion and the church that represented the most radical expressions of the Greek Enlightenment (Kitromilides 2013, 250–259). Its epigones in the revolutionary decade included the author of the pamphlet *The Seven Wounds of Greece,* published in 1827. It was probably the work of Spyridon Valetas, who had also translated Rousseau's *Discourse on Inequality* in 1818. In the new work he attacked mercilessly all those social groups whose self-seeking attitudes and behavior undermined the struggle of freedom. His language and the sociology of captivity he called his compatriots to leave behind clearly echo the ideas of the anonymous patriot of 1806.

The prerevolutionary anticlericalism and criticism of leading members of the hierarchy for corruption lingered on in the years of the revolution and can be documented by reference to two pamphlets, one a satire censuring Makarios, metropolitan of Thessaloniki, in 1828 and the other, the following year, a "defamatory epistle" against Ierotheos of Smyrna. These are just reminders of the last glimmers of the radical Enlightenment during the revolutionary decade.

The strength of the liberal democratic tradition in the politics of the Greek Revolution was expressed in the years 1828–1831 in the opposition that emerged to the policies of Governor Ioannis Capodistrias, whom they charged with authoritarianism. The ageing Korais from Paris played a leading role in the opposition by issuing a series of pamphlets that became known as his "Anticapodistrian dialogues," but other liberals, including Polyzoidis, Spyridon Trikoupis, Emmanuel Antoniadis, and Panagiotis Soutsos led the anti-Capodistrian campaign on constitutional principles. Although their criticism was at some points excessive and could be judged unfair in view of the odds and difficulties the governor had to face in building political order and laying the foundations of the new state, still the liberal opposition voiced important arguments over the fundamental principles that ought to guide statecraft and the future of Greece. Their arguments were deeply shaped by their faith in the Enlightenment's foremost political ideals, freedom and civil liberties (Loukos 1988).

The presence of the Enlightenment in the politics and culture of the Greek Revolution proved decisive in shaping the character of the political community that acceded to sovereign statehood after the ten-year liberation struggle.

The impact of the Enlightenment could be traced in many areas of collective life as an integral component of the transition to modernity. The Greek language registered this transition and the Enlightenment's impact characteristically. It is extremely interesting and revealing to observe in the literature of the Greek Enlightenment the sustained effort to produce a vocabulary suitable to express modern ideas and concepts in Greek. The intellectuals of the Enlightenment produced many neologisms, several of which were not eventually adopted in standard modern Greek, but the intellectual effort to forge the language of modernity in Greek is deeply impressive and moving. All the major figures in the Enlightenment movement we have encountered in this survey have coined new terms in order to express important new ideas: Voulgaris, Moisiodax, Rhigas, and foremost among them Korais have such a terminology to their credit (Kalokerinos 2015).

In the two decades immediately preceding and during the subsequent revolutionary decade of the 1820s, the language of modernity became the language of freedom. One important source of new vocabulary and terminology became the process of state building itself with the various documents produced by the national assemblies and other civil authorities in revolutionary Greece in their effort to lay the foundations of the new state. The needs of statecraft but also the needs of a free society in-the-making enriched the language in multiple ways. The new political science we noted above but also the new economic science, which produced among other things a Greek translation of Jean-Baptiste Say's treatise on a political economy in 1828 (Iliou and Polemi 2011, 345–346) represented such instances of the enrichment of Greek with the vocabulary of the culture of modernity. The production of a Greek terminology to serve the needs of modern politics and administration was greatly intensified under Ioannis Capodistrias with the edicts, instructions, and other government documents issued by his administration.

Language of course is the primary medium in the definition of a national community. The new Greek of the Enlightenment became the medium that forged the bonds of the national community that emerged from the liberation struggle. Ideas of a distinctive modern Greek nationhood, defined on the basis of the cultural and linguistic affinity of speakers of modern Greek with the ancient Hellenes, had been on the minds of intellectuals for centuries. It was the Enlightenment, nevertheless, through the historicization of that sense of cultural affinity that gave broader currency to the conception of identity and cultivated a distinct modern Greek historical conscience based on a connection with classical Hellenism (Kitromilides 2013, 63–88). Thus, the modern Greeks came to understand themselves as a modern nation with a distinct ancient lineage, rather than as members of a broad community of Orthodox Christians.

From the Orthodox *ecumene* the Enlightenment led to a modern, secular national community. That collective self-conception was generalized and actually was lived as a real-life experience through the liberation struggle. The idea of freedom and the sense of Hellenic identity provided meaning to the struggle and to the sacrifices it required, and turned the many individuals and groups that took part in it, with their multiple ethnic and linguistic backgrounds, into modern Greeks, members of the Neo-Hellenic nation, which, thanks to their struggle and devotion, acceded to freedom and joined the world of sovereign nations. It was primarily by providing existential meaning to the struggle that the Enlightenment proved the midwife of the birth of the modern political nation of modern Greeks.

Paschalis M. Kitromilides

References

Argyropoulos, Roxane D. 2014. *Diversité des Lumières dans la pensée grecque. Idées et innovations (XVIIIe-XIXe siècles).* Paris.

Bouchard, Jacques. 1974. "Les relations épistolaires de Nicolas Mavrocordatos avec Jean Le Clerc et William Wake." *O Eranistis* 11:67–79.

Dimaras, C. Th. 1969. *La Grèce au temps des Lumières.* Geneva.

Iliou, Philippos. 1978. "Στην τροχιά των Ιδεολόγων" [In the orbit of the Ideologues]. *Chiaka Chronika* 10:36–38.

Iliou, Philippos, and Popi Polemi, eds. 2011. *Ελληνική Βιβλιογραφία του 19ου αιώνα* [Greek bibliography of the nineteenth century]. Vol. 2, *1819–1832.* Athens.

Kalokerinos, Alexis. 2015. "Revisiting the Names: Korais' Political Cratylism." *Revue des Études Sud-Est Européennes* 53:327–371.

Katartzis, Dimitrios. 1970. *Τα ευρισκόμενα* [Surviving works]. Edited by Constantinos Th. Dimaras. Athens.

Kedourie, Elie, ed. 1970. *Nationalism in Asia and Africa.* New York.

Kitromilides, Paschalis M. 1992. *The Enlightenment as Social Criticism: Iosipos Moisiodax and Greek Culture in the Eighteenth Century.* Princeton, NJ.

Kitromilides, Paschalis M. 1994. "John Locke and the Greek Intellectual Tradition: An Episode in Locke's Reception in South-East Europe." *Locke's Philosophy: Content and Context,* edited by Graham Alan John Rogers, 217–235. Oxford.

Kitromilides, Paschalis M. 2006. "From Republican to National Sentiment. A Reading of Hellenic Nomarchy." *European Journal of Political Theory* 5:50–60.

Kitromilides, Paschalis M. 2007. *An Orthodox Commonwealth: Symbolic Legacies and Cultural Encounters in Southeastern Europe.* Variorum Series. Aldershot.

Kitromilides, Paschalis M., ed. 2010a. *Adamantios Korais and the European Enlightenment.* Oxford.

Kitromilides, Paschalis M. 2010b. "The Enlightenment and the Greek Cultural Tradition." *History of European Ideas* 36:3–46.

Kitromilides, Paschalis M. 2013. *Enlightenment and Revolution: The Making of Modern Greece.* Cambridge, MA.

Korais, Adamantios. 2018. *Σημειώσεις εις το Προσωρινόν Πολίτευμα της Ελλάδος* [Notes on the Provisional Constitution of Greece]. Edited by Paschalis M. Kitromilides. Athens.

Loukos, Christos. 1988. *Η αντιπολίτευση κατά του Κυβερνήτη Ιω. Καποδίστρια, 1828–1831* [The opposition to Governor Ioannis Kapodistrias, 1828–1831]. Athens.

Mackridge, Peter. 2009. *Language and National Identity in Greece, 1766–1976.* Oxford.

Philippidis, Daniel, and Gregorios Constantas. 1988. *Γεωγραφία Νεωτερική* [Novel geography]. Edited by Aikaterini Koumarianou. Athens.

Polyzoidis, Anastasios. 2011. *Κείμενα για τη δημοκρατία 1824–1825* [Texts on democracy, 1824–1825]. Edited by Philimon Paionidis and Elpida Vogli. Athens.

Tabaki, Anna. 2003. "Du théâtre philosophique au drame national: Étude du lexique politique à travers l'ère des revolutions. Le cas grec." In *From Republican Polity to National Community: Reconsiderations of Enlightenment Political Thought*, edited by Paschalis M. Kitromilides, 62–85. Oxford.

Velestinlis, Rhigas. 2001. *Άπαντα τα σωζόμενα* [Complete surviving works]. Vol. 1. Edited by Panagiotis S. Pistas. Athens.

Velestinlis, Rhigas. 2002. *Άπαντα τα σωζόμενα* [Complete surviving works]. Vol. 5. Edited by Paschalis M. Kitromilides. Athens.

Literature, Learning, and Print Culture

The ten years that rolled by from the declaration of Greek independence until its final acceptance by the European powers and the Ottoman Porte are a short period for issues of literary activity. But time does not always have uniform density, and characteristic of revolutionary periods are successive breaches in its weft. So, the pivotal question is whether—and to what extent—the years of the War of Independence constitute a revolutionary period also in the domain of intellectual activities. Consequent queries are: First, if the differences are considered radical, in which fields did the changes occur? In everything? In some sectors? And how were they made, gradually or abruptly? By some individuals or by some collectivities? And second, were the changes affected by political events, or had they perhaps already been set in motion earlier and independently of political transformations?

The Years of Gestation

Let us start by gathering the many strands. Taking March 25, 1821, as an exemplary moment, let us seek out the net forces on the intellectual landscape. For the overwhelming majority of the population, rural society, the folk song, the fairy tale, together with traditional readings—that is, popular chapbooks—held sway. We should bear this in mind but, since all these are phenomena subject to the *longue durée*, we leave them outside the remit of the present essay. Here, we are interested mainly in the level of literary textual tradition, in which the changes over the last decades before the outbreak of the War of Independence were significant.

One strand of the fabric of Greek culture was formed by the Enlightenment. Although its influence was confined to close circles, we know that something had changed in Greek society. The young generation, those born around 1790, were facing a different world. For more and more people the principal cohesive ideological construct of "we" meant "descendants of the ancient Greeks" rather than "Orthodox Christians." Schools were proliferating at a rapid pace, new subjects were being taught—modern mathematics, Newtonian physics—while opportunities for individuals to enrich their knowledge within the eastern Mediterranean basin began to appear. "Modern" books were translated, literary journals circulated, societies promoting the arts (*philomouses etaireies*) were founded, while during the last decade before the revolution, plays were not simply read but performed on stage. It was preeminently the merchants (especially those engaged in long-distance trade) who sustained the new trends, but the innovations rippled out in expanding circles—including ecclesiastical ones. Here we should bear in mind, on the one hand, the specific gravity of the Greek communities in central Europe and, on the other, the princely courts in the Danubian provinces of Wallachia and Moldavia, together a dynamic presence connected with the inhabitants of Constantinople in residence there. So, the East was approaching Europe, and vice versa; we should not forget the French and the British occupations of the Ionian islands, as well as the presence of European merchants in major Ottoman cities.

I spoke of limited or close circles, and I believe this is true, if we measure them by the standards of central Europe. If, however, we measure the phenomenon in relation to the previous generation, then the circles appear to have been widened to a considerable degree. The increase in the number of publications, of schools, and of subscribers to new books points to a multiplication of human resources. But there was also a hardening of anti-Enlightenment tendencies, guided methodically by the patriarchate. We should not forget that despite the numerical superiority of advocates of the Enlightenment, which may have been overwhelming, the circles of the patriarchate had begun to win, one by one, the battles they were fighting.

The second strand is the effects on literature, not simply of the Enlightenment, but of a more general affluence in the main urban centers, as well as in towns in the mountains and on the coasts. In the years around 1810, schematically, Neohellenic poetry presented signs of important transmutations. With prime movers Athanasios Christopoulos and—of lesser ambit but certainly more resilient—Giannis Vilaras, poetic expression acquired a value in its own right that could not be identified in earlier poets; the importance passed from the what to the how, from the meaning to the manner of formulation. In 1814, Vilaras published Ρομέηκη γλόσα (Vernacular Greek language) in Corfu, and in the same year and from the same printing press Christopoulos published his Λυρικά (Lyric poems). We cannot know whether the coincidence was a

conscious act, but let us consider it symbolic. Phanariot poetry in its two paramount versions was united with Septinsular poetry—this is one aspect. Second
is the pronounced presence of patriotic or battle hymns (*thourioi*), not so much
of Rhigas Velestinlis's Ὡς πότε παλικάρια (Until when pallikars), whose form
was traditional—it was after all sung to a folk tune—but of later poets (Panagiotis Andronikis, Stephanos Kanelos, Constantinos Kokkinakis), who combined
revolutionary content with modernist linguistic and metrical forms and were
attuned to European rhythms and melodies, to which the Greek ear was totally unaccustomed. The ease with which these songs were disseminated—
some in fact even penetrated into the rural populations—bears witness to a
more general receptivity to the new. The public, presumably in order to embrace the political, revolutionary content, was eager to accept even something
different in form; but the form of *thourioi* was chosen by their creators.

Before we proceed, however, we should pause at an important point: The concept of the literary man did not exist before 1821. Of poetry, yes; even of a man of
literature too, though rather more vaguely, but the concept of the poet as creator,
with poetry as his central target, as far as I know did not yet exist. Just about
everyone wrote verses, and easily too. Nonetheless, the dominant value lay in
erudition, on the one hand, and in the ability to compose verses, on the other.
Characteristically, Athanasios Christopoulos attached little weight to his poetic
works in relation to his other intellectual activities. And when Vilaras wanted to
point out the primacy of innate talent in relation to learning, in his 1814 preface
to Ρομέηκη γλόσα, he preferred a musical exemplar—after all, he saw his own
little book more as a defense of simple language and simplified grammar than of
poetry. We should not forget, furthermore, how isolated he and his circle felt, as
most literati remained oriented toward analytical discourse and education. The
literary interests of the time were few and were frequently expressed by texts
composed in a stiff archaizing language, sometimes even in ancient Greek language and meter, such as the dedicatory epigrams of books and, for instance,
Anastasios Georgiadis's Ειδύλλιον ποιμενικόν (Pastoral idyll) of 1807.

Changes in the theater were more radical. In the opening two decades of the
nineteenth century, plays, original and in translation, appeared thick and fast,
acquiring modernist content, in which the social viewpoint of the Enlightenment was combined with the nascent national visions. The principal change,
however, lies in that they crossed the difficult threshold of presentation on stage,
not of course in Greece itself but in Bucharest and Odessa. Nonetheless, thanks
to related news items published in Ερμής ο Λόγιος (Literary Hermes) and other
periodicals, the sense of the revival of theater was broadcast everywhere.

On the contrary, steps taken in prose writing were few and faltering. Perhaps in the brief interval of 1817–1821 some slight flickering was apparent; sev-

eral translations were undertaken but the revolution seems to have delayed their publication. So, since a related tradition had not managed to be created, this sector of literature, which in Europe was entering full sail into its golden age, was practically nonexistent. Equally nonexistent was the discourse around literature, with the exception of a brief anonymous commentary in *Literary Hermes* of 1820. As I see it, the absence of literary criticism reveals clearly the negligible weight attached to literature in the construct of learning.

To summarize, broadly speaking this was the situation on the eve of the War of Independence. The beginnings of radical change could already be seen; in several individual consciences and in some collective bodies perhaps they had even taken root, precisely as they had at the political level. However, from one standpoint, only the plant gives value to the seed.

It is this plant—more correctly these plants—that we shall now try to look at. Literature separately from literateness, because I believe that one of the main changes the revolution brought about lies exactly in the extrication of literature from literateness, in literature coming into its own.

Poetry

1821–1822: *The First Impetus*

The first poetic act of the revolution was the circulation of a small pamphlet with *thourioi*: Άσματα και πονημάτια διαφόρων. Εν Κοσμοπόλει (Songs and brief essays of various [authors]: In Kosmopolis). It must have been printed in February or March 1821, either in Jassy or on a small portable printing press that followed the troops of Alexandros Ypsilantis. These *thourioi* were of course written before 1821, but had been reworked so that the lyrics were related to the revolution—more correctly to their intended use, as we know nothing about their circulation. However, this intention is not without significance; Ypsilantis's revolutionary staff deemed that its troops could be enthused by this exhortative poetry:

> Greek patriots
> Brave soldiers,
> Do or die.
> Pounce like lions.
> Leap into the fire,
> Victory or death.

Songs of this kind were quite widespread even before 1821, but with the revolution they were diffused more widely, far beyond the circles of initiates or literati.

They symbolized, albeit clumsily, the struggle—and poetry undertook to serve it from the first moment.

The second poetic act was the bilingual publication of Christopoulos's *Lyrika* with a prose translation in German by Anastasios Papas, son of a leading member of the Philiki Etaireia (Society of Friends): *Der neue griechische Anakreon. Ο Νέος Ελληνικός Ανακρέων* (The modern Greek Anakreon), an elegant small-format publication which was printed in Vienna, most probably at the end of April 1821 or a little later. So, immediately after the outbreak of the revolution, a fiery patriot of the Greek communities abroad felt the need to make known to the Europeans that his compatriots had not only a militant but also a poetic face. This was an act comparable in importance to the declarations of Ypsilantis or Mavromichalis. A few months later, a new translation of nine of Christopoulos's poems, by a German literatus, appeared in a Frankfurt newspaper (January and February 1822). Before the revolution, as far as I know, only a few scattered samples of Neohellenic poetry had been published in European periodicals.

In November of 1821, we have the third poetic act: *Ο Δήμος. Ποίημα κλέφτικον* (Dimos: A klephtic poem) was printed in Paris. Its author, Spyridon Trikoupis, was about thirty-three years old. The work is now forgotten but if we read it we discern two very important elements. The first lies in the form, in the meter. Trikoupis intentionally opts for the "folk" fifteen-syllable line: "I wrote for the people; therefore, I was obliged to handle its verse." In my view, the pathway to the people, following the Enlightenment line, declares a great deal, and more as soon as we correlate it with the second element, which lies in the content. The poem does not have national content; it is purely amorous, but swathed in a martial cloak so as to be in keeping with the national circumstance. Dimos is a klepht; a rival seizes his betrothed and Dimos, in his effort to save her, is killed fighting heroically. We meet neither Turk nor national struggles, but something new is coming with this poem; love ceases to be a game, it becomes serious, and it is linked with death, on the one hand, and with valor, on the other. This is a new way of looking at the world, one closer to European mentalities, and somewhat tinged with Romanticism. We shall see that this path of poetry was not without continuation.

These are not, of course, the only metric texts of the two years; oral compositions, rhymes and folk songs, which immortalized important events, abounded—but very few were published. They represent traditional creativity which was in no way different from the years before the Revolution. What is interesting is that now the *thourioi* existed alongside it, with increasing intensity; it goes without saying that these patriotic hymns were actually sung.

1822–1826: *The Zakynthos Circle*

One more important watershed. The Ionian islands had a textual tradition all their own, much closer to folk discourse yet at the same time far more sophisticated, capable of expressing itself in both Greek and Italian. Within this creative climate, fellowship of poets emerged in Zakynthos around 1820. They were Antonios Matesis, Dimitrios Pelekasis, Georgios Tertsetis, the somewhat older Dionysios Tagiapieras, among others, as well as Dionysios Solomos. Today we know of this group almost exclusively from its supreme representative, that is, we have a distorted view; the titanic personality of Solomos has effectively silenced for us the lesser voices. However, then he was no more than primus inter pares, admittedly the most splendid figure but by no means the only one. Shortly after the revolution broke out, some members of the company ventured along a new poetic path: the written resynthesis of oral tradition, foremost in which is the klephtiko song. A poem by Pelekasis, dated 1822, begins thus:

> Resounding o'er Arcadia's flower-covered crests
>   Of a handsome young man a victory song
> —"Slaves now we are not, to Turks we pay not homage;
>   Vales, forests and caves you shall no longer hear
>   the lamentations of slavery and the weeping of desolation.
>   We shall live free in our glorious land."
>   Such were the songs of the fair-haired youth . . .

So, the resynthesis aspired to a new ideological content; no longer the dirge-like klephtiko song, but a triumphal song of victorious import, with the form and the style of the folk (demotic) song. Perhaps this turn is related to Spyridon Trikoupis's brief sojourn on Zakynthos in the winter of 1822; apart from *Dimos*, Trikoupis had composed, probably even before 1821, songs in demotic style, which were loved and sung. Tertsetis followed the same path and cultivated it more persistently. One poem is dated by himself to 1823; here the technique has advanced further:

> Tell me again, my pretty maid,
> Your dream, if you love me;
> so that always in your life
> may you meet good fortune.

Both Tertsetis and Pelekasis continued to compose folksy poems of this kind. Indeed, Tertsetis tried out other meters too, closer to Italian prose writing, and throughout his life always wrote in vernacular Greek. He proposed a totally unprecedented vision for the future of poetry, which he imagined as emanating from oral tradition, as close to the people, different from literacy and education. No matter that his proposal was forgotten after 1830–1835; he believed in it and he had conceived the value of poetry in its own right, the idea of the solitary poet-guide.

Antonios Matesis was moving in the same milieu; he was writing in vernacular Greek (*dimotiki*), perhaps with less flexibility, and was defending it theoretically. Nonetheless, it is worth noting that none of these poets had their works printed until much later, when the advocates of purist Greek (*katharevousa*) had a stranglehold on poetry. Their strand was left dangling and was forgotten after the revolution; the new needs of society were seeking different prospects.

The Intervention of the Philhellenes

On April 7/19, 1824, Lord Byron breathed his last in Mesolonghi; it was the final act of a life filled with adventures, contradictions, and glory, to which the ultimatum of death gave incalculable brilliance. This was an exceptionally symbolic event that brought Greece to the center of European attention: the poet dies for the revolution.

The movement of Philhellenism spread in many ways. One of its aims was to present the language, history, and culture of the modern Greeks. For their struggle to be legitimized in European consciences, for the petition for a nation-state to acquire support, it was not enough for the Greeks to be heroic, their existence had to receive European recognition; that would also prove their affinity to the ancient ancestors.

After all, even Solomos sent copies of his poems abroad, while in 1824 Andreas Kalvos had added a Greek-French glossary to his *Lyra* and in 1826 his *Lyrika* circulated with French prose translations on the facing page, complemented contrapuntally by poems of Christopoulos, also with translations. One further French translation of Christopoulos was printed in 1831, and in the same year a plaquette was printed with three poems by him in Italian translations. However, it was not only the self-contained publications, it was also the diverse European anthologies, sometimes inserted into calendars, textbooks for learning Greek, and the like; these collective volumes also contained sporadic samples of the contemporary literary output.

In 1824, however, a totally different poetry collection was published, for the first time, for the European (and Greek, of course) public: no longer samples of the achievements of educated Neohellenes, but quite the opposite, the oral poetry of the common people. This is the collection of Greek folk songs that had been compiled, translated, and prefaced by the Frenchman Claude Fauriel. The surprise and sentiment that the discovery of a hitherto unknown poetic continent evoked were enormous. So, the modern Greeks had not only choice representatives, worthy to rub shoulders with their European counterparts in the salons or the universities, they had as a people a highly cultivated poetic sense—what better proof of their elevated cultural level, of their right to be classed among the civilized nations?

The European lettered and scholarly public enthusiastically received these "folk songs." The reviews in the press were ecstatic and straight away, in 1825, there followed two translations of the collection into German (one was republished in 1828), one into English (somewhat abbreviated and without the Greek texts, but with a translation of Solomos's *Ymnos*), a brief selection in Russian, while a French metrical reworking of Fauriel's prose translation circulated in two volumes in 1824–1825 (and the first was republished in 1825). Meanwhile, several songs were reprinted in anthologies and similar books; even Goethe's periodical *Kunst und Alterthum* featured five poems, in fact in his own translation (1827).

Thus, in one way or another, an educated European—let us say at some moment in the spring of 1826, when it became known that "Mesolonghi no longer exists" and the philhellenic outpouring had reached its peak—was now able to cross paths with Neohellenic poetry, both literate and folk. In fact, he would have formed a much fuller picture than a Greek could have formed, either in the territories in revolt or those still Ottoman-held, because, beside all the rest, he also had some historical insights—but we shall speak of these below, when we examine the diffusion of learning.

Greek Patterns: Central Europe

Neohellenic poetry was produced mainly outside the lands in revolt—in the Ionian islands and in central Europe. This is not a singularity or a contradiction; a large part of the Neohellenic intelligentsia was living in Europe, and from the second half of the eighteenth century the Greek communities abroad had been playing a leading role in cultivating letters and fostering Enlightenment ideas, as well as in shaping national consciousness. Experiencing, now as refugees, the revolutionary climate and the new conditions, some Phanariot literati abandoned their penchant for levity and frivolity, hallmarks of their prerevolutionary poetry, and tried to attune themselves to the lofty demands of the time. Perhaps the most characteristic case is that of Iakovakis Rizos-Neroulos. A

mature man, an experienced scholar and politician, a famed poet and playwright, at the age of forty-five he changed course; henceforth, he dedicated his
abilities to the struggle and sought poetic inspiration in the pathways of the
patriotic hymns. The Ωδή εις τους Έλληνας (Ode to the Greeks) was written in
1823, and consisted of sixty-five quatrains, in which he attempted a leap in
style and manner:

> Savage tiger, powerful beast,
> of Turks sultan, by eunuchs raised,
> He rabidly sucks Greek blood,
> Blood of the old, of men, of infants.

> Instead of seizing the sword
> of his forefathers the Osmans,
> and of the Mehmeds and the Suleimans,
> he has not the mettle to hold it.

It is an indicative example of his effort to give his discourse greatness, but
also a dismal failure. But the failure reveals better the scale of the endeavor, the
distance between Neroulos's will and his abilities: he wanted, he tried to out-
strip himself—this denotes a disposition, at least, for renewal.

The next example is more low-key. In 1825, Dimitrios Mourouzis, scion of a
great Phanariot family, printed in Paris a booklet, Ποιητικαί μελέται (Poetic
studies). The title perhaps echoes the famous collection of Lamartine; the content refers to the struggle and the Muse Calliope's return home to the land of
her birth. Mourouzis tried to reshape the Phanariot tradition by enriching it
with a heavy mythological charge, which was aimed more at the Philhellenes,
and with some elements of lyricism. In the few successful verses, he echoes
Kalvos's images here and there, as well as explicitly and purposely some lines
from Solomos's Ymnos:

> In the dance sweetly circle
> the golden-haired maidens;
> On their necks are undulating
> two gilded braids.

> There, standing and watching,
> kindly, are their fathers,
> and their sons are singing
> manly songs.

[...]
The eagle of Souli
Holds a wreath and runs;
and Byron has the lyre,
he sings of you even dead.

So, the achievements of Solomos and Kalvos did not pass unnoticed by their fellow poets. As soon as their work was circulated, they began to have influence, although of course only among literary men living in Europe. Even the Europeans did not hesitate to honor the poetry of Mourouzis; indeed, one French critic considered him on a par with Kalvos—surely carried away by his philhellenic sentiments. Just as strongly affected was Panagiotis Kodrikas, who wrote a metrical Δοκίμιον περί κοινής ποιήσεως (Essay on common poetry) and dedicated it to Mourouzis: "Hail splendid Dimitrios! scion of illustrious forefathers! / You remind me of the pleasures of years past; / when I too in my youth sang odes / and plucked the one-stringed lyre with songs." The Athenian Phanariot was almost sixty-five years old, but perhaps he also wanted to remind his readers that the milieu of Constantinople, which he so honored, had some poetic credentials. We know that Constantinos Kyriakos Aristias, the prominent actor and poet who was in Corfu in 1825, took pains to acquire a manuscript copy of this work.

Remaining in the magnetic field of European Philhellenism, we come across other poetic voices of Greek communities in Europe, such as Michail Schinas, Christodoulos Nikolaidis, Angeliki Palli, Constantinos Kyriakos Aristias, Nikolaos S. Piccolos. They did not write great poetry, but they did try to infuse with lyricism the expression of their sentiments. What is of interest here is how the poetic temperature was rising overall; Angeliki Palli in fact is one more example of a turn in language, from Italian to Greek—but we notice here that Hellenism's force of attraction was weakened once the shockwave of the struggle had abated.

Greek Patterns: Insurgent Greece

It was difficult for poetry to circulate inside insurgent Greece, as minds were turned toward literacy, education, and political institutions. The tremendous change here lay in setting up printing presses and, of course, newspapers. In 1824, a long poem in rhyme was published in Mesolonghi, recounting military events in the region and accompanied by two *thourioi*. In 1825, Solomos's *Ymnos* was printed and publication was scheduled, together with an Italian prose translation. The same year saw published, in Athens, a small selection of Christopoulos's poems, at the end of which we find a new translation of the Spartan elegiac poet Tyrtaeus, now in vernacular Greek. From 1827, activity became somewhat more intensive, the printing presses of Nafplio and Ydra had been started up—in other words, it was a movement similar to that of Europe but on a smaller scale. Older literati reappeared, such as Dimitrios Gouzelis, Constantinos Kokkinakis, and Georgios Serouios, and younger ones came to the fore, such as Dimitrios Ainian. This picture is reflected in the newspapers too; some *thourioi,* some odes—and these publications proliferated as the years passed, particularly when systematic opposition to Capodistrias began, while quite a few poets kept back, hesitated or did not find the opportunity to have their works printed, such as Georgios Lassanis. It appeared that the energy of the first, impetuous period began to dissipate.

Nevertheless, a second channel existed, more folklike, more direct, closer to the political realities: oral compositions, which very often circulated in manuscript copies that had wide dissemination. More folksy *thourioi,* narrative rhymes, but also satires, sometimes acerbic in the extreme. Very little has survived from this output—after all, these works had been composed for the purpose solely of the present—either in manuscripts or in later publications. Nonetheless, the few samples are sufficient for us to imagine the climate: enthusiasm, connection to ancient heroes, naïvety, flippancy, and improvisations. The Epirot Zois Panou, kinsman of the Tzavellas family, of advanced years at the time of the War of Independence, published twenty years later some compositions of 1822:

> O Sons of Greeks, O Heroes Greek
> You should imitate also Themistocles,
> And all the admirals and this Pericles.

The most renowned folk bard was Panagiotis Kallas from Dimitsana, known as Tsopanakos, a typical example of a traditional singer. Afflicted by rickets and therefore unfit for manual work, he earned his daily bread by singing, acquiring the ability to improvise and frequently drawing on what he read or heard:

> Greeks now let's go,
> Let's take up our arms;
> the fatherland calls us
> and Rhigas commands us

or, again:

> The Greeks are waging war
> and these Super-Greeks too.
> War in Valtetsi
> where countless rifle shots were fired.

A third typical example is the Athenian Spyros Bougiouklis, also a singer, and a fiddler. Before the revolution he wrote love ditties, but then he became serious and wrote hymns for the freedom fighters. We may add, so as to complete the sampler, Georgios Kleanthis from Samos. He was more literary and was quick to have some of his compositions printed in 1832, but was unable to surpass the conventional strictures of rhetorical discourse:

> Nike running with wreaths
> the plains of Attica,
> avoiding cowardly Muslims,
> seeking tyrant-hating men
> and friends of heroic glory.

Even fewer specimens of the handwritten political satires have survived. Nevertheless, this was a thriving activity that reveals the vehement passions between groups or persons, as well as the strong social shocks of the period of the struggle, its internal dynamic. From 1826 onward, chief of the genre, indeed for many decades, was Alexandros Soutsos, the first to have his satires printed and signed with his name, in an endeavor to give them a wider audience.

Fresh Phanariot Blood and One-Dimensional Romanticism

From 1825, when Alexandros Soutsos and his brother Panagiotis arrived in insurgent Greece, they represented the generation of young literary figures who had been adolescents in 1821. They were talented, they had studied in the best prerevolutionary schools and in Paris, but at the same time they were aristocrats. They had the courage and opportunity to express themselves openly and were imbued with democratic ideas. They also had public endorsement, since their eldest brother, Dimitrios, a centurion of the Sacred Battalion, had been killed at Dragatsani.

Their first steps in literature do not set them apart from prerevolutionary learning. While he was living in Italy between 1823 and 1825, Alexandros had written five tragedies, two on ancient subjects and three with themes taken from glorious incidents of the struggle—that is, in the footsteps of Ioannis Zambelios—while his satires brought nothing new other than their boldness. Panagiotis wrote a "Song on the Fall of Mesolonghi," which was published in the *Geniki Ephimeris tis Ellados* (General newspaper of Greece) in 1826, and in 1827 he was emboldened to publish in Ydra a booklet with six hymns and odes, all in the clime and in the usual Greek style.

In the summer of 1827, the two brothers returned to Paris, from where they served the Greek cause. In 1828, Panagiotis published poems in French, and enriched the volume with the Greek poems of his previous publication, accompanied by a prose translation in French. In 1829, Alexandros published a history of the War of Independence, in French. Concurrently, they were serving an apprenticeship in contemporary Parisian romantic poetry, so that when they returned to Greece two years later, envisioning different worlds, they brought there the last word of the literary avant garde, unbridled Romanticism. In 1830, they were joined by another Phanariot, their close relative who had just come back from his studies in Munich, the highly talented Alexandros Rizos Rangavis.

The *Οδοιπόρος* (Wayfarer) by Panagiotis Soutsos and *Δήμος και Ελένη* (Dimos and Eleni) by Rangavis were printed almost simultaneously in Nafplio, in January 1831. Love, death, valor were their canvas, but the weaving was different. Unlikely situations, excessive passions, dark horizons, ghosts, suicides, but also poetry, lyricism, adroitness in handling language, and here and there also grace: a mixture of virtues and faults, as in all romantic poetry.

Prose

Prose fiction writing before and after 1821 was not original, only translated. But this output too was hardly added to during the years of the struggle, excepting a couple of works translated before the revolution, which were printed belatedly, and a few more works that were reprinted in a second edition.

In the spring of 1821, the Greek version of Salomon Gessner's *Ο Δάφνις* (Daphnis) was printed in Vienna, a short "pastoral romance" translated by Petros N. Darvaris, the continuation of a series initiated by the same translator in 1819. It had obviously been completed, perhaps before the uprising in Moldavia-Wallachia (we ascertain this from the date of the proem, March 3, 1821). Therefore, the first appearance in prose was the next contribution of Petros Darvaris, likewise printed in Vienna in 1822: two short stories by Jean-François Marmontel, *La Bergère des Alpes* and *Lausus et Lydie*, entitled *Η Βοσκοπούλα των Άλπεων. Ηθικόν διήγημα εκ των του κλεινού Μαρμοντέλη, ώ προσετέθη και έτερον εκ του αυτού συγγραφέως, καλούμενον Λαύσος και Λυδία* (The shepherdess of the Alps: A moral short story of those by the illustrious Marmontel, added also another by the same author, called *Lausos and Lydia*). Like Gessner, Marmontel was one of the favorite authors of the Greek Enlightenment; the moral objective of their short stories, their idyllic and ancient Greek themes, their moderate but steadily enlightening contemplation are sufficient to explain this preference.

Next in line is Nikolaos S. Piccolos's translation of *Τα κατά Παύλον και Βιργινίαν* (original title: *Paul et Virginie*; Paris 1824); three brief short stories by

Bernardin de Saint-Pierre followed (1825). This was a significant contribution (running through several editions in the years after the revolution), a landmark novel in European literature, with strong Enlightenment characteristics: faith in the essential honesty of men, faith in the natural life, faith in divine providence, faith in religious tolerance. The translation is well worked and fluent; it is interesting too that the desire to project to Europeans the progress of Neohellenic education and to enrich the reading horizon of the modern Greeks is consciously and vividly apparent. Nevertheless, this work too dates from an earlier period; the translation was ready in January 1821 but the outbreak of the revolution delayed its publication.

In 1824, the second edition of Antonios Koronios's translation of Jean-Pierre Claris de Florian's *Galatée* was published; it had first appeared in 1796. The same year saw the circulation in Greek of John Bunyan's *Pilgrim's Progress,* under the title *Η πρόοδος του χριστιανού αποδημητού εκ του παρόντος κόσμου μέχρι του μέλλοντος,* translated by the energetic English missionary S. S. Wilson. Normally, we would speak about the presence of a classic work of seventeenth-century English religious literature, rendered in a simple language, not lacking in freshness and charm, despite some foreign turns of phrase, which could fertilize the Greek prose-writing tradition. However, this is not the case; the work was translated for other aims and if it functioned at all, it did so differently, in the direction of theological meditation.

In December of the following year, 1825, the announcement of a new translation of Marmontel appeared in the *Ellinika Chronika* (Greek chronicles) of Mesolonghi, but the book did not circulate, while in 1826 *Ο θάνατος του Άβελ* (original title: *Der Tod Abels*) was republished. This was another work by Gessner, probably a republication of the 1795 translation. In 1827, the second important prose work of the period, Christoph Martin Wieland's *Των Αβδηριτών η ιστορία* (original title: *Die Geschichte der Abderiten*), translated by Constantinos M. Koumas, was printed in two small volumes. This is a text of the purest Enlightenment, with a satirical and didactic disposition, written in 1773; Wieland explains that even if the ancient Thracian city of Abdera no longer existed, Abderism, in other words the stupidity and political ill-judgment that destroys societies, egotism, and other human flaws, continued to reign. Koumas considered that this was a suitable partner to the serious *Die Geschichte des Agathon* by the same author, which he published in 1814. We know that he had already translated the work on Abdrites by 1815; so, here too we have a case of delayed publication.

We have come, it appears, full circle. In 1830 and 1831 three versions of *Τηλέμαχος* (*Telemachus*) were printed—one of the novels most translated into Greek—but none need, I think, occupy us here as they do not constitute a literary contribution; Wilson's translation of *Pilgrim's Progress* was reprinted too.

What is interesting is that the new trend that was now getting ready to invade the Neohellenic intellectual domain, namely the opening up of literary men also to prose writing, was based initially on very popular models. We may mention the translation by the young Antonios Kalamogdartis of *Τα κατ' Αρσάκην και Ισμηνίαν* (original title: *Arsace et Isménie*), a tender tale by Montesquieu, which was printed in Nafplio in 1831, omitting the author's name. A work written about a hundred years earlier, which still kept its freshness as a child of the Enlightenment, as well as of early Orientalism. However, I suspect that its translator read it wearing the spectacles of romanticism.

The world of the revolution had no desire to trust or to rely on prose. It needed elation, exaltation, rhetoric, poetry. Either because the cultivation of prose writing had not been organized and had not created a tradition or because society itself did not have within it the appropriate dynamic, or presumably for both reasons, the literati, the intellectuals, had not managed to find the path that would make prose writing become literature, with elation, exaltation, poetry.

Learning

If we rely on only quantitative criteria, there was a falloff in the production of books of literary content: printed editions, original or translated, decreased considerably. Nonetheless, from another viewpoint, the role of literate individuals was upgraded significantly. First, with the outbreak of the struggle, all kinds of educated people migrated to the free territories, where they were active at the political or administrative level and were involved in the conflicts that shook society. European printing presses were transported to and operated in the Peloponnese, Rumeli, and the islands, producing newspapers, government pamphlets, and a few books. Indeed, before attempting an overall assessment, we should bear in mind that before the revolution the area of Greece where the insurgency began had been extremely underdeveloped in relation to other regions. It had the fewest schools, the fewest subscribers to books, the fewest libraries—and those that existed were exclusively monastic and not, as elsewhere, school or public libraries.

From the perspective of trends and orientation, scholarly output continued the course that had been set in motion in the two or three preceding decades. This does not mean that we do not observe some important steps or some shifts, which will be pointed out; it means that the aims do not seem to have changed. Democratic governance, individual rights, the organization of a civil state remained the fixed poles to which literate persons looked, whether in warring

Greece or in the philhellenic circles of Europe. Now, of course, everything was filtered through the prism of the nation-state; the constitutions made provision, for instance, that the right of Greek citizenship was exclusive to Christians, and only Adamantios Korais considered it a blunder to deprive Muslims of this right. Even so, the reference to "Hellenism" as a value in itself—which was to swell in the ensuing decades—had not yet been imposed as a dominant trend.

Printing in the Nation-State

In those crucial years each printed document constituted, throughout Europe, a diffusion of the national "credo," a demonstration, not in the streets by crowds, but in the notional "public" space. But how public was that space in Greece? In practice, printed matter spread very little to the wide public, but in the consciousness of its authors was the feeling that they were addressing the Greeks as a whole—and indirectly Europe as well: "Look, we too are like you." Of course, printing in Greece had little leeway for development, mainly because Greek speakers were few in absolute numbers. Any development of printing was due to the voluntarism of the intelligentsia, not to the "capitalism" of businessmen (both before 1821 and during the revolution). But there is still something else that we should pay attention to. Naturally, the written Greek language and its dissemination through printing reinforced national sentiment, but its singularity in relation to what was happening in other lands lies in a special Greek "privilege": the existence of ancient texts that were revered models for the entire European world.

Books and Buyers

There was an appreciable drop in the production of Greek books immediately after 1821. As time passed, the output picked up, but only in the decade after the revolution were the curves balanced again. It goes without saying that both before and during the revolution the large numbers corresponded to ecclesiastical texts and schoolbooks, but the number of titles that might interest the literate public was reduced, particularly in the first five years of the revolution. Taking as a base line the number of books of scholarly interest that were published with the aid of subscribers: for the decade 1811–1821 there were fifty-five titles a year, with an average of 264 subscribers and 455 subscriptions per book. The corresponding figures for the decade of the War of Independence are forty-two titles (with 186 subscribers and 350 subscriptions on average). But there are two significant and important differences: the first is that the ratio between the first and second five-year periods of the revolution is one to five for titles and even bigger, one to ten, for subscriptions, and the second is that during this second five years (1826–1831) the insurgent regions were numerically prominent, whereas before 1821 they made no contribution. So, in the years under examination, Greek literateness moves from the communities abroad, the Danubian Principalities and the great cities of the Ottoman Empire to the places that were to make up the free Greek state.

Political Thought: The Contributions of Korais and the Younger Generation

Understandably, political thought now acquired particular interest for the Greeks. Korais continued to lead the field, always with his eye on the ancient literary corpus—that is, toward national consciousness—but now his interest turned to more political texts. In 1821 he published Aristotle's *Politics*, the following year *Nicomachean Ethics*, as well as Onesander's *Strategikon* (together with Tyrtaeus's "elegy," i.e., *thourios*); in 1824 Plutarch's *Politics*; in 1825 Xenophon's *Memoirs*, together with Plato's *Gorgias*; in 1826 Lycurgus's *Against Leocrates* and the *Discourses of Epictetus* as recorded by Arrian. As was his standard practice, Korais accompanied these works with a rich preface of political content, written as lightly as possible so that it was understandable to a wide readership. Concurrently, in 1823 he republished his translation of Beccaria's *Dei Delitti e Delle Penne* (Περί αδικημάτων και ποινών = *On Crimes and Punishments*), while we should not forget the letters full of exhortations that he sent either to Greeks—politicians, military men, school inspectors, all manner of individuals—or to eminent foreign personalities in order to promote Philhellenism and help the good outcome of the struggle. Last were his climactic militant manifestations, his remarks about the 1822 Constitution—the monument of an unqualified democratic consciousness—his fiery anti-Capodistrian dialogues, and, of course, the Συνέκδημος ιερατικός (Clerical traveling companion), in which (an old technique of his) the sacred texts of the Apostle Paul were used to castigate the behavior of the priesthood. Korais was indisputably the leader, accepted by all, even if the quality of his thought was so much above the usual standards that he did not manage to fertilize Greek society as much as he would have wished (see further Paschalis M. Kitromilides, "Enlightenment," in this volume).

How much, however, did the common civic concept of learning change? In the absence of reliable evidence, I shall try to elicit clues from the texts, albeit few, that were published in Greece. In both the original texts and the translated ones, I detect a breath of exhilaration and an almost absolute identification with progressive Europe. I begin with the overt interest in the concept of justice (I recall the translation of Beccaria from 1823). In 1825, a young "patriot"—as he signs himself in his preface "to the Greeks"—Spyridon Skoufos, translated *Αποσπάσματα εκ των του κυρίου Βαττέλου Περί του δικαίου των Εθνών* (Excerpts from Mr. Vattel's *The Law of Nations*). This is Emer de Vattel's celebrated work (1758) on relations which, according to natural law, should hold between nations at war: they should be merciful with the enemies, not kill prisoners of war, respect the rights of civilians, and observe humanitarian standards, as far as possible. The translator, newly arrived in Greece, obviously did not have in mind the Ottoman foe, but his compatriots, who with their cruel behavior had so often defamed the struggle. "Now, however, we are Europeans and we have to hold fast to what is legitimate according to natural law". The following year, 1826, an exiled Italian resident on Ydra, Alerino Palma, translated from the French Georg Friedrich von Martens's *Συλλογή των αρχών του και του εκ συνθήκης της Ευρώπης Δικαιώματος των Εθνών περί των θαλασσίων λειών και της ουδετερότητος* (Précis du Droit des Gens moderne de l'Europe, fondé sur les traités et l'usage), which was written in the same spirit and must have had in mind also the problem of piracy, Greek piracy too.

Similar too were the aims of the more explicitly political texts that were translated and printed within Greece. In 1824, we have the translation by Stephanos Kanellos of *Βιβλιαράκι κατ' ερωταπόκρισιν περί λογής λογιών πραγμάτων αναγκαίων μάλιστα εις την πατρίδα των Γερμανών* (Booklet of questions and answers on all manner of literary matters necessary indeed in the fatherland of the Germans) (Ydra 1824; reprints 1825 and 1830 in Nafplio); this was an intensely democratic political catechism. In 1826, *Τα μυστικοσυμβούλια και οι λαοί από τα 1815 έως σήμερον* (*Les cabinets et les peuples, depuis 1815 jusquà la fin de 1822*), by Louis Pierre Édouard Bignon (Paris 1822), circulated in Nafplio, translated by Nikolaos Spiliadis: a very important work—also a very long work, indicative of robust publishing activity. In 1828 we have some excerpts from one more cornerstone of the French Enlightenment, Volney's *Φυσικός νόμος ή Φυσικαί αρχαί της Ηθικής* (Natural law or the natural principles of ethics), translated by Constantinos Pentedekas (Aigina 1828), and, again in Aigina, *Πολιτικής οικονομίας Κατήχησις* (Catechism on political economy), by Jean-Baptiste Say, in translation by Georgios Chriseides, and the two-volume *H ηθική εφαρμοσθείσα εις την πολιτικήν* (Morality applied to politics) by Etienne de Jouy, also translated by Spiliadis (Nafplio). But I think we should pay special attention also to the presence of early Fichte, translated by his former pupil Drosos Mansolas, *Διδασκαλίαι περί του ορισμού του Ανθρώπου και του Σπουδαίου* (Teachings about the definition of man and the learned) (Ermoupolis 1829), in which it is noted that certain formulations are expressed with greater freedom in oral delivery than in censored printed matter. And the list is completed with the now complete translation of Vattel's work *Το Δίκαιον των Εθνών ή Αρχαί του Φυσικού Νόμου, . . . ελευθέρως μεταφρασθέν εις την απλοελληνική γλώσσαν από τον Γ. Α. Ράλλην* (*The Law of Nations or the Principles of Natural Law, . . .* freely translated into the simple Greek language by G. A. Rallis) (2 vols., Nafplio 1831).

This sampling concludes with three more books: in 1826 a young primate from Livadia, Emmanouil Spyridonos, a scholar who was not to follow a career as an author, undertook to draft on his own a *Σχέδιον Οργανισμού του ατάκτου Στρατιωτικού* (Plan of organization of the irregular military) and to submit it to the National Assembly of Troezen. It was a personal initiative which has left us with a sixty-page-long printed text (Athens 1826) full of information on the social upheavals brought by the sudden influx of money from the British loans. This is an excellent specimen of how creatively, clearly, and democratically inclined (explicitly toward the democratic model of the United States) were some minds of the generation that matured in the years of the struggle. The second specimen comes from a now mature literatus, member of the Philiki Etaireia, with good knowledge of prerevolution Constantinople, Spyridon Valetas: *Επτά πληγαί της Ελλάδος. Εις επτά διαλόγους δίχως Ρω* (Seven plagues of Greece: In seven dialogues without R) (perhaps Ydra 1827). This is an explicit and impassioned denunciation of the *kocabaşı*s, the princes of Wallachia and Moldavia, and of situations of flattery, obsession with titles, the English loan of gold sovereigns, ambition, and the lack of freedom of the press. The new Greece must rid itself of all these ills with which Ottoman rule had burdened it.

The third document leads us elsewhere. In 1828 a short handbook, *Μαγειρική εκ του ιταλικού* (Italian cooking), was translated and circulated in Ermoupolis, Syros. On what was a deserted shore with a safe harbor until 1822, refugees had settled and founded a new town. These were mainly merchants who had lived on Chios and in Smyrna, who had traveled to ports in the West, where they had got to know another version of Europe, that of emergent prosperity and the bourgeois habits of the great cities. They became active also in publishing, and *Mageiriki* was one of the first books produced. It seems strange, but it is a safe indication of the need for luxury, as a concept and as a usage: the subscribers included thirty-five women (something unprecedented until then).

Before we leave the inquiries around the common civic perception of literateness or learning, we should pause at something overarching and important: the concept of the "national we"—What is Greece? Who are the Greeks? In warring Greece and in analogous texts that circulated in Paris, Vienna, and elsewhere, as well as in official texts (proclamations of the national assemblies, national constitutions), Greece, the state, the "nation," was the space of battles. Nowhere was anything said about some "imagined" nation beyond the Morea,

Rumeli, the islands. If I am not mistaken, in order to encounter the notion that Greece includes all the Orthodox Christians of the Balkans and of Asia Minor we must wait until the end of the 1830s.

Here I hesitantly open a parenthesis. Most of these texts, whether originals or translations, even those issuing from the administrative machine, were written in a quite simple language, both in structure and vocabulary—only for scientific terminology do they resort to ancient or archaizing words. Even though almost all the authors moved politically in the sphere of Korais, their writings aimed at understanding not correcting the language, as happened before 1821—and as was to happen after 1835. And yet we are not in the space of a small prerevolution heretic group of pure *Luminaires* (Christopoulos, Vilaras, and their close company) (Oikonomou 1964), but before a "gentle Koraism" that would accept third declension nouns, temporal augmentations, and so on: a language that was not based on oral discourse, a language that was "written and literate," but not what we would call today "purist" (*katharevousa*). Should we include this too in the current of reversals caused by revolutionary action, those tendencies that were cancelled later when the express identification with the ancient ancestors became an indisputable need?

In order to complete the picture of the intelligentsia, let us take a look also at the view about the historical perception of events. During the struggle, Constantinos Michail Koumas completed in Trieste and Vienna the crowning piece of historiography of the Enlightenment: Ιστορίαι των ανθρωπίνων πράξεων (History of human deeds), in twelve volumes, printed in 1830–1832. Along with the events of world history it included the history of the Greek War of Independence, as well as his personal life—one of the first Greek autobiographies. From another viewpoint, Spyridon Trikoupis, also a groundbreaker, realized in time the need for a systematic recording of the events; we know that from very early on he was gathering material for the Ιστορία της Ελληνικής Επαναστάσεως (History of the Greek Revolution), which he was to complete three decades later. The Phanariots, on the contrary, were better prepared to respond to the demands of the public, and indeed that of Europe, as they had the facility to write quickly and easily. Thus, Iakovakis Rizos-Neroulos was to compile a massive *Histoire moderne de la Grèce depuis la chute de l'empire d'Orient* (Geneva 1828), while Alexandros Soutsos an equally detailed *Histoire de la Révolution grecque* (Paris 1829).

Literary Criticism and Historical Reviews

The newspapers, the most regular of which circulated twice a week, included in addition to war news, which systematically presented events from the optimistic side, the laws and decisions of the provisional administration, foreign news, and the like. They also gave readers the opportunity to read an appreciable number of political articles or news items that attested to the social progress being made and, rarely of course, some poems and, even more rarely, literary criticism. However, even the simple presence of critical discourse reveals in itself an aesthetic maturity. Poetic discourse always exists; criticism demonstrates a higher level of aesthetic culture. And in the newspapers of the revolution such texts appeared almost for the first time. One was the analysis of Solomos's *Ymnos* published in the issue of October 21, 1825, of the *Geniki Ephimeris tis Ellados* under the initials S. T., that is, Spyridon Trikoupis; a few days later, on November 4, 1825, Trikoupis's *Dimos* was published anonymously; and on November 11, 1825, a second critique of the *Ymnos,* written by Georgios Psyllas, was included in the columns of the *Ephimeris Athinon.* A fourth example is the fulsome presentation of *Nikekratos*, a very lukewarm play, but one that had been written by a girl, Evanthia Kairi, reviewed by Alexandros Soutsos in the *Philos tou Nomou* on February 7, 1827.

Psyllas's article also included a more holistic review of Neohellenic literature; he wrote about Erotokritos, Christopoulos, but also about the language question. It is significant for us to observe that the philhellenic public had an intense curiosity about reviews of this kind, which were cultivated mainly in the European environment, primarily of course by Greeks. First Carl Iken sought information; the answers came from Stephanos Kanellos in 1822, but were published in German in 1825 with the title *Leukothea.* Meanwhile, Fauriel proposed a very concise synthesis in the prolegomena of his collection of folk songs; it was too progressive to be appreciated by Greek learning. And in 1826 Iakovakis Rizos-Neroulos, now in Geneva, undertook a series of lessons on Neohellenic literateness and literature (it was published, as we have seen, in French in 1827, with a second edition in 1828). This was the most extensive attempt at synthesis, which enjoyed impressive publishing and translation success. These were not the only efforts; in order to comprehend their significance, we should remember what was noted above, where we examined the European interest in modern Greek literature.

A New World

We need one more final indicator: the limits of the dreams, of the objects of collective desire. From the beginning of the revolution the early military successes, their appeal to the European public, the sense of racial superiority, and confidence in the future created a climate of euphoria, in which all prospects appeared feasible and all European achievements could happen in Greece too.

In the school founded in Mesolonghi, French language was also taught and the monitorial method was applied in many schools; with the help of Philhellenes, scholarships were awarded for studies abroad. In Corfu a foundation of higher education was founded, the Ionian Academy, and the efforts to set up a university in Greece were also persistent. In April 1824, parliament voted to found an academy, the emblem and the oath of the academicians were defined, and contacts with corresponding European institutions were proposed. That same year in Athens it was decided to found a municipal library, a school of sciences, and a botanical garden, while Dimitrios Mostras, who had a very rich library in Pisa, wanted to donate part of it to Mesolonghi. All these intentions, whether simple and applicable or unrealistic, should be understood as a single set of possibilities, desires, and achievements, so that we can approach in some way, with imagination, but realistically, the world of the people who were living through those world-changing times.

Alexis Politis

Translated from the Greek by Alexandra Douma

References

Dimaras, Constantinos Th. 1982. *Ελληνικός Ρωμαντισμός* [Greek romanticism]. Athens.

Droulia, Loukia, and Gioula Koutsopanagou, eds. 2008. *Εγκυκλοπαίδεια του ελληνικού τύπου 1784–1974* [Encyclopedia of the Greek press, 1784–1974]. Athens.

Fauriel, Claude, ed. 1824–1825. *Chants populaires de la Grèce moderne*. Paris.

Fauriel, Claude, ed. 1825a. *Neugriechische Volkslieder. Gesammelt und herausgegeben von C. Fauriel. Übersetzt . . . von Wilhelm Müller . . . , Τραγούδια ρωμαϊκά*. Translated by Wilhelm Müller. Leipzig.

Fauriel, Claude, ed. 1825b. *The Songs of Greece, from the Romaic Text, Edited by M. C. Fauriel, with Additions*. Translated by Charles Brinsley Sheridan. London.

Iliou, Philippos. 2005. *Ιστορίες του ελληνικού βιβλίου* [Histories of the Greek book]. Edited by Anna Marthaiou, Stratis Bournazos, and Popi Polemi. Iraklio.

Iliou, Philippos, and Popi Polemi, eds., 2011. *Ελληνική Βιβλιογραφία του 19ου αιώνα* [Greek bibliography of the nineteenth century]. Vol. 2, *1819–1832*. Athens.

Kitromilides, Paschalis M., ed. 2010. *Adamantios Korais and the European Enlightenment*. Oxford.

Kitromilides, Paschalis M. 2013. *Enlightenment and Revolution: The Making of Modern Greece*. Cambridge, MA.

Mackridge, Peter. 2009. *Language and National Identity in Greece, 1766–1976*. Oxford.

Oikonomou Larisaios, Ioannis. 1964. *Επιστολαί διαφόρων* [Letters of various persons]. Athens.

Politis, Alexis. 1996. "1821–1831. Η νεοελληνική ποίηση σε επαναστατική περίοδο" [1821–1831: Modern Greek poetry in a revolutionary period]. *Ta Istorika* 13, nos. 24–25 (December): 129–138.

Politis, Alexis. 2004. "Η απουσία της πεζογραφίας στα χρόνια του Αγώνα (1821–1831)"
[The absence of prose-writing in the years of the struggle, 1821–1831]. In *Μνήμη Άλκη
Αγγέλου. Τα άφθονα σχήματα του παρελθόντος. Ζητήσεις της πολιτισμικής Ιστορίας και της
θεωρίας της Λογοτεχνίας* [In Memory of Alkis Angelou. The abundant schemes of the
past: Issues of cultural history and literary theory], 199–214. Thessaloniki.
Schott, D. A., and M. Mebold. 1824. *Taschenbuch für Freunde der Geschichte des
griechischen Volkes älterer und neuerer Zeit.* Heidelberg.

Digital sources

Anemi. The Digital Library of Modern Greek Studies. https://anemi.lib.uoc.gr/.
Iliou, Philippos, and Popi Polemi, eds. "Ελληνική βιβλιογραφία του 19ου αιώνα.
Ηλεκτρονικός κατάλογος" [Greek bibliography of the nineteenth century: Digital
catalog]. Benaki Museum. http://62.1.45.170/bibliology/search_simple.asp.
Politis, Alexis, Panagiotis Antonopoulos, Vasiliki Palaiochori, and Iro Vamvakidou, eds.
"Παρουσιολόγιο νεοελληνικής ποίησης 1801–1850" [Record of attendance of modern
Greek poetry 1801–1850]. http://anemi.lib.uoc.gr.
University of Crete. "Neohellenic Prosopography." http://argo.ekt.gr/opac2/Help
/Databases/ENU/09_Neoellhnikh_Proswpografia_EN_.html.

Popular Culture

The Greek War of Independence of 1821 found Greek traditional culture set in patterns known to us from post-Byzantine times: it was organized within the bounds of traditional communities with vital cultural memories from the Byzantine past and sometimes even from the remote early Christian period. These communities were involved with agriculture and stock raising, and the patterns of their collective life were closely related to the axes of space and time. With many variations and particularities, depending on the place where each community was organized and according to the effects of isolation of traditional communities imposed by geographical factors and the limited possibilities of communication, the manifestations of Greek traditional culture in the period were consistent with a general cultural model of partial ethnic differentiations of local cultural systems.

At the same time, there were many elements shared between the peoples of the Balkans, particularly those with the same religion, Orthodox Christianity, which is significant for understanding, given the role that religion has always played in forming both general components and partial expressions in traditional societies. This was a common Balkan substratum of mentalities, conceptions, beliefs, and values, from which the individual Balkan nationalisms subsequently emerged (Kitromilides 1996).

Needless to say, revolutionary events, military conflicts, and realignments of peoples and policies brought about a radical change in ways of life, particularly in regions that were liberated first and which eventually made up the free Greek state. These changes were not so great and decisive for those populations that, notwithstanding their revolutionary activity, continued to be part of the Ottoman Empire. Although the roots of the changes that shaped traditional daily life in Greek society after 1830 are to be found in the revolutionary period, during the actual course of the struggle phenomena of transformation and change are not attested, since the priorities lay, of course, in the military events and the consequent political developments.

So, if we want to look at the effect of the 1821 revolution on traditional folk culture of the time, inevitably we must look at the impact and the imprint of the events of the struggle on folk cultural manifestations. The issue of the wider cultural changes that the revolution triggered and which, being reliant on the economic and social differentiations that were set in motion, were to become visible at least two decades later in the folk culture of the Greek state cannot be examined here; it belongs among the phenomena of the *longue durée* and is therefore beyond the timeframe of this essay.

We should be aware too that popular culture can be described only in its general outline, since there is no full record and study of pertinent expressions, both of the intangible art of the spoken word and of folk handicraft. To a lesser extent in the first case and to a greater in the second, many of the creations of folk art either have been lost or remain unknown to us in private and still uncatalogued collections. And it is these objective difficulties that inevitably shape the examination and exposition of the subject in what follows.

One of the fields in which the revolutionary events were most responsively imprinted was the folk (demotic) song, one of the major cultural expressions of people of the period. Embedded in the heroic poetic tradition of the marchland songs (*akritika*), there developed during the years of Ottoman rule the klephtika songs, which praised persons and events associated with leading figures of the social brigandage that was flourishing in the period (Koliopoulos 2005). The klephts were role models of heroism for the people and enjoyed admiration and respect (Politis 1973 and 1974). They frequently alternated in the role of *armatoloi*, the independent armed militia who periodically assumed duties of guarding the safety of everyday life and communications in a region, in accordance with a strategic periodical and circumstantial coexistence with the Ottoman authority and its local representatives during the eighteenth century. And this was the case not only among the Greeks, but also among other peoples of the wider region, such as the Serbs and the Bulgarians.

In the related folk songs that have been written down there are references to persons and battles, exemplary heroic deaths, and forms of behavior that are underpinned by a strict code of traditional morality. Some elements of the songs, in terms of expression, versification, and ideology, can be traced back to survivals from the Byzantine and early post-Byzantine folk heroic tradition, as this is imprinted in the *akritika* folk songs (Romaios 1968).

The continuity between this kind of song and the heroic songs of the revolution is shown by similarities at the level of technique and ideology, and by the fact that in some of the better-known klephtika songs protagonists are similarly heroes of battles and martial episodes, this time in the War of Independence: for example, men of the Kolokotronis family; Dimitrios Panourgias (1759–1834), who fought in central Greece; Anagnostis Striftompolas, who was killed in the battle of Levidi (April 15, 1821); the Souliots; and Georgios Karaiskakis. Just as the klephts in the period of Ottoman rule were the core of the armed bands of the struggle, so their songs were the literary substratum upon which the folk songs about the freedom fighters and the great martial events of the 1821 War of Independence were molded. That is why there are no essential poetic, thematic, or other differences between them; they are conventionally divided according to the period to which they refer. From a poetic standpoint, they can be divided between songs with many verses or purely narrative songs, which as a rule are of inferior poetic value, and brief songs characterized by dramatic expression (Petropoulos 1958).

In 1914 Nikolaos Politis published a brief form of a song that refers to the onset of the revolution and mentions the Agia Lavra monastery, which he had cobbled together from verses of three different variations, in accordance with the editorial method he followed, which was notably criticized by later researchers (Apostolakis 1950). In the relevant literature there are published folk songs about important events in the war, such as the battle at Dervenakia in July 1822, the massacre of Kasos in May 1824, the siege of Mesolonghi and the landing of the troops of Ibrahim Pasha in late 1825, and the exodus of the city's defenders between April 10 and 11, 1826 (Academy of Athens 1962).

Songs relating to heroic figures and protagonists of the revolution have also been recorded and published, as for example about the battle at Maniaki and the sacrifice there of Archimandrite Grigorios Dikaios or Papaflessas, on May 20, 1825, in which the folk poet incorporates several dialogues that enhance the dramatic tone of his creation. Indeed, it is characteristic that Greek folk songs were created also about Turks who moved popular sentiment, such as Kiamil Bey, governor of Corinth, who had amassed great treasures before the struggle. With the outbreak of the war, he sought refuge in Tripolitsa, was taken captive on the city's fall, and in the end was sent in chains to Acrocorinth. There he was put to death by the garrison commander, Achilleas Theodoridis, during the raid by Dramali in 1822, mainly because he did not disclose where he had hidden his treasures. In this song his wife, whom Dramali married after Kiamil Bey's execution, appears weeping for him. The same applies to the captive Albanian women at Lalas in Ileia in 1821 (Politis 1914).

The folk songs about the Kolokotronis family and its freedom fighters make up a special category, which, as is well known, was a bone of contention between Sokratis Kougeas and Giannis Vlachogiannis, with the first advocating their folk authenticity and the second arguing that they had been composed by specific versifiers on commission from the Kolokotronis family (Imellos 1992–1993). Although hidden behind this dispute is the rivalry between the Peloponnese and central Greece as to the priority and the precedence of each region in the struggle of 1821, it also brought to light an indisputable fact: the folk song is initially the creation of a poet, which becomes the possession of the people and is the subject of many and successive variations in the course of its various performances and in accordance with the canons of oral folk poetry, before it reaches versions that were written down by folklorists from the late nineteenth century onward.

The popular resonance of the feats and the personality of Theodoros Kolokotronis contributed to the proliferation of original songs, with the addition of often artless compositions and improvised verses. Characteristic is the fact that in 1883 Nikolaos Politis gathered and published seventy-three related folk songs (Politis 1920). The principal songs of this category extol the pride of the Kolokotronis men, both in their family and in their contribution to the cause of freedom; they praise dramatic episodes in the family's history—captivities, betrayals, and laments—and make particular reference to the siege of Tripolitsa and the role in it of Theodoros Kolokotronis (Vlachogiannis 1922).

Imprinted too in folk songs of the Greek people are the martyrdom of the Patriarch of Constantinople Grigorios V, individual battles such as that at Levidi (1821), the siege and fall of Naoussa to the Turks and the consequent suicide of the women (1822), the death of Kyriakoulis Mavromichalis (1822), the sea battle of Gerontas and the repelling of the Turkish-Egyptian fleet from Samos (1824), the battle of Diros (1826), the deeds of families of klephts and freedom fighters, such as the Chontrogiannis family from Kalavryta, and so on.

Folk songs refer also to events and persons that were preserved in popular collective memory, such as the resistance of Athanasios Diakos at Spercheios (April 22, 1821); the struggles and death (August 8, 1823) of Markos Botsaris; the struggles and heroic deaths of Dimos Skaltsas (1824), Mitros Botaitis (1825), Grigoris Liakatas (1826), Giannis Gouras (1826), Dimos Tselios (1825), Agriogiannis (1826), Giannis Notaras (1827), Safakas (1827), Theodoros Grivas, Giorgis Kontovounisios, and Theodoros Ziakas. Indeed, it should be noted that some of these cases implicate freedom fighters of 1821 who survived the War of Independence but either devolved into robbery or came into political and armed opposition to Othon' s monarchical regime, and yet with their heroism they continued to inspire the people over time, which was expressed by the creation of these folk songs.

Nikolaos Politis dealt for many years with the case of the professional versifier of the events of the revolution Panagiotis Kallas or Tsopanakos (1789–1824), who was born at Dimitsana in the Peloponnese. Tsopanakos, an ugly man, had attached himself to Nikitas Stamatelopoulos or Nikitaras, whom he followed into battle, afterward enthusing his fellow freedom fighters with his verses, many of which praised the leading figures of the struggle and were the basis for the later creation of related folk songs. Politis classes Tsopanakos in the category of folk poets, citing various testimonies of his activity and that of other versifiers who lauded episodes of the 1821 War of Independence, some anonymous and others known, such as Gavogiannis from Thessaly and Stasinos Mikroulis from Mesolonghi, who composed a long poem about the siege of the city (Politis 1920).

From testimonies of freedom fighters such as Theodoros Kolokotronis, Theodoros Grivas, and Ioannis Makrygiannis we know too that at critical moments of the revolution or when in a state of high emotional charge, freedom fighters and even key players in the struggle who had versifying talent composed poems and verses about specific events. In fact, relevant poetic compositions frequently existed in the memoirs of freedom fighters or in records of the period. All these instances reveal how much the revolution moved the Greeks, so that they imprinted these intense emotions both in folk songs and in popular and popularizing verse that were widely disseminated among the Greek people, directly influencing the formation of its folk poetic creation and expression ever since.

These are prerevolutionary and mainly revolutionary verses in rhyme form, describing the historical facts and circumstances of certain regions, the outbreak of the struggle and some of the battles, with many interpolated elements of traditional everyday life. The prolix poem by Anagnostis Salamalekis from Samos is a case in point, while many of these poems remained unpublished in manuscripts in various archives.

Even more recent historical traditions about events of the War of Independence, are similarly shaped by legendary transmission of lived experience. Nikolaos Politis cites a typical example relating to the destruction of Psara in 1824. In another interesting case, earlier hagiological and etiological traditions and individual motifs from them were adapted by Logothetis Lykourgos to the case of Samos, so as to inspire courage in its defenders during the two attempts by the Ottoman fleet and army to capture the island, in July 1821 and August 1824. Thus, new traditions were generated, which in their turn were included in the corpus of folk mythmaking, and the researcher today may come across these being transmitted in the folk oral or written literature of our time. It is in this case characteristic that the "old wine" put in "new bottles" of newly acquired traditions succeeded in its goal as a kind of psychological warfare based on emotionally reinforcing the (spirit of the) freedom fighters by telling tales of divine assistance (Varvounis 2011).

Apart from the folk song mentioned, other kinds of artful folk discourse survived tenaciously. For example, the memoirs of the 1821 freedom fighters, which are a significant source of information on traditional daily life in the period, are full of proverbial phrases that the men used in their everyday speech (Loukatos 1957). Many cases have been recorded and studied, which show with specific examples that the events of the revolution also stimulated the creation of new proverbial phrases that have been embedded in Greek popular proverbial discourse ever since (Constas 1958, 1963–1964). The Greek people do indeed use several proverbs and proverbial phases that are said to derive from episodes in the life of the 1821 freedom fighters. Giannis Vlachogiannis collected from the oral and textual tradition of his day considerable material, which he then published in the form of historical anecdotes (Vlachogiannis 1922).

The same holds for coining nicknames, which as is well known is widespread in Greek traditional culture. Dozens of such examples have been inventoried, as well as cases of coining new place names on the basis of episodes in the War of Independence, which due to their importance and dramatic unfolding remained etched in collective historical memory (Constas 1963–1964). Last, mention should be made of the use and retelling of fables, frequently animal fables deriving from the ancient Aesopian tradition, which the protagonists of the revolution often employed when addressing the men of their armed bands. According to Georgios Tertsetis, Theodoros Kolokotronis in particular frequently used fables in his effort to boost his men's morale (Valetas 1958).

The traditional daily round in its principal forms, continued at its established pace during the years of the 1821 War of Independence. The freedom fighters came basically from farming and herding societies, closed, static, and inward looking, with stable mechanisms of production. As a rule, this stability also kept immobile or extremely cumbersome the ways of understanding the world, always at the level of folk culture (Loukatos 1974). This was in marked contrast to the deeper changes that the Neohellenic Enlightenment had brought a few decades earlier to urban populations engaged in mercantile, shipping, and entrepreneurial pursuits.

The revolution had an impact on the everyday activities of the agricultural and stock-raising communities of the period according to how close the military events approached. Animal husbandry and agriculture, maritime activities and domestic tasks, cottage industry and manufacturing, trade and every means of earning a living were practiced only in the brief interludes of peace. They were, of course, affected directly and negatively by the campaigns and all manner of military confrontations, while a large part of their products was used to keep the struggle going and for the material support of the troops. In many cases destructions due to warfare meant also the uprooting of a local tradition of productive activity: for example, the massacre of Chios spelled the end of textile production on the island, which had been at its zenith from the mid-eighteenth century onward, and the same happened elsewhere with the output of many local products.

By contrast, in matters of spiritual life the link between conservatism and observed cases of resistance was much stronger. From testimonies in the memoirs of freedom fighters (Imellos 1996–1997b) and in the accounts of certain foreign travelers who happened to be in Greece during the War of Independence and who described the habits and life of the country's inhabitants, it emerges that, as a rule, in the case of life-cycle rituals—with the three key stages of birth, marriage, and death—the traditional customs of each place were kept, to the degree of course that the turmoil of war allowed. The wedding feasts, the observance of related preclusions and superstitions associated with ensuring beneficent magical influence on the life of the newlyweds, and the ceremonial practices of all kinds relating to the care of the dead body—the ritual lamentation and the burial of the deceased—constituted islets of resistance within a generally transmuting world of insurrection in which the constants of the past appeared almost utopian.

Characteristic in this case are the descriptions of customs that pepper the memoirs of freedom fighters. Even though the value of these texts as historical sources has often been treated critically, the folklore testimonies they provide are important and certainly more reliable than the often doubtful material provided by foreign travelers in Greece in the years of the struggle (Simopoulos 1984).

Despite the more general upheavals of war, the Greek people continued to celebrate all kinds of folk religious ceremonies, particularly those associated with the annual festive cycle of the church. The religious feasts of parishes and monasteries, as well as the great feast days of saints or the cycles of the Twelve feast days of Christmas, and Easter, continued to be honored in the years of the struggle, together with patronal feasts and fairs (*panigyria*), which combined the religious event with entertainment and the reshaping of social, kinship, and familial structures. From freedom fighters' memoirs we learn about many such *panigyria*, with especial emphasis on the feast days of the soldier-saints, such as St. George, St. Demetrios, and the Archangels in the Peloponnese and central Greece.

Panigyria were occasions for social coexistence and contact, as well as for leisure and pleasure. Moreover, the revels and carousing (*glentia*) in the encampments, which are so vividly described by many memoir writers of the revolution, had their origins in religious feasts, with their communal meal and the attendant dances, as well as oracular ceremonies such as divination of the scapula—that is, extracting omens for the future of the struggle and their personal survival from signs on the scapula of a lamb, which some claimed they could read and decode (Constas 1963–1964).

In many memoirs of freedom fighters there is information about superstitions and diverse portents, as well as about dreams that had ominous importance and were frequently interpreted by specific individuals who were considered wise and knowledgeable about the associated symbolism. Many of these dreams are related to aspects of the revolutionary action of Theodoros Kolokotronis (Imellos 1991–1993), but also of Lambros Tzavelas and Ioannis Makrygiannis. Such omens were extracted also from the coincidence of chance occurrences: well known is the case of the three hares caught by Greeks before the battle at Valtetsi and which were considered a good omen (Imellos 1996–1997a; Romaios 1985) by, among others, Odysseas Androutsos. By contrast, the appearance of a black hare, according to Alexandros Kriezis, or a cuckoo's call, according to Nikolaos Kasomoulis, was considered an inauspicious sign of defeat and death (Kasomoulis 1940).

Kasomoulis describes the anxiety caused by a public curse in the encampment of Thebes (August 6, 1829) existing alongside frequent discussions in freedom fighters' texts of the concepts of martial honor and of fulfilling promises, showing us the contrast between the psychological makeup of the fighters and the conditions they found themselves in daily during the years of the struggle (Romaios 1981). And naturally, all these values survived the war, largely determining the daily life of the people in free Greece after 1830.

Characteristic too was the formation of a special customary protocol directly related to the revolution and its memory, particularly after the establishment of the official anniversary of the War of Independence on the day of the feast of the Annunciation of the Virgin (March 25), in 1838. Thus a singular public ceremonial was elaborated, which combines some of the liturgical observances from the feast of the Annunciation with the protocol of a national celebration (memorial services, panegyric orations, laying of wreaths, flying flags, and, later, parades), and which was established in the popular consciousness so that it is today one of the principal occasions of public ceremonial for the Greek people.

The sector of folk artistic creation, in the sense of handicraft and its products, has preserved many of the influences of the 1821 revolution on Greek traditional culture. Mainly these are creations in the visual arts, inspired by the struggle, its battles, and its important figures. Characteristic is the case of the folk painter

FIGURE 39   Dimitrios Zographos, *God's Just Decision for the Liberation of Greece*, 1836–1839.
Watercolor on paper. The Gennadeion Library, Athens.

Dimitrios Zographos, born in the late eighteenth century at Vordonia in Laconia, veteran freedom fighter of the revolution, and self-taught vernacular and
ecclesiastical painter in the post-Byzantine folk tradition. General Ioannis
Makrygiannis commissioned Zographos, with the assistance of his two sons,
to illustrate the important moments of the War of Independence (Figure 39);
he had previously commissioned these pictures from a European painter, but
was dissatisfied with the result (Asdrachas 1976).

As Makrygiannis himself narrates, he conceived the idea of depicting in
paintings the important battles of the revolution in the spring of 1836, when—
as head of his tetrarchy—he went together with Richard Church into western
Rumeli, in order to quash a rebellion against King Othon. After seeing once
again the battlefields on which he had fought and after reading the inaccuracies in the Othonian glut of memoirs of various freedom fighters who, in his
opinion, promoted themselves without stating the truth of the events, as
Makrygiannis puts it:

> on coming here to Athens, I took a Frankish painter and I had him make
> for me illustrations of these wars. I didn't know his language. He made a

couple, they were no good; I paid him and he left. After I'd got rid of this painter, I sent and they brought from Sparta a freedom fighter, Panagiotis [*sic*] Zographos was his name; they brought him and we talked and we agreed on the price for each painting; and he sent for and brought also his two sons; and I had them in my house when they were working. And this started from 1836 and ended in 1839. I took Zographos and we went out into the hills and I told him. . . . That's what this place is like, that's what that one is like; that's what this war was like, that's how he became leader of the Greeks, he leader of the Turks. (Asdrachas 1976, 7)

This was a particularly fruitful collaboration, resulting in twenty-five paintings on wood, measuring 56.5 × 40 cm and executed in the Byzantine medium of egg tempera. One of them, which represented the regent Josef Ludwig von Armansperg tearing out the heart of Greece, was destroyed by Makrygiannis's friends who, wishing to protect him, replaced it with a portrait of the general. These paintings were products of folk artistic expression, as they had been painted by a folk painter, which is why they satisfied Makrygiannis. The general paid for four additional sets to be made, three of which he presented to the ambassadors of Britain, France, and Russia, while one set he offered to King Othon. The good reviews he received and the enthusiasm of his fellow freedom fighters encouraged Makrygiannis to put into action his idea of publishing an album that many people could acquire.

For this purpose, he made an agreement with the schoolteacher Alexandros Isaias and in 1839 they cosigned a notarial act confirming the handing over to Isaias of the set of copies that Makrygiannis had gifted to Othon and which the general had borrowed in order to prepare the publication. Isaias promised to go to Paris, to have lithographs made of the paintings, and after carrying out some minor corrections of the locations and the persons—without moving away from the idea or altering anything from the reports of the incidents and their descriptions—to print copies. The end of this collaboration is interesting, as in Venice, Isaias made new paintings based on the tenets of the European art of his time, totally different from the originals, and he had them printed. When, in 1840, these lithographs circulated in Athens, Makrygiannis denounced them and publicly accused Isaias of adulterating his paintings and forging them.

Today we do not have all the copies of Zographos's paintings, which record the imprint of the revolution on folk painters of the period; after Isaias's death in Trieste, the whole series belonging to Othon was lost. However, in 1909 John Gennadios located it in Rome and purchased it, and so it survives today in the Gennadeion Library in Athens. The set that Makrygiannis gave to the British ambassador Edmund Lyons was handed over to the foreign secretary of Great

Britain, Lord Palmerston, who in turn offered it to Queen Victoria. From the original set that Makrygiannis kept for himself, there are in the National Historical Museum in Athens eight paintings measuring 56.5 × 40 cm, while three other copies on paper were gifted to the Historical and Ethnological Society of Greece by his son, General Kitsos Ioannis Makrygiannis, in 1927. The present whereabouts of the sets presented to the French and the Russian ambassadors are unknown.

Furthermore, the battles and personalities of the revolution steadily fueled the inspiration of folk painters, at least until the first half of the twentieth century. We mention characteristically the case of the painter Theophilos Chadjimichail, who in a series of murals, mainly at Pelion and on Lesbos, rendered in his own compositions battle scenes and typical moments of the 1821 War of Independence. In these cases, the structure and conception of each subject resemble those of Zographos, because, as Marina Lambraki-Plaka observes

> the archetypal images they had in their mind originated from the same culture; a folk but self-sufficient culture, vitalized by a rich past that had passed through its agencies, not as dry historical memory, but as life style, as handed over technique and good taste. (Lambraki-Plaka 1997, 12)

Telling, for instance, is the way in which Theophilos painted the portrait of Rhigas Velestinlis, as a folk hero. Indeed, this portrait was the model for the depiction of Rhigas in Neohellenic popular art, given that his figure inspired over time a series of folk artists and was the basis for the creation of lithographs and engravings. These prints enjoyed great popularity and were widely diffused, not without political reason, particularly during the years of the German occupation and the Greek Civil War that followed (Varvounis 2011).

Moreover, it was Theophilos again who created his own versions of compositions featuring revolutionary heroes and events of the period. These compositions had wide appeal in the popular imagination. Another characteristic case is the works by the Bavarian artist Peter von Hess, who in 1839 elaborated forty drawings on the subject of the struggle of the Greeks. These works inspired large-scale murals that graced the palace of King Othon in Athens. Indeed, von Hess's drawings were used later by Heinrich Kochler in 1852, to produce a series of lithographs, through which these compositions reached a large audience and enjoyed popular appreciation, given their widespread use for decorating classrooms and assembly halls in schools of the Greek state.

Many of these works became widely known through lithographs and more rarely by engravings, usually tinted, that hung in public spaces, schools, coffee shops, and so on. They put into pictures what ordinary people learned at school or from narrations of the folk collective memory. It is characteristic that until the shooting and screening of Greek films with subjects from the 1821 revolution, which mainly appeared in the 1970s, these prints were the principal sources through which people formed an opinion about the revolution, the battles, and their protagonists. In one sense, films and prints are varieties of popular art with wide appeal, and for decades the images of the lithographs and the scenes of the films fueled the popular imagination and contributed to the formation of other icons and impressions.

Folk pottery too was influenced by the revolution. During the nineteenth and in the first half of the twentieth century, ceramic plates and ornamental vessels with portraits or figures of freedom fighters circulated widely. These plates and the larger decorative platters, which were frequently made in foreign centers of ceramic production, usually in Italy or other countries of western Europe (Korre-Zografou 1995), were part of the traditional decoration of the folk house, and also reveal the very wide popular appeal of subjects relating to the revolution and its heroes.

In both the aforesaid categories of folk artworks the influence of the art of European Philhellenism should not be underestimated. We refer to the folk artists' practice of copying subjects, motifs, and scenes relating to the struggle, its battles, and its heroes, which were created by European painters within the fold of the philhellenic movement and which went on to become models for imitation by folk and folksy artists, and so entered the thematic repertoire of Greek folk art. Since then they have been reproduced by many and varied folk craftsmen.

Depictions of events and moments of the revolution in embroidery are rarer. Perhaps the most characteristic example is a piece of embroidery from the second half of the nineteenth century, in the Michalis and Dimitra Varkarakis Collection, which depicts the return of a freedom fighter's family to its ruined home, after the battle, with the freedom fighter himself shown in the foreground. It belongs among the philhellenic artworks and certainly does not seem to have had an influence or wider impact on folk needlework, which has no similar works in its repertoire, at least among those in museums or which have been studied and published.

The situation is different, however, in folk gold and silver working, where assorted objects, mainly cups, flasks, flintlocks, swords, and so on, are decorated with scenes of the struggle or are directly related to it. Perhaps the largest museum collections of such objects are held by the National Historical Museum and the War Museum of Athens, while numerous such works from smaller museums and private collections have been published.

A typical example is the broadsword of militia leader Diamantis Zervas, in the National Historical Museum Collection. Depicted on the upper part of its scabbard is Diamantis Zervas armed with sword and with his flintlock musket leaning against the wall. Depicted below are battle scenes, ancient gods, foliage, and other motifs, while at the tip of the scabbard is a dragon. This is a work by the silversmith Dimitrios Davaroukas from Kalarrytes in Epirus, an important center of Greek traditional gold and silver working.

Important as well as indicative are the silver cups (*tasia*) of General Ioannis Makrygiannis, which are kept in the National Historical Museum (Korre-Zografou 1988). The cups were made by specialist craftsmen, together with the yataghans (Ottoman sabers), rifles, grease cases (*medoularia*), swords, pistols, and so on, as a set of personal objects and weaponry of each freedom fighter, and these objects are referred to often in the klephtika and historical folk songs of the period (Korre-Zografou 1984). Ancient gods and heroes are represented on these cups, as well as historical scenes such as those linked with the uprising of 1843 and the granting of the Constitution by Othon. Similar wooden cups survive, whose decoration echoes the art of folk woodcarving (Korre-Zografou 1989). Diffuse in these objects, either in inscriptions or through motifs and symbols, such as the cross, the "all-seeing eye," and so on, is the expression of Makrygiannis's piety, a sentiment shared also by the rest of the freedom fighters of 1821.

Beyond the conventional floral and vegetal ornaments, these objects feature, together with figures of gods and heroes from Hellenic antiquity, figures of *foustanella*-clad fighters with their weaponry, and inscriptions with verses and sayings—usually of heroic and patriotic content—as well as buildings, often embellished with minarets (Korre-Zografou 2002). These are compositions in the Ottoman baroque style but which carry the indelible seal of the revolution both in form and in their individual artistic formulae.

One further observation should be made: the influence of the War of Independence is clearly visible also in the way in which this revolution was used in later critical and desperate times for Greek society, such as during the Greek Resistance (1941–1944) and the ensuing Civil War (1945–1949). Apart from the frequent reference in texts of the period to freedom fighters and their example, and the symbolic function of their images, particularly interesting is the attempt to project onto the revolution of 1821 political ideas of the mid-twentieth century, as can be detected in some writings of the time. Posters, works of literature and the visual arts, songs, plays, and all kinds of representations reveal that in the thoughts of people in those years the Greek Revolution and its leaders were something more than living and clear realities. Even in the recent Greek economic crisis, retrospective recoveries of revolutionary imagery are frequently encountered, primarily in theater and in song, and because they are widely diffused they could be considered manifestations of contemporary folk art.

In conclusion, we can say that the Greek Revolution of 1821, its battles, and its protagonists created a "heroic tradition" in the collective mind of the Greek people, which continues what has been characterized as a "tradition of rebellion" (Damianakos 1987), a tradition that inspired both daily life and many artistic expressions of the Greeks. It is a tradition that is drawn upon and used as an exemplar at various periods of crisis and transition, as a paradigm of heroism, patriotism, and self-sacrifice. To what degree these exemplars and paradigms correspond to reality or represent a pronounced predilection for creating myths from the past is an issue that has yet to be investigated systematically. Certainly, however, in the collective lore of Greek society the 1821 War of Independence is constantly present, permeating the expressions of folk collective aesthetics and of the social and political sensibilities of the Greeks. It is a landmark of memory and as such it is represented frequently in the discourse and in the various art forms of the Greek people.

Manolis G. Varvounis

Translated from the Greek by Alexandra Douma

References

Academy of Athens. 1962. *Ελληνικά δημοτικά τραγούδια (Εκλογή) 1* [Greek folk songs (Selection) 1]. Athens.

Apostolakis, Giannis. 1950. *Το κλέφτικο τραγούδι* [The klephtiko song]. Athens.

Asdrachas, Spyros. 1976. *Μακρυγιάννης και Παναγιώτης Ζωγράφος. Το ιστορικό της εικονογραφίας του Αγώνα* [Makrygiannis and Panagiotis Zographos: The story of the iconography of the struggle]. Athens.

Constas, Constantinos S. 1958. "Λαογραφικά του Εικοσιένα" [Folklore of 1821]. *Nea Estia* 63:382–387.

Constas, Constantinos S. 1963–1964. "Η λαογραφία της σκλαβιάς και του ξεσηκωμού" [Folklore of bondage and uprising]. *Laografia* 21:3–88.

Damianakos, Stathis. 1987. *Παράδοση ανταρσίας και λαϊκός πολιτισμός* [Tradition of rebellion and folk culture]. Athens.

Imellos, Stephanos D. 1991–1993. "Πώς στρατηγούσε ο Θ. Κολοκοτρώνης ή σχολιασμός μιας επιστολής του προς τον Γ. Καραϊσκάκη" [How Th. Kolokotronis acted as a general or commentary on a letter from him to G. Karaiskakis]. *Mnimosyni* 12:269–288.

Imellos, Stephanos D. 1992–1993. "Τα τραγούδια των Κολοκοτρωναίων" [The songs of the Kolokotronis family]. In *Πρακτικά Δ΄ Διεθνούς Συνεδρίου Πελοποννησιακών Σπουδών 3* [Proceedings of 4th International Conference of Peloponnesian Studies 3], 417–423. Athens.

Imellos, Stephanos D. 1996–1997a. "Ο Κολοκοτρώνης και οι λαγοί κατά την μάχη στο Βαλτέτσι" [Kolokotronis and the hares during the battle of Valtetsi]. *Peloponnisiaka* 22:49–56.

Imellos, Stephanos D. 1996–1997b. "Το λαϊκό στοιχείο στο έργο του απομνημονευματογράφου Φωτάκου" [The folk element in the work of the memoir writer Photakos]. In *Πρακτικά Ε΄ Διεθνούς Συνεδρίου Πελοποννησιακών Σπουδών* [Proceedings of 5th International Conference of Peloponnesian Studies], 4:195–207. Athens.

Kasomoulis, Nikolaos. 1940. *Ενθυμήματα στρατιωτικά της Επαναστάσεως των Ελλήνων 1821–1833* [Military reminiscences of the Revolution of the Greeks, 1821–1833]. Vol. 2. Athens.

Kitromilides, Paschalis M. 1996. "'Balkan Mentality': History, Legend, Imagination." *Nations and Nationalism* 2, no. 2: 163–191.

Koliopoulos, Ioannis. 2005. *Η ληστεία στην Ελλάδα (19ος αι.)* [Brigandry in Greece, nineteenth century]. Athens.

Korre-Zografou, Katerina. 1984. "Οι παλάσκες του Εθνικού Ιστορικού Μουσείου" [The flasks in the National Historical Museum]. *DIEEE* 27:197–255.

Korre-Zografou, Katerina. 1988. "Τα τάσια του Μακρυγιάννη" [Makrygiannis's cups]. *Archaiologia kai Technes* 26:64–74.

Korre-Zografou, Katerina. 1989. "Τα τάσια του Εθνικού Ιστορικού Μουσείου" [The cups in the National Historical Museum]. *DIEEE* 32:229–283.

Korre-Zografou, Katerina. 1995. *Τα κεραμεικά του ελληνικού χώρου* [Pottery of Greece]. Athens.

Korre-Zografou, Katerina. 2002. *Χρυσικών έργα, 1600–1900. Συλλογή Κ. Νοταρά* [Goldsmiths' works, 1600–1900: C. Notaras Collection]. Athens.

Lambraki-Plaka, Marina. 1997. "Εικονογραφία του Αγώνα" [Iconography of the struggle]. *I Kathimerini* (June 8): 12.

Loukatos, Dimitrios S., ed. 1957. *Νεοελληνικά λαογραφικά κείμενα* [Neohellenic folklore texts]. Athens.

Loukatos, Dimitrios S. 1974. "Λαϊκός βίος (1669–1821)" [Folk life, 1669–1821]. *IEE*, 11:273–284, 457–458. Athens.

Petropoulos, Dimitrios A. 1958. *Ελληνικά δημοτικά τραγούδια* [Greek folk songs]. Athens.

Politis, Alexis, ed. 1973. *Το δημοτικό τραγούδι. Κλέφτικα* [The folk song: Klephtika]. Athens.

Politis, Alexis. 1974. "Το δημοτικό τραγούδι" [The folk song]. *IEE*, 11:284–299. Athens.

Politis, Nikolaos G. 1914. *Εκλογαί από τα τραγούδια του ελληνικού λαού* [Selections from the songs of the Greek people]. Athens.

Politis, Nikolaos G. 1920. *Λαογραφικά Σύμμεικτα 1* [Folklore miscellanea 1]. Athens.

Romaios, Costas. 1968. *Η ποίηση ενός λαού* [The poetry of a people]. Athens.

Romaios, Costas. 1981. "1821. Οι άνθρωποι και τα γεγονότα από τη σκοπιά της Λαογραφίας" [1821: The people and the events from the viewpoint of folklore studies]. *Praktika tis Akademias Athinon* 56:90–108.

Romaios, Costas. 1985. "Βαλτέτσι 1821: δοξασίες και ψυχολογία των πολεμιστών" [Valtetsi 1821: Beliefs and psychology of the freedom-fighters]. *Peloponnisiaka* 16:403–17.

Simopoulos, Kyriakos. 1984. *Πώς είδαν οι ξένοι την Ελλάδα του '21. Απομνημονεύματα, χρονικά, ημερολόγια, υπομνήματα, αλληλογραφία εθελοντών, διπλωματών, ειδικών* απεσταλμένων, περιηγητών, πρακτόρων κ.ά. [How foreigners saw Greece in 1821: Memoirs, chronicles, diaries, memoranda, correspondence of volunteers, diplomats, special envoys, travelers, agents, etc.]. 5 vols. Athens.

Valetas, Giorgos, ed. 1958. Τερτσέτη άπαντα [Tersetis complete works]. Vol. 1. Athens.

Varvounis, Manolis G. 2011. "Ιδεολογικές χρήσεις της λαϊκής παράδοσης στη σαμιακή επανάσταση του 1821" [Ideological uses of folk tradition in the Samian revolution of 1821]. In 1821, Σάμος και Επανάσταση. Ιστορικές προσεγγίσεις [1821, Samos and revolution: Historical approaches], 381–390. Athens.

Vlachogiannis, Giannis. 1922. Τα ανέκδοτα του Καραϊσκάκη και του Κολοκοτρώνη [The anecdotes of Karaiskakis and Kolokotronis]. Athens.

The Revolution as Creative Experience

Greek literature of the revolutionary period consists entirely of poetry. The poems of the Greek Revolution can be seen as constituting the founding texts of Greek national literature, at a time when every civilized European nation was expected to have its own "national literature." In this essay I focus on the work of two poets, Andreas Kalvos (1792–1869) and Dionysios Solomos (1798–1857), the second of whom is generally thought of as Greece's national poet par excellence, partly (but by no means only) because he wrote the words that were later used for the country's national anthem. As well as presenting a critical overview of the poetry itself, I trace the processes by which Kalvos and Solomos reinvented themselves as poets of the revolution and voices of the Greek nation.

Before the Greek Revolution

Greek revolutionary songs urging the Greeks to rise up against their Ottoman masters began to appear in the late 1790s. Orally composed Greek songs had already been celebrating the exploits of rebels such as Daskalogiannis in Crete (1770) and the klephts in mainland Greece. But two important and interrelated Greek literary manifestations of the revolutionary spirit were a direct consequence of the French Revolution: the songs of Rhigas Velestinlis, first published in Vienna, and a group of poems written in the Ionian islands.

Rhigas (1757–1798) set out to convey French revolutionary ideas to the Greeks in two volumes entitled *New Political Administration* and *Military Handbook*. All copies of these books were confiscated and destroyed by the Austrian authorities, but the *New Political Administration* survived in manuscript.

This volume included a revolutionary song entitled "Thourios," while two additional revolutionary songs were included in the *Military Handbook* (all three are republished in Velestinlis 2000). Two of them, including the "Thourios," were republished in Corfu in 1798, shortly before Rhigas's death. The publicity surrounding Rhigas's execution led to the popularity of his songs, which quickly entered the oral tradition. During the first twenty years after his execution, "it was Rhigas's poetry which kept his name alive" (Woodhouse 1995, 154). I quote here the opening two lines and one other couplet from the "Thourios":

> How long, brave lads, are we to live in the narrow passes,
> lonely as lions in the hills and the mountains? . . .
> Better one hour of free life
> than forty years of slavery and prison.

The title "Thourios" (rushing, impetuous, furious) is an adjective in ancient Greek, but since Rhigas's time it has been used as a noun meaning "war song." The "narrow passes" refer to the mountain passes where the klephts lay in wait to ambush passing merchants and Ottoman officials.

Other revolutionary songs were written in Rhigas's time and shortly afterward. One of these was erroneously attributed to Rhigas by Lord Byron (1812, 223–225, 273–274), who was the first to publish it. The first two lines, "Go, children of the Greeks, / the hour of glory has come," are a fusion of the "Marseillaise" with the song sung by the Greek warriors at the battle of Salamis in Aeschylus's tragedy *Persians*: "Go, children of the Greeks, / liberate the homeland." The same poem includes the following stanza: "Wherever you lie, valiant bones of the Greeks, scattered spirits, now take breath."

Apart from Rhigas's Vienna, another important site of revolutionary songs was Corfu, where French Republican troops landed in June 1797 to take over the Ionian Islands from the now defunct Venetian empire following the Treaty of Campo Formio. During this brief French occupation, Antonios Martelaos and Thomas Danelakis on the island of Zakynthos (Zante) wrote poems celebrating the liberation of the Ionian Islands by the French and exhorting the rest of the Greeks to free themselves from the Turks. Martelaos's poems incorporate verses borrowed from "Go, children of the Greeks." Some of these songs, like those of Rhigas, were widely sung to well-known French and German melodies, including that of the "Marseillaise."

Both Kalvos, in his odes, and Solomos, in the *Hymn to Liberty*, refer to Rhigas and to "Go, children of the Greeks," while Solomos also incorporates phrases from a poem by Danelakis.

Poetry during the Revolution

Kalvos and Solomos, who were both born on Zakynthos, dominated the poetry of the Greek revolution. A third poet, born some years earlier on the same island, was Ugo Foscolo (1778–1827), whom Kalvos and Solomos greatly admired. These three writers found themselves experiencing cultural transformations and reinventing themselves in a transitional age during which the relationship between individual, community, and territory was shifting. However, whereas the Catholic Foscolo became an Italian national poet, the (at least nominally) Orthodox Kalvos and Solomos became Greek national poets. For a comparative study of the intellectual development of these poets, see the section "One island, three (trans)national poets" in Zanou (2018, 24–63). For an English translation of Kalvos's *Odes,* see Kalvos (1998). For English translations of Solomos's "The Woman of Zakynthos" and "The Free Besieged," see Solomos (2015).

Kalvos and Solomos were contemporaries of the greatest romantic poets: Giacomo Leopardi (1798–1837) in Italy; Alphonse de Lamartine (1790–1869), Alfred de Vigny (1797–1863), and Victor Hugo (1802–1885) in France; Adam Mickiewicz (1798–1855) in Poland; and Alexander Pushkin (1799–1837) in Russia. As for English poets, Kalvos and Solomos were coeval with Lord Byron (1788–1824), Percy Bysshe Shelley (1792–1822), and John Keats (1795–1821), while Solomos was born in the year that Samuel Taylor Coleridge and William Wordsworth published their *Lyrical Ballads.*

The two Greek poets were born six years apart, and some aspects of their careers are strikingly similar. Each of them moved to Italy at the age of ten; both of them became British subjects after the United States of the Ionian Islands was set up under British protection by the Treaty of Paris in 1815, and they remained as such for the rest of their lives; each of them wrote poems and personal correspondence in Italian before beginning to write poetry in Greek; each of them wrote poems on some of the same topics (for instance Byron's death at Mesolonghi in April 1824); and they made their public debut as the voices of the Greek nation within a few months of each other, in 1824, with poems in which they celebrated Greek military successes and urged their compatriots to win further victories and avoid civil strife. In each case a French prose version of their debut poems was carried out by the same translator. Both poets saw themselves as teachers of the nation, making it aware of its own history, its achievements and its destiny, and they thought of themselves as participating in the liberation struggle in their own way, through words rather than deeds.

Yet in other respects their careers were markedly different. Because of their immersion in Italian, the language of their Greek poetry was rather eccentric, but in quite different ways. There is no evidence that they met personally; once they had become aware of each other's poetry, each must immediately have viewed the other as a rival. They appear to have studiously avoided each other even while living in the same small town of Corfu, and they never mention each other's names in their extant correspondence.

Kalvos wrote all his Greek poems outside the Greek world, whereas Solomos was writing in the Ionian islands, at that time under British "protection." Kalvos published his first Greek poem in 1819, but it passed unnoticed. The *Hymn to Liberty* (1823) was Solomos's first published Greek poem, and he was already being described as the "national poet" before the *Hymn* became the Greek national anthem in 1865. He continued to write poetry in Greek—most of it inspired by the revolution—until about 1851 (after which he resumed writing poetry in Italian), whereas Kalvos seems to have stopped writing poetry altogether, in any language, after completing his second collection of Greek odes in 1826.

Kalvos

Kalvos lived in Tuscany between the ages of ten and twenty-four, first in Livorno with his father, then from 1812 to 1816 in Florence. In Livorno in 1811, at the age of nineteen, he published an Italian ode to Napoleon, which he repudiated in 1814. In Florence he met Ugo Foscolo, who became his mentor and friend. This was the period of his poetic apprenticeship to Foscolo, for whom he worked as an amanuensis. Kalvos's second earliest known publication—an Italian poem entitled "Anacreontica," replete with classical allusion and written to celebrate a wedding—dates from 1813 (Pappas 2019). In the same year, Foscolo (1954, 382) wrote to a friend that Kalvos "knows Italian like a Tuscan; he knows a little French and Greek."

While in Florence, Kalvos attended courses in declamation and theatrical arts at the Academy of Fine Arts and played the title role in a student performance of *Agamennone* by the Italian tragedian Vittorio Alfieri (Pappas 2017). He also came near to completing an Italian tragedy that he never published (*Teramene*) and planned another one (*Ippia*) that he never completed (this has been dated to spring 1821 by Vagenas 1992); both of them were strongly influenced by the plots and diction of Alfieri's tragedies (Trenti 2017, 46). Each of these Italian tragedies is set during the rule of the Thirty Tyrants in ancient Athens and is concerned with the hero's efforts to kill one of the tyrants in order to restore democracy. Also in this Florence period, Kalvos completed a third (and more original) Italian tragedy, *Le Danaidi* (The Danaids), based on an ancient myth about the daughters of a tyrannical father. In his notes on *Ippia*, Kalvos wrote that he was depicting a confrontation between "the virtue of liberty," which he identified with patriotism, and "the vice of Tyranny" (Vitti 1960, 64, 66). The antithesis liberty versus tyranny, together with the concept of virtue (by which Kalvos means martial valor as well as civic virtue), was to play a major thematic role in Kalvos's Greek odes.

In 1816 Kalvos moved to London to join Foscolo, who had been forced to leave Tuscany for political reasons. In London he gave Italian and modern Greek lessons, published *Le Danaidi,* and in 1819 married an Englishwoman, who died four months later. This tragic event in his personal life came a few months after a shocking event in the history of Greece: the British sold the town of Parga in Epirus to Ali Pasha, after which its Greek inhabitants, having disinterred and burnt their ancestors' bones, emigrated en masse to Corfu. It was probably these two events that made Kalvos wish to leave England and eventually return to his birthplace.

It was in London that he wrote and published his first Greek poem, "Hope for the Homeland" (*Elpis patridos*), which is dated November 20, 1819. The poem is dedicated and addressed to Lord Guilford, the newly appointed chancellor of the University in the Ionian Islands, which was to begin functioning in Corfu in 1824. Kalvos was always in a precarious financial situation, and one future possibility seemed to be to secure a post at the university. But "Hope for the Homeland" was not only intended to persuade Guilford to give him a job, it also expressed the hope that the foundation of the first Greek university would eventually lead to the Greeks regaining their national and political freedom (Garantoudis in Kalvos 2016, 214). Kalvos ends his poem by proclaiming his belief that liberty is interdependent with the arts and sciences: "if I do not see Liberty and the Muses engaged together in a dance before the sanctuary of Greece, I wish for death." The same belief forms the basis of his later ode "To the Muses," in which the poet welcomes the nine sisters back to their homeland after centuries of exile during the Ottoman period.

The only known extant printed copy of "Hope for the Homeland" is housed in the University of Glasgow library, where it had remained unknown until it was discovered in 2003 by Lefkios Zafeiriou. Lord Guilford seems to have received a copy, but none have been found in Greece; this was an inauspicious start for Kalvos as a Greek poet. However, he was eventually appointed to a teaching post at the Ionian university in 1827.

Much was to happen in Kalvos's life—and in Greek history—between his leaving England in 1820 and his move to Corfu six years later. First, he settled once more in Florence with the aim of continuing his writing career in a familiar environment. It was probably at that time that he was initiated into the Carbonari, an illegal revolutionary movement struggling for democratic ideals and the liberation of European peoples from tyrannical empires (Porfyris 1975; Kalvos 2014, 1:284–286; Garantoudis in Kalvos 2016, 277). Georganta (2011), who argues that Kalvos's involvement dates from his time in London (1816–1820), demonstrates that his poetry contains many key concepts of Carbonarism. His involvement with the Carbonari led to his expulsion from Tuscany a few weeks after the outbreak of the Greek Revolution. From Florence he found refuge in Geneva, which was becoming a hive of philhellenic activity. It was there in 1823 that he became acquainted with a group of 158 patriots from all over Greece who had fled from the Danubian Principalities after the defeat of Alexandros Yspilantis's troops by an Ottoman army at the battle of Dragatsani and reached Geneva after a long odyssey. His acquaintance with these people—probably the first time he had been surrounded by so many Greeks since he had left Zakynthos at the age of ten—was no doubt one of the factors that led him to write his Greek odes (Bouvier 1972, 80).

Kalvos's first collection of ten odes, entitled *I Lyra* (The lyre), was published in Geneva (and distributed in Paris) in June 1824. This collection "was primarily addressed to a . . . French-speaking public" (Garantoudis in Kalvos 2016, 230). For this reason the poet, who could take it for granted that his classically educated readers would have no difficulty understanding the ancient Greek words used in his poems, appended a "Table of words and phrases" in which modern Greek words were translated into French. Four months later, a French prose translation of the odes by Stanislas Julien was published in Paris, another great center of Philhellenism.

Kalvos moved to Paris at the beginning of 1825. His second collection of ten odes was published there in April 1826 in a volume that also contained poems by the best-known Phanariot poet of the previous generation, Athanasios Christopoulos. Christopoulos's Anacreontic poems in praise of love and wine served as a foil to highlight the virtues of Kalvos's patriotic odes; indeed, an anonymous introductory note to the volume criticized Christopoulos's "light poetry" and "frivolous songs" (Kalvos 1826, vi). One of Kalvos's odes, "On Psara," begins with expressions of Christopoulian frivolity, which are then explicitly condemned by the poet. In the Paris collection the original Greek text of the poems was accompanied by a facing prose translation in French by the romantic poet Jean-Pierre Guillaume Pauthier, who had already published a book of poems entitled *Helléniennes, ou Élégies sur la Grèce* (1825).

Some of Kalvos's odes are devoted to specific locations in Greece that played a major part in the struggle against the Turks: particularly the islands of Chios and Psara, whose Christian population was massacred, and Samos, which was the site of a Greek naval victory; but also the town of Parga, whose Greek population had felt obliged to flee; and the region of Souli, whose inhabitants were already renowned for their heroic exploits before and during the revolution. "The Ocean" and "The Volcanoes" refer to Greek naval victories, and especially to the success of Kanaris's fireships. (Perhaps because of the abundant civil strife on the mainland, Kanaris is the only living hero named in any of Kalvos's poems, while none is mentioned in those of Solomos.) Some odes are meditations on certain concepts: Glory, Death, Liberty, Victory. Others focus on particular human or divine beings: the Muses, Lord Byron, the Sacred Battalion (a group of five hundred young Greeks who fought and died at Dragatsani), the Hagarenes (i.e., the Turks), and one particular Greek traitor. Lastly, in "The Prayers" the poet tells the Greeks that God, not the European kings, is their sole protector, while in "The Specter" he presents a nightmarish scene in which Discord celebrates the erasure of the Greek people from the face of the earth. Today the odes devoted to places are generally considered to be his finest; they are less abstract than some of the others, and they include atmospheric evocations of the beauties of the Greek landscape; indeed, Kalvos has been credited with the poetic rediscovery of the Greek islands.

At the beginning of his 1824 collection Kalvos placed two epigraphs that set the scene for his own poems: the first, on the front cover, is from a French poem published about six months earlier, while the second, on the title page, is from a poem by Pindar dating from the early fifth century BCE. In this way Kalvos linked his odes both to the latest European philhellenic poetry and to the heroic poetry of ancient Greece. Delavigne's poem "Tyrtée aux grecs," the source of the first epigraph, depicts the ancient Spartan poet Tyrtaeus, "upright, lyre in hand," exhorting the Greeks to rise up against their executioners (Delavigne 1824b, 9–19). The quotation from Pindar's First Pythian Ode, declaring that "those things on land and sea that Zeus does not love are stunned with terror when they hear the songs of the Muses," implies that Kalvos's odes are divinely inspired to combat evil and dismay the unjust.

The odes themselves are prefaced by a poem in the Italian eleven-syllable meter that invokes the Muses, daughters of Memory—a sign that Kalvos's poetry is intended to commemorate heroic deeds. Virtue has at last returned to Greece, but she will stay only if she is praised by the Muses.

The title of the first ode ("O philopatris") is pregnant with symbolic meaning. "The Lover of his Homeland" (the patriot) denoted by the title is none other than the poet himself, who refers to his life of exile in Italy and England, and expresses his love and nostalgia for his native Zakynthos, which he has not seen for more than twenty years. It is significant that the title of this particular poem is not "To Zakynthos," unlike Foscolo's "A Zacinto" (written in exile in Milan in

1803) and Solomos's undated "L'isola del Zante." The Greek word *philopatris* is first recorded as an adjective in Plutarch, who applies it to several of the Greek and Roman subjects of his biographies. Kalvos was no doubt aware that Plutarch describes some of his biographees not only as *philopatris* but as *misotyrannos* ("tyrant-hater": e.g., *Timoleon* 3.4). The poem itself is a hymn to the beauties of the poet's native island, yet Kalvos's choice of title for this first ode positions himself center stage as someone determined to help save his country. It is no coincidence that in the second ode, "On Glory," the poet hurls insults at the Ottomans and expresses his wish to join in the fighting, while in the third, "On Death," he places himself most clearly at the center of the action: here he expresses his devotion to the memory of his beloved mother, whose presence on the other side of the chasm separating the living from the dead relieves him from any fear of death. In these first three odes Kalvos displays the individualism of the romantic poet (cf. Georganta 2011, 120).

Some of Kalvos's odes read like dramatic monologues. He frequently uses the verbs "I see" and "I hear," exclamations, apostrophes (phrases addressed to persons or concepts), rhetorical questions, hesitations, and self-interruptions. The difference between the soliloquies in the odes and those that appear in tragedies is that the speaker is presented as being the poet himself rather than a fictional character.

The categorization of Kalvos's poetry as either neoclassical or romantic has been the subject of controversy. Georganta devotes much of her book (2011) to arguing that Kalvos was a thoroughgoing romantic, while Tziovas (1987) and Paschalis (2013) stress the neoclassical nature of much of his diction. Yet Garantoudis (2012, 134–135) sensibly concludes that Kalvos is both neoclassical and romantic, and that, besides, the question is of little interest to most modern readers.

Kalvos's earliest surviving letters in Greek, written in London between 1817 and 1819, contain elementary errors in spelling and grammar. His Greek improved as the years went by, especially between "Hope for the Homeland" and the odes. Yet, despite his infatuation with antiquity and the reputation for scholarship that he enjoyed in his time, the Greek of his poems is characterized by spelling and grammar mistakes, as well as by abundant Italianisms, especially literal translations from phrases in Foscolo's poetry (Paschalis 2013, 165).

Some of the abstruse ancient words in his poems (most of which are decorative adjectives) would have been unfamiliar even to some of his classicist readers. Paschalis (2013, 73–86) argues persuasively that instead of alluding to the content of ancient Greek texts, Kalvos takes ancient Greek words from dictionaries and embeds them in his poems. The fact remains, however, that generations of Greek readers have often been charmed by Kalvos's choice of words;

what is important to readers is how effectively these words function within the poem.

By contrast, when Kalvos uses a hackneyed turn of phrase drawn from neoclassical poetry, his message can become so obscure as to risk misunderstanding. This occurs, for instance, when he addresses the Muses as "aoniai melissai" ("Aonian bees"; see Paschalis 2013, 33–34). Aonia was the name of the region of Boeotia, which included Mount Helicon and Mount Cithaeron, where the Muses were believed to reside. In some editions that are still in print we encounter the misprint of the adjective "aoniai" as "aioniai" ("eternal": Meraklis 1965, 86); the same word was also mistranslated as "eternal" in the English version of Kalvos's odes (Kalvos 1998, 39). The ancient Greek vocabulary used in Kalvos's poetry goes together with the plentiful allusions to ancient Greek mythology; yet he was also influenced by the language and content of the Greek Old Testament, especially after he had translated the Psalms of David into a rather archaic form of modern Greek (published in London in 1820).

In addition, Kalvos often employs neoclassical circumlocutions in an effort to lend sublimity and elegance to his diction. Examples of these are "grape-bearing roots" ("Philopatris") and "the thunderclaps of war" ("On Glory"), which he interprets in his "Table of words and phrases" as referring to vines and firearms respectively.

In his comprehensive and authoritative study of the metrical form of Kalvos's odes, Garantoudis (1995) demonstrates that the Kalvian stanza is the poet's own invention. It does not conform to traditional modern Greek metrical patterns, yet it is entirely consistent with the principles underlying Italian versification, even though no Italian poet seems to have used exactly this stanzaic pattern. Unlike most Italian poetry in stanzaic form, Kalvos does not use rhyme. The absence of rhyme brings his poems closer to ancient Greek poetic forms; but it also enabled him to compose stanzas whose lines contain a varying number of syllables and to use plentiful enjambment (the carrying over of meaning from one line to the next, often accompanied by a pause within the lines); enjambment is a particularly frequent phenomenon in dramatic poetry.

With the exception of the invocation to the Muses that prefaces his first collection, he used basically the same stanza for the entirety of his published Greek poems, from "Hope for the Homeland" in 1819 to the last ode of his second book in 1826. The only alteration that he allowed himself was that whereas the stanzas of "Hope" consist of four lines, those of the odes contain five. Each stanza consists of four so-called "heptasyllables" followed by one pentasyllable. The Italian-style heptasyllable that Kalvos employs has its final stress on the sixth syllable, which may be followed, at will, by a number of unstressed syllables (one, two, or none). The stanza finishes with a five-syllable line whose final stress falls on the fourth syllable. In any one line, before the final stressed syllable the stresses may fall on any syllable. The first stanza of the first ode may serve as an example (ˊ indicates a stressed syllable, ˘ an unstressed syllable):

Ὦ φιλτάτη πατρίς,   ˘ ˘ ˊ ˘ ˘ ˊ
ὦ θαυμασία νῆσος,   ˘ ˘ ˘ ˊ ˘ ˊ ˘
Ζάκυνθε· σὺ μοῦ ἔδωκας   ˊ ˘ ˘ ˊ ˘ ˊ ˘ ˘
τὴν πνοήν, καὶ τοῦ Ἀπόλλωνος   ˘ ˘ ˊ ˘ ˘ ˊ ˘ ˘
    τὰ χρυσᾶ δῶρα!   ˘ ˘ ˊ ˊ ˘
O dearest homeland,
o wondrous island,
Zakynthos; it is you that gave me
breath and Apollo's
    golden gifts!

The fact that some of the specific historical topics of Kalvos's odes were also treated by non-Greek writers and painters reminds us that the Greek Revolution had pan-European repercussions. I will mention just some of the scholarly and artistic manifestations of a keen and sympathetic interest in the Greek Revolution in France in 1824. The first volume of Fauriel's collection of Greek folk songs includes eight songs about the Souliots (Fauriel 1824–1825, 284–303). Delavigne (1824a) published an elegy for Lord Byron in which he addresses the late, lamented English poet, assuring him that the Greeks have sworn to free themselves and avenge his death. In the same year the painter Eugène Delacroix (an admirer of Byron born in the same year as Solomos) depicted *The Massacre at Chios,* while two years later he went on to produce his famous painting *Greece on the Ruins of Mesolonghi.*

The second collection of Kalvos's odes is prefaced by a dedicatory letter to General Lafayette, in which the poet pompously proclaims that he is about to "expose one more heart to the fire of the Muslims," implying that he feels it is now time to convert his words into actions. He did indeed travel to mainland Greece, where he spent two months in Nafplio, the seat of the revolutionary government. There is no record of why Kalvos left Nafplio for Corfu. The reason was not necessarily disillusionment: we need to remember that for many years he had been planning to settle in Corfu (Kalvos 2014, 2:325). Nor is it known why he never wrote a single poem from then on.

Solomos

Solomos's family straddled the class boundaries of Ionian society. His father was a nobleman married to a woman from a similar background, while the poet's mother was one of the countess's housemaids; she was only fourteen years old at the time she gave birth, while the poet's father was sixty. The father was bilingual in Greek and Italian, while the mother knew only Greek. On his deathbed in 1807, some time after the countess's death, the count married the poet's mother, thus rendering him legitimate at the age of nine and enabling him to inherit a share of the family estates along with the Venetian title of count; for this reason, Solomos (unlike Kalvos) did not need to work for a living (Figure 40). The year after the marriage the young Solomos was sent to Italy, where he completed his school education in Venice and Cremona before studying law at the University of Pavia. By the time he returned to Zakynthos in 1818, his native island was part of the United States of the Ionian Islands.

Solomos began writing poems in Italian while he was in Italy and continued to do so after his return to Zakynthos. These early poems, the majority of which are sonnets, display a remarkable facility in poetic composition. Most of them were written as competitive exercises: a friend would propose the theme and the rhyming words, on the basis of which the poet had to compose an appropriate poem. The only collection of poems published by Solomos himself, consisting of thirty improvised Italian sonnets under the title *Rime improvvisate*

FIGURE 40   Unknown artist, *Posthumus Portrait of Dionysios Solomos*, ca. 1858. Benaki Museum, Athens.

(Improvised rhymes), appeared in 1822 while the Greek Revolution was already under way. All the poems included in the volume were on serious subjects, most of them religious. The volume was prefaced by a dedicatory letter from Solomos's friend Lodovico Strani to Ugo Foscolo, in which he assures the older poet that while Solomos still composes such Italian poems for the pleasure of his friends, he now devotes all his attention to the formation of the modern Greek language. Partly because of his lack of instruction in ancient Greek, Solomos hardly ever bothered to follow Greek spelling conventions; instead he wrote Greek phonetically. For him, in contrast to Kalvos, Greek was primarily an oral language.

Solomos had begun writing poems in Greek, by way of exercises in various meters and on various themes, well before the outbreak of the revolution. In late 1822 he was visited by Spyridon Trikoupis, a native of Mesolonghi, who the previous year had published a romantic love story set in his native town and imitating the language and fifteen-syllable verse of Greek folk song. According to his own account, Trikoupis took Solomos in hand and set about training him to become a Greek poet. We cannot be sure exactly how much Solomos owed to Trikoupis's mentoring, but he certainly carried out a program of reading Greek texts dating from the previous three hundred years in order to enrich his knowledge of the Greek language. Solomos displays views that are diametrically opposed to those of Kalvos when he writes, like a true romantic poet: "First subject yourself to the language of the people and, if you are capable, master it" (Solomos 1955, 20). And indeed, the language of Solomos's Greek poetry is fluid and fluent in comparison with the jagged-edged quality of Kalvos's diction. Nevertheless, Solomos felt more comfortable writing Italian than Greek: he would write the first drafts of his Greek poems in Italian prose. His Greek is sometimes slightly clumsy and often influenced by Italian, though less so than that of Kalvos, since he was living in the Greek-speaking world and was able to discuss drafts of his poems with his circle of devoted Greek friends.

The *Hymn to Liberty* was written in May 1823 and was published three times in quick succession. It first appeared as an appendix to the second volume of Fauriel's collection of Greek folk songs, which is dated 1825 but appeared in December 1824; there the *Hymn* was accompanied by a French prose translation by Stanislas Julien. Shortly afterward an unsatisfactory rendering of the *Hymn* in English verse, based on Julien's translation, appeared in a translation of Fauriel's collection by Charles Brinsley Sheridan, the son of the playwright Richard Brinsley Sheridan (Fauriel 1825). Later in 1825, the *Hymn* was first published in a volume of its own, at Mesolonghi, accompanied by a reliable Italian prose translation by Solomos's friend Gaetano Grassetti. These were the only publications of the *Hymn* during the Revolution.

The *Hymn to Liberty* consists of 158 stanzas that can be divided into seven parts. The introductory first part is followed by five sections evoking five episodes from the story of the Revolution so far, while in the concluding part Liberty addresses the Greek warriors. At the head of the poem Solomos placed an epigraph adapted from Dante, thus linking himself with Italy's greatest poet. The first words of this adapted quotation, "Libertà vo cantando" ("I go singing Liberty"), is a variation on Dante's phrase "Libertà va cercando" ("He goes seeking Liberty", *Purgatorio* I.71). The use of the first person singular in the epigraph is related to the first words of the poem itself, where the poet is the subject and Liberty the object of the verb. Later in the poem his declaration that "like Pindar I utter freedom-loving songs" brings him close to Kalvos.

The introduction (stanzas 1–15) begins with these two stanzas:

> I know you by the fearful
> blade of your sword.
> I know you by your glance
> that impetuously surveys the earth.
>
> Emerging from the sacred
> bones of the Greeks
> as valiant as before,
> hail, O hail, Liberty!

The second stanza is an allusion to the stanza addressing the "valiant bones of the Greeks" (meaning the ancient Greeks) that Solomos knew from the poem by Martelaos, who had borrowed it from the song that had been erroneously attributed to Rhigas by Byron. These borrowings reveal the genealogical lineage from Rhigas (or at least Rhigas's reputation) via Martelaos to Solomos.

One or other of these opening stanzas is repeated as a refrain between some sections to indicate the transition to the following episode; elsewhere one episode simply segues into the next. The second section relates the beginning of the uprising and the reactions of foreign powers (stanzas 17–34); the third evokes the capture of Tripolitsa by the Greek insurgents in September 1821. Solomos justifies the massacre of noncombatants at Tripolitsa at the hands of Greek insurgents by showing that the ghosts of those who had been unjustly killed by the Turks had removed pity from the warriors' hearts (stanzas 35–73). The fourth section relates the defeat of the Ottoman general Dramali at Dervenakia pass near Corinth in July 1822 but finishes with a vision of dancing maidens who will suckle free heroes—a riposte to Byron's "The Isles of Greece" (in *Don Juan*, Canto III, written in 1819–1820 but published in August 1821), where a fictional poet pessimistically predicts that Greek girls will suckle slaves (stanzas 75–86); and the fifth evokes the successful outcome of the first siege of Mesolonghi in November–December 1822, during which many of the Ottoman troops who had been repulsed by the Greeks were drowned in the nearby river Acheloos (stanzas 88–121). The depiction of the last phase of that episode leads the poet to pass on, in the sixth section, to a Greek victory at sea, namely the destruction of the Ottoman flagship by Kanaris's fireships off the island of Tenedos in October 1822 (stanzas 123–138). The poet presents such naval victories as acts of retaliation for the execution of Patriarch Grigorios V, whose body was thrown into the sea on Easter Sunday, 1821. Here Solomos adjusts the historical record by stating that the patriarch had cursed any able person who refused to fight, whereas in fact Grigorios had anathematized those who took up arms against the sultan. In the final section Liberty bids the poet be silent and warns the Greek warriors against the ultimate enemy: internal discord (stanzas 139–158).

The episodic structure of the *Hymn* gives the impression that Solomos is acting like a war correspondent, and indeed much of what he relates is based on reports he had read in the Greek and international press. However, the fact that the poet addresses Liberty throughout—except when he addresses Religion in the part of the Mesolonghi episode that takes place at Christmas—gives the poem a dramatic character. As in Kalvos's case, the use of exclamations, rhetorical questions, and first-person verbs such as "I see" and "I hear" reinforces the dramatic nature of the evocations, in which the poet presents himself as an eyewitness.

Like Kalvos's odes, Solomos's *Hymn* is replete with Christian symbolism. In the Mesolonghi episode, for instance, during which the Turks launch an attack on Christmas Day, Religion addresses Liberty, thus coopting her as a Christian figure. She goes on to address the people of Mesolonghi, who have brought redemption to the Greeks just as Christ had done to humankind. The poet compares the drowning of the Turks in the river Acheloos to the drowning of the Egyptians in the Red Sea: here Solomos finds the Old Testament to be a more powerful source of mythical allusion than ancient Greek culture might have been.

The *Hymn* is written in a meter that would have been equally familiar to Italian and Greek readers, in stanzas consisting of four Italian-style "octosyllables," which alternate between eight syllables in the first and third lines and seven syllables in the second and fourth. Within each stanza the lines of equal length rhyme with each other. Vincenzo Monti had used exactly the same meter (*ottonario*) and stanzaic pattern in his patriotic poem of 1801 "Bella Italia amate sponde" (Peri 1979, 19–20). The *Hymn* is also metrically identical to some of the stanzas in "Go, children of the Greeks," the difference being that Solomos employs more frequent rhyme.

After the English poet's death Solomos wrote a lyric poem "On the Death of Lord Byron." It is in the same meter as the *Hymn,* and it is presented as a sequel to it. It reads more fluently than the *Hymn* and in some respects it is a superior poem: Solomos is better at lamenting than exhorting.

In the first stanza the poet bids Liberty to put aside her sword for a while and come and weep over Byron's body. Unlike most of Solomos's poetry, the Byron ode includes abundant allusions to mythology and to English poetry: near the beginning, for instance, the poet depicts a "melodious goddess" bidding Byron sing, whereupon the English poet utters a song whose sublimity had not been heard since Milton. Coutelle (1977, 215) traces Solomos's inspiration here to Milton's *Paradise Lost,* book 7, which identifies the Muse as Urania, the patroness of astronomy. I should add that in all probability Solomos had access to English poetry only in Italian translation. Most of the poem is devoted to an evocation of Byron's arrival and activities in Greece: he had been lamenting the absence of Liberty from the greater part of the world until he suddenly saw her fly to Greece, where he decided to join her. Solomos links Byron both to the Souliot Markos Botsaris, who was buried at Mesolonghi shortly before the English poet's arrival there, and to "the Man of the Age," namely Napoleon. Byron finds Greece in thrall to the Fury Discord, and he berates the Greeks who are driving Liberty from her own homeland. Finally, the poet sees Byron being greeted in the Underworld by the shades of the Greeks who crowd around him to enquire about their country's fate. The poem ends with his reply: if Discord is defeated, their fame will live again.

Some time after Solomos had completed an almost definitive draft of the Byron ode in 1825, complete with Italian translation, he became deeply dissatisfied with it, seeing it as too much like a chronicle of events, with insufficiently organic links between the episodes. So he began radically revising it, altering some parts of the text and jettisoning others, until finally, after a number of years, he abandoned work on it.

Two shorter poems that Solomos worked on during the revolution give contrasting pictures of what he was capable of at that time. The first, "On Markos Botsaris" (1823–1824), is an unfinished poem in which the death and funeral of the Souliot hero are likened to those of Hector in the *Iliad.* The second, "The Destruction of Psara," was written the year after the massacre and scorched-earth policy carried out by the Ottomans on the island in June 1824 as a reprisal for the successes of Kanaris, who had been born there. The poem is written in the nine- and ten-syllable anapestic verse (with stresses on the third, sixth, and ninth syllables) known in Italy as the *manzoniano* (this is the meter used in Lorenzo da Ponte's aria "Non so più cosa son, cosa faccio," sung by Cherubino in Mozart's *The Marriage of Figaro;* I reproduce the meter only in the last line of my translation):

> On Psara's blackened ridge
> Glory walks alone
> pondering on the splendid heroes
> and wearing a garland woven
> from the few blades of grass
> that remain on the desolate earth.

Despite the neoclassical personification of Glory, the density of the imagery contained in this single sentence makes it read like a piece of vividly pictorial rhythmical prose, stripped of rhetoric and decorative adjectives.

The most important of Solomos's works inspired by the revolution were conceived in 1826, around the time that Mesolonghi fell to Ottoman and Egyptian forces at the end of its third and last siege (April 1825 to April 1826), and he continued to work on them for many years without ever completing them. Delivoria (2016) shows how Solomos kept abreast of developments at Mesolonghi both through the distressing yet inspiring diary of events appearing in the newspapers published in the besieged town and through the Zakynthos Committee that was set up to gather intelligence on the progress of the war and to provide aid to the warriors.

"The Woman of Zakynthos" is a powerful work of prose fiction whose narrator, a fictional Orthodox Christian monk, presents a portrait of an unnamed evil woman who seems to symbolize those Zakynthians (particularly members of the nobility) who refused to aid the revolution. Solomos began writing "The Woman of Zakynthos" in 1826 and made a fair copy of it in 1829. As with his poem on Lord Byron, however, he continued to revise his prose narrative in such a way as to undermine the original form of the work, until at last he abandoned it (Tiktopoulou in Solomos 2017, 143–144).

In one sequence of chapters, set during the siege of Mesolonghi, when widows and orphans from the besieged town go from door to door begging for food, the Woman dismisses them violently. In another chapter (entitled "Prophecy on the Fall of Mesolonghi"), the narrator is transported in a vision to Mesolonghi during the last days of its year-long siege. Amid the darkness and the flashes of cannon fire (Solomos records that the bombardment of Mesolonghi could be heard in Zakynthos) the narrator sees a woman dressed in black and carrying "the lyre of justice." This supernatural figure, symbolizing Greece and Liberty, sings some lyrical stanzas presenting brief vignettes of the daily life of the courageous besieged, who are close to starvation.

Solomos moved from Zakynthos to Corfu in 1828. For many years after the end of the revolutionary hostilities in 1829 he worked on an ambitious poetic composition about Mesolonghi, under the title "The Free Besieged," in an effort to encapsulate the supreme courage and self-sacrifice of the town's inhabitants and the other Greek warriors who had gathered there. For Solomos, the defenders of Mesolonghi embodied a saintly aspiration to transcend every physical and mental vicissitude in order to achieve spiritual freedom. In his view, the Greeks of his time had shown themselves to be so supremely valiant that they had no need to be compared to the ancient Greeks, and that the language in which they spoke and sang was appropriate for sublime poetry. He presents the defenders as being all of one mind, in contrast to the internal dissentions that often plagued the revolution. The poem was intended not to convey historical facts but to express what Solomos felt to be the profound moral and spiritual significance of the heroic thoughts and deeds of the Greeks during the final stages of the siege, when their food supplies had run out and it had become clear to them that—on a physical plane—they could no longer hold out. The composition consists of a patchwork of vividly pictorial episodes: the romantic Solomos seems to have conceived of poetic creation as an incessant process rather than as the production of discrete and finite poems.

Remarkably, it wasn't till about 1833 that he decided to abandon the use of various rather jaunty Italian lyric meters, with their short lines, their stanza form, and their abundant rhyme, which were more suitable for songs than for national poetry. At last he adopted the traditional fifteen-syllable line of the Greek folk song, which he raised to a peak of intensity with a combination of dramatic, epic, and lyric features. Only in the last recension of "The Free Besieged" (1844–1851) did he abandon rhyme, which Kalvos had shunned thirty years earlier.

The drafts of "The Free Besieged" consist of precious nuggets of pure poetic Greek gold that shine out from among the passages of Italian prose. Unlike Kalvos and the English romantics, Solomos doesn't express his own feelings of dejection and despondency, yet he often places soliloquies in the mouths of his anonymous characters. I quote just two lines from the last recension of the poem; the words are uttered in desperation by an elderly local fisherman who sums up the overwhelming odds facing the defenders, with Egyptian cavalry, French military expertise, Turkish bullets, and British heavy weaponry marshaled together against the fragile defenses of the small town:

Αραπιάς άτι, Γάλλου νους, βόλι Τουρκιάς, τόπ' Άγγλου!
Πέλαγο μέγα πολεμά, βαρεί το καλυβάκι!

Araby's horse, France's mind, Turkey's bullet, England's cannon!
A mighty ocean is fighting to strike the tiny shack.

The Afterlife of the Poetry of the Greek Revolution

For more than 150 years the first two stanzas of Solomos's *Hymn,* in a musical setting composed in 1829–1830 by the poet's Corfiot friend Nikolaos Mantzaros, have been sung as the national anthem of Greece. The royal decree establishing the *Hymn* as the national anthem was signed by King George on June 28 / July 10 1865. The fact that he signed the decree in Corfu rather than in Athens indicates his personal interest in establishing the *Hymn* as the national anthem to celebrate the recent cession of the Ionian islands by Britain to Greece as a gesture to mark the beginning of his reign. A century later, in 1966, the *Hymn* was also adopted as the national anthem of the Republic of Cyprus, which had become independent from Britain in 1960.

Solomos's "The Free Besieged" (published posthumously together with most of his other Greek works in 1859) kept alive the tragic story of the defiant heroism of the defenders of Mesolonghi. Yet the choice of his *Hymn* as national anthem provoked a reaction from certain intellectuals in Athens, who protested against the "vulgar" (i.e., colloquial) language in which it is written. Although it nonetheless remained the national anthem, Solomos's poetry, like that of Kalvos, was little appreciated in Athens until it was rehabilitated by the poet Kostis Palamas, who had (perhaps not coincidentally) been brought up in Mesolonghi. Palamas published enthusiastic articles about Kalvos and Solomos in the late 1880s, and some of the poetry he wrote during the following decade was inspired by their work. Since then their poems have been considered classics of modern Greek literature.

In school readers today, from the third year of primary school to the first year of upper high school, Greek children continue to be familiarized with the poetry of the revolution. Thus Kalvos and Solomos have achieved their aim of commemorating the heroic feats of the War of Independence—and memorializing themselves.

Peter Mackridge

References

Bouvier, Bertrand. 1972. "Calvos in Geneva." In *Modern Greek Writers,* edited by Edmund Keeley and Peter Bien, 68–91. Princeton, NJ.

Byron, George Gordon, Lord. 1812. *Childe Harold's Pilgrimage.* 2nd ed. London.

Coutelle, Louis. 1977. *Formation poétique de Solomos, 1815–1833.* Athens.

Delavigne, Casimir. 1824a. *Messénienne sur Lord Byron.* Paris.

Delavigne, Casimir. 1824b. *Trois messéniennes nouvelles.* Paris.

Delivoria, Maria. 2016. *Ο αγώνας του '21 και η υπονόμευσή του: οι σύγχρονες μαρτυρίες και η κρίση του Σολωμού* [The struggle of 1821 and its subversion: Contemporary evidence and Solomos's judgment]. Athens.

Fauriel, Claude, ed. 1824–1825. *Chants populaires de la Grèce moderne*. Paris.

Fauriel, Claude, ed. 1825. *The Songs of Greece, from the Romaic Text, Edited by M. C. Fauriel, with Additions*. Translated by Charles Brinsley Sheridan. London.

Foscolo, Ugo. 1954. *Epistolario*. Vol. 4. Florence.

Garantoudis, Evripidis. 1995. *Πολύτροπος αρμονία: μετρική και ποιητική του Κάλβου* [Multifarious harmony: Kalvos's metrics and poetics]. Iraklio.

Garantoudis, Evripidis. 2012. "Ο Κάλβος μεταξύ νεοκλασικισμού και ρομαντισμού" [Kalvos between neoclassicism and romanticism]. In *Τριαντάφυλλα και γιασεμιά: Τιμητικός τόμος για την Ελένη Πολίτου-Μαρμαρινού* [Roses and jasmine: Festschrift for Eleni Politou-Marmarinou], edited by Z. I. Siaflekis and Erasmia-Louisa Stavropoulou, 110–135. Athens.

Georganta, Athina. 2011. *Τα θαυμάσια νερά: Ανδρέας Κάλβος. Ο ρομαντισμός, ο βυρωνισμός και ο κόσμος των Καρμπονάρων* [Wonderful waters: Andreas Kalvos. Romanticism, Byronism, and the world of the Carbonari]. Athens.

Kalvos, Andreas. 1824. *Η Λύρα: Ωδαί Α. Κάλβου Ιωαννίδου του Ζακυνθίου* [title page] / *La Lyre: Odes en grec moderne. Par A. Calbo. Avec un vocabulaire à la fin* [cover]. Geneva.

Kalvos, Andreas. 1826. *Κάλβου και Χρηστοπούλου Λυρικά μετά γαλλικής μεταφράσεως / Odes nouvelles de Kalvos de Zante suivies d'un choix de poésies de Chrestopoulo, traduites par l'auteur des Helléniennes, P. de C.* Paris.

Kalvos, Andreas. 1998. *Odes*. Translated by George Dandoulakis. Beeston.

Kalvos, Andreas. 2014. *Αλληλογραφία* [Correspondence]. Edited by Dimitris Arvanitakis and Lefkios Zafeiriou. Athens.

Kalvos, Andreas. 2016. *Έργα. Τόμος Α΄: Ποιητικά. Μέρος πρώτο: δημοσιευμένα* [Works. Vol. 1: Poetry. Part one: published]. Edited by Luigi Trenti and Evripidis Garantoudis. Athens.

Meraklis, Michalis G., ed. 1965. *Ανδρέα Κάλβου, Ωδαί (1–20). Ερμηνευτική έκδοση* [Andreas Kalvos's Odes 1–20: Interpretive edition]. Athens.

Pappas, Spyros N. 2017. "Ο Ανδρέας Κάλβος, σπουδαστής και ηθοποιός στη Φλωρεντία (1814–1815)" [Andreas Kalvos, student and actor in Florence, 1814–1815]. *Nea Estia* 1874 (September): 676–720.

Pappas, Spyros N. 2019. "Anacreontica (1813). Ένα άγνωστο ποίημα του Ανδρέα Κάλβου" [Anacreontica (1813): An unknown poem by Andreas Kalvos]. *Athens Review of Books* 104 (March): 37–39.

Paschalis, Michail. 2013. *Ξαναδιαβάζοντας τον Κάλβο* [Rereading Kalvos]. Iraklio.

Peri, Massimo. 1979. *In margine della formazione poetica di Dionisio Solomos*. Padua.

Porfyris, Kostas. 1975. *Ο Α. Κάλβος Καρμπονάρος* [A. Kalvos a *carbonaro*]. Athens.

Solomos, Dionysios. 1955. *Άπαντα, τόμος δεύτερος: Πεζά και ιταλικά* [Complete works, vol. 2: Prose and Italian works]. Edited by Linos Politis. Athens.

Solomos, Dionysios. 1961. *Άπαντα, τόμος πρώτος: Ποιήματα* [Complete works, vol. 1: Poems]. Edited by Linos Politis. 2nd ed. Athens.

Solomos, Dionysios. 2015. *The Free Besieged and Other Poems.* Edited by Peter Mackridge. Translated by Peter Thompson, Peter Colacides, Michael Green, and David Ricks. Nottingham.

Solomos, Dionysios. 2017. *Η γυναίκα της Ζάκυθος* [The woman of Zakynthos]. Edited by Eleni Tsantsanoglou. Athens.

Trenti, Luigi. 2017. "I Soliloqui di Andrea Calbo (edizione e appunti di commento)." In *Kalvos e Solomòs: Studi e richerche,* edited by Christos Bintoudis, 41–52. Rome.

Tziovas, Dimitris. 1987. "Νεοκλασικές απηχήσεις και μετωνυμική δομή στις Ωδές του Κάλβου" [Neoclassical echoes and metonymic structure in Kalvos's Odes]. In *Μετά την αισθητική* [After aesthetics], edited by Dimitris Tziovas, 151–193. Athens.

Vagenas, Nasos. 1992. "Για μια νέα χρονολόγηση του *Ιππία*" [On a new dating of *Ippia*]. *Αντί* second period, no. 510 (December 18): 12–18.

Velestinlis, Rhigas. 2000. *Άπαντα τὰ σωζόμενα* [Complete surviving works]. Vol. 5. Edited by Paschalis M. Kitromilides. Athens.

Vitti, Mario. 1960. *A. Calvos e i suoi scritti in italiano.* Naples.

Woodhouse, Christopher M. 1995. *Rhigas Velestinlis: The Proto-Martyr of the Greek Revolution.* Limni.

Zanou, Konstantina. 2018. *Transnational Patriotism in the Mediterranean 1800–1850: Stammering the Nation.* Oxford.

VII

RESONANCES

Philhellenism

Between Souliote Chiefs—German Barons—English Volunteers—and
adventurers of all nations—we are likely to form as goodly an allied
army—as ever quarrelled beneath the same banner.

(Byron 1981, 108)

So wrote George Gordon, Lord Byron, on February 7, 1824, at Mesolonghi,
where he would soon become one of the many foreign volunteers, or Philhellenes, to succumb to disease in the service of the Greek Revolution. Many more
are commemorated in the Garden of Heroes that was established as early as
1829, to honor the memory of Greek and foreign victims of the conflict. Along
with monuments to individuals, including Byron himself, the former captain
in the British Royal Navy Frank Abney Hastings, and a single Finn (Gustaf
Adolf Sass, from Juttilan), others pay tribute to contingents of Germans, Americans, Italians, Poles, Frenchmen, Swedes, and Swiss who gave their lives in or
near Mesolonghi (Florou n.d.). The garden is well tended even today, despite
the financial crisis that has decimated Greek public services since 2010. It is a
tranquil spot, that invites reflection on the quirks of destiny that brought all
these named and many unnamed individuals from all over Europe and as far
away as the United States to give their lives in a cause that, on the face of it, was
not their own. In Nafplio, the provisional capital during much of the revolution, the names of some 270 volunteers who gave their lives are inscribed on
the columns of a memorial arch in the Roman Catholic Church, dedicated in
1841 (Barau 2009, 643–644; St Clair 2008, 352, fig. 35).

Byron himself, with rueful irony, characterized them as "adventurers." His
account highlights the many divisions within this motley group, divisions of

language, religion, customs, social class, and background, and also between the Philhellenes as a whole and the Hellenes (Greeks) whose cause they had come to serve. For most of these foreign volunteers, however, it was more than a thirst for adventure that had brought them there. Directly or indirectly, they were responding to a call that gone out in the very first days of the revolution. In a "Manifesto addressed to Europe by Petros Mavromichalis, Commander-in-Chief of the Spartan Troops, and the Messenian Senate, sitting at Kalamata," the Maniat leader, better known to history as Petrobey, announced that his countrymen had taken up arms against "the insupportable yoke of Ottoman tyranny." The peroration is worth quoting in full:

> We invoke therefore the aid of all the civilized nations of Europe, that we may the more promptly attain to the goal of a just and sacred enterprise, reconquer our rights, and regenerate our unfortunate people. Greece, our mother, was the lamp that illuminated you; on this ground she reckons on your active philanthropy. Arms, money, and counsel, are what she expects from you. We promise you her lively gratitude, which she will prove by deeds in more prosperous times. (Gordon 1832, 1:183)

Whoever was in reality the author of this text, it betrays a close familiarity with the rhetoric of the French Revolution of 1789 and the Revolutionary Wars of the 1790s, as well as with an idea that can be traced back to the writings of European travelers to the European provinces of the Ottoman Empire for at least half a century: namely that the present-day civilization of Europe owed a debt to the cultural achievements of ancient Greece. Now that the Greek subjects of the Ottomans had broken their bonds, it was time for that age-old debt to begin to be repaid.

It was to this and many similar calls emanating from the theaters of war, and from expatriate Greek communities all over Europe, that the volunteers responded. This was the first time that so many individuals from so many different countries and backgrounds had left their homes to fight in somebody else's war. They went neither as paid mercenaries nor in the service of their own governments. Indeed, especially in the first years, the authorities in their countries of origin took rigorous steps to prevent them from leaving, fearing what today would be called the spread of "radicalization." It has sometimes been suggested that these volunteers, and their far more numerous supporters back home, were the pioneers of the later phenomenon of humanitarian intervention (Bass 2008; Rodogno 2012). But the truth is, as the text of Petrobey's proclamation makes clear, they went to Greece to fight for something that they believed was their own, something in which they believed that their own societies and governments ought to have no less of a stake. And in due course, that conviction and its effects would prove to be the real, long-lasting significance of the movement that has ever since been known by the name "Philhellenism."

The first part of this essay focuses on those volunteers in the field, who they were and the campaigns they fought in. The second looks at the organizations back in their own countries that supported their efforts, as well as the wider movement of Philhellenism throughout Europe. The specific forms that Philhellenism took in the United States, and the contributions of American volunteers and organizations, are the subject of a separate essay, and will be touched on here only insofar as they relate to the European movement.

Volunteers in Action

The only way to reach revolutionary Greece from western Europe was by sea. The first ship to carry foreign volunteers sailed from the French port of Marseilles on July 18, 1821. This was the vessel that had been chartered by Alexandros Mavrokordatos to convey him and his immediate entourage to Mesolonghi. Aboard were some twenty-four French and Piedmontese officers and noncommissioned officers who had previously served under Napoleon and had since been demobilized. Among their number was Maxime Raybaud, who would go on to write extensively about his experiences (Raybaud 1824, 267–270). A month later the Scottish aristocrat Thomas Gordon of Cairness would follow the same route, starting out from Paris where he had recruited a small band of French officers to accompany him. Gordon's first expedition to Greece would be short-lived, and he was unusual in being one of the very few British volunteers at this early stage of the revolution. Later he would return to serve with distinction. But Gordon is principally remembered as the author of the first, and still one of the most authoritative, histories of the conflict (Gordon 1832).

These first contingents were very small. But during 1822 the tide of volunteers swelled, with no fewer than eight ships setting out from the same port for Greece, carrying in all some three hundred personnel (St Clair 2008, 66, 357). All, it seemed, wanted to fight. But, in contrast to later, more targeted expeditions, these contained only a minority of trained soldiers or officers. Volunteers in 1822 included merchants, students, cobblers, tailors, cart-repairers, butchers, doctors, clerks, and domestic servants (Barau 2009, 297–298). After 1822, by far the largest influx came in 1826, during the months when the future of revolution hung in the balance.

Throughout, and to some extent irrespective of their individual backgrounds or training, the role expected of the Philhellenes was to form the nucleus of a Western-style regular army, and later also navy. In most wartime contexts this might seem a self-evident priority, in which case the role of the volunteers might have proved pivotal on the battlefield. But this was not how it was in revolutionary Greece. The tactics introduced by the foreigners would prove controversial almost from the start in a war in which all the victories on the Greek side were being won by irregular guerrilla tactics. Not one of the military initiatives in which Philhellenes were predominantly involved would result in either a victory or even the establishment of a corps that would last for much longer than the immediate necessity that had brought it into being (Barau 2009, 580).

The first command of such an embryo "regiment" was assigned by Dimitrios Ypsilantis to a French former Bonapartist officer called Joseph Baleste, who had been living for some years in Crete. The Régiment Baleste, made up mainly of expatriate Greeks, seems never to have numbered more than three hundred. Command passed to the Piedmontese Colonel Pietro Tarella at the end of 1821. In May 1822 a "Battalion of Philhellenes" was formed to fight alongside it (Barau 2009, 553; St Clair 2008, 26–34, 90–94). These together made up the combined force that faced the western prong of the Ottoman counterattack in the battle of Peta, fought near the town of Arta on July 16, 1822. It was one of the very few pitched battles of the entire war, fought along relatively conventional lines. The result was the near annihilation of the regiment under Tarella and the battalion commanded by General Karl von Normann, an officer from Württemburg, whose reputation had been tarnished by an episode in his native land during the Napoleonic Wars (St Clair 2008, 74–75). The damage to the prestige and influence of the Philhellenes, and of the regular military tactics associated with them, was all the greater when the Ottoman offensive on the eastern side of the country was repulsed by guerrilla action at Dervenakia and the greater part of the Ottoman force destroyed, just ten days after the disaster of Peta.

By the end of 1822, the supply of ready volunteers from the west was drying up. After the departure of the largest contingent from Marseilles in November the French authorities closed the port to further expeditions. Already, most European governments were making it more difficult to enlist. A German legion, recruited from the Swiss cantons and some of the southwestern German states, was formed at Nafplio out of the last of these expeditions. But it never saw action and was disbanded by the summer of the following year. By this time, the total number of foreign volunteers who had arrived (the majority of them then either to die or to depart again) numbered around six hundred (St Clair 2008, 121–125).

The formation of the London Greek Committee at the end of February 1823 set in train a new initiative, which bypassed the French Mediterranean ports. Lord Byron and his small band of followers set out from the Italian port of

Genoa in July. Over the next two years, no fewer than ten shipments were dispatched from London for Greece, carrying few volunteers but significant support for the fragile provisional government in the form of military supplies and, latterly, money in the form of the famous (or infamous) loans of 1824 and 1825 (St Clair 2008, 358, and see further below). Byron's expedition included such colorful eccentrics as Leicester Stanhope and Edward John Trelawny, both of whom would write at length, and polemically, about their experiences (Stanhope 1825; Trelawny 2000). But none saw action while they were in Greece. The short-lived Byron Brigade at Mesolonghi, and the plans concerted by Mavrokordatos for an assault on the nearby fortress of Lepanto (Nafpaktos) in the first months of 1824, on the face of it fit well with the general pattern of philhellenic activity (Barau 2009, 580). But the campaign against Lepanto was never more than a sideshow. The real nature of Byron's contribution was different (Beaton 2013, xvi–xviii, 211–272).

The support given by Byron's personal influence and his personal gifts and loans of money to the provisional government, between November 1823 and his death on April 19, 1824, had two effects. One, little remarked by historians at the time or since, was the lifting of the Ottoman siege of Mesolonghi at the beginning of December 1823 (Beaton 2017, 254). The other was to ensure that the provisional government and "modernizing" leaders such as Mavrokordatos gained the upper hand in the civil conflict that tore revolutionary Greece apart during 1824. The consequence was to set the revolution on a course that would lead eventually to the creation of a Western-style nation-state (Beaton 2013, 265–267, 271–272). These outcomes, it should be said, were almost entirely the result of Byron's individual contribution and his strategic decision to work closely with Mavrokordatos. The London Greek Committee and other members of his expedition were either largely oblivious to the nature of the internal conflict in revolutionary Greece or chose, like Trelawny, to lend their support to the opposite side.

The final burst of philhellenic activity in the field reached its peak during the crisis years of 1825 and 1826. Already in the summer of 1825, while Ibrahim Pasha was ravaging the Peloponnese and for a time threatened even the provisional capital, Nafplio, the provisional government turned to the recently arrived French ex-Bonapartist Colonel Charles Fabvier in a desperate attempt to reconstitute the conventional military force that had been disbanded after the disaster at Peta (St Clair 2008, 249). Instead of trying to relieve the siege of Mesolonghi, which was still going on, the embryo corps led by Fabvier made a diversionary attack on Karystos, at the southern tip of Euboea in March 1826 and was heavily defeated. Fabvier and his corps would remain a significant presence on the scene in Greece until 1829. But their effectiveness would be largely annulled by quarrels with other French volunteers, rivalry with Fabvier's British counterparts, and ultimately his falling-out with Capodistrias (Barau 2009, 560–563, 649–650; St Clair 2008, 290–291, 318–322, 329, 349). Smaller expeditions of Italian volunteers, exiles based in London, also set out for Greece during 1825. Best known of the Italian volunteers was Count Santore di Santa Rosa, who had taken the same route at the end of 1824 and would lose his life in the failed attempt to dislodge the Egyptian fleet from Navarino Bay in May 1825 (St Clair 2008, 254, 256–257). Santa Rosa is commemorated by a monument on the shore of the island of Sphaktiria, near where he fell.

The fall of Mesolonghi on April 10, 1826, sent shockwaves round the world. The name of the town had been made famous by Byron's death there almost exactly two years before. Even while the siege had been tightening, during the first months of the year, more volunteers had been setting out from Europe—once again, in the new circumstances, permitted by the French authorities to sail from Marseilles, while others set out from London. A newly founded Paris Greek Committee dispatched several expeditions. The emergency brought back to Greece the Philhellene who in the estimation of the authoritative historian of the revolution, George Finlay, was "perhaps the only foreigner in whose character and deeds there were the elements of true glory" (Finlay 1861, 2:154). Captain Frank Abney Hastings had been a rising star in the British Royal Navy until an act of insubordination led to his dismissal in 1820. Like Byron, but unlike most of the volunteers who went to Greece, Hastings possessed a private fortune, some of which he donated to the cause. Along with Thomas Gordon, Hastings had been one of the very few early British volunteers. Temporarily based in France, he had joined up with one of the contingents sailing from Marseilles in 1822. As a naval man Hastings had a quick appreciation of the strategic significance represented by the armed merchantmen, principally based on the islands of Ydra, Spetses, and Psara, that had come close to gaining control of the Aegean and Ionian Seas in the first year of the war. While other Philhellenes directed their initiatives, or were deployed by others, to build regular land forces, Hastings made it his task to build a fighting navy for the embryonic Greek state.

A justly famous memo addressed to Lord Byron and eventually passed to the Greek committee in London, written as early as 1823, outlined Hastings's two revolutionary insights. These would have consequences for the entire future of naval warfare, more far-reaching than their immediate limited impact in Greece. The first was to adapt the new technology of steam to a fighting ship; the second, to use the boilers aboard to heat lead shot that could then be fired into an enemy vessel, with a good chance of setting it on fire, in those days when ships were built entirely of wood (cited in Finlay 1861, 2:385–389). After a great deal of difficulty, and thanks to financial support from the London Greek Committee, the world's first fighting steamship arrived at Nafplio, then the provisional Greek capital, on September 26, 1826, with Hastings in command (Abney-Hastings 2011, 135–136). Built at Deptford outside London, it had been named *Perseverance* under the pretense that it was destined for the coal trade. Now raising Greek colors, its name was translated into Greek, to become *Karteria* (Figure 41). Along with other initiatives taken in the United States, the *Karteria* from that time on became the backbone of a fledgling Greek navy and carried out operations off the Greek coasts until Hastings was killed in an action off Mesolonghi in May 1828 (Abney-Hastings 2011, 200–205). By that time, the war had entered on an entirely new phase, and the significance of the role of individual volunteers had been largely eclipsed by events elsewhere.

Back in 1826, the emergency was still acute. The future of the revolution hung in the balance. North of the Isthmus of Corinth, only the Acropolis of Athens remained in the hands of the insurgents after the fall of Mesolonghi. Most of the Peloponnese had been overrun by the Egyptian troops brought to Greece

FIGURE 41   Karl Krazeisen, *The Frigate "Hellas" and the Steamship "Karteria"* (Perseverance), 1827. Watercolor. National Gallery-Al. Soutzos Museum, Athens.

by Ibrahim. More by chance than thanks to any coordinated initiative, these darkest days for the revolution brought to Greece the final waves of military volunteers. As it happened, the most prominent individuals among them were not quite volunteers, in the sense that all their predecessors had been.

In December 1826, at the same time that the newly built frigate *Hellas* arrived from the United States to strengthen the embryonic Greek navy (see Ioannis Evrigenis, "American Philhellenism," in this volume), Colonel Carl Wilhelm Freiherr von Heideck arrived at the head of a dozen Bavarian officers aboard a ship from Ancona (St Clair 2008, 322–323, 359). Heideck's efforts to recruit and train a regular corps of Greek troops were no better received by the provisional government, and no more successful in their outcome, than those of several of his predecessors had been. But though small in number, and insignificant in terms of the one (unsuccessful) military action it undertook (Finlay 1861, 2:133; St Clair 2008, 325), Heideck's expedition was the first harbinger of things to come, which would wholly change the nature of Philhellenism and its impact on the course of events in the Greek Revolution. Heideck and the men under his command were the first to be sent by a foreign government. Far from having to evade the police in his own country, or to risk disapproval or even sanctions back home, Colonel Heideck was acting directly under the orders of his sovereign, King Ludwig I of Bavaria. As we will see more fully in the next section, Heideck's little more than token expedition would prove to be the tip of a much larger iceberg, whose full contours would only begin to emerge during the months and years that followed.

Hard on the heels of the Bavarian king's initiative, two of the most high-profile British military figures to take part in the revolution arrived, within a few days of each other, in March 1827 (Finlay 1861, 2:127; St Clair 2008, 326). Both men had distinguished, and unconventional, military careers behind them. Both, in contrast to most of their predecessors, were responding to desperate and direct appeals that had been addressed to them personally on behalf of the provisional government. In all other respects, they could not have been more different from one another. The same can be said of the motives that had brought them to Greece.

Sir Richard Church had taken part in the campaign in 1809 in which the British seized six of the seven Ionian islands from the French. He had remained there for several years, recruiting and training Greek troops in the islands. In this capacity he had first come to know Theodoros Kolokotronis, who remained a lifelong friend. After the end of the Napoleonic Wars, Church had seen service in the Kingdom of the Two Sicilies, defending the restored Bourbon regime against brigands and liberal-minded revolutionaries. It seems to have been his affinity with the land and the men he had formerly trained and fought alongside, rather than ideology, that aligned Church with the Greek cause—since politically his role had been the exact opposite in Italy (St Clair 2008, 319–321).

Thomas Cochrane, later Baron Cochrane of Dundonald, was in every sense a revolutionary. Dismissed from the Royal Navy, like Hastings, for insubordination, he had gone on to enlist in the service of no fewer than three revolutionary states in South America: Chile, Peru, and Brazil. Flamboyant, unconventional, and known for his winning streak, Cochrane had established a reputation that the provisional government of Greece determined to ally to their cause. Cochrane's role would be to build up a regular navy. He, too, espoused the new technology of steam, though his ambitious plan to arrive in Greece with six steamships came to nothing. Of all the Philhellenes, only Cochrane deserves to be termed a mercenary rather than a volunteer. It was only after much haggling that he agreed to accept financial terms from the provisional government—with the result that a significant portion of the second loan raised in London to aid the Greek cause ended up in the pocket of another Briton (St Clair 2008, 303–313).

It was the Third National Assembly, which had just been convened at a place in the northeastern Peloponnese then called Damala, now known by its ancient name of Troezen, that in April 1827 conferred high commands on these two individuals: Church as *archistrategos* or generalissimo of land forces, Cochrane as "arch-admiral." Shortly afterward, the same body decided to confer the highest office of state upon Count Ioannis Capodistrias. All of these decisions would play their part in redefining the nature of the revolution (Finlay 1861, 2:138–139). For all the fanfare and the high expectations, however, neither Church on land nor Cochrane by sea had any success in their attempts to break the Ottoman siege of the Acropolis of Athens, whose garrison was obliged to capitulate on May 24, 1827, after several costly operations. Cochrane remained in Greece until 1828; Church would make his home there after the revolution was over, living until 1873 (Woodhouse 1969, 158–159).

The story of Philhellenism as a form of military intervention is in marked contrast to the aura of fame that surrounds many individual names, such as Church or Byron. Despite the often colorful character of the volunteers, the stories of heroism and endurance that have been told many times in the intervening two hundred years, and the selflessness with which many of them dedicated themselves to the cause, their contribution on the ground was almost negligible. Their total number was probably no more than twelve hundred. Almost a third of those lost their lives, either in combat or from disease (St Clair 2008, 355–356). They won no significant victories. None of the attempts that they spearheaded to build up the regular armed forces necessary to establish and maintain a functioning modern state was successful during the revolution. The creation of a national army would have to wait for the arrival of the Bavarians in the 1830s. It was not on the battlefield that the most important contribution of the Philhellenes lies, but far behind the lines, in the countries from which the volunteers set out.

Philhellenism at Home

During the 1820s, philhellenic initiatives sprang up spontaneously in most parts of Europe. Activity took a wide variety of forms: setting up voluntary committees and fundraising, reporting and commentary in the press, reflections of philhellenic themes in the arts, even (latterly) large-scale fundraising for the cause and lobbying governments at home. In these cases it is impossible to quantify the scale of participation. But clearly it was of a magnitude that goes far beyond the limited numbers who went to Greece with the expectation that they would join in the struggle there. Denys Barau, in his magisterial study of the phenomenon, sets out to trace the lineaments of what he calls a "movement," and to situate it within the dynamic of post-Napoleonic societies as they were developing across Europe at the time. "To be a philhellene," as he puts it, "was to wish to participate in history in the making" (Barau 2009, 25, 713, the latter cited). There were many other ways to do this than to take up arms in Greece. And without those whom Barau terms the "Philhellenes of the home front," it would have been impossible for the volunteers even to have set out (Barau 2009, 321–396).

Of the many philhellenic committees and societies, some were short-lived, some only ever had a handful of members. But at some point between 1821 and 1828, a philhellenic committee was established and flourished in the capital cities of Great Britain, France, the Netherlands, Sweden, Denmark, Baden-Württemberg, Prussia, Bavaria, and Switzerland. Many smaller regional centers set up their own. Of the Swiss cantons, no fewer than half were home to a committee (Barau 2009, 39–40). The Austrian and Russian empires are conspicuous, but not unexpected, absences, given the degree of political control exercised over their subjects. Spain, where the constitutionalist revolution had been suppressed early in 1823, is another—though it is notable that some philhellenes from other countries gravitated toward the Greek cause by way of Spain (including the founders of the London Greek Committee, John Bowring and Edward Blaquiere). Members tended to belong to the national or regional elite, and to share broadly liberal-national political opinions.

The London Greek Committee, founded at the end of February 1823, began with twenty-five members. Most were members of Parliament who belonged to the radical wing of the Whigs (the predecessor of the later Liberal Party).

Within a month, that number had doubled. The final list runs to just over eighty (Dakin 1955, 42–44; Rosen 1992, 305–307). The equivalent committee in Paris, whose full name was Société Philanthropique en Faveur des Grecs, founded in 1825, seems to have reached a membership of a little over five hundred, among them François-René de Chateaubriand, the art collector and publisher Ambroise Firmin-Didot, the military generals Etienne Maurice Gérard and Horace Sébastiani, and the Swiss philanthropist from Geneva, Jean-Gabriel Eynard (Barau 2009, 44, 46–47).

Money raised by these societies through subscriptions was used to support individual volunteers making their way to Greece and often to charter the ships that would take them there. During Byron's time in Greece, the London committee raised sufficient funds of its own to equip the military expedition that included the "firemaster" William Parry (best known for his memoir of Byron's last days) and a quantity of artillery and explosives (Parry 1825; St Clair 2008, 158–159). Of the Paris committee, it has been said:

> It sent men, equipment, and money to Greece in quantities which had an important effect on the outcome of the war, and was undoubtedly the best organized and most effective of all the militant philhellenic movements to arise during the war. (St Clair 2008, 267)

Despite its name, we now know that funds raised by the Paris committee came not just from the metropolitan center but from every part of France, with almost every *département* represented (Barau 2009, 164–170).

In those countries where the press was relatively free, newspapers, periodicals, and hundreds of privately printed pamphlets became the vehicles for vigorous campaigns aimed at raising public consciousness and, whenever possible, lobbying governments on behalf of the Greek cause. Once again, there was little, if any, coordination among these initiatives—although there is evidence that prominent individuals and groups among Greek expatriates did what they could to direct and control the flow of information and opinion about affairs in Greece. From Pisa the exiled Orthodox bishop of Ungrowallachia, Ignatios, and his entourage were active in this field until Ignatios's death in 1828, as was Mavrokordatos for the few months in 1821 that he remained in Pisa before embarking for Greece (Beaton 2013, 72–79). Some modern accounts give prominence to the fact that much of what was reported about the Greek Revolution in the European press was wildly inaccurate (St Clair 2008, 24–25, and passim). In part this was due to the difficulty of communication in the circumstances of the time. Much was no doubt the product of wishful thinking, or in some cases downright fabrication. But more important for our purposes than the accuracy of what was reported or how justifiable the opinions is the enormous impact that all this activity had throughout those parts of Europe where newspapers enjoyed at least some element of freedom.

Atrocities, particularly those committed by the Ottomans, were widely reported and provoked often impassioned comment. This was particularly the case with the massacre and enslavement of the greater part of the population of Chios (known at the time in English as Scio) in May and June 1822. According to the London *Times,* in its leading article on August 2 in that year, "The most civilized, cultivated, and interesting people, the flower of Greece, have been, the greater part, exterminated" (cited in Bass 2008, 71). An analysis of coverage in the French press shows that the number of articles on Greece in daily newspapers and the influential *Revue encyclopédique* peaked at just this time, which also coincided with the greatest concentration of expeditions of volunteers setting out from Marseilles (Barau 2009, 157–158, see also 92–102). According to one French pamphlet published in 1825, the huge number of publications in favor of the Greek cause that had already circulated was itself a kind of guarantee of the truth of their content (Barau 2009, 213). However questionable the argument, there is no doubt that public opinion *was* influenced. And eventually, as we shall see, this influence would extend beyond the sphere of local committees, spontaneous volunteers, or mere feelings of sympathy among readers: the time would come when the concerted influence of philhellenic publications would reach into the heart of the political establishment in Britain and France. Even in Russia, where control of the press was much stricter, "scores of pamphlets, historical essays, and booklets were published in connection with the Greek rebellion," especially during and after the final siege of Mesolonghi in 1825–1826 (Frary 2015, 32–34).

The role of the press and the role of the philhellenic committees were inextricably bound together. This was quite explicit in the case of the London Greek Committee, whose members were well placed to ensure that letters expressing their opinions regularly appeared in the daily and periodical press, particularly in 1824 and 1825. As one of their members put it in an open letter published in 1823: "there is *one empire* which they can never hope to subdue—THE EMPIRE OF OPINION, whose throne is THE LIBERTY OF THE PRESS" (cited in Bass 2008, 83). The cause of Greece and the impact of the philhellenic movement in Europe themselves constitute a chapter in the story of the emancipation of the press and the rise of modern mass media.

In the arts, poetry, drama, opera, and painting were all deeply imbued with philhellenic feeling during the 1820s. Lord Byron, surely the most famous of all the Philhellenes and at the time probably also the most famous poet in all Europe, in fact never in his lifetime published a poem that unambiguously advocated the cause of Greek independence. Indeed, his sentiments on the subject were remarkably ambivalent up to, and some would say even beyond, the fateful decision that he took in the last year of his life that would take him to revolutionary Greece (Beaton 2013, 136–139). But others were far less reticent. *Hellas,* the long poem in dramatic form written by Byron's friend and younger contemporary Percy Bysshe Shelley in the autumn of 1821 and published shortly afterward, contains the brief polemical preface in which the poet famously declared, "We are all Greeks." Shelley castigated what he termed

> The apathy of the rulers of the civilised world to the astonishing circum-stances of the descendants of that nation to which they owe their civilisa-tion, rising as it were from the ashes of their ruin. (Shelley 1943, 447)

Shelley, in the same preface, was also one of the first to build on the idea, that had first begun to circulate in Europe in the last decades of the previous century, that modern European civilization as a whole owed an immense debt to Greece. Now, according to Shelley, writing in Pisa in 1821, was the time to begin repaying that debt, while to the north of the Alps the exact same idea was being articulated in German by Friedrich Wilhelm Thiersch (Beaton 2019, 31, 113; Güthenke 2008, 100; on English philhellenic literature during the 1820s, Roessel 2002, 72–97).

In France, the rollcall of famous names who dedicated poems to the Greek cause is impressive: Alfred de Vigny, Victor Hugo, Alexandre Dumas, Jules Barbey d'Aurevilly, even the young Gérard de Nerval and the ever-popular songwriter Pierre-Jean de Béranger. Altogether more than 180 poems or collections with philhellenic content were published in France during the 1820s, many of them in the provinces (Barau 2009, 106–107). At the same time, a pioneer of the emerging discipline of folklore and the later science of social anthropology, Claude Fauriel, drew on an extensive network of expatriate Greek correspondents in different parts of Europe, to compile the two-volume *Chants populaires de la Grèce moderne,* which appeared in 1824 and 1825 and was soon translated into English and German (Fauriel 1824–1825, 1825a, 1825b). In a lengthy introduction, Fauriel painted a heroic picture of the lives and careers of the mountain brigands known as klephts, who since 1821 had become the backbone of the successful guerrilla operations that had driven the Ottomans out of most of southern Greece. Readers of Fauriel's collection of folksongs were encouraged to see in the modern klephts a revival of fighting spirit of the Greeks of old (Barau 2009, 382–394; Fauriel 1824–1825, 1:liv–lxv; Ibrovac 1966). Quite apart from its propaganda value, and the high quality of the production, with texts provided in the original Greek and an accompanying French translation,

Fauriel's *Chants populaires* would establish a benchmark for the collection and study of the modern Greek oral tradition, and also indirectly establish the folksong as one of the categories considered the most "authentic" in the definition of the modern Greek national character, both at home and abroad.

The German states and the German language had been home to the original, prerevolutionary concept of *Philhellenismus,* by which was meant a veneration for the *classical* Greek past, and especially its literature and sculpture (Güthenke 2008, 11–13; Marchand 1996, xvii–xix). This had already inspired writers such as Friedrich Hölderlin, who never visited the Greek lands, but whose novel *Hyperion,* published in two volumes in 1797 and 1799, has been described as "the Greek landscape of the German soul" (Güthenke 2008, 71–92). The revolution of 1821 brought a new topicality and an element of revolutionary fervor to bear, particularly, as elsewhere in Europe, in the publication of pamphlets (Güthenke 2008, 97–101; Marchand 1996, 32–3).

In German poetry the leading proponent of the new politicized Philhellenism was Wilhelm Müller. Best known today as the poet of lyrics set to music by Schubert, Müller never visited Greece either. But between 1821 and his death in 1827 he published a series of fifty-two poems in six slim volumes, known collectively as *Lieder der Griechen* (Songs of the Greeks). This was what today we would call "engaged," or political, poetry. Many of the songs draw the expected parallels between the great battles of antiquity, such as Thermopylae, and the struggle going on at the time in Greece. Close to the spirit of folksongs themselves, Müller's original compositions seek to promote an idea of the untutored spirit of the Greek *Volk* (people), in just the same way that the movement for *German* national unification had been doing, in seeking the roots of German national identity in folklore (Güthenke 2008, 116–139). Once Fauriel's collection of real Greek folksongs had been published in Paris, it was none other than Müller who promptly translated it into German (Güthenke 2008, 114–117).

The other arts were not to be left behind. Inspired by the massacres of Chios, Eugène Delacroix created a canvas that stands more than twelve feet high. Its full title is *Scenes of Massacres of Chios: Greek Families Awaiting Death or Slavery* (Plate 17). First exhibited in 1824, and now hanging in the Louvre, the work captures on an epic scale the sense of horror that had swept through the continent as news of the events was disseminated. No less celebrated, at the time and ever since, is the same painter's *Greece on the Ruins of Mesolonghi,* created in the immediate aftermath of the fall of the town in April 1826 (Plate 18). It depicts Greece personified as a beautiful young girl in traditional peasant costume amid a scene of utter destruction. These paintings would later provoke the horrified admiration of the poet Charles Baudelaire, among others, who declared that they "bear witness against the eternal and incorrigible barbarity of man."

Delacroix was fascinated by the exoticism of his subjects and clearly touched the hearts of his contemporaries who viewed them in France. But it has been questioned whether he can truly be called a Philhellene (Barau 2009, 349–352).

In music, the same event (the fall of Mesolonghi) prompted Rossini to adapt an earlier Italian work for the Paris Opéra. *The Siege of Corinth* had its premiere in October 1826, just six months afterward. Although its libretto is set at the time of the conquest of Greece by Mehmed II in the fifteenth century, the topical allusion was clearly not lost on audiences. The title was probably chosen because it was also the title of a poem by Byron—though the stories told in the two works are quite different and Byron's tale had been written in 1815, long before anyone thought a revolution in Greece was remotely likely.

In states ruled by authoritarian governments, notably Austria and Russia at this time, there was little prospect for such public manifestations of support for the Greek cause. It has been suggested that Beethoven's Ninth Symphony, first performed in Vienna on May 7, 1824, just a few weeks after the death of Byron at Mesolonghi, was inspired in part by sympathy for the revolution that was going on in Greece (Barau 2009, 151; Sachs 2010, 79–87). In Russia, the "national poet," Alexander Pushkin (1799–1837), celebrated the preparations by Alexandros Ypsilantis for his campaign in the Danubian Principalities with enthusiasm in the poem "War," though the poet's confident prediction of victory would soon be overturned by events (Farsolas 1991, 63–65; cf. Bass 2008, 56). In the early years of the revolution Pushkin "wrote a considerable number of letters, poems, notes, and stories inspired by or dedicated to the Greek revolt" (Farsolas 1991, 67; Prousis 1994, 135–158). Though he subsequently went on to express something of the profound disillusion with the cause that affected many volunteers in the field, Pushkin would return to the subject to celebrate the final achievement of Greek independence in verse.

Of all the activities undertaken by Philhellenes on the home front, whether by individuals, committees, or societies, the one that would make the greatest impact during the revolution, and indeed would leave a lasting legacy ever afterward, was financial. Europeans—and Americans too—were exceptionally generous with their money during the Greek Revolution. At the simplest and most local level, this took the form of modest subscriptions for membership of a society or committee, or to support a publication. Contributions of this sort seem to have come from every part of the continent where such organizations were permitted to flourish.

At the opposite end of the scale, the Swiss banker and philanthropist Jean-Gabriel Eynard, a leading member of the Paris committee, donated significant sums to shore up the tottering Greek armed forces during the crisis years of 1826 and 1827 (Figure 42). Eynard and the committee, between them, also dis-

FIGURE 42   David d'Angers, *Portrait of Jean Gabriel Eynard*, 1830.
Medallion in bronze. Inscribed *Jean Gabriel Eynard L'ami des
Grecs. David 1830.* Benaki Museum, Athens.

patched seventeen shiploads of provisions to relieve famine in the Peloponnese
(Barau 2009, 63–65, 394–396; St Clair 2008, 286, 334–335). Other prominent figures who donated funds were the Duke of Orléans in France (the future King
Louis-Philippe) and King Ludwig I of Bavaria. It has been stressed that at the
time these benefactors were acting as individuals, not as representatives of their
respective governments (Barau 2009, 244, 326). But in the case of Ludwig of
Bavaria, when the donor exercises monarchical rule over the only state in the
world that during the 1820s could be described as truly philhellenic, it is hard
to draw the line between individual commitment and the beginning of official
state aid to the Greek cause—which during the final years of the revolution
would effectively replace the philhellenic movement.

During the middle years of the decade, funding from abroad on a much larger
scale took the form of loans. This time the initiative belonged to the provisional
government of Greece. But Philhellenes abroad were central to the realization
of these plans—and far from innocent of the scandals that would result. As early
as the spring of 1823, the provisional government recognized the potential value
of cash from abroad and began to draw up plans to raise huge loans. The future
agricultural potential of lands liberated from the Ottomans was offered as

security. Several rival schemes were mooted. In the end, two loans were secured, both of them raised in London and both of them with central involvement by the London Greek Committee. In April, the sum of £800,000 was
pledged. A second, even larger, loan was floated in February 1825, and was
quickly oversubscribed, to a nominal value of two million pounds sterling.
These were not philanthropic gifts, though there were many in Greece who
thought that the issue of repayment could safely be ignored, on the grounds
that the Europeans were only now starting to repay their enormous *cultural*
debt from antiquity (Finlay 1861, 2:26; Levandis 1944, 15). Investors were motivated by promises of profit. Banks and intermediaries (including the secretary
of the London Greek Committee, John Bowring) made huge gains immediately by discounting the stock and other dubious means. Of the £800,000
pledged by the first loan, just under half reached Greece; the second was reduced, by sharp practice in London, to a mere £566,000—little more than a
quarter of the amount nominally pledged (Brewer 2001, 223, 289–290; St Clair
2008, 209–223).

Historians, from Finlay onward, have lamented the ways in which the cash
received by the provisional government was squandered, particularly in 1824
when most of it went to pay for the government's internecine war against the
warlords on its own side. But it has more recently been argued that the outcome of that internal conflict would in the long run determine the outcome of
the entire revolution (Pizanias 2011, 64). And the future debt that would hang
over successive Greek governments would be out of all proportion to the amount
actually received. That first tranche of Greek national debt would not be settled until 1878 (Levandis 1944, 27–28; cf. Finlay 1861, 2:38–44). The legacy of
indebtedness to foreign investors and governments, which would become a
constant theme throughout the history of the Greek state, down to the financial crisis of 2010–2018, began with the first international loan brokered by the
London Greek Committee in the spring of 1824.

That said, it is important in principle to separate the movement of Philhellenism from the involvement of foreign *governments* that would play such a
decisive part in the eventual outcome of the revolution. The marginal case of
Bavaria under King Ludwig I deserves more consideration than it has been
given in the literature on the subject. Bavaria was to all intents and purposes
a philhellenic state during the 1820s—as witness many of the public buildings erected then and later in its capital, Munich, and elsewhere. From a
strategic or military point of view, landlocked Bavaria could never have been
a significant player in the conflict. Indeed, it was for precisely that reason
that, when the time came for the great powers to appoint a monarch for independent Greece, in 1832, it was to Ludwig that they applied. The result was

that the underage Otto, second in line to the Bavarian throne, became the first king of Greece. During the following decade, Philhellenism, as it had flourished in Bavaria over the previous decades, would go on to play a defining role in establishing the institutions of the new Greek state. In this context, Ludwig's personal gifts of money in 1825 and 1826, and the tiny uniformed contingent he sent to the Peloponnese under the command of Colonel von Heideck, assume an importance far beyond their actual impact at that time.

Once the great powers had established the London Conference in 1826, and still more after the decisive battle of Navarino on October 20, 1827 (on which see Robert Holland, "Navarino," in this volume), the whole course of the revolution changed. No longer would the fate of Greece be determined by military action on the ground, but in the capitals of Europe and on battlefields in the Danubian Principalities and the Caucasus, where the latest in a series of wars between the Russian and Ottoman empires was fought in 1828 and 1829. In Greece, military figures who entered the conflict under the orders of their own governments, and wearing the uniforms of those countries' armed services, have ever since been commemorated as Philhellenes. Such is the case of Edward Codrington, the British admiral in command of the combined fleet at Navarino, or General Nicolas Maison, whose French force was entrusted with subduing the last remnants of Ottoman forces in the Peloponnese afterward (Barau 2009, 548–549, 650). It is in this context, too, that the claim has been made that Russia did more militarily than any other country to help the Greeks win their independence (Frary 2015, 44, 53).

But the role of these individuals and the forces in which they were enrolled was in fact quite different from that of the Philhellenes. For all the decisive importance of these military interventions, the commanders and the men who fought under them were not volunteers, as the Philhellenes had been. They did not fight under the banner of the provisional government of Greece, but of the armed forces of their own nations. Their personal sentiments, however well disposed toward the Greeks, were in that sense strictly irrelevant.

This is not the place to explore the complex series of events that brought about the shift in the attitude of the great powers to the conflict, except insofar as the actions of the Philhellenes paved the way for it and made it possible, if not inevitable. This, in hindsight, must be seen as the greatest of all the contributions of the movement of Philhellenism to the successful outcome of the Greek Revolution.

The volunteers who went to Greece were the spearhead of a far larger and more deeply rooted movement that spread throughout most of Europe and the United

States (see Ioannis Evrigenis, "American Philhellenism," in this volume) during the 1820s. It was that movement that established societies and committees throughout Europe. These proved effective in mobilizing public opinion through the press (in those countries where this was permitted) and through pamphlets financed by subscription, and consciousness-raising through the arts. The real significance of the volunteers lies not in the little or nothing that they achieved in the field, but in the propaganda value of the fact that they were there at all. High-profile acts of apparent self-sacrifice, such as the death of Byron, fueled the movement of sympathy back at home and added momentum to the pressure groups that were acting on other, less glamorous, fronts in their own countries.

Philhellenic committees and societies were at their most effective and influential when it came to channeling financial donations and raising speculative loans on behalf of the provisional government of Greece. The influx of funds and high-profile volunteers undoubtedly helped the Greeks to survive in the field during the most crucial period of the revolution, between 1825 and 1827. It was during the same period that the governments of Great Britain, France, and Russia were finally persuaded to take a hand in the conflict. Whether this could have happened without the strength of the philhellenic movement at home must be very doubtful. It was therefore individual Philhellenes, and Philhellenism as a movement, that opened the door to the *internationalization* of the Greek Revolution—with the twin consequences that the Greeks would win their battle for freedom, and that independent Greece would become established along the lines of the *nation*-state with which we are familiar throughout Europe and the world today.

Roderick Beaton

References

Abney-Hastings, Maurice. 2011. *Commander of the Karteria: Honoured in Greece, Unknown at Home*. Bloomington, IN.

Barau, Denys. 2009. *La cause des Grecs, une histoire du mouvement philhellène (1821–1829)*. Paris.

Bass, Garry. 2008. *Freedom's Battle: The Origins of Humanitarian Intervention*. New York.

Beaton, Roderick. 2013. *Byron's War: Romantic Rebellion, Greek Revolution*. Cambridge.

Beaton, Roderick. 2017. "Byron and Greece: Lessons in 'Political Economy.'" In *Byron: The Poetry of Politics and the Politics of Poetry*, edited by Roderick Beaton and Christine Kenyon Jones, 249–260. Abingdon.

Beaton, Roderick. 2019. *Greece: Biography of a Modern Nation*. London.

Brewer, David. 2001. *The Flame of Freedom: The Greek War of Independence, 1821–1833*. London.

Byron, George Gordon, Lord. 1981. *'For Freedom's Battle': Byron's Letters and Journals.* Vol. 11, *1823–1824,* edited by Leslie Marchand. London.

Dakin, Douglas. 1955. *British and American Philhellenes during the War of Greek Independence, 1821–1833.* Thessaloniki.

Droulia, Loukia. 2017. *Philhellénisme. Ouvrages inspirés par la guerre de l' indépendance grecque 1821–1833. Répertoire bibliographique.* Second ed. Edited by Alexandra Sfoini. Athens.

Farsolas, James. 1971. "Alexander Pushkin: His Attitude toward the Greek Revolution." *Balkan Studies* 12, no. 1: 57–80.

Fauriel, Claude, ed. 1824–1825. *Chants populaires de la Grèce moderne.* Paris.

Fauriel, Claude, ed. 1825a. *Neugriechische Volkslieder. Gesammelt und herausgegeben von C. Fauriel. Übersetzt . . . von Wilhelm Müller . . . , Τραγούδια ρωμαϊκά,* trans. Wilhelm Müller. Leipzig.

Fauriel, Claude, ed. 1825b. *The Songs of Greece, from the Romaic Text, Edited by M. C. Fauriel, with Additions.* Translated by Charles Brinsley Sheridan. London.

Finlay, George. 1861. *History of the Greek Revolution.* 2 vols. Edinburgh and London.

Florou, Rodanthy-Rosa. n.d. *Guide to the Monuments of the Heroes Garden of the Sacred Town of Mesolonghi.* Mesolonghi.

Frary, Lucien. 2015. *Russia and the Making of Modern Greek Identity, 1821–1844.* Oxford.

Gordon, Thomas. 1832. *History of the Greek Revolution.* 2 vols. Edinburgh.

Güthenke, Constanze. 2008. *Placing Modern Greece: The Dynamics of Romantic Hellenism, 1770–1840.* Oxford.

Ibrovac, Miodrag. 1966. *Claude Fauriel et la fortune européenne des poésies populaires grecques et serbes.* Paris.

Levandis, John A. 1944. *The Greek Foreign Debt and the Great Powers, 1821–1898.* New York.

Marchand, Suzanne. 1996. *Down from Olympus: Archaeology and Philhellenism in Germany, 1750–1970.* Princeton, NJ.

Parry, William. 1825. *The Last Days of Lord Byron.* London.

Pizanias, Petros, ed. 2011. *The Greek Revolution of 1821: A European Event.* Istanbul.

Prousis, Theophilus C. 1994. *Russian Society and the Greek Revolution.* DeKalb, Illinois.

Raybaud, Maxime. 1824. *Mémoires sur la Grèce.* Paris.

Rodogno, Davide. 2012. *Against Massacre: Humanitarian Intervention in the Ottoman Empire, 1815–1914. The Emergence of a European Concept and International Practice.* Princeton, NJ.

Roessel, David. 2002. *In Byron's Shadow: Modern Greece in the English and American Imagination.* Oxford.

Rosen, Frederick. 1992. *Bentham, Byron, and Greece: Constitutionalism, Nationalism and Early Liberal Political Thought.* Oxford.

Sachs, Harvey. 2010. *The Ninth: Beethoven and the World in 1824.* London.

Shelley, Percy Bysshe. 1943. *The Complete Poetical Works.* Edited by Thomas Hutchinson. London.

St Clair, William. (1972) 2008. *That Greece Might Still Be Free: The Philhellenes in the War of Independence.* Introduction by Roderick Beaton. Cambridge.

Stanhope, Leicester. 1825. *Greece in 1823 and 1824: Being a Series of Letters, and Other Documents on the Greek Revolution, Written during a Visit to That Country.* London.

Trelawny, Edward John. (1878) 2000. *Records of Shelley, Byron, and the Author.* Introduction by Anne Barton. New York.

Woodhouse, Christopher Montague. 1969. *The Philhellenes.* London.

American Philhellenism

Soon after the outbreak of the Revolution, on May 25, 1821, the Messenian Senate of Kalamata addressed an appeal to the people of the United States of America as that nation "above all the nations which have gained a name for liberty and laws," asking for their help in banishing "ignorance and barbarism from the country of freedom and the arts." The address, which was signed by Petrobey Mavromichalis, was brought to Paris, whence it made its way to the United States through two notable channels. First, on July 26, 1821, Adamantios Korais sent it to Edward Everett, a young American scholar whom he had met in Paris in 1817. Then, on September 15, 1821, Albert Gallatin, American minister to France, forwarded it to John Quincy Adams, the US secretary of state. Although Gallatin did not comment on the appeal and Adams was opposed to US involvement in the conflict, Korais urged Everett to transmit his zeal for Greece to his fellow countrymen and Everett appears to have obliged. By November 1821, the Messenian proclamation had been reprinted in newspapers all over the United States, with evidence pointing to Everett as the source.

Born in 1794, Everett received bachelor's and master's degrees from Harvard University and became minister at Boston's Brattle Street church. Everett had shown an early interest in Greece, having published an article on the modern Greek language in 1813 and delivered an oration entitled "On the Restoration of Greece," during his graduation in 1814. In 1815, Samuel Eliot established a professorship in Greek literature at Harvard in memory of his son, Charles, which Everett agreed to assume on the condition that he be allowed to travel to Europe first. During the next four years, he studied at Göttingen, becoming the first American to receive a PhD, and spent some time in Paris, where in addition to meeting with Korais several times he also learned modern Greek. Before returning to the United States in 1819, Everett also visited Greece.

In November 1821, George Jarvis, the European-born son of an American diplomat, left his home near Hamburg to join the Greek struggle. Jarvis arrived in Greece in 1822 and not long thereafter—with the permission of Mavrokordatos—joined other foreign volunteers and began service that would see him continuously in battle until 1826. On his very first assignment, Jarvis sailed on the *Themistocles* to Chios, where he arrived right after the massacres. His record of the aftermath may be the earliest (Arnakis 1965, 35–78). Jarvis taught himself Greek, assumed Greek dress, and came to be known as Capetan Zervos. His distinguished service on the battlefield, on land and sea, earned him the rank of lieutenant-general. Jarvis was the first of a small number of Americans who enlisted and played an active role in military operations. He fought at Palaiokastro and was imprisoned by Ibrahim Pasha, before joining Kolokotronis and Karaiskakis.

News from Greece traveled slowly to the United States in 1822, mainly in the form of reprinted stories from European newspapers and journals. By 1823, however, the press was already speaking of a "Greek fever" having spread across the United States. In July of that year, Korais began a correspondence with Thomas Jefferson, whom he had met in Paris, asking for his help and advice. In October, in what began as a review of Korais's edition of Aristotle's *Nicomachean Ethics* for the *North American Review,* of which he was editor, Everett gave an account of the state of affairs in Greece and argued for the significance of the Greek struggle for European politics. Wary of the danger of relying too much on Greece's past and eager to combat widespread caricatures of modern Greeks that emanated from travelers' impressions, Everett used Korais's learning and his decision to aid the rebirth of his nation through education as examples of a people with robust spirit and culture that had to be aided in its quest for freedom. Noting that the Provisional Constitution of Epidavros had been published in Europe but not in the United States, Everett included a translation of it in his review, in its entirety. Everett also included the proclamation of the Messenian Senate, in Greek and English, as well as the letter from Korais that had accompanied it. For Everett, taken together, Korais's Aristotle, the Hellenic Library of which it was part, and the documents from Greece made a powerful case for continuity between the country's past and present. As Everett put it, "[w]e see nothing but an enterprising, intelligent, [C]hristian population struggling against a ghastly despotism, that has so long oppressed and wasted the land; and if an animating word of ours could cheer them in the hard conflict, we should feel that not to speak it, were to partake the guilt of their oppressors" ([Everett] 1823: 418). Beyond that, Everett issued an appeal to private individuals to emulate their counterparts across Europe who both went to Greece to serve and collected funds for the struggle. New York, Philadelphia, and Washington, DC, heeded the call by forming committees, and less than two months later, on December 19, Everett and Thomas Winthrop founded the Boston Committee for the Relief of the Greeks, which became one of the main sources of American aid during the revolution. The most notable sign of American interest in the Greek cause came in President James Monroe's annual Address to Congress, on December 2, 1823. In that speech, which has become famous as the encapsulation of the "Monroe doctrine," the president of the United States repeated the hope that he had expressed in his speech the year before that the Greeks "would succeed in their contest, and resume their equal station among the nations of the earth."

Just before Monroe's speech to Congress, Daniel Webster, who had recently been elected to represent Massachusetts in Congress, wrote to Everett asking for information about Greece. A few days after Monroe's speech, on December 8, 1823, Webster introduced a resolution before Congress that read: "*Resolved,* That provision ought to be made by law for defraying the expense incident to the appointment of an agent, or Commissioner, to Greece, whenever the President shall deem it expedient to make such appointment" (*Annals of the Congress of the United States,* 1083–1084). When the House reconvened on January 2, 1824, Robert Hayne, senator from South Carolina, conveyed resolutions passed by the House and senate of his state, according to which "the State of South Carolina regards with deep interest the noble and patriotic struggle of the modern Greeks to rescue from the foot of the infidel and the barbarian the hallowed land of Leonidas and Socrates; and would hail with pleasure the recognition, by the American Government, of the independence of Greece." On January 19, Webster's resolution became the subject of vigorous debate that lasted more than one week. In his opening remarks, Webster made a powerful case for sending a signal of support to the struggling Greeks. Webster's address followed the same contours as Everett's appeal, noting that he was not moved by the need to repay the debt that the world owed to ancient Greece, but by the urgency of a struggle for freedom of a Christian people that had recently suffered the destruction of "Scio" (Chios), "a scene I will not attempt to describe—from which human nature shrinks shuddering away; a scene, thank God without parallel in all the history of fallen man" (*Annals of the Congress of the United States,* 1095). Dismissing the fears of those who wished no argument with the Porte, Webster noted that in approving his resolution Congress would merely be catching up with the nation. Fearing that Webster's resolution went too far, Joel R. Poinsett of South Carolina rose to propose a substitute that read, "*Resolved,* That this House view with deep interest, the heroic struggle of the Greeks to elevate themselves to the rank of a free and independent nation; and unite with the President in the sentiments he has expressed in their favor; in sympathy for their sufferings, in interest in their welfare, and in ardent wishes for their success" (*Annals of the Congress of the United States*, 1111). Even this resolution, however, failed to persuade those who feared interference in European affairs. While opposing official US involvement, George Cary of Georgia nevertheless encouraged private assistance. John Randolph of Virginia pointed to George Washington's advice to refrain from political entanglements with other nations, while Ichabod Bartlett of New Hampshire argued that the resolution served no purpose in expressing interest but carried dire consequences by embroiling the US in European affairs. Henry Clay of Kentucky pointed to President Monroe's repeated statements of encouragement, which were met with "universal applause" and pledged his support for Webster, but acknowledged that that support was feeble. In the absence of broader backing, the resolution was not put to a vote. Yet, the debate on the "Greek cause" crystallized the widespread sense that even those who opposed US involvement abroad had expressed their personal affection for Greek culture and history, and their belief in the justice of the Greek struggle.

Webster's sense that the American people were ahead of Congress is corroborated by the evidence of a flurry of fundraising and organizing activity in churches, colleges and universities, private and learned societies, and by various formal and informal committees of solidarity. In 1824, governors and state legislatures issued proclamations and resolutions of support for the Greeks, while grass-roots organizations raised funds and collected clothing and other items that could be sent to Greece. In 1824, it was not uncommon to find in American newspapers both advertisements for Lord Byron's works and news of his exploits in Greece. News of Byron's death, published in American newspapers in the early summer of 1824, added fuel to the "Greek fire."

In the summer of 1824, Samuel Gridley Howe, a young doctor from Boston, resolved to emulate Byron by going to Greece to offer his services (Figure 43). Armed with a letter of introduction from Edward Everett, Howe arrived at Monemvasia in the winter and, by March 1825, when he wrote his first letter home, he had already seen action in battle and begun a long service as surgeon that would eventually earn him the rank of surgeon-general of the Greek fleet and director of army hospitals in Nafplio. In that letter, Howe reported having run into Jarvis, Captain Jonathan Miller—a veteran of the War of 1812—and other American and English volunteers, but he also noted his astonishment at the fact that more "young men of fortune" would not come to Greece. In addition to writing several letters, Howe kept a journal that provides a unique perspective on conditions both within the Greek army and of life during the first years of

FIGURE 43   John Elliot, *Samuel Gridley Howe in Greek
dress*, 1876. Oil on canvas. Brown University Portrait
Collection, Providence, R.I.

the revolution (Richards 1906). Invaluable for his medical expertise and dili-
gent, Howe was criticized by those who witnessed him in action only for his
willingness to expose himself to danger. Indeed, one of several instances of
Howe's bravery inspired John Greenleaf Whittier's 1853 poem "The Hero."

Between late 1824 and 1826, and while private efforts in the United States continued, American involvement in the revolution was dominated by the so-
called frigate scandal. Advised to procure frigates for their fleet, Greek deputies in London accepted offers for two ships by American shipyards at a cost of
$250,000 each. As the project neared completion, the cost of the ships had risen
to $750,000, forcing the Greek deputies to sell one ship in order to pay for the
other. The US government bought one of the ships, albeit at a price much lower

than the Greek deputies had paid for it, thus allowing the second ship to join the Greek fleet as the *Hellas*. This affair generated a "prolonged controversy" in the United States and in Europe, leading James Madison to write to Lafayette, "the indignation of the public is highly excited; and a regular investigation of the lamentable abuse is going on," adding, "[i]n the meantime Greece is bleeding in consequence of it, as is every heart that sympathizes with her noble cause" (Earle 1927, 57–58; cf. Curti 1963, 28–29). Around the same time, news of Ypsilantis's achievements on the battlefield inspired settlers near Woodruff's Grove, in the Michigan Territory, to name their settlement after the general. The two communities joined and were subsequently incorporated as the village of Ypsilanti, which was reincorporated as a city in 1856.

The combination of the frigate scandal and news of the suffering that had befallen the Greek people in 1826–1827, especially in Mesolonghi, renewed public interest in Greece. Urged on by public appeals from Everett, Howe, and other prominent Philhellenes, American aid during this phase of the struggle focused overwhelmingly on relieving the hunger and poverty that afflicted the civilian population. Fearing embezzlement, American relief committees had stipulated that aid should be distributed by Miller, who had returned to the United States in 1826. In early 1827, the Executive Greek Committee of New York recruited Miller as its agent in Greece and dispatched him there with a ship filled with provisions (Curti 1963, 29–40). This arrangement frustrated Theodoros Kolokotronis, who, in a letter to Everett, expressed his gratitude for American relief efforts but complained that it would have been more effective if aid had been given to soldiers instead. Nevertheless, shipments continued to be directed to Miller, who in accordance with his mandate recorded his extraordinary efforts to relieve poverty and hunger during 1827. Miller, Howe, and other Americans adopted Greek orphans during this period. Among them, Lucas Miltiades Miller later came to represent Wisconsin in the fifty-second Congress.

The writings of Howe and Miller reveal their concern about the disparity between the aid and the needs of the population. Howe, in particular, began looking for longer-term solutions and as a first step redirected some aid in order to establish a hospital at Poros (St Clair 1972, 342–343). Eager to maintain momentum, both Howe and Miller returned to the United States in 1828 and engaged in vigorous campaigns on behalf of Greece. As part of these efforts, Miller published *The Condition of Greece in 1827 and 1828* and Howe *An Historical Sketch of the Greek Revolution,* which he dedicated to Carey and Everett, "the generous and untiring Philhellenes." Howe also wrote letters to committees and individuals who might help and embarked on a speaking tour. When he returned to Greece toward the end of 1828, Howe found hundreds of refugees at Aigina. He decided to hire some of them to construct a pier in the damaged harbor. Through his efforts, Howe managed to provide seven hundred refugees with employment during the winter months and Aigina with a new pier. From there, Howe went to Megara, where he helped some four hundred families procure seed for farming. Soon thereafter, he obtained permission from the government to establish a refugee colony he named "Washingtonia" at Examilia, near the Isthmus of Corinth. Leaving Greece for Paris in time for the July 1830 Revolution, Howe returned to the United States in 1831, where he began a new phase of extraordinary philanthropy. Among his many achievements during this period was his work as founding director of the Perkins School for the Blind, where he helped Laura Bridgman become the first blind person to read and write. Howe also continued his work abroad, delivering aid to Poland and, once more, to Greece during the Cretan Revolution of 1866, a cause for which he also campaigned in the United States. In 1835, Howe was awarded the Savior's Cross by the Greek government.

In her pioneering treatment of America's attitude toward Greece during the revolution, Myrtle A. Cline sees American Philhellenism as the result of the confluence of several important developments. Cline argues that chief among those were the centuries-old admiration for Greek civilization, the call to liberty inspired by the American and French revolutions, and the spirit of romanticism with its "sentimental fondness for desperate enterprises," of which Byron had become an emblem. As Cline notes, Americans were fresh from their own struggle for independence and, hence, favorable to other similar struggles (Cline 1930, 15–16). To these one should add the fact that the Greek Revolution was the embodiment of the struggle to defend Christianity from the Turk, who had so often played the role of *Hannibal ad portas*. The first and last of these factors, in particular, explain why even most of those wary of involvement in foreign entanglements nevertheless expressed sympathy and admiration for the Greeks. As such, American Philhellenism represents an excellent case study of the dynamics of American society that Tocqueville would soon thereafter describe so well. Whereas in most other countries the official policy of the government against involvement would have been the end of the matter, in the United States private individuals were able to use newspapers and associations small and large to awaken interest in and contribute to the Greek cause.

Ioannis D. Evrigenis

References

Address of the Committee Appointed at a Public Meeting Held in Boston December 19, 1823, for the Relief of the Greeks, to Their Fellow Citizens. 1824. Boston.

Annals of the Congress of the United States 41 (1823–1824). 1856. Washington, DC.

Arnakis, George Georgiades, ed. 1965. *George Jarvis: His Journal and Related Documents*. Thessaloniki.

Booras, Harris J. 1934. *Hellenic Independence and America's Contribution to the Cause*. Rutland, VT.

Cline, Myrtle A. 1930. *American Attitude toward the Greek War of Independence, 1821–1828*. Atlanta.

Comstock, John L. 1828. *History of the Greek Revolution*. New York.

Curti, Merle. 1963. *American Philanthropy Abroad: A History*. New Brunswick, NJ.

Dakin, Douglas. 1955. *British and American Philhellenes during the War of Greek Independence, 1821–1833*. Thessaloniki.

Earle, Edward Mead. 1927. "American Interest in the Greek Cause, 1821–1827." *American Historical Review* 33, no. 1 (October): 44–63.

[Everett, Edward]. 1823. "Review of *The Ethics of Aristotle to Nicomachus*, Revised and Edited by A. Coray, at the Expense of the Injured and Oppressed Sciotes." *North American Review* 17, no. 41 (October): 389–424.

Everett, Edward. 1860. *The Mount Vernon Papers*. New York.

Hanink, Johanna. 2018. "From Greece to Gettysburg: Edward Everett, American Patriot." *History Today,* April 11. https://www.historytoday.com/miscellanies/greece-gettysburg-edward-everett-american-patriot.

Hatzidimitriou, Constantine G., ed. 2002. *"Founded on Freedom and Virtue:" Documents Illustrating the Impact in the United States of the Greek War of Independence, 1821–1829*. New York.

Howe, Samuel Gridley. 1828. *An Historical Sketch of the Greek Revolution*. New York.

Larrabee, Stephen A. 1957. *Hellas Observed: The American Experience of Greece, 1775–1865*. New York.

Miller, Jonathan P. 1828. *The Condition of Greece, in 1827 and 1828*. New York.

Pappas, Paul Constantine. 1985. *The United States and the Greek War of Independence, 1821–1828*. Boulder, CO.

Richards, Laura E., ed. 1906. *The Greek Revolution: Letters and Journals of Samuel Gridley Howe*. Vol. 1. Boston, MA.

Robinson, David M. 1948. *America in Greece: A Traditional Policy*. New York.

St Clair, William. 1972. *That Greece Might Still Be Free: The Philhellenes in the War of Independence*. Oxford.

Trent, James W., Jr. 2012. *The Manliest Man: Samuel G. Howe and the Contours of Nineteenth-Century American Reform*. Amherst.

Vagenas, Thanos, and Evridike Dimitrakopoulou. 1949. *Αμερικανοί Φιλέλληνες: εθελοντές στο Εικοσιένα* [American Philhellenes: Volunteers in the 1821 revolution]. Athens.

The Visual Narration of the Greek War of Independence

The term "Philhellenism" derives from the epithet "Philhellene," used in antiquity to characterize those foreign rulers who were amicably disposed toward the Greeks, such as the Egyptian pharaoh Amasis II. During the period of the Greek Revolution (1821–1828), foreigners who endorsed the Greek struggle, whether with sword or money, pen or brush, were dubbed "Philhellenes" because the supportive climate they created contributed indirectly but essentially to the final successful outcome of the War of Independence. With reference to the arts, the definition of a work as "philhellenic" is rather wide in compass, temporally and conceptually, given that it includes works whose subjects do not coincide with the historical events taking place in Greece. This may perhaps be justified by the fact that, due to the means of communication of the period, information about these events reached Europe with a standard delay, but furthermore because its dissemination demanded a receptive intellectual, literary, and artistic milieu. Consequently, the term "philhellenic" embraces works created within the pulse and also in the resonance of the historic events of the Greek Revolution.

The term "Philhellenism" is often considered as having much in common with "antiquarianism." Antiquarian connotations are more eloquently implied in a specific pictorial genre, that of landscape painting. To European Hellenophiles, Greece had been for many centuries an idea rather than a specific geographical location. In the eighteenth century, the Age of Enlightenment, which was reexamining Europe's intellectual heritage, established a fertile climate for studying and reevaluating Hellenic antiquity. For European artists who visited Greece in the course of the eighteenth and the beginning of the nineteenth centuries, the experience of touring the land was an *anaplous,* a pilgrimage, an educational experience of seeking out their intellectual roots in a space hallowed by time (Tsigakou 1981, 26–30). This approach is substantiated by the host of "Greek" images (prints and drawings) created by European artist-travelers. Their antiquarianist frame of perception is reflected in their thematic choices, which focus on depicting ancient monuments or landscapes, with the emphasis on archeological sites, suggesting their historical and mythological dimension. Additionally, in their effort to evoke the spirituality of classical sites, the artists often "correct" or selectively recompose local features, in order to prettify the scars of destruction wrought by time and nature, securing, instead, the illusion of a "living antiquity." This resulted in the creation of Greek Views, distinguished by the absence of references to the here and now and by the marginalizing of the inhabitants of Greece, whom the painters depict as tiny figures dressed in festive costumes and invariably engaged in bucolic pursuits. Nevertheless, the inclusion of these imaginative Greek landscapes in the category of philhellenic works is not entirely unjustified, if we consider that these incredibly popular Views created by antiquarianist painters helped to link the European intelligentsia's abstract knowledge of ancient Hellas with its natural setting—that is, the space in which subsequent events unfolded. Furthermore, the reconstitution of the ancient world offered by these spectacular Views served to embed the continuity and unity of Hellenic antiquity with contemporary Greek reality in the mind of European intellectuals.

Already by the end of the eighteenth century, political developments in the Ottoman Empire and the rise of wealthy Greek communities in major European trade centers had the effect of gradually awakening Europe to the existence of a contemporary Greece that was inhabited by real people rather than by ghosts of glorious ancestors. This phenomenon led to a gradual reconstruction of the image of Greeks in accordance with historical and social coordinates. At the turn of the century, authors of travelogues attempted to draw parallels between ancient and modern Greek customs by drawing forth the country's— formerly invisible—contemporary inhabitants, while also making eloquent appeals for their liberation. A case in point is the antiquarianist representation in the frontispiece of the first volume of the three-volume publication by the French Comte de Choiseul-Gouffier, *Voyage Pittoresque de la Grèce* (1782–1822), which has been acclaimed as a precociously philhellenic statement (Plate 1). Greece is depicted as a woman in chains, seated among the ruined tombs of Pericles, Themistocles, and other Greek heroes, and behind her is inscribed in Latin *Exoriare aliquis*—"that an avenger might spring out of our bones"—the curse uttered by Dido, queen of Carthage, when she was cruelly abandoned by Aeneas (Tsigakou 1981, 43, 195). Choiseul-Gouffier's lavishly illustrated publication abounds in Views of the flourishing ports of the Aegean islands. In the illustrated travel literature on Greece published in the early years of the nineteenth century, new themes began to surface, such as samples of Greek costumes, the Greek flora, and scenes from everyday life. The eminent French romantic author Comte François-René de Chateaubriand, in his *Itinéraire de Paris à Jerusalem* (Paris 1811), summarized the entire spectrum of emotions felt by the enthusiasts of romantic Hellenism. This feeling was heightened by Lord Byron's arrival on the scene. With his poem *Childe Harold's Pilgrimage,* published in 1812 after his first journey to Greece, Byron was established as bard of a reborn Hellas. Moreover, his death at Mesolonghi in 1824, although it did not change the flow of events in Greece, nonetheless signified a new period for Philhellenism by kindling the sentiments and activities of Philhellenes everywhere (Tsigakou 1988). By painting portraits of Byron, European artists reminded public opinion of his voluntary sacrifice on the altar of the Greek struggle for liberation. In the spectacular painting by Joseph-Denis Odevaere, entitled *Lord Byron on His Deathbed,* the poet's deathbed, decorated with medallions in which the titles of his poems are inscribed, is placed under the statue of Liberty; his sword is leaning against the base and the strings of his lyre are broken (Plate 2). The dead poet's pose and his laurel-wreathed head bring to mind Jacques-Louis David's painting *Andromache Mourning Hector.* The death of the "Bard of the Hellenes," which was lamented by the entire philhellenic world, has been elevated to an image of universal significance. Byron's Greek poetry interweaves the pulsating color and mystery of the East with the current reality of the country. In the poet's verses Greece was no longer solely the deserted abode of Nymphs, River-gods, and Muses. Indeed, Byron's "Greek Women" ousted the Nymphs from the exhibition salons, while his "Palikars" and "Brave Souliots" were regarded as the incarnation of a new type of Greek male, the fearless freedom fighter, the romantic hero. "Rappelle-toi pour t'enflammer éternellement, certains passages de Byron," Eugène Delacroix noted in his diary, on May 11, 1824. His painting *The Combat of the Giaour and the Pasha,* presented in the Galerie Lebrun, Paris, in 1826, was inspired by Byron's poem *The Giaour, A Fragment of a Turkish Tale,* which recounts the Giaour's revenge for the death of his beloved Leila, who was atrociously assassinated by Hassan. The poetic scene is embodied in a phantasmagoric pictorial manner, a series of allegorical connotations, such as the battle between Christian civilization and "infidel" barbarity.

Philhellenism became a cult. The inventory of literary men and scholars who were animated by the spirit of Philhellenism is long, even though the writers' motives were varied and sometimes contradictory (Constans 1996, 84–88; Hassiotis 1972, 10–16; Tartaro 1986, 117–119; Tartaro 2000, 224–250). The list of philhellenic literature includes—apart from the authors of *Travels*—eminent

representatives of the romantic literary movement, such as the Germans Friedrich Hölderlin, Friedrich Schiller, and Johann Wolfgang von Goethe who, in
1823, translated some of the Greek folksongs collected by Werner von Haxthausen. Philhellenic feelings dominate the *Elégies* of French poet Casimir
Delavigne and the *Invocation* of Alphonse de Lamartine, the lyric poem *Hellas*
by Percy Bysshe Shelley, the *Lieder der Griechen* by the German Wilhelm Müller,
the *Canzone sulla Grecia* by the Italian Giacomo Leopardi, *I Profughi di Parga*
by Giovanni Berchet, the *Canción Guerrera* by the Spaniard Francisco Martínez
de la Rosa, and *Grecia, ó La Doncella de Missolonghi* by Estanislao de Cosca
Vayo. The philhellenic literary output revolved around the various facets of Philhellenism, mainly humanitarian feelings and propensity toward Christian
solidarity, admiration for the Hellenic past, and advocacy of freedom and emancipation. Such themes were pivotal for the philhellenic artistic repertoire,
given that they often accompany and inspire creations in the visual arts.

Not just from the literary viewpoint, but from the pictorial one too, the
Greek freedom fighters' confrontation with a far more numerous foe, their
Christian religion, and their country's classical past offered a highly promising
thematic repertoire. Ancient Greece continued to make its presence felt in
philhellenic compositions. However, the classical references were not elegies
for the glorious past but were a driving force for the revolutionary Greeks who
were defending their country with self-sacrifice worthy of their ancestors.
Based on a popular lithograph by Karl Krazeisen, *A Greek Commander and
His Pallikars in the Fight,* the oil painting by Peter von Hess depicts Greek warriors fighting with Spartan fortitude among the ruins of a Doric temple (Plate
3). Ruined temples and broken columns set their seal on philhellenic representations, denoting the presence of the classical past that fuels the protagonists'
agonistic disposition and elevates particular persons and events to images of
global import. The painting by Louis-Leopold Robert entitled "A young Geek
warrior whetting his knife on ancient marble" is an allegory of the ancient
heritage that was a driving force for revolutionary Greeks (Plate 4). The Greek
freedom fighters of 1821 were inscribed in the philhellenic repertoire alongside
the heroes of the classical pantheon, while several instances of the heroic Hellenic past were synchronized with episodes of the Greek struggle. As a result,
battle scenes featuring the greatly popular, fearless Souliot leader Markos Botsaris were skillfully tailored to fit accounts of the Spartan Leonidas, while images of Greek naval battles against the Turkish fleet were printed with the title
"Salamis."

Equally powerful as the presence of ancient Hellas was that of the Church.
Philhellenic circles, avoiding the issue of the doctrinal schism, declared
Christian solidarity in such a way that the struggle between the Cross and the

Crescent revived the spirit of the Crusades, firing Christian public opinion in Europe and America. "If our voice could be heard, the Banner of the Cross would flutter over the rooftops of Constantinople or above the Parthenon, and Hagia Sophia would function again as of old," was the outburst of the newspaper *Constitutionnel* on July 26, 1821. The religious propaganda that was addressed directly to the fellow Christian "brothers" passed into the visual vocabulary in a series of motifs, in which the Greeks were projected as modern martyrs of the faith. Inspired by Casimir Delavigne's poem "Le Jeune Diacre, ou la Grèce Chrétienne," which narrates the story of a young Greek deacon of Messenia in the Peloponnese who was shot by brutal janissaries while he was playing his lyre and singing plaintive Christian hymns, Vincent Nicolas Raverat created an astounding painting entitled *The Death of the Young Deacon* (Plate 5). The handsome young clergyman expires with his arms wide open, echoing the pose of the Crucified Christ, enveloped in a metaphysical moonlight that alludes to his divine reverence (Athanassoglou-Kallmyer 1989, 15–16). The scene is rendered with immense dignity and grandeur. Greek clerics were seen as soldiers of the Cross and their persecution by the "infidels" attracted great sympathy from Christian nations in Europe and America. Scenes with priests administering Holy Communion to freedom fighters departing for battle, pallikars waving the banner with the cross, profanations of churches, Turks humiliating venerable clerics or raping Christian maidens: all ignited fires in the souls of Europe's Christians. The image in Cesare Mussini's painting entitled *Saremo Liberi* (We shall be free) eloquently expresses the declaration in a French periodical: "The Iphigenias of modern Greece are those Christian virgins who choose death rather than be molested by infidel monsters" (Plate 6). Under the diabolic gaze of the ghastly Turk, the Greek captive is ready to kill himself with the same knife as he has just used to kill his young wife (Spetsieri-Beschi and Lucarelli 1986, 315).

In his presentation of works with Greek subjects exhibited in the 1827 Paris Salon, one French critic commented:

Happy are the peoples who seize a small piece in history; happy are those who never caught the attention of poets or painters. The monotonous existence of a peaceful people offers not the burning and exciting experiences that inspiration seeks. Those nations who were oft hymned with lyre and pen must pay for glory with their happiness. And in our days, with the price of blood and tears, Greece has acquired the right to inspire all the offspring of the Muses! The Greeks, their heroism, their destructions, their defeats offer our painters a host of subjects. (Tsigakou 1981, 49)

Philhellenism in the arts brought to the forefront a rich and imaginative production of works created mainly by European romantic artists. This was inevitable, given that the series of dramatic contrasts embodied in the Greek struggle gave wings to the romantic imagination. Philhellenic subjects were very popular with romantic painters because they allowed the artist to reenact historical events emphasizing moral and patriotic issues. Furthermore, as Greek historical events were familiar to the European public, they presented artists with the opportunity to echo or to eulogize government politics of their own country or to articulate a covert protest against current social and political agendas. Additionally, romantic artists employed these events symbolically, in order to express artistic demands and to challenge the academic establishment.

Particularly interesting is the simultaneous presence of both classical and religious elements in philhellenic compositions. Hellenic and religious motifs depicted in each other's company transform such images into manifestos of wider significance, asserting both the superiority of the classical heritage and the victory of Christian powers. In Michel Philibert Genod's painting *The Oath of the Young Freedom Fighter* (Plate 7), the young Greek takes leave of his family for the battlefield where he will presumably replace his wounded father, having sworn an oath on the wooden cross that is impacted inside the capital of an ancient column, while his father rests on another broken classical fragment (Constans 1996, 152–153). In Ary Scheffer's work *A Young Greek Defending His Father* (Plate 8), the boy's sense of duty is awakened while his wounded father is dying, breathing his last in the style and manner of the famous ancient sculpture of the *Dying Gaul*. There is no need to stress that the romantics—adulators of the dramatic—milked dry whatever offered them a violent and tragic subject. According to contemporary descriptions, Horace Vernet's painting entitled *The Defeat* shows a Greek standing over a dead Turk, ordering the Turk's servant to behead his master with his own sword (Plate 9). The cruelty of the scene was justified by the innumerable reports of the Turks' ferocity and blood lust, which innocent Greeks had suffered for centuries (Tsigakou 1981, 51, 195). Interestingly enough, this macabre subject became immensely popular and was reproduced in all kinds of philhellenic applied arts (Tsigakou 2015, 33–46). It is not accidental that the balance of the philhellenic repertoire is tipped toward the calamitous moments of the revolution, the massacres and holocausts, such as Parga, Chios, and Mesolonghi. The series of images of "Expiring Warriors," such as the one depicted in the painting by Henri Auguste Serrur (Plate 10), eloquently testify to the romantics' preference for victims rather than heroes (Constans 1996, 206–207). Romantic artists often turned to a genre style, where the historical events are remodeled with a familiarity that conveys with greater immediacy to the viewer the drama of the unfortunate protagonists. Nothing could bring more tears to the eyes of philhellenic spectators than the poignant scene in the painting entitled *A Greek Mother with her Dead Child,* in which the heartbroken father faces the devastating sight of his wife holding in her arms their dead son (poisoned by the snake depicted in the foreground; Plate 11). The mother's embrace is a reference to a religious *Pietà* (Tsigakou 2015, 22, 47). In Jean-Baptiste Vinchon's painting *Modern Greek Subject* a sorrow-stricken old man sits among the ruins of his household the day after the defeat, the burning, and the slaughter (Plate 12). At his feet lies his dead daughter, whose infant child he holds on his lap, and further away lies the body of the child's father, who still holds the knife with which he had tried to defend his family (Constans 1996, 212–213). The painting is a heartrending condemnation of the drama of innocent people caught up in the cogs of a catastrophic moment in history, an image that elevates the work to an antiwar manifesto.

Images of Greek women were also popular with the philhellenic romantic imagination. They are often depicted next to their wounded husbands and brothers, exhausted, desperate, or in the act of comforting them. But they are also frequently represented playing a leading role in battle scenes. Indeed, in a series of episodes inspired by the Greek struggle, they appear vigorously brandishing guns. Particularly popular was the image of the women of the rebellious Souliots who fervently resisted the oppression of Ali Pasha, the ruler of Epirus, for many years (1789–1804). Their dauntless spirit and legendary bravery gave rise to a number of prints entitled *The Courage of Souliot Women,* where they are depicted as warriors, marching decisively forward to the battle. The moving details in the European press on the adversities of Greek women and children, and the abduction of captive females brought tears to the readers' eyes. The painting *Greek Women in the Slave Market* by Stanislas-Henri-Benoit Darondeau (Plate 13) conveys with shocking immediacy the humiliation and desperation of the girl in the hands of the brutal slave-trader (Tsigakou 2015, 23, 55). In the Mesolonghi City Hall there is an iconic image of female heroism, *Episode from the Siege of Mesolonghi* by François-Émile de Lansac (Plate 14). As the body of her dead husband lies next to her and the Turks are fast approaching, a Greek mother, frightened yet fierce, has taken the tragically heroic decision that she will not be humiliated and that no one and nothing but death will ever take her child away from her. Her ceremonial gesture lends even more solemnity to the image that is endowed with the atemporal quality of a Byzantine icon (Constans 1996, 168–169).

It is essential to emphasize that a number of philhellenic issues corresponded to the Greek revolutionaries' political aspirations and were consequently emphasized and promulgated by the Greeks themselves, both during the War of Independence and after the founding of the Greek state. In that sense, philhellenic iconography is remarkable for its longstanding associations with national ideologies that have been propagated by modern Greeks, the foremost case in point being the exploitation of their Hellenic heritage. In 1828, having won its freedom, the country chose to model itself on its classical past. The young King Othon, who landed in Greece in 1833, and his Bavarian staff shared the belief prevalent among both Greek statesmen and intellectuals that "The Muses of the classical spirit should return to their homeland." The veneration of antiquity that determined the ideological orientation of the Hellenic kingdom fundamentally influenced nineteenth-century Greek culture, specifically Greek artists and architects, who sped to adopt and adapt imported European neoclassical models. In the painting entitled *Hellas in Gratitude* by Theodoros Vryzakis, a prominent Greek history painter (Plate 15), a group of more than fifty Greek Commanders pay their respect to the allegorical depiction of modern Greece. Depicted as a young woman with laureate head and wearing a chiton, Hellas rises on a cloud over the broken chains of her bondage, against the backdrop of a Doric temple, her arms outstretched as if to protect the men. Her pose reproduces the religious iconography of the Virgin of Mercy. In the right foreground, a musket rests conspicuously on an ancient column. To Greek spectators of the Othonian period the painting broadcast the rebirth of the Christian motherland sustained by its Hellenic heritage.

Needless to say, the Greek state that emerged after four hundred years of Ottoman rule was imbued with an amalgam of contradictions, ideological, political, social, and cultural. These were mirrored, in a way, in the actual physiognomy of the country, which was characterized by a series of striking visual contrasts, such as its quasi-Western, quasi-Oriental scenery (camels could often be seen on Greek country roads), marked by the coexistence of Turkish mosques, Byzantine churches and ruined Hellenic temples, of humble homes next to newly built neoclassical mansions. A veritable stage set that was peopled by individuals wearing plain Western-style clothes or elaborately embroidered traditional costumes. All these contrasting motifs made for a picturesqueness that delighted visiting artists. Romantic artists of the 1830s and 1840s, who witnessed these contrasts, did not just record them; they also attempted to invest them with the associations embodied in their bygone, philhellenic counterparts. Consequently, in their historical compositions they recreated scenes inspired by the Greek struggle with a nostalgic sentiment aimed at echoing the impact of historic events long gone. In addition, their images of everyday life are characterized by the presence of ancient ruins—dispersed not only in the countryside but also all over the narrow streets of the new towns—hinting at the continuity and endurance of the Hellenic heritage that enfolded the fledgling state in its arms. In *A Scene in the City of Nafplio*—the provisional capital of liberated Greece—the German Baron Carl Wilhelm Freiherr von Heideck, who accompanied King Othon as one of the three Bavarian regents, represents a picturesque scene of everyday life with beautifully dressed Greeks brimming with life and optimism (Plate 16).

As pointed out above, definitions of philhellenic artistic production in Europe are broad in scope, accommodating a series of post hoc works. An overall review of the relevant works has yet to be carried out. The summary anthology of European philhellenic production in painting and the applied arts during the first half of the nineteenth century, presented here, gives insight into the great variety and diversity of imagery that can be assembled under the heading "philhellenic pictures." An attempt has been made also to elucidate the particularities of familiarization with the philhellenic repertoire by artists of different nationalities, to define the corresponding horizon of acceptance of these works, and to reveal their cultural realities. Specific geographical regions have been selected, such as France, Italy, Germany, and Britain, on the one hand, because a greater percentage of philhellenic pictorial production is located there and, on the other, because in these regions during this period different ideological orientations and social actions developed, which had a decisive influence on the formulation of philhellenic themes in the visual arts.

Philhellenic subjects found unprecedented appeal among French artists. French Philhellenism in the visual arts is distinguished not only by its numerical superiority but also by its contemporaneity with the historical events being enacted in Greece until the end of the struggle. An exceptionally interesting and original—from the art historical standpoint—characteristic of French Philhellenism is the intellectual alliance between French supporters of the liberal opposition, made up of Orleanists and Bonapartists, and French romantic artists who were at odds with the Academy and its feeble classicism. Delacroix's *Scenes of the Massacres of Chios: Greek Families Awaiting Death or Slavery,* an archetypal romantic painting in subject, composition, and execution, was painted in six months of feverish work, to be exhibited in the 1824 Salon (Plate 17). Against a background of conflagration and destruction, Delacroix renders a hideous panorama of appalling acts of violence (Athanassoglou-Kallmyer 1989, 29–31). A totally devastated Greek sits immobile, gazing at the lamenting woman and the two girls in tight embrace at his feet, two desperate and defenseless couples await their servitude, a dead mother and child, a man struggling in vain to rescue the nude woman who is tied to the horse of the savage rider. Among this sequence of horrific vignettes sits an elderly woman; she looks outside the canvas, with a grief-stricken expression on her face. Nicknamed by contemporary critics "le massacre de la peinture," this painting not only stirred philhellenic consciences but also ruffled artistic academic waters, thanks to its revolutionary romantic style. More importantly, it fueled the Greek national imagination. To modern Greeks the elderly woman in the foreground resonates their homeland's plea to Europe's humanitarian feelings, while to Greek art historians Delacroix is the Philhellene Painter par excellence.

Equally prominent in the national imagery of modern Greece is *Greece on the Ruins of Mesolonghi* (Plate 18). Against a dreary sky and blurred crumbling city walls on which a black Oriental man holding the banner of Islam is discerned, modern Greece personified as a beautiful woman in folk attire emerges from the havoc and ruins of Mesolonghi. Kneeling upon a tombstone, she appeals for help with her arms open. Her frontal life-size figure has a majestic stature, lending vibrations of courageous decisiveness to her attitude (Athanassoglou-Kallmyer 1989, 91–100, 147–148). "This is an image of a strong spirit which although shaken by powerful blows, is never crushed," a contemporary art critic observed (Athanassoglou-Kallmyer 1989, 147). Delacroix not only created an image of universal significance but also furnished the pictorial history of modern Greece with a national image that has often been elevated to the status of a religious icon. Delacroix's painting was premiered in the exhibition *On Behalf of the Greeks,* which was organized in the Galerie Lebrun in 1826. The Lebrun exhibition opened on May 17, only a month after the fall of Mesolonghi (April 10). Among the exhibited canvases there were philhellenic works by several representatives of the romantic movement, such as Raverat, August Scheffer, Auguste Vinchon, Henri Decaisne, Horace Vernet, and Alexandre-Marie Colin. Similar exhibitions outside the official Salon, which was the bastion of academic artists, were the platform for those artists who were rejected by the formal selection committee. However, the following year, twenty-one works with modern Greek subjects were to be seen at the Paris Salon of 1827. The reason was the victorious naval battle of the allied great powers—England, France, and Russia—at Navarino (October 20, 1827), in which the Ottoman fleet was crushingly defeated and the revolutionary Greeks were vindicated. The French spectators were overwhelmed. In reviewing the works at the Salon the art critic Auguste Jal concluded: "Liberty, Liberty."

Despite the fact that the victorious naval battle of Navarino was described by the Duke of Wellington as "an untoward event," it nevertheless generated enthusiasm among the British public. Masses of people gathered in the staged panorama of *The Naval Battle of Navarino,* exhibited in the Strand in 1828. George Philip Reinagle, a painter of naval scenes and an eyewitness of the event, not only painted a number of versions of the battle (Plate 19), but also published a monumental folio of lithographs of the subject (Reinagle 1828). However, the philhellenic movement in Britain advanced at a tardy pace, given that government policy ranged from negative to hostile toward the insurgent Greeks. Even so, British Philhellenism is attested in both literature and art, thanks, on the one hand, to the special fascination for the very land of Greece and, on the other, to the charitable and romantic notions of public opinion, and certainly thanks to the poetry of Lord Byron (Tsigakou 1984). In fact, Byron's poetry is the basis of the philhellenic movement in the visual arts. Later copies of *Byron in Greek Dress* by Thomas Phillips (Plate 20) often figure prominently in philhellenic events. Though the list of British artists who tackled subjects from the Greek War of Independence is rather short, it nonetheless includes the preeminent romantic landscapist Joseph Mallord William Turner (1775–1851), who never visited Greece, yet painted the first British work of Byronic inspiration in 1812 (Tsigakou 1981, 41, 194). It is a watercolor inscribed "'Tis living Greece no more," a line from Byron's poem *The Giaour, A Fragment of a Turkish Tale:*

> Such is the aspect of this shore
> 'Tis Greece but living Greece no more!

The line is written in the foreground, where a group of two Greek women in chains, guarded by a ferocious Turk, is depicted; the Acropolis rising in the background alludes to the cultural heritage of these enslaved creatures (Plate 21). An ardent admirer of the poet, Turner contributed numerous illustrations for the *Complete Works* of Byron, published by John Murray. The historical subjects of the Greek struggle held little appeal for British artists. A rare example of a historical picture referring to the recent war in Greece is the painting by Denis Dighton *Defeat of the Turks under the Command of Ali Pasha by the Souliots* (Plate 22). While creating an authentic battle scene, the British artist was also concerned with orchestrating the composition with theatrical bravado. On the whole, British artists preferred to represent the Greeks' happier moments, rather than their tragedies, and specifically to immortalize the contribution of their own government to Greece's liberation. This explains the proliferation of scenes from the victorious *Naval Battle of Navarino,* which inundated British exhibition halls in 1827 and 1828. Sir Charles Lock Eastlake (1793–1865), president of the Royal Academy, found an eloquent pictorial way of reminding his compatriots of Great Britain's beneficent role in Greek affairs, with his oil-painting *Greek Fugitives: An English Ship Sending Its Boats to Rescue Them* (Plate 23). The work shows a group of devastated women, children, and an old man fleeing from their hometown, which is in flames, while the mounted enemy troops are fast approaching. Further to the left, a wounded man is waving a white flag toward the sea where—suddenly and miraculously—a ship flying the British flag appears, coming to their rescue (Tsigakou 1991, 66–67). The picture of the magnanimous British liberators was much admired at the Royal

Academy exhibition in 1833, the year King Othon arrived in Greece. In the 1840s and 1850s, the anemic British philhellenic output in the visual arts gave way to imaginative works of pastoral and genre orientation. In their Greek images, which incorporate a diversity of picturesque motifs, British artists invite their viewers to share their own enchantment of visiting a country rich in historical associations and pictorial qualities.

In the 1820s, the pervasive patriotism of the Italian liberals, which was intermingled with national problems and demands for emancipation, is reflected in Italian literature and the visual arts. However, Philhellenism in the visual arts of Italy is not synchronous with Greek historical events, owing to the prevailing political situation at home—that is, the Austrian domination and consequently the very strict climate of censorship, which banned Italian artists from openly expressing their personal commitment or from exhibiting explicitly dissident works in public spaces.

It was only natural that Italian artists supporting the Risorgimento would use philhellenic imagery in their attempt to reveal the deplorable situation of their country and seek parallels in their neighbors to express the vision of their own unfulfilled revolution (Spetsieri-Beschi and Lucarelli 1986, 120–127). The events of Parga in 1819, which roused public opinion, deeply moved Italian patriots who identified the Pargans' fate with the tragedy of their own political refugees. A small town on the northwest coast of Greece facing the Ionian islands, Parga shared their fate as part of a British protectorate. However, when, in 1819, the British sold Parga to Ali Pasha, the inhabitants chose to abandon their homeland rather than endure Turkish rule. Victims of the ruthless machinations of the great powers, their fate was perceived to parallel Italy's situation. It is not fortuitous that the first Italian philhellenic painting, produced on the morrow of the founding of the revolutionary organization Giovine Italia by Giuseppe Mazzini in 1831, is *The Refugees of Parga,* by the foremost Italian romantic painter, Francesco Hayez (Plate 24). This depicts the Pargans, tragic exiles, bidding a last farewell to their native land, most of them mournfully raising their eyes toward the sky. A priest in the foreground bows his head in resignation, a woman kisses the soil of the motherland: an elegiac image of innocent people subjected to cruel ordeals and exile, due to the intrigues of callous diplomacy. A number of Italian philhellenic images are allegories of the perfidy of international diplomacy, while others were purposefully constructed in order to propagate deeply felt patriotic beliefs. In his painting *The Death of Markos Botsaris,* Filippo Marsigli was inspired by the Souliot chieftain Botsaris who, as leader of the troops in Mesolonghi, died in action on August 25, 1823, trying to slow down the Turkish army's advance against the heroic town (Plate 25). A group of Greek soldiers with dignified expressions of grief cluster around their mortally wounded leader, who lies in their arms. His posture, deriving from the Lamentation of Christ, furnishes the picture with religious overtones. Two of his devoted companions, with their swords raised and stepping over the body of an expiring Turk, hold the enemy riders at bay. Their fierce and resolute gestures leave no doubt that the enemy will never take away their beloved commander. The scene pulsates with drama and patriotism. Lodovico Lipparini, an equally prominent figure on the Italian artistic scene, chose to associate Botsaris's heroism with the emblematic figure of Lord Byron, in his painting entitled *The Oath of Lord Byron on the Tomb of Markos Botsaris* (Plate 26). In August 1823, upon landing in Greece, bound for Mesolonghi, Byron had received a letter from Botsaris announcing that he was longing to meet "His Excellency," but unfortunately, Botsaris died only a few days later (*British Philhellenes,* exhibition catalog, 1971, 39). In January 1824 Byron arrived in Mesolonghi, where he died in April. In Lipparini's composition, Byron dressed in Greek costume takes the oath before the citizens and prelates of Mesolonghi, with a solemnity and sacred enthusiasm that inspires them all. The painting echoes what the poet himself called "the very poetry of politics," while the presence of young women and men and specifically the gesture of the father to his son, on the left, invest the scene with a didactic content. Memories of Botsaris's heroic death and Byron's self-sacrifice must have touched Italian nationalists as allusions to their own struggle for "Freedom or Death."

German Philhellenism in the visual arts developed in parallel with the monarchy of Othon, son of King Ludwig I of Bavaria. During the first half of the nineteenth century, fine arts in Bavaria flourished under the patronage of the classically educated crown prince, crowned Ludwig I in 1825, who, in response to Napoleon's hegemonic claims, implemented an unprecedented artistic program that evoked sentiments of national pride among his subjects. Consequently, German philhellenic imagery appears in interaction with then-current Bavarian political expediencies. Othon's enthronement attracted a great number of artists to Greece. In the 1830s and 1840s, a colony of more than twenty German artists and architects was established in the country, working under commission for either King Othon or his father. Peter von Hess, Ludwig's favorite history painter, was commissioned to execute a series of historical scenes inspired by the War of Liberation (Baumstark 2000, 306–336). The young king's arrival in Athens was spectacularly recorded by von Hess in his painting entitled *The Reception of King Othon of Greece in Athens* (Plate 27). The king is depicted rather discreetly in the middle of the composition, surrounded by a small group of Bavarians, his brother Maximilian and the members of the regency, while the rest of the foreground overflows with a large crowd of Greeks, not only high officials and the head of the Church, but common people in festive dress.

An eyewitness of the event, von Hess did not wish his picture to be a panorama of Greek costumes, but to suggest the popularity of the new king among his subjects and also to bring out the new solidarity between the two nations. At Ludwig's behest, von Hess also collaborated with his compatriot landscape painter Carl Rottmann on developing the new Greek epic in the north porticoes of the Royal Garden in Munich, where Rottmann created a significant set of Greek Views. A true romantic, Rottmann did not idealize the historically significant Hellenic sites, but rendered them in their current devastation. His Views of classical sites are expansive landscapes depicting little remains of the past glory of Hellas within a primeval environment enveloped in a radiant light that sets up a spiritual dialogue between mythology, mortal history, and eternity. In his *View of the Bay of Poros,* he has created an enchanting landscape where the natural features are silhouetted in delicate, vaporous tones that impart a lyrical feeling to the scene and suggest the artist's personal dialogue with the place (Plate 28). The opportunity to record the physiognomy of the young Hellenic kingdom under Bavarian tutelage presented visiting German artists with a noble purpose. In addition to rendering the saga of King Othon, many of them executed scenes of everyday life with philhellenic overtones, such as veterans leaning against broken columns or wounded war victims begging in the streets or sitting next to tumbledown houses. Despite their sentimentality, such pictures were not an uncommon sight to visitors to postrevolutionary Greece. Also, a number of visiting artists created unpretentious images of the scenery and everyday life in Greece, which constitute valuable visual documents for archaeologists and folklorists. Otto Magnus von Stackelberg, for instance, published a high-quality set of engravings, in which almost a complete series of Greek costumes is accurately depicted. Christian Perlberg, who was in Greece in the 1830s, took a modern Greek festive occasion as a pretext for touching upon philhellenic imagery. The title of his picture, *A Folk Festival in Athens,* refers to *Koulouma* a popular Greek festival, the celebration of the first day of Lent—Shrove Monday (Plate 29). A group of elderly yet stalwart Greek men relax on the marble foundations of the colossal temple of Olympian Zeus, the gigantic columns of which occupy one-third of the composition, while the Acropolis is perceived in the distance. Further to the left, a group of younger men are performing a spirited dance. Given the fact that in Ottoman times this same spot was used by the Turks as an open-air mosque, Perlberg did not choose it merely for its picturesqueness. The old warriors are not there just to entertain themselves but also to celebrate their recent victory and their freedom. The painting convinces the spectators of the relevance and vitality of the Hellenic legacy in modern Greece. A little-known work that may be included in the German philhellenic production is the exquisite *Portrait of Dimitrios Botsaris* by Albert Riegel (Plate 30). The sitter, the fourteen-year-old son of the heroic leader Markos Botsaris, was painted under commission from King Ludwig, when the boy was attending the Panhellenic Gymnasium in Munich, a school founded by Ludwig for the orphaned sons of Greek commanders. Set against a bare background, the boy possesses none of the attributes or the domestic surroundings normally depicted in children's portraits. A sense of innocence, purity, and dignity emerges from this simultaneously realistic and heroic portrait.

Included in the long list of philhellenic painters are some of the eminent representatives of the European romantic movement. However, philhellenic subjects did not inspire exclusively the so-called great painters of the nineteenth century. They were also used by many minor painters of the period, who purposefully turned to philhellenic imagery, given that Greece was the burning issue of the day. That explains also the prolific output of prints within the philhellenic production, which, thanks to their low cost, were used as a powerful instrument of philhellenic propaganda. The most interesting prints in terms of subject matter and quality are by Giovanni Boggi, Adam Friedel, and Karl Krazeisen, while pictorial narrations of the main battles figure in a series of lithographs by Alphonse de Neville. The thematic variety of prints is amazing and touches upon many aspects of the philhellenic repertoire. Despite the disputed accuracy and quality of their representations, philhellenic lithographs sold like hot cakes, not only in philhellenic bazaars but also in European and American stationery shops and bookstores. Current historical events, portraits of the Greek leaders, allegorical and fantastical compositions of anonymous Greek men and women bearing arms or dying in battle, and melodramatic scenes often verging on the tragicomical all cultivated public sympathy. The same characteristics are to be found in another unpredictably popular means of philhellenic propaganda: domestic and decorative goods (Tsigakou 2015, 33–46). Addressed to an audience interested in sentiment rather than the harsh realities of the revolution, Greek historical events were transformed into soft, domesticated and didactic images and were printed on all types of objets d' art or utilitarian objects, such as porcelain tableware, dinner services, tea and coffee sets, flasks for liqueurs—labeled "Missolonghi Liqueur," or "Nectar of the Valiant Greeks"—glass inkwells, an impressive range of ormolu clocks with fanciful miniature sculptural representations, bronze candlesticks, paper fans, wooden jewelry boxes, embroidered cushion covers and firescreens, wallpapers, and upholstery fabrics. These were sold in bazaars set up by philhellenic committees, which also organized dinners, balls, concerts, and theatrical performances. The philhellenic industry created a fashion that captured people of different classes and ideologies, even those barely aware or totally unaware of what was going on in Greece. Their contribution to spreading information about the Greek cause and keeping interest in it alive was not unrelated to the final outcome of the Greek War of Independence. In the period after the creation of the Greek state, amusing parodies of historical events emerge from the cartoons by the outstanding British caricaturists George Cruikshank and James Gillray, while the Frenchman Honoré Daumier created a series of hilarious lithographs relating to King Othon.

There is no doubt that the canvas of philhellenic paintings has been stretched to the limits, in order to accommodate works whose definition as philhellenic may be debated. Indeed, philhellenic artistic production in Europe raises a series of questions and doubts that the art scholar needs to explicate, because such pictures often cloud over or distort the depicted events. It goes without saying that the past is different from its narration. Consequently, in attempting to reconstruct the history of the Greek Revolution through the "Philhellenic Picture Gallery," viewers should be conscious of the fact that they are beholding the visual narration of a history that is simultaneously represented and undermined.

Fani-Maria Tsigakou

References

Athanassoglou-Kallmyer, Nina. 1989. *French Images from the Greek War of Independence, 1821–1830: Art and Politics under the Restoration.* New Haven, CT, and London.

Baumstark, Reinhold, ed. 2000. *Das neue Hellas, Griechen und Bayern zur Zeit Ludwigs I.* Munich. Exhibition catalog.

Boggi, Giovanni. 1826–1829. *Turcs et Grecs les plus renommés soit par leur cruauté soit par leur bravoure dans la guerre actuelle de la Grèce, dessinés d'après nature par Boggi.* Paris.

British Council. 1971. *British Philhellenes.* Athens. Exhibition catalog.

Cassimatis, Marilena, ed. 2000. *Αθήνα-Μόναχο. Τέχνη και πολιτισμός στη νέα Ελλάδα* [Athens-Munich. Art and culture in the new Greece]. Athens.

Cassimatis, Marilena, ed. 2006. *Exhibition Catalogue: Karl Krazeisen, The Original Figures of the Heroes of '21. Drawings, Watercolors, Lithographs, 1826–1831* [Οι αυθεντικές μορφές των ηρώων του '21. Σχέδια, υδατογραφίες, λιθογραφίες, 1826–1831]. National Gallery-Al. Soutzos Museum / Nafplion Annex. Athens.

Constans, Claire, ed. 1996. *La Grèce en révolte: Delacroix et les artistes français, 1815–1848.* Athens. Exhibition catalog.

Friedel, Adam. 1825–1827. *The Greeks: Twenty-Four Portraits of the Principal Leaders and Personages Who Have Made Themselves Most Conspicuous in the Greek Revolution.* London.

Gombrich, Ernst. 1977. *Art and Illusion.* Oxford.

Hassiotis, Ioannis K. 1972. "Ο Ισπανικός Φιλελληνισμός προ του 1821 και κατά τη διάρκεια της Επαναστάσεως" [Spanish Philhellenism before 1821 and during the revolution]. *Makedoniki Zoi* 70 (March): 10–16.

Kotidis, Antonis. 1995. Ζωγραφική 19ου αιώνα [Nineteenth-century painting]. Athens.

Krazeisen, Karl. 1828–1831. *Bildnisse ausgezeichneter Griechen und Philhellenen nebst einige Ansichten und Trachten.* Munich.

Reinagle, George-Philip. 1828. *Illustrations of the Battle of Navarin: Dedicated to H. R. H. the Duke of Clarence.* London.

Simopoulos, Kyriakos. 1972–1975. Ξένοι Ταξιδιώτες στην Ελλάδα 333 μ.Χ.—1821 [Foreign travelers in Greece, 333–1821 CE]. Athens.

Simopoulos, Kyriakos. 1979–1981. Πως είδαν οι ξένοι την Ελλάδα του '21 [How did foreigners see Greece in 1821?]. Athens.

Spetsieri-Beschi, Caterina, and Enrica Lucarelli, eds. 1986. *Risorgimento greco e filellenismo italiano: Lotte, cultura, arte, mostra promossa dall'Ambasciata di Grecia e dall'Associazione per lo sviluppo delle relazioni fra Italia e Grecia.* Rome. Exhibition catalog.

Stackelberg, Otto-Magnus von. 1825. *Costumes et usages des peuples de la Grèce moderne.* Rome.

Tartaro, Achille. 1986. "Letteratura filellenica in Italia." In *Risorgimento greco e filellenismo italiano: Lotte, cultura, arte, mostra promossa dall'Ambasciata di Grecia e dall'Associazione per lo sviluppo delle relazioni fra Italia e Grecia,* edited by Caterina Spetsieri-Beschi and Enrica Lucarelli, 117–119. Rome.

Tartaro, Achille. 2000. "Griechenbegeisterung und Philhellenismus." In *Das neue Hellas, Griechen und Bayern zur Zeit Ludwigs I,* edited by Reinhold Baumstark, 224–250. Munich.

Tsigakou, Fani-Maria. 1981. *The Rediscovery of Greece: Travellers and Painters of the Romantic Era.* London.

Tsigakou, Fani-Maria. 1984. "Έργα με ελληνικά θέματα που εκτέθηκαν σε δημόσιες αίθουσες στο Λονδίνο τον 19ο αιώνα" [Works of Greek subjects exhibited in public places in London during the nineteenth century]. *DIEEE* 27: 299–354.

Tsigakou, Fani-Maria. 1988. *Lord Byron in Greece.* Athens. Exhibition catalog.

Tsigakou, Fani-Maria. 1991. *Through Romantic Eyes: European Images of Nineteenth Century Greece from the Benaki Museum Collections.* Alexandria, VA. Exhibition catalog.

Tsigakou, Fani-Maria. 1995. *British Images of Greece from the Benaki Museum Collections.* Athens. Exhibition catalog.

Tsigakou, Fani-Maria. 2015. *Artistic Interpretations of Philhellenism: The A. and D. Varkarakis Collection.* Athens.

The Revolution and the Romantic Imagination:
Echoes in European Literature

The cultural movement known as Philhellenism has been recognized as an unprecedented example of the power of public opinion to influence government policies even in the delicate area of foreign relations. Throughout Europe, literature about (and, less often, from) Greece played an important role in inspiring a transnational solidarity movement that made substantial contributions to the cause of Greek independence (Bass 2008, 47–151). Most of this literature is now forgotten, and modern readers are likely to find fault with the often sentimental, moralizing, and derivative efforts of literary-inclined Philhellenes. However, some of their writings are still worth reading for more than historical reasons. Most importantly, this material as a whole deserves to be reassessed not only as subsidiary evidence in the historiography of the Greek Revolution, but also as original expression of a key moment in European culture when relations between aesthetics, public discourse, and politics were being redefined.

The idea of Greece was a richly coded signifier that had occupied a central place in the cultural identity of the West for centuries. But from 1821 a set of live political and intellectual issues gave new urgency to the myth of classical antiquity. The insurgency in Greece was seen as a struggle of Christianity against Islam, of democracy against despotism, of civilization against barbarism. These multiple layers contributed to activate a powerful transhistoricality that once again placed Greece at the heart of the European quest for political and cultural self-definitions. The Greek cause struck a chord with different segments of society, from the classically educated elites to middle-class Christian families, and across the political spectrum from liberal revolutionaries to reactionaries. Literature on philhellenic themes resonated with all the different and contradictory inflections of classicism, romanticism, and orientalism.

Interest in Greece also dovetailed with developments in historical and political thought. Traditionally, the ancient past had been understood within the eschatological framework of the succession of empires, which allotted minimal space to the Greek city-states. It was not until the French Revolution that Greek history emerged as an independent field, at a time when questions about the nature of political communities and rights were high on the agenda. It was in the work of British historians such as William Mitford and John Gillies (both staunch antirepublicans), and later in George Grote's defense of Athenian democracy, that for the first time "political discussion was embodied in Greek history" (Momigliano 1955, 215). In a postrevolutionary Europe marked by the experience of rupture, new narrative histories emerged that attempted to reflect in a systematic way on the differences between antiquity and modernity. Among the French Idéologues, the contrast between ancient polities (above all Athens and Sparta) and modern states founded on trade became a focal point in discussions about liberty and citizen participation (Loraux and Vidal-Naquet 1979). And while the German Romantics idealized Greece as a long-lost homeland of the spirit, classical philology became central to the system of elite higher education initiated in Prussia by Humboldt in 1810. Thus institutionalized, Philhellenism was enlisted in the German project of nation and state building (Marchand 1996).

Nineteenth-century literary Philhellenism and its later echoes live in the tension between Greece as an ideal paradigm outside space and time and Greece as an actual place with its own social and political peculiarities in ongoing historical development. As Constanze Güthenke has argued (2008, 4), among the most lasting features of what she calls "political Philhellenism" is "its fascination with Greece's materiality, not as it opposes but as it is inseparable from its ideality." This structural interdependence is visible in the recurring contrast between ancient and modern Greece, with its attendant dialectic of transcendence and temporality, resurgence and decline, attraction and disillusionment. What follows will look at manifestations of Philhellenism in literary productions that respond to and interact with the Greek Revolution and its aftermath; among such productions, travel writing, folk songs, and poetry loom large.

Travel to Greece, fueled by the eastward extension of the Grand Tour in the late eighteenth century, gained new momentum from the revolution itself. Members of the London Greek Committee such as Edward Blaquiere shared with "romantic pilgrims" such as François-René de Chateaubriand and classical scholars such as Friedrich August Ukert a tendency to find echoes of the past in the present. On being offered roasted meat in a mountain village, Blaquiere is ecstatic to find that "it differed very little . . . from those which Homer describes in the first book of his immortal epic" (Blaquiere 1825, 59). Others take a more cautious approach to the question of continuity. Spurred by his "love of antiquity," Ukert sets out to "discover whether the race he encountered [in his journey] . . . could still be said to resemble the ancient Greeks" (Ukert 1810, x). More often, travelers were ill-disposed toward the heterogeneous world of modern Greece that contaminated the purity of the classical landscape with "contemporary structures, which, like the Greek language, betrayed foreign influences" (Augustinos 1994, 184). In a misguided attempt to locate the ruins of Sparta in present-day Mystra, Chateaubriand tells of his dismay when confronted with "a town absolutely modern, whose architecture exhibited nothing but a confused mixture of the Oriental manner, and of the Gothic, Greek and Italian styles, without one poor little antique to make amends" (Chateaubriand 1814, 95). Self-mockery at the ambitious traveler's archaeological illiteracy cannot completely efface the underlying sense of disappointment and anxiety at the hybrid reality of contemporary Greece, more eastern and Mediterranean than classical.

By contrast, some politically active Philhellenes had little patience for cultivated nostalgia and fanciful expectations. William Parry, with Byron at Mesolonghi, describes as "nonsense" the infatuation of the London Greek Committee with "the classic land of freedom, the birth place of the arts, the cradle of genius, the habitation of the gods, the heaven of poets" (Parry 1825, 188). Giuseppe Pecchio, one of the "Carbonari counts" who became involved in the Greek Revolution while in exile in England, went to Greece with Count Gamba shortly after Byron's death on behalf of the committee (St Clair 2008, 251–262). An experienced revolutionary, he warns against the overoptimistic predictions of Greek revival trumpeted in London and Paris: "the Greeks sit cross-legged like Turks (and will keep doing that for a long time still) . . . eat Turkish pilaf, smoke long-stemmed pipes, write from left to right . . . greet, sleep, and laze around like Turks" (Pecchio 1826, 14). As with Italy's former greatness, the ancient glory of Greece is buried deep in the past, too far removed to be a short-term political goal and achievable only through a slow process of social and cultural transformation.

Travel literature contributed in fundamental ways to turning traditional Hellenism into a politicized Philhellenism that acknowledged the Greeks as a living people. However, as far as literary responses to the Greek Revolution go, a key textual strategy, which has still not received sufficient critical attention, was the recording (and sometimes the rewriting) of Greek folk songs. Interest in the popular poetry of modern Greece fits in the wider context of romantic ideas about oral folk traditions as constitutive of national identity, from Homer to the present. This intersection of politics and philology, as well as its cosmopolitan reach, is most vividly illustrated by the figure of Claude Fauriel, whose

Chants populaires de la Grèce moderne were published in Paris in 1824–1825 and widely translated or adapted thereafter. When Napoleon became consul for life, Fauriel, an active Jacobin during the revolution, resigned from public office and devoted himself to literature, joining the group of the Idéologues and befriending Manzoni. It was through Manzoni that Fauriel met Andrea Moustoxydis, a historian and philologist from Corfu who had settled in Italy and became a key collaborator in Fauriel's project, facilitating contacts with informers in the Greek communities of Venice and Trieste. Fauriel also credits Korais and the paleographer Charles Benoît Hase as contributors of material.

Fauriel's was not the earliest attempt to collect Greek folk songs, but his *Chants* were the first to appear in print and enjoyed immediate success. Some songs had already been recorded in travel accounts, and Werner von Haxthausen's collection, which garnered Goethe's approval, was abandoned on the publication of Fauriel's (Beaton 1980, 3). In Vienna, a south Slavic connection was established by Vuk Stefanović Karadžić, who had been translating Serbian and Greek songs into German on the encouragement of Jacob Grimm (Ibrovac 1966, 70). In the Francosphere, the historian Sismondi, a member of the Coppet circle which hosted the first meeting of the Swiss Philhellenic Committee, had enlisted Moustoxydis's help as early as 1804, for a projected volume that likewise came to nothing. Moustoxydis himself was contemplating such an edition in 1820 (Zanou 2018, 174, 204). Evidently, Fauriel captured the Zeitgeist, and it is thanks to him that "the cause of Greek folk poetry and that of Greek nationalism became inseparably linked" (Beaton 1980, 7).

Fauriel was well aware of Herder's reflections on folk poetry, and echoes of Wolf's research into the oral genesis of the Homeric epics are evident in the prefatory essay to the *Chants* (Espagne 2005, 66–67). In fact, Fauriel never set foot in Greece and his sources were mostly literate Greeks living in Europe, making his access to this idealized *génie du peuple* heavily mediated at best. The collection, Fauriel explains, intends to refute the view of present-day Greeks as "something incongruous and profane thrown in the midst of the sacred ruins of ancient Greece, only to spoil the scene . . . for the worshipping scholars that visit them from time to time." Greece is still alive with the "energy" and "passionate love of liberty" that the learned people of Europe admire in its classical past, even if these virtues lie crushed under the "Turkish yoke" (Fauriel 1824–1825, 1:viii). Fauriel's lament for the lost "genius of paganism" sounds another radical note, one which also accords with the emphasis on non-Christian mythic and heroic tales of the romantic Nordic revival, from Ossian to the *Eddas*. Modern Greek lore also had the advantage of uniting two great aspirations of the romantic movement: on the one hand, the search for a classically conceived universal poetry that would speak of, and to, an ideal version of the human condition; and on the other hand, the historical investigation and active recuperation of particular national cultures and their authentic, unique features. This coincidence of aims clearly underpins Fauriel's assertions that the folk songs represent "a veritable national history of modern Greece," while also being the natural continuation of "the dead language of Homer" (Fauriel 1824–1825, 1:xxv, ix).

The image of Homer is of course central to the articulation of this new historical awareness. Fauriel pays tribute to the anonymous "blind rhapsodes" who travel rural Greece to "collect, memorize, and disseminate pieces they haven't themselves composed," as well as weaving new songs out of current events. Like their ancient counterparts, they are "the popular historians of Greece," and the klephts whom they memorialize are the modern equivalent of Homeric heroes (Fauriel 1824–1825, 1:xcii–xciii). Fauriel would have found the idea that Homer was "the first historian of pagan antiquity" in Vico, together with the insight that insofar as the *Iliad* and *Odyssey* had been compiled from the repertoire of popular stories, "these Greek peoples were themselves Homer" (Vico 1999, 387, 382). It is no surprise, then, that the first and longest section of the volume is dedicated to klephtic songs.

And although Fauriel makes little direct reference to the ongoing war, the inclusion of contemporary poems in the Greek demotic by Rhigas and Solomos clearly signals sympathy for the radical, cosmopolitan patriotism embodied in their texts. In keeping with the documentary spirit of the collection, Rhigas's *Hymne de guerre* (Battle hymn) is reproduced in the historical section of the second volume not for its literary merits, of which Fauriel is less than appreciative, but because of its wide dissemination. Rhigas's hymn had been able to reach even illiterate laborers (Fauriel tells in his introduction), thereby earning its place in folklore. Solomos's *Dithyrambe sur la liberté* appears instead in a separate appendix as a contrastive example of learned poetry.

Fauriel's volume spawned a series of translations and adaptations, including instant versions by Wilhelm Müller in German and by Charles Brinsley Sheridan in English (both 1825). Paul Joss capitalized on the philhellenic market with his *Specimens of Romaic Lyric Poetry* (1826), and the following year saw the publication of the first of five volumes of *Neugriechische Volkslieder,* Theodor Kind's more scholarly endeavor (1827–1861).

That the European reception of Greek folk song as part of the revolutionary atmosphere comes about in very culture-specific ways can be discerned through Sheridan's *The Songs of Greece* (Fauriel 1825b). The editor and translator made numerous changes to Fauriel's French-language versions. Among these are the employment of verse translation in the ballad idiom for which English readers had acquired (but were by now losing?) the taste; the removal of supposedly weak verses and even entire songs; and, especially, the insertion of intrusive and partisan editorial comment drawing out the political implications. It is not that Fauriel had ignored these—he mentioned, for example, the significance of Athanasios Diakos as now a name known all over Europe, unlike that of the earlier klephts—but Sheridan, whose volume was produced in aid of the Society for the Promotion of Education in Greece, went further. A characteristic intervention comes in his version of "The Night Journey" (better known as the "Song of the Dead Brother") where the marrying off of the sister is not just a narrative device—marriage abroad in Babylon (Baghdad)—but conjures up a par excellence Orientalizing spectacle (Fauriel 1825b, 207):

> Fearing the Pasha's gloating eye
>   And unrelenting hand!
> Oh! send her, mother, as a bridge,
>   To Europe's happier land.

Here a song close to the Greek heart to this day is endowed with a message of quite another kind, and the kind of activism behind Sheridan's enterprise—the belief that, as he oddly puts it, the Greeks might become "the recipient and conductor of moral electricity" (Fauriel 1825b, lxv) rather than simply crusading all the way to Constantinople (xlv n)—comes through. A further interesting point is that, while Sheridan's subtitle refers to "the Romaic text, edited by M. C. Fauriel," he later disavows the term: "I have avoided the word 'Romaic,' and such other terms, as hang about Greece, like badges of shame and suffering" (lix). Greek identity, preserved by the klephts in their mountain fastnesses, must issue forth as truly Hellenic.

In 1842, the Dalmatian intellectual Niccolò Tommaseo published his own *Canti del popolo greco* (as part of a wider anthology of South-East European folk songs), which borrowed freely from the *Chants*, as well as from the works of Kind and Joss and from the expert advice of Moustoxydis, Solomos, and other Greeks. The presentation of the texts follows Fauriel's by then paradigmatic format, with parallel text, literal versions in prose, and a substantial apparatus of notes and commentary, often translated verbatim from the *Chants*. The free exchange between these scholars was carried out in the eighteenth-century tradition of antiquarian research, but the circulation of these songs in multiple translations and retranslations points forward to the emergence of a new world literary space, where Greek folk songs became simultaneously an object for international consumption and a building block of Greek national identity.

Tommaseo, who went on to become an influential figure of the Risorgimento and of Italian letters, was an overseas Venetian, born in Dalmatia just after the fall of the republic to Napoleon and the loss of its territories in the Mediterranean. His Greek songs are part of a larger work which gathers together Tuscan, Corsican, and Illyrian specimens. Here, the rhetoric of purity and authenticity is reserved exclusively for exaltations of rustic virtue and spontaneity, and tirades against the corrupt academic poetry of "printed books" read on "green velvet armchairs" (Tommaseo 1841–1842, 1:v). A strict moralist on matters of religion and sex, Tommaseo can be refreshingly open in his outlook on the relations between nations. Unlike Chateaubriand, he delights in the melting pot of cultures that is the Balkans, starting from his native Dalmatia, "a mixture of different peoples and histories." He berates the Greeks for looking down on their Orthodox "brothers" in the region and ends his preface to the last volume with a plea for the "united glory of both Greece and Serbia, two elect members of the human family" (Tommaseo 1841–1842, 4:20, 24).

Tommaseo's project is comparative in spirit, and the copious notes accompanying the texts highlight thematic and phraseological similarities across the corpus, as well as loanwords and etymologies from the Turkish and from Slavonic languages (though the corrupting influence of modern French worries him). Time and again, Tommaseo singles out for praise imagery or style he judges authentically Greek, as in this gloss on a lament: "only Greece can fasten together so powerfully imagination and feeling, serenity and sorrow, society and nature" (Tommaseo 1841–1842, 3:291). More often, however, Tommaseo relies on the reader's instinctive empathy for what he understands as universal human sentiments, which are rendered in Italian in an archaizing language that owes much to the Tuscan part of the anthology punctuated with expressions and figures of speech lifted from Dante—Italy's own "bard." This is done in a spirit of ecumenical Christianity but also of political internationalism inspired by Mazzini's doctrine of a "cosmopolitanism of nations." Throughout Europe, Mazzini declared on the eve of 1848, a battle is being fought by "millions of men . . . having a language of their own, as well as specific manners, tendencies, traditions, and national songs," but whose "end is doubtless the same: Liberty" (Mazzini 2009, 194).

In Tommaseo's mind, as in those of many Italian Philhellenes, Italy and Greece had a special bond cemented by their common classical heritage and victimization at the hands of imperial powers. In this vein he addressed the following (unpublished) lines to Greece in 1832: "Look now, Italy turns to you and passionately / Calls you her ally and her sister." The same geopolitical argument is implicit in the structural choice of placing Greek songs side by side with those of other peripheral European nations in the *Canti*: Greece should heed the call of her Italian sister and look west to the Adriatic world where she belongs, and resist falling "within cutting range of the Russian sword" (Tommaseo 1974, 25; on links between the Greek Revolution and the Italian Risorgimento, see Spetsieri-Beschi and Lucarelli 1986). While heavily indebted to Fauriel, Tommaseo's collection reflects a transformed political landscape where the issue at hand was no longer the armed struggle for emancipation but the growing Russian and Eastern Orthodox influence over the new Greek state.

Significantly, the klephts did not occupy pride of place in Tommaseo's volume. Only a small selection of klephtic songs from Fauriel appears in the section on "Death," together with folkloric materials unconnected to war, and the richest offerings fall under the domestic rubrics of "Love," "Family," and "God." In his version of the "Sterghios," one of the most famous of the klephtic songs popularized by Fauriel, Tommaseo repeatedly translates "Turks" by the generic "enemies." And where the last line, "rather than living with the Turks," gets an anti-Muslim spin from Sheridan ("rather than share with the Turks the mosque"), Tommaseo speaks simply of "living with the unrighteous" (*ingiusti*), opting to stress the immorality of foreign domination rather than religious differences (Fauriel 1824–1825, 1:129; Fauriel 1825b, 43; Tommaseo 1841–1842, 3:376). The days of valiant outlaws and barbarous infidels were over—or at least had gone out of fashion.

The romantic fascination for Greek folklore also reverberates through original poetry composed around the years of the revolution. Wilhelm Müller, who translated Fauriel into German, was also the author of *Lieder der Griechen* (1821–1826), fifty-two poems that sealed his fame as "Griechen-Müller." The majority are dramatic monologues written from the perspective of stock Greek characters such as "The Souliot Woman" and "The Maniot Boy" or that commemorate revolutionary heroes such as Kanaris and Byron. Müller consciously inscribed them in the pan-European folk tradition by adopting the fifteen-syllable line the standard meter of Greek popular (and other narrative) poetry, as well as the rhyming couplet typical of German ballads (Güthenke 2008, 130). The first slim volume appeared in October 1821, only seven months after the start of the revolution, and was soon out of print. Five more installments followed, none of which quite matched the sales rates of the first, until publication was stopped by the censor.

Though Müller had been a favored student of Wolf in Berlin, his Philhellenism was not of the scholarly kind. In 1818 he proclaimed Goethe's injunction to imitate the Greeks "the ne plus ultra of banality and presumption," and while in Rome he distanced himself from the arch-classicism of German artistic circles to chronicle popular customs and manners (Werner 1969, 135). His interest in Greece was similarly geared toward the present and the political and, like many liberal Philhellenes, he saluted 1821 as the continuation of the revolutionary struggle that had been stamped out by the Restoration in Europe. In a poem addressed to the "friends of antiquity" ("Die Griechen an die Freunde ihres Alterthums"), Müller imagines the Greeks of his day taking apolitical Hellenists to task:

> Don't you recognize free Greece?
> Alas, friends, so you were only playing with names! . . .
> What was old has become new, what was distant has gotten closer . . .
> It's knocking at your door—and you shut it in its face.
> Does it look so different from what you dreamed of?
>
> (Müller 1906, 183)

Müller attacks the solipsistic aspects of aesthetic and philosophical classicism, which make it possible for the great powers of Europe to see themselves as the rightful heirs to ancient civilizations while failing to intervene in support of the Greek Revolution. What they didn't understand was that the true message of classical learning was a radical one: "Be free!" ("Die letzen Griechen," Müller 1906, 224).

Metternich's policy of appeasement toward the Ottomans is a particular target. It is no use for Greece to plead with Europe: "Don't ask a lord's help against vassalage, / Even the sultan's divan is for Europe a sacred throne" ("Griechenlands Hoffnung," Müller 1906, 189). In this way, the Greek war loses its political specificity and becomes an ersatz revolution conducted against reactionary governments at home. Müller did not join the Philhellenes' battalion (although he gave money to the cause), and apart from a brush with censorship he did not suffer unduly for his political convictions. But it would be unfair to write off his Greek poems as empty posturing. Their raw anger and violence aspire to shock his readers into action, or perhaps donation. One of the most outspoken is "Die Verpestete Freiheit" (Pestilential freedom) of 1822. It pours scorn on the selfish indifference of the "Pharisees" of Europe to the humanitarian crisis in Greece, hitting a nerve that is still relevant today:

> They shout: block the ports, quick, secure with quarantines
> borders and shores from boats and ships! . . .
> Freedom itself, as they call it, has been struck by the plague,
> And now flies to the West with all her children . . .
> These days she comes in many disguises:
> One moment she's a woman, then a man,
> Then a mere child, then she's wrinkled with age.

So make sure don't let in any refugee from Greece,
That freedom might not spread its plague in your fine lands!
(Müller 1906, 217)

Metaphors of contagion denounce Europe's abject fear of the foreign outcasts
that threaten its wellbeing. The disease they bring, says Müller, is the infectious
love of freedom, by which European society post-Waterloo has been untouched.
Though they espouse the simple aesthetics of folk song, the *Griechenlieder* reflect in complex ways on the power imbalance between European readers and
Greek fighters and civilian victims on the ground. The strongly performative
and subjective slant of the poems enacts the dialectic of distance and proximity
inherent in philhellenic culture, and, at their best, ask difficult ethical questions
about passive spectatorship and engagement, testing the limits of political art
and action.

The failure to intervene on behalf of the oppressed Greeks is also at the
center of the controversy around the cession of Parga, an affair which cast a
long shadow. Part of Venice's Ionian possessions for three centuries, the coastal
town fell under French control in 1797 and became a British protectorate in
1814. In 1819, however, Britain ceded Parga to Ali Pasha. Greek patriots and
Philhellenes everywhere regarded this as a disgraceful betrayal, and the plight
of the town's inhabitants, who chose exile rather than submitting to Ali, made
an enormous impression on international public opinion. The "sale of Parga"
became the subject of countless newspaper articles, pamphlets, poems, paintings, and melodramas. There are numerous examples in Droulia's (2017) bibliography, and a further four are recorded in Caccia (1951). A forged Byron
poem with the title "Parga" also circulated in the 1820s (Cochran 2000). Parga's cession was taken as a tragic case of realpolitik crushing legitimate aspirations to freedom, and offered particular points of comparison with the obstacles
placed by the great powers to Italian unification. From his London exile, Ugo
Foscolo, the Italian-Greek poet and intellectual, wrote an article for the *Edinburgh Review* called "In Parga," in which he denounced it as "one of the most
flagrant instances of impolicy and oppression of which history has preserved
any record" (Foscolo 1964, 96). Foscolo also wrote a book on the topic entitled
Narrative of Events Illustrating the Vicissitudes and the Cession of Parga (now in
Foscolo 1964, 171–377, alongside his other writings on the Ionian islands). It was
hastily withdrawn from publication either for fear of repercussions or because
Foscolo had started to doubt the reliability of testimonies coming from Parga.
Either way, his perceived lack of nerve in this instance cost him his reputation
among Italian liberals, with Tommaseo his harshest critic (Muoni 1907, 6).

Foscolo's article helped crystallize the main outline of the story. The cession of Parga, in itself a minor episode, thus became a symbolic site where British values and the role of Britain in the Mediterranean were put to the test—as was, by extension, the Greeks' relation to the great European powers. Castlereagh's claim that Britain was acting within the terms of an international treaty is systematically dismantled in Foscolo's article, and the fictional figure of the "Pargiot elder" delivers the final thrust of the argument, urging his fellow citizens not to rely on England, a country of "merchants" who will not hesitate to "sell" them in exchange for "commercial advantages in [Ali's] harbours" (Foscolo 1964, 89). The old man's prediction comes to pass, and the inhabitants of Parga give an exemplary display of unflinching patriotism:

> Every family marched solemnly out of their dwelling, without tears or lamentation; and the men . . . proceeded to the sepulchers of their fathers, and silently unearthed and collected their remains, which they placed upon a huge pile of wood. . . . They then took their arms in their hands, and, setting fire to the pile, stood motionless and silent around it, till the whole was consumed. (Foscolo 1964, 102)

No one was better placed than Foscolo, whose own poem *Dei sepolcri* revolves around tombs as sites of memory and civic identity, to depict the scene of the townspeople burning the bones of their ancestors to preserve them from desecration, which was to become a powerful trope of philhellenic propaganda.

Another Italian exile in London, Giovanni Berchet, turned his attention to the Parga affair in his narrative poem *I profughi di Parga* (The refugees from Parga), first published in 1823 in Paris, with a French translation by Fauriel. Berchet's democratic ideas extended to matters of versification, and *I profughi* is written in a version of the medieval *romanza* form that aims for a formulaic structure, simple language and strong emotional impact. Drawing on reports by Foscolo and others and protesting factual accuracy, the poem in fact imagines the encounter between a survivor from Parga who attempts suicide by jumping off a cliff and Arrigo, the Englishman who saves him. There is no shortage of conventional motifs: Ali Pasha is devious and bloodthirsty, and the anonymous Greek a paradigm of manly virtue, driven to madness (*furor*) by grief and humiliation. The main outline of the incident is set by now: the people of Parga stoically accept the fate of exile, but not before exhuming and incinerating "the reliquiae of the forefathers" (Berchet 1911, 16).

A new element is the ambiguous characterization of Arrigo as himself a victim of Britain's unscrupulous foreign policy. His melancholy, a trait associated, from de Staël onward, with British travelers, is here reinterpreted not as a matter of temperament but as the burden of empire: disgusted with his country and himself, Arrigo roams around Europe in self-imposed exile, but finds no peace. Wherever he goes he is hounded by

> The laments of countless peoples,
> Of all the peoples that England betrayed
> Of all the peoples that England sold off.
>   (Berchet 1911, 23)

This emphatic conclusion drives home the idea that Parga is just one of Britain's many victims, representative of the fate of smaller and weaker nations at the mercy of more powerful ones. But, through Arrigo, it also registers the point that a disconnect might emerge between individual citizens and their conservative national governments, which could be exploited to advance the cause of justice and freedom and create transnational solidarity networks. Here we see dramatized the possibility that adversarial free speech (in this case a poem) and grassroots opposition can shrink the distances between peoples and push governments to respond. It is to such sentiments that Berchet appeals in his foreword to the French edition, where he insists that "the peoples of Europe are not and cannot really be enemies, least of all today when [their common] suffering combines with reason . . . to develop among them a sentiment of European nationality that is beginning to draw them closer together" (Berchet 1911, 4).

While Italian and German Philhellenism was mostly coded in classicizing terms or in the popular forms of militant romanticism, French responses to the Greek Revolution also felt the lure of the East, and in the Byronic vein. Philhellenic and Orientalist themes merge most spectacularly in Victor Hugo's *Les Orientales* (1829), a collection of odes and ballads that appeared as the revolution was drawing to a close and Greek independence seemed firmly within reach. The majority of the forty-one poems deal in some manner with the war, and the brutality of violence and destruction is often described and aestheticized with relish. In "Les Têtes du sérail," the severed heads of the Greek martyrs captured at Missolonghi are impaled on stakes outside the harem, and speak in turn of their death or humiliation at the hands of the Turks. And Navarino is celebrated as an epic battle in which "Africa [is] defeated" and "the true God tramples the false prophet underfoot" (Hugo 1912, 658). Generally, though, Hugo is more interested in points of contact and symmetries rather than in the clash of civilizations. In a calculated provocation, he ends the preface by hinting that "perhaps the old barbarism of Asia is not as devoid of superior men as our civilization would like to believe." As an example he cites the universally reviled Ali Pasha, calling him a "man of genius" in the same class as Napoleon (620).

Most of the poems are uncontroversially pro-Greek, but a few swap sides and give a voice to the Ottoman leaders and their armies:

> We shall retake you, city whose domes are made of pure gold,
> Sweet Setiniah, which in their coarse language
> The barbarians call Athens!
> ("Cri de Guerre du Mufti," Hugo 1912, 661)

Just as the binary of barbarism and civilization is relative and reversible, so Hugo's Orient is not a remote heterotopia but exists at the periphery of Europe: Greece, but also the Danube and Moorish Spain. Orientalist tropes abound (fantasies of the harem, extravagant atrocities, *djinns,* and other magical creatures), and take hold of Western sympathizers, too. In the grip of philhellenic frenzy, the poet cries out: "To Greece, my friends! Revenge! Liberty! / A turban on my brow! A sword on my side!" ("Enthousiasme," Hugo 1912, 648).

Hugo never went to Greece, and openly admits that the poems are a creation of the imagination inspired by the recent surge of interest in the Orient. Still, he suggests this cultural trend foreshadows an actual geopolitical shift. Chateaubriand's architectonic metaphor returns in Hugo's preface, where he compares his work to a medieval Spanish town, where the great gothic cathedral stands at a short distance from "the oriental mosque." This rich hybrid aesthetics might provide a model for European politics, and it is on this basis that Hugo attempts a political prognosis: "For empires as well as in literature, the Orient will soon perhaps be called to play a role in the West. The historic war in Greece has already brought everyone's attention on that part of the world. Now, the balance of Europe is about to break. . . . The whole continent is tilting east" (Hugo 1912, 619–620).

Such a tilt east, as concerns imaginative literature in English, had been made decisively by the work and life of Byron; and this generates certain paradoxes. On the one hand, the presence of modern Greece in the modern European mind owes much to Byron's own works, as of course to the cult of his memory, starting in 1824, when the War of Independence had years to run. (A striking example, from a poet whose study of ancient Greek poetry was deep and whose later influence on modern Greek poetry was formative, was Tennyson [1987, 1:159–160], who wrote a teenage effusion, "Exhortation to the Greeks," in 1827, but never returned to the subject.) On the other, as David Roessel (2002, 8) shrewdly observes in the authoritative study of the topic, significantly entitled *In Byron's Shadow:*

one of the main reasons that so little of the mass of philhellenic writings from the Greek War of Independence has lasted is that the canonical texts of the Greek Revolution were written by Byron before the Greek Revolution had even started. With the "scripture" of the Greek uprising intact, later works functioned more as commentary and interpretation.

One danger, then, was that Byron's influence would overwhelm all later literary production, even in Greece itself: the poet and critic Kostis Palamas, who thought hard about all this and who had absorbed philhellenic currents of many kinds into his own writing, wrote in 1896 of the Greek romantic period as an "age of Byron-mania" (Georganta 1992, 11). Writers, especially but not only in Byron's own language, would find it hard to find a place outside his shadow. The cult of Byron was Europewide (Cardwell 2004), and to some extent it squeezed out other preoccupations, certainly in the field of poetry. Palamas, an astute observer, was to comment that "In France alone have poetry and prose been for any duration inspired by the Greek land and soul" (n.d., 230).

Palamas's instinct was right: Roessel (2002, 91) notes the number of Greece-inspired French novels as compared with English (and the same point could be made about painting and music). Perhaps more importantly, the cult of Byron was longer-lived in the European south (including Greece itself, where Byron is still a common Christian name) than in Britain (Holland 2018, 93). But there is a further point of importance: the Greek poetry of the revolution was shaped by foreign, and especially French, poetry, at least as much as it shaped the latter. Georgia Gotsi, in a full case study, draws attention, for example, to the influence of the French poet and academician Casimir Delavigne on Andreas Kalvos's ode honoring Kanaris, "The Volcanoes" (1826), a poem which, as Palamas correctly surmised, later came to influence Hugo's Les Orientales through its French translation (Gotsi 2010, 43–44). In turn, Hugo's "Canaris," in particular, came to influence a wide range of Greek poetry (25–88).

In all this there is a certain selectivity: revolutionary writings (think of Carlyle) tend to revolve around hero-worship. As Palamas noted (n.d., 231): "In 1827 two names stand out in the admiration of Philhellenes. Dioscuri of heroism: Botsaris, Kanaris." But it is striking to note just how far Kanaris, in Hugo's poem that bears his name, functions as a mere emblem of the freedom struggle rather than bearing much historical detail; in "À Canaris" some years later, this fervor has been replaced by a tenderness toward a (supposedly) now neglected figure treated as akin to the toppled Napoleon (Gotsi 2010, 26). At any rate, Hugo remained an author who, to the gratitude of the Greeks, would at later points in his career be heard defending Greek national claims.

But Hugo was just one of a number of French poets, most of them forgotten today, who was inspired to verse by the figure of Kanaris; Gotsi (2010, 36–37) lists another fifteen French poems on this hero. The theme was tailor-made for romantic poetry: a naval victory against overwhelming odds, echoing the battle of Salamis. (As Roessel notes, events of the '21 were often brought into specious harmony with the Persian Wars [2002, 84].) So far is this true that Kanaris is addressed also in Hugo's "Navarin," despite his (and the Greeks') absence from the crucial engagement of 1827 (Gotsi 2010, 56–57). Kanaris is thus coopted to Hugo's own political engagement; and the wider scope of *Les Orientales,* with its attention to and sympathy for the Ottomans as well as the Greeks, is both more elusive and less obviously *engagé* than the run of philhellenic poetry from the period. Hugo's formulation, "Grèces de Byron et d'Homère," illuminatingly glossed by Roessel (2002, 43–44), is less a statement about cultural continuity than a claim coming from a poet who aspires to a voice which can synthesize these two entities into a new poetic frame. And what Holland (2018, 93) notes as "something too simply equivocal about modern Greece," as a subject for romantic mythmaking, is precisely what brings out the most in Hugo the poet.

The Greek Revolution in poetry can give us the same sense that it offers itself as a personal subject more than an object of empathy: Landor's poem "Regeneration" (1824) is a good example. Holland (2018, 92) notes of Shelley's oft-quoted statement from his last poem, *Hellas* (1822), "We are all Greeks," that "the declaration had to do with universal mind and spirit, not actual events"; and so the Greek Revolution seems to have been for Landor. The core idea of his poem is an arresting one: that, despite Homer's greatness, the subject of the *Iliad* was a petty domestic quarrel between squabbling monarchs when compared with recent explosive events, and in particular with Kanaris's first great exploit with his fireships off the coast of Chios in 1822. The modern poet addresses Homer:

> When on the Chian coast, one javelin's throw
> From where thy tombstone, where thy cradle stood,
> Twice twenty self-devoted Greeks assailed
> The naval host of Asia, at one blow
> Scattered it into air . . . and Greece was free
>   (Landor 1964, 153–155)

What is interesting to note about Landor's (over-long and over-Miltonic) poem is that its real focus was less on Greece than on the Italy where the poet now resided, and more still, perhaps, on the England he had left behind. It is not the oppressed Greek, the *rayah,* who represents the truly servile culture which requires to be reborn in this age of revolution: no, it is the rest of the world that stands in need of the bold message that comes from the regenerated Greeks: "Thou recreant slave / That sittest afar off, and helpest not, / O thou degenerate Albion!" Revolutionary Greece for Landor, Adam Roberts argues (2014, 67), is the cure for an "individual melancholia."

Perhaps the very absence of Kanaris's name from "Regeneration" is significant here: contrast a poem which we find noticed in the innocently antiquarian pages of the *Classical Journal* in 1823: "Canares, a Poem in Modern Greek" by a student of Trinity College, Cambridge (and seemingly a native of Ithaka), one Nicholas Maniakes. This assiduous young man composed a mini-epic, centered on Kanaris's exploits, in a form of the language mingling spoken Greek with Homeric idioms. The reviewer commends the effort and the authorship but scorns the modern Greek meter. And he begins his review with words which show caution (he is thinking of the massacres at Tripolitsa in the previous year): "Notwithstanding the excesses with which the Greeks have in some instances stained the glory of their victories [. . .]" ("Review" 1823, 350). This ambivalence does not mark all works which dwell on the Greek Revolution, by any means— think of Hugo—but it contributes to the "certain sourness" which Holland (2018, 183) sees as lingering in British views and affecting the reception of such late-flowering revolutionary poems such as Swinburne's "Ode to Candia" (1867), better received in Greece than it ever was in Britain.

Now, when we speak of echoes of a revolution, we might imagine that they would persist, even out of mere nostalgia and allowing for the distance in time from the events, and also for the fact that the Philhellenes who participated on the ground were diverse and often noteworthy, but numerically few. Yet the flame of revolutionary ardor for the Greeks was soon dimmed by the Greek acquisition of a state and then by a pervasive disappointment with that state—and with the Greeks themselves—across much of Europe. Acton, least poetic of historians, spoke for such people when he wrote in 1862 that "The Greeks neither deserved their independence nor acquired it themselves" (1952, 456).

Memories of revolutionary ardor could be fanned into flame, notably at the time of the (disastrous) war of 1897 with its Garibaldi connection. But this itself could provide a ready target for the Oxford classical scholar and popular versifier A. D. Godley (1899, 54–60). In "The Road to Renown" he counsels the would-be politician as follows: "You must come on the scene as a bold Philhellene, and a foe to the Turk and the Tyrant! / You may cheerfully speak of assisting the Greek 'gainst the foes that his country environ: / 'Tis improbable quite you'll be wanted to fight, and the phrase will remind them of Byron." "Graeculus Esuriens" goes a step further in imagining the Greeks thinking beyond Crete and annexing the Isle of Wight, having influenced British public opinion not to fight "The men of Homer's gifted line—the sons of Socrates!" It was only in the graver circumstances of the Great War and Greece's entrance on the side of the Entente Cordiale that the force of Greece's revolutionary literature would return: Kipling (2013, 1384–1385) was asked in 1918 by the Greek legation in London to translate the national anthem (the opening stanzas of Dionysios Solomos's *Hymn to Liberty*), and he did so in a vigorous idiom:

> From the graves of our slain
>> Shall thy valour prevail
> As we greet thee again—
>> Hail, Liberty! Hail!

The Greek Revolution found an echo in many contemporary hearts—most commonly, those many hearts receptive to the glamor of Byron—and the phenomenon which Roessel wittily calls "klephtomania" (2002, 86) is of no small interest. Yet its lasting contribution to the literature of Europe is a minor one. That is not for lack of material: Loukia Droulia's catalog (2017) of philhellenic productions—defined as works inspired by the Greek War of Independence and issued between 1821 and 1833—is both rich and diverse. Furthermore, a case study such as Georgia Gotsi's on Kanaris shows that there is room for further analysis of such material and what it tells us about what may be called the Greek Revolution effect (cf. Perovic and Mucignat 2018), a complex phenomenon of reciprocal influences. A survey chapter of the present kind has had for reasons of space to concentrate on major literatures, and especially on verse production, and to leave the rather different case of Russia (Ilinskaya 2001) to one side; and there is a further story to be told about revolutionary Greece's presence in Western musical settings in the spheres of art song and popular song (for an intriguing suggestion about Schubert, see Johnson 2014, 3:277–278; see Katerina Levidou, "Sounding the Greek Revolution," in this volume). But the presence of the Greek Revolution in the canon of European poetry beyond Byron is surprisingly thin.

In Robert Holland's wide-ranging study (2018) of how the Mediterranean shaped the British imagination, the Greek Revolution is but a minor theme; and not because that theme is one unfamiliar to the author. And in his well-nigh comprehensive study on modern Greece in the English and American imagination, David Roessel (2002, 90) is unsentimental in his assessment:

> When we survey the enormous output of philhellenic literature in Europe and America during the Greek War of Independence, now admirably catalogued in the bibliography of philhellenic writing by Droulia, one

is immediately struck by the fact that almost none of it has lasted. Delacroix's paintings. Hugo's *Orientales,* and Halleck's "Marco Bozzaris" are about all that stand out.

Roessel contrasts the impact of the Spanish Civil War on the literature and art of the twentieth century: an apposite contrast, because the Greek cause was always harder to see in terms of a dividing line with pan-European appeal. And if we are considering a longer run of engagement with another story of nation-building, territorially and spiritually, then it is clear that the importance of the Italian Risorgimento is of more pervasive importance for nineteenth-century English poetry (Reynolds 2001) than the Greek Revolution. Roderick Beaton (2013, 266) has drawn attention to Byron's own words from March 1824:

I cannot . . . calculate to what a height Greece may rise. Hitherto it has been a subject for the hymns and elegies of fanatics and enthusiasts; but now it will draw the attention of the politician.

Revolutionary Greece preoccupied the statesmen of Europe, as, intermittently, would the Greece of the economic and political crises that have followed at intervals. Meanwhile, most of the literary echoes have gradually died away.

Rosa Mucignat and David Ricks

References

Acton, John. 1952. *Essays on Church and State.* Edited by Douglas Woodruff. London.
Augustinos, Olga. 1994. *French Odysseys: Greece in French Travel Literature from the Renaissance to the Romantic Era.* Baltimore, MD.
Bass, Garry. 2008. *Freedom's Battle: The Origins of Humanitarian Intervention.* New York.
Beaton, Roderick. 1980. *Folk Poetry of Modern Greece.* Cambridge.
Beaton, Roderick. 2013. *Byron's War: Romantic Rebellion, Greek Revolution.* Cambridge.
Berchet, Giovanni. 1911. "I profughi di Parga." In *Poesie,* edited by Egidio Bellorini, 3–5. Vol. 1 of *Opere.* Bari.
Blaquiere, Edward. 1825. *Narrative of a Second Visit to Greece.* London.
Caccia, Natale. 1951. "L'episodio di Parga in alcuni componimenti poetici francesi e inglesi." In *Studi sul Berchet pubblicati per il primo centenario della morte,* edited by Alfredo Galletti, 387–418. Milan.
Cardwell, Richard A. 2004. *The Reception of Byron in Europe.* London.
Chateaubriand, François-René de. 1814. *Travels in Greece, Palestine, Egypt and Barbary, during the Years 1806 and 1807.* Translated by Frederic Shoberl. New York.

Cochran, Peter. 2000. "The Sale of Parga and *The Isles of Greece.*" *Keats-Shelley Review* 14: 42–51.

Droulia, Loukia. 2017. *Phihellénisme: Ouvrages inspirés par la guerre de l'indépendance grecque, 1821–1833. Répertoire bibliographique.* 2nd ed. Athens.

Espagne, Michel. 2005. "Le philhellénisme entre philologie et politique. Un transfert franco-allemand." *Revue Germanique Internationale* 1–2:61–75.

Fauriel, Claude, ed. 1824–1825. *Chants populaires de la Grèce moderne.* Paris.

Fauriel, Claude, ed. 1825a. *Neugriechische Volkslieder. Gesammelt und herausgegeben von C. Fauriel. Übersetzt . . . von Wilhelm Müller . . . , Τραγούδια ρωμαϊκά.* Translated by Wilhelm Müller. Leipzig.

Fauriel, Claude, ed. 1825b. *The Songs of Greece, from the Romaic Text, Edited by M. C. Fauriel, with Additions.* Translated by Charles Brinsley Sheridan. London.

Foscolo, Ugo. 1964. *Prose politiche e apologetiche (1817–1827), parte prima: Scritti sulle Isole Ionie e su Parga.* Edited by Giovanni Gambarin. Florence.

Georganta, Athina. 2001. *Αιών Βυρωνομανής* [A century of Byronomania]. Athens.

Godley, Alfred Denis. 1899. *Lyra Frivola.* London.

Gotsi, Georgia. 2010. *Η διεθνοποίηση της φαντασίας* [The internationalization of the imagination]. Athens.

Güthenke, Constanze. 2008. *Placing Modern Greece: The Dynamics of Romantic Hellenism, 1770–1840.* Oxford.

Holland, Robert. 2018. *The Warm South.* New Haven, CT.

Hugo, Victor. 1912. *Œuvres completes.* Vol. 24, *Odes et Ballades, Les Orientales.* Paris.

Ibrovac, Miodrag. 1966. *Claude Fauriel et la fortune européenne des poésies populaires grecques et serbes.* Paris.

Ilinskaya, Sonia, ed. 2001. *Η Ελληνική Επανάσταση στον καθρέφτη της ρωσικής ποίησης* [The Greek Revolution in the mirror of Russian poetry]. Athens.

Johnson, Graham, ed. 2014. *Franz Schubert: The Complete Songs.* New Haven, CT.

Kipling, Rudyard. 2013. *The Cambridge Edition of the Poems of Rudyard Kipling.* Edited by Thomas Pinney. Cambridge.

Landor, Walter Savage. 1964. *Poems.* Edited by Geoffrey Grigson. London.

Loraux, Nicole, and Pierre Vidal-Naquet. 1979. "The Formation of Bourgeois Athens." In *Politics, Ancient and Modern* by Pierre Vidal-Naquet, 82–140. Cambridge.

Marchand, Suzanne L. 1996. *Down from Olympus: Archaeology and Philhellenism in Germany, 1750–1970.* Princeton, NJ.

Mazzini, Giuseppe. 2009. "The European Question: Foreign Intervention and National Self-Determination (1847)." In *A Cosmopolitanism of Nations: Giuseppe Mazzini's Writings on Democracy, Nation Building, and International Relations,* edited by Stefano Recchia and Nadia Urbinati, 193–198. Princeton, NJ.

Momigliano, Arnaldo. 1955. "George Grote and the Study of Greek History." In *Contributo alla storia degli studi classici,* 213–231. Rome.

Müller, Wilhelm. 1906. *Gedichte.* Edited by James Taft Hatfield. Berlin.

Muoni, Guido. 1907. *La letteratura filellenica nel romanticismo italiano.* Milan.

Palamas, Kostis. n.d. "Ο Βίκτωρ Ουγκώ και η Ελλάς" [Victor Hugo and Greece]. In *Άπαντα,* [Complete works], vol. 10, 221–262. Athens.

Parry, William. 1825. *The Last Days of Lord Byron*. London.

Pecchio, Giuseppe. 1826. *Relazione degli avvenimenti della Grecia nella primavera del 1825*. Lugano.

Perovic, Sanja, and Rosa Mucignat, eds. 2018. "The French Revolution Effect." Special issue, *Comparative Critical Studies* 15, no. 2 (September 1).

"Review of Nicholas Maniakes, 'Canares.'" 1823. *Classical Journal* 27:350–355.

Reynolds, Matthew. 2001. *The Realms of Verse, 1830–1870: English Poetry in a Time of Nation-Building*. Oxford.

Roberts, Adam. 2014. *Landor's Cleanness*. Oxford.

Roessel, David. 2002. *In Byron's Shadow: Modern Greece in the English and American Imagination*. Oxford.

Roth, Tobias. 2015. "Mit scharfen und mit zerbrochenen Zithern. Wilhelm Müllers Kriegslyrik, die Lieder der Griechen und der Kampf um Griechenlands Antike." In *Wilhelm Müller und der Philhellenismus,* edited by Marco Hillemann and Tobias Roth, 19–43. Berlin.

Spetsieri-Beschi, Caterina, and Enrica Lucarelli, eds. 1986. *Risorgimento greco e filellenismo italiano: Lotte, cultura, arte, mostra promossa dall'Ambasciata di Grecia e dall'Associazione per lo sviluppo delle relazioni fra Italia e Grecia*. Rome. Exhibition catalog.

St Clair, William. 2008. *That Greece Might Still Be Free: The Philhellenes in the War of Independence*. 2nd edition. Cambridge.

Tennyson, Alfred. 1987. *The Poems of Tennyson*. Edited by Christopher Ricks. 2nd ed. London.

Tommaseo, Niccolò. 1841–1842. *Canti popolari, toscani, corsi, illirici e greci*. Venice.

Tommaseo, Niccolò. 1974. *Un affetto: Memorie politiche. Testo inedito*. Edited by Michele Cataudella. Rome.

Ukert, Friedrich August. 1810. *Gemälde von Griechenland*. Königsberg.

Vico, Giambattista. 1999. *New Science*. Translated by David Marsh. London.

Werner, Hans-Georg. 1969. *Geschichte des politischen Gedichts in Deutschland von 1815 bis 1840*. Berlin.

Zanou, Konstantina. 2018. *Transnational Patriotism in the Mediterranean 1800–1850: Stammering the Nation*. Oxford.

Sounding the Greek Revolution: Music and the Greek War of Independence

The Greek Revolution of 1821 struck a chord particularly in Europe and North America and, before long, it inspired many composers. The ground for engagement with the Greek War of Independence in music was fertile for both political and cultural reasons. There was the wider political context shaped, on the one hand, by the successful revolutions in North America and France, and, on the other, by the ongoing struggle for independence and national unification of other nations, such as Italy, Poland, and Germany. At the same time, it was the widespread European Philhellenism associated with the Enlightenment's interest in Greek antiquity that made it easy for other European nations to sympathize with the revolt of the people considered to be the true descendants of the ancient Greeks. A composition that elegantly captures this atmosphere and the fusion of the ancient and modern Greek scenes in European imagination, and, in a way, prepares the ground for works with references to the Greek War of Independence, is Beethoven's *The Ruins of Athens,* op. 113 (1811), incidental music for August von Kotzebue's theatrical play. In Kotzebue's play, the Greek goddess Minerva (Athena), whom Zeus had cast into eternal sleep, wakes up and visits contemporary Athens. She is disillusioned to witness the destruction of the ancient culture by the Ottomans and the poor living conditions that the modern Greeks had to endure under the invaders' rule. But she is subsequently relieved to know that the ancient Greek civilization had fed into contemporary European culture. Beethoven's music highlights the contrast between the civilized West (Christian Europe) and barbarous East (Muslim Ottomans), a theme that also underlay European sympathies with the Greek cause. Once the Greek Revolution broke out, Western composers made more direct references to contemporary events—for instance *La Grèce,* a *scène lyrique* with music by Jacques-Auguste Delaire (performed in Paris in 1826) expresses concerns that Greece will perish (Amandry 1981, 30; Romanou 2011, 146). The responses of Greek composers, though, appeared later, starting in the second half of the nineteenth century, due to the belated development of art music in the country. Quite often, composers did not restrict themselves to the events that took place around 1821, but drew from a wider thematic pool that encompassed references to the Ottoman occupation and cases of resistance that predated or followed the events of the Greek War of Independence.

Philhellenism in Western Music

The Greek Revolution sparked a massive response among composers particularly in Italy and France, but also in England, North America, Russia, Germany, and the Netherlands (Constantzos 2016, 8). Many of them have now fallen into oblivion, but were quite successful in their time (Romanou 2003), while many works, particularly songs, were composed by amateurs (Constantzos 2016). A great number of pieces inspired by the Greek War of Independence were published, especially in Paris (Droulia 2017; Romanou 2003) and were adorned with lithographs by famous engravers (Constantzos 2016). Such scores were sold, and earnings were meant to contribute to the Greek cause. Money was also raised at soirées specifically organized for this purpose as well as intended to recruit volunteers, where the works presented were mostly songs. This is not to say that all works on this topic were popular; for example, the premiere of Hector Berlioz's *La Révolution grecque, scène héroïque* in Paris in 1828 was such a failure that the composer destroyed the manuscript (Romanou 2003). It should also be noted that several of the surviving compositions are anonymous, a practice that is explained by contemporary politics since, officially, European countries recognized the sultan's sovereignty over the region for some years after the outbreak of the Greek Revolution. In this political context, certain works were censored, especially in France, as was the case with *Le dernier jour de Missolonghi* (1828), a *drame héroïque* by Georges Ozaneaux with music by Ferdinand Hérold (Everist 2002), while Rossini's French opera *Le siège de Corinthe* (1826), which depicted the last hours of Corinth before it fell to the Turks in 1458, could easily work as an allegory for the siege of Mesolonghi (Gerhard 1998; Walton 2007).

Compositions inspired by the Greek War of Independence naturally drew on historical events and certain personalities. Among those, the Greek hero Markos Botsaris (who became known for serving in the French army) and the siege of Mesolonghi were the two most popular themes. For instance, Botsaris inspired compositions as diverse as: *Hymne auf den Tod des Marco Botzaris* for voice and piano or guitar (1843) by German composer Johanna Kinkel; *Marco Bozzari,* a *grande scena* by Maltese composer Vincenzo Napoleone Mifsud (published in Trieste in 1849); and the opera *La Fidanzata di Marco Bozzari* by Italian composer Martino Frontini (performed in Catania, Sicily, in 1863). As regards Mesolonghi, a popular reworking of Hérold and Ozaneaux's *Le dernier jour de Missolonghi* appeared in Italy: Antonio Cortesi's ballet *L'ultimo giorno di Missolungi,* with music by Luigi Maria Viviani, was performed in Venice in 1832–1833 and remained in the repertoire for over thirty years. Byron's residence and death in Mesolonghi, specifically, gave rise to Rossini's cantata *Il pianto delle muse in morte di Lord Byron* (1824), while a trio entitled *Byron au camp des Grecs,* signed by Nicoris (possibly the Greek composer Constantinos Agathophron Nikolopoulos—known in Paris as Constantin Nicolopoulo de Smyrne) was published in Paris in 1826. Other historical events that were captured in musical compositions include: the resistance of Souli (*Ultimi giorni di Suli,* an opera by Giovanni Battista Ferrari on Giovanni Peruzzini's libretto, produced in Venice in 1842); the destruction of Psara (the ballets *La caduta di Ipsarà* composed by Luigi Astolfi and *La caduta di Psarà* by Antonio Guerra, both performed in Italy in 1836); and the battle of Navarino (the *opera seria La Battaglia di Navarino* with music by Giuseppe Staffa on Giovanni Emanuele Bidera's libretto, premiered in Naples in 1838, and *Bataille de Navarin,* op. 132, a *fantaisie brillante* for piano with violin or cello accompaniment by Austrian composer J. [Hieronymous] Payer, which was premiered in Paris in 1827).

Historical persons and heroes, as well as characteristic figures of the Greek Revolution (e.g., the klepht and Greek women, especially mourning mothers or female warriors) also fed into musical compositions. Giovanni Galzerani's pantomime *Alì Pascià di Giannina,* with music by Antonio Mussi, was premiered in La Scala, Milan, in 1832 (Leotsakos 2003, 33). Moreover, the figure of Germanos, bishop of Old Patras, inspired Gennaro Fabbrichesi's opera *Il Giuramento di Germanos* (published in Athens in 1842; Leotsakos 2003, 33) and Vincenzo Mifsud's opera *Il giuramento di Germanos, ovvero, La liberazione della Grecia,* which was published in Rome in 1849. At the same time, Greek women were depicted in works such as Giovanni Pacini's *Mères, endormez vos enfants: Chant de Missolonghi,* dedicated to French women protecting Greeks (which was known since 1826); Louis Jadin's romance *La Veuve du Grec Botzaris à l'autel de Marie* (1825); *Chant d'une mère Souliote* by Isidore Milhès; and the romance *Une Veuve grecque au berceau de son fils* (1829) by Ferdinando Paër. We also encounter songs that parallel Greek warriors with their Greek ancestors, bearing titles that refer to Spartans and Macedonians (Constantzos 2016).

A large number of compositions inspired by the Greek War of Independence are songs, or small-scale works for piano or small musical ensembles, although larger-scale works also exist, such as operas and ballets, as we have seen. Most of those works are, technically speaking, rather simple, and use standardized musical means (Romanou 2011). However, Rossini's *Le siège de Corinthe* is a notable case of a composition based on the Greek Revolution that sought to bring about a musical revolution (Gerhard 1998; Walton 2007). It provided a model for the engagement of French opera with historical events in the wider context of historicism (Gerhard 1998, 71–76). Moreover, the opera's ending, marginalizing the role of the heroine as well as that of the choir, enables the depiction of ugliness on stage through a new aesthetics of horror articulated by the orchestra (Gerhard 1998, 76–80). Finally, the role of the choir is elevated overall: it becomes one of the dramatis personae, with an active part in the drama—a political statement about the power of the People (Gerhard 1998, 81–85). Noteworthy is also the *folie-vaudeville Le Dilettante; Ou Le siège de l'Opéra* by Emmanuel Théaulon, Théodore Anne, and Jean-Baptiste Gondelier, which appeared as a response to *Le siège de Corinthe* (it was staged in 1826, less than a month after the premiere of Rossini's opera), with numerous couplets in support of the Greek cause (Walton 2007, 108–109). Last but not least, apart from the composition of original works, a popular practice was the setting of new pro-Greek verses to existing famous military and revolutionary tunes, such as the "Marseillaise" and "Chant du départ," which appeared in collections such as *Hymnes patriotiques des Hellènes, Chansons militaires sur nos airs nationaux les plus remarquables. Dédiés au Colonel Fabvier et à ses braves compatriotes armés pour la même cause,* published in Paris in 1827 (Romanou 2003, 347; Walton 2007, 126).

Greek Musical Responses to the Revolution

The practice of setting popular patriotic tunes to new words is also encountered among Greeks living either in western European cities or in territories that would gradually be incorporated into the Kingdom of Greece. Verses by intellectuals of the Greek diaspora were used and the resulting songs were disseminated as marches by Greek and philhellenic troops or as popular songs at secret gatherings (Constantzos 1993; Kardamis 2019). For example, "La Marseillaise" and "La Carmagnole" were set to Greek verses by Rhigas Velestinlis (Romanou 2003, 347). The setting of the former tune became popular even in the taverns of Constantinople and Thessaloniki, while adaptations of Greek songs to the tune of the "Marseillaise" could be heard in the streets of Athens during King Othon's reign (Kardamis 2019, 66). The main route through which such settings were disseminated in those areas was through the Ionian Islands, which were under French rule in 1797–1779. Patriotic songs by the

Greek, Paris-based, composer Constantinos Agathophron Nikolopoulos (such as "Hymne à l'Éternel pour les Grecs" and the religious and war aria "Le chant de Germanos, archevêque de Patras"), as well as other Greek revolutionary songs were published in western Europe, especially Paris, but also in Belgium (Romanou 2003, 347). The first Greek publication of patriotic songs seems to be in the music volume entitled *Euterpi,* which appeared in Constantinople in 1830 and is in Byzantine notation (Romanou 2003, 347).

The outbreak of the Greek Revolution found areas that would later be incorporated into the Greek state in a very different situation—as far as music is concerned since they were culturally a province of western Europe. Exposure to the tradition of Western art music effectively came through the Ionian islands, which, having been under European rather than Ottoman rule, could maintain musical contact with neighboring Italy. Ionian composers later played a decisive role in the development of Western art music in the Greek mainland, starting in the second half of the nineteenth century. Opera was the predominant musical genre in the Ionian islands, and a music theater had existed in many of them since the eighteenth century. The most famous musical venue was the San Giacomo theater in Corfu, built in 1720, where opera was first staged in 1733 and was more systematically introduced into the annual program in 1771. The outbreak of the Greek Revolution did not really affect this theater's program for over a decade (Romanou 2003, 353–354).

With the exception of Nikolaos Mantzaros, Greek composers born in the Ionian islands were too young to produce any works around 1821 (Romanou 2011, 157). Mantzaros's response to the Greek Revolution was modest—at least until his father's death in 1843—due to his noble descent and his family's status (Romanou 2003). His most emblematic composition, though, is *Hymn to Liberty,* a setting of Dionysios Solomos's poem (which was inspired by the Greek Revolution)—popular settings already existed in Zante, based on the local vernacular polyphonic practices. The first version of *Hymn to Liberty* dates from 1829–1830, and soon it became so popular that its first two stanzas were chosen in 1865 to become the Greek national anthem. The patriotic character of Solomos's poetry, traced both in the Greek language and subject, marked Mantzaros's setting, which includes elements of revolutionary anthems and martial rhythms (Kardamis 2011). The first version of the *Hymn* (at least another three were to follow), which was published in London in 1873, is the "popular" one (i.e., in a style most accessible to the wider public), while the second version (1842–1843) is more elaborate through the use of polyphonic techniques, and Mantzaros dedicated it to the Greek king Othon in 1844. Other patriotic compositions by Mantzaros include a setting of Rhigas Velestinlis's "Thourios" as the thirteenth of his *16 Arie Greche* (1830) (Romanou 2003), as well as "Ode on the Death of Lord Byron," on Solomos's poetry, composed after 1829. The latter became particularly popular at least after 1840 and was used to refer to political developments in Greece (Kardamis 2019, 68). Mantzaros also set to music various excerpts of Solomos's poem "Lambros," whose hero joins the Souliots' fight against Ali Pasha.

The younger generation of Ionian composers was keen to make overt references to the Greek War of Independence, and opera was the primary musical means employed. In fact, Italian operas inspired by the Greek Revolution became their prototypes (Romanou 2003, 346–347). Their works, though, were met with the suspicion of the authorities of being associated with anti-British sentiments (Kardamis 2014b, 356). Here again, the figure of Markos Botsaris attracted the attention of a number of composers, including: the Zantiot Frangiskos Domeneginis, who had taken part in the Greek Revolution (an excerpt of his patriotic opera *Markos Botsaris* was first performed on Zakynthos in 1849); the Corfiot Iosif Liveralis (his opera was composed before 1852); and the Cephalonians Nikolaos Tzannis Metaxas (his opera premiered in Cephalonia in 1873) and Georgios Lampiris. The most famous opera on this topic, though, is undoubtedly that by Pavlos Carrer, from Zakynthos, completed in 1860. It incorporates Carrer's song "O Gero Dimos" (on Aristotelis Valaoritis's poem) and is in the style of klephtiko traditional (*dimotika*) songs. It became so popular that for some time it was considered to be truly a traditional song, while Nikos Skalkottas made an arrangement for string quartet possibly in the late 1940s. Carrer composed one more song in the style of klephtiko, "The Condemnation of the Klepht" (1859), as well as the operas *Kyra-Frosyni* (1868) and *Despo* (1875). An opera on the latter topic also exists by Domeneginis: *Despo, Heroine of Suli* (1850). Liveralis composed two more operas on patriotic themes: *Rhigas Feraios* (completed before 1852) and *The Return of Kanaris* (written before 1852). His piano piece *Le réveil du Klepht: Souvenirs des chants populaires de la Grèce*, (composed in 1849) should also be mentioned as the earliest known work to use Greek folklore elements (Kardamis 2014a). Finally, Spyros Samaras's operetta *I Kritikopoula* (The Cretan girl) (1916), although referring to the revolt against the Venetians, was inspired by Cretan revolutions toward the end of the nineteenth century and the island's incorporation into Greece in 1913.

An important corpus of works drawing on the Greek Revolution exists by Nikolaos Lavdas (1879–1940). Those were presented by the Athens Plucked Orchestra (Athenian Mantolinata), which he founded in 1900 and subsequently directed with the aim of popularizing Western music in Greece. Lavdas's compositions, which were often performed at the Mantolinata's concerts celebrating the anniversary of March 25, include: *Greek Rhapsody* (on the theme of the demotic song "Enas aitos kathotane" (An eagle was perched), which refers to

Greek warriors of the revolution); *Oi adikoskotomenoi* (Those killed in vain) (poetry by S. Matsoukas); *Cretan Dance* (referring to warriors on Mount Psiloritis); as well as harmonizations of the *dimotika* songs "Tou Kitsou i Mana" (Kitsos's mother), "Pantrevoun tin agapi mou" (They are marrying away my beloved), and "O Dimos." Other works included in the Mantolinata's repertoire, performed at such anniversary concerts are: the Cephalonian Dionysios Lavrangas's *I klephtiki nyktodia* (Klephtic nocturne) from his *Suite Hellénique,* his arrangement of the *dimotiko* song of Macedonia "O pligomenos kapetanios" (The wounded captain), and *Introduzione e fuga* (based on the *tsamiko* song "Tourka dernei"). Another two patriotic works that often featured on such programs are by the Italian Philhellene Raffaele Parisini: *To Arkadi* (1866), inspired by the heroic fall of the Cretan monastery, and *O ethnophylax* (The national guard), which was reportedly sung in Athens in the second half of the nineteenth century.

The founding father of the so-called national school of composers in Greece, Manolis Kalomiris, also expressed an interest in the Greek War of Independence through his works: songs for choir "Enas aitos" (An eagle) (1920) and "I leventia" (Valor) (1939) (both based on *dimotika* songs); *Oi eleftheroi poliorkimenoi* (The free besieged) (1926, with poetry by Solomos, for voice, choir, and orchestra); *I katastrophi ton Psaron* (The destruction of Psara) (1949); *I exodos ton Pargion* (The exodus of the Pargians) (composed in 1911 or 1912, possibly an excerpt from music for Spyros Peresiadis's theatrical play, which has been lost); and *O thanatos tou klephti* (The death of the klepht) (1911) (on verses from the *dimotiko* song). Although composed as a response to the German occupation, his symphonic poem *O thanatos tis andreiomenis* (The death of the valiant woman) (1943) employs the famous *Choros tou Zaloggou* (Zalongo dance) as its main theme, thus drawing a parallel between the country's occupation by the Ottomans and the Germans, and expressions of resistance in both cases. Among the best-known works by composers of the so-called national school is Petros Petridis's *Klephtik Dances* (1922), while Georgios Sklavos composed music for Georgios Aspreas's theatrical play *Kyra-Frosyni* (1921). Another composer who used the theme of the Greek Revolution to refer more generally to various forms of political resistance is the leftist Alekos Xenos, from Zakynthos, for instance in "25 Martiou 1821–25 Martiou 1946 'Ymnos sti Dimokratia'" (Hymn to democracy) (1946) from *Three Songs for Voice and Piano,* on poetry by Angelos Sikelianos. He also composed: the symphonic sketch *Neoi Souliotes (26 April 1941)* (New Souliots), on the outbreak of the war against Italy; the cantata *Eleftheroi poliorkimenoi* (The free besieged) (1968–1978), on Solomos's poem; and music for Spyros Melas's theatrical play *Rhigas Velestinlis* (1962). Renewed interest in the theme of the Greek Revolution has emerged on the occasion of its bicentennial. In this context, certain Greek institutions such as the Athens Concert Hall and the Greek National Opera have commissioned works from composers, including the symphonic overture *The Death of Lord Byron* (2019) by Philippos Tsalachouris.

To sum up, the Greek Revolution proved a powerful source of inspiration for composers, first primarily in other parts of Europe (where Philhellenism was widespread, and the Greek War of Independence encouraged other peoples' revolutionary aspirations) and, following the development of art music in Greece in the second half of the nineteenth century, for Greeks themselves. The initial surge of interest in topics associated with the Greek Revolution outside Greece did not outlive the end of that century. As regards Greece itself, an interest in themes relating to the Greek struggle against the Ottomans went hand in hand with the cultivation of art music in the country through the work of the Ionian composers. Representatives of the national school of music, however, with very few exceptions, were much less attracted to this subject. By the end of the twentieth century, and with the growth of modernism in Greek art music in postwar Greece, interest in such themes had waned, and its revival has been associated mostly with anniversary celebrations.

Katerina Levidou

This project has received funding from the European Union's Horizon 2020 research and innovation programme under the Marie Sklodowska-Curie grant agreement No 745631.

References

Amandry, Angélique. 1981. "Le Philhellénisme en France: Partitions de musique."
   O Ernanistis 17: 25–45.
Constantzos, George. 1993. Ίτε παίδες Ελλήνων. Τραγούδια για την Επανάσταση του 1821
   [Onward sons of the Greeks: Songs on the revolution of 1821]. Pella 609, CD liner notes.
Constantzos, George. 2016. Φιλελληνική Μούσα. Παρτιτούρες Γαλλικών φιλελληνικών
   έργων [Philhellenic Muse: Scores of French philhellenic works]. Athens.
Droulia, Loukia. 2017. *Philhellenisme. Ouvrages inspires par la guerre de l' independance grecque
   1821–1833. Repertoire bibliographique.* Second ed. Edited by Alexandra Sfoini. Athens.
Everist, Mark. 2002. *Music Drama at the Paris Odéon, 1824–1828.* Berkeley.
Gerhard, Anselm. 1998. *The Urbanization of Opera: Music Theater in Paris in the Nineteenth Century.* Translated by Mary Whittall. Chicago and London.
Kardamis, Kostas. 2011. "From Popular to Esoteric: Nikolaos Mantzaros and the Development of His Career as a Composer." *Nineteenth-Century Music Review* 8:101–126.
Kardamis, Kostas. 2014a. "Liberalis, Iosif." Grove Music Online. https://www.oxford
   musiconline.com/grovemusic/view/10.1093/gmo/9781561592630.001.0001/omo
   -9781561592630-e-0000049861.

Kardamis, Kostas. 2014b. "The Music of the Ionian Islands and Its Contribution to the Emergence of 'Greek National Music.'" In *Ionian Islands: Aspects of Their History and Culture,* edited by Anthony Hirst and Patrick Sammon, 340–366. Newcastle upon Tyne.

Kardamis, Kostas. 2019. "Odes, Anthems and Battle Songs: Creating Citizens through Music in Greece during the Long Nineteenth Century." In *Music, Language and Identity in Greece: Defining a National Art Music in the Nineteenth and Twentieth Centuries,* edited by Polina Tambakaki, Panos Vlagopoulos, Katerina Levidou, and Roderick Beaton, 63–74. New York.

Leotsakos, Giorgos. 2003. *Παύλος Καρρέρ. Απομνημονεύματα και εργογραφία* [Pavlos Carrer: Memoirs and list of works]. Athens.

Romanou, Katy. 2003. "Μουσική εμπνευσμένη από την Ελληνική Επανάσταση" [Music inspired by the Greek Revolution]. *INE:* 345–360.

Romanou, Katy. 2011. "Ο ιταλικός φιλελληνισμός και η επτανησιακή σκηνική μουσική εμπνευσμένη από την Ελληνική Επανάσταση" [Italian Philhellenism and Ionian stage music inspired by the Greek Revolution]. In *Επτανησιακή όπερα και μουσικό θέατρο έως το 1953* [Ionian opera and musical theater until 1953], edited by Joseph Vivilakis, 145–160. Athens.

Walton, Benjamin. 2007. *Rossini in Restoration Paris.* New York.

Historiographical Traditions and Debates

The Greek uprising of 1821 was the seminal event of the period between the end of the Napoleonic era and the outbreak of the revolutions of 1848. It broke the legitimist consensus of 1815 dealing a body blow to Metternich's "system" and legitimated the principle of nationality as an expression of freedom.

The French Romantic Paean to the "Nation"

The idea of the sovereign nation was the most explosive legacy of the French Revolution. The Restoration colored it with the healing hues of Christianity, while liberal romanticism once again charged it with some of its former élan. French writing about the Greek revolution exhibits these emphases in varying proportions.

The most influential account by far was François Pouqueville's *Histoire de la régénération de la Grèce* (Pouqueville 1824). Pouqueville was the diplomatic representative of France with Ali Pasha from 1806 to 1816, and the consul of France at Patras from 1816 to 1821. His intimate knowledge of the language, mores, history, and geography of the country was already established by the publication of his *Voyages de la Grèce* (Pouqueville 1826–1827), first published in 1805 with a dedication to the emperor. He now stepped forward as an ardent herald of the Greek revolutionary cause. He purported, in the manner of Herodotus, to immortalize the divinely sanctioned mission of the oppressed nation to cleanse Europe of Turkish "barbarity." His language is rhetorically inflated. The deeds of the revolutionaries are framed by a halo of antique heroism combined with invocations of their Christian zeal. "Victory to the Cross" is the paean sweeping his historical landscape. This verbal pathos surrounds a largely accurate depiction of the uprising (to 1824). This web of facts, however, is embellished with flourishes of the imagination as well as selective emphases.

Pouqueville's *Histoire* is introduced by a lengthy account of the career of Ali Pasha of Ioannina. This is the authoritative source for anyone writing on the subject. It is based upon personal acquaintance and repeated conversations with this formidable leader, as well as many of the personalities associated with him. He is exhaustively familiar with the physical surroundings and the circumstances attending Ali's rise and fall. And he is right in judging that Ali's rule, and finally rebellion, was a vital precondition for the Greek Revolution.

In describing the opening stages of the revolt, Pouqueville is the inventor of its most emblematic scene, namely the blessing by Archbishop Germanos of Patras of the banner of Freedom in the monastery of Agia Lavra in the presence of the assembled captains and fighters of the Morea. He has the prelate deliver an inspiring address explaining the religious significance of the uprising and the expected opposition of the European courts. This event is not corroborated by any other historian. Germanos did indeed bless the revolutionary Cross on March 25, but this was in the city of Patras. Still, the romantic reenactment by Pouqueville, breathing the fearless air of the mountains and replete with the full pomp of ecclesiastical authority, did indelibly register in the popular imagination and has been taken up by nationalist writing ever since.

Pouqueville's target of choice is the British consul in Patras, Philip Green, whom he accuses of actively aiding the Turks in putting down the nascent rebellion. Throughout his history he portrays the agents of Britain as militarily and diplomatically undermining the Greek struggle. He notes that not a single Briton was among the Philhellenes who died at Peta. He does not note the diplomatic sea change signaled by the advent of Canning. Only Byron receives his praise at the end of the story.

Pouqueville is not silent about Greek atrocities but he relativizes them as an inevitable outburst after centuries of oppression. Concerning the carnage in Tripolitsa, he is, to his credit, categorical that it cannot be "justified" by reference to the massacres of Greeks in Constantinople, Smyrna, and Kydonies, among others. Still, his description is rather cursory. In the case of the massacre by the Greeks of the garrison of the Acropolis in the summer of 1822, he does indeed excuse it by invoking Turkish brutality in Chios and the approach of the Ottoman army from the north. Pouqueville is also candid about the dissensions among the Greeks. He lays the blame for the civil war upon the military captains of the Peloponnese, who wanted to make political authority dependent "upon the sword." In a famous indictment he accuses Kolokotronis of aspiring to become the "Ali Pasha" of the Morea, but he also excoriates the "political faction," the winners of the first civil war, of misusing their victory for the promotion of the interests of the naval islands. All in all, Pouqueville's work set the standard for nationalist iconography and popular, journalistic, and educational rhetoric in Greece.

Pouqueville's work was widely disseminated in Italy. A *Continuation* of the history by Stefano Ticozzi also appeared, with the venue of publication given simply as *Italia*, thus indicating the vision of Italian unity aroused by the example of Greece. Mario Pieri also published a *Compendio della storia del Risorgimento della Grecia* (Pieri 1825). The author declares that the Greek struggle offers to the "philosophical observer" an example, "unique and full of passion," of the impact that "the general enlightenment of our century" can have on the resolution of a people to break the chains of "a barbarous and ferocious government." Another *History of Greece* by Giuseppe Rovani covering the years 1824–1854 appeared in Milan (Rovani 1854). It is also infused with philhellenic ardor: this is the story, says the author, of civilization resurgent against "decrepit barbarism." The work of Gervinus was also translated into Italian. It is clear that the example of Greece inspired Italian patriots for their own epic struggles later in the century.

One of the sources of Pouqueville was the memoirs of Maxime Raybaud. He was a French military officer who arrived in Greece on the ship hired by Alexandros Mavrokordatos in Marseilles. He was a member of the latter's staff throughout his stay in the country, and was personally devoted to him. His *Mémoires sur la Grèce* (Raybaud 1824) is an accurate and dispassionate record of the first two years of the war. It is devoid of religious zeal, despite constantly referring to the Turks as "infidels." It is introduced by an essay by Alphonse Rabbe, which summarizes the history of the country from the Roman conquest down to the outbreak of the revolution. Rabbe discusses at length the organization of the Church under the Ottomans, with detailed reference to its finances. Despite the corruption of the hierarchy, it was the framework for national unity. Still, for all the privileges accorded to the subjugated populations, the Ottoman system was one of arbitrary oppression, with no security of life or property. Since the Peloponnesian insurrection of 1770, the nation was in a state of alert, heightened by the diffusion of letters, which "Dr. Coray, littérateur respectable établi à Paris" had brought to the attention of the European public.

Raybaud assumed the command of the rudimentary Greek artillery. He was instrumental in the siege of Tripolitsa and was an eyewitness of its capture and the horror that followed. He recounts this horrific event blow by blow, with an accuracy and lucidity that allow the reader to relive it. His description of the murderous fury of the victors makes one cringe. All restraints of humanity had been lifted. He tried to save some innocent victims, only to see them mercilessly butchered under his eyes. He notes the depths of historical resentment and suggests that the Greek chiefs had lost control of the soldiery. But his disgust at this barbarity is palpable. Raybaud left to rejoin the staff of Mavrokordatos in western Greece, which he did after a sojourn of a few weeks in Athens. The Acropolis was then under siege by the Greeks, but it was conducted in a rather lackadaisical manner. Raybaud visited the French consul in Athens, the renowned Dr. Fauvel, whose house was filled with a treasure of antiquities. And in the company of this highly cultivated personality (who was not sympathetic to the cause of the Greeks and gently mocked the naïveté of the Philhellenes) he made excursions in the countryside. These are the most charming scenes of his account. It was springtime and his evocation of the blooming serenity of the Attic plains is infused with genuine poetic sensibility. This was an interlude before another scene of horrors. Raybaud rejoined Mavrokordatos during his ill-fated incursion into Epirus. He describes with his usual vividness and precision the camp of the Greek regulars, the Philhellenes, and the klephtic bands at Peta, the heroic but hopeless expedition of Markos Botsaris to relieve Souli and the treachery of Bakolas that caused the annihilation of the Greek army. He himself escaped with his life, only because on the eve of the battle he had been sent on a mission for reinforcements. The end of the story of this worthy man is a lament at the prospect of civil war then looming. He too blames Kolokotronis, who "supported by his brutish soldiery had lit the flame of this sacrilegious struggle."

Other memoirs by foreign participants in the Greek struggle also appeared around the same time. Olivier Voutier was a French naval officer who had previously been involved in the discovery of the famous Venus de Milo and its transport to France; he arrived in revolutionary Greece in 1821 in the entourage of Thomas Gordon. His *Mémoires sur la guerre actuelle des Grecs* (Voutier 1823) was severely criticized by Raybaud and others as full of fabrications for the purpose of self-glorification. The memoirs of Claude Denis Raffenel entitled *Histoire des événements de la Grèce* (Raffenel 1822–1824) were more substantial and informative. Raffenel was an official of the French consulate at Smyrna at the time of the outbreak of the revolution. He had been the chief editor of the *Spectateur oriental,* the mouthpiece of the Francolevantine merchants, which was opposed to the Greek aspirations. He justified this as a necessity since he was operating under the supervision of the Ottoman government. Eventually he joined the French corps of General Fabvier in Greece and was killed in 1827 defending the Acropolis against the besieging Turks of Mehmed Reşid Pasha, Kütahı.

Raffenel rebuts the argument of the opponents of the Greek struggle that in recent years the Ottoman rule had become milder, thus rendering a revolution pointless. Even if true in some areas like the islands, this loosening of the bonds depended on the whim of the rulers and could be arbitrarily revoked. The annual tour of the Ottoman fleet in the Archipelago in order to collect the tribute was marked by frightful exactions. Raffenel was an eyewitness of the massacres of the Greeks of Smyrna after the outbreak of the revolution. His account of the terror that seized the Greek inhabitants and their rush to board ships as hordes of inflamed Turks from the hinterland massed at the entrance of the city is full of pathos. He describes numerous corpses floating in the harbor in scenes prefiguring what was to transpire in 1922. During the night, the blood-curdling scream of "kill the Greeks" filled the empty streets. He himself barely escaped with his life, when a group of Turks who had pinned him against the wall with a pistol piercing his chest suddenly abandoned him to pursue a group of unfortunate Greeks whom they proceeded to slaughter. His information about the situation in the Archipelago is also factual. He notes the frictions between the Roman Catholic and Orthodox inhabitants of the islands, and reports the mass volunteering of the Jews of Thessaloniki for the Turkish army to join in the suppression of the revolt in Macedonia. But Raffenel's account of the revolution in the Morea and Rumeli is sketchy and marred with inaccuracies. He erroneously describes, for instance, Dimitrios Ypsilantis as in charge of the siege of Tripolitsa. He also claims that hundreds of Greeks were killed in fighting among themselves for the distribution of the booty, and that the Albanians who were allowed to leave after an agreement with Kolokotronis were later massacred crossing the mountains to the north. These claims are untrue.

A piece of French writing that also deserves note is by Armand Carrel, one of the most prominent personalities of liberal romanticism and a leader of the revolution of 1830. His *Résumé de l'histoire des Grecs modernes* (Carrel 1825) is not an original presentation, as the author relies primarily upon Pouqueville, Raybaud, and Raffenel, but there is a strikingly new tone of voice. Carrel's interpretation is inspired by Fauriel's epoch-making collection of the demotic songs of modern Greece, which so impressed European literary opinion at the time. In them he discerns an ethos of struggle which had shaped Greek society. It was this perennial preoccupation with freedom that exploded in the present uprising and its heroes, like Efthymios Vlachavas and Markos Botsaris, should be revered by all progressive Europeans. It was to the lasting shame of European monarchies that they had conspired with a retrograde and mind-stifling despotism to deny the Greek people the deserved fruits of their bravery. In Carrel, the aspirations of an ongoing French revolutionary movement are welded together with those of the Greeks to fashion an ideal of freedom and progress meant for all the nations of Europe.

The British Perspective: Government of Law and
Social Order of Freedom

British writing on the Greek Revolution is soberly factual and, for all its phil-hellenic commitment, devoid of ideological declamation. It does recognize, on the strength of empirical observation, the continuity of the Greek people, even connecting it to Hellenic antecedents. But its central concern is to investigate the prospects for the foundation of a society of free citizens placing individual interest under a common purpose and capable of finding its place alongside the other civilized nations.

William Martin Leake's *An Historical Outline of the Greek Revolution* (Leake 1826) is a work of expertise and reflection. His profound knowledge of the history, topography, language, and customs of the Greek-speaking world eminently qualified him for an assessment of the Greek struggle which still retains its validity. Leake writes as a member of the British establishment that shares the overall goals of official diplomacy. But he acknowledges both the justice of the revolutionary cause and the inevitability of its success. He begins with the extraordinary statement that "there is no nation . . . that has so little changed in the long course of ages as the Greeks" (1). This he attributes primarily to the continuity of the language, which once political freedom has been attained will enable them to reacquaint themselves with the wisdom of their forefathers. The present struggle between Greeks and Turks, he adds, is just the latest episode in the conflict between Europe and Asia, which has lasted "since the earliest records of history." In this contest, the preponderance seemed to lie on the side of Turkey, but this was illusory. The Greeks as the nautical and commercial nation had managed to grow economically and intellectually, and their appropriation of European lights ensured their eventual success. Europe would in time come to embrace the cause of Greek independence as her own. European travelers generally disparaged the character of the modern Greeks, because they had no access to the mountains and the islands where the vivacity of spirit and the taste for freedom of old Hellenism had been well preserved. Leake then provides a summary of the main events of the first four years of the war, concluding that Turkey could not put down the revolution with its own forces. She must accept Greek independence, realizing that she would benefit more from Greece as a free and prosperous friend rather than as a downtrodden slave. As for the Greeks, the task before them now was the construction of a free polity. The British loan and the change in British foreign policy through the recognition of the Greek blockades provided the means to achieve this. It required the curbing of the anarchic license of the local warlords (τὸ στασιῶδες, as he expresses it in Greek) by a functioning constitution and the organization of a regular army. He judged that the most appropriate form of government would be that of a "federal republic." Such a state must then proceed to put down piracy in the Greek seas and integrate itself in the international system. Its territory would of necessity be only a part of historical Hellas, but this initial nucleus of national existence would be the focal point for the eventual unification of all Greek lands. Writing about a quarter of a century later, Leake had to concede that none of his republican hopes had come true. Foreign protection for the independent state had brought only despotic rule in the form of the Bavarian monarchy, while the British blockade of the Piraeus in 1850 had ruined the country's commerce (Leake 1851).

The masterpiece of British historical writing on the Greek war was General Thomas Gordon's *History of the Greek Revolution* (Gordon 1832). Gordon was a Scottish Philhellene with significant participation in the revolution and later in the military affairs of the independent kingdom. He arrived at the Greek camp before Tripolitsa in the summer of 1821 and was member of the staff of Dimitrios Ypsilantis. He was not present at the sacking of the city, because he followed Ypsilantis in his ill-judged expedition to the northern shore of the Morea while the siege was in progress. He returned to Tripolitsa nine days after its capture, protested the atrocity, and left Greece. He was later persuaded to return and was placed in charge of the operation to relieve the Acropolis in May 1827. He captured the hill of Phaliron (Kastella), but the attempt ended in disaster. After independence he was made a general of the Greek army by King Othon.

His work, a complete account covering events until the arrival of Capodistrias, exhibits the same virtues of clear-eyed factualness and unbiased judgment that we saw in Leake. It displays extraordinary knowledge of the terrain, the disposition of forces, the plans and circumstances of the belligerents, even down to the direction of the wind in naval engagements. Gordon is reticent only about his own role. His championship of the Greek cause was firm and sincere, having spent a large part of his personal fortune to support it. He was, however, unrelenting in his censure of the faults of the Greek political and military class. He too considered the Greek people as the descendants of the old Hellenes. They had preserved the core of the ancient virtues of spirited enterprise, love of freedom, and intellectual curiosity, albeit crusted over with the duplicity, deceitfulness, and servility requisite for survival through generations of crushing oppression. The question whether the revolution could or should have been postponed he considers pointless. The Ottoman Empire was falling apart, and if the Greeks had not revolted, its disintegration would have been managed by the great powers without taking Greek interests into account. In his sociological analysis of revolutionary society, he describes the notables (*ḳocabaşıs, proestoi*) as petty tyrants interested in overthrowing Turkish rule only in order to establish their own oppressive "oligarchy." The ecclesiastical hierarchy, equally venal and power hungry, were allied to them. The military captains were men of violence opposed to political order. Despite his undoubted military prowess, Kolokotronis is indicted for "sordid avarice and mean ambition" that "severely scourged" his nation. The patriotism of the various leaders, he says, rarely extended beyond the boundaries of their own districts or coteries, and a concern for the public good never took hold. In a famous summation, Gordon concludes that those who managed public affairs, especially after the disbursement of the loans, were just robbers of the public purse. His description of the Greek rampage at Tripolitsa, although damning, is not emotionally inflamed. He is primarily interested in the political dimensions of the event. The conduct of the military chiefs, especially the Maniots, was loathsome. Each was bent upon securing for his person the greatest possible amount of the loot, contemptuous of the claims even of their own soldiers. Not a single cent of the tremendous treasure captured found its way to the public coffers. The Greeks should have restrained the "meanness, ferocity, and treachery" of their vengeance, because their excesses alienated public opinion in Europe. Gordon shows particular revulsion at the slaughter of the sick and dying Turks who surrendered at Athens, for it was a crime committed on a fortnight of premeditation and not in the heat of battle, as in Tripolitsa. He says, with a dash of hyperbole, that if one were to compare Greek cruelty to that of the Turkish pashas the "palm of humanity" might as well be awarded to the latter. But the word humanity does not really apply to this conflict, because it was a war of mutual extermination from the start. All this, however, does not distract from the fundamental justice of the Greek cause. Gordon rails against the collusion of the European courts with the Sublime Porte and is scathing about the conduct of the British government during the Castlereagh period. He is particularly damning about the conduct of Sir Thomas Maitland, whose pretended neutrality amounted to provisioning the Ottoman fleet in Ionian ports, expediting their communications through British facilities, and aiding the Austrians in breaking the Greek blockades. With respect to the civil disturbances in 1823–1824, Gordon considered them inevitable given the fragmentation of Greek society and the wide divergence of interests. The extreme republicanism of the Constitution of Epidavros was simply a pretense, behind which the depredations of the local lords and chieftains could unfold without hindrance. Faced with this anarchic chaos, where "all crime went unpunished," the common people as well as sensible politicians such as Mavrokordatos longed for a constitutional monarchy. Revolutionary Greece failed in erecting a functioning government of laws and a regular army under its direction. In the concluding stages of the war the actions of foreign Philhellenes (including the two British loans, despite their onerous conditions) were crucial in keeping Greek freedom alive. The factual accuracy and sociological perspicacity, illuminated by a constant moral flame, render the work of Gordon an unsurpassed historical achievement.

George Finlay, also of Scottish descent, was an associate of Gordon's who elected to settle in the independent kingdom. His *History of the Greek Revolution* (Finlay 1861) is a work tinged with Gibbonian contrarianism, probably fed by deep personal resentments. Finlay obstreperously dismantles the "myths" of Philhellenism, together with the shibboleths of modern Greek nationalism. This is an idiosyncratic piece of dissenting Philhellenism. It does espouse the Greek cause, but on condition of full candor about the dysfunctions of the Greek character and society: ὀρθὸν ἀλήθεια ἀεὶ (the truth is always right) is his motto. Of the descent of the modern Greeks from the Hellenes of old he does not hold much store. Religion and not nationality was the cement of Greek society under Ottoman control, and the Church did nothing to promote national aspirations. The vaunted municipal institutions, praised as enduring foci of freedom, were in reality arrangements for the extraction of ruinous taxation. They were inherited by the sultans from the effete East Roman Caesars. The Ottoman system was oppressive but it weighed upon both the Christian and the Muslim populations. The image of the klephts as a heroic national militia was a recent literary invention. In reality they were "highwaymen and sheep-stealers." "There is nothing to eulogize in the conduct of criminals," Finlay asserts. The Greeks suffered as much from the klephts as the Muslims, and the larger klephtic bands were a mixture of Greeks, Turks, and Albanians. As Kolokotronis himself says, the Maniots believed only in money: "Οἱ Μανιάται λησμονοῦν ὅλα διὰ τὰ γρόσια" (The Maniots forget everything for the kurus). The naval islands, to which Greek freedom was largely due, were populated by Albanians. Education flourished more in Ioannina under the tyranny of Ali than in the Morea under the Greek *koçabaşıs*. The influence of the ideas of the Enlightenment is absent in Finlay's account. His description of the revolutionaries' atrocities at Navarino, Tripolitsa, and Athens follows Gordon. It is laced with the biting observation that their intense devotion to their religion did not instill in them feelings of humanity. Diverging from Gordon, he claims that the Constitution of Epidavros, laudable in its declarations, was in fact meant only to deceive European public opinion. Finlay pronounces a blanket condemnation of all Greek leaders thrown up by the revolution as vile self-servers. This applies not only to Kolokotronis, whom he blames in the standard fashion for the first civil war; but also to Mavrokordatos, whom he accuses of both incompetence and intrigue. The great failure of Greek society was precisely its inability to produce politicians with the common good in view. The British loans should not have been extended, because they were used for private enrichment and internecine carnage. On this he again differs with Gordon—and, to my mind, he was wrong. Thus, according to Finlay, the two civil wars "created a new race of tyrants as despotic as, and far meaner than, the hated Turks." And in all this the common people suffered extreme depredations, while they also carried the burden of the war in its most dangerous phase after the invasion of Ibrahim. The real heroes of the Greek Revolution, the ones who carried the prize of independence, he concludes, were the anonymous masses. Finlay challenges received orthodoxies and his iconoclastic assertions are a stimulant to critical thinking.

A significant contribution of Irish historiography is also James Emerson's *History of Modern Greece from Its Conquest by the Romans in 146 B.C. to the Present Time* (Emerson 1830), the second volume of which deals extensively with the social condition of the Greek people under Ottoman domination. It contains the standard philhellene account of Turkish rapacity through the medium of the *kocabaşıs*, who are named "the absolute reptiles of despotism." This work also contains a lengthy discussion of the development of modern Greek literature from medieval to modern times, which is still of value. The resurgence of letters prior to the revolution and the dissemination of the ideas of the Enlightenment are discussed in depth.

German Historicism: Greece and the Spirit of the Age

German culture was permeated with the Hellenic ideal, hence interest in the Greek uprising was a natural consequence. German historiography had a strong philosophical foundation. The revolution was seen as bringing to the fore the underlying tendencies of historical development, thus presaging a political and cultural culmination for the peoples of Europe. It is liberal and democratic in its convictions.

Johann Wilhelm Zinkeisen wrote a history of Greece from antiquity to his own time, in which the revolution is seen as the organic outcome of the long tribulations of the Greek people. The first volume covers the period from Hellenic antiquity to the incursions of the Normans into Greece (Zinkeisen 1832). Its most significant contribution is the refutation of Jakob Fallmerayer's "Slavic theory." Zinkeisen shows in great detail that the historical record does not support the claim of the disappearance of the Hellenic population in the Peloponnese. The second volume, on the condition of the Greeks under the Franks and the Ottomans, was never written. Volumes 3 and 4 are an account of the revolution, which, however, is a German translation of the history of Thomas Gordon (Zinkeisen 1840).

The first important work of synthesis is the history of the Greek insurrection by Georg Gottfied Gervinus. Gervinus was one of the noblest political personalities of the German nineteenth century. He supported the revolutionary movement of 1848, but the failure of the liberals pushed him in a militant democratic direction. He denounced Bismarck and his "blood and iron" policies, arguing that this manner of German unification presaged future disasters. He considered history as an instrument for moral instruction and the practical regeneration of society. He had contempt for mere "fact gatherers," a stance that earned him a condemnation by the chief representative of scientific history, Leopold von Ranke (Craig 1972). His account of the Greek Revolution is embedded in a general history of the European nineteenth century since 1815 (Gervinus 1866). It is presented as the consummation of a grand movement for popular emancipation against corrupt despotism. A distinctive feature of Gervinus's perspective is his constant comparison of the Greek case with the struggle of the Latin American peoples to shake off the yoke of Spain. The Greek insurrection, however, was a far more difficult project, for it faced the concentrated might of an enfeebled but vast empire in whose midst it was attempted. Gervinus bases his account on Zinkeisen and Gordon, but more significantly on the history of the Revolution by the Greek historian Spyridon Trikoupis. In standard fashion he outlines the brutality of Ottoman oppression and the outstanding economic and intellectual achievement of the Greeks around the turn of the nineteenth century. He rebuts the apologists of Turkish power (such as David Urquhart, the British diplomat under Stratford Canning in Constantinople) who argued that its abuses were due to the arbitrariness of local officials. This was a natural outcome of Ottoman despotism. Its principle was the separation of the *rayah* as a foreign body upon which any kind of arbitrary compulsion could be exercised. Thus, it was not a political form of government but a violent imposition devoid of moral content. Whatever signs of improvement one might detect in the empire were due to the commercial and the intellectual activity of the Greeks. Gervinus reprises Zinkeisen's refutation of Fallmerayer, but with a more theoretically pregnant line of argument. The point is not blood, but "spirit." The ancient Hellenes were also a racial mixture, but they managed through their love of freedom and intellectual acumen to vivify culturally the populations among whom they took residence. Their history was also tainted with brutality, corruption, and civil violence. All this was also true of the modern Greeks. But their "elasticity" of perception, propensity for education, economic dynamism, and taste for independence as evinced by the ethos of the mountain warriors eminently qualified them as historical descendants of the former. Gervinus's chapter on the general meaning of the Greek struggle is a remarkable document of historical perspicacity. The revolution was the act of self-assertion of a people deformed and brutalized by slavery. Hence it was unavoidably a mixture of moral greatness and human depravity. Gervinus does not hide, nor does he justify, the misdeeds of the Greeks. He notes that at the beginning there was mutual restraint and even respect among Greeks and Turks. But then on the signal given by the massacres in Constantinople, Smyrna, Kydonies, Cyprus, and so on, the war became one of extermination. The instincts of the "blood-thirsty slave" were released in the insurgents. This was facilitated by the fact that the Greek side was just a rough-and-tumble agglomeration of wild bands. Still, there were personalities who displayed superior moral and political qualities. He praises Alexandros Mavrokordatos who, in a country "with a modicum of civilization," would be the first choice for leader. But he is not overly critical of Kolokotronis, whose memoirs he often cites as an expression of that fearless élan that propelled those "children of nature." The institutions of Epidavros were a commendable attempt to combine the rule of law with popular sovereignty. Given the historical forces arrayed at this key juncture in the struggle of the peoples of Europe, Gervinus concludes, it was clear from the beginning that the revolt of the Greeks could not be defeated. Gervinus's work was a philhellenic document of significant intellectual weight, tying together the achievements of the Greeks with the dearest aspirations of German democrats.

Gervinus's reconstruction placed the Greek insurrection firmly within a European historical teleology, and the same was done by Anton von Prokesch-Osten's *Geschichte des Abfalls der Griechen vom Türkischen Reiche im Jahre 1821* (History of the secession of the Greeks from the Turkish empire)—but from a directly opposed interpretative standpoint (Prokesch-Osten 1867). Prokesch was an Austrian diplomat serving under Metternich, ambassador to Athens from 1834 to 1849, and later ambassador to Constantinople. He was the most knowledgeable Orientalist of his time. His work is the most thoroughgoing account of the diplomatic background of the Greek conflict, based upon a great wealth of confidential documents. It was for this reason that it was banned as it was about to be published in 1853, and authorized only in 1867. It stands to reason that Prokesch was committed to defending the official Austrian position on the Greek revolt, which in his mind was also founded on solid historical sense. Only a few years before, united Europe had managed to put down a mighty attempt to destroy its traditional political order, something that had plunged it into bloody chaos. Now, the "party of subversion" hiding behind the Greek rebels was resuming this effort. It was therefore imperative that the principle of legitimacy, only just restored, be defended at all costs. Turkish power had been recognized by solemn international treaties, and therefore the Porte was within its rights to treat its Greek subjects under its internal laws without external powers interfering. Prokesch reconstructs the logic of the Porte's responses to diplomatic protestations especially after the bloody reprisals of April 1821. The patriarch was a public official who had violated his oath of allegiance and therefore he was legally punished—after all, the British had decapitated their king. The anti-Christian excesses had been put down by the authorities, and the distinction between the guilty and the innocent clearly upheld. If the Irish had rebelled against it, what would the British government say to Turkish offers of "mediation"? This line of reasoning is cogent, if you accept the initial premise (of "lawful authority") and you overlook its misrepresentation of facts—for the Turkish authorities only rarely tried, or wished, to restrain the murdering mobs. It must be noted that neither British nor Austrian official papers, and much less Prokesch himself, denied the oppression inflicted by Ottoman officials on the *rayahs*. These abuses must be remedied. But this would have to be a sovereign initiative undertaken by the sultan himself and not the result of foreign imposition. The Porte, of course, obliged by offering "amnesties" and "paternal mercy." Thus, diplomatic appearances were saved, as the Ottoman forces on the ground pursued their "Greek hunts."

Prokesch is superb in reconstructing the diplomatic tangle that arose from the Greek rebellion. Austria had to prevent war between Russia and Turkey, but at the same time support the former's demands in the Danubian Principalities so that the European Concert would not break up. The immediate victim of this was Count Capodistrias. However, the pressure of philhellenic opinion in Russia was intense, and this led to the Russian proposal in January 1824 that Greece be divided into three autonomous principalities under the suzerainty of the sultan. This amounted to the creation of three Russian vassal states. Austria was adamantly opposed, and so was the fledgling Greek government because it would permanently preclude independence. The Porte also rejected it as unwarranted interference. To everyone's astonishment, Austria now indicated that under the circumstances the only solution was either the military defeat of the rebels or *complete Greek independence*. This amounted to a radical reversal of the diplomatic situation, not because Metternich *desired* independence (he did not, expecting the victory of the Turks), but because independence was now on the table even as a mere theoretic possibility. The advent of Canning in Britain and Tsar Nicholas in Russia accelerated the momentum in favor of some kind of imperative intervention by the European powers. With Austria now isolated, the Treaty of London of July 1827 *demanding* a cessation of hostilities led the way to Navarino and the final triumph of the Greek cause. Prokesch shows masterfully that the "Greek problem" was lodged right in the heart of European international order. Against this background, his treatment of Greek military and political affairs is rather summary but still based on intimate personal knowledge of events and persons. His insight into Greek society is also sharp and intimate. He identifies an incompatibility between traditional norms and mores, founded on religion, and the Enlightenment values of Greeks with a European background that prevented the construction of a functional polity.

In a lengthy critical note, Karl Mendelssohn-Bartholdy (Mendelssohn-Bartholdy 1867) praises the high quality of Prokesch's work, but chides him for his support of Metternich's approach. Austria was working against a mighty historical trend. A groundswell of opinion in Europe was behind the Greeks. Greek freedom was supported by both the liberals and the legitimists, and Austria thus lost the opportunity to be at the head of a powerful popular movement. Turkey's domination of Greece was not lawful. International treaties cannot legitimize power based on raw force alone. The Turks never managed to give a moral basis to their rule. That is why the Greek insurrection was both justified and also fated to win, as it expressed the aspirations of all freedom-loving classes in Europe.

Karl Mendelssohn-Bartholdy's *Geschichte Griechenlands von der Eroberung Konstantinopels durch die Türken bis auf unsere Tage* (History of Greece from the conquest of Constantinople by the Turks to the present) is the supreme achievement of German historiography on the Greek Revolution (Mendelssohn-Bartholdy 1870). Mendelssohn-Bartholdy (the son of the famous composer) was Gervinus's research assistant, and his work is an application of the guidelines of his master. But the result is far superior. Mendelssohn-Bartholdy mastered modern Greek, visited the country four times, read all the available sources, Greek and foreign, and had access to the archives of the foreign ministries in Vienna and Berlin. His, therefore, is the definitive account, methodologically impeccable, albeit suffused with intense philhellenic rhetoric occasionally reminiscent of Pouqueville. His story is introduced by a refutation of Fallmerayer, mixing historical argument and personal invective. With respect to the evaluation of the historical sources, Mendelssohn-Bartholdy relies on Karl Hopf. But the emphasis is now on the ability of the Greeks to "assimilate" culturally the populations around them. Thus, since the middle ages the Slavic and Albanian settlers had become Greek in religion, language, and manners. The customs of the people display an unmistakable continuity with the Hellenic past. Their virtues and vices (i.e., independence of spirit and thirst for knowledge, on the one hand, anti-social egotism, on the other) were the same as those of the Hellenes of old. The revolution was the result of the prodigious increase in commercial and intellectual activity of the nation, supplemented by the decomposition of the Ottoman state. Kolokotronis, as the archetypical klepht, is the symbol of the urge for freedom that mobilized the people. His greatest gift was to communicate instinctively with the uneducated masses. Mendelssohn-Bartholdy praises the political ability and the urbanity of Mavrokordatos, although he censures his tendency to intrigue.

He also emphasizes that the first preference of the assembly of Epidavros, echoing the widespread wishes of the people at large, was for a constitutional monarchy. Since in 1822 it was not possible to establish one, the republican arrangements were an expedient expressing the anarchy of a fragmented society. Both the instigators (the military captains) and the victors of the civil wars were unworthy of the nation. The Greek atrocities are condemned, but only the massacre of Tripolitsa is described in extensive detail. After 1824, Philhellenism became a Europewide movement with the character almost of a religion. Mendelssohn-Bartholdy also provides a thorough reconstruction of the diplomatic background that led to the Treaty of London in 1827. The battle of Navarino was not an accident, whoever may have fired the first shot. It was the necessary consequence of the decision of the three powers to intervene in the affairs of the East against the will of the Porte if necessary, thus breaking the principle of legitimacy. In this the governments were bending to the will of a massive popular movement. Mendelssohn-Bartholdy's work acquired instant acclaim. Unfortunately, during the last two decades of his life he was mentally incapacitated, unable to complete his magnum opus.

The last major German work on the Greek Revolution was by Gustav Friedrich Hertzberg (Hertzberg 1879). This was a competent summation of the conclusions of historical research up to that time.

The American Coda: Revolutionary Humanism

After 1821 American Philhellenism became a nationwide movement, spurred on by the efforts of prominent individuals such as Edward Everett, who had come to know Korais in Paris. It was called the "Greek wave" in the press. Its political highpoint was the address delivered in the House of Representatives in January 1824 by Daniel Webster, a superb display of parliamentary oratory (Webster 1851). Webster lambasted the self-declared "right" of the Holy Alliance to intervene by force to put down "revolution" in foreign countries. He then reviewed the progress of the Greek nation in seaborne commerce and education, and denounced Ottoman oppression, with special emphasis on the massacre of Chios. The uprising of the Greeks was, thus, morally justified and deserved the support of the Christian world. The Greeks had set up a popular assembly (Congress), just like the Americans in their revolution, indicating that they were pursuing a similar enterprise of popular freedom. But they did it under extremely adverse circumstance, whereas the Americans already had a long experience of self-government behind them.

Of all the Philhellenes, the person who arguably benefited the Greek nation the most was Samuel Gridley Howe, humanitarian, revolutionary, abolitionist, and advocate of the blind. He was one of the noblest personalities to grace the atrocious history of his times. Howe graduated from Harvard Medical School in 1824 and upon hearing of the death of Lord Byron resolved to travel to Greece to join the struggle for which his idol had sacrificed his life. Enlisting under Captain Hastings, he became the chief surgeon of the Greek navy. However, his attention was drawn to the plight of civilians in the ravaged land. He founded a hospital and organized projects for the relief of these unfortunates who had been reduced to starving and bleeding animals. His activities regenerated interest in Greece, which had been flagging in America since the earlier days of romantic Philhellenism (St Clair 2008, 288; Trent 2012, chap. 2). Howe also wrote *An Historical Sketch of the Greek Revolution* (Howe 1828). This was a substantial, if not original, contribution. His sources were Leake and Raybaud. He recapitulated the standard philhellene story of the commercial and intellectual resurgence of Greece as against the decaying Ottoman despotism. But his synthesis is also enlivened by sharp personal insight. At the beginning of 1825 it seemed that a glorious chapter was commencing. The regenerated nation was beginning to be organized under liberty. The mutiny of the military chiefs had been suppressed and the government was the epitome of the country's best talent. But the promise was not fulfilled. The new rulers misused their power in order to benefit narrow interests. Greece, Howe explains, is a fragmented society, traversed by deep cultural and economic rifts. The naval islands, in particular, that were now in control were considered alien by the other provinces. They were Christian Albanians who spoke their own language and pursued their distinct material interests. In the cold light of Howe's experiences on the ground, the Bartholdy thesis of "assimilation" thus suffers substantially.

The American Philhellenes saw the Greek struggle as a continuation of their own revolution, a conviction reiterated with emphasis by Cornelius Conway Felton, another president of Harvard, four decades after Webster (Felton 1867). The community of destitute refugees that Howe founded near Corinth was named Washingtonia. But Greece was not after all "Americanized" as the Benthamite companion of Byron, Colonel Stanhope, had dreamed. "Democracy" was the cover under which the local strongmen camouflaged their feudal rule. In the face of this, the people longed for the imperious presence of a national αὐθέντης (master). Capodistrias and the Bavarians provided this, but the sociological malaise was not healed.

Postscript: Perspectives from Greek Historiography

A general characteristic of Greek historical writing about the revolution of 1821 is the determination to justify it as a just struggle fulfilling a national longing for freedom through the long centuries of foreign subjugation. This is a view from within, and has the aim of forging an active national consciousness. In a century marked by a general outbreak of national feelings this was a necessary task. To be sure, the political and ideological means to achieve this were diverse and the various factions whose voices color the historical accounts remained at loggerheads with regard to their respective choices. Beyond this discordant stridency, however, one can discern the conviction of each separate actor that their commitments would best serve the ultimate aim of national restoration, which was common and "sacred" to all.

The first historical reconstruction of the revolutionary period consists of the personal reminiscences of the participants and protagonists, about forty-five texts in all. These are invaluable as a source but also a potential impediment to sound judgment. For each author is primarily concerned to justify his own personal conduct and defend himself against perceived slanders and slights coming from rival factions. The accounts of the Peloponnesians in particular are woven around the belief that the Peloponnese was the cradle of the Greek nation and hence its political claims overrode those of other parts.

Three sets of memoirs deserve special mention. The first is by Kanellos Deligiannis, written in the 1850s but published only in 1957. Deligiannis was the chief member of the most prominent family of potentates or primates (*proestoi*) of Arcadia. This social stratum was subjected to criticism for its accommodation of Turkish rule and for allegedly aspiring to succeed the Turks in the despotic government of the nation. Deligiannis rebuts these accusations by claiming that after the failure of the revolt of 1770, in which the *proestoi* had participated, a functional modus vivendi under the vengeful Ottoman government was unavoidable. In doing this the primates had both secured the physical survival of the Greek people and also nurtured their unextinguished desire for freedom. Later they joined the Philiki Etaireia and provided the political leadership of the armed uprising. In the course of the War of Independence they also made immense sacrifices in blood and wealth.

The dictated reminiscences of Theodoros Kolokotronis, the most famous of the Peloponnesian military chiefs, are entitled *An Account of Events Concerning the Greek Race.* They were published posthumously in 1846 and offer an instructive counterpoint to Deligiannis. His is the unadorned voice of the klephts, the segment of the oppressed peasantry that took to the mountains. These "primitive rebels," as Eric Hobsbawm dubbed them, engaged in brigandage often affecting not only the well-defended Turkish enclaves but equally the helpless Christian populations. But in this manner they kept alive a reckless courage that eventually provided the raw physical impulse behind the revolution. The klephts and the *proestoi* were rivals. The Kolokotronis and Deligiannis families in particular were bitter enemies, although they briefly reconciled during the second civil war. Kolokotronis provides a proudly blood-drenched account of the klephtic past of his family: in a famous scene he depicts his mother giving birth to him under a tree. He describes his escape to the Ionian islands, his service in the British army and his joining of the Philiki Etaireia. His account of the revolutionary events naturally emphasizes his own glorious deeds: the capture of Tripolitsa (with a distressingly frank description of the massacre) and his defeat of the massive Turkish invasion of 1822 at Dervenakia. These accomplishments, he says, excited the envy of his enemies, who conspired to humiliate him and diminish his freedom of operation. It is in this connection that he pronounces his biting verdict that "the Maniots are prepared to do anything for money." In the civil wars that followed he was defeated and imprisoned, but he remained certain that his countrymen would again appeal to him to lead them. They did under baleful circumstances, following the invasion of Ibrahim which well-nigh strangled the revolution. Kolokotronis was released and made once again commander-in-chief, providing dogged resistance with his hastily mobilized irregulars. Toward the end he plaintively regrets the internecine hatreds that almost ruined the Greek cause from within.

The memoirs of General Ioannis Makrygiannis is a document whose significance extends beyond the nineteenth century. Written in the 1850s it was published at the beginning of the twentieth century. Since then its political and cultural aperçus have come to dominate the collective consciousness of Greek society. Makrygiannis was a minor figure in the revolution. He was a Rumeliot, invading the Peloponnese with the troops of continental Greece to put down the local antigovernment forces during the second civil war of 1824. More usefully for his country he participated in the successful defense of the road to Nafplio that forced Ibrahim to turn away from the last fortress in Greek hands, as well as in the campaigns to secure as much of Rumeli as could be saved after the fall of Mesolonghi. Yet the significance of his writing does not lie in the account of these events, but firstly in the language in which he expressed himself. Makrygiannis was illiterate and he taught himself the rudiments of writing just for the purpose of jotting down his reminiscences and ruminations. The result is a mode of expression that reflects popular speech and sensibility. He thus became the symbol of cultural regeneration, especially in the eyes of the poets of the "generation of the thirties." But there is also a pungent political message in his text. Makrygiannis describes the aftermath of the revolution, and in this epoch he detects the supremacy of social forces that were the direct opposite of the revolutionary ideals as he understands them. Under the Bavarian autocracy Greece has been invaded, he claims, by alien manners and values. Those who fought for freedom are now beggars, and power is in the hands of foreign-dressed and foreign-minded youth mimicking "the Franks." Makrygiannis participated in the military uprising that forced King Othon to grant a constitution in 1843. Of an intensely religious disposition, he believed that a constitution was a God-mandated government under which the genuine voice of the people would be heard and foreign domination chased away. The notion that Greece had been colonized by foreign cultural and political "interests" became entrenched in the Greek public mind over the twentieth century, and Makrygiannis's memoirs lent it ideological legitimacy by linking it with the "betrayed" ideals of 1821.

Systematic historical writing with a serious claim to factuality and interpretative plausibility began to appear in the 1850s. The first of such syntheses, which still retains the status of an indispensable work of reference, was that by Spyridon Trikoupis entitled *History of the Greek Revolution*. It was published in London beginning in 1857, when the author was serving as Greek ambassador to the Court of St. James. Trikoupis was the scion of a prominent family of Mesolonghi. During the revolution he played an active role in local and national affairs. He was a member of the revolutionary executive after 1826 and following independence he served briefly as the first prime minister of the new kingdom in 1833. Mesolonghi was the power base of Alexandros Mavrokordatos with whose liberal and anglophile orientations Trikoupis identified throughout his life. On the side of Mavrokordatos, Trikoupis welcomed Lord Byron to Mesolonghi in early 1824 and he was the one pronouncing the eulogy during the great man's funeral a few months later. In his work he attributes the deep causes of the revolution to the domination by force of a culturally and economically progressive nation by one stagnant and retrograde. The tension had been building up for at least a century. The armed attacks against Ottoman tax collectors in March 1821 were not in themselves revolutionary, but they provided the spark that detonated the longstanding situation. Trikoupis declares his intention of describing "the good and bad deeds of both Greeks and Turks" (in a phrase echoing the opening lines of Herodorus). His description of the siege and sack of Tripolitsa is detailed and unsparing. He does not intend to justify the inhuman behavior of his compatriots. But he warns Europeans not to be judgmental, for their past history is also full of similar horrors. Besides, the Greeks had learned violence at the school of Turkish despotism. As "slaves of slaves," they had no other means of physical survival vis-à-vis brutal oppressors except cringing subservience, dissimulation, and lawless violence. The rampage at Tripolitsa had come at the first flush of rebellious rage and in the anarchic conditions of the Greek camp there was no undisputed authority to curb the violence.

The overall protagonists in Trikoupis's story are Mesolonghi, Mavrokordatos, and George Canning. He praises his mentor for the efficient organization of the affairs of western Greece and the fortification of Mesolonghi, which enabled it to repel the first Turkish siege in 1822 and to mount the resistance that astounded the world during the doomed one of 1826. The Constitution of Epidavros was also Mavrokordatos's deed, but he saw it as a temporary expedient. He believed in constitutional monarchy, in accordance with the general wishes of the people at the time. But since no candidate for the throne was then available, he opted temporarily for republican government, which he knew that the European liberal public approved, and fought against the oligarchy promoted by the notables. Trikoupis places the blame for the civil war on the Peloponnesian military chiefs, who would not accept any political supervision of their conduct of operations and thought that the only duty of the politicians was to organize supplies for their bands. In times of war, Trikoupis ruefully commends, the sword has the strongest voice. Mavrokordatos's activities in foreign affairs were also beneficial for Greece, because through the loans floated in London he de facto engaged England on the side of the revolution. This was consummated through the accession of Canning at the helm of British policy in 1822. Trikoupis expatiates at length about this crucial turning point, underlining Canning's sincere but wisely pragmatic Philhellenism. His recognition of the Greek naval blockades was in fact an acknowledgment of the definitive separation of Greece from the Ottoman state. His diplomacy, through his nephew Stratford Canning, appointed as ambassador to Constantinople, was the first to address the Greek chiefs as a "provisional government." Finally, we have to note the account of the two sieges of Mesolonghi. Trikoupis was a native of the place, with intimate knowledge of the terrain, the personalities of the fighters, and every last detail of the tactics of the opposing armies. His masterful recitation brings to life an epic confrontation which fired the philhellenic sentiment that safeguarded the sputtering revolution. On King Othon's reaching his majority Trikoupis suggested to him that he immediately grant a constitution, but he was not heeded.

In contradistinction to Trikoupis, the work of Ioannis Philimon is suffused with a Russophile sentiment. Philimon was a longtime adherent of the Ypsilantis family in Constantinople. And, when Prince Dimitrios Ypsilantis arrived in Greece in June 1821 as the plenipotentiary of his brother Alexandros fighting in the Danubian Principalities, Philimon was by his side as his personal secretary. Thus, he eventually got hold of the archive of the Philiki Etereia and the papers of his master. As a result his *Historical Essay on the Greek Revolution* (1859–1861) has exceptional methodological significance, because it rests upon documentary evidence which the author publishes in lengthy appendices at the end of each volume. The first volume of the work is an account of the Philiki

Etaireia, purporting to reestablish its credit as the prime mover of the revolution, disputed during the revolution and especially afterward. Philimon argues that the claims by the *Philikoi* that their insurrectionary designs had the support of Emperor Alexander and Count Capodistrias were not empty boasts, although this support could only be intimated privately given the international constraints. He also defends Alexandros Ypsilantis for the conduct of the campaign in the principalities. It may have been haphazard and uncoordinated, but still it drew substantial Turkish military forces to this theater, which would have been otherwise deployed to defeat the insurrection in the south. It was also of capital moral and political importance, for its proximity to Constantinople showed that this was a movement of the entire Greek nation and not just a local revolt. The true historical date for the commencement of the Greek revolution, Philimon argues, is February 24, the day Alexandros Ypsilantis crossed the Pruth river and issued his appeal to the enslaved Christians of the empire. The date of March 25, fixed by legislation in 1838, should of course be accepted for its symbolic import. It was after all also the target date set by the Philiki Etaireia itself, but this ought not to serve as a pretext for claiming the revolution as the deed exclusively of the "natives" of the southern provinces. Philimon is enraged by the injustice of this "nativism" (*autochthony*) which dominated public life in the kingdom after 1844. After his defeat in the first National Assembly and the suppression of the emblems of the Philiki Etaireia as the national coat-of-arms on the instigation of Mavrokordatos, Prince Dimitrios Ypsilantis devoted himself to the military struggle. As a result, Philimon's account of the war on the ground is exemplary, although naturally from the point of view of the military party toward which the prince gravitated.

Of great symbolic and emotional significance is the lengthy chapter that Philimon devotes to the description of the massacres and general terror inflicted on the Greek population in the areas of the empire that had not revolted: from Constantinople through Smyrna to Cyprus. A small part of the Greek nation, he says, rose against the military forces of Turkey, but as a response the whole of the Turkish nation declared a war of extermination upon all the Greeks, whether they had revolted or not. He insists that the atrocities were officially condoned and orchestrated, whatever the Porte might claim to the ambassadors. His description of the hanging of the patriarch and the anti-Christian horrors in Smyrna is a pathetic story brimming with inhuman depravity. His estimate of the victims in the capital alone is around ten thousand. Dimitrios Ypsilantis fought the last battle of the revolution, a victorious engagement at Petra in 1829 that drove the Turks from Rumeli as the Russians battered them in Thrace. This symbolically enhances Philimon's conviction that the liberation of all the Greek lands will necessarily occur under the beneficial influence of

Russia, but also that the revolution thus ending had achieved only a small part of its aims, and that in the future the struggle would inevitably resume.

The crowning achievement of Greek historiography in the nineteenth century, and arguably to the present time, is the grand synthesis by Constantinos Paparrigopoulos entitled *History of the Greek Nation* (1860–1874). This covers the history of Greece from prehistoric times down to his days. Paparrigopoulos was a Constantinopolitan Greek of Peloponnesian origin, whose father, brother, and other relatives were massacred in the terror unleashed by the janissaries and the *ulema*s in April 1821. The family found refuge in Odessa, before eventually returning to liberated Greece. He became professor of history at the University of Athens. The assumption underlying his magnum opus is the continuous existence since remote antiquity of a Greek people assuming different characteristics at each historical age (e.g., the adoption of Christianity) which, however, did not alter its enduring cultural identity. The history of the revolution of 1821 appears in the last volume of the work as the culmination of this grandiose narrative. The revolution's historical necessity is grounded on the yearning for freedom to experience and to express this identity. This yearning had acquired tangible forms under Ottoman rule through the autonomous existence of local communities and also through the expansion of commerce and learning in the eighteenth century. But although the revolution is presented as a climax, it is also paradoxically a subdued one. Paparrigopoulos's standpoint is a strictly *national* one. He is determined, that is, to stand above all factions, assessing with searing frankness the contribution of each as well as the damage it inflicted on the general cause. The business of history, he explains, is neither absolutely to justify nor to condemn the various actors, but to judge their actions by reference to the objective facts. This, together with his decision to write primarily a *political* history of the revolution, is the reason for the marked pessimism pervading his account. For the politics of the revolution were indeed lamentable on the whole, and it was during the revolutionary period that the evils which subsequently marred the public life of the independent kingdom, such as factionalism, favoritism, and only hypocritical regard of the public interest, took root.

Paparrigopoulos adopts Philimon's conclusions as to the tacit support of the Philiki Etaireia's designs by Count Capodistrias and Emperor Alexander and the diversionary value of the campaign in the principalities, but he is scathing with regard to Alexandros Ypsilantis's conduct of the operations. He calls him the most inept person that could be chosen to lead the campaign, inflicting pointless repression upon innocents and neglecting elementary tasks of military planning while devoting weeks to the organization of a theater troupe. He is, further, damning concerning the form of government instituted at Epidavros.

He concurs that this was the work of Mavrokordatos, who, however, was motivated by his personal animus against Dimitrios Ypsilantis. The latter was excessive in his claiming general overlordship concerning the affairs of Greece on the remit of his soon-to-be defeated brother. Still, the prince had the right ideas about effective government, arguing as he did in favor of a strong executive unhampered by the interference of the legislature. Mavrokordatos, seeing that he would not lead it, pushed instead for the ruinous system of "polyarchy or even anarchy." Mavrokordatos, Paparrigopoulos says, was the most gifted political leader of those years. But internally although he was reputed to be an anglophile, he rather acted "as a Frenchman," namely as a subverter of strong government if he could not be in command. He was excellent in diagnosing the defects of existing structures, but incapable of constructing functioning alternatives. And his self-aggrandizement collided with another immovable political object, namely Kolokotronis's adamancy in considering the Peloponnese as his personal domain.

It was in the international relations of the revolution that Mavrokordatos exhibited his beneficial genius. Paparrigopoulos quotes approvingly from his 1820 Memorandum on the state of Turkey and from his correspondence with Metternich's confidant Friedrich von Gentz. There it is argued firstly that Turkey can no longer play a constructive role in the affairs of the East and that a renascent Greece as a dynamic and progressive nation will necessarily take its place. In addition, Turkish rule in Greece rests on brute force and not on any free contract between ruler and subject or on international treaties, as the "legitimist" position had it. Finally, the insurrection of the Greeks had nothing to do with the Carbonari, or any other revolutionary society that had caused the recent troubles in Spain and Italy, but rested on the same principles of Christianity and constitutional liberty as the civilized governments of Europe. Paparrigopoulos also commends Mavrokordatos for the decision to raise loans in London, for he envisioned this as a political act that forced official Britain to buy stock, as it were, in an independent Greece. With his appeal to Canning for British protection in 1825 he laid the foundation for the foreign intervention that finally secured independence. For the rest, the proceeds from the loans were squandered on factional favoritism by an outrageously corrupt and incompetent government. So, on the eve of Ibrahim's invasion the fleet had not been supplied and lay idle, and the army had disintegrated into rude and untrained gangs strutting about in their gold-plated pistols. With anguish and even disgust, Paparrigopoulos recounts the "calamitous years 1825, 1826, and 1827," during which good—or indeed any—government had disappeared and only the desperate harassment of the triumphing Ottoman armies by Kolokotronis and

Karaiskakis kept the revolution flickering. This collapse rendered in a sense necessary the transition to authoritarian rule under Capodistrias and the Bavarians. But the legacy of failure encumbered public life long after independence. In this very somber assessment, the revolution also emerges as an unfinished project, not only because there were still Greek lands to be liberated but also, and perhaps chiefly, because the Greeks had not managed to learn to govern themselves as a free people.

During the twentieth century the rising influence of Marxism led to a reinterpretation of the revolution from a "materialist" standpoint. The most influential attempt was *The Social Significance of the Greek Revolution of 1821* by Yannis Kordatos, appearing in 1924, an application of the scheme of economic determinism and the class struggle. According to this, the "real" contest of the revolution was between the peasants and the landowning *proestoi,* functioning as the effective agents of Turkish oppression and aspiring to succeed them in power when the revolution became unavoidable. The bourgeoisie, thriving primarily abroad and still a progressive force, fought for their ideals of liberal government, but their "true" historical aim was the establishment of their own version of class exploitation under the control of European imperialism. In this scheme the national ideals and the religious feelings animating the revolutionaries are dismissed as a facade for underlying economic interests. The heroes of 1821 are said to be the irregular military bands giving vent to the social aspirations of the peasantry, those people's fighters excluded from the distribution of the spoils after independence. This picture bends the record for ideological purposes. The first two triumphant years of the revolution, for instance, were exclusively financed by the personal wealth of the *proestoi* and the shipowners of the nautical islands. The rule of the military leaders over the peasantry could be just as ferocious in its rapacity, as the conduct of Gouras in Attica shows. And finally, the deals and arrangements of the military chiefs with the Turks were numerous and calamitous for the cause of Greek freedom, as the cases of Georgios "Gogos" Bakolas, Odysseus, and Karaiskakis himself testify. Still, the claims of Kordatos did stimulate a heightened sensibility about the social background of military and political events that had dominated traditional historiography. The conventional wisdom about the Greek revolution was codified in a new twelve-volume synthesis by Dionysios Kokkinos entitled *The Greek Revolution* appearing in the 1950s. The merit of this work is its elaborate discussion of political affairs during the years of civil strife. It is also enlivened by the reproduction of actual conversations between the participants.

Pericles S. Vallianos

References

Carrel, Armand. 1825. *Résumé de l'histoire des Grecs modernes*. Paris.

Craig, Gordon. 1972. "Georg Gottfried Gervinus: The Historian as Activist." *Pacific Historical Review* 41, no. 1 (February): 1–14.

Diamandouros, Nikiforos P. 1976. "Bibliographical Essay." In *Hellenism and the First Greek War of Liberation, 1821–1830: Continuity and Change*, edited by Nikiforos P. Diamandouros, Peter W. Topping, and John Peter Anton, 193–230. Thessaloniki.

Dimaras, Constantinos Th. 1986. *Κωνσταντίνος Παπαρρηγόπουλος* [Constantinos Paparrigopoulos]. Athens.

Emerson, James. 1830. *The History of Modern Greece from Its Conquest by the Romans in 146 B.C. to the Present Time*. London.

Felton, Cornelius Conway. 1867. *Greece Ancient and Modern*. Boston.

Finlay, George. 1861. *History of the Greek Revolution*. Edinburgh and London.

Gervinus, Georg Gottfried. 1866. *Histoire du dix-neuvième siècle*. Vols 11–13. Paris.

Gervinus, Georg Gottfried [Georgio Goffredo]. 1863. *Risorgimento della Grecia*. Milan.

Gordon, Thomas 1832. *History of the Greek Revolution*. Edinburgh.

Hertzberg, Gustav Friedrich. 1879. *Von der Erhebung der Neugriecher gegen die Pforte bis zum Berliner Frieden (1821–1878), Geschichte Griechenlands seit dem Absterben des antiken Lebens bis zur Gegenwart*. Vol. 4. Gotha.

Howe, Samuel Gridley. 1828. *An Historical Sketch of the Greek Revolution*. New York.

Leake, William Martin. 1826. *An Historical Outline of the Greek Revolution*. London.

Leake, William Martin. 1851. *Greece at the End of Twenty-Three Years' Protection*. London.

Mendelssohn-Bartholdy, Karl. 1867. "Die orientalische Politik des Fürsten Metternich." Edited by Heinrich von Sybel. *Historische Zeitschrift* 18: 41–76.

Mendelssohn-Bartholdy, Karl. 1870. *Geschichte Griechenlands von der Eroberung Konstantinopels durch die Türken bis auf unsere Tage*. Leipzig.

Pieri, Mario. 1825. *Compendio della storia del Risorgimento della Grecia*. Italy.

Pouqueville, François. 1824. *Histoire de la régénération de la Grèce*. Paris.

Pouqueville, François. 1826–1827. *Voyage de la Grèce*. 2nd ed. Paris.

Pouqueville, François. 1836. *La Grecia di Pouqueville*. Translated by Francesco Falconetti. Venice.

Pouqueville, François. 1838a. *Istoria della Grecia dal 1740 al 1824*. Naples.

Pouqueville, François. 1838b. *Storia della rigenerazione della Grecia*. Lugano.

Prokesch-Osten, Anton von. 1867. *Geschichte des Abfalls der Griechen vom türkischen Reiche im Jahre 1821*. Vienna.

Raffenel, Claude Denis. 1822–1824. *Histoire des événements de la Grèce*. Paris.

Raybaud, Maxime. 1824. *Mémoires sur la Grèce*. Paris.

Rovani, Giuseppe. 1854. *Storia della Grecia negli ultimi trent'anni (1824–1854)*. Milan.

Sakellariou, Michail V. 2011. *Θέματα νέας ελληνικής ιστορίας* [Issues in modern Greek history]. 2 vols. Athens.

St Clair, William. (1972) 2008. *That Greece Might Still Be Free: The Philhellenes in the War of Independence*. Introduction by Roderick Beaton. Cambridge.

Ticozzi, Stefano. 1827. *Storia della rigenerazione della Grecia per servire di continuazione a quella di Pouqueville*. Italy.

Trent, James W., Jr. 2012. *The Manliest Man: Samuel G. Howe and the Contours of Nineteenth-Century American Reform*. Amherst, MA.

Voutier, Olivier. 1823. *Mémoires sur la guerre actuelle des Grecs*. Paris.

Webster, Daniel. 1851. "The Revolution in Greece." In *The Works of Daniel Webster*, 3:60–93. Boston.

Zinkeisen, Johann Wilhelm. 1832. *Geschichte Griechenlands*. Vol. 1. Leipzig.

Zinkeisen, Johann Wilhelm. 1840. *Geschichte Griechenlands*. Vols. 3–4. Leipzig.

Anniversaries

Since the outbreak of the Greek War of Independence in 1821, the Greek people have celebrated three major anniversaries: the 50th, 100th, and 150th anniversary dates of the inception of this revolutionary war that led to sovereign statehood after nearly four centuries of Ottoman rule. These three jubilees, each with its own legacy, have come to represent three different ways of celebrating Greek statehood that have, nonetheless, much in common. The celebrants considered the festivities to be in the best interests of the Greek state, and of its younger generations especially, but many ceremonies—and subsequent state rituals— displayed a more self-serving political culture or nationalist ideology as well. Through 1971, Greek political and religious nationalisms represented two sides of one coin, and they tended to reinforce each other through historicizing parades and other displays of unbroken cultural (if not religious) continuity. They posited a linear and authentic progression from Greek antiquity through postclassical, Byzantine, and post-Byzantine (Ottoman) times. Thus, the celebrations and reenactments, with their commemorative events and symbolic images, acquired a prescriptive character, which further advanced their aim to educate youth in state-promoted nationalism.

In anticipation of the bicentennial of Greece's independence, it may prove helpful to study the earlier celebrations, their main themes and agendas, the imaginary nation to which they appealed, and some of the images and reports they left behind. We expect to find the years 1871, 1921, and 1971 as the key anniversary dates, but we are immediately struck by an important exception: the grand celebrations of the centenary of 1921 were "postponed" due to political and military circumstances. Besides, the Greeks looked forward with great anticipation to a more wide-ranging series of events that was scheduled for 1930, the centenary of the year in which the Greek state was formed. Thus, past and present, and even the unknown but projected future, affected the making of the anniversaries of Greece as a product of a revolution and as a nation. Also, the various anniversaries offer up a potent reminder that, on each occasion, the nation's process of becoming was yet to be completed. The year 1871 preceded the Balkan Wars (1912–1913) and the ensuing territorial gains by a few (turbulent) decades. The crisis of 1921–1922 signaled a reduction in the Greek territorial expanse and an even greater blow to Greek political and cultural self-confidence. The year 1971, which fell about halfway through the dictatorship period of 1967–1974, was used by the military regime to affirm "revolution" and "independence," but by the antidictatorship opposition to question the extent to which the long-suffering state had been genuinely sovereign and democratic. The question now remains what the anniversary year of 2021 holds in store for a nation that has seen a dozen years of a crisis economy and several natural disasters (the tragic fires of July 2018 being just one of them).

The Fiftieth Anniversary, 1871

The celebratory year of 1871, or the marker of the fifty years since the Greek Revolution, was much anticipated. A few events raised the stakes in the lead-up to the anniversary year. Russia had been holding the relics of Ecumenical Patriarch Grigorios V (1746–1821), who, as the leader of the Orthodox Greek religious minority living under the Ottoman Empire, had been killed shortly after the outbreak of the Greek revolt. The Sublime Porte retaliated against the "traitors" among the members of the Greek elite who served in prized clerical and administrative positions. It considered the then patriarch, despite his calls for caution and even for submission, to be one of them. Upon his assassination, Patriarch Grigorios's remains had been taken to Odessa. Half a century later, the Greek state arranged to have these relics brought home to the new nation and to rebury them, with due pomp and circumstance, in the Metropolitan Cathedral of Athens. The conspicuous involvement of the royal couple, King George I and Queen Olga, marked the interment as a nationalist and Atheno-centric occasion (Exertzoglou 2001). The Greek state also arranged to have the patriarch's honorific statue erected in front of the central building of the University of Athens. This statue was sculpted by Georgios Fytalis but was unveiled with a slight delay (Mykoniatis 1984, 355, 364–365). As a religious symbol, the statue joined that of another ethnomartyr, Rhigas Velestinlis or Rhigas Feraios (1757–1798). The tribute to this precursor-champion of the revolutionary struggle was the work of sculptor Ioannis Kossos, who acknowledged Rhigas's enlightened and secular political philosophy and also the postrevolutionary idealization of his person and aspirations. Historian Thomas Gallant has characterized the ideology behind the 1871 jubilee ceremony and the erection of the statues as "the wedding of Orthodoxy to the Revolution" (2016, 91). Significantly, too, the plan to create two statues of revolutionary martyrs superseded an earlier proposal to erect statues of ancient deities. The two statues tied the revolution to the new institutions of the modern, nationalist Greek state, in particular to the University of Athens with its classicizing ethos (Karamanolakis 2014, 117–118). Both statues were executed in a conventional style, which did not assert a new aesthetic but affirmed, rather, an existing code of classicizing.

In 1875, the statue of Adamantios Korais (1748–1833) was set up in the same general location, outside the central building of the University of Athens. Korais left a rich intellectual legacy to the Greek state. He had made his permanent home in Paris, where he shared in French Enlightenment theory and in radical thought (Kitromilides 2013, especially chap. 10). He laid the foundations of a Hellenic Library of editions of seminal classical texts, with which to instruct the younger Greek generations. This Hellenic Library functioned as a secular vehicle for transmitting Western cultural ideals, which inculcated in the Greek reading public an awareness of one of its most valued possessions: remnants from antiquity. The concern for the younger Greeks' education was a recurrent theme also in the subsequent anniversary celebrations, whose pageantry was modeled after French revolutionary prototypes. All of these initiatives exemplified the deliberate creation of new cultural and social beings in young (male) Greeks, who would cultivate patriotism. They became identified with the nationalist-didactic ideology of Korais as the revolutionary Greek expatriate who inspired many others. Uses of Greek texts and monuments alike, of symbolic imagery and of a normative ideology in subsequent anniversaries strengthened the classicizing ethos that the three statues of the 1871 jubilee had first come to embody. But the anniversary celebrations remained more limited in scope than, for instance, the broader nineteenth-century Greek impulse to organize knowledge and nationalism: knowledge about (and power over) the ancients and their artifacts began to overlap with the creation of national museums, printed collections, libraries, theater stages, and the educational infrastructure of the modern Greek state at large.

The three statues, of Rhigas Feraios, Patriarch Grigorios, and Korais (in the chronological order of their making), embodied the fusion of antiquity, Byzantium, and the modern era; they captured the power of religion to augment nation-building (and vice versa), as well as the potential of language and patrimony. Taken together and with the University of Athens as their backdrop, the statues showed the Greeks' commitment to the blending of all of these facets of the modern Greek nation. Thus, the 1871 anniversary celebration signaled an early call of achieved success, even though major struggles of religious integration, territorial expansion and defeat, linguistic debate and reform, and overall institutional (re)structuring still lay ahead (Gallant 2016, 90–91; Makrides 2009, 180; Vovchenko 2016, 151–153; and especially, Mykoniatis 1984).

The seminal model of Greek historical continuity underpinned the five-volume *History of the Hellenic Nation* (1860–1874; second edition 1885–1887), the influential nation-building work of Constantinos Paparrigopoulos. Paparrigopoulos had proposed five eras of Hellenism (the epochs of ancient, Macedonian, Christian, medieval, and modern Hellenism), but his work has been remembered in terms of three eras only: ancient, Byzantine, and modern Hellenism (Kitromilides 1998, 29). These three ages of Hellenic civilization congealed in a "form of teleology for the Greek state," which underpinned its irredentist and Byzantine ambition of the Great Idea (*Megali Idea*) (31). They became staples of nearly all Greek nationalist celebrations and their visual and verbal rhetoric.

Decades prior to 1871, the initiative had been raised to stage Greek history as a continuum of male athletic prowess inherited from antiquity and to strengthen national reawakening in that manner. In January 1835, Ioannis Kolettis (1774–1847), minister of internal affairs to King Othon, published a proposal (in French) for athletic games and festivals to commemorate, at public expense, the major events and battle sites of the 1821 War of Independence and also the spirit of national unification that its advocates had propounded (Decker 2006). Significantly, the celebration of March 25 as the anniversary date of the Greek Revolution (coinciding with the Christian feast of the Annunciation to the Virgin Mary) was established in 1838, or three years after Kolettis had issued his plan (Skopetea 1988, 215). The events proposed by Kolettis were modeled after the panhellenic athletic games and other festivals of Greek antiquity, such as the famous Olympian, Pythian, Nemean, and Isthmian games, but also the classical religious festivals of the *Panathenaia*, the *Eleusinia*, the *Thesmophoria*, the Great *Dionysia*, among others. Kolettis singled out the particular advantages of such pageants for the newborn Greek state: the international resonance of such festivals, their role in strengthening the royal house, and the tremendous ethical benefits ("d'immenses avantages moraux") that they would deliver and that promised to bring modern Greece closer to ancient Greece (Diamantis 1973, 313). Kolettis summed up: "Tâchons que le Grec moderne approche de l'ancien, que le fils réproduise le père" (Let us try to make the modern Greek approach the ancient Greek, to make the son reproduce the father) (324). The vision of Kolettis to recreate aspects of the athletic competitions and religious feasts that took place in antiquity was instrumental in designing the state-sponsored pageantry of Greece in the twentieth century, including its anniversary spectacle. The ideal of bestowing a renaissance on the Greek nation through ancient sports and their ethos drove the nineteenth-century Zappas Olympics (1859, 1870, 1875, and 1888–1889), two occurrences of which closely met the creation of the three honorific statues in time and space (again in central Athens). However, the 1896 revival of the Olympic Games proved to be the most important catalyst in the process of establishing the Greek heroic pageantry of cultural continuity. Through the era before the First World War, Greece was eager to claim and secure its guardianship over the "authentic" ancient athletic tradition, which would become more significant as the modern Olympic movement gained wider local and Western support (Hamilakis 2007, 1–7, 203–204; Kitroeff 2004; Koulouri 2006, 2012; Mackridge 2008, 310–311; Young 1996). Historicizing pageantry, tied to symbolic dates and locations, drew from the Enlightenment philosophy and the praxis of the French Revolution, which espoused the edifying value of mass public spectacles, dynamic bodies moving through dramatic spaces, ancient or ancient-style monuments, and the arts. In Greece, however, the heroic pageantry of continuity and syncretism acquired a life of its own and determined nearly all subsequent types of historical reenactments in the nationalist vein.

1921 Becomes 1930: A Centenary of the Revolution or of Nationhood

The aftermath of the First World War and Greece's own political and military predicament prevented the year 1921 from being the celebratory centenary that it could have been. The Cretan statesman Eleftherios Venizelos (1864–1936) dominated the national and even the international scene. For some, he gave all to the fight against the Greek oligarchy and monarchy of the early years of the twentieth century. Leader of a prolonged struggle against the royalist elite, Venizelos's star shone bright through 1920. As prime minister of Greece, Venizelos traveled to Paris in 1919, to represent his country at the Paris Peace Conference. There, he secured Allied consent for Greece to occupy the region of Smyrna (Izmir) and its hinterland in Asia Minor. Venizelos then pursued the signing of the Treaty of Sèvres (August 10, 1920), which postulated settlement terms between Greece and the Ottoman Empire and sanctioned the Greek occupation of Smyrna and its environs. Thus, he became the executor of Greece's irredentist aspirations of the Great Idea. At the peak of his power, Venizelos was proclaimed the architect of "Greater Greece," or of "Greece of the two continents and the five seas." In mid-September of 1920, he staged his partisan-patriotic victory celebrations at the Panathenaic Stadium (that is, the old

Olympic Stadium or Kallimarmaro Stadium in downtown Athens). Venizelos's own triumphal procession provoked reactions that ranged from uncritical adulation to shock and outcry (Van Steen 2010).

Venizelos did not shy away from self-promotion and the relentless quest for patriotic prestige. After he lost the November 1920 elections, however, he went into self-imposed exile and temporarily disappeared from the Greek political scene. By March 25, 1921, the Greek army had suffered the first military setbacks in the battle against the new Turkish nationalist forces. The sense of danger, of loss and catastrophe, would soon be borne out by the Smyrna Disaster of mid-September 1922 (on the burning of Smyrna's quarters that housed ethnic minorities, the resulting compulsory exchange of populations, and the rise of the new Turkish state, see further Llewellyn Smith 1998). The post-1922 era may have been ripe for a reconsideration of the irredentist Great Idea, but in March 1921 the time to rethink the propagandistic use of mass pageantry had not yet come. Did 1921 as a jubilee date go by unnoticed then, because of the shadows cast over it by current events? Not at all. The year 1921 saw modest ceremonies that again placed the emphasis on honoring the revolutionary martyrs. As Dora Markatou has noted (2008, 311), Spyridon Lambros spearheaded the centenary commemorating the War of Independence. He envisioned festivals that would be supervised by other historians, archaeologists, and folklorists. The 1921 celebrations offered up a modest blend of historical reenactments, and they prompted the erection of war memorials and the foundation or restoration of monuments and other prestigious public venues (such as the Herodes Atticus theater). Venizelos himself saw in the muted 1921 anniversary a means to again bolster the political and military project of a Greater Greece, the quest to consolidate Greek territories in Asia Minor, to annex new ones, and to recapture Constantinople. This backdrop transformed the 1921 parade into a Venizelist rally, not unlike the triumphal procession of mid-September 1920. Thus, Venizelos tapped a powerful wellspring of personal prestige and (party-)political propaganda, and he tied the performative quality of military expeditions and parades to the spectacle of official representation: both codified patriotism and institutionalized nationalism in his own conception. Classicizing festival pageantry was mined for its political capital as well as for its cultural capital (to use notions established by Pierre Bourdieu). The Venizelist production of the leader's personal triumph marked the public euphoria about the Greeks' military, territorial, and diplomatic gains.

On March 25, 1921, it was far too early to claim victory in the Asia Minor campaign. At Venizelos's instigation, the Greeks had ambitiously occupied Smyrna and its hinterland for many months, during which Turkish ratification of this or any other Greek territorial expansion into Asia Minor had not been forthcoming. The Turkish victory, the Greek rout, and the Smyrna Disaster of September 1922 meant that the history of 1821 was being reversed, that the centenary of 1921 was unraveling. Venizelos's grand scheme and the entire vision of the Great Idea collapsed in the ashes of Smyrna. The dream of the grand celebration of Greater Greece, of the final realization of the Great Idea, was forever crushed. Critics of the Anatolian adventure had feared the Greek overreach all along. Once the battle sites were no longer those of historical defense but had become those of military hubris, the scars of defeat were harder to explain and took much longer to heal. The surviving ethnic Greek populations of Asia Minor were forced to leave for an uncertain future in Greece, which, as a country with very limited resources or infrastructure, had already been straining under the burden of prolonged war. It took Greece at least through the interwar years to recover.

Venizelists strategically blamed King Constantine I and a group of military commanders for the Smyrna Disaster of 1922. But Venizelos himself had risked Greek territorial integrity and political sovereignty in the historical gamble of the Asia Minor campaign. The consequences were deeply divisive politically and affected culture and commemoration as well. In another act of overreach, the Greeks postponed the big celebrations of their country's centenary, to commence on the symbolic date of March 25 of the year 1930. The delay of the centenary festivities was motivated by the once again unrealistic expectation of new gains to celebrate by 1930. This new centennial would celebrate the actual formation and recognition of the independent Greek state, which was founded in 1830. When the grand centennial of 1930 finally came around, the atmosphere was still subdued in and around Athens, again the geographical center-point of the festivities. Venizelos's last administration of 1928–1932 oversaw the celebrations, which explains their self-congratulatory tone and ethos. Once more, politics, the military, religion, and ideology blended together in mass spectacles of the state staging itself. Lambros again inspired the celebrations, which reaffirmed the idea and ideal of national continuity and the medium of outdoor mass festivals emboldened by the contemporary moral and didactic ideology. As in 1921, an organizing committee in which academics and archaeologists, especially, assumed key positions designed and scheduled the events—one month full of events. In addition to historicizing parades, these events included the ceremonial raising of the flag and the firing of cannons, ample occasions for speech making, and also religious services. Notably, the centennial also recreated the Panathenaic Procession in an archaizing and nationalist spirit. Athena's new *peplos,* however, was substituted by the Greek flag, which, according to plan, would be changed annually on top of the Acropolis, and each year a different Greek city or region would be responsible for this flag ceremony (Markatou 2008, 311–312). Thus, archaizing public spectacle merged with the modern Greek demand for regional as well as national unification. The Tomb of the Unknown Soldier on Syntagma Square, begun in 1929 and meant to deliver yet another symbolic message of moral strength and continuity, was, unfortunately, not ready to be unveiled in time (not until March 25, 1932). But the completion of the restoration works on the Acropolis was included in the formal centenary program (Markatou 2008, 311). In 1930, too, Venizelos rededicated the bronze statue of the revolutionary war hero Kolokotronis, who had been imprisoned by King Othon's administration, thus placing himself in a popular genealogy that was antiroyalist as well as revolutionary.

As in 1921, the 1930 centennial celebration of Greek statehood raised reservations about Venizelos hailing his personal return to politics. Also, the prominence of Cretan culture was pervasive, given that the prime minister was from Crete. Venizelos further drew extensively from the structure and the aesthetics of the mass events organized by the Lyceum of Greek Women and held at the Panathenaic Stadium. It was the Lyceum that had first added the Minoan age to the parade of the canonical three eras of Greek history, in the "great national festival" of 1926 at the stadium. The staged representation of the "Bloodless Sacrifice from the Minoan Period," too, was a creation of the Lyceum (Van Steen 2010, 2139). In 1930, it was again the Lyceum that brought the parade of heroes and heroines of the Greek War of Independence to the stadium. Significantly, the embodied display of the four eras in the life of the Greek nation, now including the Minoan age, became part of subsequent mass events (Fournaraki 2011; Koulouri 2012; Markatou 2008, 313; Zervas 2017). Thus the War of Independence and the formation of the Greek nation were symbolically linked to Byzantium, Greek antiquity, and to Crete. The past had to infuse the present in an unbroken continuum of patriotic spirit and resiliency. The latter, the message of the indomitable spirit of the Greek people and its fighters, and thus of the "Greekness" of the centenary, was both prominent and poignant given the recent collapse of the irredentist dream and the ensuing mass refugee problem. Notably, too, hyperbolic Greek festival pageantry, held at the Panathenaic Stadium, predated the dictatorship of General Ioannis Metaxas (who ruled 1936–1941), with whose regime (and fascist sympathies) we all too often associate it.

1971: The Self-Celebration of a Military Regime

Metaxas or the colonels of the dictatorship of 1967–1974 did not invent their parade festivals and athletic contests, but they made them their own by expanding and militarizing them. The architects of the latter regime's events had before them a series of canonical templates and a performative repertory from which to choose in accordance with the prevailing state priorities. The strongmen of the coup of April 21, 1967, had certain technical advancements working for them as well. Thus, Georgios Papadopoulos propped up his public celebrations with "suitable" (read: censored) television and other media coverage, whose rote praise was the illusionary equivalent of the rote applause in the Panathenaic Stadium.

By 1971, the year of the 150th jubilee of the Greek Revolution, the dictators had sought and found an "authentic" tradition of origins and a "valid" genealogy for their own military intervention, their self-styled "regenerative Revolution." Thus, the cult of the revolutionary past came to serve a cult of much-advertised new but undemocratic beginnings. The "Revolution of April 21, 1967" was far removed from the kind of liberalizing sociopolitical reform that Greece badly needed. The colonels also posited the anniversary date of their own take-over as a new national holiday. On the regime's first anniversary, Papado-poulos concluded his address to the nation with statements that underscored his will to graft the army's intervention onto the Greek tradition of revolution resulting in "morally superior" victory:

The Revolution of April 21 represents the greatest and most serious attempt to restore, reorganize, and cure Greece since it regained its National Independence. And the Revolution will succeed, because it bespeaks the necessity of the historical imperative. ("April 21 Has Proved to Be a Landmark in the History of Our Country," *To Vima*, April 21, 1968)

Papadopoulos's casting of the revolution of 1821 as a grand analogue for his own military aggression smacked of propagandistic distortion. The 150th anniversary of the revolution and the anticipated nationwide festivities were announced with a similar, hubristic degree of fanfare (Athanassopoulos et al. 1971; Golia 2011, 43–45, 144–162, 303; Katsapis 2011, 292). The jubilee's specific events were planned at a large meeting held in the Old Parliament, in September 1970. Papadopoulos himself gave the directions, but top officials of the political and ecclesiastical hierarchy participated as well (Katsapis 2011, 289). The attendees decided that the celebrations should last throughout 1971, which was named as the "Year of Hellenic National Freedom." The organizers also shared an important concern, to stage a series of unusual events, many so hyperbolic as to become caricatures.

For the dictators, the theatrical communication through displays of military culture was one of tradition, supremacy, and proven authenticity. The junta relentlessly promoted the values of the country's rulers, ancestors, and roots by grounding them in a proud, "authentic" history, in an unchanging geocultural territory, and in unshaken diachronic time. Moreover, the dictators presented the battles against interior and exterior communists of the past and present alike as interrelated parts of a single "holy war" in defense of the nation. Their official rhetoric, bolstered by the protracted state of martial law, was rife with calls for "patriotic" loyalty to the nation's "protectors" and for vigilance and suspicion of fellow Greeks. Thus the 1971 jubilee and other junta festivals emptied out or "erased" the past of the Civil War, especially, and the leftist sympathies and forces of resistance that lived on. Not surprisingly, the official rhetoric of ethnic pride and of the strong national family appealed to the patriotic sentiment of those Greeks who sought stability after many years of military and political turmoil. For some, the regime's stagings of historical continuity were gratifying precisely because they were long familiar. Plenty of others, however, realized that the junta was reducing Greek valor to purebred military character—and, even then, more to muscle power than to military genius. More outspoken critics saw a farcical spectacle and a transparent concoction of propaganda.

Obviously, the monumental junta festivals did not come about without the planning and cooperation of many more people, in other realms of cultural production as well. James Paris, a Greek-American entrepreneur, became the colonels' favorite producer of patriotic films, to which the armed forces readily contributed. Paris's morale-boosting war epics did their part to support the dictators' "revolution" and, like the festivals, they featured the typical purple passages of Greek history and also stories of personal sacrifice for the good of the collective. The genre generated movies such as *The Souliots* (1972, directed by Dimitris Papakostantis) and *Papaflessas, Hero of the Greek Revolution* (1971), which, directed by Errikos Andreou, became the genre's best-known film. Paris himself goes often unmentioned: his work as an architect of the propagandistic junta festivals has not recommended him to posterity. In the late 1960s, however, the experience that Paris had gained in the United States lent a—spurious— legitimacy to his work.

The regime's exaggerated displays of military prowess at the 1971 jubilee and on many other occasions were meant to (re)shape the people's knowledge of Greek history and to inspire their pride for being "racial descendants" of the ancient Greeks. Thus, the junta festivals picked up where the practice of school history lessons and their nationalizing mission had left off, teaching sacrifice-oriented "patriotism" and conformism in the name of Greek continuity. From the nineteenth and well into the twentieth century, instruction in Greek history in primary and secondary schools, preferably highly structured, was marked and marred by its relentless emphasis on the "patriotic" national past. Ancient Greek language and literature, too, were often taught in tedious, ethnocentric ways, presenting the symbols of classical culture as sacred cows.

For decades, "patriotism" had been performed in Greek school teachings, in the teacher's lecturing, and in the student's regurgitating of historical content that was to be idealized but never reinterpreted. The junta festivals joined traditional pedagogy in using youths and adults as prime material for nationalist subject formation. To be sure, the nationalization of the masses through formal history lessons or through festivals that display the nation's bodily performance or that invent national "traditions" is a widely shared process in constructing modern nation-states. However, the Greek dictators' manipulation of the past was an extreme case in the long course of the state's appropriation of national history, whether through the official discourse that addressed the adult population or through the poor teaching of history in the public school and university system.

Among the sharpest detractors of the regime's spectacles were students and youth, who mocked all officialdom, its bombast, its victory festivals and military parades. They resented the artificial cultivation of "sound morality," especially. Greek history's heroes appeared as *exempla virtutis* in a morality play, out of touch with the progressive spirit and changing mores of the late 1960s. The spectacle of 1971, too, instilled a rigid essentialism, which proved far removed from the fluidity of Greek history in 1821. The 1971 jubilee was a commemoration of the past; at best, it was a hypocritical legitimation of an undemocratic present. Its events did not leave any notable artistic or architectural legacies; they only affirmed past and outdated commemorative modes. Thus, the anniversary was detached from contemporary cultural developments as well as audiences and failed to look forward to a new era. Ever since the collapse of the dictatorship, the critiques of the misuse of history by the colonels and by other authorities have been more vocal. They have rallied against the historicizing and anticommunist pageantry, especially, which lasted through the early 1980s (Kourniakti 2018; Van Steen 2015a; 2015b, 178–179).

The productive but also troubled realm of Greek historical celebrations and of mass pageants has, for decades now, been central to the formation of Greek identity. For the greater purpose of instilling national sensibilities, the Greek state has put itself on display on the occasion of landmark anniversaries. The performative dimensions of anniversary parades, with their typical sequences of heroic episodes through the canonical ages of Hellenic civilization, had to model proper ideals and modes of conduct for Greece's young people, especially. Three major events have marked the nation's celebration history of the outbreak of the War of Independence in 1821. The domestic political culture and ideology of the three major anniversary dates—namely 1871, 1921/1930, and

1971—could hardly have been more different. Nonetheless, the execution as
well as the objective of these jubilees of the past converged as they resorted
to classicizing statues and mass pageantry to mark the Greek state's public
and formal use of history. Surveying these anniversaries has proven to be a
fruitful exercise in anticipation of a critical evaluation of the bicentenary of
the year 2021.

The Greeks of the three anniversaries of the revolution had not yet reached
a consensus about how to present recent Greek history, but many had come to
realize that the true interest of the national past lay in how it constituted and
conditioned the future. Their monuments and festivals served the national interest and also the goal of political cohesion; they projected the idea of progress along a historical and cultural continuum, and they posited a survival,
revival, or even resurrection of a Greek patriotic ethos. The sustained continuity model that linked the past to the present was, undoubtedly, engaged in
national mythmaking. Also, this model kept suggesting a paradoxical kind of
parthenogenesis of Greek culture, as if Greek culture moved forward in a controlled vacuum, from one military victory to the next, and was only ever driven
by male leaders. The last jubilee of 1971, in particular, marked an intense era in
Greek politics and culture when truth, authority, Greek history, destiny, and
collective identity were the subjects of a public standoff that played out in the
old venues. Perhaps for the last time, this jubilee tried to solidify a national
master narrative that reasserted the political and socioeconomic status quo. In
hindsight, it failed to once more crystallize the national myth. Let us hope that
the bicentennial celebrations of 2021 will build on a critical reception of the past
jubilees and will prove to be meaningfully different.

Gonda Van Steen

References

Athanassopoulos, A., E. Alexiou, N. Anagnostaki, M. Anagnostakis, K. Antypa, et al. 1971.
    "Manifesto on the Occasion of the 150th Anniversary of Independence." In *Free Greek
    Voices: A Political Anthology,* edited by Helen Vlachos, 142–143. London.
Decker, Wolfgang. 2006. *Praeludium Olympicum. Das Memorandum des Jahres 1835 von
    Innenminister Ioannis Kolettis an König Otto I. von Griechenland über ein Nationalfest
    mit öffentlichen Spielen nach dem Muster der antiken panhellenischen Agone.*
    Hildesheim.
Diamantis, Constantinos A. 1973. "Πρότασις καθιερώσεως εθνικών επετείων και
    δημοσίων αγώνων κατά το πρότυπον των εορτών της αρχαιότητος κατά το έτος 1835"
    [Proposal of the year 1835 for instituting national anniversaries and public games
    modeled on the festivals of antiquity]. *Athina* 73–74: 307–325.

Exertzoglou, Charis. 2001. "Πολιτικές τελετουργίες στη νεώτερη Ελλάδα. Η μετακομιδή των οστών του Γρηγορίου Ε΄ και η πεντηκονταετηρίδα της Ελληνικής Επανάστασης" [Political rituals in modern Greece: The transport of the bones of Grigorios V and the fiftieth anniversary of the Greek Revolution]. *Mnimon* 23:153–182.

Fournaraki, Eleni. 2011. "Bodies that Differ: Mid- and Upper-Class Women and the Quest for 'Greekness' in Female Bodily Culture (1896–1940)." In *Sport, Bodily Culture and Classical Antiquity in Modern Greece,* edited by Eleni Fournaraki and Zinon Papakonstantinou, 49–85. London and New York.

Gallant, Thomas W. 2016. *Modern Greece: From the War of Independence to the Present.* 2nd ed. London and New York.

Golia, Paraskevi. 2011. *Υμνώντας το έθνος· Ο ρόλος των σχολικών γιορτών στην εθνική και πολιτική διαπαιδαγώγηση (1924–2010)* [Glorifying the nation: The role of school festivals in the national and political education process, 1924–2010]. Thessaloniki.

Hamilakis, Yannis. 2007. *The Nation and Its Ruins: Antiquity, Archaeology, and National Imagination in Greece.* Oxford.

Karamanolakis, Vangelis. 2014. "The University of Athens and Greek Antiquity (1837–1937)." In *Re-Imagining the Past: Antiquity and Modern Greek Culture,* edited by Dimitris Tziovas, 112–127. Oxford.

Katsapis, Kostas. 2011. "Perceptions of the Past by the Dictatorship of April 21st: The Concept of 'Bravery' and the Exploitation of 1821." In *The Greek Revolution of 1821: A European Event,* edited by Petros Pizanias, 287–294. Istanbul.

Kitroeff, Alexander. 2004. *Wrestling with the Ancients: Modern Greek Identity and the Olympics.* New York.

Kitromilides, Paschalis M. 1998. "On the Intellectual Content of Greek Nationalism: Paparrigopoulos, Byzantium and the Great Idea." In *Byzantium and the Modern Greek Identity,* edited by David Ricks and Paul Magdalino, 25–33. Aldershot and London.

Kitromilides, Paschalis M. 2013. *Enlightenment and Revolution: The Making of Modern Greece.* Cambridge, MA.

Koulouri, Christina. 2006. "The First Modern Olympic Games at Athens 1896 in the European Context." *European Studies* 5:59–76.

Koulouri, Christina. 2012. "Γιορτάζοντας το έθνος. Εθνικές επέτειοι στην Ελλάδα τον 19ο αιώνα" [Celebrating the nation: National anniversaries in Greece of the nineteenth century]. In *Αθέατες όψεις της ιστορίας· Κείμενα αφιερωμένα στον Γιάνη Γιανουλόπουλο* [Invisible facets of history: Essays dedicated to Gianis Gianoulopoulos], edited by Despoina I. Papadimitriou, Serafeim I. Seferiadis, and Dimitris Bacharas, 181–210. Athens.

Kourniakti, Jessica. 2018. "The Classical Asset: Receptions of Antiquity under the Dictatorship of 21 April in Greece (1967–73)." PhD diss., University of Oxford.

Llewellyn Smith, Michael. 1998. *Ionian Vision: Greece in Asia Minor, 1919–1922.* 2nd ed. Ann Arbor, MI.

Mackridge, Peter. 2008. "Cultural Difference as National Identity in Modern Greece." In *Hellenisms: Culture, Identity, and Ethnicity from Antiquity to Modernity,* edited by Katerina Zacharia, 297–319. Aldershot.

Makrides, Vasilios N. 2009. *Hellenic Temples and Christian Churches: A Concise History of the Religious Cultures of Greece from Antiquity to the Present.* New York and London.

Markatou, Dora F. 2008. "Archaeology and Greekness on the Centenary Celebrations of the Greek State." In *A Singular Antiquity: Archaeology and Hellenic Identity in Twentieth-Century Greece,* edited by Dimitris Damaskos and Dimitris Plantzos, 309–320. Athens.

Mykoniatis, Ilias G. 1984. "Οι ανδριάντες του Ρήγα και του Γρηγορίου Ε΄ στα Προπύλαια του Πανεπιστημίου της Αθήνας και το πρώτο κοινό τους" [The statues of Rhigas and Grigorios V before the Propylaia of the University of Athens and their first public]. *Ellinika* 33, no. 2: 355–370.

Paparrigopoulos, Constantinos. 1860–1874. *Ιστορία του Ελληνικού Έθνους.* [History of the Hellenic nation]. 5 vols. Athens.

Skopetea, Ellie. 1988. *Το "Πρότυπο Βασίλειο" και η Μεγάλη Ιδέα. Όψεις του εθνικού προβλήματος στην Ελλάδα (1830–1880)* [The "Model Kingdom" and the Great Idea: Aspects of the national problem in Greece, 1830–1880]. Athens.

Van Steen, Gonda. 2010. "Rallying the Nation: Sport and Spectacle Serving the Greek Dictatorships." *International Journal of the History of Sport* 27, no. 12 (August): 2121–2154.

Van Steen, Gonda. 2015a. "Parading War and Victory under the Greek Military Dictatorship: The Hist(o)rionics of 1967–74." In *War as Spectacle: Ancient and Modern Perspectives on the Display of Armed Conflict,* edited by Anastasia Bakogianni and Valerie M. Hope, 271–290. London.

Van Steen, Gonda. 2015b. *Stage of Emergency: Theater and Public Performance under the Greek Military Dictatorship of 1967–1974.* Oxford.

Vovchenko, Denis. 2016. *Containing Balkan Nationalism: Imperial Russia and Ottoman Christians, 1856–1914.* New York.

Young, David C. 1996. *The Modern Olympics: A Struggle for Revival.* Baltimore and London.

Zervas, Theodore G. 2017. *Formal and Informal Education during the Rise of Greek Nationalism: Learning to Be Greek.* New York.

Symbolic Commemorations and Cultural Affiliations

National anniversaries are rarely innovative. Being called upon to reproduce officially standardized ideas, they usually tend to follow strictly preordained patterns. It is not surprising therefore that with the lapse of time most commemorative venues seem to develop into predictable and sometimes boring rituals. Organized under the auspices of the state, or other official institutions like the Church, they end up as internalized domestic affairs reproducing ossified stereotypes. The narration and renarration of the national past, the faithful adherence to national traditions and myths, and the reenactment of largely fetishized ceremonials are integral components of a discourse intended to emotionally motivate rather than to rationally persuade or convince. It is therefore no wonder that national commemorations are rarely "exportable" to wider audiences. With the notable exceptions of the universal significance attributed to American independence (1776), the French Revolution (1789), and the Russian Revolution (1917), most national anniversaries tend to be conceived and enjoyed as "family affairs."

The Internationalization of the "Greek Issue"

There is no reason to suppose that, under normal circumstances, this should not be true in the case of the oncoming anniversary of the Greek Revolution of 1821. But the current situation can hardly be thought of as normal, Indeed, Greece is preparing to celebrate the bicentennial of its historical emergence as an independent country in a time of an unprecedentedly deep crisis, at a moment in which its future appears to be hanging by a thin thread. And, ironically, this is not the first time that historical circumstances seem to be conspiring to deprive Greeks of enacting their inalienable right to celebrate their past in relative quiescence. It should be remembered that the celebration of the first hundred years of Greek independence coincided with the Anatolian war that was to change the nation's destiny forever. Similarities, however, end here. Indeed, the events that took place in 1921–1922 were mainly determined by exceptional domestic considerations. At least in retrospect, it seems clear that, whatever the context of all the crucial decisions of the period, Greece could have avoided the Anatolian adventure that brought about the disappearance of the flourishing Greek communities of the eastern Mediterranean and ended by sealing its fate. Indeed, henceforward, for better or for worse, Greece was bound to think of itself in terms of a circumscribed national state among many others. In a certain sense therefore, the all-round effects of the crisis may be thought of as historically cathartic.

In full contrast, the present crisis is directly connected with uncontrollable international developments. The thin thread from which the country now seems to be hanging is not spun by unwarranted domestic choices but by dire global necessities. Indeed, Greece is no longer free to define its options or choose its international alliances and allegiances: it is increasingly clear that the country's destiny is by now irrevocably tied to the future of Europe within a rapidly changing globalized system. In this new context, therefore, the historical ingredients of the current Greek crisis and its eventual outcome can hardly be conceived of in purely domestic terms. As is the case for many small countries, the broad lines of Greece's destinies are being traced in an undefined "elsewhere"—in the chancelleries of the powerful European countries, the European Central Bank, the International Monetary Fund, and the ubiquitous organized creditors.

It is precisely for these reasons that international opinion is more crucial than ever before. And this element is all the more important in that for the last ten years the image of Greece has been subjected to systematic and often unwarranted attacks. Indeed, far from being interpreted as a side effect of the international financial crisis, Greece's exceptional situation is often interpreted in terms of presumably intrinsic national deficiencies: its social system is often described as hopelessly anachronistic, its inhabitants as lazy, corrupt, ineffective, and untrustworthy, and its "culture" as largely incompatible with standard "Western" norms. Implicitly, for many Europeans, an eventual "Grexit" was, and still is, conceived as an open issue.

This is not the place to argue against such unsubstantiated allegations. But some questions must be made clear. And within this context, the bicentennial may provide an excellent opportunity to present an alternative image of Greece to broad international audiences. Obviously, an enlightened public opinion

cannot "save" Greece from the nefarious effects of the economic crisis. But it
might mitigate some of its most flagrant side effects. To the extent that it becomes clear that the destiny of the country is intimately and irrevocably linked
with that of Europe, the European "image" of Greece must shape its future.

Taken in itself, this is hardly new. Although often neglected, European
opinion has played a significant role in the historical emergence, consolidation,
and evolution of modern Greece ever since the first day of independence. And
in some respects, the conditions prevailing at the time of the War of Independence present striking analogies with the current situation. Once more, the
future of the country is largely dependent on decisions taken in Europe. Once
more, the international "image" of the country seems to be instrumental in the
shaping of its destiny. Once more, wide segments of an ever-fluid European
opinion seem to resist dominant mainstream attitudes regarding the future of
the entire continent. And once more the final outcome may well depend on the
potential of general ideas and values to modify and eventually to change the
prevailing balance of powers. In much the same way that Greece's independence
occurred in spite of a Holy Alliance opposing all actual or potential threats
to established power equilibria, the future of Greece may be shaped in spite
of a new Holy Alliance aiming to forestall any radical modification in the
internalized regulations of international integration. In a certain sense, the
conservative norms of political stability invoked at the Congress of Vienna are
historically equivalent to the norms of financial and economic stability spelled
out in the so-called Washington Consensus. Indeed, if modern Greece originally emerged as a result of a radical change in the principles underlying the
formation of public opinion, a process aptly referred to as "birth of modernity," the future of Greece may well depend on a radical change in the normative foundations of current political ideas.

The celebration of the Greek Revolution should therefore be seen in terms
of the broader international and European dimensions of the conflict. Indeed, in the present context it is important to substantiate that Greece was
born and developed as an integral component of the European system. It is
hardly an accident that ever since the first day, the new country opted for
endowing itself with European democratic institutions. As early as 1822, less
than a year after the outbreak of the war, a constituent assembly unanimously adopted a liberal and representative democratic constitution, largely
inspired by the French revolutionary constitution of 1793. And it is also no
accident that the country participated in all major European wars and suffered the consequences of its entanglements. In this sense, the official participation of Greece in the European Union should not be seen as merely a
simple (and logically reversible) result of a deliberate political option occur-

ring within a particular context. The historical, ideological, and symbolic links are indissoluble.

A National Name with Universal Connotations

However, the Greek perception of Europe is only a mirror image of a European perception of Greece intimately linked with the conceptualization of the entire European civilization. Indeed, the emergence of the independent country in modern times is clearly connected to this unique Western conception of "Greekness." In the same way that the idea of Europe cannot disclaim its symbolic heritage, the perception of Greece cannot possibly escape the universal connotations and the symbolic aura the *word* Greece is endowed with. Indeed, the meanings evoked by the name are unique. In contrast to all equivalent national characterizations, this word did not simply serve to invoke a *particular* society, country, nation, or state. Above and beyond its concrete spatial, geopolitical, and geocultural connotations, the word was also endowed with an aggregate of *universal* meanings. In this sense, the semantic implications of Greece and its synonym Hellas—together with most of their derivatives—literally seem to transcend the concrete geopolitical entity that rightfully carries the time-honored historical name. Even in our present demystified world, the vague notion of "Greekness" may still occasionally refer to an idealized perception of the quintessence of Western civilization.

The implications of this inherent semantic overlapping between the particular and the universal should not be underestimated. Indeed, the unique symbolic connotations of the national name are immediately felt when it comes to the country's exceptional *visibility*. For better or worse, events in Greece seem to hit the international headlines with exceptional regularity. It is probably no accident that, unlike most other countries of comparable power and size, Greece's *international image* is an object of constant debate. Like movie stars, the country seems to breed good or bad news in all conceivable circumstances. And this can be explained only in terms of its inalienable brand name.

Hellenolatry and the Emergence of Culture as an Autonomous Notion

It is obviously impossible here to examine the historical foundations of Western "Hellenolatry." It should however be pointed out that the *cultural* (and by extension political) importance of "Greekness" was finally crystallized as a side effect of the *new perception of culture as an autonomous notion* which emerged in Europe in the seventeenth century. Although often neglected and unclear with respect to its historical origins, this ideological rupture carried immense implications. Though the question cannot be addressed in detail, one is entitled to surmise that the new ideas were connected to the overall evolution of the historical context. Indeed, the emergence of a "modern world system" was founded on an institutionalized balance between separate established "powers," none of which could ensure its permanent hegemony over the others. In such a context, the rationalization of the emerging collective European supremacy vis-à-vis the rest of the world—later conceived in terms of an identifiable but fragmented "West" versus an unspecified "Rest"—appeared as an aggregate of numerous antagonistic political entities. Even before it developed into a set of recognizable national states, the new "system" was being conceived as a clearly definable yet fragmented "whole" split into separate and allegedly permanent components or "parts."

Inevitably, under the circumstances, the issue of the relations and institutional balances between these separate powers became the object of systematic deliberation. But many questions remained unanswered. Indeed, any potentially "shared" world domination called for a consensual construction of a rudimentary set of "rules of the game." And this became even more obvious once the distinction between the West and the Rest could not be explained away on exclusively religious grounds. The gradual advance of rational secularism had brought about a relative erosion of the ancient opposition between faithful and infidels. Thereafter, European dominance could not ground its collective imagination on the true faith monopolized by an eternal *Universitas Christiana;* new, additional forms of discursive rationalization had therefore to be invented. And it was precisely in this context that the notion of a commonly defined *superior but fragmented European entity* entered the scene. To all intents and purposes, collective European superiority was seen as an historical function of a common "superior culture."

This new idealization of culture represents a crucial rupture in the history of ideas. It was the first time that the idea of *"culture" was conceived as a separate, named, and systematically idealized "level"* of social reality and social organization. Even more importantly, this conceptual autonomization of culture paved the way for the emergence of a new *general taxonomic matrix.* For the first time, together with "culture," the state, organized power, and at a later stage the market, the economy, and whatever was implied by the new term "society," were being thought of as separate "levels" of reality and as distinct objects of discursive specialization.

One cannot overestimate the long-term implications of the emerging "modern" taxonomic practices, whereby wholes must be distinguished from their constituent parts on the basis of preestablished functional criteria. Indeed, within a premodern world where "collectivities" were conceived in terms of organized power or of religious affiliation it would have been as pointless to conceive of a common culture as it would have been to propose the notion of "society." This is obviously true not only of all self-contained imperial entities (such as Rome, Byzantium, and China), where the unity and coherence of the dominant entity were taken for granted, but also for most less developed communities, where the main discursive distinction consisted of the opposition of "us insiders" to "them outsiders."

In this sense, the emergence of the autonomous and heavily charged idea of a common culture is decidedly novel. Be that as it may, it is precisely in this context that "Hellenolatry" and the ensuing "Hellenology" emerged as an essential feature of the collective European imagination. Indeed, this newly conceived common European "culture" could not be explained away as having come out of the blue. If it were to appear discursively plausible and historically traceable, it would first have to be *defined* in terms of its intrinsic values, its main conceptual ingredients, its practical and ideological implications, and its *historical origins and development.* Not surprisingly under the circumstances, the unique civilization lying behind European supremacy was seen in terms of its cultural foundations. The particularity of the politically fragmented European system was gradually being conceived as ideographically indistinguishable from the semiotics of its common descent. Within what can be thought of as a gigantic exercise in *metonymic rationalization,* modern Europe was being provided with impeccable common historical and symbolic credentials equally shared by all concerned parties. It was precisely in this context that ancient Greece (and, to a significantly lesser degree, Rome) emerged as the undisputed symbolic founding kernel of the new dominant civilization. Even on the level of current terminology, the cultural implications of Hellenolatry are ubiquitous to the present day. Even today, in most European languages many words used to denote the modes of perception of social organization (polity, democracy, autocracy, autonomy, history, economy, ecology, etc.), of the natural world (physics, chemistry, biology, mathematics, optics, acoustics, geometry, geology, geography, topology, pathology, electricity, electronics, magnetism, etc.), of knowledge (theory, praxis, epistemology, philosophy, idea, ideology, idol, organic, etc.), and of narrowly cultural phenomena (theater, drama, comedy, tragedy, poetry, plastic arts, music, symphony, cinematography, etc.) are Greek. Such etymological persistence cannot possibly be attributed to a simple lexicographical inertia. All the more so that many of these words emerged only in response to the needs of modernity.

The International Importance of the Greek Revolution
within a Highly Explosive Environment

Obviously, the particular events leading to the independence of Greece cannot
be explained in the sole light of the unique transhistorical aura of classical antiquity. But this does not imply that these events should be seen as confinable
to their local dimensions. Indeed, even if indirectly, the very fact of the nominal connection of Greeks to their venerated forefathers proved instrumental
in shaping the outcome of their own struggle. It is no accident that in the eyes
of a large number of Europeans—and by extension of many Greeks—the War
of Independence seemed to inaugurate a "revival" of the historical relevance of
what had been the cradle of civilization. But this observation is beside the point.
The main defining feature of the Greek Revolution does not consist in the simple
fact that it took place. Nor is it particularly significant that the Greek struggle
proved to be the first successful "war of national liberation" on the European
continent. Strictly speaking, the only "unique" characteristic of the Greek War
of Independence consists in the fact that it was largely conceived in terms of a
revival of the idealized aura of "Greekness," a vindication of an eternal idea, a
cultural debt to be paid to the symbolic foundations of European culture. Indeed, albeit "accidentally," the main factor that ultimately led to the historic
success of the revolutionary venture must be traced down to the ubiquitous
cult of cultural ancestry. In the last analysis, even if waged by means of arms,
the struggle for Greek independence was eventually won by means of symbols, values, and ideas.

However, the causal relations between events in Greece and European developments can only be seen as mutually interactive. Indeed, if the contribution of European policies to the independence of Greece proved to have been
instrumental, the same is true of the increasing contribution of the Greek war
to the shaping of a perennially volatile European opinion, at a time when the
intellectual and cultural situation was already explosive. Within a totally hostile geopolitical environment circumscribed by the Holy Alliance, an increasing
number of Europeans were now being mobilized in increasing numbers in the
name of the revolutionary ideas that had been stifled by post-Napoleonic reaction. In the beginning of the 1820s, the libertarian issues raised by the Enlightenment were once again reentering the political and intellectual scene. Not
more than five years after the proclamations of the Congress of Vienna, the
eternal institutional landmarks seemed to be crumbling. After the Latin American wars and a series of rebellions in Italy and elsewhere, the Greek War of
Independence presented growing challenges to that short-lived status quo.
Broad movements of solidarity emerged across a newly defined "progressive"

Europe mobilized in the name of the values first raised by the Enlightenment. Once more, the issue of progress against reaction was becoming the object of widespread critical debate.

The "Philhellenic" Movement

It was in this context that a new movement labeled "Philhellenism" entered the scene. This was the first time that an international and collectively self-conscious *civil society* sharing universal principles and values was beginning to emerge all over the continent. Within a common struggle for liberty, reason, democracy, autonomy, and progress for all mankind, widespread collective initiatives aimed to practically reenact some of the revolutionary ideas that had been repressed by the post-Napoleonic conservative reaction. In the words of Claude Lévi-Strauss, most European civil societies seemed to be "warming up": by becoming actively conscious of their autonomous capacity to carry their ideas and to shape their own history, large segments of the rising bourgeoisie and the intellectuals were committing themselves to take their destinies and those of the world in their own hands, in spite of and against the will of empowered rulers.

The philhellenic movement proved particularly durable and effective. In the eyes of many intellectuals, active solidarity with the fighting Greeks must have been enhanced by fantasies inspired by antique glory. It was natural that the unequivocal rational rejection of all forms of reactionary and irrational authoritarianism should run hand in hand with the veneration of classical antiquity as the cradle of civilization and democracy. Abstract normative principles seemed to be converging with symbolic historical continuities. It should be kept in mind that in this brave new industrial world, everything seemed to be changing overnight for the better but also for the worse. Unprecedented technological achievements marched hand in hand with unprecedented plight. Under these circumstances, therefore, it was inevitable that the fundamental modern notion of "rational progress" would become an object of fiery debates. Suddenly, the whole European world seemed plunged in agonizing political and moral dilemmas. Within an increasingly educated population, issues pertaining to the future of the world, the modes of emancipation of mankind and the role and moral responsibilities of the free individual in the process of social change were reaching ever broader audiences. It is no accident that political *utopias* were increasingly being transformed into intellectually coherent social alternatives, eventually crystallizing into massive collective political *movements* like anarchism, nihilism, communism, and socialism. The yearning for "that which does not *yet* exist" (to use Ernst Bloch's words) led to the emergence of a plethora of vague doctrines and unidentifiable "unknown Gods."

However, it was perhaps inevitable that nascent radicalism should bring about increasing waves of intolerance and strong political reaction. Unprecedented repressive measures were imposed by newly organized *police states*. It was therefore natural that in counterreaction "antisystemic" movements should be deliberately organized as *secret societies*. Indeed, it seems reasonable to assume that the spectacular proliferation of "lodges" and sects like the Freemasons, the Illuminati, and the Greek *Philikoi* was intimately related to the new forms of intellectual and moral solidarity between responsible free individuals who took it upon themselves to contribute to changing the face of the world in spite and against all established powers. Within this context, intellectual and political *nonconformism* was gradually permeated by new forms of individual and collective *activism*.

The cultural implications of such antisystemic ideas proved to be even wider than anyone could have possibly anticipated. Indeed, unleashed individualist reactions against mainstream ideas became generalized. Far from restricting themselves to questions pertaining to the organization of social and political power, radical ideas tended to become an aim in themselves. Individual commitment to higher principles and causes was henceforward seen in terms of existential options and moral duties. Nonconformism was becoming a "way of life." Not surprisingly therefore, *radical ideas tended to penetrate the separate realm of cultural activities*. Artistic and intellectual creativity were increasingly characterized by unrestricted intellectual and moral autonomy, active disrespect of internalized norms, and constant formal innovation. One hundred years before Dadaism and surrealism, literature, the visual arts, and even music seem to have joined philosophy in taking strong stands in most current social issues. Utopian projections and political radicalism were giving birth to what was later considered a cultural avant-garde.

Geocultural Considerations, Semantic Transmutations, and Taxonomic Antinomies

In view of the above, it would seem that at least some of the issues raised by the Greek War of Independence go far beyond the national level. Indeed, it would be no exaggeration to maintain that many significant ideological and cultural mutations leading to the shaping of modern Europe were first crystallized within this context. All the more so that since its forceful emergence, the idea of nationalism had led to a radical reorganization of the *normative* content of political power. Established (or even imagined) "nations" were increasingly perceived as being the only self-evident and "naturally" given collective entities. And obviously these novel ideas entered into direct conflict with all "traditional" dynastic conceptions of political legitimacy. It was therefore inevitable that the ideas of national collective liberty, autonomy, and "self-determination" should provide the main intellectual and normative framework with new forms of collective self-awareness. The radical rupture with the past proved to be historically far-reaching. Indeed, the overwhelming appeal of nationalism was destined to gradually eradicate the "natural" principles of "interdynastic peace," objective stability, respect of the status quo ante, and conformity to internalized institutional realities. The radical redefinition of "rightful" historical "subjects" entailed even more radical mutations in the modes of perception of the new "international" order. The principles underlying the "Eurocentric" world system would have to be redefined.

However, the idea of nationalism was not conceived as universally applicable. "Rightfully" established collective national entities and by extension legitimate emerging *Volksgeists* were acknowledged *only within the areas included within the "civilized" West*. In significant contrast, these ideas appeared essentially inoperative within the "barbaric," irrational, uncivilized, or simply immature "Rest." Despite their alleged universality, most newly fundamental principles, values, and norms defined by the Enlightenment were considered pertinent only for those who seemed culturally and historically "worthy" of them. The applicability of fundamental normative principles was far from universal. Thus, it was obviously being taken for granted that Europe must be intrinsically "different" with respect to what was to become the "Orient" at large, at all conceivable levels. It would seem that, like power and military prowess, higher principles and abstract norms were also invented for the chosen few.

Obviously, this radical geocultural distinction had immense implications in shaping the self-awareness of all parties concerned. While "Orientals" would have to find ways to cope with their innate inferiority, "Westerners" felt free to boast of their collective cultural superiority perceived as a given "historical right." But this is not all. For this taxonomic bias entailed further logical implications. Indeed, for lack of any other rational grounds, the intrinsic collective "superiority" of the European West would now have to be substantiated on "essentialist" grounds. And this implied that the "*entire* barbaric Orient" should be intrinsically distinguishable from the *entire* civilized West by definition and *on principle*. An assumption that can be held as tenable only if "both" worlds may be seen, albeit tautologically, as endowed with an indelible cultural essence and by extension a minimum of "internal" cultural homogeneity. In the same way that the "others" are defined as bearers of their intrinsic common barbarity, Europeans had to be defined by their posited common supremacy.

This is precisely the reason why internalized European ideas and principles are seen as valid and applicable all over the Western world. In full contrast with the non-Western peoples who are thought of as totally impervious to Western rationality and values, *all* European peoples were called upon to claim their inalienable human rights, to invent their proper *Volksgeist,* to strive for their collective autonomy and to institutionalize their own independent polity. Ideally at least, *all* members of advanced civilized communities should be endowed with elementary human rights and *all* civilized peoples should be able to claim collective self-determination. Very characteristically, however, this "natural" and allegedly universal right does not extend to the unnamable "others."

The role of the Greek War of Independence in consolidating these profound ideological mutations proved pivotal. Indeed, it was probably the first time that the notion of "national liberation" was generally invoked. And obviously the magic of the name must have been, once more, instrumental. Venerable transhistorical values born in ancient Greece like autonomy and democracy were endowed with their modern counterparts of individual liberty and national liberation. Not surprisingly, the two value systems seemed to complement and reinforce each other. It seemed to be taken for granted that, if *all* self-aware civilized nations should be given a right to their political autonomy, those who were called upon to embody the idea of civilization could not be plausibly deprived of the rights their own ancestors had given birth to. In a certain sense, the independence of Greece was ensured on the basis of a historical and symbolic "credit."

However, there is more to it than that. As already mentioned, the conceptual and practical interrelations between universal abstract principles and concrete historical realities are not always smooth. Thus, paradoxically, if the Greek War of Independence contributed to the crystallization of the conceptual and ideological separation of the civilized "West" and the barbaric "Rest," it also served to blur the dividing lines between these two worlds by complicating an otherwise clear taxonomic imagery. If the clear distinction between actual or prospective European colonial "powers" and the inferior peoples of the East provided the elementary pattern underlying colonization as an expression of immutable and implicitly "natural" geocultural and geopolitical realities and balances, the real world seemed to defy all simple classificatory matrices. Indeed, the emergence of new independent states in the European periphery seemed to be announcing a much more complex system of global relations and hierarchies. The Greek example showed that the simple and self-evident taxonomic dualism would have to be enriched and qualified. Even the most unconditional of Philhellenes did not and could not ignore (and

occasionally deplore) the fact that, on the level of cultural practices and attitudes, the vast majority of fighting Greeks appeared to be more "oriental" than
"European." And this became even more obvious as soon as Greek chieftains
assumed responsibility for their collective fate.

The struggle for Greek independence brought about further changes in the
geopolitical perceptions of the international power game. Indeed, if the impending dissolution of the Ottoman system was seen in terms of an emerging
"Eastern question," it was also obvious that its eventual substitution by new formally independent national states would necessarily bring about a *significant
translocation of the geographic and symbolic borderlines* separating civilized European and barbarous Ottomans. Even if there could be no question of direct
colonization of territories and peoples lying within the geographical and symbolic limits of Europe—the French and later the British colonization of the
Ionian islands being one of the last historical example of "intra-European"
colonization—it was predictable that the still *unnamed* states and societies lying
between the West and the East that would eventually see the light of day threatened to be politically and culturally as untrustworthy as their prospective
names were unpronounceable. Nevertheless, albeit reluctantly, these emerging
political entities would have to be integrated within a single intelligible cognitive
pattern. European powers would therefore be obliged to invent new institutional
forms, terms, and discourses ensuring the continuing indirect domination over
formally independent states.

It is probably no accident that by the middle of the nineteenth century, this
taxonomic disarray led to the concoction of novel institutionalized conceptu-
alizations such as protectorates, entities with "limited sovereignty"—clearly a
contradiction in terms—nonindependent autonomy, and various forms of
quasi-sovereign dependencies. More to the point, it also led to the spectacularly negative symbolic transmutation of a geographical connotation of wider
intermediate regions like the "Balkans" into synonyms for archetypically hybrid, unfixable, and unclassifiable excrescences of originally "pure" European
forms and, by extension, into an untrustworthy and unpredictable set of entities lying on a permanently mobile threshold of the West.

Predictably enough within this context, "modern" Greece was not immediately conceived as an unequivocally full-fledged European nation. Indeed, it was
more than obvious that the living embodiments of classic perfection did not
dress, think, talk, or act in ways reminiscent of their idealized forefathers. It
was therefore inevitable that both the self-appointed godfathers of the unequaled
ancestors and their hapless offspring should find themselves entangled in insoluble discursive traps. However, if Europeans could easily escape by simply
shrugging their shoulders, Greeks could not possibly escape occasionally

glancing at their collective selves in a distorted "Lacanian" mirror. They could neither act as detached realists by deliberately looking at their reflected face nor escape reality by romantically refusing to believe their own eyes. Hence, there is a cognitive and taxonomic disarray that seems to have persisted down to the present day. The futile quest for pinning down the new nation's historical "essence" remains a going concern. It is highly characteristic that the quest for a transhistorical cultural "essence" is a permanent object of an ongoing Kulturkampf. Indeed, most major Greek poets have proposed their own versions of this insoluble issue. George Seferis talked of a mysterious historical process, while his fellow Nobel laureate Odysseas Elytis insisted in the autonomous effects of a nature imposing its own terms to all cultural manifestation including the language. Despite its senselessness however, the issue is far from being settled. Even today, Greeks are widely thought of (and sometimes think themselves) as split among the rational "Apollonian," Western-oriented "Hellenes" and the irrational, sensual, "Dionysiac," and Eastern-oriented "Romioi."

Romanticism, Neo-Classicism, Greek Revivalism

Whatever the impact of the Greek War of Independence on European geopolitical perceptions, its cultural side effects were even more important. In this respect, the philhellenic movement seemed to reflect one of the most conspicuous as well as insoluble contradictions of the quest for progress. This fundamental feature of modernity is clearly connected to a new perception of history as an agency projecting the present into a "better" open-ended future: henceforward, yearning and searching for "that which does not *yet* exist" became a central object of self-awareness and imagination, both on the collective and on the individual level. The newly defined "promethean" vision introduced by the Enlightenment led to new forms of existential options and individual morality. Henceforward, rational free individuals were called upon to responsibly choose their principles, to take their destinies in their own hands and to fight for their beliefs regardless of consequences. Modern man would be quintessentially both rational and agonistic. As epitomized in Goethe's *Faust,* this might indeed be seen as the cornerstone of existential dramas in modern times.

It is in this context that the historical importance of the Greek issue appears to have been pivotal in shaping and synthesizing contradictory intellectual currents. Indeed, the philhellenic movement seemed to seek inspiration in various cultural foundations. On the one hand, the active support of the Greek struggle was obviously circumscribed by the prevailing archeolatry. The emblematic figure of Lord Byron who finally met his death among the fighting men defending Mesolonghi was not alone in going back to ancient texts and myths.

The same is true of poets like Keats, Shelley, Blake, Pushkin, Goethe, Schiller, and Hölderlin, and intellectuals like Chateaubriand, James Mill, Bentham, Fichte, and Jefferson. Enhanced by the neoclassical revivalism characteristic of the Napoleonic (and post-Napoleonic) era, unconditional cultural and esthetic Hellenolatry was rapidly penetrating wide segments of the educated classes. Furthermore, even if seen as an aim in itself, the revival of eternal harmony and perfection appeared both increasingly pointless and practically unattainable. Shelley's famous dictum "We are all Greeks" was qualified and effectively reversed by his contemporary the German painter Philipp Otto Runge's lament "We are not Greeks anymore. We can no longer feel the sense of wholeness." Inevitably, the self-sufficient optimism of the revivalist dream was being tainted by widespread cognitive ambivalence, normative doubt, and practical disarray.

It is precisely this contradictory cultural conjuncture that circumscribed the philhellenic movement. The Greek struggle for independence was imbued both in classic revivalism and in undisguised romanticism. A large number of committed intellectuals seemed to be facing an impasse. Far from providing answers or adequate "solutions" to the gathering political and cultural storm, the romantic movement (aptly named *Sturm und Drang* in Germany) often appeared as an inarticulate cry of agony. The intellectual and moral burden of facing the intrinsic political and historical limits and antinomies of the rational project of the Enlightenment was sometimes unbearable, with many genuine thinkers being appalled at the sight of the ubiquitous victims of the new industrial age. In Walter Benjamin's words, what we insist on referring to as "progress" is nothing else than the storm propelling us to a future to which our back is turned, while the pile of debris is steadily rising toward the sky. In this context, an increasing number of responsibly self-conscious rational individuals found themselves constantly tossed from one intellectual and moral extreme to the other. This indeed was the "double life" (*Doppelleben*) described by Goethe in his fundamental work *Dichtung und Wahrheit*. Clearly, the first decades of the nineteenth century inaugurated the most relentlessly persistent painful and insoluble existential dilemmas of modern times.

Something similar may well be occurring in these first decades of the new millennium. In a certain sense, history may well be repeating itself. Indeed, for the first time in many decades, it would now seem that the course of history is being increasingly detached from the idea of progress as conceived by the European Enlightenment There is increasing intellectual and political opposition to the dogmatic mainstream assumption that there can be no rational alternative to an uncritical acceptance of a quasi-automatic reproduction of the status quo. Once again, history appears both as a source of inspiration and a guideline for action.

This is obviously not the place to provide a blueprint for the commemoration. It is however possible to trace some of the main issues and the broad contours that should be taken into consideration. Indeed, quite apart from the discernible effects of the Greek Revolution on the evolution of political and geopolitical ideas, it will be necessary to cover its influence on cultural trends and events. To the extent that, as mentioned, the novel perception of culture as an autonomous "field" seems to have been instrumental in shaping the image of Greece, it seems obvious that the main object of the commemoration should be centered on literally "cultural issues." In this respect, I have already referred to the contradictory ways in which neoclassical revivalism and nonconformist romanticism were articulated. Indeed, the philhellenic phenomenon should be seen independently from the struggle for Greek independence, as a crucial development in European intellectual history. This general conceptual framework should be substantiated by concrete examples in particular fields of cultural action. The visual arts provide the most obvious illustration of this general trend. Indeed, the Greek War of Independence is directly present in a number of works of Delacroix, while, for all their differences, artists like Géricault, Runge, Constable, Blake, Caspar Friedrich, Turner, and Böcklin tirelessly indulged in antique memories and ancient ruins. Similar questions can be addressed with respect to the incomplete "fragments" of beauty, truth, and harmony provided by remnants of the golden age, fragments that cannot possibly and must not be restored to their original integrity. Characteristically, approaches to the past in its unsurpassed glory were increasingly seen as an integral part of an actual "natural" cultural environment of the West; the past is to be cherished and preserved not only for what it evokes but also for what it stands for. One is tempted to think in terms of the postmodern and resolutely "postromantic" "end of grand narratives."

Architecture and urban planning are promising fields of reference. Indeed, it is no accident that the doyens of German architecture, after having actively participated, together with their younger Greek colleagues, in the neoclassical revival in Berlin, Munich, Washington, DC, Odessa, and St. Petersburg, concocted a series of elaborate plans for Athens, the new capital of Greece, centered around the Acropolis. It would be interesting to examine these plans in a comparative perspective. Similar reflections on current cultural and political issues are to be detected even in the most "abstract" of arts, music. Beethoven's *Fidelio* is a clear cry against autocratic police methods, Mozart's *The Magic Flute* is an explicit glorification of secret societies, while Rossini's *The Siege of Corinth* was directly inspired by the Greek events.

The close affinities between the Greek war and western European cultural agendas is even more evident in historiography. It is noteworthy that modern national histories followed in the path of Greek histories, which reached unsurpassed peaks of uncritical glorification of antiquity. Very characteristically, following in the steps of his more careful predecessors, the eminent German historian Ernst Curtius went as far as to maintain that if among other peoples beauty was the exception, among Greeks it was the general rule. Under the circumstances, it is no wonder that it was exactly within this period that archeology and museology appeared as distinct cognitive fields. The increasing political rivalry between European nations led to new fields of professional antagonisms relating to the effective cultivation of a cultural heritage common to all. The general cult of antiquity seemed to be running hand in hand with the opening chapters of liberal modernity in Europe.

Historical Analogies in Critical Retrospect

On the basis of the above, it seems that the effective celebration of the bicentennial of the Greek Revolution should be thought of in terms of its historic contribution to reconfiguring the evolution of European politics and culture. Indeed, both the national liberation war and the unique phenomenon of Philhellenism brought about significant historical ruptures in the prevailing forms of political culture. The events that were taking place in the early nineteenth century seem to condense the ever-lurking dialectical interaction between conservation and change, between historical continuity and discontinuity, foreshadowing Lampedusa's dictum that if things are to remain as they are, everything must change. Never before had it been so evident that any kind of historical "transition" is literally a leap into the unknown.

In this sense, Greek independence is the pure, condensed product of a period of political, cultural, and normative transition. And it is precisely in this context that one may discern some striking analogies to the actual situation. Indeed, once more today, while the "old" seems to have exhausted its historical perspectives, the "new" has not yet clearly emerged. Once more, internalized principles and images appear increasingly detached from an apparently incoherent reality that seems to defy all acceptable taxonomic matrices. Once more, it is hard to distinguish between the possible and the impossible, between that which must be accepted as irrevocably given and that which might happen instead. Once more ideas, values, and principles seem to be developing in uncontrollable and unpredictable ways. Once more we are obliged to face the seemingly insoluble choice between utter conformity, resignation, and acceptance of what "is" and a utopian leap into the unknown. Once more the modern world seems engulfed in insoluble promethean dilemmas. And once more, ironically, to Greece seems to be attributed a pivotal symbolic role. In the same way that Philhellenism raised political and moral issues that proved crucial for the future of Europe, the "eccentric" development of current Greek affairs may indirectly contribute to reshaping and eventually to relaunching the tottering European project. Ironically, if the "image" of classical Hellas emerged as a key notion in the battle of ideas in the early nineteenth century, the wide (and often bitter) debates over the "image" of modern Greece may have served to sharpen insoluble political and cultural dilemmas. It may well be that, once more, the bells that appeared to be tolling for Greece are also tolling for Europe.

In a certain ironical sense, the whole Western world might conceive the on-going commemoration as an opportunity to reimburse the universal symbolic debt owed to the venerable fathers of civilization. All the more so that, in Marcel Mauss's words, gifts must always defy the laws of economic rationality. And this is precisely the reason why moral debts can never be immediately restituted. The functional and symbolic links between the parties concerned suggest that a certain amount of time should elapse between the original gift and its symbolic restitution. Arguably, two hundred years may be seen as amply sufficient.

Constantinos Tsoukalas

Summary Chronology: The Greek Revolution, 1814–1834

All dates in the Chronology are in the Julian Calendar (Old Style), the calendar in force in Greece at the time of the Greek Revolution. Revolutionary events and other developments in Greece are recorded in that calendar. Diplomatic events and other events of international significance, such as Lord Byron's death at Mesolonghi or the naval battle at Navarino bay are given in the Gregorian Calendar (New Style) since they are generally known and recorded in international historiography in that calendar.

1814

September 14   Conventional date of the foundation in Odessa of the secret society Philiki Etaireia (Society of Friends) by three diaspora Greek merchants, Nikolaos Skoufas, Emmanouil Xanthos, and Athanasios Tsakalov, to prepare a revolution for the liberation of Greece from Ottoman rule.

1815

June 9   Congress of Vienna concluded. Restoration of dynastic legitimacy imposed on Europe.

November 17   The United States of the Ionian Islands ceded by the Treaty of Paris to Great Britain as a protectorate.

1818

Headquarters of Philiki Etaireia moved to Istanbul.

1819

April 15   Parga sold by British administration of Ionian Islands to Ali Pasha of Ioannina. The inhabitants leave their native town for Corfu, carrying with them only the ashes of their ancestors.

1820

Insurrection of Ali Pasha of Ioannina against his Ottoman sovereign.

1821

January 26–29   Peloponnesian ecclesiastical and lay notables and members of the Philiki Etaireia meet at Vostitsa (Aigio) to plan the proclamation of the revolution.

March 14   Revolutionary action initiated at the village of Agridi, Kalavryta.

March 17   Revolution proclaimed by Maniots at Aeropolis.

March 17   Revolution proclaimed at Kalavryta. Local Ottoman officials besieged at three fortresses at Kalavryta.

March 23   Greeks led by Petros Mavromichalis (Petrobey), Theodoros Kolokotronis, and Grigorios Dikaios (Papaflessas) liberate Kalamata from Ottoman rule.

March 23–25   Messenian Senate convenes and issues an appeal to the European courts, declaring the Greeks are determined to be free or die.

March 25   Revolution proclaimed at Patras. Archbishop of Old Patras Germanos raises the standard of revolt and revolutionaries take an oath to fight for liberty or die.

March 27   Ottoman reprisals in Istanbul. Ottoman authorities decapitate leading Greek Phanariot dignitaries.

April 10   Patriarch of Constantinople Gregory V and senior prelates martyred in Istanbul on Orthodox Easter Sunday.

April 18   Revolution proclaimed by Constantis Lachanas at Vathy, Samos.

April 22–24   Athanasios Diakos fights against superior Ottoman forces at Alamana bridge, is wounded, captured and executed at Zitouni (Lamia).

May 7	Proclamation of revolution at Milies, Mount Pilion by Anthimos Gazis and Kyriakos Basdekis.
May 8	Odysseas Androutsos at Gravia defeats Ottoman troops, interrupting their march to the Peloponnese.
May 8	Revolution proclaimed by Lykourgos Logothetis at Karlovasi, Samos.
May 12–13	Victory of Greek revolutionaries at Valtetsi.
May 18	Revolution proclaimed at Karyes, Mount Athos and at Polygyros, Chalkidiki by Emmanouil Papas.
May 26	Regional assembly at Kaltezon Monastery in Arcadia establishes Peloponnesian Senate.
June 7	Defeat of Sacred Battalion under Alexandros Ypsilantis at Dragatsani, Wallachia.
June 14	Revolution proclaimed in Crete.
June 24	Violent Ottoman reprisals in Crete. Metropolitan Gerasimos of Crete with five bishops and scores of civilians martyred in Iraklio (Candia).
June 25	Revolution proclaimed at Syrrako and Kalarrytes in Epirus by Ioannis Kolettis and Ioannis Rangos.
July 5–8	Massive attack by Ottoman navy and attempt to land at Karlovasi, Samos turned back by Samiots.
July 9	Archbishop Kyprianos of Cyprus, the island's three bishops and more than 100 ecclesiastical dignitaries and lay notables executed by Ottoman governor in Nicosia, Cyprus.
July 14	Victory of the Greeks at Vrysakia, Euboea.
July 23	Monemvasia fortress surrenders to the besieging Greeks.
August 26	Victory of the Greeks at Vasilika in Boeotia.

September 8   Final defeat of Greek revolutionary movement in Moldavia at Secu Monastery.

September 22   Commercial fleet of Galaxidi (about seventy boats) destroyed by Ottoman forces in the harbor of this important maritime town on the northern coast of the Gulf of Corinth.

September 23   Tripolitsa, administrative capital of the Morea, captured by Greek revolutionaries under Theodoros Kolokotronis after a long siege.

November 4   Regional assembly convenes at Mesolonghi and votes for the Statute of the Senate of Western Continental Greece.

November 15   Regional assembly of eastern continental Greeks convenes at Salona (Amphissa) and votes the Legal Charter of Aeropagus.

December 20   First National Assembly of revolutionary Greece convenes at Piada (New Epidaurus).

1822

January 1   First National Assembly votes the Provisional Constitution of Greece. On January 15 it issues the Declaration of Greek Independence.

January 17   Ali Pasha defeated by Ottoman forces and killed on the island in Ioannina Lake.

February 19   Revolution breaks out in the city of Naousa in western Macedonia.

March 8   Revolution breaks out on Mount Olympus (Eleftherochori).

March 10   Rising incited on Chios by revolutionaries from Samos.

March 30   Massacre of Chios by landed Ottoman naval forces. Massacre provoked international outrage. French painter Eugène Delacroix eventually recorded this in an imposing painting depicting the events.

April 6	Massacre and burning of Naousa by Ottoman forces.
May 16	Souli surrenders to the Ottomans; Souliot fighters and civilians evacuated to Ionian Islands.
June 6	Constantinos Kanaris burns flagship of the Ottoman navy at Chios harbor. Ottoman admiral Kara Ali dies in the explosion.
June 9	Ottoman garrison of the Acropolis surrenders to besieging Greek forces.
July 26	Crushing defeat of Ottoman army under Mahmud Dramali Pasha by Greeks led by Kolokotronis at Dervenakia.
July 4	Ottoman forces at Peta overwhelm Greeks and Philhellenes led by Alexandros Mavrokordatos.
August	Under George Canning as foreign secretary of Great Britain, reorientation of British policy on the Greek Question begins.
October 25	First siege of Mesolonghi begins.
October 28–29	Kanaris burns the second flagship of the Ottoman navy at the straits of Tenedos.
October 30	Victory of the Greeks at Nafplio. The fortress of Palamidi taken by Staikos Staikopoulos.
December 2	Congress of Verona condemns the revolt of the Greeks.
December 31	Seige of Mesolonghi by Omer Vrioni and Kütahı Pasha lifted.

1823

January 15	Victory of Greeks under Georgios Karaiskakis over strong Ottoman forces at Saint Vlasios, Evrytania.
January 18	Nafplio selected as the capital of revolutionary Greece.
March 25	Britain recognizes the Greeks as combatants, providing de facto recognition of revolutionary Greece.

March 30   Second National Assembly convenes at Astros, Kynouria. On
               April 13 it votes to confirm the Law of Epidavros, a revision
               of the Provisional Constitution of Greece of 1822.

July 12   Lord Byron arrives in Argostoli, Cephallonia. On Christmas
               eve he arrives in Mesolonghi to an enthusiastic welcome.

July 8–9   Markos Botsaris falls in battle at Kephalovryso, Evrytania. His
               heroic death stirred the peoples of Europe profoundly and
               captured the imagination of Byron, Delacroix, and Dionysios
               Solomos.

1824

January 9   Russian plan on the Greek Question provides for establishment
               of three autonomous principalities under Ottoman suzerainty.

February 21   First Greek loan contracted in London.

March   First civil war of the revolution breaks out, largely a conflict
               between civilian and military leadership groups.

April 19 (N.S.) Death of Lord Byron at Mesolonghi. Dionysios Solomos
               mourns his death in a long ode.

Late May   Hussein Pasha leading Egyptian forces quells revolution in Crete.

May 27–30   Destruction and massacre on the island of Kasos by Turkish-
               Egyptian navy.

June 20–24   Destruction, massacre, and burning of Psara by Turco-
               Egyptian navy. The tragic event is commemorated in a
               famous epigram by Dionysios Solomos.

August 4–5   Attempt of Ottoman naval forces to land on Samos turned back.

August 29   Naval battle at Gerontas bay. Greek navy under admiral Andreas
               Miaoulis causes considerable damage to Turco-Egyptian fleet.

November   Second civil war breaks out, marked by strong localist
               antagonisms between Rumeliot and Peloponnesian notables
               and military chiefs.

1825

January 26	Second Greek loan contracted in London.
February 12	Turco-Egyptian forces under Ibrahim Pasha land at Methoni.
April 15	Second siege of Mesolonghi begins.
April 26	Turco-Egyptian forces land and occupy the island of Sphaktiria at Navarino bay.
May 20	Heroic death of Papaflessas at Maniaki, Messenia, draws the admiration of Ibrahim Pasha.
May 20	Naval victory of the Greeks under Sachtouris at Cape Kaphireas (Cavo d'Oro) at southeastern Euboea. At least three enemy ships destroyed by Greek fireships.
June 2	Greek navy under Andreas Miaoulis attacks Turco-Egyptian fleet at Suda bay in Crete and blows up enemy corvette.
June 5	Odysseas Androutsos killed at the Acropolis of Athens on instructions of rival commander Ioannis Gouras. He was the last victim of the civil wars of the revolution.
June 10	Ibrahim Pasha retakes Tripolitsa from the Greeks.
June 13	At the battle of Myloi on the Argolid coast Greeks under D. Ypsilantis and I. Makrygiannis inflict serious defeat on the forces of Ibrahim Pasha.
July 24	Greek appeal to Great Britain to take under its exclusive protection the cause of the liberation of Greece. The appeal is rejected by British government to avoid diplomatic complications in the Concert of Europe.
July 29	Attempt of Greek squadron under Kanaris to burn Egyptian fleet in Alexandria harbor fails on account of contrary winds.
July 31	Revolution revived in Crete.
August 13	Greek victory at Trikorfa.

November 18	Greek victory under Karaiskakis at Distomo.
December 18	Ibrahim Pasha and his troops cross over to Rumeli and join Ottoman forces laying siege on Mesolonghi.

1826

April 4	Protocol between Great Britain and Russia, signed at Saint Petersburg, provides for mediation by the two powers for the establishment of an autonomous Greek state under Ottoman suzerainty.
April 6	Third National Assembly convenes at Epidavros; following the exodus of Mesolonghi on April 10–11, it suspends its sessions.
April 10–11	Exodus of Mesolonghi. The city taken by enemy forces.
June 22–24	The Maniots turn back fierce attacks by Turco-Egyptian forces at Verga.
June 22–23	Attempt by Turco-Egyptian naval forces to land at Diros in Mani turned back by Maniots. Maniot women play decisive role in repelling enemy using harvesting sickles.
July 16	Naval battle off Karlovasi, Samos turns back Ottoman navy.
August 3	Ottoman troops under Mehmed Reşid Pasha (Kütahı) take Athens. Gouras and his men are besieged in the fortress of the Acropolis.
August 6–8	Greeks under Karaiskakis and Colonel Fabvier resist occupation of Attica at Chaidari.
November 11	Greek government moves seat from Nafplio to Aigina.
November 22–26	Greeks under Karaiskakis defeat enemy advance at the battle of Arachova.

1827

January 27	After a hard battle Greeks defeated by Ottoman forces at Kamatero, Attica.

January 30	Greeks turn back Ottoman forces at Castella on the Saronic coast.
February 5	Greeks led by Karaiskakis score a victory over enemy forces at Distomo.
March 2	Karaiskakis leads Greeks to victory at Keratsini, Attica.
March 19	Third National Assembly reconvenes at Troezen.
April 2	Third National Assembly elects Ioannis Capodistrias first head of state of free Greece.
April 22	Georgios Karaiskakis mortally wounded at a skirmish outside Athens. He dies on his nameday (feast day of St. George), April 23.
April 24	Crushing defeat of Greeks and Philhellenes at Analatos, southeast of Athens.
May 1	Third National Assembly votes the Political Constitution of Greece.
May 25	Besieged Greeks on the Acropolis in Athens surrender to Ottomans.
July 6	Britain, France, and Russia sign in London the Treaty for the Pacification of Greece, reaffirming terms of St. Petersburg Protocol of the previous year. The treaty provides for active military involvement of the three powers to bring about a settlement of Greek Question.
September 10	Admirals Codrington and de Rigny notify Ibrahim Pasha that no more military movements on Greek territory are allowed.
September 18	Naval battle in the gulf of Itea. Captain Hastings in charge of the frigate *Karteria* destroys seven Ottoman naval vessels.
October 20	The united navies of the three powers, Britain, France, and Russia, destroy Turco-Egyptian fleet at battle in Navarino Bay.

1828

January 8   Governor Ioannis Capodistrias arrives in Greece. He sets up
                 his Provisional State Administration in Aigina on January 18,
                 1828.

January 31   Alexandros Ypsilantis dies in Vienna.

February 2   National Finance Bank set up; the phoenix established as the
                 national currency.

April 14   Russia declares war on Ottoman Empire.

May 18   Battle at Frangokastello, Crete.

July 19   The three powers sign in London a protocol providing for
                 French military mission under General Maison to be sent to
                 Peloponnese to help expel Ibrahim's troops.

August 17   French military mission lands at Petalidi in Messenia.

September 4   Beginning of evacuation of Egyptian forces from the Morea.

September 20   Ibrahim Pasha departs from the Morea.

1829

July 11   Fourth National Assembly convenes at Argos.

September 12   Last battle of the revolution fought at Petra, Boeotia. Greeks
                 led by Dimitrios Ypsilantis defeat Turkish troops.

September 14   Treaty of Adrianople signed between Russia and the Ot-
                 toman Empire. By the Treaty of Adrianople the Sublime
                 Porte recognizes all earlier international agreements on the
                 Greek Question.

1830

February 3   The three great powers sign the Protocol of London, establishing
                 an independent Greek state within a continental boundary
                 running from the sources of Acheloos to Spercheios River and
                 including the islands Euboea, the northern Sporades, and
                 the Cyclades.

1831

September 27   Governor Ioannis Capodistrias assassinated at Nafplio.

December 5   Fifth National Assembly convenes at Argos. It eventually
                introduces a monarchical form of government for the new state.

1832

May 7   London Convention between the great powers and Kingdom
                of Bavaria establishes the Kingdom of Greece and offers the
                crown to Prince Otto of Wittelsbach. Greece recognized as
                an independent and sovereign kingdom.

1833

January 25   King Othon arrives at Nafplio.

March 20   The fortress of the Acropolis taken by a Greek garrison.
                Bavarian officers Paligan and Neeser receive the keys of
                the Acropolis from the last Ottoman commander, Osman
                Effendi. The Greek flag flies on the liberated Acropolis.

1834

September 18   Athens officially becomes the capital of the Kingdom of
                Greece.

Contributors

Nicos C. Alivizatos, National and Kapodistrian University of Athens

Stavros Th. Anestidis, Centre for Asia Minor Studies

Eleni Angelomatis-Tsougarakis, Ionian University

Roxane D. Argyropoulos, Institute of Historical Research / National Hellenic
Research Foundation

Roderick Beaton, King's College London

Constantinos C. Chatzopoulos, Democritus University of Thrace

Maria D. Efthymiou, National and Kapodistrian University of Athens

Ioannis D. Evrigenis, Tufts University

Lucien Frary, Rider University

Katerina Galani, Institute for Mediterranean Studies / FORTH (Foundation for
Research and Technology-Hellas) and Hellenic Open University

Basil C. Gounaris, Aristotle University of Thessaloniki

Mathieu Grenet, University of Albi / Federal University of Toulouse

Gelina Harlaftis, University of Crete

Robert Holland, King's College London

H. Şükrü Ilıcak, Institute of Mediterranean Studies, Rethymnon

Markos Karasarinis, Historian, Independent Scholar

Paschalis M. Kitromilides, National and Kapodistrian University of Athens /
Academy of Athens

Kostas Kostis, National and Kapodistrian University of Athens

Phokion Kotzageorgis, Aristotle University of Thessaloniki

Christos Landros, General State Archives, Samos

Katerina Levidou, National and Kapodistrian University of Athens

Dimitris Livanios, Aristotle University of Thessaloniki

Peter Mackridge, St Cross College, University of Oxford

Slobodan G. Marković, University of Belgrade

Dimitris C. Mavroskoufis, Aristotle University of Thessaloniki

Vasilis Molos, New York University Abu Dhabi

Rosa Mucignat, King's College London

Dimitrios Papastamatiou, Aristotle University of Thessaloniki

Andrei Pippidi, University of Bucharest / Romanian Academy of Sciences

Alexis Politis, University of Crete

David Ricks, King's College London

Vaso Seirinidou, National and Kapodistrian University of Athens

Ioannis D. Stefanidis, Aristotle University of Thessaloniki

Fani-Maria Tsigakou, Benaki Museum, Athens

Constantinos Tsoukalas, National and Kapodistrian University of Athens

Dionysis Tzakis, Ionian University

Pericles S. Vallianos, National and Kapodistrian University of Athens

Gonda Van Steen, King's College London

Manolis G. Varvounis, Democritus University of Thrace

Acknowledgments

Both editors feel deeply grateful for the honor our former colleague at the University of Athens and former president of the Hellenic Republic, Prokopios Pavlopoulos, has done to our project by contributing a foreword to the *Critical Dictionary*. We feel obliged to acknowledge his unconditional support for this project, which has enabled us to carry it to its completion more effectively.

Our project to mark the bicentennial of the Greek Revolution by coordinating and editing the present *Critical Dictionary* has met with the support of many institutions, organizations, and individuals. The *Critical Dictionary* is published as the contribution of the Hellenic Culture Foundation to the bicentennial of the Greek Revolution. Its coordination and production have been supported by the Hellenic Culture Foundation and its services. Valuable support has been received from Ilias Nicolacopoulos who took care of the practical needs and problems arising and from Andromachi Marouda and Vassilis Tzoulis. My coeditor, Constantinos Tsoukalas, as president of the Board of the Hellenic Culture Foundation, has facilitated my work on the *Critical Dictionary* in every possible way. I am deeply grateful for his enthusiasm and his friendship.

Substantial financial support for the project has been received from the Stavros Niarchos Foundation and Hellenic Petroleum. We are very glad to acknowledge the help and support of our sponsors, whose generosity has made it all possible.

We wish to thank the following museums and art collections for graciously making available to us free of charge high-resolution photographs of works of art from their collections:

Brown University Portrait Collection, Providence, R. I., and Curator Nicole Wholean

Musei Reali-Palazzo Reale, Torino, and director Dr. Enrica Pagella
Museo Civico, Treviso
Pinacoteca Civica Tosio Martinengo, Brescia
National Gallery-Alexandros Soutzos Museum, Athens, and director
    Professor Marina Lambraki-Plaka
National Historical Museum, Athens, and director Dr. Efthymia
    Papaspyrou
History Museum, National and Kapodistrian University of Athens and
    director Evangelos Papoulias
Benaki Museum, Athens, and academic director George Manginis
Gennadeion Library, Athens, and director Dr. Maria Georgopoulou
E. Averoff Museum of Modern Greek Art, Metsovo and Mrs Tatiana
    Averoff, Chair of the Board
Museum of the City of Athens and Mr. Antonis Voyatzis, Chairman of the
    Board, and Dr. Stephanos Kavallierakis, director
Municipal Gallery, Mesolonghi
The Abbot and Brotherhood of Machairas Monastery, Cyprus
Oxford and Cambridge Club, London
The Thanassis and Marina Martinos Collection, Athens
The Michael and Demetra Varkarakis Collection, Athens

Fani-Maria Tsigakou, a great authority on European art history and philhellenic art, has expertly helped with the collection of the illustrations. Valuable
assistance with the collection of illustrations for the volume has also been offered by two other distinguished art historians, Marilena Cassimatis and
Dimitris Pavlopoulos.

The maps documenting the narrative of revolutionary events in the *Critical
Dictionary* have been drawn with great skill, expertise, and patience by Nopi
Ploutoglou and Elpida Daniil at the General State Archives of Greece. I wish
to express my sincere appreciation and thanks to them both for their excellent
contribution to this volume and to the General State Archives of Greece–
Historical Archives of Macedonia–Cartographic Heritage Archives and its
director Mr. Nestor Bamidis my gratitude for the support they have extended to our project. The production of the maps has been based on cartographic infrastructure which is available at Geodata.gov.gr, http://geodata.gov
.gr/Hellenic Republic / Ministry of the Interior and Administrative Reconstruction / Creative Commons Attribution 3.0, and Open Street Map, https://
planet.openstreetmap.org/Creative Commons Attribution-Share Alike 2.0 license (CC BY-SA 2.0), to which the Cartographic Heritage Archives has
added the special data required by the present project. In the production of

the map of Mesolonghi, valuable assistance was received from Mrs. Rodanthi Florou, president of the Mesolonghi Byron Society, while the mapmakers have also drawn on the work by P. D. Doulis on Engineer Michael P. Kokkinis (Athens 1976).

The mapmakers also wish to record their debt to cartographic information in *History of the Greek Nation* (1976) for the map of the Danubian Principalities and *History of Modern Hellenism* (2003) for the map of the Battle of Navarino, and in *The New Cambridge Modern History Atlas,* ed. by H. C. Darby and Harold Fullard (Cambridge 1970).

The production of the final manuscript has been supported in multiple ways by the Centre for Asia Minor Studies in Athens. Maria Mougkaraki has offered invaluable assistance.

Alexandra Douma has rendered an essential service to the project by translating a number of texts originally written in Greek. Katerina Gardikas has been an outstanding collaborator to the difficult editorial work required by the collection. Her help has been inestimable and her presence in the project has been a great source of relief to the anxieties of editorial work.

A very special debt is owed to Vasilis Panagiotopoulos, the country's foremost authority on the history of the Greek Revolution, on whose wisdom I repeatedly drew at various stages of the project.

Several other colleagues and friends have offered the editor or individual contributors the benefit of their scholarly help and advice. It is a great pleasure to record here my gratitude to Stavros Anestidis, Eleni Angelomatis-Tsougarakis, Roxane Argyropoulos, Jennifer Betts, Christophoros Charalambakis, Maria Constandoudaki, Myrto Economides, Maroula Efthymiou, Stratos Efthymiou, Tim Engels, Kallia Kalliataki-Mertikopoulou, Yorgos Kallinis, Kostas Kardamis, Constantinos Karkanias, Helen Katsiadakis, Michael Kitromilidis, Kostas Kostis, Nathan Medici, Constantinos Nianios, John Robertson, Katy Romanou, Katerina Tiktopoulou, Dionysis Tzakis, Pericles Vallianos, Gonda Van Steen, Nasos Vayenas, George Vlastos, Ioannis Xourias. Some of them have acted as peer reviewers, others have offered advice and information or supplied source material, still others have helped with the collection of illustrations, all of which has greatly facilitated our collective work.

Last, but far from least, I wish to express my deep gratitude to my editor at Harvard University Press, Kathleen McDermott, for her invaluable advice, guidance, and support. It is a rare privilege to have worked with her.

P.M.K.

Index